MODERN

CHARLES P. LOOMIS
Research Professor
Michigan State University

ZONA K. LOOMIS
Research Assistant
Michigan State University

THE VAN NOSTRAND SERIES IN SOCIOLOGY

Edited by
WILBERT E. MOORE
Professor of Sociology, Princeton University

MARTIN H. NEUMEYER—Social Problems and the Changing Society

M. BERGER, T. ABEL AND C. H. PAGE—Freedom and Control in Modern Society

MARTIN H. NEUMEYER—Juvenile Delinquency in Modern Society, 2nd Ed.

OLIVER M. BUTTERFIELD—Planning for Marriage

MELVIN J. VINCENT AND JACKSON MAYERS—New Foundations for Industrial Sociology

DON MARTINDALE—American Society

ROSE K. GOLDSEN, MORRIS ROSENBERG, ROBIN M. WILLIAMS, JR., AND EDWARD A. SUCHMAN—What College Students Think

CHARLES P. LOOMIS—Social Systems: Essays on Their Persistence and Change

CHARLES P. LOOMIS AND ZONA K. LOOMIS—Modern Social Theories: Selected American Writers

JACK P. GIBBS—Urban Research Methods

Additional titles will be listed and announced as published.

SOCIAL THEORIES

SELECTED AMERICAN WRITERS

D. VAN NOSTRAND COMPANY, INC.

PRINCETON, NEW JERSEY

TORONTO   NEW YORK   LONDON

D. VAN NOSTRAND COMPANY, INC.

120 Alexander St., Princeton, New Jersey (*Principal office*)
24 West 40 Street, New York 18, New York

D. Van Nostrand Company, Ltd.
358, Kensington High Street, London, W. 14, England

D. Van Nostrand Company (Canada), Ltd.
25 Hollinger Road, Toronto 16, Canada

Published simultaneously in Canada by
D. Van Nostrand Company (Canada), Ltd.

PRINTED IN THE UNITED STATES OF AMERICA

TO

BETSY, LAURA, AND VERA

PREFACE

The present volume grew out of a one-term graduate course in modern social theory taught for some years by the senior author. Despite his preference for assignments from original sources, a dilemma seemed to mark each course taught principally from the works of modern theorists. Highly selective readings yielded the student a mastery of only a fragment of essential materials while wider readings from the voluminous output of modern theorists gave little more than an overview with limited mastery. Although the sociological readers which offer special facets of the works of various of the theorists represented in this volume proved to be useful, there seemed to be a need for summarizations and analyses of the type made available in the present volume. This need was all the more urgent in view of the availability of the orienting exposures to the works of other theorists such as MacIver, Riesman, and Znaniecke. Chapters 2 through 9 of the present volume were developed to meet that need. In mimeographed form they have been used in a course on Contemporary Social Theories, where they have undergone changes in various versions in response to criticisms and suggestions from the students for whom they were required reading. Used by the student in conjunction with a wide and thorough exploration of at least one major theorist for which each student was responsible, the present chapters have proven useful in resolving the dilemma of learning too little about a great number of concepts, or learning much about too few.

Student criticism of the chapters in their various versions has not only improved their final form, but has led in a few instances to a formal collaboration. It was by such a route that Robert C. Bealer became junior author of Chapters 6 and 8 and Robert Holloway the junior author of Chapter 5. Their sizable contributions are deeply appreciated as was their willingness to give high priority to the work at different stages of the enterprize despite the pressures of other compelling commitments.

While the presentations were being refined and improved by actual class use, the co-author's long standing interest in social theory and her extensive and intensive reading in the field was admirably suited to the task of collaborative writing and of codifying the many books, journal articles, monographs and other materials into the organizational framework which is the chief distinction of the present chapters. That organizational framework (called the Processually Articulated Structural Model or PAS Model) was developed in an earlier companion volume, *Social Systems.* The concepts of the theorists whose works comprise the content of the present volume contributed significantly to the development of the PAS Model. None the less it was found that the concepts as set forth in the PAS Model varied considerably in exactness of "fit" as they were matched with the concepts of the theorists whose works are presented here. It is, therefore, a tribute to the individual theorists treated here that they without exception, gave cooperation, encouragement and support to a presentation of their works in a form which in many respects is distinctly different from their own conceptual arrangements. In addition to providing a common denominator by which variously termed concepts could be examined for content and analyzed for meaning, the analytical endeavor resulted in not a few cases in the theorist's discovery that his works contained strains and implications of which he had been unaware.

Each theorist read the draft as prepared, made marginal comments, and later discussed these and other relevant matters in tape-recorded interviews, most of which lasted from six to eight hours. The transcriptions of these together with the marginal notes furnished the basis for the final revision of the manuscripts. Since the theorists did not have the opportunity to read the final versions of the chapters they must, of course, be absolved of any ultimate responsibility for their present form and content. Although the present authors have attempted to give a faithful presentation of each theorist and to incorporate into the final product all of the suggestions offered by each one, they have no illusions of complete success. The fallibilities inherent in interpreting the meanings of others as well as the space limitations in an endeavor of this sort must be recognized as factors which may render the product faulty in some respects. For example, the comparative feature made possible by casting the concepts of each theorist in the common phraseology provided by the PAS Model seemed one of the most exciting prospects in the project as it was originally conceived. It was abundantly clear at the completion of Chapter 8 that full-scale comparisons must be severely restricted. Chapter 9, consequently, compares the concepts of the preceding chapters in respect only to cognitive mapping and to social change. This shortcoming is partially offset by the rather detailed indexing which should facilitate the task of comparisons among the theorists on other dimensions.

The authors are indebted to John A. Hostetler, James B. McKee, and John T. Gullahorn who read earlier versions of Chapters 1, 2, and 4, respectively. Also deserving of special mention are Clyde R. McCone, Eugene C. Erickson, and Warren Sower who in the early stages of writing, assisted with Chapters 2, 4, and 8 respectively. Donald Clelland checked references and Elizabeth Nall assisted with manuscripts as used in seminars before the final rewrite. Margaret Holloway and Marilyn Jesser performed the laborious task of transcribing the lengthy author interviews while Robert Holloway and Clinton Jesser assisted in the editing of these transcriptions. The authors relied heavily on Vera Krause who was ably assisted by Dorothy Tervo for many rush jobs of typing, mimeographing, and other services. Wilbert E. Moore, editor of the Social Science Series, was a valued advisor in the planning stages.

Finally, as in the case of the companion volume, *Social Systems*, indebtedness to the Division of Hospital and Medical Facilities of the United States Public Health Service and to the Carnegie Corporation of New York for financial support must be acknowledged. Under the aegis of these two sources of support, vital field investigations elsewhere reported have been carried on which proved to be closely associated with the development of the conceptual scheme here used. Work undertaken at the behest of the United States Public Health Service under Project W 108, Anglo-Latino Relations in Hospitals and Communities, while clearly directed toward a focus on aspects of health finds broader ramifications not only in the health themes which are particularly apparent in Chapters 3, 5, and 6, but also in the minority group theme present in all chapters, but notably discernible in Chapter 8. Investigations supported by the Carnegie Corporation of New York specify a wide latitude of social research which is reflected in the pervasive theme of cultural-societal exchanges and in the frontier work of boundary exchanges as expounded in Chapters 6 and 9. Without the support of these two organizations the present endeavor would have been impossible.

CHARLES P. AND ZONA K. LOOMIS

East Lansing, Michigan
October 1961

CONTENTS

The Elements, 3. The Processes, 3. Social Change—
Conceptualization of Static and Dynamic Aspects of
Social Systems, 6. Conditions of Social Action, 7. A
Change Resistant Social System—the Old Order
Amish, 8. Conditions of Social Interaction for the
Amish, 9.

ELEMENTS AND ELEMENTAL PROCESSES, 10.

Knowing, 10. Belief (Knowledge) as an Element,
10. Cognitive Mapping and Validation as Process,
10.

Feeling, 11. Sentiment as an Element, *11.* Tension
Management as Process, *11.* Communication of Sentiment as Process, *11.*

Achieving, 11. End, Goal, or Objective as an Element, *11.* Goal Attaining and Concomitant "Latent"
Activity as Process, *12.*

Norming, Standardizing and Patterning, 12. Norm as
an Element, *12.* Evaluation as a Process, *12.*

Dividing the Functions, 13. Status-role as a Unit Incorporating Both Element and Process, *13.*

Ranking, 13. Rank as an Element, *13.* Evaluation of
Actors and Allocation of Status-roles as Process, *13.*

Controlling, 13. Power as an Element, *13.* Decision
Making and its Initiation into Action as Process, *14.*

Sanctioning, 14. Sanction as an Element, *14.* Application of Sanctions as Process, *14.* Notes, *17.*

Editorial Introduction

The language of sociology is subjected to intermittent criticism by various literary types, who assume in their ignorant arrogance that if the sociologist does not communicate with them he has nothing worthwhile to say at all. To the man who thinks he already understands everything about human nature and social behavior—and many people harbor this comforting illusion—the technical concepts of the sociologist may be regarded as so much "double-talk." I do not mean to condone bad syntax or empty virtuosity in conceptualization of phenomena that are imaginary or insignificant. It is, however, time to recognize that analysis of the complexity of social behavior, the rendering of nuances of interpretation into predictive propositions, of vague categories into reliably identifiable ones, of common sense into valid or erroneous allegations, require a degree of linguistic precision (and occasional inventiveness) that surpasses the vocabulary of the person with a "general" education.

This book is not for beginners in sociology, to say nothing of literary critics, who have their own exotic tongue, but a different one. Charles and Zona Loomis have set about a systematic exposition of the sociological concepts and propositions developed by seven leading practitioners of the dark art of theory in contemporary American sociology. Since sociological concepts *are* to a degree unstandardized, and the phenomena that excite theorists into calling them names are somewhat selectively drawn from the rich mass of social experience, a comparative analysis of the works of the seven theorists presented substantial difficulties. This problem has been alleviated to a remarkable degree by virtue of a conceptual model developed by Charles Loomis in a related volume, *Social Systems.* In each chapter of the present volume devoted to a contemporary theorist, an initial summary of the man's main concerns and orientations is followed by a more detailed and systematic exposition of concepts and conclusions according to the uniform analytical scheme. The result is not a sociological theory that is truly singular; there is little reason to suppose that any science can indeed achieve such a goal, which therefore constitutes a kind of useful myth. The similarities as well as differences do stand in sharp focus by this procedure. The sociological apprentice, more interested in being expert in analysis than an authority on leading men, can take his shopping list for concepts and approaches and find the shelves clearly labeled.

This Introduction is not the occasion to write another book of theory, but I do want to take the opportunity to make a few comments on our current state. In particular, I should like to offer some thoughts on the use of an "equilibrium model" of social systems, and on the analysis of social change.

Several of the theorists whose works are analyzed by the Loomises give explicit testimony that their view of societies or smaller social structures rests on the notion of an equilibrium. Now such a "model" of orderly social phenomena has substantial disadvantages if it is taken seriously. The notion is relatively harmless, but also unnecessary, if it simply means that sociological analysis must deal with *systems* if it is to yield predictive propositions of any consequence, if, that is, the study of social phenomena is to go beyond endless and tiresome descriptions of events and entities.

Human acts, groups, rules of conduct, and goals or values are interrelated, not isolated and autonomous variables. The interrelationships constitute the major data for meaningful description or analysis of social systems. They underlie so-called functional analysis, which asks the systemic consequences of given patterns of action. By their predictability, their persistence, they constitute a major source of order, of reliability in social affairs that makes life tolerable if not wholly without risk and uncertainty. The establishment of the relationships among social phenomena, the attempt to achieve precision in concepts for elements and processes and to achieve precision in measuring the degree of predictability from one set of variables to another, have been the major concerns of contemporary sociology. Inevitably, some of the results have supported the cynical accusation that sociology is the art of saying what everybody knows in terms that nobody can understand. At worst, however, the guilt is not unique, for any science incorporates and makes precise things already known to the layman by crude experience. But experience can also be a false teacher, for many scientific principles are contrary to common sense, and many more are contrary to the unrepresentative experience, the poor sample, of single individuals.

The equilibrium model, I am suggesting, is relatively harmless when it provides a kind of constant reminder of the systemic qualities of social phenomena, including the circumstances that actions produce consequences and even reactions, and indeed that systems may provide significant self-regulating mechanisms. The mischief begins when the model is followed rigorously.

Besides the orderly persistence of interrelated patterns of action, there are also ample sources of disorder in social systems, of tensions and conflicts, of *intrinsic* sources and paths of change. All social systems, and particularly those loose confederations that we call societies, display evidence of openness and "gaps" in connections, and degrees of relative autonomy of actions or groups or larger systems. If an equilibrium model is taken at all seriously, these circumstances are downright embarrassing.

It is the function of theory to impose order on what might appear to be chaos, and it does so by being in some measure abstract. Yet the predictive test is *de rigeur* in any theory claiming scientific authenticity. It is not surprising that the several sociological theorists represented in this book who are still very active in the quest for models with a better fit to data should be looking at processes like tension-management and decision-making or initiation of action, which allow both disorder and purposive change to have space in the house of society. The senior author of this book has made a notable advance by inviting in these former strangers. It is widely recognized that a major next step is to put the house on rollers and permit it to move, while furnishing the interior with flexible and movable partitions and occasionally discordant inhabitants.

The theorists whose works are expounded and analyzed here

are, on the whole, highly cognizant of men's goals and sentiments, their beliefs and rules. There are here no radical behaviorists, who "have made up their windpipes that they have no minds," or attitudes and aspirations. Yet they strike me as a rather "conservative" group with regard to the larger shape of things social. Fearing, perhaps, the "group mind" fallacy, the theorists seem to depict society as a kind of by-product of mindless functional necessities plus mindful and motivated individual actions almost solely at the interpersonal level. The "common value system" attributed to societies seems to have no politically powerful spokesmen, although we know better. And the values seem not to include deliberate, planned, and large-scale social change. The reality of such change tends to be treated as "exogenous," an unpredicted datum, and the equilibrium model used to trace through systemic consequences. The pursuit of consequences is not a trivial kind of labor. However, it does fall short of large issues—issues of scientific predictability as well as such practical questions as human survival and the capacity to tolerate change at explosive velocities —presented in the factual world of contemporary experience. Social revolutions no longer just happen, if they ever did. They are planned and executed, despite the real resistances that equilibrium models of society help to identify but not to protect.

I do not mean to issue a call to revolutionary action, but only to scholarly contemplation of the realities of large-scale and rapid change in social arrangements. It is comforting that the theoretical minds explored in this book are indeed turning to that contemplation.

WILBERT E. MOORE

Princeton, New Jersey
September 1961

CHAPTER 1

THE ANALYTICAL CONCEPTS AND THEIR DEFINITION

Before undertaking the study of the sociological theories of the writers whose works are reviewed in the following chapters, a conceptual scheme was developed which will be followed chapter by chapter throughout the book. This conceptual scheme and its background have been elaborated in considerable detail in the volume, *Social Systems: Essays on Their Persistence and Change.*[1] The purpose of the present chapter is to acquaint the reader with the terms of that conceptual scheme. Two procedures will be employed. First, pertinent excerpts and definitions from *Social Systems* will be presented. Second, a summary description of a particular social system—that of the *Old Order Amish* community in Lancaster County, Pennsylvania—organized in terms of the pertinent concepts will be given to introduce the concepts and illustrate their use in analytical application. The consistent organization of the sociological theories which comprise the content of the present volume facilitates point by point comparison of the various theorists' works. The scheme which provides that organizational device is called the Processually Articulated Structural Model, hereafter referred to as the PAS Model.

As the first step in familiarizing the reader with that model the following excerpts from *Social Systems* are presented.[2]

"*The frame of reference of sociology.* Activity may be defined as any event involving the use of energy. It is thus a generic term. The social sciences in large measure limit their frame of reference to human activity and approach its analysis by use of

1

the 'action' frame of reference which, although similar to some usages of the behavioral frame of reference in that it concerns what people do, avoids some of the limiting connotations of stimulus-response 'behaviorism.' Social action is the activity of social units.[3]

"Interaction, the core datum of sociology, has been defined as any event by which one party tangibly influences the overt actions or the state of mind of the other.[4] It is a reciprocal and interdependent activity, designated as having the quality of complementarity or double contingency.[5] Reciprocal activity or interaction that is repeated and persists comprises *social relations.*

"Interaction tends to develop certain uniformities over time, some of which tend to persist. As they are *orderly* and *systematic,* they can be recognized as *social systems.* Because the *social system* is composed of identifiable and interdependent parts it is said to possess *social structure.* Sociology, like other sciences, is concerned with the *orderliness* or *uniformities* involved in its particular class of phenomena, and it finds this order in the *social system.* It is very much concerned with two very different kinds of order found in interaction. On the one hand it is concerned with order resulting from factors in the situation over which the members of a given social system have no control or order imposed from what may be called the conditions of action. An example of this type of order is that imposed by man's limited physical mobility as related to the factor, geographical space which makes it impossible for an actor to be at two geographical points at the same time. On the other hand sociology is concerned with norms which determine what is evaluated as just or unjust, true or false, and beautiful or ugly and what are considered appropriate responses to these evaluations.

"The *social system* is composed of the patterned interaction of members. It is constituted of the interaction of a plurality of individual actors whose relations to each other are mutually oriented through the definition and mediation of a pattern of structured and shared symbols and expectations.

"A means of delineating a social system is furnished by the more intense and frequent occurrence of *specific types of interaction* among members than among non-members, within a situation having both physical and symbolic aspects. However, this simplified means of delineating social systems requires accurate use. It has been observed, for instance, that actors of a given family whose members are scattered about in an industrial society may retain solidarity as a family but interact less frequently with family members than with non-members on the job and in other places. Because there is a difference in the type of interaction and resulting bonds among the family and non-family members, the phrase 'specific types of interaction' in the definition is important. Among the dimensions that may determine the type of interaction are extensity, intensity, duration, direction (i.e. whether solidary or antagonistic), and nature and extent of integration.[6]

THE ELEMENTS

"An element is simply one of the constituent parts of some larger whole. Thus in chemistry an element is one of a limited number of distinct varieties of matter which, singly or in combination, compose every material substance. An element, then, is the unit of analysis employed in explaining interaction from the point of view of a given discipline. An explanation of social interaction calls for the examination of the elements of the social system. It is not implied here that there is in sociology the same universal agreement as to what the elements are as in chemistry, but it is maintained that in the accumulative work of sociologists certain analytic aspects of interaction have been consistently used. From among these aspects those that are considered elements are 1) belief (knowledge); 2) sentiment; 3) end, goal, or objective; 4) norm; 5) status-role (position); 6) rank; 7) power; 8) sanction; and 9) facility. At any given moment in time the structure of a given social system may be described and analyzed in terms of these elements.

THE PROCESSES

"The elements that stand in a given relation to each other at a given moment do not remain in that relation (except by abstraction) for any length of time. The processes mesh, stabilize, and alter the relations between the elements through time; they are the tools through which the social system may be understood as a dynamic functioning continuity—a 'going concern.'[7] The concept, process, is commonly employed in various of the sciences. A mere listing of such processes as osmosis, metamorphosis, succession, or evolution indicates the diversity of the specialties to which the term is applicable. Regardless of the diversity, each process is characterized by a consistent quality of regular and uniform sequences and is distinguishable by virtue of its orderliness. This same orderliness is the essence of any social process through which transition from one social condition to another is accomplished. For the present purposes the social processes may be classified under two headings: the specialized elemental processes by which the separate elements are articulated and the comprehensive or master processes by which several or all of the elements are articulated or involved. Those of the first category, along with the elements that they respectively articulate are:

1) cognitive mapping and validation by which the element belief (knowledge) is articulated
2) tension management and communication of sentiment by which the element sentiment is articulated
3) goal attaining and concomitant 'latent' activity as process by which the element—end, goal, or objective is articulated
4) evaluation by which the element norm is articulated
5) status-role performance by which the element status-role (position) is articulated
6) evaluation of actors and allocation of status-roles by which the element rank is articulated
7) decision making and its initiation into action by which the element power is articulated
8) application of sanctions by which the element sanction is articulated
9) utilization of facilities by which the element facility is articulated.

"The structural-functional categories shown in Figure 1 are handy names by which any structural element and its particular functional process (both being ingredients of the structural-functional category) may be designated as a closely connected bundle of phenomena. In the sections of this chapter which follow, and in subsequent chapters the elements and the specialized processes by which the elements are articulated will be treated together. The comprehensive or master processes by which many or all of

FIGURE 1

ELEMENTS, PROCESSES AND CONDITIONS OF ACTION OF SOCIAL SYSTEMS
THE PROCESSUALLY ARTICULATED STRUCTURAL MODEL (PAS MODEL)†

Processes (*Elemental*)	*Structural-functional Categories*	*Elements*
1) Cognitive mapping and validation	Knowing	Belief (knowledge)
2) a) Tension management and b) Communication of sentiment	Feeling	Sentiment
3) a) Goal attaining activity and b) Concomitant "latent" activity as process	Achieving	End, goal, or objective
4) Evaluation	Norming, Standardizing, Patterning	Norm
5) Status-role performance	Dividing the functions	Status-role (position)
6) a) Evaluation of actors and b) Allocation of status-roles	Ranking	Rank
7) a) Decision making and b) Initiation of action	Controlling	Power
8) Application of sanctions	Sanctioning	Sanction
9) Utilization of facilities	Facilitating	Facility

Comprehensive or Master Processes		
1) Communication	3) Systemic linkage	5) Socialization
2) Boundary maintenance	4) Institutionalization	6) Social control

Conditions of Social Action		
1) Territoriality	2) Size	3) Time

† For a more detailed version of this figure see Figure 1 in Charles P. Loomis *Social Systems, op. cit.,* p. 8. For the relation of the above concepts to the *Gemeinschaft-Gesellschaft* continuum see Ibid., pp. 61 ff.

the elements are activated will follow. These are communication, boundary maintenance, systemic linkage, social control, socialization, and institutionalization. Both the elemental and comprehensive processes discussed later are those that have been found by many investigators to be of general utility in the analysis of social action and particularly in the development, persistence, and change of social systems.

SOCIAL CHANGE—CONCEPTUALIZATION OF STATIC AND DYNAMIC ASPECTS OF SOCIAL SYSTEMS

"Sociologists like other scientists have been plagued with substantive and methodological difficulties in the analysis of change. To obviate these difficulties it is important that process or change itself be made the focus of observation. It is clear that the elements and processes noted in Figure 1 emphasize both structure and function through time. By linking the important elements of social structure to the processes crucial for the articulation of the structure through time, it is hoped that some contribution may be made to 'our knowledge of structural imperatives . . . and . . . knowledge of many processes of change . . .' .[8] It is in an effort to break through some of the difficulties imposed by the static aspects of the equilibrium model in the analysis of social change that this model is presented.[9]

"Clearly a society or a sociology department as going concerns involved in action can be analyzed by means of the construct, the social system. The construct in application must reflect the achievements, failures and altered goals of the members of the group being analyzed. Its use as an action-involved tool emerges as various of the elements and processes come into greater or less prominence depending upon the nature of the activity. Independent scientists have repeatedly observed that a given collective of individuals interacting within a given social system evinces varying patterns of relations determined by the conditions of the situation and/or the functions of the relations for the system. One discernible pattern of relations will be referred to as 'external'; a correlate pattern will be called 'internal.' [10]

"Viewed analytically a pattern of a system which exists as a response to a group's adjustment to its environment and the attainment of its goals is an *external* pattern. This pattern's primary structural-functional categories are 1) *achieving*, with *end, goal,* or *objective* as an element and *goal-attaining activity* as process; and 2) *controlling*, with *power* as an element and *decision making and initiation into action* as process. An external pattern of interaction then is marked by adaptation and goal-achievement.

"A group through its internal pattern establishes non-adaptive and non-goal directed relations which focus upon the expression of the system members' sentiments toward one another. The most crucial structural-functional category in this pattern is *feeling* with *sentiment* as an element and *communication of sentiment* as process.

CONDITIONS OF SOCIAL ACTION

"The elements and processes constitute the working components, the parts and articulating functions, of the social system. Not all aspects of social systems are encompassed in these concepts but the components as presented constitute the central core of social structure. Some components are partly systemic; that is, partly structured and partly not. Space, time, and size are such components. Both space and time are to a certain extent utilized as systemic attributes, as facilities, but they are never completely controlled by the system's members and are, therefore, arbitrarily classified as conditions.

"*Territoriality.* The setting of the social system in space is called its *territoriality*. Since actors are biological organisms limited in energy and mobility the actors of all social systems are influenced by spatial considerations. Territoriality determines within limits, how much space each person or group may have, the frequency and intensity of interaction within the group and the probabilities of systemic linkages between groups.

"*Time.* Time like space may be a facility, but as a factor in action it generally is inexorable and cannot be made to stand still or be completely controlled by man. It is, therefore, a condition of action. Even though man bridges the generations through the transmission of culture in a manner not possible among other animals, he is none the less time-bound. The inability of social groups to control time accounts in part at least for patterns of change.

"*Size.* Insofar as size of social systems is not controlled by the actors, it may be discussed as a condition of social action. Although inventions which improve man's efficiency in the use of energy tend to increase the size of certain systems, various subsystems in different organizations, societies, and epochs are remarkably similar.[11] Ordinarily the number of actors supervised directly by one authority is not less than four or five or more than 20 or 30.[12] Sorokin recognized that in terms of operation, 'There seems to be an optimum size of a given type in given circumstances. A great deviation from such an optimum size either in the direction of overgrowth or undergrowth, seems to be negatively correlated with the longevity of the institutions of the same kind.' [13] Such considerations mean that size cannot be controlled at will by actors of a system and must be considered at least in part as a condition of action in systems."

Of course, an ultimate objective in the development of such concepts as those discussed in the preceding paragraphs is that of facilitating scientific explanation and prediction. To this end propositions involving such variables as goal attaining potential and goal attaining efficacy for instrumental organizations and social solidarity (or cohesiveness as the variable is called by some) for all pluralities have been developed for various ongoing investigations not reported in the present volume. These propositions have assisted in the development of hypotheses of the "x varies as y" variety (See Chapter 4) involving these variables and/or those represented by the concepts of the PAS Model. The use of these concepts in the present volume is, however, confined in large part to codification and comparison.

A CHANGE RESISTANT SOCIAL SYSTEM— THE OLD ORDER AMISH

The substantive treatment of the Old Order Amish in the pages to follow is a greatly attenuated version of a more substantial presentation.[14] The original presentation had as its purpose a systematic exploration of the Old Order Amish community viewed as a social system; the organizational means employed was the PAS Model. The presentation in this chapter reverses the intent. The purpose of this presentation is to give the reader in as succinct a form as possible a working knowledge of the concepts of the PAS Model; the means employed is to demonstrate their use by actual application to an empirical community viewed as a social system.

The effort to acquaint the reader with the terms of the PAS Model is a consequence of the authors' conviction that understanding and appraisal of various social system analyses must be based upon common denominators which will insure categorical treatment of comparable phenomena. The common denominators constituted of the elements and processes of the conceptual scheme and tabularly presented in Figure 1 owe their origin to a large number of writers, both "dynamicists" and "structuralists." The scattered parts of this conceptual whole have here been synthesized, enlarged, and arranged [15] in such a manner that theories of social system and social change (as well as empirical systems) can be examined, analyzed, and compared. Needless to say, the present chapter will tell the reader all the fine points of neither the Amish nor of the PAS Model. Should his interest in either of these subjects exceed the offerings of this chapter, he is referred to a fuller treatment in a companion volume.[16] The paragraphs immediately to follow should serve the purpose of initiating the reader into an organizational framework with which he will be very familiar by the time he finishes this book.

CONDITIONS OF SOCIAL INTERACTION FOR THE AMISH

Territoriality. The area of this Amish community encompasses roughly 150 square miles, with thirty-three church districts and about 6,000 people. Interaction between members is much greater than between members with non-members. Boundary maintenance among the Amish results in land in the center of the settlement having higher value than that on the outside where exposure to the "gay" world is easier. Similar sects in other counties which have adopted the automobile have almost overnight "moved out of the neighborhood." In few American social systems is space more important than among sects which organize their activities on a territorial basis and without the use of modern transportation.

Space as a condition and, therefore, uncontrolled is a continuous concern of the Amish. The settlement is small and densely populated and many "swarmings" to other areas have resulted in new settlements.

Time. Time as a facility is reflected in the sequence of events in church ritual and other ways. Time as a condition and uncontrollable by man is reflected in the conceptions of eternity and the concern that each accomplish as much good as possible before he dies.

Size. The size of the various subsystems of the Amish, with the exception of the family, is to a considerable extent controlled. Obviously the limited land available and the consequent migrations from the Lancaster site have made the community less powerful than if all could have been retained.

ELEMENTS AND ELEMENTAL PROCESSES

KNOWING

Belief (knowledge) as an element. A belief is any proposition about the universe which is thought to be true. The Amish [17] believe that each individual is responsible for his own salvation and that the Amish are a chosen people. Like other Protestant groups the Old Order Amish believe in the supremacy of the Bible and the necessity of living and worshipping as prescribed by the Bible as they themselves interpret it. Likewise, the Amish believe no salvation can come through sacraments mediated by formally trained or ordained priests.

Cognitive mapping and validation as process may be defined as the activity by which knowledge, or what is considered true and what false, is developed. For the Amish nothing is more important than the Bible in cognitive mapping and validation. Whether an agricultural practice will make more money or reduce effort is of less importance than what the Scriptures are interpreted as saying. Many farmers claim and some believe that the use of tractors, which is forbidden by the norms, would decrease profits. These beliefs are surprising and contrary to fact. This indicates that in the process of cognitive mapping and validation, Amishmen can neglect some pieces of evidence and overemphasize others.

FEELING

Sentiment as an element. Whereas beliefs embody thoughts, sentiments embody feelings about the world. An Amishman feels reverence, awe, and holiness in the conduct of religious services. But he also feels piety as he works the fields, tends the livestock, sells his wares, and converts his savings into capital gains.

Tension management as process. Tension management may be defined as the process by which the elements of the social system are articulated in such manner as to 1) prevent sentiments from obstructing goal-directed activity and 2) avail the system of their motivating force in achieving goals. Among the Amish various rites of passage operate at potential tension points of the family cycle. The baptismal ceremony, for example, inducts young people into the fellowship of the church from ages 16 to 18 and up to 20 for those who give evidence of "true conversion." Rites of intensification, such as family and community prayer, regularly accompany crises such as impending legislation threatening to their way of life. Institutionalized methods of dealing with the deviant reduces the tensions of "not knowing what to do" when someone has driven a forbidden automobile, or indulged in a too-short hair cut.

Communication of sentiment as process. Communication of sentiment is the process by which members of a social system may be motivated to achieve goals, to conform to norms, and to carry out systemic action through transfer of feeling by symbols. The tabooing of paintings, family pictures, radio and other means of mass communication, and of many forms of self expression leaves the process of communication of sentiment almost entirely to personal precept and example. The cultivation of the sentiment of feeling "different" probably is assisted by the true horror tales in the widely owned *Martyr's Mirror* which communicates the in-group feelings of a persecuted people.

ACHIEVING

End, goal, or objective as an element. The end, goal, or objective is the change (or in some cases the retention of the *status quo*) that members of a social system expect to accomplish through appropriate interaction. Eternal life is the highest goal of the Amishman. Although families strive to increase yields, incomes, and success in farming, these are secondary goals.

Goal attaining and concomitant "latent" activity as process. Whether one attains the goal of salvation never can be proven nor disproven. However, when all Amishmen are motivated toward this goal by becoming active in particular ways, their united activity is palpable in the greater society. The processes comprised of all this united activity are called "latent" because their consequences are unintended and unrecognized.[18] Thus, as thrift, industry, and careful stewardship became activities which gave proof of goodness, the average income and property values of these farmers became for a period the highest in the nation.

NORMING, STANDARDIZING, PATTERNING

Norm as an element. The rules which prescribe what is acceptable or unacceptable are the norms of the social system. The most highly visible norms among the Amish are those of grooming and dress which hark back to bygone periods—beards, long hair, and other differentiating features. Only farming or farm related occupations are permissible. Most norms support the Biblical injunction for separation from the world and non-conformity to it.

Evaluation as a process. Evaluation is the process through which positive and negative priorities or values are assigned to concepts, objects, actors, or collectivities, or to events and activities, either past, present, or future. A most crucial evaluation is made by the whole congregation each time that it must deliberate on reported moral shortcomings of members. Whether a practice such as using an electric fence is moral or not, or whether the group must consider leaving the country, as other similar groups have done to seek freedom, requires evaluation.

DIVIDING THE FUNCTIONS

Status-role as a unit incorporating both element and process. The two-term entity, status-role, contains the concept of status, a structural element implying position and the concept of role, a functional process. Both are important determinants of what is to be expected from an incumbent and how it is performed by him as he occupies any social position. Among the most important Amish status-roles are those which differ by sex and age, with the accompanying sharp differentiation in grooming, clothing, and behavior. The smooth-shaved face of the youth at marriage becomes the bearded face of the man in the new status-role of head of a household. His open buggy, used during courting days, is replaced by the closed family-style buggy.

RANKING

Rank as an element. Rank or standing represents the value an actor has for the system in which the rank is accorded. Age as well as success in farming, church duties, and leadership are important determinants of rank. Amish youth often line up by age to march into church service, and of the sixteen bishops the five oldest are the most important.

Evaluation of actors and allocation of status-roles as process. The community gives high evaluation to the successful Amish farmer who also demonstrates church leadership. Honor and high standing are accorded to those whose lives exemplify Godliness, humility, and "full fellowship." High rank is accorded those successful farmers whose houses are large enough to hold two hundred persons in church meetings.

Rank by achievement and by ascription is shown by the allocation of the status-role of minister. All baptized members of the congregation participate and any man who receives as many as three votes is entered as a candidate for minister. The bishops place on a table Bibles of similar outward appearance, one for each candidate. A slip of paper is hidden in one Bible. Candidates file past the table and pick a Bible. The one picking the Bible with the paper has been chosen by God to take this great responsibility and honor.

CONTROLLING

Power as an element. Power is the capacity to control others. It has many components which may be classified as authoritative and non-authoritative control. Authority is the right as determined by the members of the social system and built into the status-role to control others, whereas unlegitimized coercion and voluntary influence are nonauthoritative. Influence may rest on personal characteristics, social capital, and many other bases. In the Amish family the husband and father is the chief authority figure, and the ministers, deacons, and bishops exert more control over community affairs related to the church than do ordinary members. Proven wisdom and honesty characterize the Amish influential both in and out of office. Unlegitimized coercion among Amishmen is indeed rare, but vivid memories of the unbelievable coercion practiced upon their forebears are kept alive by oral tradition and by familiarity with the *Martyr's Mirror*, a book which recounts the sect's persecution during the days of the Reformation.

Decision making and its initiation into action as process. Decision making is the process by which the alternatives available to the members are reduced. It can be illustrated by the after-church sessions held to decide what is to be done in the case of outside threat, or to decide what sanctions should be applied to individuals who have violated the norms. In the latter case, the deacon repeats the charge after all unbaptized persons have left. Unanimity of decision concerning the sanction to be applied to the offender is the ideal; with few exceptions it is attained. Majority vote means that the members are acting upon the recommendation of the ministers and deacons who are, it is believed, chosen by divine influence. Often the bishop is slow to arrive at a decision, but once he nods his head in approval, the opinions of the congregation are likely to coalesce in agreement. Thus, "the bishop's nod" has come to be practically synonymous with ultimate decision. The execution or initiation into action follows.

SANCTIONING

Sanction as an element. Sanction may be defined as the rewards and penalties used to attain conformity to ends and norms. The most interesting and powerful sanction among the Amish is negative—the *Meidung* or the practice of shunning. The *Meidung* shuts off the violator from any communication whatsoever with anyone of the congregation—his family, his friends, his neighbors. Persons subjected to it have been known to lose their memories and even to commit suicide.

Application of sanctions as process. After evaluation and decision making have assigned the sanction, amends are usually required in order that the sanction be lifted. The Lord's Supper and full fellowship may be refused the deviant until public repentance and discontinuation of the deviancy is made. Usually the family member who is being shunned must eat alone and remain apart from the rest of the family, but a certain amount of affection, especially from the mother, during the period is inevitable although forbidden. Failure to recant can result in permanent *Meidung* and rejection from the group.

FACILITATING

Facility as an element. A facility is a means used within the system to attain the members' ends. One of the characteristics of the Amish as non-conformists is that facilities of worship and facilities of everyday life are limited. No churches or other intermediary facilities between man and God are permitted and many "worldly" things of the home and farm, of "gay people" or non-Amish, are forbidden.

Utilization of facilities as process. Consistent with the relative unimportance of facilities as articles of worship is the highly institutionalized use of the straight backless long wooden benches which serve as congregational seats and which are moved from home to home as the place of service shifts every fortnight. Likewise they tolerate no improvisation of the Bible or the *Ausbund*, the hymn book, which is claimed to be the oldest unchanged hymnal in use. In farm production the very avoidance of most normal agricultural facilities or equipment has led to ingenious improvising to increase the utility of permitted facilities.

COMPREHENSIVE OR MASTER PROCESSES

Communication. Communication is the process by which information, decisions, and directives pass through the system and by which knowledge is transmitted and sentiment is formed or modified. Such media as the radio, television, and the telephone are taboo. Only farm magazines, religious literature, and newspapers are generally permitted. Amishmen speak a German dialect known as Pennsylvania Dutch, Biblical High German, and English. The High German used in sermons, singing, and reading of religious literature may have a special place in interaction, particularly with God, but intimate interaction among kin, friends, and neighbors is carried on in Pennsylvania Dutch.

Boundary maintenance. Boundary maintenance preserves the solidarity, identity, and interaction pattern within the system. So much of the energy of the Amish goes into this process that it is difficult to single out illustrations. The hypothesis has been advanced that the norms which are most observed and obeyed, and which are insured by the most severe sanctions, are those which protect the Amish social system against the "gay culture." Thus introduction of electricity might bring radio and television. The automobile would expose members to the temptations of the outside world, and the discontinuance of distinctive dress and grooming would render less conspicuous that Amishman who dared dally with worldly ways.

Systemic linkage.[19] This is the process whereby the elements of at least two social systems come to be articulated so that in some ways and on some occasions they may be viewed as a single system. Whereas the processes previously discussed deal chiefly with interaction within a system, systemic linkage relates members of at least two systems. The Old Order Amish attempt to minimize linkages with other organizations but are unable to maintain complete isolation. Compulsory school attendance laws, draft laws in time of war, governmental agricultural programs, marketing transactions, and medical and legal services result in some interaction with the non-Amish and a degree of systemic linkage.

Institutionalization. Through institutionalization human behavior is made predictable and patterned, social systems are given the elements of structure and the processes of function. As each invention or practice is accepted or rejected as a part of Amish life, institutionalization of relationships concerning it takes place. The comparatively static Old Order Amish social system is replete with institutionalized practices; compared with the rapidly changing world which surrounds it, few areas of life are not predictable and patterned. When changes are made, the new practice rapidly becomes patterned. One such contingency arose over the threat of school consolidation. The Amish, who were earlier prohibited by their own norms from voting, began to vote in defense of a self-contained school system, a form of organization evaluated more highly than that of political non-participation. Voting on this one issue is becoming institutionalized.

Socialization. Socialization is the process whereby the social and cultural heritage is transmitted. Amish children play mother, father, farmer and farmer's wife. The only approved occupational role-model of the boy is the farmer, of the girl, the farm wife.

Social control. Social control is the process by which deviancy is counteracted. Most pressure among the Amish toward deviancy is toward the norms of the larger society. For this reason the processes of social control and boundary maintenance tend to merge. There are no police arrests of Amishmen by Amish officers. Controls are built into the system so that the deviant is deprived of "full fellowship" by informal procedure if not through formal *Meidung* or other procedures.

The reader has to this point been introduced to the bare essentials of the concepts of the PAS Model. The elaborations which may occur as that model is used in the following chapters must be explained as the need arises. It is hoped that this introduction will provide the necessary background, so that the reader's attention in the pages to come may not have to be diverted from the content of the theorists whose works are the subject of the remainder of the book.

NOTES

1. Charles P. Loomis, *Social Systems: Essays on Their Persistence and Change* (Princeton, N. J.: D. Van Nostrand, Inc., 1960).

2. *Ibid.*, Essay 1.

3. Social action for Florian Znaniecki stressed conscious performances, "i.e., those in the course of which the agent, the X who acts (whoever he may be), experiences the data included in his performance, and is aware of the changes which he is producing." *Cultural Sciences* (Urbana: University of Illinois Press, 1952), p. 187.

4. Pitirim A. Sorokin, *Society, Culture and Personality: Their Structure and Dynamics—A System of General Sociology* (New York: Harper and Brothers, 1947), p. 40.

5. Talcott Parsons, "The Social System: A General Theory of Action," in *Toward A Unified Theory of Human Behavior*, edited by Roy R. Grinker, (New York: Basic Books, 1956), pp. 55-56. Here Parsons gives Robert R. Sears credit for the term, "double contingency."

6. Pitirim A. Sorokin, *Social and Cultural Dynamics* (Boston: Porter Sargent Publisher, 1957), p. 444.

7. Sorokin has perhaps provided the most comprehensive definition and description of process: "By process is meant any kind of movement, or modification, or transformation, or alteration, or 'evolution,' in brief any change, of a given logical subject in the course of time, whether it be a change in

its place in space or a modification of its quantitative or qualitative aspects." Original in italics. *Social and Cultural Dynamics, op. cit.,* p. 53. Sorokin says, that the study of process must specify the unit involved, the time and spatial relations and the direction. *Ibid.* Various writers have related process to function. Parsons has developed "four functional problems or exigencies" of action systems in general. See "Some Comments on the State of General Theory of Action," *American Sociological Review,* Vol. 18, No. 6, December, 1953, p. 625. Earlier Robert E. Park had delineated three such problems: In "Sociology and the Social Sciences" Robert E. Park and Ernest W. Burgess, (eds.), *Introduction to the Science of Sociology,* (Chicago: University of Chicago Press, 1921), p. 46. From Park's earlier article "Sociology and the Social Sciences; The Group Concept and Social Research," *American Journal of Sociology,* Vol. 27, No. 2 (September 1921), pp. 169-183.

8. Talcott Parsons, *The Social System* (Glencoe, Ill.: The Free Press), 1951, p. 486. See also Wilbert E. Moore, "A Note on the Measurement of Social Change," *Social Science Research Council Items,* Vol. 12, No. 4, December, 1958, pp. 42 and 43 and "A Reconsideration of the Theory of Social Change," *American Sociological Review,* Vol. 25, No. 6, pp. 810 ff.

9. Florian Znaniecki saw the necessity of incorporating the dynamic in sociological analyses and this led him to use the concept, system. In Herbert Blumer, *Critiques of Research in Social Sciences, I—An Appraisal of Thomas and Znaniecki's "The Polish Peasant in Europe and America,"* (New York: Social Science Research Council, 1939), p. 95.

10. George C. Homans, *The Human Group* (New York: Harcourt, Brace and Co., 1950), Chapters 4, 5, and 6.

11. W. Fred Cottrell, *Energy and Society: The Relation Between Energy, Social Change and Economic Development* (New York: McGraw-Hill, 1955).

12. Wilbert E. Moore, *Industrial Relations and the Social Order,* (New York: The Macmillan Company), 1951, p. 75.

13. Pitirim A. Sorokin, *Society, Culture and Personality, op. cit.,* p. 533.

14. For a more complete description, analysis and bibliography see Charles P. Loomis, *Social Systems, op. cit.,* Essay 5.

15. See Charles P. Loomis, *Social Systems, op. cit.,* A special schematic outline is presented in Charles P. Loomis, "Systemic Linkage of El Cerrito," *Rural Sociology,* Vol. 24, No. 1, March, 1959. The senior author, whose conceptualization this is, first presented the rudiments of the construct in "The Nature of Rural Social Systems: A Typological Analysis," Presidential Address for the Rural Sociological Society, 1948. Published in *Sociometry,* Vol. II, No. 3, Aug. 1948. For later usage in writings by the senior author and associates see Charles P. Loomis and J. Allan Beegle, *Rural Social Systems,* (New York: Prentice Hall, 1950), and *Rural Sociology: The Strategy of Change,* (Englewood Cliffs, N. J.: Prentice Hall, 1957).

16. Charles P. Loomis, *Social Systems, op. cit.,* Essays 1 and 5.

17. See Charles P. Loomis, *Ibid., op. cit.,* Essay 5. The best empirical study of the Amish was made by Walter Kollmorgen under the direction of Carl C. Taylor. The investigation was supervised by Charles P. Loomis who lived with an Amish family during part of the field work. See *Culture of a Contemporary Rural Community, the Old Order Amish of Lancaster*

County, Pennsylvania, Rural Life Studies, Washington: U.S.D.A., September, 1942. See also Charles P. Loomis and J. Allan Beegle, *Rural Social Systems, op. cit.,* pp. 11 ff.

18. Robert K. Merton, *Social Theory and Social Structure,* (Glencoe, Ill.: The Free Press, 1957), pp. 60 ff.

19. For the development of the concept, systemic linkage, see Charles P. Loomis, *Social Systems,* op. cit. pp. 53 ff. footnotes, 62-66 and pp. 32 ff. See also Charles P. Loomis and Douglas Ensminger, "Governmental Administration and Informal Local Groups," *Applied Anthropology,* Vol. 1 No. 2, Jan.-March 1942. For recent application of systemic linkage in analysis see Robert C. Hanson, "The Systemic Linkage Hypothesis and Role Consensus Patterns in Hospital Community Relations," *Abstracts of Papers, 56th Annual Meeting of the American Sociological Association,* St. Louis (New York, 1961). Used in conjunction with the other elements and processes of the PAS Model the concept, systemic linkage, has many advantages. As a generic term it may serve to articulate various concepts used in the interrelations of systems. Parallels of meaning are suggested, for example, by the "relationship between the formal and the informal aspects" of organization; the "professional protagonist" who carries on "institutionalized procedural" and "structural disputes" in arbitration, negotiation, mediation, strikes and/or lockouts; "competitive" and "cooperative strategy" involving "*bargaining, co-optation* and *coalition.*" Such varied concepts and approaches used respectively by Amitai Etzione, Robert Dubin (using conflict in the tradition of Herbert Blumer and others) and McEwen and Thompson (see A. Etzione, *Complex Organizations: A Sociological Reader,* New York: Holt, Rinehart and Winston, 1961, pp. 130 ff., 285 ff., p. 177 ff.) might well be submitted to comparative study by the kind of generic common denominator provided by such a concept as systemic linkage. Other studies embodying approaches possessing a common central core of meaning and hence analyzable by a generic concept such as systemic linkage are numerous. The following are examples: the "corruption of authority" as prison guards establish "linkage" with inmates—G. M. Sykes, *Ibid.,* p. 198; *bureaucratization* and *debureaucratization*—S. N. Eisenstadt, *Ibid.,* pp. 268 ff.; the observation that the Communist "party does not merely link itself to the masses, but in a significant sense 'creates' them!"—Philip Selznick, *The Organizational Weapon* (New York: McGraw-Hill, 1952), p. 114; an organization by linking itself to its environment "loses its purity as an abstractly or ideally envisioned entity . . . in a living community; it becomes institutionalized."—Selznick, in Etzione, *op. cit.,* p. 357; "Supplementary organizations" in industrial societies which foster "traffic in favors among business men and between business men and community [which] is a lubricant [providing] on the spot prestige returns"—Peter H. Rossi, *Ibid.,* pp. 304-305; and relations of staff and line—M. Dalton, *Ibid.,* pp. 212 ff. The concept systemic linkage as used on the PAS Model has been given perhaps the greatest formal specificity through the term *bridge* and *articulation point* as applied by Frank Harary and R. Z. Norman in *Graph Theory as a Mathematical Model in Social Science* (Ann Arbor: Institute for Social Research, U. of Michigan, 1955), pp. 8-9.

CHAPTER 2

HOWARD BECKER—
TYPOLOGICAL ANALYST

Howard Becker from the beginning of his sociological career maintained an extraordinarily comprehensive perspective. Few others have used and cited such a breadth of subject matter and drawn upon the conceptual schemes of so many scholars. In his writings few schools of sociological thought were left uncovered and few segments of life did not yield material for his analyses.

Early in his career, while working with Robert E. Park and others at the University of Chicago, he came under the influence of German sociology. His first book-length publication, appearing in 1932, was an "augmented" adaptation of Leopold von Wiese's *Beziehungslehre und Gebildelehre*.[1] After this Becker refused to confine himself to any one school or to the trend within any one country, but drew heavily upon the leading masters of both Europe and the United States. Among others, Becker noted his indebtedness to Toennies, Max Weber, Simmel, Tarde, Durkheim, Wiese, Robert E. Park,[2] and Znaniecki.[3] He also acknowledged influence from W. I. Thomas, Pitirim Sorokin,[4] G. H. Mead, and Everett Hughes.[5]

Never a withdrawn scholar, his erudition savors of his widely varied experiences: in factories as a shop mechanical engineer; in the military, operating in the field where his speciality was intelligence; in governmental and academic administration; and in extensive travel. His writing, with its expressive sparkle, reflects the vigor of participation no less than the love of knowledge. One unusual feature is his interspersing of jaunty headings throughout an otherwise profound and dignified text—the one typical of the gifted conversationalist and master of apt quotation and repartee, the other typical of the man of letters. Thus a penetrating discussion of the origin of capitalism is studded with such headings as "Profiteers as Sinners," "The Protestant Monkey-Wrench," while "High Power Stuff" heads a section on religion.[6]

Some of his earlier criticisms may seem overly harsh today, such as his criticism of positivism, but it must be remembered that at the time they appeared positivism in sociology was itself somewhat dogmatized. His avoidance of positivism has, however, not been coupled with any enchantment with intuitive sociological interpretations. Rather, he favored a quantitative approach, although he was never a statistical sociologist nor did he make extensive use of statistics. "The goal is as precise a statement as possible of functional relations (in the mathematical sense) among constructs."[7] He emphasized the detached point of view, holding prediction as the final objective. He disparaged the particularizing, historical procedures of some writers as well as the normative, judgmental, and prophetic tendencies of others.

This chapter can do no more than present from his voluminous writings the unique, the distinctive, and the most important aspects of his work. Basic to the analytical section of the present chapter is Becker's concept of system and the pertinent supporting concepts.

System analysis. Becker accepted the separation of personality, social, and cultural systems, viewing them as "not only analytically separable but also as mutually irreducible."[8] However, he did not emphasize differentiations which render some concepts applicable only to the personality system and others applicable only to the social and culture systems. Rather, he saw the three systems articulated to each other by social interaction, which he termed more specifically "sociation," including both association and dissociation. Sociation, for Becker, meant *social* interaction, i.e., association and dissociation with others *as others,* or reciprocal interaction. In simple terms, reciprocity means that the individual, in carrying out an action, takes into account the expectancies of others—what others will think of his action or how they will respond to it.

Sociation, with its implication of action, reciprocal interaction, and expectancies, articulates all three systems: cultural, social, and personality. Its conceptual development replaced the taxonomic phase of sociology which was apparent in Becker's earlier work as specified in Wiese-Becker. At that point he wrote, "sociology . . . must deal with interhuman relations without immediate reference to ends, norms, or purposes; it involves a wholly different kind of abstraction" than other studies of culture such as economics.[9] Fifteen years later he had come to regard the formal taxonomic categories as representing lesser phenomena of sociation, the central meaning of which must be sought in value-need components:

Closely related to the increased attention given to value-system analysis was the changed emphasis in the study of sociation. Where once it was thought sufficient merely to classify and rank in order of intensity the various associative and dissociative relations, it became increasingly evident that social interaction of every variety had so large a value-component that very little predictive utility could be attached to researches that ignored it or treated it as secondary . . . Pairs, "sets," and like groupings, for example, could not be adequately analyzed without direct heed to the value-systems in which they were incorporated.[10]

Since the core of sociation is value and need, and since sociation articulates the cultural, social, and personality systems to each other, value and need are embedded in the three mutually irreducible systems. An interweaving of values and needs is the stuff of culture, is defined by culture, and is transmitted throughout the society by the process of sociation between actors whose personalities are constituted by the roles socially assigned them. Although sociation transmits culture it is not the sole determinant of culture; such a position "would amount to complete sociological determinism of cultural *content,* and this in turn to a sociological variety of solipsism." [11]

Becker's emphasis upon process is consistent with the key position accorded sociation, involving as it does, social action. Culture "is not a state or condition only but a process: as in *agriculture* or *horticulture* we mean not the condition of the land but the whole round of the farmer's year, and all that he does in it: 'culture,' then, is what remains of men's past, working on their present, to shape their future." [12] He stated elsewhere that societies take shape only out of the process of social action. "Convenience alone prescribes the use of 'society' as a noun." [13]

Becker's treatment of what he sometimes called plurality patterns and sometimes social systems was influenced mostly by contributions from Wiese and Park. Following Wiese, social relationship or social process became the basic unit. These are summarized in Figure 1, Appendix A. From the common-human social processes (association and/or mixed) emerge social structures, social systems or plurality patterns. These latter were described in terms of two dimensions; namely, their duration and degree of abstractness. In these terms he examined concrete crowds, which are visible but short-lived; abstract crowds, which even if invisible may have long duration; groups, such as the dyad, triad and others; and abstract collectivities, such as the state and church.

Becker employed various devices to illustrate the existence and importance of group structure:

Let's say [an engineer is] building a foot bridge in a public park . . . for people to stand on or pass over . . . while look[ing] at a regatta, boat race, or something. . . . For practical purposes [one can] replace the [people] with sacks of sand, they're just so much weight. He's interested in an aggregate but he's not interested in them as a crowd. . . . However, . . . the engineer does have to take into account certain social considerations. . . . You design a bridge in a public park differently if you're going to have to calculate with bodies of troops who are not appropriately instructed to break step in crossing the bridge . . . or if you get people who are cheering in unison. You've got to design your [bridge or] bleachers differently; otherwise the bridge [may] collapse.[14]

Some parts of the Wiese-Becker volume are Becker's exclusive work. One such section which Becker claimed to have keyed to the lectures and dissertation of Robert E. Park, is entitled "the connection between concrete and abstract crowds":

The abstract crowd is related to the concrete as the molten interior of the earth is to the lava of the active volcano. . . . One type of crowd is a necessary complement of the other; . . . the occurrence of concrete crowds continually reinforces the neuropsychic patterns upon which the abstract crowd is based . . . concrete crowds cannot arise when there is no abstract basis of any kind.[15]

That early work, directed toward an understanding of differences in kinds of pluralities including crowds, anticipated an interest in values which even then may have been dominant but which certainly was destined to become so in the decades to follow:

What is your abstract crowd going to be like? Has [it a] holy value system . . . loyalistic value system, a consequent value system [making it ruthless] or a comfortable value system? [16] [See Figure 1 p. 48.]

In Becker's view, the more abstract a plurality, the greater the importance of ideological influences. "The word abstract is ambiguous, but in the present context it means only great distance from the concrete human being. The crowd is the least abstract, the closest to the human being, of all plurality patterns . . . Groups . . . achieve a fairly high degree of abstractness . . . Abstract collectivities are the most abstract forms of plurality patterns possible." [17]

Becker was usually careful to specify the referent from among the three operationally interrelated but analytically separable systems. He suggested that they be distinguished thus: "By culture we shall mean everything that man has made by hand or tongue; by society, a collection of persons who in interaction constitute an ongoing social system; and by personality, all the consequences of culture and society that when absorbed can be viewed as forming particular specimens of our species." [18] His actual usage of the terms culture and society, as with most other theorists treated in the present volume, suggests however, that he would concur with Levy: the "claim to supreme mana of each of [the] two concepts" now functions in such a manner as to make a rigorous separation difficult. [19]

Since for Becker, culture *is* process and the ongoing social system is a product of process, neither can be static. Novelty, innovation and deviation in society were introduced by Becker through the use of George Herbert Mead's "I," even though the "I" concept for him was a residual category requiring refinements. [20] It is in this context that Becker criticized Parsons' use of habit as "a mechanism" applicable to the personality system. Becker proposed that this usage is inconsistent with most contemporary psychoanalytic theory as well as the work of Kardiner and others on basic personality structure. A "habit as such" defined as a "mechanism" is a circular argument, he contended. Becker would substitute "attitude" for "habit" and would impute to this attitude/ habit the motivating force characteristic of "prime-movers." As attitudes/habits are transmitted through sociation they acquire "heavy normative content" which imperceptibly grades into moral codes and ethical precepts. The usage of "habit" was not trivial for Becker, for his famous continuum of sacred and secular societies is differentiated in large part on "the normative content of some action patterns," [21] and varieties of the "habit" component coincide with gradients of the continuum.

Becker's construct is premised upon systems possessing common characteristics: they display action patterns, are articulated by the process of sociation, reflect the values of the past, accommodate to the needs of the present, and determine in part the needs and values of the future. The key to differentiation and hence to prediction of human behavior lies in the variability of values among systems. The variations represent infinite gradations in respect to abstractable characteristics which at their polar points were designated by Becker as sacred and secular. As this model is juxtaposed against the PAS Model elaborations of Becker's theories will emerge.

ELEMENTS AND ELEMENTAL PROCESSES

KNOWING

"It would be quite proper always to speak of human activity as essentially 'knowing-desiring-norming,' " Becker wrote.[22] The convergence of Becker and other social scientists on this point has been noted elsewhere.[23]

Belief (knowledge) as an element. The cognitive aspect of action, sometimes termed belief by Becker, is found throughout his writings. His treatment of beliefs connected with religion, for example, relates the cognitive component to the total action pattern in the tradition of Weber. Among the many available presentations of the Weberian theory of the origin of modern capitalism one of the most readable is to be found in Becker's *Man in Reciprocity.*[24] The same work develops his interpretation of belief as it relates to the origin of the state. In general he deprecated the search for origins *per se*, indicating that it usually is "a fruitless one, the source of man's non-material culture being buried so far in the debris of the past that there is little hope of recovering them. [Nevertheless, the beliefs from the past embodied in the applied theories of the present] determine the attitudes we ultimately take toward contemporary political institutions." [25] Becker distinguished two theories of the origin of the political state: the theory of external conflict and the theory of internal conflict. The theory of external conflict recognizes the state as being an accretion of many groups which at one time or another were in conflict with each other, but which by subjugation, exploitation, regulation, and absorption developed into a more or less solidary whole—a whole which exhibits for a very long period of time stratification patterns reminiscent of the differential statuses characteristic of the conquest periods.[26] The theory of internal conflict (expounded by Marx and logically based on Hegel) recognizes the state as the weapon fashioned by the rich with which to protect their possessions and to further exploit the poor.[27] Although Becker noted weaknesses as well as strengths in both theories, his purpose in exploring them was to demonstrate that the cognitive antecedants of a society determines to a large degree how its members will perceive reality. He said to his students, "Had you been brought up under the appropriate influences you would now be mouthing Communist slogans with great gusto. You don't like to think that, but from all we know about social psychology, it's true." [28]

Becker's works of course reflect his own cognitive orientation; his scholarship is admirably demonstrated in the volume *Social Thought from Lore to Science* [29] in which he joined Barnes and others in the description of the belief systems of the world. His major contributions in that work cover a wide range of subjects including summaries of sociological thought in such diverse places as Italy, Russia, Latin America, India, and several other countries. Most pertinent to this section is his exposition of social thought as it prevailed in the ancient far East and near East, as well as its prevalence among preliterate peoples. The very extensive treatment is summarized in terms of broad sociological themes in *Man in Reciprocity*. In purposefully over-simplified typological constructs, the religions of ancient China and Egypt are characterized as extreme examples of social monism; [30] those of the Hindu, of the Hebrew, and Greek are presented as dualistic, by which more or less separate recognition is accorded the world of the spirit and that of the flesh with interconnections of various kinds between the two. The religious prescriptions among the ancient Hebrews not only specified man's way of life, but provided him with "the notion that Jehovah likewise observes something like this tribal *ethos*. This ethos we can best label with the Hebrew term *mishpat*, equating it with the *dharma* of the Hindus, the *maat* of the Egyptians, and the *tao* of the Chinese." [31] In the monistic religions the belief concerning the "ought" was inseparably fused with what "was, is, and will be." In the dualistic religions, the belief concerning the "ought" is separate and different from what "is" but possible of attainment in the "will be," a belief which forms part of the tradition of the Western world. [32]

In terms of the PAS Model, although not specified by Becker, cultures dominated by a monistic belief system display a fusion of the elements—ends, norms, and facilities—and of the respective articulating processes. Since the "ought" is synonymous with what "is," restraints for keeping power figures in check are relatively nonexistent. In contrast, cultures dominated by dualistic religious beliefs which perceive the "ought" to be different than that which "is" furnish a climate favorable to government by laws rather than by individuals and one in which the rationality of science can be applied. Social change is clearly more possible in the cultures with dualistic religions than in those with monistic religions, or dualistic religions such as Hinduism which are "the same [in these respects] as that of social monism . . . [in which] social conduct . . . remains rigidly static. Social change does not occur; or if it does . . . at very slow rates . . . and usually is induced only by some terrific shock from without." [33] Becker's own orientation toward belief imperatives bordered on, what in terms of Figure 1, Chapter 1 is called cognitive mapping.

More and more man has been coming to the conviction that knowledge of his society is going to have to be acquired the hard way. . . . If he is to learn very much about the way he *should* behave, he must first find out something about the way he *does* behave. He's got to take account of the split between "ought" and "is." . . . *The discovery of the future, in other words, is man's major enterprise,* and in particular, man's major enterprise in the social world. [34]

Cognitive mapping and validation as process. To understand Becker's work it is necessary to understand something of his epistomological position, his own system of cognitive mapping and validation as it were. As he understood cognition, man's mind is no *tabula raza* automatically written on by the empirical world. For Becker cognition involved interaction between mind and the empirical which he characterized as a relation between "the given [data]" and "the taken [capta]." As Becker put it, "using Kantian language loosely, percepts call forth concepts and concepts call forth percepts in a reciprocal process having no ascertainable beginning nor end." [35]

None of the theorists discussed in the present volume follow the positivistic practice of allowing the facts to speak for themselves, but none are as vocal as Becker was in denouncing positivism and raw empiricism. He said that "even a bad theory, if it enables you to think . . . is a value as a starting point." [36] In the same vein he maintained that "we *construct* the instruments through which we cope, well or poorly as the case may be, with ourselves and the world around us." [37] And again, "man makes his 'laws of nature' he does not merely discover the formulas of a Divine Mathematician." [38]

Becker defined science as *"the systematic statement of the probability of the hypothetical or actual recurrence of phenomena that for the purposes in hand are regarded as identical."* [39] As for defining *social* science, he would maintain that it or any other science "is determined by its general approach, its angle of focus, and not by its specific subject matter." [40] Thus sociology as a discipline has certain characteristics not shared by all disciplines. The sociologist like other scientists "is not interested in the unique *as such.*" [41] He has no need or desire to gather all the facts as advocated by anthropologists of the Boas type. Such endeavors, completely unsuited to scientific prediction "cause anthropologists of this school to bog down in the particularistic swamp and, unaware of their frog's-eye view, to deride all efforts at generalization by croaking, 'Exception'." [42] Given his definition of science as systematic statements of probability, it follows that "the sociologist wishes to be able to say, 'Given such and such circumstances, these consequences will follow.' " [43] History, based upon interest in the particular consequently stands far removed from sociology in objective and method. Becker would insist, however, that the sociologist should deal with history, albeit not idiographically after the manner of some orthodox historians. He regretted that only a few distinguished sociologists had not "fought shy of history," naming Barber, Eliot, Hertzler, MacIver, Meadows, Merton, Nisbet, Teggart, and Sorokin.[44]

Becker considered that one of the sciences most analogous to sociology was geology. Like sociologists, geologists generally validate their theories not by experimentation but by accurate predictions, such as the location of ore deposits. The scientific method leading to such predictions are not dissimilar to that of sociology. Another science similar to sociology is philology in which, Becker maintained, the methods employed for prediction of such occurrences as vowel shifts resemble those of sociology. Of course Becker was in agreement that the sociologist's necessity for handling the subjective poses difficulties which do not confront the geologist or philologist.

. . . if the investigator's constructs are to possess any degree of analytic utility, they must be constructs imputing a certain "state of mind" to the actor which is meaningful in the light of the actor's own personality traits, the elements of the situation, and the over-all value-system (or systems) within which those traits and elements function and from which they derive their ulterior significance.[45]

An article subsection with the expressive heading "Who Says What?" commends the practice of separating the actor's "definitions of the situation" from those of the investigator. Although the investigator "need not be Hesiod in order to understand Hesiod," he "must ultimately say what's what, but he can do so only when he is fully aware of what's what for the subject." [46] (To a similar observation by Weber that one need not be Caesar to understand him Merton retorts that some sociologists think it is not even necessary to *study* Caesar to understand him, an adverse judgment clearly shared by Becker.) In attacking positivism and supporting what he called interpretative sociology Becker made a happy combination of George Herbert Mead's "taking the role of the other" and an approach adapted from Max Weber's *Verstehen:*

Here, reduced to its barest, most obvious terms, is what is meant by interpretation, no more and no less: the interpreter puts himself in the place of the actor as best he can, and the degree to which he views the situation as the actor views it determines his success in predicting the further stages of the conduct.[47]

The constructed type. For Becker "the only way out of formless historicism"[48] was the constructed type, which was his chief methodological tool. The type was extracted from the culture case study which he designated as "a selective description of relatively unique societal phenomena designed to return a tentative answer to a question about the relationships of social actions and norms that, in principal at least, admits of predictive solution."[49]

Becker's constructed types are somewhat similar in concept to Max Weber's ideal types. After 1940, however, he used the term "constructed" for various reasons,[50] one of them being the possibly misleading connotation of the word "ideal." The modifications which he introduced into typological procedures make his product different in important essentials from that of Weber, another factor which indicated the wisdom of a distinctive name for the type. Becker's modifications of typological procedures represent an attempt to bring ideal/constructed types into "line with modern probability logic and with the logic of experiment as well," thus rendering them capable of portraying quantified data.[51] The essential features of the ideal-typological procedure as well as the culture case study procedure were developed early in Becker's professional career.

To begin with, the construction, *on the firm basis of previous culture case study,* of an ideal type wherein the phenomena denoted by the problem are at a *minimum* would yield a heuristic fiction that would establish the necessary conceptual limit in one direction. One point thus fixed by this marginal ideal type, it would then be necessary only to construct another, *also on the firm basis of previous culture case study,* in which the phenomena denoted by the problem are at a *maximum,* and two points of reference would be established.[52]

Almost immediately after the appearance of this statement concerning "these *Grenztypen* or marginal types," Becker in the early thirties launched the establishment of the "isolated sacred" and "accessible secular" types. In the ensuing years, he increased and improved the scale of gradients between the types and explicated their criteria with the result that the current sacred-secular theory embraces practically all facets of sociological thought. Becker stated that predictions from constructed types were never absolute but insisted on their predictive power. "All that the constructive typologist ever says is that 'if and when' certain factors, which have been isolated as significant, recur in configurations which can be regarded as identical for the purposes in hand, then this in turn will probably ensue." [53] The constructed type never includes all particular cases. "If construct and 'reality' exactly correspond, you are in the morass of the particular. . . . The belief that the constructed type is rendered useless because exceptions to it can be found is childishly naive." [54] The constructed type is "designedly a heuristic construct . . . and is never exactly duplicated in any concrete instance." [55]

Although Becker wrote in detail along this line on the construction and use of types,[56] shortly before his death he gave the authors a manuscript on the subject prepared by colleagues at the University of Wisconsin and recommended that it be used as a statement of his thinking for the present chapter. This formulation by Holzner and Rhoads,[57] will, therefore, be briefly summarized here. It begins by indicating what types are not:

1) They are not simple classes based upon such clearcut properties as maleness or femaleness.[58]

2) They are not hypotheses offered as a conditional explanation of the relationships which result in an event and which must be tested before explanation or prediction are demonstrated.[59]

3) They are not variables which, like group cohesion, permit ordering entities on the basis of how much or how little of this they have. (Actually a type is more complex than a variable but under certain conditions may be translated into a variable.)

4) They are not theories. A theory is a deductively related set of laws (verified hypotheses) in which some laws, namely, the axioms imply the others, the theorems. "Theories [like hypotheses] are testable and verifiable; types as types are not." [60]

5) Types are not models if a model is to be defined (as it is by some)[61] as a theory the laws of which have the same logical structure as another theory making for isomorphism. (With less stringent requirements for the concept, model, a type might be considered a model, and Becker did on occasion equate the terms.)[62]

In summary, although types "can be used as tools in the accumulation of substantive knowledge . . . one of the principal uses . . . [being] that they can be built into hypotheses,[63] they are not hypotheses, theories, classes, variables, nor models as above defined.

Becker's constructed type, the sect, determines a given unit's place on the dimensions of a) membership criteria, b) exclusiveness, and c) presence or absence of a professional clergy. In general, types are not merely a list of properties in terms of such dimensions. All the properties of a type are combined into one descriptive whole called a "configuration" in which the properties are related. Much of the objection to the type as a research tool is provoked by the vagueness or lack of specifications of the interrelatedness of the properties in the configuration. However, "much of the utility of types derives from the fact that for comparative purposes it is *not* necessary to specify the relationships of interdependence in the type, i.e. the type remains a configurational concept." [64] However, types need not be constructed so that the interdependence of properties remains unspecified. Although the nature of Becker's constructed and Max Weber's ideal types are determined in large measure by the purpose for which they are used and although for the most part they are of the configurational variety in which the interrelations of properties are not expressed in rigidly prescribed logical or mathematical terms, these types may be compared with "three kinds of type concepts—extreme types, configurational concepts, and determinative systems." [65]

1) Extreme types [66] such as Jung's description of the extrovert and the introvert and other psychological types stress endpoints of scales built out of one or more dimensions. The typologist using this form emphasizes "the placing of the constructed types based upon empirical study at the endpoints of the scale." [67] The continuum type rather than the polar type was Becker's specialty.

2) Configurational concepts are essentially descriptive. Although not systems by rigid rules of logic they may, when applied to concrete instances, have a built-in classifier function such as Weber's types of authority: charismatic, traditional, and rational or legal. Such configurational concepts may specify a "complex," referring to the concrete individual or instance in terms of all relevant classifiers. How such complexes may be articulated with

one another is of considerable importance. In this regard Becker, Holzner, and Rhoads stress the importance of the articulation of the type with the empirical referents. Becker has been particularly emphatic concerning the importance of the empirical:

The way to valid abstract conclusions does not lie through the phantom valley of abstractions: we must walk with our feet on real ground, among real people.[68] . . . I am not at liberty to construct an Airedale with a cast-iron stomach. . . .[69]

Becker maintained that the requirement imposed upon the constructed type that there always be an empirical referent removed it from the realm of such logically consistent but non-empirical constructs which at most can only achieve "objective possibility." His empirical requirement, he maintained, provides the type with the "objective probability" of being matched in reality. This insistence on empirical referents leads to the conclusion that his "configurational concepts are constructed with a view to their possible transformation into determinative systems."[70]

3) Determinative systems[71] differ essentially from configurational concepts. Whereas the former are explanatory the latter are descriptive concepts. Determinative systems are constituted of sets of interrelated propositions that are subject to empirical verification. In the social sciences they are subject to the same forms of logical and empirical proof as in the natural sciences. Through various tests concerning the internal structure of a system it is possible to determine whether or not it is logically entitled to the status of a determinative system. Once their status as determinative systems is legitimized the boundary conditions may be formulated and tested. When this has been accomplished "we may then use [a given] constructed type [thus tested] as components of hypotheses about boundary conditions."[72] Although the use of the constructed type in accordance with rigorous standards of analytical investigation requires that attention be given to its internal structure, it should be kept in mind that "the utility of type constructs for sociology derives largely from the possibility of using configurational type concepts for purposes of comparison as a stage preliminary to their transformation into determinative systems."[73]

Typology was the core of Becker's own cognitive mapping, and in his hands it was an effective tool for analyzing the process of cognitive mapping as it is carried on by members of diverse social systems. The rational and nonrational types as distinguished by Max Weber, Toennies, and others were used freely by Becker.[74] Likewise different types of cognitive mapping are differentiated on his sacred-secular continuum. In several instances he followed Znaniecki in perceiving the social situation to be constituted of "four distinguishable analytic elements: the social object, the social method, the social instrument, and the social response." [75] Situational definitions in terms of these concepts and in terms of the concept of the reflected self as perceived by the actor were used in the analysis of the German youth movement.[76]

As the historical sociological researcher perceives a "tentative answer to a problem initially posed" by culture case study data, he frames an hypothesis which may be universally applicable under specified conditions. Becker propounded ten tests to determine whether the "hypotheses [are] applicable to other cases;" his tests converged at many points with Merton's paradigm for the logic of procedure for functional analysis which interestingly enough is represented by ten categories. One of the convergences specifies the necessity for differentiating the situation as perceived by the participant from its interpretation by the observer.[77] He would emphasize extreme care in determining the level of abstraction at which the hypothesis is cast since its utility coincides with the degree to which it "serves to guide the researcher safely between the extremely idiographic and nomothetic poles." [78] Except for this problem of abstraction to which Becker gives considerably more attention than does Merton, the procedures for scientific investigations enunciated by them are very similar.

FEELING

Becker used the term conation to distinguish what has been called feeling from cognition. He avoided "cathexis" as used by Freud and Parsons, because that term "involves commitments to a body of psychoanalytic theory" of which he was "quite skeptical." For the sake of verbal flexibility he used "desire" as the equivalent of conation, "to conate" and "a conation" seeming to him stiff.[79] The term desire as used by Becker covers not only feeling but some part of achieving as those terms are used in the present volume.

Sentiment as an element. The values which mark the scalar gradients of Becker's continuum (Figure 1) manifest the component of sentiment in varying degrees. The pole representing the extracted sacred is heavily saturated with evaluations charged with sentiment. Piety and awe, for example, accompany high evaluations of the holy; loyalty, allegiance, and patriotism accompany high evaluations of clan, nation, or other identifying membership group; and intimacy, friendship, and good faith prevail when bonds of intimacy are cherished. Strong emotional responses attach to the familiar domestic environment and to the place of birth. Distress, fear, and strain accompany change or the suggestion of change to which there is emotional resistance. The pole representing the extracted secular is not without its charge of sentiments of a nature compatible with the highly evaluated items anchored there. Unlimited expediency often manifested by ultrarapid change would presumably not be emotionally sterile; zeal, emergency-borne exhilaration, fanaticism, and insecurity are situationally indicated. He specified as characteristic of the extreme secular type the values of comfort and thrill, the indulgences of which are hedonistically gratifying and hence emotional. Thus, for Becker both poles of the constructed type exhibit the greatest manifestations of sentiment; the intermediate gradient points on the scale (Figure 1) exhibit lesser or no sentiment.[80] In this respect the Becker types differ from the PAS Model on which sentiment clusters only at the *Gemeinschaft* pole, affective neutrality being characteristic of the *Gesellschaft*. An application of the typology to religious groups distinguishes the cult-sect-denomination-ecclesia stages and types which display religious sentiment decreasingly from cult to ecclesia. The early Methodists, for example, "studying at Oxford . . . [found] the established Church of England . . . too external, too cold, too formal." [81]

Tension management and communication of sentiment as process. In Becker's culture case studies, he reported many instances of tension management and communication of sentiment. Although these terms were not systematically used by Becker he acknowledged the hazards to both the individual and the group of uncontrolled emotions, of tension-fraught situations, and of excessive or meager sentiment expression. He also recorded practices which presumably reduced the hazards for the pertinent individuals and groups. Thus he described the collective responsibility-collective guilt constellation of the ancient Hebrew tribe as one which exerted great social pressure on all members. The sin of one person resulted not only in punishment of that individual by his fellow tribe members, but also, so it was believed, in God's "cosmic boycott" of the whole tribe. But "once a year everybody in the clan got together, unloaded the clan's sins on the head of a goat (the familiar scapegoat) who was chased out into the wilderness, bearing with him all the sins of the tribe as a whole and of all the individual members as well." [82] Among the castes constituting basic Hinduism, relative deprivations were extreme. Contentment with one's lot, however, was maintained by a number of mutually reinforcing beliefs among which was reincarnation. Far from being ambitious to win "divine promotion" into a higher caste, the individual was constrained from envy and discontent by the belief that anything short of complete acquiescence would result in demotion. "You might return as a grasshopper or a goat or something." [83]

The more sacred ceremonials Becker characterized implicitly as communication of sacred sentiment; explicitly as reinforcements of the sacred; the somewhat less sacred ceremonials appear to have a tension managing function. Among them might be numbered "forms such as 'small talk,' avoidance of 'talking shop,' and accepted ways of 'breaking the ice.'" [84] The intense emotional stress under conditions in which comfort and thrill are dominant values is eventually resolved through archaism or futurism. [85] The latter, to be effective, requires a leader of unusual gifts, a circumstance which led Becker to a discussion of the charismatic leader. The "emotionalized obedience" rendered the charismatic leader represents a degree of control over sentiments [86] which may be dangerously diminished upon the death or retirement of the charismatic figure. Becker did not differ essentially from Max Weber and from Parsons as he addressed himself to the institutionalization of cults and the routinization of charisma; his employment of the sacred-secular typology gave a slightly different slant to the explanation, however.

Thus in the German Youth Movement although "traditional and affective nonrationalities became more and more standardized in their modes or expression . . . charismatic leadership, at first highly spontaneous and unpredictable, became increasingly standardized and indeed virtually traditional. [Note here that tradition is not broken.] They expressly rejected the expedient rationality of *Festlegung*, best paraphrased as 'planning toward determinate goals.'" [87] This is the description before Hitler came to power. True "routinization" took place after his rise to power when "membership in the Hitler Youth and the League of German Girls had become compulsory for all young Germans between the ages of ten and eighteen." [88] "The Hitler Youth, at first only a handful of brutally fanatic devotees led by maniacally cunning perverters, successfully transformed their new faith into the dogmas of what is in all essentials a great State Church. . . ." [89] Thereafter, as in the ecclesia, the *charisma* of persons was transposed into the offices and other components of the system. "Youth groups . . . began to be pervaded by a considerable degree of expedient rationality . . . [Figure 1] 'Youth for youth's sake' bodies failed to increase or actually declined . . . centralized and routinized office staffs usually drew personnel from among those who had begun to pass out of the movement . . . needs of the central organization soon came to seem more important than the preservation of traditional forms. . . ." [90]

Becker utilized some interesting devices to achieve as precise a measure as possible of intensity of sacredness. One to be treated later, for example, correlates the degree of sacredness with the extremity of the negative sanction against its violation. Of interest in sentiment communication is a similar correlation: the "amount of sacredness may be defined in important respects by chills of fright, throbs of joy, qualms of nausea, and thrills of ecstasy, as well as by furrowed brows, quickened pulses, contorted mouths, beaming eyes, and rapturous chest heavings." [91] Such a catalog, although appearing in a recent work which is a remarkably compressed bit of writing, is suggestive of the formalism characteristic of the Wiese-Becker period when ordered and detailed comprehensiveness prevailed. (See Figure 1 Appendix A.)

ACHIEVING

End, goal, or objective as an element. Throughout most of Becker's writings the four wishes of W. I. Thomas are used as the basic ends of man. (After 1950 he avoided the term "wish").

As the scientist sees him, man's strivings for his supreme ends are classifiable as search for 1) security, 2) response, 3) recognition and 4) new experience. Moreover, these strivings, classified in this *general* way, are inseparable from the ends themselves; no useful working distinction is possible, and none will hereafter be made. 'End' will signify both. Further, all discussion of ends here presented is on the assumption that they are *always* culturally defined. What men want is what they *learn* to want.[92]

The specific content of each of the four wishes or goals may have almost infinite range. To know where the next meal is coming from qualifies as a security goal no less than "eternal peace in God"; [93] what food is dreamed of by the hungry and what heaven by the weary will be culturally determined. Satisfying affective relations with family members, friends and lovers are the ordinary goals represented by Becker's category, response; culture will likewise determine what ingredients will render them satisfying to the individual actor. Napoleon's arduous pursuit of military fame and the American clubwoman's aspiring to space in the society column are examples which Becker used to illustrate the goal of recognition.[94] (Becker's implication that the goal of recognition parallels the actor's aspiration to rank achievement or maintenance suggests that the same phenomena would appear on the PAS Model under the element rank and the process of actor evaluation.) Becker's fourth goal, the search for new experience, he acknowledged to be more limited in range than the others, but nevertheless to be found in every type of society. The restless adventurer, the scientist, the gourmet, or the fashion faddist exemplify at different levels the search for the new.[95]

Goal attaining and concomitant "latent" activity as process. The means-ends schema is most clearly seen in Becker's adaptation of the four types of action developed by Max Weber. He arranged these on his sacred-secular continuum and called them traditional nonrationality, sanctioned rationality, expedient rationality, and affective nonrationality. (Figure 1) As the process oriented typologist, Becker was appropriately interested in these goal categories only to the extent that the social action involved in their pursuit might be classified as predictive criteria especially as such criteria might be related to constructed types. Unfortunately,

Few if any social actions are classifiable with reference to any single end. . . . The most that can be said, where concrete instances of end-seeking activity are concerned, is that greater emphasis is laid on one end as over against another. *If, in a given context,* a high proportion of social actions can be successfully predicted by directing attention toward demonstrable concentration by the actors upon certain ends, to the relative neglect by those same actors of other ends, the purpose of the classification has been achieved.[96]

A high proportion of the social action in sacred societies is devoted to security, response, and recognition goals, with action directed at security probably predominating. In such a society the activities pursued in earning a living are traditional and non-rational. "Apprenticeship" in learning the skills requires long years of training of the young by the old. The extended personal contact during the training period bequeaths to the young not only the crafts and skills but a constellation of values and action patterns which impinge on all other aspects of life. The fields, the live-stock, and the methods by which they are exploited are not viewed as impersonal means but as possessing a sacred identity of their own. As Becker remarked, " 'the old home-stead' is not simply so-and-so many acres, for the reason, among others, that 'the old oaken bucket' is not simply a wooden pail." [97] To depart from tradition in respect to any action connected with them would be as desecrating as the secular handling of any sacred object. Specialization of task is slight, and each actor tends to be a jack-of-all trades.

Activities pursuant to the second goal important to the sacred society, those directed at response, are again nonrational and traditional. They are clearly not classifiable as exclusively directed toward response, but suffuse other goals. Isolated and inaccessible, the sacred society is marked by intense response among its members, each act being particularistic and unique. The importance of all the fused activities which accomplish the goal of response is indicated by kin nomenclature. "Some dwellers in folk [proverbial] societies [Figure 1] have as many as three hundred ways of labeling their various relatives." [98] Activities directed at achieving recognition are likewise nonrational and traditional. The ascribed characteristics of sex, age, and family are greater determinants of the recognition accorded an actor than are his specific activities engaged in for that purpose.

Societies qualifying for placement near the secular pole pursue the ends of new experience, recognition, and response.[99] Although Becker omitted security as a goal of this society type (not actually denying its existence of course, but revealing by its omission the relatively greater importance of the other three ends), he described the activities which comprise earning a living. He characterized them as competitive, highly specialized, technical, and dependent upon the written word for skill transmission. Economic activity is not integrated with other action patterns and consequently the latter may remain the same even though the action patterns involved in economic pursuits undergo drastic change; or the reversal of this shift may be true. New experiences invited by the typical actor of the polar secular society include contact with strangers, particularly exotic strangers; interaction with cosmopolites; new clothes, new friends, new marital partners. The activities pursuant to the end of new experience incidentally provide fulfillment of the goal of recognition, for since the new is valued, he who achieves it is correspondingly elevated. Social action pursuant to the goal of response is directed toward kin "to an everdwindling degree in secularizing societies; the rapid shrinking of kinship vocabularies is a consequence." [100] The nuclear family plays a necessarily greater part in response achievement, because there is little stability among other groups from whom satisfying response could come. Neighborhoods change, friends move, families live in a succession of places.

Becker saw few social acts as being exclusively directed toward specific ends; accordingly there are frequent examples in his works of what is called "latent" activity above in Chapter 1. "Latent activity" is presaged in a chapter heading: "Economic Institutions Aren't Economically Determined," and is revealed therein, along with manifest activity (Chapter 1, above), in dramatic form. Interpreting a scene from Malinowski's *The Argonauts of the Western Pacific,* Becker described activity manifestly directed toward trade.

Queer armlets carved out of mussel shell are being passed back and forth, and around the circle in another direction long necklaces made of discs of spondylus shell . . . travel from hand to hand. As you investigate more closely . . . you discover that the swapping is apparently not governed by "value received" . . . you find that what is actually at work here is nothing more nor less than considerations of prestige. The man who is friendly, [a] . . . wise . . . successful fisherman . . . skillful with his hands or voice may be given a great many *kula* gifts, and his prestige is thereby enhanced.[101]

Insofar as the actors consider the activity as yielding "value received," it has been in part "latent" as that term is here used. The oft-interpreted Calvinistic creed as it relates to economic institutions (in the tradition of Max Weber) was offered by Becker with characteristic verve.

It might be thought that such a creed would naturally predispose people to lie back on their oars. . . . If you're saved, why you're saved . . . but . . . the Calvinist has to have the assurance of salvation . . . to *know* that he is saved. . . . How do you get more than inward assurance? You naturally expect to show "the outward signs of inward grace." . . . From . . . this it follows . . . that the Calvinist will automatically save a great deal . . . invest his surplus . . . so they waxed fat and prospered exceedingly.[102]

Insofar as their prosperous condition assured the Calvinists that they were among the chosen, the activity directed toward this attainment was in part "latent."

NORMING

Of the "knowing-desiring-norming" triad, which Becker viewed as constituting the essentials of human activity, there are obvious parallels between the first two and the structural-functional categories knowing, feeling, and achieving of the PAS Model. An even greater convergence occurs on the third of his triad, norming, with the similarly designated category on the PAS Model. Norming, a term invented and developed by Becker,[103] is intimately connected with evaluation which he defined as "choice between norms, which necessarily involves symbolic interaction." [104] The distinction between values, which for Becker were always objects, and norms is a difference in level of abstraction.[105] "The range of values is far wider than those issuing in actual conduct," the latter always representing normative judgments in which more than one actor is involved. Apart from the abstractions of the typological level in which the use of the abstract "value" is appropriate, on the human level, "it would be possible to handle the issues involved in such a way as to require frequent use of the term 'norms.' "[106]

Norm as an element. The sacred-secular continuum is Becker's abstract representation of human activity which he saw as constituted by the knowing-desiring-norming triad; of the triad components it is the norming-evaluating activity which is uniquely human and which is the core of the sacred-secular model.[107] Beginning with the abstractions which designate the two poles and give the model its name,[108] there are the *sacred* and *secular,* terms which do not represent values in themselves but rather "designate certain kinds of orientation . . . toward values."[109] The construction line connecting the polar types represents the "reluctance and readiness to accept or initiate social change"[110] with greatest reluctance (as measured by willingness to sacrifice human life) being located at the sacred pole and greatest readiness to accept or initiate change (as measured by the same criterion) at the secular pole. The model would now look like this:

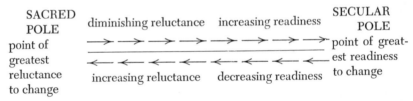

SACRED POLE   diminishing reluctance   increasing readiness   SECULAR POLE

point of greatest reluctance to change   increasing reluctance   decreasing readiness   point of greatest readiness to change

Values for which martyrdom is most readily exacted, or for the violations of which death to the violator is most often demanded, are those belonging at the sacred pole. Becker offered as most capable of commanding martyrdom or the death penalty the *holy* values (those imputed to the supernatural) and *loyalistic* values, those imputed to allegiance, patriotism, and identification with "race, class, faction, party, or what not."[111] He believed that throughout history the holy has been somewhat stronger in this respect than the loyalistic and for this reason he placed from left to right on the continuum the value *holy* followed by that of *loyalistic* as representing values that are most highly resistant to change and therefore sacred.

Next among the values that do not yield readily to change are the bonds of intimacy. The ties between family members, friends, mates, and other close affective ties are represented in the value termed *intimacy*, which by its resistance to change and the sacrificial zeal it evokes is rendered sacred.

Intimacy is followed on the scale by the *moralistic* by which Becker meant "enjoined or forbidden types of conduct specifically distinguishable from the total personalities of those engaged therein." [112] Piecemeal parts of behavior, highly condoned or highly censured and considered to be more compelling than fitting behavior, but less than holy or loyalistic, and upon occasion having life-death power, is what constitutes the moralistic.

Of considerably less intensity is what Becker termed the *fittingly sacred:* good form-bad form, decent-vulgar, and the like, arousing not indignation but at the most contempt, but nevertheless possessing a high degree of reluctance to change and therefore somewhat sacred in nature. Of even less intensity is the value of *appropriateness* which is not particularly resistant to change and the violations of which are not very seriously regarded. At this point in the continuum "the shift to the secular is close at hand." [113] The model would now look like this: [114]

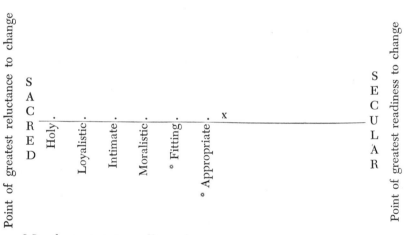

* See these categories on Figure 1.

An overall aspect of sacred conduct applicable to all the above values designated on the continuum is the ceremonial (considered in Chapter 1 as communication of sentiment). Becker's term ceremonial is differentiated from the ritual which he reserved for the holy ceremonial. He also differentiated it from the commemorative which, as a part of the ceremonial, exerts a powerful socializing influence as well as a significant influence on the perpetuations of evaluations. The values designated as sacred can be shown to be reinforced thus, with the left part of the brackets indicating points of greatest intensity.

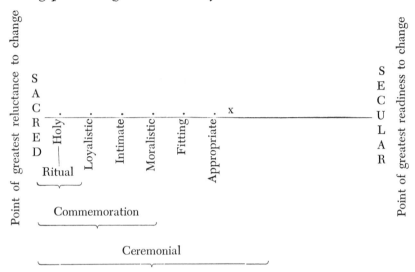

The first value appearing on the secular scale was termed by Becker the *pursuant*. Change, as predictable in light of this value, "is viewed as both possible and desirable" [115] insofar as it is congruent with important abstract principles which are conceived as being sufficiently broad to be applicable by interpretation to a wide range of circumstances. Ideally, the accepted principle is held as unalterable and the proposed innovation is adopted or rejected by its compatability with or pursuance of the principle. Actually, the principle is often manipulated by interpretation so that it will seem to support the innovation. If such manipulations result in innovations which are too incongruous with the principle, one of two results is probable: values pursuant to the principle will be reaffirmed by a reversion to a more sacred representation or they will be abandoned for limited expediency.

Consequent or *unlimited expediency* is the next value cluster on the secular part of the scale. [116] Although there is no inherent contradiction between action in accordance with expediency and action pursuant to a principle, [117] the likelihood is remote that unlimited expediency will always conform to *a priori* principles.[118] The values represented by consequent expediency permit the achievement of ends by any available means so long as they are not regarded as self-defeating.[119] As both ends and means become completely unprincipled, or at least not systematically limited by the principle to any appreciable degree, the final stage of secularity is reached.

Comfort and finally *thrill* are extreme secular values. Ends that yield comfort and thrill, achieved by means that are comfortable and thrilling result in a fusion of means-ends characterized by an uncritical acceptance of and desire for the new experience. So transitory are values at this stage that they scarcely represent a "system." The values of the comfortable and thrilling at their zenith, unlike those marking the foregoing part of the secular scale, share with the sacred values the ability to exact forfeiture of life for their maintenance. This, coupled with their instability, imparts a full-circle aspect to the continuum. Both the extreme sacred and the extreme secular, although literally poles apart as concerns the reluctance and readiness to change, exhibit the "extinction" criterion, aspects of the ceremonial, and the concrete and particularistic, all of which except readiness to change are absent from other secular values. The model would now look like this:

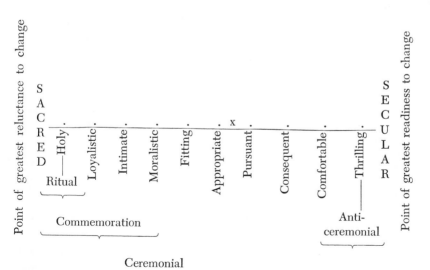

This, then, is the core of Becker's sacred-secular value scale. It represents a wider range in its entirety and a purer concentration in its parts than is ever represented by the empirical value judgments and choices of individuals and groups. In this respect Becker was careful to reiterate that all groups exhibit commitments to values which ideally fall at different points on the scale. There is no society which is so sacred that it does not have some secular attributes, and no society so secular that aspects of the sacred are not observable. The articulation of the values was called evaluation by Becker in very much the same way that articulation of norm is termed evaluation on the PAS Model.[120]

Evaluation as a process.[121] Societies which subscribe to values represented by the abstractions holy, loyalistic, and intimate and thereby are the most sacred of societies voice their values in sayings or proverbs.[122] The proverbs *in toto* often express meanings that are inconsistent. One bit of wisdom is applicable to one situation; another "truth" is applicable to another, although completely contradictory to the one just uttered. Each separate situation of life is capable of evoking a severely limited number of modes of behavior which yield or have yielded in the past, to an evaluative process, and are thereby rendered amenable to a particularistic judgment unique to that situation. "Proverbs are seldom if ever arranged in such a way as to constitute a creed or a coherent ideology. . . . [They] are likely to be implicit in content and connection, primarily uncodified, and almost always accrete"[123] (initially separate, but finally fused into an inseparable whole).

With few if any *generalized* rules of behavior, the *proverbial* society (Figure 1 p. 48) as it was aptly designated by Becker, has little wherewithal for adapting to the new.[124] Nurtured solely by tradition, it values the old for the sake of the old. Its modes of evaluation are traditional and nonrational. The traditional and nonrational nature of evaluations characteristic of the proverbial society are illustrated by Becker's Hebridean Scottish Sacred Society of 1800 or thereabouts.

. . . the Hebrideans are Presbyterians. But though they are Presbyterian and though our friend Donald is an elder of the church and hence has a very responsible position, he still is a pagan in the sense that he firmly believes in the wee folk, in the fairy people. . . . Along with such animism you also find some folk animatism or dynamism ... the ashes from burnt-out fires at certain places must be very carefully avoided by the unmarried young women because of the fact that these ashes blown about freely by gusts of wind may bring on pregnancy. . . . Christianity has nevertheless made a deep mark. It is indeed a dull elder of the Presbyterian church who doesn't know his Bible inside out, even though he has got most of his knowledge by word of mouth and not by reading.

. . . Just over the hill, a little distance away . . . are other people with a slightly different dialect, with a slightly different way of celebrating Pentecost or Whitsuntide, and who as a consequence are in many respects quite inferior. The farther you get away from home base, the more and more strange does the out-group become, until finally, as in the case of the Greeks. . . . Stranger and enemy [are] the same. . . .

We have seen that the inhabitants of these islands, with their feuds, with their blood-thirsty customs of premeditated revenge, with their primitive diet, with their crude clothing, with their simple plows and like tools, were a folk very much like the inhabitants of the same islands in pre-Roman times . . . [and this] in areas inhabited by Mac-Leods and MacLeans and MacFarlanes and all the rest of the kilted crew [where] you found conduct that according to our present ideas was savage, primitive, barbaric, outlandish, yes—and kindly as well.[125]

Proverbial societies are not alone in dependency on tradition as the mode of evaluation. Those societies primarily subscribing to the values of intimacy and moralism (although the types of values held are never unmixed as Becker frequently warned) also are highly traditional. Their application of the traditional mode of evaluation differs significantly from that employed by proverbial societies. The items evaluated highly are codified, are cast into creeds, are reduced to catechisms, and are explicitly stated in injunctions. Behavior for countless situations is prescribed; hence they are named *prescriptive* societies. (Figure 1 p. 48). He viewed their codified orderliness as representing the first step toward deductive systematization. There are no priorities among the prescriptions. Each is equally sacred and inviolable. As wholes and in respect to their parts, they are viewed as unalterable. With the semblance of systemization has come the semblance of rationality. Good defenses can be made for the prescriptions, albeit many of the reasons for their validity are

FIGURE 1

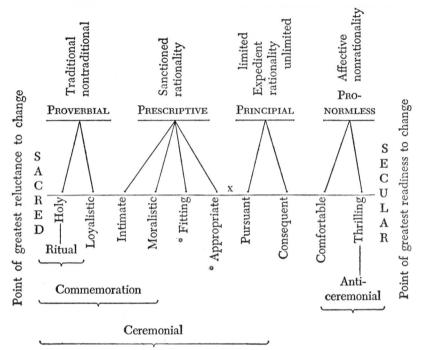

* The categories fitting and appropriate were telescoped into the category, conventional, in the definition of "Sacred Society" for the *UNESCO Social Science Dictionary.*

ex post facto justifications rather than *a priori* reasons. "Concisely, proverbial formulations are implicit, uncodified, unintentionally accrete, and traditionally nonrational; prescriptive formulations are explicit, codified, in some degree intentionally accrete, and at least formally rational or even apparently deductive." [126] Examples of evaluations cast in the prescribed mode are "sets of prescriptive evaluations such as the Eightfold Path, the Torah, the Code of Justinian, the Apostles' Creed. . . ." [127] The nonrational traditionalism of the proverbial society to a large extent prevents even the consideration of new issues. The somewhat more rational traditionalism of the prescriptive society (the sanctioned rational) at least examines the new in light of the prescriptions, and although much is rejected by virtue of incongruence with the prescriptions, the door to change has been opened, and the resistance to it modified. Traditionalism tempered by rationality is revealed in Becker's sketch of a German Sacred Society *circa* 1800:

Marriage was an excellent thing; "it is not good for man to live alone." Hadn't Saint Paul said, "It is better to marry than to burn?" H'm, it wasn't as bad as that—sounded almost like Schopenhauer, that *Hagestolz,* that disquieting cynic! Nobody knew much about him, and he had few readers—good, good. Luther was a heartier fellow; he believed that marriage was necessary and right, and he practiced what he preached. . . . Luther stuck pretty close to the customs, in spite of some of the things his followers did. Hadn't he said that "God Almighty hath made our princes mad, but mad or sane, they must reign"? The sermon in Horb last Sunday was just what was needed, for although everything seemed to be quiet one could never tell what notions might get into people's heads. It was a good text, too: "The powers that be ordained of God, and whoso resisteth the power, receiveth unto himself damnation." That was the pure doctrine; something ought to be done about those wild-eyed Silesian sectarians who were talking about the end of the world and the community of goods. [Here the schoolmaster interrupted his reflections to chat with the peasant Goodman Baumann who is telling him:]

"The three-field system was good enough for father and it's good enough for me; all these new fancy crops and planting-times will lead to no good. . . ."

"Well, that may be," rejoined the schoolmaster, "but they're talking about a railroad all the way from Kehl to Stuttgart. . . . Maybe you could sell your crops and livestock to an honest German if you could send them farther than Horb."

"Bosh! I mean—saving your respected presence, sir—we'll only get smoke and dirt and squashed geese and a kettle of travelling scum. Here we have lived for many generations, and we want to be let alone. Let the Britishers have their railways and steamboats and new fangled farming. They're a gadabout people, anyway. When they fought the French, where would they have been without the Germans?" [128]

Lest the sanctioned rational [129] seem to savor of remote and by-gone days, Becker pointed out that from "the Russian illustration it is plain that prescribed societies must not be thought of as being of interest to antiquarians only." [130]

Considerably greater modifications in respect to change occur among *principial* societies, (Figure 1) the least secular of the secular societies, in which, as the name denotes, evaluations are cast in terms of general broad principles.[131] In contrast to proverbs and prescriptions which "are so concrete that they are tightly bound to their immediate manifestations in conduct," [132] principles are sufficiently abstract that their application to a wide range of conduct is feasible without violation of the principle, which is still viewed as sacred in that the values it embodies are unalterable. In actual practice, however, the principle may be so modified by amendment, or it may initially be cast at such a high level of abstraction that behavior said to be condoned by the principle bears little relation to the evaluation it purports to uphold. If the principle and the proposed innovation are actually consistent, the abstraction still may not be understood by the rank and file of society. In order that it be a guide to actual conduct, then, either the principle must change by reverting to a less abstract or more prescriptive formulation, or the behavior (and, of course, the values by which it is determined) must change in accordance with the non-controlling principle which so meagerly represents the sacred values. "When prescriptive evaluation gives ground to the principial variety, expedient rationality has begun to operate. However, it has only begun, for it is still limited by persisting reluctance to change the core of the abstract principle or principles. . . . In such societies, there must always be something to which rationality can be pursuant." [133] In addition to the American "natural rights" principle, Becker cited among other examples that of the British limited constitutional monarchy "in which the sovereign is not much more than 'a human flag.' " [134]

How effectively principle had become dominant over prescription was shown by the abdication of Edward VIII, forced by a mere commoner, Stanley Baldwin. Protests there were, issuing from adherents of both proverbial and prescriptive conceptions, plus other protests deriving from a good deal of comfortable and even thrilling nonrationality, but the pursuantly secular won out. [See Figure 1 p. 48.]

In spite of this, however, any observer thinking that the sacred core of the monarchical principle had been eliminated would be in serious error. It triumphantly survived the abdication of the sovereign who had now become the feckless Duke of Windsor, to find a focus in devotion to a legitimate and earnest successor, George VI, and at his death there resounded the shout, "The King is dead—long live the Queen." [135]

Becker generalized from the British example that "normlessness does not necessarily follow drastic innovations if the principial society within which they occur is possessed of principles abstractly sacred manifested in changes concretely secular." [136]

Relative normlessness *does* follow in the wake of some drastic innovations, however, and to describe this kind of society Becker originally used the term "normless." Such a society could be expected to be in a constant state of flux and not to be perceptibly controlled by enunciated principle, prescription or proverb. In recognition of the inevitable functioning of *some* norms he later adopted the term "*pronormless* societies—that is, . . . societies having value systems *favoring* an extremely free-and-easy state of affairs, and that are therefore *pro*normless in this sense." [137] The mode of evaluation in the pronormless society (Figure 1 p. 48) resembles that employed by the proverbial society in that it tends to be nonrational. Large numbers of actors in such a society are dedicated to extremely emotional ends (comfort and thrill being the dominant values); the means of achieving are fused with ends and are similarly emotional. The result is a mode of evaluation which is "strikingly irrational, which is to say *counter-rational*, rather than merely nonrational." [138] Evaluations fraught with self-indulgence are common whether it be the "I like it because I like it, and what's to stop me?" variety, or that represented by "The Roman slogan 'Bread and the Circus.'" [139] Pursuits saturated in the thrilling are highly valued by large groups who seek "Gratifications . . . from rabid spectatoritis," or by the lone actor who commits murder "for the hell of it." In the pursuit of the new for its sensational value, proverbial, prescriptive, and principial limits are flouted and individual whim is given a higher priority than controlling norm. Such a tendency, according to Becker, can easily be overstated, however, for "needs and their correlative values are never utterly discrete, never wholly 'private,' never completely at random, never without functioning system." [140] Nonetheless in the pronormless society the articulation of values to social actions result in the extinction of life. As the glutton demonstrates, even a craving for the comfortable when gratified unlimitedly, represents a higher evaluation upon particular comforts than upon longevity. The evaluations given high priority by the "flame-divers," the "hell-drivers," and drug addicts, examples used by Becker, demonstrate a similar evaluative choice among the thrill-seekers, although these last represent only a small part of a population. The desire to watch such spectacles, although not jeopardizing the life of the spectator, nevertheless Becker saw as destructive of many parts of the value system with resultant instability; "avid delight in gladiatorial spectacles together with craving for increase in their cruelty, for example, are not usually regarded as having fostered the coherence of Roman society." [141] Ceremonial which so adequately reinforces all of the sacred values and the least secular of secular values, is also employed to reinforce the thrilling, but Becker sees it as a bogus ceremonial or anti-ceremonial.

. . . the "ceremonial" that may accompany a strip-teaser's conduct, for instance is not ceremonial *per se,* for it may be freely changed "to give the bald-headed row a bigger bang." So likewise with ceremonial in some "luxury" restaurants; the waiters may be garbed as Arabs during one season and as Robin Hood yeomen the next. Hence, "ceremonial" may be essentially anti-ceremonial if it has no proverbial, prescriptive, or principial halo." [142]

Abstractions from the sacred or even from the less secular values "have become so attenuated that they have virtually disappeared," and hence contribute very little to the guiding norms with high priority. "The concrete again is dominant—*but* as non-traditional or even anti-traditional." [143] The above model showing the value abstractions may now have an over-lay (Figure 1) which will show in relation to those values the societal types which ideally exhibit those values as well as the modes of evaluation which prevail in each societal type.

Becker's extracted values and typed societies would be incompletely presented without mention of his "situational criteria," which in a sense seek to aid the investigator in the ultimate question of "whence values." Becker posited that *isolation* and *accessibility,* attributes which obviously relate to possibility of change, display vicinal, social, and mental aspects. Vicinal isolation signifies "physical absence of or separation from other societies in the vicinity . . . of any society so situated." [144] For Becker this was a situational criterion; it is represented on the PAS Model by one of the conditions of social action, namely territoriality where it will be appropriately elaborated. Insofar as it was not a condition (i.e., controllable by humans) it was amenable to change by technology, the pertinent aspects of which will be elaborated under facilities and their utilization. Social isolation differs from vicinal isolation as evidenced by "the fact that [because] other societies can easily be reached does not mean that there will be an effort to reach them. . . . At bottom social isolation roots in failure, for whatever reason, of effective communication." [145] The present chapter, insofar as it reports lack of communication is partially devoted to social isolation. Mental isolation for Becker, was in some respects similar to social isolation. Nonetheless, there may exist between two societies which are by no means socially isolated from each other a mental isolation "kept intense if not intact by more or less clearly outlined ideas." [146] Under boundary maintenance as a master process this kind of isolation is treated as are also aspects of social isolation. Suffice it to say here, then, that Becker's "situational criteria" made substantial contributions to his typing of societies, especially in reference to the basic question that might be stated thus: "Granted that a proverbial society (or any other type) tends, as it evaluates, to attach high priority to certain beliefs, sentiments, ends, norms, etc. and granted that it tends to use predictable modes of evaluation, what are the factors which cause this tendency? What imparts the value to the value?" A mere summary of his extracted societal types with their most frequently dominant criteria of isolation-accessibility follows: [147]

Proverbial: *vicinal isolation* common; when absent is compensated for by social and mental isolation
social isolation common; often intensified by occasional contacts with others
mental isolation common; intensified by prevalence of other two types of isolation

Prescriptive: *vicinal isolation* common; tending to stem from paucity of culture, especially its technological aspects
vicinal accessibility when present not necessarily destructive to value system, at least for a long time

social isolation common; often deriving from such factors as lack of common language, offensively different personal habits, and the like

mental isolation common; ideological conflict common

Principial: *vicinal accessibility* common
social accessibility common
mental accessibility common

Pronormless: *vicinal accessibility* extremely high
social accessibility high
mental accessibility high, with tolerance reflecting indifference to principle

Societal types extracted from values displayed by many societies are among the most ambitious of Becker's typologies; however, it would be a mistake to leave the impression that type extractions are limited to societies. Becker's typing of religious groups as the cult, sect, denomination, and ecclesia exemplifies one of his better known institutional type constructs.[148] Each type (exemplified by the Buchman cult, the Jehovah's Witnesses sect, the Methodist denomination, and the Episcopal church respectively) is extracted from actual religious bodies as they manifest their distinguishing characteristics in structure; hence it was called by Becker a structural-institutional typology. The structural abstractions were made at a lower level than were the value abstractions marking gradient points on the sacred-secular continuum (consistent with his less universalistic content of religious phenomena which is restricted to "associational patterns of religious persons in Western civilization").[149] It could easily be fitted into the more general abstractions of the sacred-secular continuum, however, as may be evident from the following partial resumé of sect-ecclesia characteristics.[150]

SECT	ECCLESIA
Withdraws from rest of world; is in opposition to it	Supportive of existing social, political, and economic institutions; closely identified with *status quo*
Membership policies are exclusive, elective	Membership policies are inclusive

SECT	ECCLESIA
Radicalism of a sort	Eminently conservative
Relatively untrained leaders	Erudite, well trained religious functionaries
Non-compromising	Adaptive to ethic of modern world
Little ecclesiastical hierarchy	Elaborate ecclesiastical hierarchy
Non-resistance evaluated highly	Militancy to same degree as is greater society
Lower class adherents	Middle and upper class adherents

Becker termed the denomination "the sect grown old," and as such at least for the observer it is more secular than the sect, more sacred than the ecclesia. High secularization of the ecclesia tends to promote the growth of cults composed of dissenters within the ecclesia which under propitious circumstances develop into schismatic sects most of which begin the long developmental road to the ecclesiastic state (although quite unwittingly) but few of which arrive.

Such circuitous development from cult to sect, to denomination, to ecclesia, and back to cult has its parallel in societal sacralizations which are insufficiently represented in the above presentation; for it should not be erroneously implied that changed values move only from left to right on the sacred-secular continuum. Becker was careful to point out that among societies the reverse direction is common.

Moreover, secularization in well-marked form is not only evident in the remoter record but, in addition, has been repeatedly followed by its reverse, sacralization. At many times and places we encounter a "normative reaction to normlessness" that not only puts a stop to ultra rapid secularization but also introduces and/or reinstates reluctances to change that soon take on, or attempt to take on, the features of stabilizing value-systems.[151]

Examples of sacralization may be found in the Protestant Reformation, the Catholic Counter-Reformation, the Fascist and Nazi seizures of power, various revivals of the Ku Klux Klan, and the founding of Methodism;—historical events employed by Becker to illustrate his theme.

DIVIDING THE FUNCTIONS

Status-role incorporating both element and process. Becker's use of the concept role appears to give greater attention to the personality system than to the social system. Much of his use of the concept involved the process of socialization. In the tradition of George Herbert Mead he portrayed the child as playing postman, father, puppy dog, and other characters,[152] and maintained that the actor who learns to play adequately any one position on the baseball team is the one who has successfully taken "the role of the other" in regard to each other positional player on the team.[153] Although he used the idea of role in the development of seven personality types,[154] the resulting typological abstractions are on a more generalized level than those commonly employed to describe status-role as it relates to division of function. However, he occasionally related the personality type to the kind of status-role with which it might be compatible (e.g. personality types congruous with different kinds of religious leaders)[155] and clearly stressed the impact of group membership upon the personality or self in much the same manner as does Sorokin. The impact of a status-role within an economic organization displaying a specialized division of labor induces segmental conduct (the segmental being one of his personality types):

. . . you develop a special technical vocabulary; moreover, you live in a little world apart, and you develop ethical standards that apply on weekdays, but that don't apply on Sundays. You regularly fulfill your due quota of tasks, and as long as you are "a faithful employee" in terms of the standard expectations of your place of employment, no further questions are asked. In other words, your private life may be what it will as long as you meet the expectations of your place of employment, and the consequence of this frequently is that we have doubly, or triply, quadruply, or even more minutely divided personalities that attempt in one way or another to find substitutes for gratifications and channels of expression that in a sacred society would be automatically provided.[156]

The pronormless type of society, in Becker's view, in part has its genesis in specialized status-roles.

Status-role also has basic implications for societal integration. The "of one-piece" character of the sacred society offers a limited number of roles to its members, but most members can play practically the whole range of those available. Everyone is doing virtually the same thing as everyone else thereby reinforcing societal integration. The highly specialized society offers an almost unlimited number of roles to its members, but most members can play a very few of them; if an actor performs his specialty, he has little time to play at or learn about other roles. Integration in such a society comes about through the meshings and interlinkings by which each specialty (and likewise, each incumbent) teams up with others to create a whole product from their varied processes.

The status-role of stranger appears frequently in Becker's writing. Two ideal types of stranger are constructed, the *secular stranger*, "the man habituated to abstraction . . . equally at home everywhere—but . . . not very much at home anywhere," [157] and the *sacred stranger* "habituated to nothing but the concrete and personal." [158] Keyed as it is to similarly typed societies, the typology permits a four-way comparison: the sacred stranger to both the sacred and secular society, and the secular stranger to both the sacred and secular society. To a considerable extent the early work in the analysis of the processes of secularization involved these status-role types, and his situational criteria of accessibility and isolation were in part specified by characteristic sociation patterns with the stranger.

The pairs and sets, characteristic of his earlier work by their very nature specify roles for the actors. Thus most social relations are a mixture of the processes of association and dissociation (Figure 1, Appendix A) and these are divided into those constituting the pair (which by definition would involve primary relations), and into those which constitute the set (which by definition would involve secondary relations since three or more persons are necessarily involved.) [159] Similarly role is implicit in associative processes (advance, adjustment, accordance, and amalgamation) and in dissociative processes (competition, contravention, and conflict). [160] (Figure 1, Appendix A). Here as elsewhere the structural and functional aspects are rarely differentiated explicitly, and here as elsewhere the functional aspects are emphasized almost to the exclusion of the structural which is occasionally represented, however, by implication only.

He at no point gave much attention to the typical bureaucratic arrangements for division of labor, although he noted the church hierarchy: "All of these churches have well-developed administrative staffs, arranged in ranks and grades so that you pass on down from higher to lower officials—let us say, from patriarchs and metropolitans or from popes and cardinals or from archbishops to bishops, elders, deacons, on down until finally you reach the simple laymen, the infantryman of the church militant, as it were." [161]

In accordance with Becker's attention to personality development he perceived the unfortunate results of role incongruencies stemming either from roles defined in terms of value systems inconsistent with that of the incumbent or from separate but conflicting roles played by the same incumbent. The social worker, for example, whose basic values specify sympathetic rapport with clients, and who in fact may have become a social worker as an enunciation of those values, will find it difficult to work with the emotional detachment specified by that role A judge whose political values render him less than judicial is in a similar position. Even the most versatile role-incumbent, however, has to allow some of his potentialities to atrophy. He cannot be all things, a point frequently reiterated by Becker who had a favorite quotation from William James which he used to underline his meaning:

Not that I would not, if I could, be both handsome and fat and well-dressed, and a great athlete, and make a million a year, be a wit, a *bon-vivant*, a lady-killer, as well as a philosopher; a philanthropist, statesman, warrior, and African explorer as well as a "tone-poet" and saint. But the thing is simply impossible.[162]

RANKING

Rank as an element. Rank as an element of a social system, one would infer from Becker's works, was in the nature of a given that need not be established; to the degree that it did figure in his analysis of social action it did so obliquely. A few illustrations may make this clear. He said, for example that "in a secular society the range of social roles is very great—all the way from the garbage collector to the Supreme Court justice and back again." [163] This statement, cast in role terms and used in the context of personality types, obviously shows Becker's assumption that members of a society are differentially ranked. Characteristically, he was interested in the action aspect of social distance, and developed the theme of different sociative patterns on the assumption that society is stratified. To be a rival, for example, "usually you are a member of much the same ethnic group and essentially the same class. . . . Prince and pauper, in spite of story books, don't often meet." [164] Competition, one of the dissociative processes, (Figure 1, Appendix A) takes place everywhere but its range differs from society to society. One respect in which it differs is on the dimension of stratification rigidity characteristic of given societies.

Some societies display rigid stratification and Becker often injected fascinating detail from Hindu caste society to illustrate a point. His analysis in this respect, however, was focused not on the differential rank component, but on the belief-value system which in order to persist, demands a specification of many life styles each of which is the predestined lot, an endurance test so to speak, of a particular caste. (This is in striking contrast to other treatments of the caste system, notably that of Kingsley Davis, who analyzes it in relation to its function in getting differentially important societal jobs done by differentially qualified groups.) Some societies display relatively open stratification patterns which enable not only the individual actor to change his rank within the many groups of which he is a member, but which also enables a relatively continuous organization to be ranked differently at different stages of its existence as its members manifest beliefs, sentiments, and norms in varying degrees of conformity to those prevailing in the greater society. Such is the essence of the developmental stages of the sect, to denomination, to ecclesia to which Becker gave attention considerably before the late 1930's and early 1940's when sociological interest in stratification was at its peak. Discussing the Oxford Methodists he observed that they "would have won no following had they not offered the poor a type of faith and religious life which met their needs. . . . The characteristic features of the new sect also marked it off as especially adapted to the poor." He also noted the rise of the Methodists to middle class respectability, as well as John Wesley's cognizance of the consequences of this shift. [165] Class was also recognized as a component in the development of bureaucratic capitalism. He repeated Weber's phrase: "In some countries a middle-class ecclesia, in some countries a middle-class sect, but middle-class in tendency everywhere." [166]

The Marxian doctrine dedicated to classlessness, emerged from the middle class (both Marx and Engels having shared that background) and continues to recruit, in the United States at least, not from the proletariat whose cause Marxism claims to be sponsoring, but from the "younger generation of the American urban middle-class, especially of college age . . . [who] substitute [it] for a traditional religion" [167] wherewith they can shock their staid and stodgy elders.

Although Becker did not say so, they may be demonstrating their need for recognition, one of the four ends specified by Becker. The need for recognition in some ways approximates the actor's recognition of differential rank and his desire to do something about it. The marginal personality, for example, "who lives on the margin of two or three or more social worlds that don't overlap in any real way" [168] often does not know to which world he belongs. The resultant introspection, self-consciousness, and insecurity often are expressed in an obtrusiveness which may have rank-changing consequences.

Interesting, to say the least, is the fact that many of the leaders of the Nazi movement, from Hitler down, or up—as the reader prefers—were clearly marginal: an Austrian house-painter, a champagne salesman trying to crash into "society," a limping art historian who failed to get a professorial appointment, the son of a German businessman living in Egypt, a flier who had lost status because of drug addiction, and so on.[169]

An interest in the lack of status crystallization or congruence, and its consequences, so preoccupying to a large number of sociologists in the late 1950's , thus seems to have been anticipated by Becker.

a) Evaluation as a process in ranking and b) Allocation of status-roles. Of the four components which comprised for Becker the "circumscribed social processes" (Figure 1, Appendix A), the differentiative processes specify action which most nearly resembles what is specified on the PAS Model as evaluation as a process

in ranking. A "rise of inequalities or the growth of disparities" [170] attend the differentiating processes. Some of these rank
disparities Becker saw as having a biological root—"differences
in reaction time, differences in stature, differences in intelligence,
differences in emotional range." [171] Some of these biological variations may, for given circumstances, account for differential performance and thus give rise to differential evaluations in respect
to these biological differences. In Becker's colorful language,
"The biological root . . . bears little proportion to the social tree
. . . that grows out of it," [172] for rank is only to the smallest extent
attached to an individual because of his demonstrably biological
characteristics. The differentiating processes of gradation and
stratification are often based on individual or group variations
which may be unrelated to achievement and are not functionally
based. Skin color is the most notable example. The process of
selection, another of the differentiating processes, may result in
rank designation based on present occupancy of position on the
socio-economic ladder, although another such process, individuation may result, especially in an open class society, in rank determination directed solely to the individual without respect to
his family, guild, caste, etc. from which he may have separated
himself.

The elite as a group to whom high rank has been accorded is
implicitly made up of those chosen for certain qualities which
are highly evaluated. "They may be superior only with regard to
the keenness of their eye for the main chance, but often times
they *are* in that sense superior." [173] In any modern democracy
and in fact in any open class society "the makeup of this controlling elite changes very rapidly. The circulation from top to bottom goes on vigorously." [174] Wherever this phenomena is possible
competition as a form of sociation (Figure 1, Appendix A) is the
"all-pervasive and general rule," and ranking ideally is done
chiefly in relation to differential achievement in the competitive
situation.[175] In the rigidly stratified society, of which the Hindu
society is an example, competition in the form of striving may
lead within the caste to a superior rank accorded to those who
excel "in conformity to the special *dharma* that is incumbent upon
the entire caste." [176]

Among the integrative processes (as distinguished from the

differentiating processes) uniformation or uniformization (Figure 1, Appendix A) are processes by which aggregates of actors are assigned a common rank as in the army. Illustrations of this kind of dual evaluation are given which show a summation of status-role requirements which are variously ranked and a summation of an individual's possession or lack of possession of matching capabilities. The chants, songs, and poems of the Mahabharata are an important means of culture communication, and their recitation which can last as long as three weeks at a stretch, requires a good memory. A child who has a slightly better memory than his peers is evaluated highly in respect to this one trait; he is given slightly deferential treatment on account of it. Various assignments are given him which make use of his memory which by constant use and training as well as by the importance attached to it as a rank indicator, is developed to the point where the small initial memorizing superiority he showed becomes phenomenally great. He becomes the bard of the tribe. The self that develops, then, is as much the product of taking over fortuitously or almost fortuitously assigned roles the successful execution of which leads in adult life to allocation to status-roles highly suggested by early experiences.[177] By the same token many potentials atrophy, an observation made frequently by Becker and one which suggests the "talent erosion" concept developed at the University of Wisconsin and often associated with the works of William Sewell.

Although not related to a specific status-role, a similar process occurs among the Zuñi who highly evaluate the quiet and unobtrusive man who never gets on anyone's nerves. "Consequently, I make bold to say, there is competition for success in conforming to that particular type of personality, even though such competition may not be recognizable if we persist in thinking of it in terms of our bustling, jostling, elbow-crowding variety of competition."[178] If the Zuñi society specifies a status-role which is defined by requirements of this trait to a marked degree, it would be consistent with Becker's thesis that the actor who had most successfully internalized the highly valued model behavior would be considered as a natural incumbent.

Still another way in which status-roles are allocated, although not considered in those terms but rather as one of the "destructive processes" (Figure 1, Appendix A) by Becker, is favoritism, bribery and nepotism. No attempt is made under the application of these processes to match the requirements of the status-role with the capabilities of the incumbent.

We know what happens when Son-in-law Dabbles is given a position in the manufacturing firm of Cosy and Co. that his intellect does not enable him adequately to fill, and you know what happens to Cosy and Co. if too many Son-in-law Dabbleses and their country club friends get into key positions. Cosy and Co. is totally destroyed as a result of favoritism. . . .[179]

CONTROLLING

Becker's closest approach to the phenomena designated on the PAS Model as controlling appeared under the processes of domination and submission (Figure 1, Appendix A). Aspects of controlling also appear with certain of the Wiese-Becker categories under common-human processes.

Power as an element. Differential power was viewed by Becker as a natural concomitant of differential rank. Its relative distribution as well as its normatively approved modes of manifestation are frequently revealed in the social action directed toward goal attaining and the means used therefor.

For example, if the social action is combat and the need is annihilation of the opponent, the value may be defined in such a way that, as it were, "no holds are barred." Anything from poison to terroristic inducement of insanity may be held suitable.[180]

Although it was not so specified by Becker, the "no holds barred" use of means suggests a value system of the consequent expedient rational type. In a power struggle of the combat type just cited, adherents of the consequent rational (unlimited expedient) would almost certainly have an advantage over otherwise equally powerful opponents who subscribed to a value system which limited the choice of means (Figure 1 above). Pursuant rationality (limited expedient) which specifies "economy of effort, efficiency, and absence of undesirable consequences" (as well as conformity to a limiting principle) would modify the power potential of its adherents. Becker reported that in their first encounters with the Japanese in World War II, the proclivity of American soldiers to "give the guy a break" appropriate to their conception of a fair fight led them to refrain from thrusting a bayonet into a Japanese lying face downward. The Japanese, subscribing to a different value system, did not hesitate to explode a grenade thereby killing himself and the American who a few seconds before could have killed him.[181] The same limitations on power are present in situations in which Christian objectives are relinquished if violent means are required in their achievement. Augmentations of power similar to those accruing to the Japanese in the above instance are afforded the Mohammedans whose "religion of the sword" sanctions the means of physical coercion.[182]

Subjugation by conquest (or by other social action) yields power to the conqueror and poses the problem of control of the conquered. Again, power manifestations are determined by the value system of the conqueror. Becker reported that from the observer's viewpoint the Italian Fascist regime practiced violence for its own sake; the Russians have subjugated and controlled in the name of the Marxian dialectic; the Americans have used "truthful propaganda, free elections, and due process of law based on [the principle of] 'natural rights'" as measures toward spreading democracy as a way of life.[183]

Although Becker regarded the heyday of conquest as having past, physical coercion in the political state still remains as the ultimate manifestation of power:

No matter how "automatic" obedience to law may become, no matter how well-recognized are the established agencies of the state, the various governmental bureaus and governmental officials, somewhere there remains the threat of the policeman's club, the bayonet, the machine gun or the cell . . . the hangman's noose, or the ax—direct physical coercion.[184]

Coercion is an effective means of subjugation only in the short run; in the long run there must be consent. *"The state reserves for itself the monopoly of the use of force"* [185] and in addition maintains a balance of sorts between groups within it which are differentially endowed in such matters as family prerogatives, prestige, property rights, political privileges, and such. The ultimate power which resides in the state necessarily represents vested interests and is dedicated to the maintenance of the *status quo.*[186]

Two theories of the institutionalization of power were examined by Becker under what he termed theories of external and internal conflict. External conflict is marked by power demonstrations which may assume any or all of six methods: extermination, tribute-taking, tribute-receiving, occupation, regulation and amalgamation.[187] The first three methods in decreasing order utilize physical coercion for their effectiveness; the last three in increasing order depend upon some aspect of consent, although as Becker warned, coercion always must be possible, or the power holder will be displaced. Internal conflict, according to the theory which is essentially Marxian, starts from the indisputable fact that "the accumulative capacity, the acquisitive drive, of one portion of a social organization as over against another portion is the rule, not the exception."[188] With possessions come power held by a small minority within the group who use their power to defend their possessions from assault by the proletariat. In this they are powerfully reinforced by the state, a device established by the rich for the systematic exploitation of the poor. When inequalities become unbearable a revolution once more levels ranks and redistributes power and another cycle toward ultimate differential distribution is begun.

Although Becker subscribed to the "Marxian assertions that the majority never rules . . . that actually a relatively small ruling group holds power at any given time,"[189] he would emphasize that the composition of the controlling elite is constantly changing in any modern democracy or other open-class society; in fact, that a circulating elite is a characteristic of Russia also. The state everywhere reflects the struggles which attend the deposing of one power elite and the accession to power of another. "It may not be . . . that the Supreme Court follows the election returns, but nevertheless, the way in which the uppermost law of the land is interpreted slowly changes. Those changes do in some measure tend to correspond with overall shifts in ideology and public opinion."[190] Inequitable power distribution is not a serious problem, Becker maintained, so long as the competent are free to rise and the incompetent free to fall. The newly elevated will shift the advantages and disadvantages in different directions than their predecessors.

On a less global scale Becker also examined power as it was

manifested in the processes which he termed domination-submission (Figure 1, Appendix A) exemplified by paired situations in which domination-submission behavior typically shifted from one person to the other; and by employer-employee relations in which the same shift was observable. The authority of the office, or that afforded by status-role, was noted by Becker although not in those terms. The carpenter yields to the lawyer on legal matters, but the reverse is true when a stairway to the attic is going to be built.[191] The influence aspect of power, especially that stemming from personality was likewise recognized as in the domination-submission shifts mentioned above; he noted that even in the patriarchal societies where the father's peak position is reinforced by law and religion, there still are hen-pecked husbands.

Decision making and initiation into action as process. Becker did not single out power as a separate component of social action and address himself to it specifically. What appears above emerges from his considerations of values, of the state as an institution, and of general categories of processes which are observable in the patterns of sociation. Nevertheless, he did say a good deal about power, and with him it was implicit that decision making and initiation into action were carried on by the power holder but correctable by one means or another by the less powerful. His value-types also are pertinent to decision making. Especially does the pursuantly rational (Figure 1) impose on the societies which subscribe to it the necessity for decisions which ideally should have all the attributes of the rational, all that is permissible of the expedient and further, should conform to a principle which defines and restricts permissible ends. Decision making for societies subscribing to consequently expedient evaluations need only to apply rationality to the question: "Will it work, and if so, is it the course of action that will work best?" Instrumental efficiency need be the only criterion. Becker's sacred-secular typology has as its core the decision demanding question "Shall we change?" and in a sense all the preceding parts of this chapter delineate the extracted answers, the processes which yield the answers and modes by which the pertinent factors are weighed. The predictive capacity of the typology could probably be most easily tested by its application to a group in the throes of making an important decision, given the circumstance of broad and intimate knowledge of its commitment to the knowing-desiring-norming aspects of social action.

SANCTIONING

Sanction as an element and application of sanctions as process. Becker treated sanctions on many different levels, and although the attention he gave to punishment and reward is not quantitatively great only social change is as fundamental to his whole value typology. Sacrificial extinction, either of themselves or their fellows, it will be remembered, is the basic criterion by which degree of dedication to a particular value is determined. Societies predominantly dedicated to the holy value as defined by Becker (or proverbial societies) are most willing to exterminate those who defile the value. (Martyrdom is most frequent among these societies too, but being self-chosen, it will not be treated here as a sanction; whatever the rewards and punishments accruing to martyrdom it can scarcely be thought of as an inducement to normative behavior.) There are instances in proverbial societies where ultimate punishment is left to God but the violator may become an outcast which may virtually amount to death, "or, less frequently, may be allowed to remain a member of the society, albeit at the lower levels." [192] Sanctions supernaturally applied, however, are conceived to be very real by members of the proverbial and prescriptive societies (Figure 1 p. 48). The fear on the part of the Hindu that reincarnation might bring regression in caste status, or worse, a nonhuman form of life was a powerful deterrent to noncomforming behavior, as was the collective guilt belief of the Hebrews, or the rewards of Heaven and the punishments of Hell to the Calvinist. [193]

Dedication to the loyalistic value carries with it in almost equal measure the willingness to take the lives of those who threaten the value. Becker cited a report on an Indian tribe in which differential sanctions were noted between those applied to the religious deviant and those applied to the patriotic deviant and in this instance the loyalistic-inspired sanctions were the more severe, involving banishment and death. [194] He might have added that even in a modern society of the atomic age, incarceration and death are inflicted upon the disloyal.

Outraged bonds of intimacy similarly provoke passionate re-

taliations which latter are viewed as justifiable or at least extenu-
ated even in societies governed by highly formalized and codified
laws, while violations of moralistic sacredness visit at the very
least, moral indignation upon the perpetrator. Contempt is
levelled at the violator of fitting behavior, whereas a measure of
amused disdain is the usual reaction to the inappropriate act.[195]
(Figure 1 p. 48)

Becker never claimed that the application of the negative
sanction is *the* most effective factor in stabilizing a value system;
rather he implied that the intensity of the sanction bears a direct
relation to the priority of the value and to the intensity to which
it is subscribed. A slight modification of that statement perhaps
should be made because of a characteristic of value observance
in the proverbial and prescriptive societies the value systems of
which, it will be remembered are accrete. Since the value systems
"as wholes and in their minutest parts"[196] are regarded as unalterable, presumably no value priorities could prevail and the
sanctions would be applied no less for a violation of the minutiae
than for the violation of the whole. One must infer that "Let the
punishment fit the crime" is a sanctioning procedure favored by
the more secular societies.

On the secular scale, as values are abstracted from proverbs
and prescriptions into formulations "functioning as ethical, governmental, professional, and similar principles,"[197] the social action which they condone or prohibit must similarly be removed
from the language of the concrete and cast in general terms. Pursuantly rational interpretations and their application, therefore,
render sanctions less inexorable and less precise than is the case
with values stated by prescription and proverb. Becker was primarily concerned, of course, with the sanction of death to the
offender, that being his criteria for value intensity. Since both
martyrdom and the death penalty are both infrequent and difficult
to attach to action which defies an expedient value of either the
pursuant or consequent variety, he was necessarily much less
specific about sanctions as they are conceived and applied in
secular societies than he was about their application in sacred
societies. Certain institutions which were typed by Becker in
accordance with his value typology yield relevant sanctioning
patterns which do illustrate secular sanctions, however. The ec-

clesia, for example, which never from the subjective view of the actor but often from the observer's point of view is the most secular of religious organizations differentiates between venal and mortal sin and extracts pennances accordingly. Here, in contrast to the sacred sect which makes no compromises, formalized value priorities are bolstered by a kind of sliding scale of sacrifices by which absolution can be gained. Many specific sanctions employed by the ecclesia and by scientific bodies are revealed in this short allegory:

The Church of Science, moreover, applies "pressures." If a scientist strays off the straight and narrow path by injecting other preferences and ultimate values into his supposedly scientific work, he will soon find that his books are no longer in the Holy Canon, his articles can be published only in journals which lack the Imprimatur and Nihil Obstat, and eventually he may discover that all his writings are in the Index Expurgatorius or even the Index Librorum Prohibitorum. Worse still, the institution with which he is identified may suffer Interdict, and he himself may be visited with Excommunication.[198]

The pronormless society may demonstrate that the deterring power of the inevitable sanction is not primarily responsible for normatively controlled behavior, although this speculation was not pursued by Becker. Such a society is fully equipped with legally pronounced sanctions which are formulated and applied through an elaborate system of legislative, judiciary, and law-enforcing institutions; nonetheless crime, deviancy, and vagrancy flourish. "You can't outlaw crime" seems to be a particularly apt truism when comfort and thrill are the prevailing values. It is in connection with the pronormless society that Becker gave some attention to the efficacy of positive sanctions. The promise of a better day or the return to the good old days, especially when promulgated by an inspired leader and expedited by a first-rate executive assistant, is one of the common accompaniments to a resacralization of values. The "normative reaction to normlessness" [199] which Becker frequently noted, is itself a kind of delayed sanctioning process requiring the renunciation (for oneself) and the denunciation (in respect to others) of comfortable and thrilling indulgence; it requires the commitment instead to a more exacting set of norms/values and to sanctions by which they will be in part preserved.

FACILITATING

Facility as an element and utilization of facilities as process. Any treatment of facilities is by definition a treatment of means, and must therefore distinguish between phenomena which expedite goal achievement (facilities or means) and the end itself. Many items which in less polarized societies would qualify as facilities are automatically eliminated as such in the polarized sacred and polarized secular societies as posited by Becker, in which means and ends merge. Fields, crops, livestock, and dwelling are holy to the sacred society just as surely as are God, kith, and kin; they are valued for their own sake and therefore are ends, not means. Similarly, in the polarized secular society, the "wine, women and song" or their counterparts come to be valued as objects in a way which is quite indistinguishable from the cathectic moment of consummation which may originally have been conceived as the end.

Means-ends differentiation on the other hand is the essence of principial evaluation, although the respective importance of the means as vs. the ends is designated quite differently by the mode of pursuant rationality than by the mode of consequent rationality. At the risk of repetition, it should be established that pursuant rationality perceives the *principle as end.*[200] Everything supportive of the principle (or what official interpretation or public opinion renders as supportive of the principle) is a means. Ideally in such a society many otherwise attractive and situationally appropriate measures will be rejected as means because they will be interpreted as inharmonious with the principle as end. Becker suggested however, that in actual practice and up to a point, the adopting of new measures is dictated by the exigencies of the situation. Apparent discrepancies between the new measure and the principle are often rationalized by reinterpretations of the flexible, abstractly stated principle. In this respect prescriptive societies which have well-worked out rationales for the prescriptive code (although many of the arguments advanced are *ex post facto* rationalizations) bear a reasonable resemblance to pursuantly rational principial societies.

The consequent rational principial societies have dropped the ultimate principle as goal; goal instead has become the successful meeting of crises and emergencies many of which have come about or have been intensified by the abandonment of principle. Means, and thus facilities, can be chosen from the total range of possibilities with no limitations except that they work. Since many of the most distasteful kinds of social action have been done in the name of expediency—and Becker mentioned "anything from gas-chamber extermination to brain-washing" [201]—he felt impelled to point out that "much of what is ordinarily called progress" including the contributions of science in all its pure and many of its applied forms is of the consequent secular type, in which utilization of *any* facility will be condoned so long as it is effective. Pure science, of course, does not subscribe to any principle other than the principle of science. The implications of its theories and its validations no matter how opposed to the *status quo* they may be, is the only compelling truth to the scientist. The scientist who eschews certain means of establishing scientific truth (e.g. human vivisection) is evincing at that moment subscription to values other than those embodied in science in which only prediction and control are values.

In a completely different vein, Becker distinguished between a *standard* of living (with standard used in the sense of some kind of guide or ideal or goal) and a *level* of living (with level describing an achieved life style in respect to the use of what is here called facilities.) Becker's presentation shifted the emphasis from the usual supposition that common ends are held by a great number of groups in competition with each other over limited means, to another quite different supposition: that lavish use of means engenders more means so that the cultivation of the attitude of unlimited needs becomes the goal:

The "unnecessary needs" that really help to raise the standard and thereby the level of living are felt needs for finery, for guitars mounted with mother-of-pearl, for the chance to see the really big bullfights in the larger towns. Men work for all kinds of such "extras" and not merely for economic needs in the narrow sense. Mankind is pushed as much if not more by a demand for the frivolous as by the demand for the wherewithal to keep body and soul together.[202]

COMPREHENSIVE OR MASTER PROCESSES

The comprehensive processes of the PAS Model are to be found in some measure in the articulation of all the above elements; "Prince and pauper . . . don't often meet" [203] is an evidence of boundary maintenance fully as much as it designates differential ranking. Further, the comprehensive processes reinforce each other; socialization, for example, could not take place without communication. The following treatment of the comprehensive processes, therefore, will indicate only those aspects of the respective processes which were uniquely approached by Becker, or which do not seem to be adequately represented above in the main body of the analysis of his works.

Communication. Contacts with other human beings is the essence of sociation (Becker's comprehensive term for association and dissociation); they are mediated by symbolized gestures, the most significant of which is speech.[204] In addition to speech there are other symbolic contacts the meanings of which are less precise. Among them are the primary contacts "directly mediated by our ordinary sensory equipment—contacts through the eye, the ear, the nose, and the sense of touch." [205] Becker speculated that sensory impressions of which the recipient actor is not necessarily aware may influence his evaluation of the contact. It seemed to him a possibility, for example

. . . that we are continually attracted to and repelled by persons in ways that, as we say, we can't get our hands on . . . may it not be that we are responding to subtle odors of which we are not aware but which none the less are impinging upon our sense equipment all the time, and which are constant forces leading to association and dissociation? There is no reason in the world why this *could* not be true.[206]

Secondary communication, in addition to the type represented by letter, radio, telephone and others which are not *vis-a-vis*, include those of face-to-face or even bodily contact in an impersonal setting. The impersonality of the contact can be highly desirable, as in a crowded subway train, or it can be undesired and demoralizing when it defies efforts to establish meaningful communication.

Conditions favorable to extensive communication (sociation)

are evinced in what Becker termed vicinal, social and mental accessibility; societies flourishing under such conditions (extensive communication with other societies) tend to be of a secular nature. Conditions favorable to limited communication (sociation) are evinced in vicinal, social and mental isolation; societies flourishing under such conditions (limited communication with other societies) tend to be of a sacred nature. Accessibility and isolation are defined above under the heading evaluation, and as indicated there, they represent phenomena which are in part treated below respectively under systemic linkage and boundary maintenance.

Boundary maintenance. The sacred-secular continuum, specified as it is in terms of reluctance and readiness to change, almost automatically shows progressive boundary maintenance as the sacred pole is approached. The burden of Becker's whole value presentation in a sense can be said to revolve around what on the PAS Model are called boundary maintenance and systemic linkage. Isolation in all its forms is in part a "given"; the culture in which a particular isolated society flourishes is replete with characteristic isolation components. Its actors are born to it, so to speak.

"We" are the people; all "others" are inferior. There is a "we" group and an "other" group, or an "in"-group, the group to which we belong, and an "out"-group, the group to which others belong. *We* speak as men speak; the others are jabberers; *we* act as men should act; *we* are human beings.[207]

Vicinal isolation encourages such ethnocentrism, but the latter may persist without the physical separateness from other societies implied by this kind of isolation. Social isolation, represented by such factors as differences in color, language, personal habits, a rigid ranking system and the like, persistently marks one group off from another. Even when these barriers do not exist, mental isolation stemming from a dedication to ideas which are different from those held by other groups is sufficient to maintain a group's identity. Becker's prime example of a group separated from others by a mental boundary is the gypsy. Always on the move, the gypsy knew no vicinal isolation; enjoying a brisk trade with his host society, he knew a social isolation that was by no means complete; he did, however, subscribe to ideas consistent with his value system which rendered him a virtual mental isolate.

Elsewhere in this volume the Old Order Amish are described for illustrative purposes. The boundary maintaining devices attributed to that society in Chapter 1, were composed in Becker's terms of a self-imposed and cherished vicinal isolation which is partial; a social isolation cultivated by highly visible costume, other highly visible facilities and a trilingual ability which conveniently can be used for social accessibility when desired or for social isolation when preferred; and finally, a high level of mental isolation which preserves the sacred value system by which separation from the world is prescribed. Becker's own culture case study of the sacred Scottish society of the outer Hebrides attributed just such boundary maintaining characteristics to his Scots, with the important exception that the vicinal isolation of the latter was not self-imposed but encouraged by its geographic location.

Although the degree and kind of isolation prevalent for a given society is to a large extent culturally determined, Becker was by no means a cultural determinist in this respect. Changes in the intensities of isolation (and hence boundary maintenance) occur, sometimes from somewhat fortuitous and unavoidable exposure to other cultures, but also they arise out of the social actions of the society itself. Those social actions represented by his term common-human processes (Figure 1, Appendix A) are particularly applicable in some respects to the phenomena of boundary maintenance. Becker viewed some common-human processes as tending to decrease social distance; these he designated as associative. Others he viewed as tending to increase social distance; these he designated as dissociative. For convenience they are tabulated here:

Associative processes	Dissociative processes
1. Advance	1. Competition
2. Adjustment	2. Contravention
3. Accordance	3. Conflict
4. Amalgamation	

The associative processes as suggested by their names, designate social contact from its stages of first tentative approach (advance), to the stage of setting up some means of getting along together (adjustment), to the stage of being in agreement on many vital points (accordance), to the ultimate stage of complete and common identity (amalgamation). From Becker's writings it would appear that within a designated social system, the associative processes as exhibited by member interaction are clearly boundary maintaining as system integration is increased thereby. However, when associative processes are at work between members of different social systems, it would appear that boundary maintenance is weakened. The first of the dissociative processes, competition, may be boundary maintaining for members within a given system, as when these members are confronted with a competition from members of another system. Competition among members of a single social system, however, weakens the integration of that system. Boundary maintenance is equally apparent as a result of contravention, (the second type of dissociation) a limited kind of opposition exemplified by Becker by Her Majesty's Opposition, in which a minority group conforms up to a point. Conflict (the third and last type) is opposition which has passed from the passive to the active state; war is one of its best known manifestations, and of course is always boundary maintaining.

In the case of the circumscribed processes (Figure 1, Appendix A) whether or not boundary maintenance is or is not indicated is much more definite. Although eschewing any ethical connotations for differentiation, integration, destruction, and construction, the following differentiation between destruction and construction leaves no doubt of their relevance in differentiating boundary maintaining from other processes.

Does the process concerned tend to build up the group by making it more closely knit (or larger), or does it tend to tear down the group by making it more loosely woven (or smaller)? . . . Other sociologists use either these terms or current equivalents such as "functional-malfunctional" or "eufunctional-dysfunctional." [208]

The process of integration varies with the norms and processes of evaluation. Becker noted that "the more differentiated a society becomes, the greater opportunity is there for the adoption of a secular value-system or value-systems." [209] Introducing the section called "Tightening up the weave," he made the following observations:

There are three subheadings under our category of integration . . . First [there] is uniformation . . . the making of the members of a society more uniform, more like each other. . . . Next [there is] ordination, the arranging of the members of a society in certain specific ways . . . [under which] we'll distinguish superordination, subordination, and coordination. . . . Finally, among these integrative processes we have what we may term harmonization, which is the growth of "we" feeling, the growth of "in-group" sentiment, the growth of solidarity in a group. . . .[210]

Systemic linkage. Just as the sacred-secular continuum (indicating as it does the reluctance or readiness of a group correctly placed on it to change) shows progressive boundary maintenance as the sacred pole is approached, so does it indicate progressive systemic linkage as the secular pole is approached. The astute reader will anticipate quite correctly in this section a repetition of the boundary maintenance section above, except that the converse terms and types are here indicated.

Accessibility in all its forms is largely culturally determined, and is characteristic of the secular society.

. . . frequent trips to Athens made even the Attic shepherd, for many purposes, a representative of urban standards of political conduct, if nothing else, and "Sears Sawbuck" and "Monkey Ward" notably assist the denizens of the American countryside in imitating, although a trifle belatedly, the styles of Hollywood and "Gay Paree." In urban centers *per se*, strangers usually are physically present in large numbers and are often accepted with little question. Those native to the society either travel freely themselves, or through the mass communications that an advanced culture affords, vicariously participate in travel . . .[211]

Vicinal accessibility is reinforced by a high level of social accessibility which provides among other things, a welcome for the stranger, and by mental accessibility which ranges from a mild philosophical relativism to tolerance which is facile to the point of indifference to principle.

Culture, society, and personality, however, were steadfastly for Becker in a state of reciprocity. With the accessible society as with the isolated, the social actions of the actors, although affected by the cultural past, have a part in determining the present. The marginal man and the segmented man in terms of personality types as employed by Becker may be both the instigators and the victims of systemic linkage.[212] The secular stranger is generally an instigator; the sacred stranger may be a victim.

Both associative and dissociative processes are operative in systemic linkage as they are in boundary maintenance, but in reverse direction so to speak. To the degree that the associative processes characterize social action *between* (in contrast to *within*) groups, other things being equal, those groups will tend to establish systemic linkages. (A logical corrolary of this, although not specified by Becker, is that to the degree that the associative processes characterize *inter*group interaction, the less will it characterize *intra*group interaction with a resultant lowered group solidarity, greater accessibility, and greater probability of systemic linkage.) To the degree that the dissociative processes characterize social action *within* (in contrast to *between*) groups, other things being equal, the lower will be the groups' solidarity, and the greater the likelihood that systemic linkage will be established.

It may be necessary, or at least wise, to note here that neither systemic linkage nor boundary maintenance as such were terms used much if at all by Becker. He did not correlate the ideas embodied in them with the processes he has designated as common-human, nor does he use these processes in connection with change. Nevertheless the concepts as they have been developed here seem consistent with Becker's whole treatment of social change to which he gave so much attention, and of which his cult-sect-denomination-ecclesia types are well developed examples. In whatever terms, his discussion of the development of the sect either into a denomination or an ecclesia is essentially a discussion of the development of a group preoccupied with boundary maintenance to a group bent upon systemic linkage.

The ecclesia . . . is closely allied with national and economic interests; as a plurality pattern its very nature commits it to adjustment of its ethics to the ethics of the secular world; it must represent the morality of the respectable majority.[213]

Social control. Even the pronormless society is not free of restraints, and most societal types exhibit a wide array of restraining influences. A summation of the evaluative modes of societal types and the characteristic casting of the respective guides to normative behavior constitutes at the same time the varieties of social control observed by Becker. (Figure 1). In review they are:

1) the guides to behavior preserved in *proverbs*, extracted from approved means of dealing with situations and embodied in the *proverbial societal type*, applied under the *traditional nonrational mode*, facilitated by completely *primary contacts*, articulated by expectations of *complete conformity* to *unchanging* and well-defined *situations* and *sanctioned* by "general aversion, indignation, and traditional and spontaneous verbal or corporal chastisement" reinforced by gossip.[214]

2) The guides to behavior preserved in *prescriptions*, in part at least extracted from proverb and applied under the *traditional rational mode*, embodied in the *prescriptive societal type*, facilitated by contacts which are almost completely *primary* but able to withstand the occasional impersonal, stranger, or other contact, articulated by expectations of complete *conformity* to *very slowly changing* but well-defined situations, *sanctioned* by punishments explicitly and concretely related to violations, and reinforced by gossip.

3) The guides to behavior preserved in *principles*, extracted from proverb and prescription and applied under the *pursuant rational mode*, embodied in the *pursuant principial societal type*, adaptable to contacts which are to a large extent *impersonal*, articulated by expectations of *varying degrees of conformity* to a fairly complex, *steadily changing* and not always defined situation, *sanctioned* by formally and legally codified punishments, with some reinforcement by informal controls.

4) The guides to behavior preserved in *principles* which have become *attenuated*, applied under the *rationally expedient mode*, embodied in the *consequent principial societal type*, adaptable to extremely *impersonal contacts*, articulated by expectations of a wide range of *conformity-nonconformity* to values/norms which have little specificity in *speedily changing*, ill-defined situations, *sanctioned* by formally and legally codified punishments in which

both guilt and punishment are subject to interpretation, with little reinforcement by informal controls.

5) The guides to behavior almost *formless,* saturated with *thrill* and *comfort* pursuits but with some *vestigial principial traits* applied under the *nonrational expedient mode,* embodied in the *pronormless societal type,* adaptable to *primary* but *short-lived contacts* in an unstable world of *kaleidoscopic change, sanctioned* by unpredictable emotional reactions consistent with the *unstructured normative order;* frequently interspersed by *cults* and *sects* which are provided *charismatic social control* and charismatic leadership.

Becker's treatment of power (see above) also presents essential features of social control. Summation here of a few of the processes specified by Becker as being pertinent to power relations will suffice: domination-submission, superordination-subordination, gradation and stratification; also pertinent may be the processes of conflict: extermination, tribute-taking, tribute-receiving, occupation, regulation and amalgamation. Other processes designated by Becker will be observable on Figure 1, Appendix A, as operative in normative integration; particular attention is called to those with positive designations such as the integrative and constructive. Becker virtually specified that although naked force is the ultimate resort for social control, the restraints imposed by societal structure and the expectancies of value-conforming social action constitute the very foundation of social control. Thus he noted that "the state rests upon a mixture . . . of force and consent; but . . . force is never quite absent." [215]

Socialization. Value is the core of Becker's social interpretation. Socialization is hence accorded an appropriately important emphasis, since it is by this process that value is transmitted to new generations. The relatively value-less states exhibited by the consequent principial and pronormless societal types must logically be viewed as capable of resulting not only from greatly enlarged accessibility and change-induced crises and emergencies but also from failure of the socializing process to instill internalized values (although these two variables are by no means independent.)

Becker posited that "the initial stage of any human activity is a more or less vague impulse, craving, or longing which manifests itself in restless trial-and-error seeking." In other words, these are "raw needs." A learning process takes place whereby the initial impulse is defined and the raw need becomes a "prepared need." [216] Here it must be remembered that Becker defined values as "any objects of any needs." [217] Thus Becker was saying that values only become defined through the process of socialization.

Becker was critical of the theory which would relate adult personality attributes solely, or even chiefly to infant-rearing practices.

Those phases of juvenile conduct escaping the oversight of guardians of the general proprieties of the society as a whole tend to be patterned by the examples of older age-groups. This, incidentally, is one of the many reasons why "diaper determinism" is nonsense.[218]

If the Germans, Russians, and Japanese are aggressive because of early tight diapers how were the Italians, without benefit of tight diapers, conditioned to *their* aggressiveness? [219]

The process of socialization which Becker subscribed to, in the manner of George Herbert Mead and Charles Horton Cooley, is a development of the self in social interaction with other human beings. Children do not merely learn mechanical routines but actually internalize the role behavior of others as they observe it in social interaction. In other words, they become objects to themselves by internalizing the role of the other. The role models provided by descriptive disciplines such as ethnography and history covers a very wide range; furthermore, the spread of individual personality presents an infinite range, since no two are identical. Despite these hazards to generalization, Becker drew personality types which he himself regarded as nothing more than very rough guides. His interest is not primarily in the personality type itself, but in "what might be called the general form of the transmutation of the self as it occurs in rapid change from societies having a primarily sacred sort of value-system to societies with a primarily secular sort of value-system." [220]

In looking for the "form of the transmutation" he perforce had to use personality types which he accompanied by admonitions regarding the validity and applicability of such types, not only as developed by himself but as developed by others. The psychologically conceived personality type promulgated as a prediction, an explanation, and final cause of social behavior has been seriously expounded and often popularly accepted. Becker's warning that it is a very poor predictive tool unless it is given specific social setting is pertinent.

It may be that an aggressive personality will remain an aggressive personality from early childhood onward, but it may make a lot of difference as to whether that aggressive personality develops in . . . one of the centers of "ganging" on Chicago's South Side, or whether it develops in reciprocity with an American small town where there are generally approved channels through which these aggressive states can work themselves out harmlessly. In the one case you may get a very able and aggressive gangster, and in the other case you may get a very able and aggressive executive or community leader.[221]

Becker not only attempted to provide characteristic social settings but to imbue them with the dynamic quality of fairly rapid change to which predictable responses by particular personality types might be hypothesized. Consistent with his constant theme of reciprocal effects between the personality, the society, and the culture, Becker's development of human personality revealed it as both a product of and a molder of society.

Excerpts and summation of two types will be given here: the segmental type which Becker regarded as perhaps more common in modern American society than any other; and the marginal type which Becker viewed as being oriented more than any other toward change.[222]

Segmental type: extracted from characteristics exhibited by actors who play many social roles each of which is compartmentalized and thus involves the actor in self-contained groups which have little or no connection with other groups in which he participates. *Type of social situation:* elaborate division of labor in economic organization the standards of which are applicable only to that facet of life; available activities for noneconomic or spare time and leisure are highly commercialized, and competitive, with the result that there is an "ever-mounting crescendo of appeal"; impersonal contacts prevail and the individual actor remains anonymous in much of his interaction; vicarious experiences supplant participating experiences to a large extent. *Type of behavior:* normatively restricted behavior on the job; relatively or wholly unchecked behavior in other compartments of activity; few checks and balances from overlapping membership groups which would force consistency from one role to another; behavior not subjected to evaluative judgments of others, since others are anonymous, impersonal; "anything goes" by way of behavior is the result; escape reading, "spectatoritis," being a "fan," etc. used as vicarious experiences; other forms of vaguely expressive conduct include going just to be going, participation in vaguely therapeutic cults, indulgence in petty crime, etc. *Instances of extreme segmentation:* Loving husband and father who supports his family by organized crime; businessman who uses cutthroat competition in his business but who passes the plate on Sunday; *Reciprocal effects of personality type—social situation:* Integration accomplished to a degree by "water-tight compartments" of personality so that inconsistencies of role are minimized in the awareness of the individual; further "it may well be that because of the difficulty of achieving this type of personal unity in a society like our own we get the periodic return to one or another sort of supernaturalistic doctrine."[223]

Marginal type:[224] extracted from characteristics exhibited by actors who live on the margin of two or three or more social worlds that don't overlap in any real way. *Type of situation:* the individual is brought up with one set of standards found not to be appropriate to a new situation which demands the adoption of another set of standards. The dilemma is always present of either subscribing to the point of view to which one was socialized, or rejecting it and all the meaningful others of that early period and adopting currently appropriate standards. The dilemma occurs frequently among groups of "high visibility" such as minority groups of various kinds, children of newly arrived immigrants, or children of parents dedicated to an ancestral faith which no longer seems appropriate. *Type of behavior:* The marginal individual is always in doubt about which world to identify himself with; as a result he is self-conscious, and perhaps confused and introspective; insecurity leads to obtrusive behavior; or, lacking adequate outward expression, he may develop fantasy environment the ultimate of which is insanity. *Instances of marginal men:* Hitler and many other leaders of the Nazi movement; leaders of cults and sects—religious, economic, political; when possessed of great expressive ability poets or artists, Dante, Heine, Burns, Shelley, and Poe. *Reciprocal effects of personality type— social situations:* type speeds up social change, for the inferiority feeling demands it; type represented by "permanent neophiliacs" who not only respond favorably to the new but also aggressively initiate it, positively, by new movements, and negatively, by vigorous criticism of existing conditions; "they are likely to be vigorous critics of both foes and friends; the sacred-to-secular shift is sometimes difficult to understand if the role of the marginal man is overlooked." [225]

Other social situations and other personality types have different mutual effects upon each other, but the up-shot of the total survey led Becker to conclude that "clearly, a thoroughly integrated self can appear only in adulthood, and there, only in a society which is highly integrated, which has an accrete or fused rather than a discrete or scattered value system." [226]

Becker examined value transmission or socialization particularly as it occurs in the proverbial society, since it is here that the process is accomplished in such a way that maximum integration develops. Its most distinguishing feature in such a society is that not only do living members of the society provide role models but all of the past members are socializing influences. This aspect of socialization was touched upon by Mead but few of those following him have elaborated upon it. Becker noted:

If departed ancestors, as far back as memory can reach, are commemorated and their virtues systematically extolled, a very great deal of the past may remain to work on the present. Not only parents and other living relatives and custodians directly influence offspring as they are reared, but also a host of departed worthies, "actively" participate in socialization.[227]

Institutionalization. In the Wiese-Becker volume "institutionalization, professionalization and liberation" (Figure 1, Appendix A) are specified as the "constructive processes" in circumscribed relations. It is noted that "institutionalization and standardization are . . . complementary" [228] and may be accompanied by ceremonial, tradition and other means of legitimation.[229]

Institutionalization may always be put in terms of more or less. Something is more or less an institution in terms of the carrying out of

activities that maintain, preserve, and extend other so-called institutions. . . . An institution is always something that takes in the washing
of some other institution. . . . A family . . . organizes, extends, maintains a church, by training children to become adequate members of
religious organizations. It institutionalizes a political unit, in that it
trains children in such ways that they become responsible citizens. . . .
Conversely the political institution institutionalizes the family . . . in
that at least it provides protection. . . . The economic organization . . .
in those countries where there is a family wage system . . . institutionalizes the family [providing] maintenance of the family. But an organization such as the family, insofar as it rears children . . . may
institutionalize and in this sense extend itself.[230]

Becker himself defined as institutional, "any mode of human conduct . . . if that conduct goes on for some time and if it helps to
keep other conduct moving along the accustomed channels." [231]
His emphasis, thus, was upon the "functionally interdependent
nature of a great part of our social life." As noted above much of
what he called institutionalization may be called systemic linkage.
What is conceptualized above in Chapter 1 as system and subsystem was in part for Becker institution and in part plurality
pattern.[232]

Functioning institutions and functioning society amount to the same
thing. . . . As long as a society is in some sense a "whole" it has working
"parts"; these "parts" are reciprocally connected or there would be no
"whole." The indispensable interconnections are provided by the institutionalizing function of the family, church, school, state, factory,
office, club, professional association, and other social institutions.[233]

These latter, in terms of Chapter 1 above, are systems or subsystems according to the point of view or the focus of the analysis, and their *institutions* would number marriage, confirmation,
degree conferring, private property, initiation, state board examinations and others. Prescribed and accepted modes of legitimation which is the heart of institutionalization on the PAS Model
is upon occasion explicitly accepted by Becker who did state for
example, that "not all customs become regulative institutions;
they are often characteristic but not necessarily obligatory. . ." [234]
The specificity of legitimizing procedures is a constant theme, of
course, in Becker's sacred-secular continuum; more than any other
theorist, perhaps, he emphasized the concrete legitimations of

behavior characteristic of the proverbial and prescribed societal types and their decreasing specificity as the secular pole is approached. That he did not choose to dwell upon their particulars nor to label them (very often at least) institutions of course does not vitiate in the least their true analytical nature. As he says in respect to institutions as he uses the term:

in any case . . . we are not looking at sharply distinct phenomena; the social world is like a great prism with numerous facets that reflect activities in many ways. We can look at the prism from this angle and that and see these flashes of light, and from that angle, those flashes, and from still another angle, still other flashes; but it is still the same prism and still the same light. The changes that have occurred have been changes in our perspective, in our modes of analysis.[235]

CONDITIONS OF SOCIAL ACTION

Territoriality. Becker recognized geographic position and spatial conditions as factors which have an effect upon sociation but quickly underlined the point that their function and primacy as determinants of behavior varies, fluctuating with cultural inventions which reduce or increase their importance. He warned against the danger of reifying the "notion of 'natural' area . . . extensively exploited by the . . . Chicago school" [236] and accepted Guenther's statement that "The boundary is just as much a spatial datum with sociological effects as it is a sociological datum that takes a spatial form." [237] His careful distinction between geographical location provided by nature and vicinal position provided by culture permits a much more precise estimate of the relative isolation-accessibility condition of a given society than can possibly be afforded by the geographic location alone.

The idea of fixed geographical location and its effects upon societies located therein has a sort of opposite counterpart in human or social ecology—"that is, the movement of persons to and from through physical space." [238] Becker acknowledged that there is merit to the claim that "the more mobile the area in which the person concerned lives, the more likely he is to be in some degree personally disorganized—because the mobile area in which he lives is likely to be socially disorganized." [239] Ongoing community life is virtually impossible in urban areas of high transiency

(rooming house areas, flop-house joints, etc.) He concluded however, that such movement and its characteristic attributes "is not
movement through physical space, but changes in social isolation
and social accessibility." [240] Some groups such as the gypsies are
highly mobile in the physical sense, but nevertheless maintain a
highly stable social organization. "It therefore does not do to
talk about *mobility* as if it were a merely physical phenomenon.
It is a social phenomenon, and it is a mental phenomenon." [241]

Size. Generally Becker in his own writings gave limited attention to size as one of the conditions or aspects of group existence.[242] In the Wiese-Becker volume considerable attention is
given to numerical size of groups. Small, medium, and large-sized
groups each is found to "manifest essential differences as well as
common features." [243] Also in this publication extended attention
is given the dyad, triad, and other groups including the "anti-
pair" one of sociology's early descriptions of the phenomenon of
human alienation. "Exploited, helpless, irritated, and disillu-
sioned persons release upon their companion in misery all the
impulses toward retaliation . . . [toward] the world outside." [244]
Simmel's and Wygodzinski's treatments of the optimum size of the
group are put in perspective. Although size is recognized as important to specific groups: ("Is the group becoming too large?
[has it] too great a number of 'outsiders'?" etc.) the optimum depends on the balancing of such factors as are represented in the
elements and processes of Figure 1, Chapter 1.

There is no possibility of fixing an optimal number of human beings
that holds good under all conditions; the number will . . . vary depending upon whether the group in question is a sect, a conspirital band, a
college fraternity, or a squad of soldiers. . . . Not only this . . . the optimal number will necessarily vary in every specific, empirical example. . . .[245]

Time. Becker acknowledged time as a conditioning factor in
at least two respects. One is in relation to the social scientist's
purpose as he arrays the data which is the focus of his attention
and constructs appropriate methodological tools with which to
deal with the data. Becker's distinction between the methodology
of the historian and that of the other social scientists has been
dealt with under cognitive mapping, as has been his own prefer-

ence for the long-range relatively timeless type construction epitomized in his sacred-secular continuum which nevertheless is not absolutely "timeless," possessing, as everything must, a degree of "historical saturation."

The other respect in which Becker recognized the time factor is very similar to, but less elaborated than his treatment of space as a factor.

Physical space is always a factor in any social science equation, but it is not to be equated with social space, any more than time in the physical sense is the same as time in the social or social-psychological.[246]

Chronological time as measured and social time as experienced may seem very different to persons engaged in various kinds of social action. The social symbols which fill the passing of the chronological minutes may, depending upon their nature, make any given unit of chronological time seem like a second or like eternity. Social duration, then, must always be taken into account as separate from physical time although closely allied to it.[247] It is but another aspect of the definition of the situation which must always accompany the focal social phenomena if the latter are to yield any predictive results. As previously noted as between the static and dynamic considerations in analysis Becker's concern was primarily with the latter. "The dynamic emphasis . . . [is] the most frequent; 'social process' is our chief category."[248]

SOCIAL CHANGE

From the beginning a major emphasis in Becker's work was the analysis and prediction of change. Writing for undergraduates he stated: "I think that when we have got through with a course of this kind we want to be able to say what is likely to happen next with regard to some kinds of human conduct. . . . The effort, then, is an effort at prediction, and by the same token, at control."[249]

The various methodologies employed, constructed types, cultural case studies, and all social analyses have their final evaluation in their utility as aids to prediction. After reviewing and criticizing some dozen or so analyses of social change Becker came to what he termed "A Usable Theory of History."[250] Here he mentioned the formulations of Shotwell, Robinson, Durkheim as well as those of Toennies and Teggart as offering less than those of Max and Alfred Weber.[251] The analyses by Max Weber, particularly those resulting in ideal types such as "rational man" and "economic man" as well as his development of the charismatic leader, the Protestant ethic and others, he accepted with little adverse criticism.

Becker's works show the marked influence of Max Weber but little of Alfred. The scant notice Becker gave Alfred Weber includes the following laudatory comment: "A signal service to historical sociology, in our estimation, has been performed by Alfred Weber in setting out this threefold classification" of society, civilization, and culture. Becker doubted, however, that "cultural" happenings and products are as unpredictable as Alfred Weber maintained.[252]

Pareto's "circulation of the elite," and the alternation between the *speculators* and *rentiers* is described with little adverse criticism. Among the theorists using large-scale cycles Spengler receives the most negative criticism, bolstered by judgments of Toynbee, Max and Alfred Weber and others who regard the *Decline of the West* as "nothing more than a *tour de force* executed by a man of undeniable literary ability and considerable erudition." [253]

Sorokin's "large-scale theory" was given more praise than disapproval but receives some of both. Becker objected that Sorokin 1) leans considerably on categories generalized in advance, 2) uses the illustrative method in propping his arguments, 3) is supported by a type of quantitative procedure which many statisticians do not condone and 4) rests only on the Greco-Roman and Western European cultures with only "forays into Egyptian, Arabic, Chinese, and Babylonian cultures." Becker also contended that "the principle of limits" which is at the base of the reversal of trends in Sorokin's types, ideational, idealistic and sensate cultures "has a dialectic flavor (although elsewhere Sorokin scoffs at Hegelian-Marxian notions) . . . [of] definitely *a priori* character." [254] He further maintained that Sorokin verges on an extreme functionalistic position based on the assumption that the socio-cultural units with which he deals are tangibly integrated in both the logico-meaningful and causal-functional senses with each isolatable part integrated as a whole forming a part of a larger whole. Sorokin's statement that "even systems of truth and knowledge, including so-called science, are but manifestations dependent upon the type of culture," if applied to Sorokin's own system of truth and knowledge would mean that he "has painted himself into a corner." [255] In this connection Becker stated that he preferred Max Weber's confidence in scientific systems which, although relevant to values, are not necessarily determined by value judgments.[256]

The cornerstone of Becker's own theory of change rests upon his faith in the predictive power of the human mind equipped with effective tools or concepts. His most dependable and frequently employed tool was the "constructed type" and most of his types are related to what he called sacred-secular theory. This sacred-secular continuum as employed by Becker implies as its basic component differential evaluation of the system itself (or society viewed as a system) and particularly of various of its components (which in Chapter 1 above are represented by elements and processes.) This is best illustrated by two of Becker's statements. "Sacred, sacredness, and sacralization . . . all designate . . . orientation on the part of members of a society toward values . . . held to be worthy of being made or kept inviolate." [257] "Secular, secularity and secularization . . . designate . . . orientation on the part of members of a society toward certain values . . . held to be worth pursuing regardless of entailed changes in the values themselves . . . or other changes . . ." [258] The designations, it may be noted, do not represent opposites as do so many typologies. The evaluations emerging from these orientations have been treated in previous parts of this chapter. The continuum is most frequently applied to societies, and time as related to social change is its focal theme. "A sacred society is one bringing its members to be unwilling or unable, in whatever measure, to accept the new *as the new is defined in that society*." [259] "A secular society is one bringing its members to be willing and able, in whatever measure, to accept or pursue the new *as the new is defined in that society*." [260]

As revealed elsewhere in this chapter but notably in the sections devoted to boundary maintenance and systemic linkage, one of the great achievements in Becker's continuum is the fact that the processes of social change are built into it. However, one of the major problems in using it in the analysis of change is that by definition sentiments toward change are the central focus and related factors such as isolation, accessibility, and sentiments toward the system so far as other processes are concerned, are secondary. The typology based upon reluctance vs. readiness to accept change obviously avoids much of the difficulties created by some static equilibrium models. However, those seeking answers to practical questions involving means for increasing the rate of change must look to what might be called the secondary characteristics of the typology in order to avoid the tautological considerations involved. In analysis it is necessary to turn to these secondary characteristics to avoid begging the question.

Becker accepted the importance of internal forces such as class conflict as well as external conflict and various other forces such as crises as being important in initiating change. Although not so dependent upon the concept of equilibrium as some social scientists the idea is used:

The most stable social organization, the most isolated sacred society to be found empirically, is but a moving equilibrium maintained by the equal action of relatively slow processes of disorganization and reorganization, and within such societies some social personalities are, relatively speaking, always undergoing a process of disorganization which may or may not be succeeded by reorganization.[261]

Moreover, in Becker's thinking "societal dissolution . . . rarely if ever occurs." [262] Like Toynbee for whom "challenge and response" are important and like W. I. Thomas who relied considerably on crisis to explain change, Becker used conquest and similar disrupting events in the explanation of change. Types of crises listed are "exhaustion of game, defeat in battle, floods, drought, pestilence and famine." [263] He agreed that "in the realm of the mind, at least, 'Conflict is the father of all things'." [264]

For Becker inventions, crises, and population movements produced change. However, although he did not use the term systemic linkage, he implied that it was required if inventions or population movements are to produce change.

Pastoral nomads do not change because of movement, nor do they change because of conflict; only when there is conquest, settlement among the conquered, and genuinely social rather than symbiotic interaction [systemic linkage] does the nomadic culture pattern undergo alteration.[265]

Whether described as taking the role of the other or in terms of various processes involving the common-human and circumscribed relations, interaction must take place if change is to come from contact. Although more attention is given to changes which move societies toward the secular pole in the process of secularization, the opposite process, sacralization, was also frequently discussed by Becker.[266] "Here mention can be made . . . of the Germans 'turning back the clock' from the Weimar secularity to Nazi sacredness." [267] "In crisis situations we regress, in some measure, to earlier types of societal organization." [268] Elsewhere Becker wrote, ". . . the path from one polar societal type to the other is not a one-way street; all around us can be seen evidence of the fact that societies, even 'modern societies,' can journey from secular to sacred." [269]

Becker was always remindful that *"there are costs of change. Every society undergoing fundamental and rapid change pays the price in the greater or lesser disorganization of some of its members. . . . When you rapidly change from the sacred to the secular mode of value-orientation, some personalities pay a price. You may feel that the price is worth paying . . ."* [270]

BIBLIOGRAPHICAL KEY

CCSAGH—Howard Becker, "Culture Case Study and Greek History," *American Sociological Review,* vol. 23 (October, 1958).

CSST—Howard Becker, "Current Sacred-Secular Theory," *Modern Sociological Theory,* ed. by Howard Becker and Alvin Boskoff (New York: The Dryden Press, 1957).

IFLIC—Howard Becker, "Interpreting Family Life in Context," in Howard Becker and Reuben Hill, eds., *Family, Marriage and Parenthood* (Boston: D. C. Heath and Co., 1955).

ISACT—Howard Becker, "Interpretive Sociology and Constructed Typology," *Twentieth Century Sociology,* ed. by Georges Gurvitch and Wilbert E. Moore (New York: Philosophical Library, 1945).

Holzner and Rhoads—Burkart Holzner and John Rhoads, "The Logic of Type Construction," unpublished manuscript.

MIR—Howard Becker, *Man in Reciprocity: Introductory Lectures on Culture, Society and Personality* (New York: F. A. Praeger, 1956).

NRN—Howard Becker, "Normative Reactions to Normlessness," *American Sociological Review*, Vol. 25, No. 6.

POS—Howard Becker, "Processes of Secularization," *Sociological Review* (British), Vol. 24, (1932).

Sac. S.—Howard Becker, "Sacred Society," UNESCO, *Dictionary of Social Science*, forthcoming.

SS & L.v.W.—Howard Becker, "Systematic Sociology and Leopold von Wiese," *Sociometry and the Science of Man*, ed. by J. L. Moreno (New York: Beacon House, 1956).

STFLTS—Howard Becker and Harry Elmer Barnes, *Social Thought from Lore to Science* (Washington, D. C.: Harren Press, 2nd ed. rev., 1952).

TVTSI—Howard Becker, *Through Values to Social Interpretation* (Durham, N. C.: Duke University Press, 1950).

Wiese-Becker—Howard Becker, *Systematic Sociology—on the Basis of the Beziehungslehre and Gebildelehre of Leopold von Wiese* (New York: Wiley, 1932).

For a more complete bibliography see the footnotes below, and the bibliographic appendix at the end of the volume.

NOTES

1. See Howard Becker, "Systematic Sociology and Leopold von Wiese," *Sociometry and the Science of Man*, ed. by J. L. Moreno (New York: Beacon House, 1956), p. 263. See Footnote 9 below for the reference to the "augmented version of the Wiese publications." This will hereafter be designated as S.S. & L.v.W.

2. Howard Becker, "Current Sacred-Secular Theory," *Modern Sociological Theory*, ed. by Howard Becker and Alvin Boskoff (New York: The Dryden Press, 1957), p. 181. This will hereafter be designated as CSST.

3. CSST, pp. 183-4.　　　　4. *Ibid.*, p. 180.

5. *Ibid.*, and taped recording of interview, May, 1960.

6. Howard Becker, *Man in Reciprocity: Introductory Lectures on Culture, Society, and Personality* (New York: F. A. Praeger, 1956), pp. xvii, 316, 317, 330. This will hereafter be referred to as MIR. Becker describes this as "a lightly edited series of lectures given in introductory courses." Notes on original manuscript.

7. Howard Becker, "Culture Case Study and Greek History," *American Sociological Review*, vol. 23 (October, 1958), p. 491. This will hereafter be designated as CCSAGH.

8. *Ibid.*

9. Howard Becker, *Systematic Sociology: on the Basis of the Beziehungslehre and Gebildelehre of Leopold von Wiese* (New York: Wiley, 1932), p. 11. See the writing specified in Footnote 1 above for Becker's relation to this work. Here his own contributions are noted. Also in MIR, p. 451, it is noted that the work is "not a translation, but an augmented adaptation." The work is hereafter designated as Wiese-Becker.

10. Howard Becker, "Sociology From 1937-1946," *Ten Eventful Years*, special issue of the *Encyclopaedia Britannica*, 1947, vol. 4. p. 113.

11. Howard Becker, *Through Values to Social Interpretation* (Durham,

N. C.: Duke University Press, 1950), p. 252. Hereafter this work will be designated as TVTSI.

12. Howard Becker, "Culture Case Study," *UNESCO Dictionary of Social Science*, forthcoming. Hereafter this work will be designated as UNESCO. Here he accepts J. L. Myres' definition.

13. MIR, p. 115.

14. Transcription of unpublished and unedited lectures for courses more advanced than those in MIR.

15. Wiese-Becker, pp. 458, 463.

16. Tape recorded discussion, May, 1960.

17. Wiese-Becker, pp. 420-421.

18. MIR, p. 1.

19. Marion J. Levy, Jr., "Some Questions About 'Concepts of Culture and of Social System,'" *American Sociological Review*, Vol. 24, No. 2, p. 247. For Levy "'cultural' refers to patterns of social action considered *qua* patterns. [These] patterns form parts of various social systems when they are considered *in operation* rather than *qua* patterns." *Ibid.*, p. 248. A "formalistic" approach which makes of sociology a taxonomy of structure and processes is in some ways a reversal of Levy's approach. See his *The Structure of Society* (Princeton, New Jersey: Princeton University Press, 1952).

20. TVTSI, p. 20 and MIR, p. 113.

21. *Ibid.*, p. 14.   22. CSST, p. 140.

23. Charles P. Loomis, *Social Systems: Essays on Their Persistence and Change* (Princeton, New Jersey: D. Van Nostrand Co., 1960), Essay 1.

24. MIR, Ch. 22.   25. *Ibid.*, p. 265.

26. *Ibid.*, Ch. 19.   27. *Ibid.*, Ch. 20.

28. *Ibid.*, p. 298.

29. Howard Becker and Harry Elmer Barnes, *Social Thought from Lore to Science* (Washington, D. C.: Harren Press, 2nd ed. rev., 1952). Hereafter designated as STFLTS. Becker is senior author of the third edition by the Dover Press.

30. MIR, Ch. 2.   31. *Ibid.*, pp. 33, 34.
32. *Ibid.*, pp. 29-36.   33. *Ibid.*, p. 31 and 32.
34. *Ibid.*, p. 39.   35. CSST, p. 176.
36. MIR, p. 284.   37. CSST, p. 136.
38. *Ibid.*, p. 136.   39. TVTSI, p. 97.
40. MIR, p. 327.   41. TVTSI, p. 96.
42. *Ibid.*, p. 120.   43. *Ibid.*, p. 106.
44. CCSAGH, p. 489.   45. TVTSI, p. 196.
46. CCSAGH, p. 497.

47. Howard Becker, "Interpretive Sociology and Constructed Typology," *Twentieth Century Sociology*, ed. by Georges Gurvitch and Wilbert E. Moore (New York: Philosophical Library, 1945), p. 72. Hereafter designated as ISACT. Shortly before his death Becker in conversation with the authors emphasized his preference for the word "Interpretative" in place of "Interpretive" as used here. In this conversation he stressed how he had "come more and more to make a real working distinction between the process of acquiring culture and the process of developing sociation . . . Self-and-other differentiation in the child becomes genuinely capable of sociation . . . [which] may not appear until three to three-and-a-half. Prior to this time [there] is socialization and inculturation, but it is not actual sociation. This

is as it appears in MIR and this is a development of only about the last five years . . ." From taped recording of interview, May, 1960.

48. TVTSI, p. 172.   49. CCSAGH, p. 495.

50. Howard Becker, "Constructive Typology in the Social Sciences," *American Journal of Sociology*, Vol. 5, (February, 1940), pp. 40-55.

51. TVTSI, p. 160.

52. Howard Becker, "Processes of Secularization," *Sociological Review* (British), Vol. 24, (1932), pp. 139-140. Hereafter designated as POS.

53. TVTSI, pp. 120-121.   54. TVTSI, p. 120.

55. *Ibid.*, p. 172.

56. For a bibliography see John C. McKinney, "Constructive Typology and Social Research," *An Introduction to Social Research* ed. by John T. Doby and others (Harrisburg, Pa.: Stackpole Co., 1954), Ch. 7. See also John C. McKinney, "Methodology, Procedures and Techniques in Sociology," in Howard Becker and Alvin Boskoff, *op. cit.*, Ch. 7. In TVTSI, p. 359 Becker briefly evaluates McKinney's treatment of dimensions on which typologies may be built.

57. Burkart Holzner and John Rhoads, "The Logic of Type Construction," unpublished manuscript. Hereafter designated as Holzner and Rhoads.

58. Becker notes that types are "not necessarily averages, although every average in the special technical sense of the mean (not the mode or the median) has some of the attributes of a constructed type." TVTSI, p. 219.

59. TVTSI, p. 220.   60. Holzner and Rhoads, p. 4.

61. May Brodbeck, "Models, Meaning, and Theories" in *Symposium on Sociological Theory*, ed. by Llewellyn Gross (Evanston, Ill.: Row, Peterson and Co., 1959), p. 378.

62. From tape recorded discussion, May, 1960.

63. Holzner and Rhoads, p. 3.   64. *Ibid.*, p. 8.

65. *Ibid.*, p. 18. Martindale maintains that "ideal types are neither experiments, mathematical models, nor theories but *devices intended to institute comparisons as precise as the stage of one's theory and the precision of his instruments will allow.*" "Sociological Theory and the Ideal Type," L. Gross, *op. cit.*, pp. 58-59.

66. C. G. Hempel and Paul Oppenheim, *Der Typusbegriff im Lichte der neuen Logik: Wissenschaftstheoretische Untersuchungen zur Konstitutionsforschung und Psychologie.* (Leiden, Holland, 1936).

67. Holzner and Rhoads, p. 10.

68. Howard Becker, "Forms of Population Movement," *Social Forces*, Vol. 9 (March, 1931), p. 361.

69. From tape recorded discussion, May, 1960.

70. Holzner and Rhoads, p. 17.

71. Kurt Grelling and Paul Oppenheim, "Der Gestaltbegriff im Lichte der neuen Logik," in *Erkenntnis*, Vol. 7 (1937-38).

72. Holzner and Rhoads, p. 14.   73. *Ibid.*, p. 17.

74. TVTSI, p. 197. See pp. 162 and 163 for a demonstration of the importance of the use of the rational model in judging the non-rational.

75. ISACT, pp. 81-82.

76. TVTSI, pp. 232 ff.

77. Robert K. Merton, *Social Theory and Social Structure* (Glencoe, Ill.: The Free Press, 1957), p. 60. See also CCSAGH, p. 504.

78. CCSAGH, p. 499.   79. CSST, p. 139.

80. *Ibid.* The following is largely based on CSST which differs from an earlier article entitled, "Forms of Sympathy: A Phenomenological Analysis," *Journal of Abnormal and Social Psychology* Vol. 26, No. 1. (April, 1931). Here various types of "sympathy" are distinguished following Max Scheler as presented in the latter's writings and in lectures at the University of Cologne which Becker attended. At this early writing Becker notes the importance of sentiment for "social personality" and "character attitudes" in sacred society. He writes, "They are built upon a basis of emotional solidarity, . . . far closer than can be found anywhere outside of the isolated sacred society." POS, p. 271.

81. MIR, p. 345.   82. *Ibid.*, p. 34.
83. *Ibid.*, p. 31.   84. CSST, p. 151.
85. *Ibid.*, p. 174.   86. TVTSI, p. 31.
87. *Ibid.*, pp. 238-239.   88. *Ibid.*, p. 246.

89. Howard Becker, *German Youth: Bond or Free* (New York: Oxford University Press, 1946), p. 200.

90. TVTSI, pp. 242-3.   91. CSST, p. 152.
92. MIR, 126.   93. TVTSI, p. 35.
94. *Ibid.*, p. 38.   95. *Ibid.*, p. 40.
96. *Ibid.*, p. 42.   97. *Ibid.*, pp. 52-3.
98. *Ibid.*, p. 48.   99. *Ibid.*, p. 68.
100. *Ibid.*, p. 70.   101. MIR, pp. 301-302.
102. *Ibid.*, pp. 320-322.

103. Before Becker's CSST appeared in which he first used the term "Norming," the senior author used the terms "standardizing and patterning" to designate what he now calls norming after Becker. See Charles P. Loomis, *Social Systems—Essays on Their Persistence and Change, op. cit.*, pp. 16-19.

104. Howard Becker, "Value," *UNESCO*. Here "valuation," is differentiated from "evaluation." " 'Valuation' may be defined as the reciprocal interrelating of needs and values at any level, nonsymbolic or symbolic." *Ibid.*

105. Loomis, *Social Systems, op. cit.*, p. 18.

106. CSST, p. 140.

107. Becker like Parsons began his career in sociological theory and research with a high evaluation of the general constructs of Ferdinand Toennies', *Gemeinschaft* and *Gesellschaft*. He also like Parsons became aware of their limitations due to their blanket, global, and general meaning. Becker writes, "Toennies has had a great deal to do with our guiding concepts of the sacred and the secular, as well as with the allied ideas of mental immobility and mental mobility." STFLTS, p. 878. In CSST Becker gives Everett C. Hughes credit for being the first to use the concepts, sacred and secular, in the tradition of Robert E. Park. Here he likewise mentions Robert Redfield's "folk-urban dichotomy" as having the same origin. CSST, p. 180. Writing about the concept, sacred society, Becker states that "R. E. Park seems to have referred to it in his lectures [in the 1920's] . . . as a rough equivalent of Toennies' *Gemeinschaft,* Durkheim's *société mécanique,* Maine's *society with status . . .*" Howard Becker, "Sacred Society," UNESCO, forthcoming. Hereafter designated as Sac. S. See Figures 2, 3, and 4, Appendix A for the relationship of Becker's types to those of other writers.

108. Wiese-Becker, p. 429. In consideration of Becker's sacred-secular continuum and its relation to Toennies it is of special interest to note that

Becker originally preferred to translate *Gemeinschaft* as "isolated sacred structure" and *Gesellschaft* as "accessible secular structure." *Ibid.* More recently Becker has translated *Gemeinschaft* as communal and *Gesellschaft* as associational, TVTSI, p. 258. He notes here that "This is only one of many possible translations."

109. CSST, p. 134. The following section relies heavily on CSST.

110. *Ibid.,* p. 141.   111. *Ibid.,* p. 145.

112. *Ibid.,* p. 146.   113. *Ibid.,* p. 149.

114. The conventionally sacred is designated as including both the fitting and the appropriate in Sac. S. Elsewhere, the sacred is split into holy, ceremonial, loyalistic, intimate, commemorative, moralistic, fitting and appropriate. "This roughly represents an intensity range from zeal for martyrdom in defense of the holy to quiet humor on behalf of the appropriate." MIR, p. 138. The first four of the eight types mentioned above "show a 'positive' self-other orientation . . . an emotionalized reluctance to change favorable or potentially favorable relations . . . A worshipper clings to his god, a patriot to his nation, a husband to his wife, and a mourner to the departed." The last four types "are not so clearly self-other-oriented . . . [and] chiefly refer to certain of the ways in which reluctances to change are kept in force . . ." MIR, p. 143.

115. CSST, p. 156.

116. Becker's dynamic classroom description of this form, shaped from Max Weber's *Zweckrational,* is as follows: "It is technical, instrumental, efficient, unbiased, calculating, dispassionate, detached, impersonal, unemotional, calm, 'objective', scientific . . . 'Nothing sacred' . . . is the watchword." MIR, p. 174.

117. "Rationality of this kind continually presses hard against the limits of principle . . . Often, heroic efforts are made to show that principle still prevails . . ." MIR, pp. 184-185.

118. ". . . Much of what is ordinarily called progress is directly attributable to consequent secularity. Science . . . is consequently secular . . ." CSST, pp. 158-9.

119. "Conservatives hoping to sacralize along prescriptive lines, and radicals (of either right or left) hoping for sweeping secularization, beleaguer the upholders of principle on every side." MIR, p. 186.

120. Becker notes that "man is a valuing animal." TVTSI, p. 6.

121. Becker's modes of evaluation resemble Max Weber's four types. Becker notes that his "formulation does not occur in the writings of Max Weber: the four-fold classification does although with some important differences." TVTSI, p. 200. See also Howard Becker, "Interpreting Family Life in Context," in Howard Becker and Reuben Hill, eds., *Family, Marriage and Parenthood* (Boston, D. C. Heath and Co., 1955), p. 14. Hereafter the latter article is referred to as IFLIC. See Becker's analysis of 1) expedient rationality, 2) sanctioned rationality, 3) traditional nonrationality, and 4) emotional or affective non-rationality. TVTSI, pp. 22 ff.; MIR, p. 116.

122. For a comparison of the sacred-secular continuum with Redfield's folk-urban dichotomy see MIR, pp. 168 and 176. For a criticism of the folk-urban dichotomy see TVTSI, p. 257. See also a criticism of the Sorokin trilogy, ideational, idealistic, and sensate, TVTSI, p. 74.

123. CSST, p. 153.

124. Sac. S. See CSST, fn. 83, p. 183. Becker's first acceptance of and

later shifting away from Redfield's folk-urban typology may be noted in various publications. See POS, p. 138 and pp. 144-45. See Footnote 122 above.

125. MIR, pp. 52-54, 61, 65. "Prescriptions are often not much more than systematic verbalizations of tradition . . . [They] may be the result either of gradual systematization or sudden charismatic reformulation of older conceptions . . ." IFLIC, pp. 31 and 32.

126. CSST, p. 154.   127. *Ibid.*

128. MIR, pp. 74-6.   129. *Ibid.*, p. 155.

130. *Ibid.*, p. 156.

131. TVTSI, p. 277. Becker observes that "P. A. Sorokin . . . exerted influence [on his own thinking], partly because his polemic against 'sensate' societies, forced [him] to reflect on the relations of principial and pronormless societies." CSST, p. 180.

132. CSST, p. 156.   133. *Ibid.*, p. 169.

134. *Ibid.*   135. *Ibid,* p. 170.

136. *Ibid.*

137. *Ibid.*, p. 171. Howard Becker, "Normative Reactions to Normlessness," *American Sociological Review,* Vol. 25, No. 6, pp. 803 ff. Hereafter designated as NRN. For Ruth Useem's unique contribution to this change from the use of the concept "normless" to that of "pronormless" see the text of Ch. 9 below. Tape-recorded discussion with Becker, last quotation before fn. 195.

138. CSST, p. 159.   139. *Ibid.*

140. *Ibid.*, p. 160.   141. *Ibid.*, p. 162.

142. CSST, p. 163.   143. *Ibid.*, p. 163.

144. *Ibid.*, p. 164.   145. *Ibid.*, pp. 164-5.

146. *Ibid.*, p. 165.   147. TVTSI, pp. 166-172.

148. MIR, pp. 328 ff. In Wiese-Becker all four types are used to explain the origin and development of Methodism, pp. 624 ff.

149. *Ibid.*, p. 333.

150. *Ibid.*, Ch. 23. Becker notes that he is more indebted to Reinhold Niebuhr in the development of his cult-ecclesia continuum than to Weber or Troeltsch. He notes that the latter two did not deal with denomination or cult in any detail. Tape recorded interview, May, 1960.

151. CSST, pp. 173-4. NRN.

152. MIR, p. 197. Becker when differentiating between role expectancies and actual role behavior prefers the terms assigned role and enacted role respectively. He gave an interesting account of how at the University of Wisconsin, Linton came to use the terms status and role from Kimball Young's interpretation of G. H. Mead's use of the term role. Taped discussion, May, 1960.

153. MIR, p. 106.

154. The types are: 1) the unmoral or amoral man, 2) the demoralized man, 3) the segmental or immoral man, 4) the marginal man, 5) the regulated man, 6) the decadent man, and 7) the liberated man. MIR, pp. 198-199. In terms of the PAS Model the marginal man is important in the master process of systemic linkage.

155. MIR, pp. 352-355.   156. *Ibid.*, p. 215.

157. Wiese-Becker, pp. 322 and 325.   158. *Ibid.*, p. 323.

159. MIR, p. 399. Wiese-Becker, pp. 132 ff. Although the text of both

these references indicates a special meaning of primary and secondary different from that of the followers of Cooley, Becker did not apparently intentionally deviate from the latters' interpretation. "When I say primary and secondary contacts . . . these are [respectively] direct and indirect . . . Secondary contacts are those that are transmitted through telegraph, telephone, [etc.] . . . If you are treated like a sack of potatoes by a subway guard, this might be [secondary]." Tape recorded discussion, May, 1960.

160. MIR, p. 398. For a systematic arrangement of these processes between selves and status-roles as well as systemic linkage of plurality patterns, see Wiese-Becker, pp. 118-119 and 124. Becker in 1960 had a manuscript index of several dozen places in Wiese-Becker in which the terms structure and/or function were used.

161. MIR, p. 332.

162. *Ibid.,* p. 421, TVTSI, p. 302. William James, *Essays on Faith and Morals* (New York: 1943), p. 401.

163. MIR, p. 373.   164. *Ibid.,* p. 410.

165. Wiese-Becker, pp. 630-641.

166. Wiese-Becker, p. 632. Becker says that the quotation is "not Weber's phrase" but only a hint of Weber's. Notes on the margin of the original of the present manuscript. Becker notes that "ascetism of the sect is quite different from the asceticism of the ecclesia. The latter may be called extra-worldly, whereas the former is intra-worldly." *Ibid.,* p. 634.

167. MIR, pp. 292.   168. *Ibid.,* p. 217.

169. *Ibid.,* p. 218.   170. *Ibid.,* p. 419.

171. *Ibid.,* p. 420.   172. *Ibid.*

173. *Ibid.,* p. 293.   174. *Ibid.*

175. *Ibid.,* p. 425. Here it is noted that "almost two-thirds of the next generation will be the offspring of the lower half of the socio-economic ladder of this generation."

176. *Ibid.,* p. 413.   177. *Ibid.,* p. 420.

178. *Ibid.,* p. 410.   179. *Ibid.,* p. 428.

180. TVTSI, p. 24.   181. *Ibid.,* p. 25.

182. *Ibid.,* p. 26.   183. *Ibid.*

184. MIR, p. 267.   185. *Ibid.,* p. 269.

186. *Ibid.,* p. 268.   187. *Ibid.,* Ch. 19.

188. *Ibid.,* p. 287.   189. *Ibid.,* p. 292.

190. MIR, pp. 293-4.   191. *Ibid.,* pp. 421-2.

192. CSST, p. 144.   193. MIR, Ch. 3.

194. CSST, p. 145.   195. *Ibid.,* pp. 143-9.

196. CSST, p. 154.   197. *Ibid.,* p. 155.

198. TVTSI, p. 298.   199. CSST, p. 173.

200. *Ibid.,* p. 156.   201. *Ibid.,* p. 158.

202. MIR, p. 307.   203. *Ibid.,* p. 410.

204. *Ibid.,* p. 197.   205. *Ibid.,* p. 385.

206. *Ibid.,* p. 388.   207. *Ibid.,* pp. 271-2

208. *Ibid.,* p. 419. In SS & L.v.W., p. 267, Becker observes, "As any reader can plainly see [construction and destruction] are equivalent to Merton's function and dysfunction or Levy's eufunction and dysfunction."

209. MIR, p. 417.

210. *Ibid.,* pp. 425-426. It will be noted that the process of harmoniza-

tion here has taken the place of socialization as it appears in Figure 1, Appendix A, from Wiese-Becker.

211. CSST, p. 172.   212. MIR, pp. 214-219.
213. Wiese-Becker, p. 625.   214. MIR, p. 192.
215. *Ibid.*, p. 269.   216. TVTSI, p. 84.
217. CSST, p. 134.   218. IFLIC, p. 7.
219. *Ibid.*   220. MIR, p. 198.
221. *Ibid.*, p. 202.

222. The other five types were as follows: 1) the unadjusted or unmoral, 2) the maladjusted or demoralized, 3) the uncritically adjusted or regulated, 4) the sophisticatedly, called fretfully in IFLIC, p. 43, adjusted or decadent and 5) the tight-rope walker-adjusted or liberated. MIR, pp. 207-224. Concerning these he states, "I was carried away in part by Thomas in the discussion of what I first called the amoral personality [1] above] . . . The so-called liberated personality type . . . is an uneasy mixture of Wiese . . . [and] my own modification." Tape recorded discussion, May, 1960.

223. MIR, p. 217. Becker notes that the segmented type "comes directly from Faris." Tape recorded discussion, May, 1960.

224. Becker states that "my own treatment of the marginal man certainly owes 80 percent to Park's suggestions . . . but it does not wholly square with Park's later treatment . . . nor [does it square exactly] with Stonequist's." Tape recorded discussion, May, 1960. Reference is made to Becker's Ph.D. dissertation in which it was first developed in 1930. "Ionia and Athens: Studies in Secularization," University of Chicago.

225. MIR, p. 219.   226. TVTSI, p. 15.
227. CSST, p. 150.

228. Wiese-Becker, p. 406. Becker notes that "professionalization is merely an aspect of institutionalization. Many institutions [require personnel which are] more interested in serving the ends of the total system than . . . serving their own personal ends . . . A professional man cannot be wholly paid for his services in dollars and cents; if he can be so paid then he does not belong to a profession." Transcription of unpublished lectures for courses more advanced than those appearing in MIR. Those readers who, like the present authors, wonder about the process called liberation, as it appears in the constructive relations, will be interested in Becker's comment concerning the tight-rope walker—adjusted or liberated type of personality. See above in footnotes on socialization. "This is an uneasy mixture, of Wiese in his discussion of liberation . . . I felt a little uneasy about it because it has a little too much of Wiese's philosophical anarchism in it." Tape recorded discussion, May, 1960.

229. Wiese-Becker, pp. 406-7.

230. Tape recorded discussion, May, 1960. The same ideas are expressed in the transcriptions of unpublished lectures for courses more advanced than those appearing in MIR. Manuscripts made available in May, 1960.

231. MIR, p. 239.   232. *Ibid.*

233. *Ibid.*, p. 239. For the student who wants to study the details of Becker's analysis of the relation of the whole and its parts as manifest in concepts such as society, separate plurality patterns and individuals, Becker recommends Wiese-Becker, Chapter 4. Tape recorded discussion, May, 1960. Here he notes, "We cannot produce this phantasm [*one* universal structure called 'society'] by addition—state+church+trade union+club . . .

We can only *abstract* the social . . . The process of sociation, not the entity of 'society,' furnishes the data for sociological research." *Ibid.*, p. 79. "There is nothing that is only 'individual' and nothing that is only 'society,' just as there is nothing that is only part and only whole." *Ibid.*, p. 84.

234. Wiese-Becker, pp. 403-4.   235. MIR, p. 240.

236. Wiese-Becker, p. 436.   237. *Ibid.*, p. 437.

238. MIR, p. 394.   239. *Ibid.*

240. *Ibid.*, p. 395.   241. *Ibid.*, p. 396.

242. Howard Becker and Ruth Hill Useem, "Sociological Analysis of the Dyad," *American Sociological Review*, Vol. 7, (Feb., 1942), pp. 13-26.

243. Wiese-Becker, p. 499.

244. *Ibid.*, p. 518. Becker noted that he coined the terms "dyad" and "triad" in Wiese-Becker, (from notes on the margin of the original manuscript of the present chapter). The phrase "companions in misery" is also used by Homans. See fn. 145, Ch. 4 below and text related thereto.

245. Wiese-Becker, pp. 500-501.   246. MIR, p. 396.

247. *Ibid.*, p. 397.   248. Wiese-Becker, p. 55.

249. MIR, pp. 17-18.

250. TVTSI, p. 158. He agrees with Toynbee's conclusion "that antlike or machine-like perfection of adaptation acts as a check on change." He is very critical of many of Toynbee's conclusions but states "that Toynbee has given to sociologists a magnificent example of the possibilities of culture case study in historical sociology." TVTSI, pp. 152-4.

251. Becker notes that "Toennies built his entire theory of social development as set forth in *Geist der Neuzeit* as well as in earlier writings, in terms of the transition from 'community' to 'society,' joining to it, as an inseparable corollary, a shift from 'essential will' to 'arbitrary will'—or in terms used earlier in the chapter [by Becker] from mental immobility to mental mobility." TVTSI, p. 159.

252. *Ibid.*, p. 168.   253. *Ibid.*, p. 180.

254. *Ibid.*, pp. 181-2.   255. *Ibid.*, p. 185.

256. *Ibid.*, pp. 181-5.   257. Howard Becker, Sac. S., UNESCO.

258. Howard Becker, "Secular Society," UNESCO.

259. Howard Becker, Sac. S., UNESCO.

260. Howard Becker, "Secular Society," UNESCO.

261. POS, p. 266.   262. CSST, p. 160.

263. Howard Becker, "Conquest by Pastoral Nomads," *Sociology and Social Research*, Vol. 15, No. 6, p. 522. See also TVTSI, p. 152.

264. TVTSI, p. 185.

265. Howard Becker, "Pastoral Nomadism and Social Change," *Sociology and Social Research*, Vol. 15, No. 5 (1931), p. 427.

266. MIR, p. 373.   267. *Ibid.*, p. 171.

268. *Ibid.*, p. 373.   269. IFLIC, p. 45.

270. MIR, pp. 441-42.

FRAME OF REFERENCE FOR THE SYSTEMATICS OF ACTION PATTERNS

Part I. Common-Human Relations

Prerequisites of Processes: Contacts (Socio-Psychological)

A. Processes of Association					B. Processes of Dissociation				M. Mixed Processes	
General Processes of Association	a. Advance	b. Adjustment	c. Accordance	d. Amalgamation	General Processes of Dissociation	a. Competition	b. Contravention	c. Conflict	Primary	Secondary
Concrete Data: Single Social Actions or Processes	Concrete Data: Single Social Actions or Processes	Concrete Data: Single Social Actions or Processes	Concrete Data: Single Social Actions or Processes	Concrete Data: Single Social Actions or Processes	Concrete Data: Single Social Actions or Processes	Concrete Data: Single Social Actions or Processes	Concrete Data: Single Social Actions or Processes	Concrete Data: Single Social Actions or Processes	Concrete Data: Single Social Actions or Processes	Concrete Data: Single Social Actions or Processes

A Processes Predominant - Associativeness, etc.   B Processes Predominant = Solitariness, etc.

Conditions Arising from Common-Human Processes;

A + B + M Processes = Genesis of Plurality Patterns

Part II. Circumscribed Relations

C. Differentiation					D. Integration			E. Destruction						F. Construction		
a. Genesis of Disparities	b. Domination and Submission	c. Gradation and Stratification	d. Selection	e. Individuation, Separation, and Estrangement	a. Uniformation	b. "Ordination," Super-ordination, and Subordination	c. Socialization	a. Exploitation	b. Favoritism and Bribery	c. Formalism and "Ossification"	d. Commercialization	e. Radicalization	f. Perversion	a. Institutionalization	b. Professionalization	c. Liberation
Concrete Data: Single Social Actions or Processes	Concrete Data: Single Social Actions or Processes	Concrete Data: Single Social Actions or Processes	Concrete Data: Single Social Actions or Processes	Concrete Data: Single Social Actions or Processes	Concrete Data: Single Social Actions or Processes	Concrete Data: Single Social Actions or Processes	Concrete Data: Single Social Actions or Processes	Concrete Data: Single Social Actions or Processes	Concrete Data: Single Social Actions or Processes	Concrete Data: Single Social Actions or Processes	Concrete Data: Single Social Actions or Processes	Concrete Data: Single Social Actions or Processes	Concrete Data: Single Social Actions or Processes	Concrete Data: Single Social Actions or Processes	Concrete Data: Single Social Actions or Processes	Concrete Data: Single Social Actions or Processes

g. Outcome of E: Deterioration

d. Outcome of F: Reconstruction

* From Wiese-Becker, op. cit. p. 124.

APPENDIX A FIGURE 2

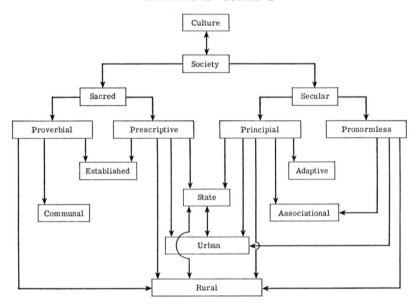

RELATIONS OF SOME CURRENT TWOFOLD CLASSIFICATIONS

Figure 2

    Established -- adaptive, Elton Mayo
    Folk -- State, Howard W. Odum
    Folk -- urban, Robert Redfield
    Rural -- urban, nobody in particular, but widely used
    Communal -- associational, Ferdinand Tönnies
        (this is only one of the many possible translations of Gemeinschaft --
        Gesellschaft; the writer personally prefers fellowship -- affiliation).

From TVTSI *op. cit.* p. 258.

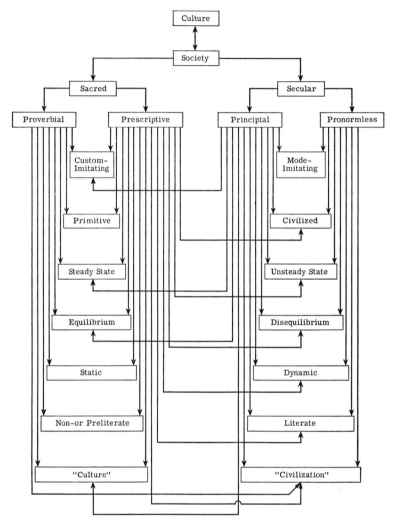

RELATIONS OF SOME MORE TWOFOLD CLASSIFICATIONS
(size and position do not indicate any estimate of relative importance)

Figure 3

Custom-imitating -- mode-imitating, Gabriel Tarde
Primitive -- civilized, nobody in particular, but once widely used
"Steady state" -- "unsteady state," Gregory Bateson
Equilibrium -- disequilibrium, many, but especially Carleton Coon and Eliot Chapple
Static -- dynamic, nobody in particular, but frequently used by many English writers
Non- or preliterate -- literate, many, but especially Ellsworth Faris
"Culture" -- "civilization," R. M. MacIver and many German writers

From TVTSI *op. cit.* p. 259.

CHAPTER 3

KINGSLEY DAVIS: GENERALIZING AND SPECIALIZING ANALYST

Kingsley Davis had already begun to specialize in demography when he wrote of his major work *Human Society* that it "intends to raise only those questions that concern social systems as wholes." [1] Indeed, one of the distinguishing features of Davis' remarkable sociological career is this mastery of demography, the most quantitative, objective, and positivistic of the sociological specialties, and of sociological theory which by its nature must be vastly less empirical. In his contributions to social science through such special fields as demography, social stratification, the sociology of the family and urbanization, interest in sociological theory and broad sociological analysis is maintained.

Employing analytical tools freely from sociology,[2] social psychology,[3] and anthropology,[4] his basic concepts involve what he calls "four fundamental approaches": 1) "social norms—the folkways, mores, laws, and institutions"; 2) the social positions or status-roles occupied by members; 3) the "means-ends schema," including the actor, the ends, means, and conditions in terms of which the norms and statuses enter the motivation of each individual; and 4) "the processes of interaction—conflict, competition, and cooperation." [5] The first two components "have to do primarily with social structure," [6] and the last two, with the dynamic and processual aspects of systems.

Although originally committed to the "functional-structural approach to sociological analysis . . . [as] basically an equilibrium theory," he has more recently renounced what he now calls the

104

"functionalist movement." Functionalism, originally seen as the explanation of "social organization and behavior from a disinterested observer's point of view," has, he now believes, proved itself unable to "see purposes and sentiments as objects of explanation," and unable "to remain detached." [7] This abandonment of functionalism according to Davis has nothing to do with the alleged inadequacies of functionalism in dealing with social change. In fact in *Human Society* "the terms sociological and functional analysis [were used] synonymously," each symbolizing for Davis the appropriate central area of interest for the sociologist and avoiding the influence of various "reductionist theories." However, in 1959 upon reviewing the relevant literature he came to the conclusion that some writers use the term, functional analysis, "as if it were something different from sociological analysis." [8] Thus, admitting that "doubtless the *feeling* behind the separation of functional and causal analysis has some basis," [9] and that some usages of functionalism including his own make it equivalent to sociological analysis, to avoid "confusions and discussions that have grown up," he decided to drop the term and speak only of sociological analysis.

No doubt the controversy about functional and non-functional analysis in its present form will pass; but it is probable that the distinctions stressed by Davis will persist. The core of systemic analysis is to be found in his distinctions between the factual and the normative; [10] between the externalized and internalized norms; [11] between that which is right and that which will work; [12] between the actor's subjectively conceived ends and those as seen by the observer; [13] between the structural and the dynamic aspects of social action; [14] and between the study of whole societies and of certain aspects of that whole, such as population. Whether those who consider these distinctions scientifically call themselves nonpositivists, functionalists, or just sociologists is less important than the distinctions.

Of the theorists treated in the present volume Davis shares with Becker the use of the conflict, competition, and cooperation forms of interaction as developed by the so-called "Chicago school of sociology." He alone, however, gives a detailed analysis of the results of non-interaction. His articles on extreme isolation of the child contribute uniquely to the development of knowledge of the sociological components of socialization. He and Warner early used the latter's distinction between the family of orientation and the family of procreation, a distinction which greatly facilitates the analyses of the family [15] and of society in general.[16] The means-ends schema pervades all of the work of Davis, in whose hands it becomes a powerful analytical tool.

Convergences with the PAS Model are to be anticipated by the most casual reading of Davis' work. Sentiment, evaluation, norms and ends for example, emerge together as follows:

the same attitude of respect that is directed toward the ultimate values, superempirical entities, and sacred objects is also directed toward the mores. . . . Sacred objects . . . symbolize the things of the unseen world, and . . . [this] gives the actor a source and final justification for his group ends—ends that he shares with other members of society.[17]

The major convergences as well as the major distinctions are elaborated as Davis' model is juxtaposed on the PAS Model.

KNOWING

Belief (knowledge) as an element. Although Davis does not identify belief or knowledge as a basic social element he acknowledges that "the distribution of knowledge and ignorance according to position in the social system is a definite part of the social system itself. . . ." [18] His two structural approaches, the norms and the status-roles or positions, accordingly exhibit aspects of cognition. Thus, "the normative order can never be completely deduced from knowledge of the factural order, nor vice versa. . . . The normative order makes the factual order of human society possible." [19] Folkways, constituting a part of the normative order when "repeated often enough become habits—habits of thought as well as of action—and they come to form the unstated premises in our mental life." [20] Law, another part of the normative order, "is a product of conscious thought and planning, of deliberate formulation and voluntary application." [21]

Division of labor with its consequent status-roles is similarly cognitively based. The specialties of each status-role are in a sense specializations of knowledge. "Putting to work the part they do learn, [individuals] perform useful functions for the entire group on the basis of their special knowledge." [22] Specialized knowledge held by incumbents of different status-roles assures human society that its main-stream of knowledge is being perpetuated despite "the finite capacity of the single individual to learn." [23]

Belief as a component of social organization is perhaps most specifically identified in Davis' exposition of religious institutions, although it is of course, here submerged by the emphasis given sentiment, evaluation, and ritual.

Resting on this subjective attitude [sentiment and evaluation] are two different aspects of the holy—namely, belief and ritual. Religious belief is the cognitive aspect of religion; it attempts to explain the nature and origin of sacred things and implicitly assumes that they exist. It refers in the first place to the superempirical world . . . [relating it] to the one we actually live in. . . . In the second place . . . religious belief tells us also what the nature of sacred objects is and how these objects relate to the superempirical world. . . . The belief rests upon an attitude, not upon observation. . . . There is nothing to distinguish a sacred cow from any cow, except the faith of those who regard her as sacred.[24]

Religious belief and health practices and beliefs are related. "Folk theory through human history has practically always regarded disease and death as caused by spiritual—religious, magical, and moral—forces." [25] Non-religious creeds, such as those subscribed to by "healing cults" are equally compelling for their advocates. "The practitioners have a vested interest in their particular creed. If it is found invalid, their livelihood no longer exists. It is this closed-mindedness, this devotion to a particular belief which justifies the title 'cult' or 'sect' for all these groups." [26] Scientific medicine sustains some non-scientific beliefs too.

A popular twentieth-century misconception is that science has replaced magic and superstition in the field of medicine. But when thinking of something as having "replaced" something else in human culture, it is wise to ask what were the functions once performed by the thing supposedly replaced. . . . It seems clear that scientific medicine cannot fulfill all the functions which religio-magical medicine can . . . [and] we find in our midst today an important body of religio-magical medicine.[27]

The processual aspect of cognition can be distinguished as the actors and groups comprising the religious systems, health systems, and other major social systems engage in interaction and pursue goals by a variety of means.

Cognitive mapping and validation as process. The term rationality for Davis may be equated to one form of cognitive mapping and validation. He maintains that both in the determination of ends and in the adapting of means to the end, the knowledge and skill at the disposal of the actor are used. Although "there is an element of rationality or attempted rationality in all human action" [28] at least four factors militate against completely rational behavior.

(1) The pursuit of transcendental goals by its nature excludes the employment of demonstrably effective means, or facilities. The actor who employs a means to salvation undoubtedly believes there is a connection between the means used and the ends to be gained, but that connection cannot be tested. His validation is by "arbitrary tradition." "He simply accepts the connection on faith rather than on evidence." [29]

(2) "Haziness of goal" likewise hinders the application of maximum rationality. Among the imperfectly conceived goals are those representing the "wish for new experience" (after Thomas and Znaniecki) based upon the unvalidated supposition that *any* future state will be preferable to the status quo; those which fail to assess the future state as it is likely to be without the application of effort; and those, the pursuit of which will yield consequences other than the desired one.

(3) Ignorance, stemming from misconception or from not having learned or having forgotten an available means, decreases the rationality of action.

(4) There are normative restrictions upon choice of both goal and means. The actor may be able to marshall all pertinent and available beliefs and knowledge in the definition of his objective and in its pursuit, but be dissuaded from the course of action suggested by such a reconnoitering because of normative restrictions. "To this extent normative regulation and rationality are opposed." [30] Although the net result of all human action is far from maximally rational, for the actor it has the "illusion of rationality." The ability of the actor to validate false belief and to rationalize irrational action protects both the actor's ego and his society for "No social order could be composed of persons willing to use any means whatever to gain their ends." [31]

The processual aspect of belief and knowledge receives Davis' attention as he analyzes various social systems. Organized education, for example, has been "rationalistic in the sense of assuming the sole significant orientation to the world to be one of cognition." [32] Educational agencies flounder when educators emphasize "real life situations" to the virtual exclusion of abstract knowledge upon which modern culture is based. ". . . To confine all instruction to the applied and concrete would soon produce stagnation." [33]

The dynamics of beliefs are demonstrated in the demographer's sphere of vital statistics—fertility, life, and death. "Human beings who have been smart enough during thousands of centuries to build fires, fashion weapons, employ speech, and regulate behavior have also been smart enough to separate sexual pleasure from procreation." [34] The high evaluation of virility is often accompanied by a false validation of belief: that "a sure proof of one's virility is the number of one's children." [35] A compelling universal goal such as health need not be supported by myth and dogma; scientific means to achieve the goal are consequently readily introduced.[36] An interesting functional comparison of mythology is developed in this connection.

The greatest social mythology is required not for the preservation of life but for its sacrifice; whereas the greatest mythology is required not for the sacrifice of fertility but for its maintenance. In the postponement of death the search is for the proper means of achieving the goal, not for the means of maintaining the goal itself.[37]

Davis' presentation of his own material, like that of the other theorists treated in this volume, demonstrates the process of cognitive mapping. He posits necessary conditions for the existence of "every kind of society from insect to man," [38] categorizing biosocial systems based on hereditary patterns and socio-cultural systems based on culture patterns. Human society, the only society characterized by both patterns, strictly speaking, should be designated as "bio-socio-cultural." The unique trait of human society is its system of symbolic communication. This latter, not being uniform the world over, makes mandatory a study of many different human societies if a general science of society is to be built. Systematic knowledge so abstracted and generalized that it can be used for social prediction requires adequate investigative techniques designed to minimize the hazards of social analysis. Among the hazards are reliance on the purely descriptive or historical accounts, the position of the social scientist as simultaneous member and observer of the social system, the logical fallacy of misplaced concreteness, the neglect of either theory or empirical data, and problems of differentiation between cause-effect and/or ends-means relations.

In his treatment of demography, Davis demonstrates some of the pitfalls of cognitive mapping in social science and the kind of inventiveness by which mistakes can be corrected. Observing that "innovations in demography, or in other social sciences, are determined mainly not by the inner development of science itself but by the impingement of historical events," [39] he cites the example of faulty population predictions resulting from reified demographic models. A long decline in fertility was causally associated with such trends as urbanization, class mobility, and the decline of family functions. These latter trends were still operative when a spectacular rise in fertility took place. "It was clear that demographic theory and technique were defective, that abstractions gave no predictive power . . . that too simplified a view of human reproduction had been followed." [40] An improved theory and technique resulted in ". . . a more complex and faithful demographic analysis of reproductive behavior than had been used before." [41] Among the corrections used were a differentiation between current and cumulative fertility ratios (the cohort idea) and the inclusion of such components as attitudes and motives.

It is perhaps appropriate here to mention Davis' early understanding and conceptualization of the modern phenomenon which is variously called the demographic transition, vital revolution, demographic revolution, and other terms. Davis was perhaps the first to use the terms "population explosion," [42] which has come into rather popular usage, and "demographic transition," [43] which is considered by some as a model to be used in interpreting population change. It has been applied to those societies which in the past have displayed a long run balance between mortality and fertility rates but which are moving into a period of imbalance. A rapid decline of mortality with no corresponding drop in fertility rates may be observed for a while after which a balance may be reestablished. To the extent that the balance-transition-balance idea is used as a model, Davis believes that it is not without its dangers of reification. An unwary demographer, for example, who thought in terms of the transition model, might reason:

"India . . . is in the early stages of demographic transition. . . . In fifty years or so it will complete the transition." The interesting thing about India or most underdeveloped areas today is not the similarity of their situations with that of the West in an earlier period [which with Japan and similar societies form the basis of the model] but the differences. . . . [It is fallacious to expect] that they are going to follow the course of Japan . . . conditions have changed.[44]

FEELING

Sentiment as an element. Davis does not treat sentiment as an element of the social system although it is specified in the last chapter of *Human Society* as being one of the elements composing the socio-cultural level.[45] Despite its not being accorded an elemental position in the bulk of the work, at no time is sentiment viewed as unimportant.[46] Its relation to norms, as elaborated under that heading, is indispensable; and it is virtually the underpinning of such basic concepts as value which too is accorded an elemental position on the socio-cultural level.

The source of the value in turn lies chiefly in the *sentiments*, broad backgrounds of feeling which make some things seem valuable, others not valuable. Such feelings arise partly from organic urges, partly from internalized norms. The transition from sentiment, to value, to end is one of increasing specificity. In a sense the end is the particular application of a sentiment or value to a given situation as perceived by the actor.[47]

Feeling and cognition are interrelated: "In every human situation there are two elements—the facts and the attitude or sentiment toward the facts . . . among the societal requirements, the necessity of ideological and sentimental cohesion, or solidarity is outstanding."[48] The importance of sentiment in boundary maintenance will be discussed further below. Davis accepts Radcliffe-Brown's position that the sentiments in the minds of the system's members conforms the individual to the needs of the society, but observes that such sentiments "prove more effective if they are not scientifically understood by the average person. One of the functions of religion is to justify, rationalize, and support the sentiments that give cohesion to the society." [49] Ambiguous and uninstitutionalized situations are characterized as tension producing, a position which resembles Malinowski's analysis of the uncertainties present in deep sea fishing and Parsons' analysis of medical practice.

Many situations accompanied by jealousy likewise produce tension. Davis sees these as provoked by conflict situations, the content of which vary from culture to culture. Jealousy is for Davis "an emotion which has a function as a part of an institutional structure." [50] Whether the conflict situation involves sexual property, romantic love and courtship, marriage between racial castes, youth-parent conflict, or divorce-produced stress for the child, the aroused sentiments support the norms, functioning not only in terms of ". . . emotional balance but also with reference to social organization." [51]

The major social systems are illustrative of sentiment as it is related to other basic social components. Religious and family systems are particularly sentiment-laden.

In every society there is a sharp distinction between the holy, the ordinary, and the unholy. . . . Clearly the holy and the unholy are closely related because of the highly emotional attitude toward them. They both stand in contrast to the ordinary. . . . For this reason the usual distinction between the sacred and the profane is ambiguous. . . . A threefold distinction therefore seems preferable. . . . The unholy generally consists of an unauthorized contact between the ordinary and the holy. This is what is meant by "profanation." [52]

In situations which are irreversible and upsetting, such as that involved in the case of death of a loved friend or relative, cognition is insufficient. "Our emotional equilibrium has been upset, our hopes and desires frustrated. We need . . . an interpretation in terms of sentiments and values." [53]

The positive sentiments associated with courtship and marriage have their counterpart in negative sentiments associated with some forms of sex behavior.

A part of our horror of prostitution apparently derives from our customary association of sexual contact with affection, and the significance of the "kiss of Judas" would be utterly nil without a similar association of kissing with affection.[54]

A combination of circumstances heightens tensions for American youth over what youth in most other parts of the world encounter. In contrast to most peoples, American youth is normatively denied premarital intercourse, but nonetheless is often denied early marriage. Also in contrast to youth in many other cultures, American youths at marriage experience a precipitous independence from their parents. They choose their own mates and upon marriage establish separate households with normative expectations that the new family of procreation be independent from both sets of parents to whom the respective partners were dependent and subordinated before marriage.

Tension management as process.[55] For Davis social structure is an important source of tensions as well as a factor in the prevention and reduction of tensions. The two types of allocation of rank and status role—1) ascription and 2) achievement, elaborated under appropriate headings below—contribute to societal balance and to individual tension management.

It may well be questioned . . . how far a society can dispense with ascribed status and nonrational belief, and still survive. . . . There is every reason to believe that the individual could not stand the insecurity, conflict, and turmoil which such a changeable and disparate society would produce.[56]

A basic assumption for Davis is that the dynamic aspect of human social life emerges from the basic tension-reduction provisions of society. In a broad sense those aspects of social structure such as status-role, norm, and convention ". . . eliminate trial and error and hence confusion in human interaction"[57] and may be regarded as tension managing devices. Custom performs this function and "people feel insecure, confused, and angry when established custom is 'flouted' or 'outraged.'"[58] Davis does not use the concepts formal and informal groups as central concepts in the manner that Robin Williams, C. I. Barnard, and some others do. Instead he prefers the concepts primary and secondary group and repeatedly presents evidence that intrinsically secondary or *Gesellschaft*-like characteristics, found predominantly of course in secondary groups, are themselves tension managing in their functions.

The nearest approach to total predictability is found in formal occasions, when the behavior is minutely regulated according to convention and when any deviation from the prescribed pattern is carefully avoided.[59]

Even the fact that ". . . the urbanite treats the myriad of strangers he meets in daily contact as animated machines rather than as human beings," [60] and that the cues which permit these urbanites to exist in ". . . dependence upon others . . . confined to a highly fractionalized aspect of the others' round of activity" [61] in this secondary form of interaction may be viewed as providing tension management. It is, of course, in the primary group where sentiments are communicated most freely.

Demonstrations of societal provisions for the reduction of tension are found as Davis examines some of what he calls the major institutions. Religion (or magic), for example, "furnishes the individual with a cushion whereby the frustration, fear, anger, and insecurity growing out of failures in this world can be compensated for." [62] The provisions for health, ranging in specifics from the witch doctor to the cheery bedside manner, are replete with mechanisms which relieve tensions common to the sick, the afflicted, and the bereaved. The family similarly provides societal provisions for managing tensions. Specific positive controls, such as the encouragement "of sexual intimacy within specific customary relations, such as courtship, concubinage, and marriage" and negative rules which absolutely prohibit sexual relations under certain specified conditions (such as those prohibited by incest taboos) work together as tension managing devices "by banishing the disruptive forces of sexual competition from the family group." [63]

Similar to the incest taboos in effect are the inter-class marriage restrictions. As class ties are bonds which facilitate interaction, class barriers are impediments which strain interaction. Thus the formal and informal bans against marriage between persons of unequal status protect not only the marriage partners but their families both of procreation and orientation from stressful interaction.[64]

There are some tensions within the family which are not societally managed at the present time. One such is the tension inherent in the position of the child of divorced parents. So inexorable is the process of societal adjustment, however, that Davis predicts an easement if the strains are sufficiently great to need one. "It may be that America will eventually have a divorce rate that will seem astounding by present standards. If so, it is safe to assume that the present chaos concerning the children will not then prevail. Some social mechanism will have been evolved for taking care of them." [65]

Governmental social systems with their prerogative on power are in potential conflict with other systems with power prerogatives, e.g. the priestly caste. Various societal mechanisms have been evolved to minimize such tensions. The combination into one group of the sacred and the secular power wielders under highly institutionalized norms is one such technique; rigid separation of the two functions with little mutual interference is a second technique.

Communication of sentiment as process. Spontaneous communication of sentiment is great in the primary groups characterized as *Gemeinschaft*-like, which are small, intimate, inclusive, and of long duration in terms of relationships. Such affective communicative contact appears to be necessary in the development of the self,[66] in the development of attitudes of loyalty and identification essential to the existence of secondary groups,[67] and in the development of commonly held ends. Close intimate personal contact is also the vehicle for communication of painful sentiments. "A careless gesture, an idle remark, may be sufficient to start a quarrel. Events are not important in themselves but rather as symbols of subjective attitudes that each is taking toward the other." [68]

The religious system provides an institutionalized channel of sentiment communication. "Ritual . . . enables [the individual] to give expression to his religious sentiments and thereby to achieve an emotional catharsis. Ritual is especially effective if performed by several individuals, . . . then . . . group stimulation (plus dramatic continuity) heightens the emotionality. . . ." [69]

Despite the unquestionably functional nature of sentiment communication, the truth is that every society is of necessity inimical to the full expression of primary association. If it is to control individuals, it must control their relationships. [Thus, such systems as boys' gangs and sexual liaisons, well adapted as they are to sentiment communication are limited by society.] It recognizes in the voluntary unregulated liaison an anarchic force.[70]

ACHIEVING

End, goal, or objective as an element. The element end, and the means-end schema are the focal and key components of social system for Davis. It is in terms of goals and means to goals that the forms of interaction emerge and that the institutional aspects of social action are explained. In fact nowhere else in sociological literature is the means-end schema as developed by Max Weber, Talcott Parsons, and others, as clearly and usefully employed as by Davis. For Davis the means-ends schema is constituted of four indispensable, inseparable, and irreducible elements of human action: 1) an actor, 2) an end, 3) a set of conditions, and 4) a set of means. On the PAS Model the actors (Item 1 on Davis' model) are assumed to be incumbents of status-roles; the set of conditions (Item 3 on Davis' model) is treated under Conditions of Social Action; and a set of means (Item 4 on Davis' model) is treated under facilities and their utilization (to the extent that means and facilities are identical). The present section deals with *end,* Item 2 on Davis' model. Of the element end, Davis writes:

The end that the self conjectures is the "x" factor in the algebraic equation of social action. . . . The end, strictly defined, is that part of the future state of affairs which would not eventuate if the actor did not want it and did not exert himself to attain it.[71]

Davis clearly differentiates end from function which is ". . . defined as a contribution to the existence of a given structure, be it a personality, an institution, or a society," [72] and from "sheer resultant" which may appear to the actor to be the result of his efforts, but which actually is not.

Although Davis recognizes that ". . . not all activity of the human organism is motivated in the sense of having an end in view . . ." [73] he maintains that ". . . a useful device is . . . to analyze behavior as if it were motivated and to formulate a theoretical system on that basis, realizing, of course, that in keeping with all scientific theory this device represents an abstraction from concrete reality and hence, taken alone, is not adequate for complete explanation." [74]

Davis takes special care to obviate the difficulties commonly encountered by those who attempt to cast all of human action into the means-ends schema. In sociological analysis his conception of ends requires that the ends individuals hold for themselves and those they hold for their groups be differentiated, and further that ultimate and instrumental ends not be confused.[75] In connection with the latter he identifies the short-term end (a sharp razor for example) as one purely instrumental to a longer-term end (a clean-shaven face). Such ends are without sentiment, and the means of their accomplishment determined solely by their efficiency. Davis uses the concept "technological integration" to designate the ideas involved in the meshing of the thousands of separate acts constituting a person's behavior which do not involve the evaluative procedure of balancing independent ends against each other, either in terms of their cost or other considerations, except their efficiency.

Involving only somewhat less instrumentality and only somewhat more evaluation are those ends termed by Davis as "economically integrated." Money for example represents an end which is instrumental, but never solely to one other end; rather it is instrumental to several different ends at the same time. Its distribution is made by some order of preference.

Both technological and economic integration are compounded in complexity when they are extended from the individual to the community or to society. Whereas the individual can subjectively determine the relative importance of competing ends, there is no such collective subjectivity by which society may be guided. Ends by their very nature are highly subjective and individualistic. On the purely technological or economic level, conflict between the ends of a number of individuals cannot be resolved without normative integration involving power and/or commitment to nontechnological and noneconomic ends. It is not surprising then that political integration of ends is another category of integration noted by Davis.

The most non-instrumental of ends, the most evaluative, and

the most ultimate are those designated by Davis as religio-moral. Despite the genuinely competitive nature of ends held by individuals, there is a sense in which even these competing individuals share a set of common ends; further, these common ends are "shared by the whole community and are known to be so shared." [76]

Davis, with cogent logic and clear presentation, thus develops the concept of ends to an extent unacceptable by such theorists as Sorokin or Homans. He is not unaware of the hazards involved in the employment of the means-ends schema, and openly acknowledges that as the concept of ultimate ends is approached the convergence of normative and evaluative components with ends is great. For the theorist who strives for relatively discrete elemental categories, the concept end might seem ambiguous or insufficiently separable from other elements.

Common ends oriented with reference to the action of others are virtually identical with the mores. . . . The behavior called for in the mores and the enforcement of the mores by the members of the community at large would not take place unless the mores stood in the minds of the people as ends to be achieved. [77]

As he addresses himself to the task of determining the origin of the common ends, Davis uses the term "end" as practically synonymous with value—as an important part of societal integration, as rationalized by religious belief and symbolized in religious ritual, and as almost ultimate in social control.

We hold that the possession of common-ultimate values by the members of different societies arose in the process of societal evolution. . . . The important thing was not so much the particular content of the ends but rather the fact of having ends in common. . . . It seems generally true that religious belief explains and makes real the common-ultimate ends, and that religious ritual strengthens and renews these ends in the minds of the participants. . . . The very feeling of profound conviction that surrounds these values is itself religious in quality. [78]

Most of the theorists treated here favor a particular elemental concept upon which to load the heaviest content of social phenomena in the process of analysis. The place of law-norms for Sorokin; sanctions for Homans; value or norms for Parsons, Williams, and Becker is taken up by ends in the case of Davis. So long as definitions are tightly constructed and adhered to fairly rigidly, such a practice is legitimate scientific method. The reader will not be confused by the use of end to signify a sharp razor at one point and a profound religious belief on the other, if Davis' definitions are kept in mind and his graduated levels of ultimacy remembered. Through the PAS Model, the attempt is made to specify more discrete elemental concepts, but it may well be that norm and the process of evaluation in that model will seem to have the same pervasiveness that end has in the Davis schema.

The less instrumental the conceived ends, the less precisely can the ends be isolated. It follows that in those social systems with *Gemeinschaft-like* attributes, in which the typical relations between individuals are themselves ends of the individuals, the goal is nebulous, difficult of precise statement, but nonetheless existent and widely diffused in the minds of a great number of actors. Some social systems would seem more resistant to analysis by the means-ends schema than others, or for that matter, more resistant to any form of analysis. As Davis comments, the scholar whose subject matter is instrumental (the industrial corporation, e.g.) is accepted in a way seldom true of the scholar whose subject matter is non-instrumental (the family, e.g.).[79] Social scientists are accordingly more inclined to analyze instrumental social systems which involve phenomena which can be "deliberately manipulated to achieve accepted ends. Family affairs, however, are not instrumental but final or ultimate. Love is a supreme emotion, not a means to an end. The obligations of parents, of husbands and wives, are among the highest in the moral hierarchy. The idea of analyzing them from a scientific point of view seems repellent or perhaps ridiculous."[80] The education system and the political system, being more instrumental and less ultimate than the family, have ends which are more readily identifiable. Organized education in the United States, for example "has stated its goal to be the scientific study and efficient satisfaction of the child's needs, has minimized ritual, and has skirted those of the nonrational norms that could not be somehow rationalized as 'science.'"[81] The government figure, vested with power, although having the right to coerce another actor into a certain line of conduct, may not have the right to do so for the pursuit of his own ends but rather only for group ends. "Were he to utilize his posi-

tion simply to pursue his private ends, the result would be absolute coercion beyond any legitimate limits, and the basis of his
position would soon deteriorate." [82] The ends of members of religious systems, in contrast, are similar to the ends of family members in that religious behavior becomes an end in and of itself,
and in that the ends of such behavior are not instrumental but
ultimate, not private but group. Davis seeks the source of these
most ultimate of all group ends.

The ultimate ends are not inherited. They are not found in external
nature. They must, therefore, arise as a cultural emergent. They must
spring from the dynamics of communicative interaction . . . they have
a subjective and a transcendant quality—an existence only in the in-
doctrinated mind. [83]

Goal attaining activity as process. As limited means are
adapted to the achievement of ends, activity takes place which
may involve the actor in situations of conflict, competition, and
cooperation. The adaptation of means or facilities is handled below in Utilization of Facilities as defined above in Chapter 1.
Since in Davis' model there are relatively few substantive limits on
what may be included in means (just as the concept end may be
used in any substantive context), much of the action and interaction pertinent to Davis' concept means is irrelevant in Utilization of Facilities, and for purposes of comparison is best handled
under what is specified in the PAS Model as Goal attaining activity. [84]

The dynamics behind the effort which is poured into goal attainment springs from organic tension; goal attainment implies
release of that tension. Here Davis distinguishes, however, between the pursuit of goals having an organic origin and the striving after goals which are socially learned. He contends that
release from tension immediately attends the achievement of the
goal of organic origin (as is true of the sex act, for example), but
such unequivocal tension release does not accompany goal
achievement of the socially learned goals. "The rivalry for prestige and esteem, for example, is never-ending." [85] In connection
with the latter, "particular subgoals may be attained, with some
relief of tension; but always there is the realization that one's own
prestige and esteem are eclipsed by others." [86] Since socially

learned goals have primacy over organic goals, to some extent inhibiting and suppressing the latter, there is a double tension attached to the socially learned goals—the tensions demanding their own realization and the tensions stemming from the more suppressed organic goals. The individual's driving power toward a goal springs from these urges.

Davis notes that "conflict is an ever-present process in human relations." [87] Its pervasiveness can be accounted for by the nature of the ends of human action, which, since they are mental rather than biological, are highly variable. A tendency to consider one's own ends as being "better" than other ends immediately allows disagreement; and the willingness to fight to preserve or extend these ends allows for conflict. Not all conflicts are openly expressed; many are latent activities suppressed or smoothed over by various social mechanisms such as humor, avoidance, making harmony the greater value, etc. The element of conflict is never completely removed from the social situation "because the ends of different individuals are always to some extent mutually exclusive." [88] While an actor engaged in conflict tries to destroy the opposition, an actor engaged in *competition* tries to outdo the competitor while still functioning within the "rules of the game." Here there are not different ends as in conflict, but a race or struggle in the attainment of some one end. As there is no such thing as unrestricted competition, there is also no such thing as a total lack of competition—there is only the relative presence or absence of this form of interaction. *Cooperation* is not, according to Davis, the opposite of competition; rather controlled and institutionalized competition ". . . is presumably a means by which the cooperation of all is accomplished." [89] The three forms of interaction are, however, interdependent and ever-present—". . . any concrete situation will manifest all three in a complex and intertwined manner." [90]

Whether in conflict, competition, or in cooperation, the employing of means always signifies the pursuit of a goal. The all-encompassing nature of that process is suggested by its fluidity: "What is a means for one actor may be a condition for another. In the same situation one man, for example, may feel obligated to tell the truth while another will feel privileged to tell a lie." [91] On the PAS Model, the decision to lie or not to lie would place primacy on norms and evaluation irrespective of the reference system involved, whether instrumental or not. Davis' frequent reference to the instrumental use of another person for the accomplishment of one's goal is an aspect of status-role and/or power on the PAS Model. Although Davis tends to incorporate more into the concepts end and means than any other theorist treated in this volume, he does not, at least overtly, incorporate that one aspect of goal-achievement which is central to Homans' scheme as presented in *The Human Group*, the concomitant generation of affective, meaningful personal relations. By inference, goal achievement is seen by Davis, however, as an integrating force.

Since the interlocking system of tasks, assigned on the basis of sex and age, turns the farm family into a close-knit productive unit, it is small wonder that about ten per cent more of farm than of city people get married, or that the average farm couple marries about a year earlier than the average urban couple, that they are about twice as fertile, and that they are about twice as likely to remain married.[92]

Concomitant "latent" activity as process. The importance of unrecognized and unintended functions is frequently stressed by Davis. The actor's perception of his environment is so limited that it is impossible for him to know the consequences of his activity, which may have functions unknown to him.

It is doubtful whether a man who makes a sacrifice to his god would make the sacrifice if he knew the social function of his act, because the situation to which his end is oriented would be altered and the end itself would disappear. Some of the ends that are farthest from any knowledge that a social function is being performed are of the greatest functional importance.[93]

Much goal-directed activity, especially that which is highly normative, accomplishes latent results for the actor and for society. Many of the tension-reducing techniques treated above under sentiment—formal behavior, compliance with incest taboos, and segmented interaction with other actors in the *Gesellschaft*-like system—involve activity which produce what are for the actor, latent results, his chief goal in the activity being something other than tension management. What might be on the conscious level a dysfunction can actually be societally functional, although, of course, latent.

If the medicine men kill off a certain number of their patients and thus save the community from the conflict and demoralization contingent upon starvation, they have made an unintended communal contribution and at the same time have reinforced the sentiment in favor of prolonged life.[94]

NORMING, STANDARDIZING, AND PATTERNING

Norm as an element. Of the various writers treated in the present volume only Sorokin gives the concept, norm, more attention than Davis. The subject is introduced as drawing heavily upon William Graham Sumner, a contributor of one of the ". . . several different but mutually supplementary points of view"[95] adopted by Davis. Although Davis regards his use of norm as the "first and broadest" of his concepts, his means-ends schema absorbs parts of what is included in norms in the PAS Model. The merging of goals and mores occurs particularly as utilitarian ends are superceded by more ultimate ends, and as individual ends are superceded by common ends.[96] For Davis societal integration is dependent upon norms, "any violation [of which] is punished by some negative reaction, be it slight or great."[97] Thus, Davis like Homans and Sorokin, conceives sanctions to be an integral part of the normative order.

Defining norm as a "rule" which implies a sense of obligation and effort, Davis subscribes to a familiar classification of norms as folkways, mores, customary and enacted laws, and institutions. Folkways, "regarded as obligatory . . . but not absolutely obligatory" are enforced by informal social control.[98] Mores, more fundamental than folkways, "represent the hardest core of the normative system . . . [they are] morally right, their violation is morally wrong."[99] Taboos are mores stated in negative form. Mores become laws when they "have some special organization for their enforcement."[100] An institution such as marriage is ". . . a set of interwoven folkways, mores, and laws built around one or more functions."[101]

Norms are not consciously adopted, but ". . . arise unwittingly as a result of societal necessity in an exacting environment."[102] Once having arisen, they permeate existence because "they are to a high degree internalized." [103] Conscience, guilt, and a constellation of sentiments result from internalized norms. Although Davis distinguishes between the norms, which for the most part actually control behavior, and the ideals, which are recognized as desirable but are rarely lived up to, these two are sometimes fused. "In order to get what is needed a society asks for more than it expects, in much the same way that a mother requests better behavior from her child than she really expects or desires. . . ." [104]

Normative expectations for actors in primary relation to each other prescribe that the relations are ends in and of themselves. A friend, who uses his friend for the pursuit of ulterior ends and the marriage partner who has married for money both violate the norms which are considered proper for an intimate and affective relationship. *Gemeinschaft*-like or primary groups are composed of a network of relations in which the relation is normatively regarded as the proper end.

The *Gesellschaft*-like secondary social system has within it small clusters of actors in primary relation to each other, but each has many more relations which are segmented and utilitarian. The behavior for these, too, are normatively prescribed, but the overt behavior and the internal state of the actor are not expected to coincide.

The urbane person has mastered the art of external conformity, of superficial politeness, which hides rather than reveals the internal motivation and state of mind. He has learned how to lead different lives in different contexts, to take advantage of anonymity and of special friendship as the occasion arises. [105]

To the individual actor, the norms can represent something desirable in themselves or an obstacle which prevents him from pursuing certain ends. It is imperative for the personality integration of the actor as well as for the maintenance of the society that he not be an extremist in either direction. He must neither be too conforming nor too deviant. How he resolves this potential dilemma is treated in the present book under evaluation.

Evaluation as a process. For Davis as for Sumner ". . . the profoundest measuring rod of right and wrong is found precisely in the mores, which fact has given rise to the expression that the mores can make anything right or anything wrong." [106] The processual aspect of norms is treated by Davis on two interrelated levels: on the individual level and on the community or societal level. On both levels the very existence of norms carries with it an obligation on the part of actors, individually and collectively that effort be put forth according to a stipulated pattern. Although there is some leeway concerning certain modes of behavior, normative considerations generally result in the effort being directed by one pattern rather than by another.[107]

On the individual level, Davis relies heavily on G. H. Mead. The self, being built out of the attitudes of the generalized other, necessarily highly evaluates the attitudes of others, especially those of approval and disapproval. "It is only through the approval of others that the self can tolerate the self." [108] Norms can be either desirable ends in themselves for the individual actor or obstacles which stand between him and his goal. Those norms that are evaluated as desirable ends must be reconciled with the actor's other goals so that the goals themselves will not be at cross-purposes. He must observe or pretend to observe those norms that seem to be goal obstructions, so that offended others will not jeopardize his goal achievement.[109] Actors, thus, not only pass judgments upon their own acts; they judge the very norms which prompted the action in the first place.[110] Over a period of time the norms do change in response to what appears to Davis as an ironical normative evaluation of the norms themselves. "A society in which everyone suddenly conformed strictly to the norms would not only be utterly static and incapable of adjusting itself to changing circumstances, but it would make impossible demands on the individuals composing it." [111] The avoidance of over-conformity as well as compulsive violation of norms constitutes an evaluative procedure in which the actor is aided by "keeping in mind the principles or general goals behind the specific normative rules; by correctly conceiving himself and his situation in the eyes of others so far as observance of the rules is concerned; and by bringing all the elements of his personality . . . into one central picture of himself." [112] The central fact of the self's being a product of interaction demands that a high value be placed on social relations. Davis' absorbing account of social isolation [113] reinforces his view that "A society that did not teach its members to value the social relationships constituting its structure would be missing a necessary aid to social cohesion. Indeed, since the main forms of interaction in a society are laid down in the mores, these forms are *ipso facto* valued by the societal members as ends in themselves." [114]

Although the individual will not necessarily pursue ends which are in complete conformity to ultimate values, he is judged in terms of those values, just as he judges others in those terms. He tends to limit his own competitive ends by this consideration. "His hierarchy of ends is therefore individualized yet subordinated to the common ultimate values." [115] This process of integrating the self with society is seldom conscious. The actor simply pursues certain ends, "of which the most general is the good opinion of others or conformity to the standards of the generalized other." [116] The integration is accomplished by subjective preference, although three influences assist in the evaluation of choices: "(1) models in those around him, especially those with whom he identifies himself; (2) cultural patterns of preference; and (3) the fact of social compulsion." [117]

All the lesser ends held by individuals are judged according to the standards of the common-ultimate ends. "In fact, we tend to define a society or at least a community as a collection of persons adhering to the same set of ultimate values and pursuing the same set of common ends." [118] Community and societal ends consequently transcend specific group ends, and are "more remote, more nebulous, and more pervasive." Nevertheless, they have to be given a concreteness, easily related to physical reality because they have the very real job of controlling the needs, drives, capacities and environmental conditions of society's members. The too remote, the too nebulous, would not help the ordinary actor much in the job of sorting out his individual ends. The ultimate values must seem real and profoundly convincing for a sustained integration of individual ends, without which society would fall apart. The symbol, the physical reality, standing for the nebulous, nonphysical value—such as nation or God— bridges the physical world to superempirical values. To an observer, the ultimate values might seem unreal, and their symbols may have the appearance of any other non-sacred object. To the actor the ultimate values are real, and the symbols, fraught with superempirical meaning, are sacred. In the last analysis, then, the religious system charged with the affairs of the superempirical world and replete with symbols of that world "furnishes through its sacred objects a concrete reference for the values and a rallying point for all persons who share the same values." [119] The mores, like the values themselves, receive their final justification and rationalization in terms of the superempirical world." [120]

Any kind of activity can be evaluated in terms of the ultimate values, but precision about what is being measured is necessary. Scientific activity, for example, has often been charged with being amoral or immoral. Davis argues that it might have very moral aims. "The conflict really becomes acute only when the search for empirical truth becomes an ultimate value too and therefore competes with religious and moral values. . . . In this circumstance the scientist is likely to collide with the theologian, the moralist, and the common man, all of whom are less emotionally bound to empirical truth." [121]

Among the instances of evaluation of almost universal application in Davis' works are the following drawn from various writings, each of which might be used as hypotheses for future research:

1. Isolation and limitation of social contact is negatively evaluated.[122]
2. Longevity is more highly evaluated and hence requires less elaborate cultural apparatus to support it than procreativity.[123]
3. "The greatest social mythology is required not for the preservation of life but for its sacrifice; whereas the greatest mythology is required not for the sacrifice of fertility but for its maintenance." [124]
4. Farm families place higher evaluation upon children than urban families.[125]
5. "Serious illness becomes an occasion for examining social relationships, and its treatment an instrumentality of social control." [126]
6. ". . . strongly individualistic desire for health and life is made the unconscious instrumentality for group cohesion and efficiency." [127]
7. ". . . in so far as health is accepted as a supreme value it implies a degree of individualism which is socially disintegrative." [128]

8. "Rulership is in the last analysis *de facto* rather than *de jure*. . . . Its avowed purpose is the furtherance of the collectivity. . . . In an effort to clothe itself in legitimacy and hence to acquire very necessary popular support, it generally *proclaims* that it is pursuing those ends [conceived by the citizens to be desirable for society.]" [129]

9. "The love relationship, unlike other property relations, is an end in itself" [130] and as such provides two dangers for the owner: "the first is that somebody will win out over him in legitimate competition . . . the second is that somebody will illegitimately take from him property already acquired. This is the danger of trespass." [131]

10. "Perhaps the outstanding characteristic affecting the family patterns of the American Negro is his consciousness of skin color. In his choice of a mate the Negro is strongly influenced by this consideration. . . ." [132]

11. Much conflict between parents and adolescents is due to cultural change placing "not only . . . parent and child, at any given moment, in different stages of development, but [making] the content which the parent acquired at the stage where the child now is . . . a different content from that which the child is now acquiring." [133] "To change the basic conceptions by which . . . [the parent] has learned to judge the rightness and reality of all specific situations would be to render subsequent experience meaningless, to make an empty caricature of what has been his life." [134]

12. "Since divorce is sinful, the child's lot must be painted as badly as possible in order to make the sin (in its consequence for the *innocent* offspring) seem as terrible as possible. Thus the moral stigma attached to divorce not only makes the child's position worse than it would otherwise be, but also requires that it be depicted as even more tragic than it actually is." [135]

13. "One thing that makes any stepchild situation difficult is the mystical importance our culture attaches to biological parenthood. A 'real' son or daughter must be one's 'own.' When the stepchild is the offspring of a person still living, who once had and (even worse) may still have the primary affection of one's mate, then the difficulty of loving the child is increased." [136]

14. "Our dynamic, competitive, mobile, and heterogeneous society places a heavy burden on the individual. . . . The individual is forced to develop toward others the same kind of attitude that

his agricultural ancestor developed toward tree stumps, rocks, and insects; an instrumental, impersonal attitude." [137]

15. "In its ultimate religious and moral evaluation, the democratic society has traditionally held all individuals to be intrinsically equal . . . There is evidence that the notion of ethical equality places some limit upon actual inequality—as against slavery and suffering—and that, translated into political terms, it rationalizes the view that each citizen, regardless of social position, should have one vote, basic issues being settled on the basis of the largest accumulation (the majority) of such votes." [138]

16. In population policy and practice increased mortality as a policy ". . . does not rest on its economic effects. It rests on the fact that human life, except under extreme group necessity, is viewed as an end in itself and not as a means to an end. This reason explains why official domestic policy with reference to deaths is nearly always in one direction . . . limitation." [139]

17. "The promotion of birth control as an official population policy has been rare in human society . . . Public funds have been liberally expended for public health, including medical research, education, treatment, and prevention. These efforts have yielded large dividends in the saving of lives. But the idea of lowering birth rates by similar expenditures has met either with hostility or with indifference in official circles. The reason for this extreme contrast in public policy is rather clear . . . Throughout human history the societies that managed to control their deaths reasonably well and to have at the same time a high birth rate were the ones that continued to exist. The others fell by the wayside. As a consequence, the customs and institutions of the surviving societies express both a high evaluation of health and longevity and a high evaluation of fertility." [140]

18. "Of the . . . sexual institutions . . . those which facilitate the task of procreating and socializing the young" [141] receive the greatest support from law and mores and are the most sacred. The more threatening any form of sexual activity is to these sacred institutions the more extremely and rigidly it will be tabooed.

19. "Because coitus . . . has come to symbolize the *Gemeinschaft* type of relation present in the family" as well as the biological perpetuation of society itself, anything such as prostitution or illegitimate sexual intercourse which may degrade the values of

these things will be more seriously condemned than flirtation, coquetry, and petting which do not constitute such threats. [142]

DIVIDING THE FUNCTIONS

Human society depends upon the division of labor or what in the present volume has been called dividing the functions to maximize the utilization of effort and facilities. As Davis notes:

a socially determined division of labor allows different persons to acquire different parts of the cultural heritage. Putting to work the part they do learn they perform useful functions for the entire group. . . . A man does not have to know carpentry in order to have a house, or to understand combustion motors in order to drive a car.[143]

Status-role incorporating both element and process. Davis' concept of position is equivalent to the positional aspect of status-role on the PAS Model. It is a more generic concept than the Davis concepts, status, and office. Position defines a minimum of obligatory behavior for the incumbent and for Davis is ". . . almost synonymous with Linton's term status." [144]

For Davis society seen as a system of social positions is the second avenue of entry to sociology following the normative approach. The social situation, comprising the mutual expectations of the participants, is derived in part from the applicable social norms and in part from the identities of the interacting individuals. Identity in this sense, refers to the "positions" held in society; the positions may be classified as statuses and offices.

The term status would then designate a position in a general institutional system, recognized and supported by the entire society, spontaneously evolved rather than deliberately created, rooted in the folkways and mores. Office, on the other hand, would designate a position in a deliberately created organization, governed by specific and limited rules in a limited group, and more generally achieved than ascribed.[145]

The incumbent of the *office* finds his job defined by a fixed and organized set of expectations of others concerning that particular office. Although fraudulent representations of status and office are possible—such as the pretense of being single when actually married, the impersonation of a doctor by a layman and so on—mores and laws condemn such fraud and punish the pretenders.[146] The designation "professor" applied to an individual is a designation of *status;* the specification "professor of government at X university" is a designation of office.[147]

While status and office define obligatory behavior for the incumbent, there will be a range of effectiveness in fulfilling the obligation varying from individual to individual. "How an individual actually performs in a given position, as distinct from how he is supposed to perform, we call his role." [148] Although role is the "dynamic aspect of status," and in this respect resembles the use of the term on the PAS Model, it may seem to fall on the factual side of the dichotomy of factual vs. normative which runs throughout Davis' writings.[149] To the extent that this is true [150] it differs from the usage in Figure 1, Chapter 1, as well as from that of other theorists in the present volume for whom the role is the expected behavior of incumbents.[151] It seems quite possible, however, that Davis' definition of role as *actual* performance in a given position (as contrasted with the normative expectation of what the performance *should be*) has been overemphasized by Levy, Gross, Mason, McEachern and others; [152] or conversely, that Davis' modifications which specify that actual performance is molded by normative expectations have been underemphasized. For example: "The term 'role' is meaningless without the implication that the individual is *trying*, or is expected to try, to carry out the minimal requirements of his status. In one sense, the role is the particular way in which a given individual *falls short* of performing the stipulated patterns. If the individual falls completely short, he does not occupy the position at all. The very fact that he does not fall completely short is due to the normative elements inherent in the status." [153] The heavier lodging of the normative component in status than in role for Davis, ought not in the view of the present authors, to negate the normative aspects of the role performance itself which is attested to by this and other statements by Davis.

Another demonstration that normative considerations are applied both to the structure and the process occurs as Davis distinguishes between *prestige, "the invidious value attached to any given status or office, or combination of them,"* and *esteem* which refers to *"the invidious value attached to any given role or combination of roles."* [154] Davis argues that a person occupying a high prestige position might be accorded little esteem because of his behavior in that position. "If in various positions he be-haves at variance with the expectations" [155] he is not esteemed but will probably be called derogatory names. Although Davis insists that the societal expectations are related to the position itself, his agreement that esteem stems from the "success or fail-ure in carrying out the stipulations of the position" [156] suggests that his concept of role is more semantically different than it is actually different from that concept as held by other theorists.

A little noted Davisonian contribution to sociology is his early attempt to formulate "the relation of personality structure to social structure." [157] Elaborations of his view on status-role are the basis for this formulation. For Davis, the relation between the personality system and the social system is based on three abstractions of the former. An individual's *positional personality* is *"the person in so far as he is a product of the sum-total of posi-tions which he occupies."* This structural aspect of his personality is augmented by his *role personality* which is *"the individual as the sum total of roles which he plays."* Based first on the posi-tions which the individual occupies, his role personality is sec-ondly a product of his cumulative experience, and thirdly, of his genetic make-up. His *genetic personality* is *"the person as the sum-total of his physically inherited traits."* Whereas the posi-tional personality and genetic personality are analytical abstrac-tions, the role personality most nearly represents the concrete individual. The study of society and the study of personality are mutually dependent.[158] Written in 1942, this antedates some of the other formulations of the relations between the personality, social, and cultural systems discussed within the present volume and now generally accepted.

The positional aspect, in contrast to the role aspect, also has a relative permanency.

The total system of positions in the entire society or group must be reasonably well integrated. Otherwise the society or group could not carry on its existence. . . . One of the things that is perpetuated, of course, is the system of positions itself. . . . Basically the positions tend to remain the same; it is mainly the occupants of the positions who change.[159]

RANKING

Rank as an element. Rank for Davis refers to the evaluation of a position and represents ". . . *a rung in a prestige scale.*" On the other hand a point in the scale of evaluation of role performance ". . . *in an esteem scale* [is] *rating*" in Davis' terminology.[160] According to Davis many of the critiques of his early article and of a later one by him and Wilbert E. Moore fail to note these distinctions which are crucial to systemic analysis.[161] Davis uses the term station to designate the ". . . cluster of statuses and offices that tend to be combined in one person as a locus and are publicly recognized as so combined in a great many cases." [162] One of the major occupations constituting a station may furnish the name for a station as in the case of the "landowning class." Again the name for a class of positions such as those designated as "professional" may provide the collective term for the station covering positions such as doctor, lawyer, and professor.

To designate rank in a hierarchy of strata Davis uses the term, stratum, which he specifies as ". . . *a mass of persons in a given society enjoying roughly the same station.*" [163] Positional rank which furnishes the basis for stratification results from evaluation of the position's significance in society and the scarcity of the attributes necessary for the occupation of the position. The first of these is of "differential functional importance"; the second represents "differential scarcity of personnel," resulting from rarity of talent and/or costliness of training.

Davis does not restrict the concept stratification, to the inheritance of social position by individuals, but concentrates upon social differentiation and hierarchical organization. These are reflected in ". . . institutionalized inequality of rewards as between broad strata." [164] The process of stratification as related to inheritance is analyzed through articulating it to familial organization in which stratified and non-stratified offices or statuses are differentiated.

Those positions that may be combined in the same legitimate family—viz., positions based on sex, age, and kinship—do not form part of the system of stratification. On the other hand those positions that are socially prohibited from being combined in the same legal family—viz., different caste or class positions—constitute what we call stratification.[165]

Davis' consideration reiterates two basic questions: "a) Why are different evaluations and rewards given to different *positions?*" and "b) How do *individuals* come to be distributed in these positions?". The distinction between these two considerations is elaborated in sections below under Application of Sanctions, Evaluation of Actors, and Allocation of Status-roles. Davis emphasizes that "our theory was designed to answer the first question by means of the second. But much confusion results . . . if the term 'stratification' is used in such a way as to overlook the distinction between the two." [166] His analysis has been criticized on the grounds that such an explanation of ranks and strata holds only for societies in which there is competition for positions. In refutation Davis maintains that his schema is concerned with the system of positions, not individuals occupying these positions; further, that "the functional necessities responsible for stratification do not operate to the exclusion of all other functions." [167] Within the system of positions, certain positions in all societies have lower ranks than other positions. Even in the most competitive societies the "broad outlines of status are laid down by ascription" and even in the most ascribed societies "many specific statuses are open to achievement." [168]

The institutional functions of religion, government, economic activity, and technology are all discussed in relation to the "two determinants of differential reward—namely, functional importance and scarcity of personnel." [169] This analysis is made against the background assumption that "any particular system of stratification . . . can be understood as a product of the special conditions affecting [these] two . . . grounds of differential reward." [170]

The crucial status-roles or positions in each of the institutional spheres are subjected to critical analysis; thus, the importance of religious functionaries such as priests in providing ". . . integration in terms of sentiments, beliefs, and rituals" [171] of the society is discussed much as Parsons and others have discussed them. That priestly classes or castes do not more frequently outrank top governmental, economic, and technological status-roles is explained by virtue of the difficulty of monopolizing channels of entry and the relative ease of preparing for the operations necessary for the priestly function.

Government which ". . . organizes the society in terms of law and authority" [172] and, in contrast to religion, deals with the actual rather than the foreseen world, is likewise limited in the prestige and power society accords its functionaries.

Economic and technical performance yield to the status-holder in those fields a prestige which is expressed in rights to facilities, but since the contribution of the technical positions is concerned ". . . solely with means, a purely technical position must ultimately be subordinate to other positions that are religious, political, or economic in character." [173] Intense specialization tends to differentiate rank, accentuating both high and low ranks.

Extreme division of labor tends to create many specialists without high prestige since the training is short and the required native capacity relatively small. On the other hand it also tends to accentuate the high position of the three experts—scientists, engineers, and administrators—by increasing their authority relative to other functionally important positions.[174]

Davis delineates five modes of variation in stratification systems which also involve power differentials:

(1) The degree of specialization, which produces two types, the specialized and the unspecialized;
(2) The nature of the functional emphasis, which produces such types as familistic, authoritarian (theocratic or sacred, and totalitarian or secular), and capitalistic;
(3) The magnitude of invidious differences, which produces the types equalitarian and inequalitarian;
(4) The degree of opportunity, producing the types, mobile (open) and immobile (closed);
(5) The degree of stratum solidarity producing the polar types, class organized, and class unorganized.

Stratification is influenced also by the following "external conditions": (a) the stage of cultural development; (b) situation with respect to other societies; (c) the size of the society.[175] Although Davis is aware of the dangers of classifying whole societies as caste, feudal, or open class systems, *Human Society* carries a very effective analysis of the Indian caste system, caste in the United States, and open class stratification. The stratification component has been used by Davis, of course, in his extensive publication in the field of demography. A "fatalistic" attitude toward family size, for example, is seen to vary by class, religion, and place of residence among Bengali women. Those holding such an attitude numbered: rural section, 86.8 per cent; lower middle urban (Muslim), 91.0 per cent; lower middle urban (Hindu) 46.3 per cent; and upper urban (Hindu), 30.1 per cent.[176]

Evaluation as a process in ranking. Davis and Moore have observed "It is one thing to ask why different positions carry different degrees of prestige, and quite another to ask how certain individuals get into these positions."[177] In the well-known article "Some Principles of Stratification," Davis is joined by Moore in a discussion of "the relationship between stratification and the rest of the social order."[178] Here the postulate is made that evaluation of actors and status-roles is in largest measure in terms of functional utility and scarcity. They say, "in most complex societies the religious, political, economic, and educational functions are handled by distinct structures not easily interchangeable." Most important for our purposes here, it is further hypothesized:

The absence of such specialization does not prove functional unimportance, for the whole society may be relatively unspecialized; but it is safe to assume that the more important functions receive the first and clearest structural differentiation.[179]

In answer to Tumin's criticism that functional importance is unmeasurable, Davis replied as follows:

Rough measures of functional importance are in fact applied in practice. In wartime, for example, decisions are made as to which industries and occupations will have priority. . . . In totalitarian countries the same thing is done in peacetime, as also in underdeveloped areas attempting to maximize their social and economic modernization. Individual firms must constantly decide which positions are essential and which not.[180]

Davis observes on the one hand that a classification of needs tacitly underlies functional evaluation; that, "there is a sense . . . in which the need . . . for medical attention is greater than the need for tonsorial attention. . . . There is a sense in which society has a greater need for the priest than for the salesman. . . ." On the other hand he acknowledges that all parts of a system, being interdependent, are less differentially important than is commonly believed. The scavenger is perhaps as important to public health as the doctor; the woman is as indispensable to society as is the man. Differential evaluation in itself does not necessarily coincide with functional priority. Scarcity of appropriate personnel for the position must be given equal consideration. Scarcity may arise from the amount of technical knowledge required and from the amount of innate talent needed. It can be "enhanced in adventitious ways." The requirement of waiting a long period, with no intrinsic need for such a delay may increase the scarcity of qualified personnel, or the same result may be achieved by the requirement of a great deal of technical knowledge which will not be used on the job. "Such adventitious limitations sometimes have symbolic significance (emphasizing the importance of the position) and sometimes a competitive significance (appearing when, for some reason, an important position is overcrowded with qualified persons)." [181] The evaluative process which makes the positional ranking system workable is always, for Davis, a complex of function and scarcity. When positions have the same prestige they are said to be separated horizontally in social space; when they are evaluated invidiously and assigned ranks appearing at different points on a prestige scale they are said to be separated in vertical social space.[182] Of course, not only the positions are evaluated, but also the actors, which brings up the second part of the question posed by Davis and Moore, ". . . how [do] certain individuals get into these positions?" [183]

Allocation of status-roles. Allocation of actors to positions underlies both the phenomena of vertical mobility, generally characteristic of the achievement-oriented society and the filling of inherited positions, generally characteristic of the ascription-oriented society. Something of the latter occurs in every society, due to the need for immediate commencement of socialization of each newborn child, the responsibility for which must be clearly assigned to designated persons possessing definite responsibilities and rights in connection with the child. "Such assignment, such arbitrary connection of the child with persons who already have a status in the social structure, immediately gives the infant mem-

bership in the society and a specific place in the system of statuses." [184] Ascriptive aspects of allocation attend the newborn
child, then, not only by sex, age, and race but by family placement. Usually "the broad outlines of status" are determined by
ascription, and this occurs in the achievement-oriented as well as
in the ascription-oriented society. However, in both "many specific statuses are open to achievement." [185] The degree of achievement orientation in a society such as that of the United States is
sometimes thought of as more extensive than it is in fact. In
courtship as in economic activity, for example, the individual's
own attributes rather than his involuntary social background is
generally conceded to determine the level of his achievement.
". . . since the courtship process is highly competitive, he has a
chance to attain a different result according to his personal charm,
skill, and achievements. . . . Yet . . . most Americans marry
within their own social class." [186] Similarly, although it is always
possible that the office of the presidency of the United States will
in fact be able to be won by anyone not constitutionally barred
from that office, the fact remains that "No woman, no Negro, no
Oriental, . . . no Jew has ever been president." [187]

Just as the society which is relatively achievement-oriented
nonetheless allocates many of its status-roles by a specie of
ascription, so too the society which is relatively ascription-
oriented allocates some of its status-roles by achievement, for
achievement not only fills important jobs by qualified people, it
also stimulates effort. Not even the most rigid caste society can
afford to pay the rewards of prestige without reaping the fruits
of activities adequately carried out. Nor can it assure the inherited transmission of position which requires arduous training
without counter-assurance that the heir-incumbent will so train
himself. "A king who rules by divine right must nevertheless
know something about the behavior required of a king." [188]

Despite the position of a given society on the ascription-
achievement scale, people are always assessing each other, and
to the talented and energetic, others give their allegiance and
support. Although the extremely cunning actor will achieve by
fair means or foul, the level of achievement for most ordinary
actors is influenced by the institutionalized means provided by a
society for the recognition of achievement. The society rich in

such legitimated methods of recognizing superiority minimizes illicit achievement, encourages maximum use of average talents, and "by providing for an orderly change of status . . . can prevent the filling of high positions by incompetents. . . ." [189] The kinds of status-roles most likely to be thrown open to incumbency by achievement include those requiring the possession of unusual talent, those "depending on the informal and spontaneous approval of the populace" including the expressive activities of "the theatre . . . the sports . . . the rostrum, and the printed page," and finally, those "requiring such long and costly education that private resources cannot supply it and hence necessitating public provision of training." [190]

Actors protect themselves from complete competition, a form of action essential to achievement. The security similar to that afforded by ascribed status is sought in the barriers erected against unlimited competition. In fact Davis observes that intense specialization and unlimited status achievement results in loss of solidarity which "will reach the point where an internal revolution by a militant cohesive minority or an external conquest by a militant cohesive rival will turn [society] back in the direction of institutional rigidity." [191]

Through the dual processes of the evaluation of both position and actor, the efficient society attempts to match the requirements of the one with the potentials of the other; to set up rewards which are portrayed as rights of position, in order to induce actors to perform conscientously in status-roles suited to their talents. One such inducement for the incumbency of certain status-roles is power.

CONTROLLING

Power as an element. Davis defines power as ". . . the determination of the behavior of others in accordance with one's own ends." [192] For him as for other writers reviewed in the present volume, the government monopolizes force for regulatory purposes. Although other agencies use force, and the government delegates force to other agencies, government ". . . has the right, or the obligation, to suppress an unauthorized use of force by an individual or a particular group. Any nongovernmental agency which succeeds in using force on a large scale becomes itself a *de facto* government and automatically acquires at least a limited legitimacy." [193] Davis, like Parsons, maintains that the "monopoly of force always resides, ultimately, in a territorial unit." [194]

Early in his career Davis differentiated "two pure and concretely nonexistent types: exchange and coercion" as modes of influencing people. [195] These were not used extensively; but the first, exchange, bears an interesting resemblance to its use by such theorists as Simmel and Toennies as well as by Homans in his more recent works.

What Davis calls structural or positional power he designates as authority, that which is determined by one's status or office. The other kinds of power he refers to as "naked or unauthorized power." [196] The following characterization of these two forms indicates that they are not different from what in the present volume, as components of the PAS Model, are called authoritative and nonauthoritative power:

Social distance (especially of the vertical sort) bolsters structural authority at the expense or personal power; intimacy, on the other hand bolsters personal power at the expense of structural power as indicated by the saying that familiarity breeds contempt. [197]

Concerning the power of nations Davis concludes that a powerful nation ". . . is one that has a large population, a rich and extensive territory, an industrial economy, a high proportion of its people in nonagricultural pursuits, a high degree of urbanization, a low agricultural density, a great amount of public education, and a balance of low fertility and low mortality." [198] Ultimate authority backed at some point by force is the province of government which exercises checks and restraints on the governed in order that help and protection can be rendered against threats from within or without the society. The exercise of such checks and restraints is the processual aspect of power examined here under decision making and initiation into action.

Decision making and its initiation into action as process. There is little in Davis' work that actually converges with the concept decision making as employed in the PAS Model. A careful reading of Davis' writings suggests that some aspect of decision making exists in the choice among alternative goals and the means to the goals. However, subjectively held goals and limited means for goal fulfillment are the object of competition and conflict. The resultant discord is handled by institutionalized power, the ultimate of which is political and governmental, and the function of which is to arbitrate disputes and to make and interpret the rules.

Decision making, which is implicit in the integration of conflicting objectives, always means that "there *must* be a poltical organization and there *must* be people in authority. A society can exist with a tyrant, a king, an elected president, or a gangster at the top; it cannot exist with nobody at the top. . . ." [199]

On those rare occasions when Davis actually uses the term decision, he consistently does so with the idea of its execution being exercised by few over many. Despite the large number of governmental personnel in bureaucracies, for example, the government

. . . is dominated at the top by an infinitesimal group who make the ultimate decisions and bear the final responsibility. The reason for this is that the thinking and planning necessary to guide the whole society can be only done, like all thinking and planning, by one or at most a few individuals. This is true no matter how large the population to be governed. . . . The separation of administration from policy determination receives its expression in the civil service, where governmental personnel is expected to be strictly nonpolitical.[200]

The involvement of the great mass of actors who constitute a system is seen by Davis as the source of public opinion, a sort of composite opinion which represents the entire public. The great bureaucracies "reach and get favorable action from millions of people." [201] Complex and many-faceted problems are usually phrased for public-opinion purposes in dichotomous terms—"war or peace, protection or free trade, prohibition or saloons, freedom or slavery." [202] Obviously the decisions which are actually initiated into action by those who possess both organized power and a fairly complete range of pertinent facts are more refined and detailed than the crude composite of public opinion can ever be although the latter, as indicated by Davis and Blumer, is watched carefully for omens of trends.

It is clear that the existing social system takes care of the fundamentals. The issues are mostly on the surface, although a trend in the solution of issues as they arise can and does gradually influence the character of social organization. When an issue is solved and the solution becomes part of the social organization, it is no longer in the forefront of the public consciousness. At that point public attention has moved on to something else.[203]

SANCTIONING

Sanction as an element. Sanctions for Davis are inextricably connected with other elements of the social system, especially stratification, norms, and status-role. The essence of the rewards and punishments themselves, however, does not differ markedly from other presentations found here. For Davis, rewards which are at the disposal of society are used as inducements. Society's task is to distribute these rewards "differently according to positions. The rewards and their distribution, as attached to social positions, thus becomes a part of the social order; they are the stratification." [204] A normative order always requires effort on the part of the actor; sanctions induce this effort for Davis. Sanctions also are a rule-of-thumb means of differentiating the norms. "Some rules are supported merely by mild disapproval of the violator, while others are supported by physical force." [205] Although the sanctions of the folkways are mild, they are also cumulative, becoming more severe for the actor who persistently violates one or a set of norms or who is known to violate a large number of different norms.[206] Concerning rewards and status-role, Davis concludes, "In a sense the rewards are 'built into' the position." [207] Besides the rights which are functionally related to the position there often are many subsidiary rights which have no functional connection and little symbolic connection with the specified duties, "but which still may be of considerable importance in inducing people to seek the positions and fulfill the essential duties." [208]

Some of the sanctions of all of the important subsystems may help to sustain societal integration. Those characteristic of the religious system are outstanding in this respect. The subordination of organic desires and the primacy of group ends are encouraged by the belief system of the religion, by the communication of sentiments among members and by the endless sanctions which God can visit upon man.[209] Beliefs about sanctions encourage certain behavior whether the sanctions are applied or not. A definite belief system of rewards and punishments encourages fertility, for example, in the familistic society. Among the rewards of progeny are salvation of the soul, the security of old age, the production of goods, the protection of the hearth, and the assurance of affection. "This articulation of the parental status with the rest of one's statuses, is the supreme encouragement of fertility." Among the ideas which act as punishments for infertility are the dread of impotence, sterility, miscarriage, and stillbirth. Active societal disapproval is extended to practices that jeopardize fertility such as nonmarriage, contraception, and abortion. In contrast to the familial society, the modern western society has withdrawn most of the connections of the parental bond with the rest of society. The sanction myth has consequently changed so that children may be regarded a burden. "The difference between primitives and ourselves is not that they procreate by 'instinct' and we by 'plan' but that their society rewards reproduction more abundantly than ours." [210]

Application of sanctions. Prestige, stemming from the actor's positions, and esteem stemming from his performance, are rewards. Actors who are rewarded similarly constitute a stratum which tends to be in an unstable state of flux as long as upward mobility by competitive means is permitted in the society. Denied this possibility, the actors who constitute the stratum have a tendency toward solidarity which takes two forms: militant revolutionary solidarity, if societal emphasis is upon prestige rewards; and peaceful solidarity if societal emphasis is upon the esteem rewards. "Esteem alone tends to produce a static society, prestige a mobile one." [211] Conditions conducive to class solidarity are almost equated with a societal reward in itself. "Although the city's competitively induced inequalities are great, ranging from the highest of the high to the lowest of the low, there are nevertheless limits peculiar to the city itself. One of these is the fact that the city gives greater voice as well as greater opportunity to the bottom strata. It brings a large number of lowly persons together and often segregates them in particular neighborhoods, where spatial juxtaposition strengthens common interest in creating class solidarity." [212]

Just as sanctions are conspicuously related to norms, so is their application related to evaluation. Davis follows Thomas in describing the application of punishment to thieving and lying among a primitive tribe. To punish for lying ". . . the people begin to pile twigs and branches near the place where the offense occurred, and always thereafter all passersby throw their contributions of sticks on the heap. Some of these 'liars' heaps' are very old, but the name of the offender is not forgotten, living on in perpetual disgrace as the name of his monument of shame." [213] Some sanctions are believed to befall the offender automatically without the need for application on the part of other members of the social system. Among some peoples the breaking of taboos, for example, is supposed to produce serious consequences; bad luck or undesirable turns of events are the lot of the deviant without any active attention to punishment on the part of the community.[214]

A very widespread evaluation is the positive one on social integration and the corresponding negative evaluation on isolation. So universally is isolation disvalued that society can use it as a negative sanction. "Its occasional use as severe punishment implies that for the time being the person is beyond the pale of society, an object of desire to nobody else, permitted to live only in a physical sense." [215] Variations on the theme of isolation are banishment, excommunication, and ostracism.[216]

Rewards and punishments as they are applied represent a system of checks and balances. In the following excerpt those actors who are relatively over-rewarded by holding power, can upon certain contingencies be shorn of their rewards by the relatively under-rewarded.

If a few must govern and the rest must obey, one form that equality can take is the opportunity of the masses, at their own desire and out of their own ranks, to replace the rulers. This exposes the rulers to the most effective kind of accountability, the risk of losing office. . . . [Thus] the threat of deposition is the most powerful restraint upon governmental corruption and the opportunity of replacement the greatest form of political equality . . ." [217]

The least demonstrably applicable of sanctions are those of a superempirical nature. Yet it is by the thought that such sanctions are ultimately applied that religion helps to maintain the dominance of sentiment over organic desire, of group ends over private interest, for "it provides an unlimited and insuperable source of rewards and punishments—rewards for good conduct, punishments for bad." [218]

FACILITATING

Facility as an element and the Utilization of Facilities as process. What is designated as facility within this book is for Davis subsumed under the concept means, a much broader term than facility. A sampling of items which are designated as means at one time or another by Davis includes speech, a factory, telling a lie, the knowledge of how to operate a machine, social power, instrumental ends, and other indivduals. In our treatment only the factory is a clear-cut facility separable from the other elements in most situations. Others of the list may under certain conditions and from certain points of view also be facilities. The task of the present section will be to examine those of Davis' chapters and articles which have as a central theme the economic and technological, and select from them all that in the PAS Model sense is actually facility. Since means for Davis is one of the elements of action, the processual aspect of facilities is uppermost in Davis' treatment. Consequently the element and process involving facilities will be treated together.

Some generalizations about means underlie their elaboration. 1) "What is a means for one actor may be a condition for another." [219] Not only the nature of the facility effects its definition and utilization; the capacity of the actor has a similar effect. An implement which in the hands of one who knows how to use it is an effective tool, becomes a bothersome obstacle in the hands of one who lacks that skill. "Those aspects of the situation that the actor may control are his means and those that he cannot control are his conditions." [220] 2) What are means from the long run point of view can be ends in the short run. In our treatment this idea might be represented by a situation in which actors held as a goal the acquisition of a particular facility, e.g. a dam; once in possession of the dam, it might be viewed as a means of accomplishing a more basic goal such as flood control, or irrigation of crops. 3) Available means are both decreased and increased by norms. Davis' examples demonstrate this claim sufficiently. Available means for Catholics, for example, are decreased as they limit their utilization of means of birth control for normative reasons. In contrast, the hungry man can in no society use the simple and direct means of grabbing whatever food he sees. His possible means must be increased by considering work, begging, borrowing, or social ingratiation, all normative means of acquiring the food. In our treatment none of these last mentioned means would be labelled facilities, although each of the goal attaining activities involved might be implemented by appropriate facilities. The actor who decided to work might use a wheelbarrow; the one who decided to beg might need a hand organ or a cup and so on. 4) ". . . control over others is a particularly valuable aid to the satisfaction of one's ends." Other actors can be conceived purely as means; the total interaction can be viewed "in terms of economic exchange wherein each person, by giving up something that someone else wants, gains something in return." The interaction, as an exchange, becomes something less than voluntary when the parties to the exchange have unequal power. Actors whose behavior is conditioned by institutions governing economic exchange may seek to remove from the exchange flagrant use of coercive power. In our treatment this whole generalization concerning means would scarcely involve facilities, but rather, power, status-role, rank, norms and institutionalization and the elemental processes involved would constitute the concepts by which the phenomena would be explained.

Davis' use of means approaches that of facilities as employed in the PAS Model as the distinction between "material" and "nonmaterial" culture is examined and found wanting. "Material objects [such as axes, knives, and spears] are not parts of culture because they are "material" but rather because they are comprehended, desired, altered, thought about, and used by human beings. . . . Physical nature merely furnishes the materials for technology; culture furnishes the knowledge and patterns of use." [221] Thus, in both our treatment and the Davis model the utilization of facilities, not the facilities themselves, furnish important clues by which attributes of a social system can be gleaned. Technology is the term Davis uses to define that end which is purely instrumental in contrast to science, the end of which is ultimate

—the search for truth, and in contrast to economic and political actions which balance competing ends and arbitrate between them. Technology, because it is always utilitarian, is limited "precisely by the limitations of its goals." [222] It can only develop in societies in which utilitarian goals flourish; such goals may not exist in societies which are morally opposed to the utilitarian goal, or which give primacy to more ultimate goals. Davis tellingly cites the case of the improved drainage system in Bengal which made an immediate improvement in the health conditions of the locality. A hasty resolution for its removal, however, resulted from an evaluation voiced by the Hindu president of the board: "The river—you mean Ganga Ma? . . . The sacred river, our Ganga Mata, to receive malodorous stuff from the jute mills?" [223] Of course, Bengal as every other society has made a cultural adjustment to its environment and therefore possesses a technology of sorts; the response to the hygienic drainage system demonstrates the extreme differences which exist between technologies, or in terms of the PAS Model, the utilization of facilities. Following Chapple and Coon, Davis describes four elements involved in any technique, "the type of implement, the kind of operation, the source of power, and the nature of the social interaction required." [224] The variations of these four elements account for much of the almost infinite variation of techniques from society to society. Davis concludes with Chapple and Coon that "the techniques which people practice, therefore, have much to do with the determination of the complexity and character of their institutions" [225] and adds that the reverse is likewise true: namely, that institutions influence utilization of facilities.

A given level of technology (or the way in which facilities are utilized) does not determine the societal forms, but it flourishes under certain conditions which preclude certain societal forms. The poor communication and relative isolation of a society of hunters requires different social organization than that required by a society of farmers who by virtue of their more efficient land use made possible by superior technology has "more cultural interchange and a more extended political organization." [226] Davis offers four institutional factors which foster technological development: 1) social values, including the climate of opinion toward change. (The relative degree of open-mindedness with which the utilization of new devices is greeted, determines to some extent technological innovations); 2) social organization, of such a nature that there exist institutional methods for rewarding the inventor and diffusing his techniques; 3) specialization, to such a degree that the specialist not only can be differentiated from the non-specialist, but also from other specialists; 4) methods of storing and transmitting ideas, including writing, printing, and libraries.[227]

Davis also considers those institutional factors which hinder technological change. He notes that all societies need stability, and therefore are cautious about entering arrangements which will bring unlimited change. However, some societies can tolerate considerable change while others cannot. The societies which are intolerant of change are likely to be concerned with "diffuse otherworldliness," a view which tends to reduce the material world to symbols of transcendental realities, thereby curtailing interest in the material world. This state is seen by Davis to spring chiefly from isolation.[228]

Primitive technology thus characterizes primitive societies, small, sparsely settled with undeveloped hinterlands. The small, sparsely settled subsystems of a technologically advanced society have little in common with the primitive societies; the former are always urbanized somewhat and consequently less isolated. As technology advances, the hinterland is able to produce a surplus which is the stuff by which the life in cities is maintained. A technology sufficiently advanced to produce the surplus and to transport it to the urban centers is thus a prerequisite of cities.[229]

COMPREHENSIVE OR MASTER PROCESSES

Communication. Davis' unique contribution to the elaboration of the communication process occurs in his presentation of the cases of extreme isolation. The biogenic and sociogenic factors which under ordinary circumstances of observation must be analytically separated were in these instances able to be concretely separated, since the life histories of the isolated children were sharply divided into two phases, the first devoid of communicative interaction and the second in which the purely biogenic stage was supplemented by the introduction of social factors. His work on these rare cases of extreme isolation verifies his observation that sensory contact must contain subjective meaning for the persons concerned in order to be social in the human sense. "Human interaction . . . is communicative interaction." [230] The ability of man alone among the animals to use symbolic communication enables him to transmit attitudes and knowledge from generation to generation.[231]

The reciprocal expectations of status-roles, the essentials of normative integration, as well as all forms of systemic interaction presuppose communication, and commonly shared goals could not exist without it. On a less abstract level, primitive societies are primitive in large measure because they have no system of writing which permits the storage of ideas. Scientific specialization can be built from this stored knowledge and writing intensifies the extent of specialization.[232] Communication becomes the core of civilization,[233] is the keystone of socialization,[234] and, Davis observes, the slower the communication in a given community the more restricted the area within which people are identified.[235]

Boundary maintenance. Integration and solidarity is a central theme in all of Davis' work. The solidary social state springs from commonly held mores, beliefs, attitudes and sentiments. It flourishes in a state of isolation or semi-isolation, whether the reference group be a subgroup within a society or a society as a whole which is relatively isolated. All devices which protect and bolster the partial isolation of the system in question are procedures for maintaining the boundaries. Taboos against inter-class and inter-caste marriages help to maintain the classes and castes in their differential societal positions; taboos, such as the incest taboo which control male and female association and sex relations, help to maintain the family in a solidary state. A common device for securing partial isolation is residential segregation whether arising from free market competition for housing, from undirected ethnocentric attitudes, or from legal prescription. Expulsion, banishment, excommunication and ostracism, by their sanctioning effects on the deviant members within a solidary system, either rid the system of the offender or persuade him to conformity.

Whether the threat to solidarity comes from the foreigner outside the society or from criminals within the society, boundary maintenance devices are applied in a similar fashion.

Whatever our attitude toward war, homicide, lynching, and execution, the fact remains that practically every society is prepared to defend itself against enemies without and criminals within, even to the point of taking lives. In every case the killing is conceived to be a means to an end, either legally or illegally. Thus the very forces that preserve social order and therefore life and property also act to take away life.[236]

In the same vein, Davis views the commonly held ends so vital to an integrated society as the seeds of discord between societies.

It is hard for absolutes to dwell together in peace. The glory of Japan, the glory of Germany, the glory of Russia, the glory of France, the glory of America—these cannot be pursued indefinitely without getting in each other's way. . . . Internal harmony and external conflict are therefore opposite sides of the same shield. This is why war is held to be inevitable in a world of soverign nations.[237]

Religion, which "helps to widen the meaning and strengthen the apparent reality of common values among believers, and to motivate behavior favorable to these values" [238] must, for maintenance purposes, throw up barriers against the intrusion of conflicting values and the loss of members to competing religious systems. "Intermarriage . . . not only threatens the sect with the possible loss of an adult member, but the possible loss of new child members. For this reason intermarriage must either be forbidden or so regulated that the allegiance of the children is guaranteed." [239] Despite the protective force of religious endogamy as a boundary maintaining device, the boundaries become less impervious as isolation decreases and mobility increases. It would appear for example, that the more open the social organization in the United States, the less effective both the Jewish and the Christian endogamous rules against intermarriage has been.[240]

Writing in a pre-space conquest period, Davis speculates concerning the concept of a world state:

Boundary disputes have used up an enormous amount of national effort. The world-state, on the other hand, will be entirely devoid of the function. It will have no other wars than civil wars, and no other boundaries than internal ones.[241]

That even the vision of a world state could exist in the minds of man is due to the next considered process, systemic linkage.

Systemic linkage. In the development of civilization localism breaks down and contacts increase; the process is accompanied by an interlocking and linking of the affected systems. In this respect the undifferentiated primitive community is unlike the "modern community . . . [which] cannot be understood in terms of itself alone. Each segment may be more closely linked with similar segments in other communities than with dissimilar segments in the same community." [242] Davis sees the political structure as performing, through legal and symbolic means, a service which guards societal ends in the face of competing interests. Government and society are linked by symbols "that connote prestige and power, and that attest the right of particular persons to occupy different positions." [243] The articulation of status-roles is one of the most common vehicles of linkage. "Ordinarily the various statuses—occupational, familial, political, religious—are so bound together in terms of interlocking rights and obligations that their manifestation in behavior gets things accomplished and the collectivity is perpetuated." [244]

The familial status-roles as linkages between the families of orientation and the families of procreation are given rather elaborate attention by Davis.

It is plain that the extended kinship universe is composed of interlocking families. The chain of connection always involves the three basic relationships—marriage, parenthood, and siblingship—and the family units are the cells out of which the larger whole is constructed.[245]

Positing two polar types of family structure, "the one in which the family of orientation completely dominates the family of procreation and the other in which such dominance is completely absent," [246] Davis demonstrates that different patterns of linkages between societal subsystems prevail as the society varies by family type. In the familistic form of linkage "The emphasis of all institutions . . . [including economic exchanges and inheritance patterns] is upon the perpetuation of the clan or family lines." [247] In the non-familistic or individualistic form of linkage, there is "a variegated system of achieved vertical mobility, necessitat[ing] long years of formal education which separate youth from adulthood, theory from practice, school from life." [248]

Because the incest taboo almost universally prohibits sexual intercourse between members of the central core and others of a given kinship group, except spouses who are linked in marriage, births usually result from systemic linkage of different kinship groups.[249] Although Davis does not use the concept systemic linkage, the idea pervades his analysis and "systemic differences"[250] become the crucial consideration in the monograph "Social Structure and Fertility: An Analytical Framework."[251] In fact this is perhaps the most insightful discussion in the field of "comparative sociology of reproduction,"[252] which successfully ties the fields of demography and sociology together. This monograph, to which limitations of space permits only a brief reference, attempts to explain differences in fertility in industrialized and underdeveloped societies as well as differences among the latter through 11[253] "intermediate variables." These vary in one way or another in accordance with the various elements and processes involved in boundary maintenance of the family of orientation and function in linking families of orientation with families of procreation. The 11 variables are classified under three headings: 1) Factors affecting exposure to intercourse, 2) Factors affecting exposure to conception, and 3) Factors affecting gestation and successful parturition. It is maintained "that *any* cultural factor that affects fertility must do so in some way classifiable under one of [the] . . . intermediate variables."[254]

Although the analysis makes "sexual union" rather than "marriage" its focus, it is noted that "marriage has a high value for the individual,"[255] especially in pre-industrial societies and is, therefore, the crucial form of systemic linkage so far as fertility is concerned. Although most of the elements and processes of the PAS Model are involved in the explanation of the negative or positive effect of the variables on fertility, only a few will be singled out for attention here.

The element "facility" in the form of property, including property rights or utilization of facilities, is a crucial variable as the "joint household and/or clan system"[256] are contrasted with the nuclear family organization. Both facilities, in the form of property, and authority make for differences in the boundary maintenance processes of families of orientation and these affect age of marriage, extent of permanent celibacy, extent of post-widowhood celibacy in nuclear as compared with extended systems.

The emphasis on marital rather than filial solidarity, on neolocal rather than patrilocal residence, which appears to have delayed marriage in Ireland and Northwestern Europe, contrasts sharply with the forces operating to precipitate marriage in an extended family system. In a truly joint household the authority of the elders continues *after* marriage; the marital bond is therefore subordinate to the filial bond and does not require economic independence on the part of those getting married. . . . In the Chinese case, the father . . . need not fear the marriage of his son as a threat to his authority, and therefore, unlike the Irish father, has no motive (at least in this regard) for postponing such marriage.[257]

Just as in the above references the elements "power" and "facility" from the PAS Model fit into the explanation of variations in fertility, so most of the other elements and the processes by which they are articulated, especially belief (knowledge), norm, end, rank and sanction are explicitly or implicitly involved.

The necessity of exchange of goods and services is implicit in a cultural adaptation based upon division of labor and specialization. The economic institutions of property and contract govern, to a large extent, the inevitable linkages which accompany such an exchange. "The interdependence of specialized groups requires a certain precision in the coordination of efforts"[258] and as the individual's needs increasingly must be filled by specialties about which he has no knowledge there grows a dependency upon the "honesty, diligence, promptness, and good management of others."[259] Societal reliance upon a "natural identity of interests" is misplaced if any sizeable number of parties of the interlocking systems are fraudulent or monopolistic. Government controls which seek to maintain the societal good emerge, which links yet another system to those already inextricably connected by mutual need and bound together by a series of contracts "specifying obligations and rationally negotiated."[260] Of three major internal needs cited by Davis—"the enforcement of norms, the balancing of ends, and the planning and direction of collective action," the last two are likely to be necessities to the extent that systemic linkages are common in the society.[261]

Social Control. Davis divides order in social action in the traditional manner into the normative and the non-normative. Accordingly

In human society there is what may be called a double reality—on the one hand a normative system embodying what *ought* to be, and on the other a factual order embodying what *is*. In the nature of the case these two orders cannot be completely identical, nor can they be completely disparate. . . . This becomes plainer when we realize that the norms often (though not always) conflict with biological inclination. They are *controls*.[262]

The basis of social control lies in the internalization of the norms by the great bulk of society's members. In the simple, small society where the intimacies of behavior and possessions are known to all, the spontaneous application of sanctions upon the breach of norms is for the most part enough to control society's members. Even in the simple society, and certainly in the large, complex society there is the possibility that the controls won't work for everyone. "There is required a more sinister control, exercised by an agency that pays no attention to how the individual feels about the rules but requires conformity nonetheless." [263] This ultimate control, vested with the authority of coercive force, is generally called law. All civilizations have law and so do many primitive bands and peasant communities.[264]

Socialization. Davis' treatment of socialization relies heavily upon the symbolic interaction theory of George Herbert Mead. It is, therefore, not greatly different from that of Howard Becker, although perhaps more influenced by Jean Piaget. Very early in life the infant learns to take the role of the other; it plays at assuming family roles. "As time goes on . . . the child increasingly adopts the attitudes of others toward himself," [265] acquiring these from those who are in authority over him, and those who are his equals. Here Davis follows Piaget in assuming that from these two, respectively, come the morality of constraint and that of cooperation. The status-roles represented by the authority figure and by the peer figure are ascribed, not achieved. Those with authority over the child usually are older; those who are equals are usually of about the same age. "What the child absorbs at first is largely a morality of constraint. . . . Ultimately . . . societal morality is not a matter of rational understanding but a matter of felt obligation. The official socializer—be he parent, educator, or master—is the representative of the greater authority of society." [266] More difficult to explain in Davis' estimation is the equalitarian element in socialization. However, the fact that peers are related by similarity of status, and thus, similarity in relation to authority, may give to them an understanding of the reasons for expecting a certain type of response; thus the basis for reciprocity is laid.[267] Even though the child cannot learn as much in one sense from another child as he can from an adult, there are types of learning that the adult cannot give him, but which come to him in interaction with other children. He learns rules as part of cooperation, he learns "to stand up for his rights" without protection and without dependence.[268]

Davis' presentation of cases of extreme isolaton illuminates the process of socialization no less than the process of communication, in which section it was briefly considered. His reiteration at various points throughout his work, that the vital process of socialization must be begun immediately at birth for maximal effect no doubt springs from his unique opportunities to observe the results of delayed socialization.

Institutionalization. According to Davis, "The quickest way to envisage the total social order of a society is to understand its major institutions and the relations between these institutions." [269] He defines an institution as ". . . a *set* of interwoven folkways, mores, and laws built around one or more function." [270] Like MacIver, he uses marriage as an example of an institution. Folkways embraced by marriage, according to Davis, are showers, wedding rings, honeymoon, rice throwing, etc. Mores embraced by marriage are post-marital fidelity, premarital chastity, taking of vows, obligation of support, etc. Laws embraced are license, proper age, absence of prohibitive kinship relationships, etc.

All of these norms taken together form a definite structure—the institution of marriage—which has meaning as a whole and which when operative in behavior, results in the performance of certain social and individual functions such as production and child rearing on the social side, sexual gratification and affection on the individual side.[271]

Economic, political, religious, and recreational institutions are similarly composed of a distinguishable set of folkways, mores and laws which taken together, facilitate the performing of distinct functions.

Apparently the term, institutionalization, is used by Davis in

much the same sense as employed in the PAS Model. He refers
to processes such as socialization as having been institutionalized;
so important is the process that it is not left to accident but "has
always taken place within an institutional framework and been
controlled through institutional channels." [272]

Davis has done much work dealing with relations which are
uninstitutionalized and ambiguous. Examples are suggested by
the following titles, which in most cases deal with conditions in
the rapidly changing social scene of the United States but usually
carry a cross-cultural emphasis: "The Sociology of Prostitution";
"Mental Hygiene and Class Structure"; "Illegitimacy and the
Social Structure"; "The Forms of Illegitimacy"; "The Child and
the Social Structure"; "The Sociology of Parent-Youth Conflict";
"Intermarriage in Caste Societies"; "Children of Divorced Parents"; "Adolescence and the Social Structure"; etc. He subscribes
to the belief that when important relationships, by their ambiguity, constitute a sufficiently acute problem, some form of institutionalization will take place. He foresees, for example, that
some social mechanism will in time evolve to lessen the stress on
the child of divorced parents.[273] It is the lack of institutionalized
prescriptions for the gradual lessening of parental authority over
the child which contributes greatly to conflict between parents
and adolescents in western industrialized society.[274]

Institutionalized behavior is given expression in the conception of social position and status-role which a member may occupy. The internal attitude of the incumbent does not always
match the expectancy as prescribed by the institution. When such
divergences exist for a large number of people in relation to a
specific status-role "institutionalized evasion of institutional prescriptions" is said to prevail. There is less strain for the evader
under such circumstances than for the lone actor who finds himself in conflict with a prescribed situation. His attempts at evasion
are not institutionalized and are often accompanied by strain,
guilt, mental disorder and similar phenomena.[275]

Davis agrees with Malinowski, Kardiner, and Linton in assuming a differential in the relation between actor and social system
as reflected in institutionalization.

The conclusion may be drawn that societies differ in the degree to which their members are forced to play incompatible roles, to engage in disquieting scenes, and to submit to inconsistent norms—in short, they differ with respect to the conflict of ends which their members according to their statuses and situations require.[276]

Societies so organized that the member is subjected to stress of long duration such as the society of United States which requires life-long achievement and competitiveness, usually have institutionalized means for lessening the stress. In the United States

The individual is protected not only by his ascribed statuses but also by his rationalizations for failure and by various aids extended to him by friends, relatives, and the community at large. In short, a competitive system has its own integrated system of values which helps it avoid the fatal consequences of its own competitiveness.[277]

CONDITIONS OF SOCIAL ACTION

A set of conditions is for Davis one of the four elements of social action, the others being the actor, an end and a set of means. The obstacles to an actor's achieving his end may be of a nature which can be overcome by appropriate means, or they may be insuperable. The latter are conditions.[278]

Territoriality. As an illustration of the manner in which space enters the means-ends schema as a condition the following excerpt is pertinent:

If a traveler wishes to reach a distant city, he cannot by a wave of the hand reduce the distance until it reaches zero. He must take the distance as a given condition and compensate as best he can for it with other means.[279]

Certain physical conditions are more conducive than others to the primary or *Gemeinschaft*-like relationship. Physical proximity is the first of such conditions. Close friendships, the primary relations of the neighborhood, the community, the family and kinship groups all possess a territorial component. Physical proximity does nothing more than provide an opportunity for the development of primary relations. The cultural definition of the situation determines whether anything comes of that opportunity. Physical proximity does not promote primary and affective relationships, for example, if those in proximity to each other are barred from intimacy by class or caste restrictions, by sex barriers, or by normative restrictions applicable to the situation, such as is the case on "a packed subway, a crowded restaurant, or a public lavatory." [280] Physical proximity is controlled by proscribing and prescribing the situations in which it is likely to occur.

Of those social systems with major territorial components, "The community is the smallest territorial group that can embrace all aspects of social life." [281] Density of population is mistakenly, according to Davis, equated with urbanism. The ratio between population and land (density) must be combined with absolute population and absolute area for a realistic appraisal of its degree of urbanity. Populations never spread evenly over an area. They cluster for contact, for protection, and for group integration and organization. The more rapid the means of interaction, the greater the tendency for the area to be less restricted, and the greater its likelihood that secondary relationships prevail.

Besides the summary which Davis gives of ecological characteristics of social systems, their relation to each other in space and of such phenomenon as the distribution of mental disorder,[282] he makes substantial original contributions. Of particular interest are his observations on the ecology of cities in Latin American countries.[283] Spanish and Portuguese instituitions transplanted to Latin American environment accentuated a number of factors which led to the growth of large separated singular metropolitan centers in agricultural regions in Latin America. Only recently has Latin America shown the spatial arrangements more common to industrialized countries in which the metropolises radiate out from a center through myriads of satellites and shoe-string-along-the-highway settlements.

The importance of territoriality to the family and kinship group is noted in various considerations. Davis reviews several studies of the relations between propinquity and mate selection in marriage, noting that "the urban society of today has no rules prescribing exogamy or endogamy on the basis of local area; but marriages occur most frequently between those who have a high degree of proximity to each other." [284] A consideration much debated among rural sociologists, namely, the consequences of isolated farm family holdings compared with nuclear settlements, is decided by Davis in a rather positive manner.

Whereas in Europe the usual mode of agricultural settlement had been the village, in America it was the open farm which the frontiersman had cleared himself. . . . Eventually, therefore, [in the United States], the farm family showed many signs of individualism which have typified urban middle-class family life for years.[285]

Size. Smallness of size, like physical proximity, is a condition favorable to the development of primary relations. In considering primitive or peasant communities thus characterized, Davis observes: "In these societies, often embracing only a few dozen or at most a few hundred individuals, the people know each other well, and anything that happens receives the attention of the whole community." [286] Generally speaking, the smaller the group the more intimate it is.

As the group becomes larger each person counts less as a unique personality but more as a sheer cipher or unit . . . With very small groups even the addition of one more member makes a difference. Thus a group of three is notoriously different from a group of two, and a group of four is different from one of three . . . With very large groups . . . it requires a great addition to change the character of the group. There is not much difference between a city of 100,000 and one of 125,000 but there is a big difference between either of these and a city of 500,000.[287]

He accepts Linton's statement that the upper limit for agricultural communities with no reliance on trade and manufacture is 350 to 400 inhabitants; an average is of some 100 to 150 inhabitants. Bands of hunters and food-gatherers are usually much smaller, but units of herding peoples with effective transportation to provide frequent movements may be as large.

Contending that "much ink has been wasted in trying to define 'urban' " [288] he observes that "almost anyone will admit that a man living in a city of several million is, at least demographically, more urban than one living in a town of 10,000." [289]

As Davis relates the size of nations to power, he finds that the total population of nations manifests greater variability than other factors such as territorial size or income. In fact, the distribution of nations by size forms a pattern not unlike the distribution of land in various sized holdings in countries with a rich landowning class.[290] He maintains that although a large population does not

guarantee power, if a nation is to be a top ranking country when
it does not have colonies (which are the result and not the source
of power), "a country must have a large population—at least sixty
million as of the midpoint of the twentieth century." [291] A strong
case is made for the importance of size as a factor in industrial
development. "The very creation of a modern economic system
is much easier if there is a sizeable population within the national
borders to furnish manpower for all the specialized pursuits required and to provide mass consumption for the goods and
services produced." [292] "A small society limits . . . functional specialization . . . degree of segregation . . . and magnitude of inequality." [293]

Jack P. Gibbs and Davis, from an analysis of available statistics, conclude that "the proportion of people who live in [small
places of 2000 to 5000] is not a function primarily of economic
development or per capita wealth, but a function of the pattern
and density of rural settlement," [294] there being in India a relatively rural, and in the United States a relatively urban nation,
17 and 5 per cent respectively in such places composed of agglom-
erations or clusters of population without regard to official boundaries. "Actually, the best cutting point [for the rural-urban
distinction] probably does not lie even in the 5,000 to 10,000
range. If a lower limit to the size of places to be called urban is
to be adopted for international comparison, we believe that it
would best be set at nothing less than 10,000 population." [295]

Time and Social Change. Since Davis relies heavily upon the
means-end schema and since "ends always relate to the future," [296]
time is built into his analysis providing "a more dynamic view of
social phenomena." [297] Also, since the primary or *Gemeinschaft*-
like group requires the conditions of frequency, intensity, and
duration of interaction, time is taken into account in consideration
of major groups.

The final chapter of *Human Society* which deals with social
change, although a tentative statement, has been one of the most
balanced statements found in a short presentation; it discusses
briefly such problems as direction, form, source and duration of
change. Central to the case Davis makes against various deter-
ministic theories of change—such as the Marxist claim that the
mode of production determines social, political and intellectual

action—is his reliance, following Pareto and Parsons, upon the conception of ". . . the social system as a moving equilibrium." [298]

One can say that in the absence of outside interference a society will manifest a trend in a direction determined by the state of the socio-cultural variables at a given moment. Furthermore this equilibrium is in part self-restoring; it resists deflection.[299]

In the consideration of "The Demographic Foundations of National Power" which carries a level of analysis somewhat less abstract than his theoretical articles, he notes that the leading personalities of epochs who often receive credit for change are actually less important in determining change than such factors as growth or decline of population, changes in technology, and economic development which "set the stage and write the script for the military and political actors." [300] This is especially true of social action considered in the long run.

Although stating his basic theory in what he called "the functional-structural approach to sociological analysis [which] is basically an equilibrium theory," he ends his discussion with the statement that "the exposition of it . . . [*Human Society*] is frankly tentative and incomplete . . ." [301] As previously noted Davis has discontinued use of the term functional analysis but not, however, on account of the ineffectiveness of functional analysis as he employed it.

The so-called cultural lag theory is given short shrift. When the variants such as "material" and "non-material" components are compared he likens the comparison to the question: Does ". . . a giraffe move faster than a cell divides . . ." [302] His reliance upon the equilibrium model leads him to conclude that ". . . over a long period the rate of change in two different parts of culture cannot be very different." [303]

In understanding the relations between the chief variables determining the social equilibrium [and, therefore, change], we naturally focus on the stresses and strains. But these stresses and strains are what they are precisely because of the character of the entire social order: they are, in short, stresses and strains *of* the whole social system. We also focus on any impingements from outside which may alter equilibrium either permanently or temporarily, and we give careful attention to the forces within the society tending to restore the equilibrium.[304]

BIBLIOGRAPHICAL KEY

CAS–Kingsley Davis, "A Conceptual Analysis of Stratification," *American Sociological Review*, Vol. 7, No. 3 (June, 1942).

DFONP–Kingsley Davis, "The Demographic Foundations of National Power," in Morroe Berger, Theodore Abel and Charles Page, eds., *Freedom and Control in Modern Society* (New York: D. Van Nostrand, 1954).

HS–Kingsley Davis, *Human Society* (New York: The MacMillan Company, 1949).

MAS–Kingsley Davis, Harry C. Bredemeier and Marion J. Levy, Jr., eds., *Modern American Society, Readings in the Problems of Order and Change* (New York: Rhinehart & Company, Inc., 1949).

PI&P–Kingsley Davis, *The Population of India and Pakistan* (Princeton: Princeton University Press, 1951).

Reply–Kingsley Davis, "Reply" to "Some Principles of Stratification: A Critical Analysis," by Melvin M. Tumin, *American Sociological Review*, Vol. 18, No. 4 (August, 1953).

SOP–Kingsley Davis, "The Sociology of Prostitution," *American Sociological Review*, Vol. 2, No. 5 (October, 1937).

SPOS–Kingsley Davis and Wilbert E. Moore, "Some Principles of Stratification," *American Sociological Review*, Vol. 10, No. 2 (April, 1945), pp. 242-249.

For a more complete bibliographical selection see notes which follow and the bibliographical appendix at the end of the volume.

NOTES

1. Kingsley Davis, *Human Society* (New York: The MacMillan Company, 1949), p. ix. Hereafter referred to as HS.

2. He notes that "the masters of sociological theory who are most responsible for the ideas expressed are Emile Durkheim, Max Weber, Vilfredo Pareto, Georg Simmel, Talcott Parsons, Robert K. Merton, Charles H. Cooley, Robert E. Park, and Robert M. MacIver," *ibid.*, p. x.

3. "In social psychology the main authors drawn upon are George H. Mead, Ellsworth Faris, Jean Piaget, Prescott Lecky, the psychoanalysts such as Karen Horney, and psychiatrists such as Roy R. Grinker," *ibid.*

4. "In social anthropology the main authors drawn upon are A. R. Radcliffe-Brown, Bronislaw Malinowski, W. Lloyd Warner, Ralph Linton, E. E. Evans-Pritchard, Margaret Mead, and Ruth Benedict," *ibid.*

5. *Ibid.*, p. 168. Elsewhere the "necessary preliminaries to considering the social system as a moving equilibrium" are given. The chief elements composing the socio-cultural level were specified. "Among these were 1) the elements of social action—sentiments, values, and ends; means; and conditions; 2) the different kinds of action in which these elements are combined —technological, economic, political, religio-moral, expressive, etc.; 3) the normative prescriptions regarding the application of these kinds of action in varying situations—folkways, mores, laws and institutions; and 4) the proc-

esses of interaction that manifest and maintain these principles—contact, conflict, competition, accommodation, etc.," *ibid.*, pp. 633-634.

6. *Ibid.*, p. 168.

7. Kingsley Davis, "The Myth of Functional Analysis as a Special Method in Sociology and Anthropology," *American Sociological Review*, Vol. 24 (December, 1959), p. 765.

8. *Ibid.*, p. 762. "The scientific problems of functional analysis are the same as those of sociology in general."

9. *Ibid.*, p. 768. Davis notes that "sociologists who have learned the techniques of empirical research come to feel that functionalism is a crank method, and they are encouraged in this by functionalists themselves who say they are engaged in noncausal analysis, whatever that is."

10. HS, p. 52.   11. *Ibid.*, p. 132.

12. Kingsley Davis, "Political Ambivalance in Latin America," *Journal of Legal and Political Sociology*, Vol. 1, No. 1-2 (October, 1942), p. 127. See also HS, p. 135.

13. HS, p. 132.   14. *Ibid.*, p. 168.

15. Kingsley Davis and W. Lloyd Warner, "Structural Analysis of Kinship," *American Anthropologist*, Vol. 39, No. 2 (April-June, 1937), pp. 291-313. Davis gives Warner credit for the distinction. From taped discussion, June, 1960.

16. HS, p. 417.

17. *Ibid.*, pp. 528-529. The influence of Durkheim and Parsons is, of course, seen here.

18. *Ibid.*, p. 130.   19. *Ibid.*, p. 53.
20. *Ibid.*, p. 58.   21. *Ibid.*, p. 67.
22. *Ibid.*, p. 45.   23. *Ibid.*, p. 46.
24. *Ibid.*, pp. 533-534.   25. *Ibid.*, p. 569.

26. *Ibid.*, p. 575. The quote from within the quotation is from Luis S. Reed, *The Healing Cults* (Chicago: University of Chicago Press, 1930), pp. 2-3.

27. HS, p. 575.   28. *Ibid.*, p. 128.
29. *Ibid.*, p. 129.   30. *Ibid.*, p. 132.
31. *Ibid.*, p. 133.   32. *Ibid.*, p. 221.
33. *Ibid.*, p. 228.   34. *Ibid.*, p. 556.
35. *Ibid.*, p. 562.   36. *Ibid.*, p. 564.
37. *Ibid.*   38. *Ibid.*, p. 30.

39. Kingsley Davis, "The Sociology of Demographic Behavior," in Robert K. Merton, Leonard Broom and Leonard S. Cottrell, Jr., eds., *Sociology Today* (New York: Basic Books, Inc., 1959), p. 316.

40. *Ibid.*, p. 317.   41. *Ibid.*

42. Kingsley Davis, "The World Demographic Transition," *The Annals of the American Academy of Political and Social Science*, Vol. 237 (January, 1945) pp. 1-11.

43. *Ibid.* and Kingsley Davis, "Fertility Control and the Demographic Transition in India," in Milbank Memorial Fund, *Interrelations of Demographic, Economic, and Social Problems in Selected Underdeveloped Area* (New York: Milbank Fund, 1954), proceedings of the 1953 Annual Conference of the Milbank Fund. See also HS, p. 414. The change from an extended family to a nuclear family system is called "the great transition."

It is prophesied that all mankind will follow the family organization found in the United States.

44. From tape recorded discussion, June, 1960.

45. HS, p. 633.

46. "While [sentiments] may enter into an explanatory context . . . [they] are not ultimate desiderata for a sociologist. . . . Take jealousy, for example. My interest in jealousy was not to explain some social mechanism as a consequence of jealousy but to explain the configuration of jealousy in terms of social organization. . . . This element can be variously characterized as sentiments, values, ends—we do use those terms almost interchangeably. . . ." Thus the psychologist not the sociologist will specialize in the study of sentiments. "As a value or goal it is in the whole scheme." Tape recorded interview, June, 1960.

47. HS, p. 124.   48. *Ibid.*, p. 47.

49. *Ibid.*, p. 519.   50. *Ibid.*, p. 192.

51. *Ibid.*, p. 175.

52. *Ibid.*, p. 520. The last two sentences of the quotation come from a footnote keyed to the other sentences.

53. *Ibid.*, p. 517.   54. *Ibid.*, pp. 291-292.

55. Davis makes his thinking regarding the process called tension managing clear. "I never used [the concept], I'll tell you why. That carries a highly rationalistic connotation. . . . In consciously and deliberately organized systems you may make some allowance for possible tensions and try to arrange the mechanisms to lower tension. . . [The concept implies] somebody planned it all out. It's too rationalistic for me." Tape recorded discussion, June, 1960.

56. HS, pp. 221-2.   57. *Ibid.*, p. 74.

58. *Ibid.*, p. 76.   59. *Ibid.*, pp. 84-85.

60. *Ibid.*, p. 330.   61. *Ibid.*, p. 331, after Louis Wirth.

62. *Ibid.*, p. 544.

63. Kingsley Davis, "The Sociology of Prostitution," *American Sociological Review*, Vol. 2, No. 5 (October, 1937), p. 747. Hereafter referred to as SOP.

64. Kingsley Davis, Harry C. Bredemeier, and Marion J. Levy, Jr., eds., *Modern American Society, Readings in the Problems of Order and Change* (New York: Rinehart & Company, Inc., 1949), pp. 610-611. Hereafter various citations to this work written by Davis will be identified by the initials MAS.

65. *Ibid.*, p. 574.   66. HS, p. 300.

67. *Ibid.*, pp. 303-304. Parallel observations will be found in chapters in the present volume devoted to Parsons and Homans.

68. *Ibid.*, p. 297.   69. *Ibid.*, p. 534.

70. *Ibid.*, pp. 299-300.   71. *Ibid.*, pp. 123-124.

72. *Ibid.*, p. 124. Since the end as above specified is from the observer's and not the actor's point of view, it can easily be fused with function; this may be one reason for Davis' ambivalence toward the concept function. He states: "A farmer may want it to rain next week, but whether or not it actually will rain is beyond his control. Rainfall next week is not, therefore, one of his ends," *ibid.* If the farmer carries out operations he assumes will produce rain—whether these involve modern "rain-making" which intrinsically relates means and ends, or various rituals—in the PAS Model the rain is an

end for the farmer in the means-end schema operating in the farmer's mind as analyzed during this operation. The scientific observer may note that various ritualistic activities which actors believe will produce rain actually produce social integration. The observer using the PAS Model may designate activities which either do or do not result in their manifest end but have unintended and/or unrecognized consequence as "latent."

73. *Ibid.*, p. 123.   74. *Ibid.*, pp. 123-124.

75. *Ibid.*, p. 135. Davis notes "I have tried—I may not have always been successful—never to refer to goals or ends as of anyone but persons. . . . When you talk about group goals or society's goals you are committing the group-mind fallacy. . . ." Tape recorded discussion, June, 1960.

76. HS, p. 141.   77. *Ibid.*, p. 142.
78. *Ibid.*, p. 144.   79. *Ibid.*, p. 393.
80. *Ibid.*, p. 392.   81. *Ibid.*, p. 221.
82. *Ibid.*, p. 494.   83. *Ibid.*, p. 526.

84. Davis notes: "I would think of something like means . . . as just a concept and the limitations of it lie within the other concepts within the framework. Viewed in that way, it refers to nothing substantive. . . . Almost anything can be a means for some actor in some situation. It's a purely analytical concept." Tape recorded discussion, June, 1960.

85. HS, p. 261.   86. *Ibid.*
87. *Ibid.*, p. 157.   88. *Ibid.*, p. 161.
89. *Ibid.*, p. 166.   90. *Ibid.*, p. 167.
91. *Ibid.*, p. 126.   92. MAS, p. 575.
93. HS, p. 125.

94. *Ibid.*, pp. 580-581. Presumably this is an example of the more speculative aspect of functionalism which Davis rejects in his more recent writings. In his more recent thinking he would no doubt separate out various aspects of the statement as hypotheses to be tested. Each hypothesis might be stated in the familiar, "If x then y" form.

95. *Ibid.*, p. 167.   96. *Ibid.*, p. 142.
97. *Ibid.*, p. 11.   98. *Ibid.*, p. 57.
99. *Ibid.*, p. 60.   100. *Ibid.*, p. 65.
101. *Ibid.*, p. 71.   102. *Ibid.*, p. 487.
103. *Ibid.*, p. 55.   104. *Ibid.*
105. *Ibid.*, p. 317.   106. *Ibid.*, p. 60.
107. *Ibid.*, pp. 56-57.   108. *Ibid.*, p. 213.
109. *Ibid.*, p. 246.   110. *Ibid.*, p. 54.
111. *Ibid.*, p. 246.

112. *Ibid.*, p. 247. Davis' concept of value may be compared with that of other writers whose works are treated in the present volume. "I think where you find differences of value from a sociological point of view, you can't take these as in any way a final explanation, because you then have to ask: Why the values? . . . [For instance] low evaluation of life. . . . You have to go back into . . . the conditions, situations, lying behind these. . . . I don't think the analysis is complete until you've gone into why the value may exist. I never like to take values as a kind of ultimate in explanation; and I have a lot of trouble with sociology students today because they . . . tend to do that. . . ." From taped discussion, June, 1960.

113. HS, pp. 153-156.   114. *Ibid.*, p. 152.
115. *Ibid.*, p. 244.   116. *Ibid.*, p. 245.

117. *Ibid.*   118. *Ibid.*, p. 143.
119. *Ibid.*, p. 529.   120. *Ibid.*
121. *Ibid.*, pp. 437-438.   122. *Ibid.*, pp. 151-153.
123. *Ibid.*, p. 563.   124. *Ibid.*, p. 564.
125. MAS, p. 576.   126. HS, p. 572.
127. *Ibid.*, p. 581.   128. *Ibid.*, p. 582.
129. *Ibid.*, p. 490.   130. *Ibid.*, p. 181.
131. *Ibid.*, p. 177.   132. MAS, p. 579.
133. *Ibid.*, p. 636.   134. *Ibid.*
135. *Ibid.*, p. 677.   136. *Ibid.*, p. 678.
137. *Ibid.*, pp. 711-712.   138. *Ibid.*

139. Kingsley Davis, *The Population of India and Pakistan* (Princeton: Princeton University Press, 1951), p. 223. Hereafter referred to as PI&P.

140. *Ibid.*, pp. 225-226.   141. SOP, p. 747.
142. *Ibid.*, p. 748.   143. HS, p. 45.

144. Kingsley Davis, "A Conceptual Analysis of Stratification," *American Sociological Review*, Vol. 7, No. 3 (June, 1942), p. 309. Hereafter referred to as CAS.

145. HS, pp. 88-89. " 'Status' is not used here in the sense of general standing in the community, but rather in the sense of a specific position. A person's general standing is a product of all his positions. . . ." CAS, p. 310.

146. HS, p. 86.   147. *Ibid.*, p. 89.

148. *Ibid.*, p. 90.

149. As Levy has noted, this usage leads to specific problems of generalization. If roles are the actions of specific individuals it is difficult to build abstractions from them. Marion J. Levy, Jr., *The Structure of Society* (Princeton: Princeton University Press, 1952), pp. 158-159.

150. Davis evaluates this as "a brilliant point. . . . Thus a politician may be getting graft . . . and he is not supposed to. . . . Even to violate norms in society you always have to do it from the standpoint of a position in that society. . . . In order to get political graft, it helps to have a political position. . . . The legitimate position is often the very best way to make an illegitimate gain." Tape recorded discussion, May, 1960.

151. In this usage an interesting convergence with Howard Becker is noted. Davis equates what G. H. Mead calls the "me" with the internally perceived position and the "I" as the actual behavior in the position, CAS, p. 311. It will be noted that Becker uses the Meadian "I" as a means of avoiding what he calls "socio-cultural" determinism. See Howard Becker, *Man in Reciprocity* (New York: Frederick A. Praeger, 1956), pp. 112-113.

152. Levy, *op. cit.* See also Neal Gross, Ward S. Mason, and Alexander W. McEachern, *Explorations in Role Analysis* (New York: John Wiley & Sons, 1958). That Davis has been misunderstood is indicated by the following: To illustrate actual performance "let's take the business of a baseball player playing a certain position on the team, say it's first base. You'll have in the baseball records, a record of his actual performance. . . . How many errors? . . . Notice that this is not a complete description of his behavior. . . . It's a highly abstract account of his performance from the standpoint of what he is supposed to do in that position." From taped discussion, June, 1960.

153. CAS, p. 311.   154. *Ibid.*, p. 312.
155. HS, p. 94.   156. *Ibid.*
157. CAS, p. 311.   158. *Ibid.*, pp. 311-312.

159. HS, p. 88.

160. CAS, p. 312. In the present writers' judgment, this article and another, written with Wilbert E. Moore, contain more important subject matter and concepts in restricted space (13 in 8 pages in the CAS article) than any other writing with which they are acquainted. Actually in these two important articles relatively few significant concepts and considerations in the field of sociology are not touched upon. The article with Wilbert Moore has been the source of considerable controversy, but its basic tenets have not been disproven. See Kingsley Davis and Wilbert E. Moore, "Some Principles of Stratification," *American Sociological Review*, Vol. 10, No. 2 (April, 1945), pp. 242-249. Hereafter referred to as SPOS.

161. Kingsley Davis, "Reply" to "Some Principles of Stratification: A Critical Analysis," by Melvin M. Tumin, *American Sociological Review*, Vol. 18, No. 4 (August, 1953), p. 397. Hereafter referred to as Reply. See also Davis' "The Abominable Heresy: A Reply to Dr. Buckley," *American Sociological Review*, Vol. 24, No. 1 (February, 1959), pp. 82-83. Some of the misunderstanding manifest in these and other exchanges would have been avoided if the writers had always specified both the units and pertinent referents to which the concept rank or other similar concepts were applied. For an attempt to develop some specification along this line, see Charles P. Loomis, *Social Systems: Their Persistence and Change* (Princeton, N. J.: D. Van Nostrand, 1960).

162. HS, p. 92.   163. CAS, p. 310.
164. Reply, pp. 395-396.   165. HS, p. 364.
166. Reply, p. 395.   167. HS, p. 370.
168. *Ibid.*, p. 117.   169. SPOS, p. 244.
170. *Ibid.*, p. 244.   171. *Ibid.*, p. 246.
172. *Ibid.*   173. *Ibid.*, p. 247.

174. *Ibid.*, p. 248. In answer to Tumin's point ". . . that the unskilled workmen in a factory are as important as the engineers," Davis agrees but again emphasizes the theory ". . . that the rating of positions is not a result of functional importance alone but also of the scarcity of qualified personnel. Any concrete situation is a product of both." Reply, p. 395.

175. SPOS, pp. 248-249.   176. PI&P, p. 228.
177. SPOS, p. 242.   178. *Ibid.*
179. *Ibid.*, p. 244.   180. Reply, p. 395.
181. CAS, pp. 317-318.

182. This differentiation as indicated in the chapter of the present volume dealing with the works of Sorokin was developed by the latter. See Pitirim A. Sorokin, *Social Mobility* (New York: Harper & Brothers, 1927), Chap. 1. Davis notes that "the analogy brings out certain truths, but if taken literally leads one astray," HS, p. 94. He notes that the use of the term "social space" is like talking of a "mechanical horse."

183. SPOS, p. 242.   184. HS, p. 97.
185. *Ibid.*, p. 117.   186. MAS, p. 611.
187. HS, p. 117. The original quotation contained, "no Catholic."
188. *Ibid.*, p. 117.   189. *Ibid.*, p. 114.
190. *Ibid.*, pp. 115-116.   191. *Ibid.*, p. 223.
192. *Ibid.*, pp. 94-95.   193. *Ibid.*, p. 491.
194. *Ibid.*, p. 492.   195. CAS, p. 319.
196. HS, p. 95.   197. *Ibid.*

198. Kingsley Davis, "The Demographic Foundations of National Power," in Morroe Berger, Theodore Abel and Charles H. Page, eds., *Freedom and Control in Modern Society* (New York: D. Van Nostrand, 1954), p. 241. Hereafter referred to as DFONP.

199. HS, p. 141.   200. *Ibid.*, p. 495.
201. *Ibid.*, p. 361.   202. *Ibid.*, p. 359.
203. *Ibid.*, p. 358. Here Davis credits A. Lawrence Lowell, *Public Opinion in War and Peace* (Cambridge: Harvard University Press, 1923), pp. 87-94, as contributing to his ideas.

204. HS, p. 367.   205. *Ibid.*, p. 57.
206. *Ibid.*, p. 59.   207. *Ibid.*, p. 367.
208. *Ibid.*   209. *Ibid.*, p. 529.
210. *Ibid.*, p. 562.   211. Reply, p. 397.
212. HS, p. 333. See fn. 244 Ch. 2 and fn. 145 Ch. 4 for convergence of this formulation with that of Becker's and Homans' "companions in misery."

213. *Ibid.*, p. 63.   214. *Ibid.*
215. *Ibid.*, p. 153.   216. *Ibid.*, pp. 153-154.
217. *Ibid.*, pp. 496-497.   218. *Ibid.*, p. 529.
219. *Ibid.*, p. 126. The ownership and use of capital goods is differentiated from symbolic wealth as a source of power, SPOS, p. 247.

220. HS, p. 127.   221. *Ibid.*, p. 435.
222. *Ibid.*, p. 438.   223. *Ibid.*, p. 447.
224. *Ibid.*, p. 440.   225. *Ibid.*, p. 441.
226. *Ibid.*, p. 442.   227. *Ibid.*, p. 149.
228. *Ibid.*, pp. 447-448.   229. *Ibid.*, pp. 318-319.
230. *Ibid.*, p. 149.   231. *Ibid.*, p. 44.
232. *Ibid.*, p. 47.   233. *Ibid.*, p. 44.
234. *Ibid.*, p. 205.   235. *Ibid.*, p. 310.
236. *Ibid.*, p. 567.   237. *Ibid.*, pp. 159-160.
238. Kingsley Davis, "Introduction" to William J. Goode, *Religion Among the Primitives* (Glencoe, Ill.: Free Press, 1951), p. 16.

239. MAS, p. 614.   240. *Ibid.*, p. 615.
241. HS, p. 504.   242. *Ibid.*, p. 315.
243. *Ibid.*, p. 489.   244. *Ibid.*, p. 88.
245. *Ibid.*, p. 399.   246. *Ibid.*, pp. 416-417.
247. *Ibid.*, p. 417.   248. MAS, p. 639.
249. The original conceptualization of the process called systemic linkage used marriage as one of the examples. See Charles P. Loomis, *Social Systems: Essays on Their Persistence and Change* (Princeton, N. J.: D. Van Nostrand, 1960), pp. 32 ff.

250. Kingsley Davis and Judith Blake, "Social Structure and Fertility: An Analytic Framework," *Economic Development and Cultural Change,* Vol. 4, No. 3 (April, 1956), pp. 211 ff.

251. *Ibid.*   252. *Ibid.*, p. 211.
253. The 11 intermediate variables are as follows:

I. *Factors Affecting Exposure to Intercourse ("Intercourse Variables").*
   A. Those governing the formation and dissolution of unions in the reproductive period.
      1. Age of entry into sexual unions.

2. Permanent celibacy: proportion of women never entering sexual unions.
3. Amount of reproductive period spent after or between unions.
    a. When unions are broken by divorce, separation, or desertion.
    b. When unions are broken by death of husband.
B. Those governing the exposure to intercourse within unions.
4. Voluntary abstinence.
5. Involuntary abstinence (from impotence, illness, unavoidable but temporary separations).
6. Coital frequency (excluding periods of abstinence).
II. *Factors Affecting Exposure to Conception ("Conception Variables").*
7. Fecundity or infecundity, as affected by involuntary causes.
8. Use or non-use of contraception.
    a. By mechanical and chemical means.
    b. By other means.
9. Fecundity or infecundity, as affected by voluntary causes (sterilization, subincision, medical treatment, etc.).
III. *Factors Affecting Gestation and Successful Parturition ("Gestation Variables").*
10. Foetal mortality from involuntary causes.
11. Foetal mortality from voluntary causes. Ibid.

254. *Ibid.*, p. 213.   255. *Ibid.*, p. 222.
256. *Ibid.*, p. 215.   257. *Ibid.*, pp. 217-218.
258. HS, p. 473.
259. *Ibid.*, quoted from John R. Commons, *Legal Foundations of Capitalism* (New York: MacMillan, 1924), p. 204.
260. HS, p. 473.   261. *Ibid.*, p. 486.
262. *Ibid.*, p. 52.   263. *Ibid.*, p. 486.
264. *Ibid.*, pp. 61 and 64.   265. *Ibid.*, p. 214.
266. *Ibid.*, p. 217.   267. *Ibid.*
268. *Ibid.*, p. 218.   269. *Ibid.*, p. 72.
270. *Ibid.*, p. 71.   271. *Ibid.*
272. *Ibid.*, p. 215.   273. MAS, p. 687.
274. Kingsley Davis, "The Sociology of Parent-Youth Conflict," *American Sociological Review*, Vol. 5, No. 4 (August, 1940), pp. 523 ff.
275. HS, p. 263.   276. *Ibid.*, pp. 275-276.
277. *Ibid.*, p. 278.   278. *Ibid.*, p. 125.
279. *Ibid.*   280. *Ibid.*, p. 292.
281. *Ibid.*, p. 312.   282. *Ibid.*, pp. 278-279, 310 ff.
283. Kingsley Davis and Ana Casis, *Urbanization in Latin America* (New York: Milbank Memorial Fund, 1946). Reproduced in Olen E. Leonard and Charles P. Loomis, *Readings in Latin American Social Organization and Institutions* (East Lansing, Mich.: Michigan State University Press, 1953).
284. MAS, pp. 611-612.   285. *Ibid.*, pp. 575-576.
286. HS, p. 61.   287. *Ibid.*, p. 293.
288. *Ibid.*, p. 315.
289. Kingsley Davis and Hilda Hertz, "Urbanization and the Development of Pre-Industrial Areas," *Economic Development and Cultural Change*, Vol. 3, No. 1 (October, 1954), p. 7.
290. DFONP, p. 217.

291. *Ibid.*, p. 223. Other factors such as military discipline, natural resources, economic efficiency, and governmental stability must be present.

292. *Ibid.*, p. 210.

293. SPOS, p. 249.

294. Jack P. Gibbs and Kingsley Davis, "Conventional versus Metropolitan Data in the International Study of Urbanization," *American Sociological Review,* Vol. 23, No. 5 (October, 1958), p. 510.

295. *Ibid.*, p. 511.	296. HS, p. 270.
297. *Ibid.*, p. 168.	298. *Ibid.*, p. 633.
299. *Ibid.*, p. 634.	300. DFONP, p. 206.
301. HS, pp. 634-635.	302. *Ibid.*, p. 627.

303. *Ibid.*, p. 627. This is illustrated in PI&P. "Population change and economic development are interlinked. . . . It seems somewhat unrealistic to attempt to do something on the economic side and yet do nothing on the population side," PI&P, p. 222.

304. HS, p. 634.

CHAPTER 4

GEORGE C. HOMANS —
INTERACTION THEORIST

The social phenomenon of most interest to George C. Homans is man's "ordinary, everyday social behavior." [1] Typically, the small group has been his research site and the attempt to state propositions of the " 'x varies as y' " [2] variety, his strategy. Much of modern sociological theory is rejected by Homans on the grounds that it consists only of "systems of categories, or pigeonholes . . . or conceptual scheme[s]," [3] which neglect general propositions by which relations between the categories might be established, thereby, in his opinion, sacrificing explanatory or predictive power. Of his second major work, *Social Behavior: Its Elementary Forms*,[4] he writes: "If a conceptual scheme and anatomical propositions are enough to constitute a theory, this book is not a book of theory. Instead it is a book of explanation." [5] Few sociologists, however, would remove the name of George C. Homans from the list of contemporary sociological theorists on the basis of this quasi-repudiation. Whatever the semantics of the word "theory," his first major work, *The Human Group* [6] which he calls "a book of theory," [7] firmly establishes him as an important social analyst, a position augmented by the volume, *Social Behavior: Its Elementary Forms* which followed a decade later.

Homans specifies the similarities and differences between the subject matter, the methods of procedure and the intellectual aims of the two volumes. Whereas *The Human Group* is addressed to the analysis of "five detailed field studies of human groups, ranging all the way from a group of industrial workers to an entire town," [8] the groups dealt with in *Social Behavior* are generally much smaller and include experimental laboratory groups as well as real-life small groups, all possessing the following characteristics. "First, the behavior must be social, which means that when a person acts in a certain way he is at least rewarded or punished by the behavior of another *person,* though he may also be rewarded or punished by the nonhuman environment. . . . Second, when a person acts in a certain way toward another person, he must at least be rewarded or punished by *that* person and not just by some third party, whether an individual or an organization. . . . Third, the behavior must be actual behavior and not a norm of behavior. . . . Its subject matter is, then, the actual social behavior of individuals in direct contact with one another." [9]

Procedurally, for *The Human Group* Homans examined the five field studies, observed uniformities and classified them accordingly as the elements,[10] sentiment, activity, interaction and norm. Then from the five studies he observed the relations which exist between the four elements, and these he cast into propositions which were shown to hold good in more than one of the studies.[11] Procedurally, for *Social Behavior,* Homans borrowed from behavioral psychology and elementary economics a set of general propositions,[12] extrapolated them somewhat for sociological purposes,[13] and from them deduced less general sets of empirical propositions the validity of which was tested against research evidence.[14]

The procedural differences of the two works are a key to the different intellectual aims of the two volumes. *The Human Group,* with its genesis in the empirical studies from which emerge the general propositions, is a prime example of inductive reasoning. The sequence is from the particular-empirical to the general-empirical, instructively descriptive but, in Homans' view, not explanatory. The second volume represents "the inevitable next step"—the attempt to "ask why the empirical propositions should take the form they do, and this is to ask for explanations." [15] "Explanation" has for Homans a specified meaning: "the process of deriving the empirical propositions from the more general ones I call *explanation,* and this *is* the explanation of the philosophers." [16] Since this is also the process of deduction, the two—

explanation and deduction—become synonymous. "To deduce [empirical propositions under specified conditions from more generally stated propositions] successfully *is* to explain them." [17] *Social Behavior,* then, endeavors to explain *why* the relationships between the observed variables obtain.

For the purposes of this chapter the sequence displayed in his two major works will generally be observed as Homans' work is analyzed in the chapter sections which form the organizational scheme of the present book. Observations about *The Human Group* will usually precede those about *Social Behavior.* This organization will work very well for the many themes which are present in both volumes. It does not work so well for important themes carried by the first work but dropped in the second, or for equally important themes central to the second work which were unforeseen or undeveloped at the writing of the first work. A few of these non-continuous points of emphasis will be examined here.

Homans' famous differentiation of patterned relationships, the one the external and the other the internal, which was central to *The Human Group* is not as apparent in *Social Behavior.*[18] As developed in *The Human Group,* the one emphasizes the relations characteristic of the group as it survives in its environment: "We call it external because it is conditioned by the environment; we call it a system because in it the elements of behavior are mutually dependent." [19] (The latter characteristic: i.e., its systemic nature based on a mutual dependency of elements as universally existent and demonstrable, Homans repudiates for reasons which will appear shortly.) The three main aspects of the environment to which each group such as a factory unit responds are 1) the physical, such as space; 2) the technical, such as tools; and 3) the social, such as supervisors and family members.[20] The other, the internal, emphasizes the sentiments among group members. As the group members work together in order to survive, there is a "build up" of cooperative effort which produces sentiments among them beyond that which is necessary for the work at hand. This excess of sentiment is expressed as the internal system. It provides a "feed back" which contributes to the external system. Thus are the two systems mutually reinforcing, although "the internal system builds itself upon the foundations

of the external system. . . ." [21] Thus, unlike some of the polar
typologies which they superficially resemble, the internal-external
systems as developed by Homans, are mutually dependent, each
being continuously reinforced by the other. "The external system,
plus . . . the *internal system,* make up the total social system." [22]
(The present writers, in free and frequent use of Homans' ideas,
prefer to use the terms internal *pattern* and external *pattern* of a
given *system,* to avoid semantic confusion.) The integrated [23]
social system tends to display a merging of the internal and external as in Tikopia (one of the five case histories upon which
The Human Group is based) where the work pattern is "(a) effective in enabling the group to survive in its environment, and (b)
carried out as an expression of social sentiments. The external
and the internal systems are fully merged." [24] The less integrated
social system tends to display a general withering of both the
external and internal systems as in Hilltown:

It is clear that in the course of Hilltown's history, *the number and
strength of the sentiments that led members of the group to collaborate
with other members had declined. . . . As the frequency of interaction
between the members of a group decreases in the external system, so
the frequency of interaction decreases in the internal system.*[25]

In *Social Behavior,* Homans equates his *givens* of the physical
and social environments in time and space with what he had
earlier called the *external system.* "I now think this is too pretentious a term and suggests what is not true." [26] He now believes
that although the environmental givens sometimes constitute a
"system" in that they bear a relation to each other, this is not
always so.[27]

Homans illustrates what he means by *givens* by selecting from
the many pertinent environmental factors, three consistently recurring classes frequently noted in field studies of social behavior.

First, features of the physical or functional proximity of men to one
another that make them likely to enter into exchange [in the present
chapter treated under territoriality]. Second, features of the past histories, or backgrounds, of men that make them likely to hold similar
values [in the present chapter treated under evaluation]. And third,
features of the positions men hold outside the group in question that
make them particularly well able to reward their fellow members

within the group [in the present chapter treated under systemic linkage].[28]

A device Homans recommends for marking out what is going to be scrutinized is that of drawing an imaginary line around it.[29] Whatever lies outside the line, by whatever name it is called—parameter, boundary conditions, background factors—constitutes the givens which the investigator takes to be constant during the period of time under consideration, and which, even though he is able to do so, he does not have to explain. What he must concentrate upon is that which lies inside the line—the problem he has staked out for himself. In *Social Behavior* that problem is explaining elementary social behavior as defined above. The concepts Homans finds most useful for his purposes come from behavioral psychology and to a lesser extent, from elementary economics. The basic paradigm from behavioral psychology is drawn from an experimental pigeon which typically explores its environment by pecking. By chance it hits a round red target upon which it is fed grain by the psychologist conducting the experiment. Immediately, the probability of the pigeon's pecking the target again has increased.

. . . the pigeon's behavior in pecking the target is an *operant;* the operant has been *reinforced;* grain is the *reinforcer;* and the pigeon has undergone *operant conditioning.* Should we prefer our language to be ordinary English, we may say that the pigeon has learned to peck the target by being rewarded for doing so. However, if we use ordinary English we must take care to remember the actual events our words refer to.[30]

Two variables determine the rate of emission of the target pecking activity, the state of the animal (whether deprived or satiated) and the rate of reinforcement. The target pecking activity is extinguished over time if reinforcement is withdrawn, i.e. if grain does not follow its pecking the target. If, however, frequent or intermittent reinforcement follows the activity for a period of time, a very long period of non-reinforcement would be required before the pigeon would cease the target pecking activity. An activity never reinforced is never emitted, but an activity often reinforced is often emitted, the highest rates of emission being obtained by intermittent reinforcement at a variable ratio. The

two factors—rate of reinforcement and the relative state of deprivation or satiation of the pigeon can be balanced in such a way
that a rate of reinforcement can be established which "will just
allay the pigeon's increasing deprivation and keep him pecking
at a maximum rate. The pigeon will do most work looking for
food if he is just a little hungry all the time." [31] This activity-
reward combination may be further varied by a conditioned response to various stimuli, for example, the ringing of a bell at the
time of reinforcement. The pigeon will also encounter punishments or negative reinforcers, such as fatigue induced by stretch-
ing for grain, or such as the discomfort of being doused by a
bucket of water triggered by the target pecking. "Punishment
that the pigeon cannot avoid if it is to emit activities positively
reinforced we may call the *cost* of these activities." [32] Cost tends
to depress the rate of emission of a particular activity and to raise
the rate of emission of some alternative activity. The withdrawal
of positive reinforcements is a punishment just as is the presentation of aversive conditions. Unlike the operant behavior of target
pecking, "emotional behavior can only be released by a particular
stimulus-situation." [33]

Extrapolating from this paradigm of pigeon and psychologist
and the variables of frequency of emission and the state of deprivation of the pigeon, Homans tries to cast the paradigm in
human terms. In part following a lead taken from Peter Blau's
book, *The Dynamics of Bureaucracy*,[34] he posits Person, the un-
skillful worker who frequently needs help from Other, a skilled
and experienced worker. Other gives help to Person, and in exchange Person gives thanks and approval to Other. Giving help
and giving approval are viewed as two different *activities*. Those
activities which are viewed as symbolic of attitudes and feelings
are for Homans' present purposes, *sentiments*. ". . . when an activity (or sentiment) emitted by one man is rewarded (or punished) by an activity emitted by another man, regardless of the
kinds of activity each emits, we say that the two have interacted." [35]

These two—activities and interaction—comprise the descriptive terms of human exchanges, and they are subject to the variables of quantity (which corresponds to the variable of frequency
in the pigeon paradigm) and of value. For measuring social in-

teraction, the quantity variable can best be expressed in units of time: minutes and seconds. Unlike the psychologist who watched to see how many times the pigeon pecked at the target, the sociologist studying social activity will try to discover "how many minutes did Other spend giving help to Person, and how many minutes of approval did Person give Other in return?" [36] The second variable is value. The interaction is an exchange of units —a unit of help for a unit of approval. "The *value* of the unit he receives may be positive or negative; it is the degree of reinforcement or punishment he gets from that unit." [37]

Homans proposes that "The measurement of value is practically a problem of comparison, which may take two forms: Does a man find a particular kind of reward more valuable on one occasion than on another? And, on the same occasion, does he find a reward of one kind more valuable than one of another?" [38] Thus formulated, the state of deprivation or satiation can be taken into account (as with the hungry pigeon, Person may be expected to need more help if he has been without help for a long time than if he has lately received a great deal); also the vagaries of human choice may be reckoned with, as for example, the person "who is too proud to ask for help, one for whom pride has a higher value than being helped." [39] Only in the past history of each man will be found the clues that will have utility in prognosticating the choice he will tend to make. Since individual case histories are expensive and difficult to come by, it will be assumed that individuals of similar background will generally share similar values, although any such grouping of individuals will inevitably yield some probability of error. Homans sees one last difficulty with the variable of value; it is subject to change by the individual who emits the valued unit. Its value is judged by the recipient, but the intrinsic worth of the unit of exchange is rendered constant or inconstant by the emitter. "Accordingly, though we take Person's scale of values, the things he finds more or less rewarding, as temporarily constant, this does not mean that the value of what he gets need be constant; for Other may change his behavior and give Person a kind of activity that stands higher or lower in Person's scale." [40] With this all too incomplete background, the general propositions may here be recounted, from which Homans derives a large number of less general empirical generalizations which finally are tested against empirical cases. The propositions are thus basic to all else in *Social Behavior*.

(1) If in the past the occurrence of a particular stimulus-situation has been the occasion on which a man's activity has been rewarded, then the more similar the present stimulus-situation is to the past one, the more likely he is to emit the activity, or some similar activity, now.[41]

(2) The more often within a given period of time a man's activity rewards the activity of another, the more often the other will emit the activity.[42]

(3) The more valuable to a man a unit of the activity another gives him, the more often he will emit activity rewarded by the activity of the other.[43]

(4) The more often a man has in the recent past received a rewarding activity from another, the less valuable any further unit of that activity becomes to him.[44]

(5) The more to a man's disadvantage the rule of distributive justice fails of realization, the more likely he is to display the emotional behavior we call anger.[45]

(In the interests of brevity, these may upon occasion be referred to respectively as: 1) the stimuli proposition; 2) the success proposition; 3) the deprivation or value proposition; 4) the satiation proposition; 5) the justice proposition.) Before introducing his fifth proposition, Homans offers economic concepts which he has extrapolated into a form appropriate for social analysis. He deals with cost: "a cost may be conceived of as a value forgone. . . . For an activity to incur cost, an alternative and rewarding activity must be there to be forgone." [46] He proceeds to profit: "We define psychic *profit* as reward less cost, and we argue that no exchange continues unless both parties are making a profit. . . . Profit is the difference between the value of the reward a man gets by emitting a particular unit-activity and the value of the reward obtainable by another unit-activity, forgone in emitting the first." [47] Although there are many ways in which an exact parallel between elementary economics and elementary social behavior falls short, "the similarities in the propositions of the two subjects shine through the differences in conditions." [48] Although discussed in greater detail in later sections of the present chapter, the following quotation may suffice to present the subject of distributive justice [49] referred to in Proposition 5:

A man in an exchange relation with another will expect that the rewards of each man be proportional to his costs—the greater the rewards, the greater the costs—and that the new rewards, or profits, of each man be proportional to his investments—the greater the investments, the greater the profit. This means that unless the investments of the two men are greatly different, each man will further expect the following condition to hold good: the more valuable to the other (and costly to himself) an activity he gives the other, the more valuable to him (and costly to the other) an activity the other gives him. Finally, when each man is being rewarded by some third party, he will expect the third party to maintain this relation between the two of them in the distribution of rewards.[50]

The over-arching propositions of *Social Behavior* are of such broad generality that *many* lower order propositions can be derived including some from *The Human Group* as well as a series of additional ones not found in that work. Although *The Human Group* is a forerunner, in a sense, of *Social Behavior,* and although some of its content is explainable in terms of the latter, *The Human Group* is in no sense a determinant of the later book's content. No point by point comparison is intended, or possible, although continuities will be noted between the two whenever pertinent, as the works are juxtaposed to the PAS Model.

COMPARATIVE ANALYSIS IN TERMS OF THE PAS MODEL

KNOWING

Belief (knowledge) as an element. When Homans explains elementary social behavior, he very deliberately does not use the concepts belief, knowledge, rationality, intelligence, or any other term which implies conscious reasoning. If the cognitive component were to play a part in Homans' explanations, its place in the logical scheme would derive from proposition 1, the "stimuli proposition." One might logically expect that knowledge, belief, or cognition is a component part of man's ability to classify present stimuli-situations as being like or unlike past ones which have occasioned his receiving a reward. Homans is quite aware that for whatever reason a man " 'perceives' the situation as one in which thanks may be forthcoming," he is discriminating between situations on *some* basis.[51] "With a man the discriminations may be the result not only of his everyday experience but also of his formal education, his reading, and the verbal arguments he may have listened to. They may be unconscious or the result of conscious reasoning." [52] The important point, for Homans, is that man's behavior could be and often is in accordance with the conditions stipulated in the "stimuli proposition" without any conscious awareness. The question of whether or not the behavior is rational is irrelevant. (Homans believes the term rational to be of dubious value in the study of behavior.) Whether an individual increases his chances for greater rewards by acquiring knowledge and making calculations, as might the strategist who uses the Theory of Games as a guide and the social climber who uses implicit knowledge of elementary social behavior, or whether he behaves "irrationally" with respect to the acquisition of rewards, no allowance for calculation (or the cognitive element) is made in the five propositions "which are to this extent incomplete." [53] Calculated behavior is not ruled out nor ruled in for two reasons, first that it is rarely needed to explain the matter which is the concern of *Social Behavior,* and second, it "is the exception and not the rule." [54] That is not to say that men choose foolishly—"that is, at random—but only in the way our propositions say they do. All we impute to them in the way of rationality is that they know enough to come in out of the rain unless they enjoy getting wet." [55]

If the purpose of the present book were limited to a faithful condensation of the seven theorists' major works nothing beyond this would have to be said about *belief (knowledge) as an element.* It is designed, however, to serve the additional purpose of comparison and contrast. For this reason, some of the phenomena which Homans deals with, although he quite justifiably does not call them cognitive, must be included here, because others dealing with similar phenomena have imputed cognitive aspects to them. For example, Homans offers evidence that *belief,* whether or not well-founded, affects the kind of activities emitted by members of some of the experimental groups which he cites. As the reader reaches the chapter devoted to Robert Merton, he will find there that what Merton calls the "self-fulfilling prophecy" is in certain important ways not unlike what Homans is reporting.

Some of the groups, for example, were differentiated by the degree of "liking" or social approval sub group members shared with each other, even though such liking or lack of it was based on nothing more than being told that they would or would not like each other. One case is typical: "It is true that the subjects did not receive . . . [social approval] directly from the other members of their groups. Instead the investigator told them they were receiving it, and they seem to have believed him." [56] The result of this belief for which the subjects had not firsthand evidence and which was no more "true" than the belief of other subjects that they were not getting social approval, was sufficient to affect their behavior as the research results clearly show.[57] For Homans the belief in this case was a stimulus.

Cognitive mapping and validation as process. The significance of the process of cognitive mapping in Homans' works is limited by the same conditions by which rationality as a component of activity was neither ruled out nor in. An instance of validating beliefs by group members who subscribe to a belief is provided as Homans examines the practice of restriction of output by work groups in factories. The worker would have no difficulty in marshalling reasons to support the practice of pegging production at some figure:

If he or his fellows much increased the number of pieces each put out, management would cut the price paid per piece so that he would be doing more work for the same pay. He may well be mistaken: a modern management, watched by a modern union, might do no such thing . . . Or he might argue that in the absence of restriction the faster workers would show up the slower ones like himself, and bring down upon them the wrath of management. Even more important, if restriction had been practiced for any length of time, any conspicuous change in output might draw management's attention to what has been going on and lead to a drastic shakeup. And the workingman would never be at a loss to find other good reasons for restriction.[58]

It is as a philosopher of science, however, that Homans makes his most outright use of the process which in the PAS Model is labeled cognitive mapping. Perhaps more than any other social theorist he enlists the reader and the student in the inductive and deductive processes which his two major works so well exemplify. As Robert Merton says in his Introduction to *The Human Group*, "Homans lets the reader in on his method of analysis . . . [producing a] document which the student of group behavior can *use*, not merely cite." [59] Insofar as the one-way communication of the written word can involve the writer and the reader in common experience, the readers of Homans' works constitute with him a quasi-social system. "We here—and this is the collaborative, not the editorial *we:* . . . are learning together" [60] he says in *The Human Group*. The theme is repeated in *Social Behavior:* "At this point I give up the competitive 'I' and we, my readers and myself, assume the collaborative 'we.' " [61] The procedural differences between his two major works as discussed in the beginning of this chapter may stimulate the student to refer to the originals for a first-hand account of Homans' cognitive mapping in which "The world and its meaning are always negotiating with one another, with experience as the go-between." [62]

FEELING

Sentiment. In *The Human Group* Homans concludes that sentiment is one of the elements of human behavior, although he marshalls some very good reasons for not being sure of what sentiment is. He leans, however, toward imputing to the word sentiment the internal states of the human body the changes in which might be measurable as various sentiments are displayed. To the affective states of sympathy, affection, respect, pride, antagonism, scorn, and nostalgia, he would also add such words as fear, hunger, and thirst to the "full range of things we propose to call sentiments." [63] Homans in *The Human Group* is far from dogmatic about what sentiment actually is. He raises the pertinent question of whether actual bodily changes need accompany some of the milder sentiments, such as friendship. He points to the unreliability of the words, gestures, tones of voice, and other overt behavior by which the sentiment which is an internal bodily state can be observed.

Admittedly unreliable though the observation of another's sentiment may be, since there seems to be no better way, Homans recommends the everyday practice of gauging sentiment by noting the signs which have come to signify particular sentiments.

"The signs may be slight in that the physical change from one whole to another is not great, but they are not slight so long as we have learned to discriminate between wholes and assign them different meanings. And that is what we do." [64] As an additional practical reason for dealing with sentiment as he does in *The Human Group*, Homans points out that he is committed to dealing with the field studies upon which his work is based, and that those same field studies "give names to such things as sentiments of affection, respect, pride, and antagonism." [65] As a precursor of what is to come ten years later, he is mindful of his task, often neglected by social scientists, that sentiments must be related to activities and interactions. "Some psychologists study attitudes alone. In the future, fruitful results will come increasingly from using several methods in conjunction with one another. If social fact must be analyzed as a mutual dependence of many elements in a whole, then we shall have to investigate social fact with mutually dependent methods." [66]

Ten years later Homans writes in *Social Behavior:*

Sentiments are not internal states of an individual any more than words are. They are not inferred from overt behavior: they *are* overt behavior and so are directly observable. They are accordingly, activities. Because people say that they are the outward and visible signs of internal states—of the attitudes and feelings men take toward other men —we find it convenient to call them by a special term. But in their effects on behavior, they do not differ from other activities: we need no special propositions to describe their effects, and unless we have some special reason for emphasizing the distinction we shall use the term *activity* to include sentiments.[67]

Here, then, is the first step toward that greater generality and hence the explanatory potential of the propositions as constructed in *Social Behavior*. If the variables of social behavior relate to sentiment in the same way that they relate to all other activities, the propositions obviously apply to a much wider range of phenomena if they are cast in terms of activity. To understand the five propositions, each of which relates *activity* to something, it probably will be helpful to recall that activity is a term which expresses " 'kind of behavior' . . . in the exchange between Person and Other we shall refer to giving help and giving approval as two different activities." [68] Since the number of things men do, or their activities, are innumerable, they are identified by Homans only as different kinds of activity as the need arises. Propositions 2 and 3, the "success" proposition and the "deprivation or value" proposition, respectively relate activity to the variables, *frequency* and *value*. From these two propositions can be derived a proposition which establishes "that the frequency of *interaction* between Person and Other depends on the frequency with which each rewards the activity of the other and on the value to each of the activity he receives." [69] This immediately suggests a basic hypothesis which appears in *The Human Group: "If the frequency of interaction between two or more persons increases, the degree of their liking for one another will increase, and vice versa."* [70]

In *The Human Group* some of the conditions which make the hypothetically stated relations inoperative are also noted: "Two persons that interact with one another tend to like one another only if the activities each carries on do not irritate the other too much. . . . Interaction and friendliness are positively associated, not on the assumption that the element of activity is out of the concrete phenomenon, for we know it comes in, but rather that this element is at least emotionally neutral." [71] "Again, interaction and friendliness are positively associated only if authority is not one of the 'other things' [which must be assumed to be equal] and does not enter the situation being considered." [72]

Homans reports in *Social Behavior* that of all the propositions which *The Human Group* set forth, none was so widely attacked as was this basic hypothesis linking degree of liking with frequency of interaction. Few readers remembered the carefully drawn auxiliary hypotheses each of which provides a condition under which the original hypothesis would not be valid. "Every reader, it appeared, could think of people, including himself, who interacted often with others and yet did not like them." [73] Accordingly, in *Social Behavior* Homans recapitulates the variables which sometimes invalidate the hypothesis, and he does so by using an " 'economic' argument to explain exceptions to a proposition itself derived from an 'economic' argument." [74] For by this time, the old proposition of *The Human Group* had found a near parallel in *Social Behavior*, derived from two more general propositions which are as follows: "The more valuable to Person a unit of activity Other gives him, the more often he will emit activity, including sentiment, rewarded by Other's activity." [75] And "the more valuable to Person is the activity Other gives him, the more valuable is the approval or liking Person gives Other." [76] A possible consequence of these two propositions is the following: "the more valuable to Person the activity Other gives him, the more valuable the approval he gives Other *and* the more often he emits activity, including sentiment, to Other." [77] The parallel between this proposition, deductively arrived at and the basic hypothesis from *The Human Group* inductively conceived from the field study evidence, is obvious. Thus equipped with what he regards as explanatory conceptual tools, Homans again turns his attention to the "other variables" that would sometimes make his original *Human Group* hypothesis fail. He suggests two situations in each of which the partners to the interaction are free to terminate the relationship. In the first, each of the two interacting men finds the activity of the other to be rewarding; in this case "each is apt to like the other and go on with the interaction." [78] In the second, at least one of the two interacting men finds the activity of the other not rewarding or perhaps even punishing; "he will sooner or later, if he is free to do so, look for some alternative source of reward. If he finds it, he will decrease interaction with the other man and give him little approval." [79] Both of these situations are covered by the derived proposition mentioned above.

Now Homans turns to situations in which at least one of the men in interaction is not free to break off the interaction and defines what is meant by "free" in this connection. As in the illustrative case in which two rivals for promotion are asked by their mutual boss to work together on a problem, and in the course of their working together find the interaction punishing, their not being "free" to break off the interaction "mean[s] of course that if either did, and thus disobeyed his [the boss's] orders, he would have to forgo the rewards he might otherwise have received from his boss and the firm. Accordingly the two go on interacting frequently, but they will probably not like, and may even come to despise, each other." [80] In the belief that other exceptions to the derived proposition will fall into the same class as this illustration, Homans posits this conditional argument: "When the costs of

avoiding interaction are great enough, a man will go on interacting with another even though he finds the other's activity punishing; and far from liking the other more, he will like him less." [81]
This argument and the one appearing in *The Human Group* which
conditions the basic proposition of that work by the proviso that
interaction will increase only if the activities each carries on do
not irritate the other too much are parallel, but the more recently
derived proposition has tighter specifications and greater generality.

Another of the hypotheses modifying the original sentiment-
interaction proposition of *The Human Group* was stated thus:
"The greater the inward solidarity the greater the outward hostility." [82] In *Social Behavior*, Homans approaches this relationship
with his new propositions garnered from psychology and economics. He attends first to relations between individuals: "People
who compete with one another are in a position to deprive one
another of rewards, and the withdrawal of a reward stimulates
the emotional reactions of hostility and aggression." [83] So with
groups: "competition between groups . . . is . . . likely to increase
the hostility members of one group express toward members of the
other." [84] Previous friendships existing between members of the
now competing and therefore increasingly hostile groups, are
likely to suffer and fellow members of the competing groups "will
be more apt to express social approval for fellow members of
their own group." [85] As one of the groups surpasses the other in
competitive activity, "the members of the group have rewarded
one another and will therefore tend to increase their expressions
of liking for one another: the greater the reward, the greater the
liking." [86] "The members of the unsuccessful group have been
deprived by the members of the other, and therefore will be hostile toward them: the greater the deprivation, the greater the
hostility. And therefore, again, the greater will be the probability
that they will express liking for fellow members of their own
group. Accordingly, both reward and deprivation may increase
within-group choice." [87] This last result of group success is remindful of the differently stated proposition from *The Human
Group:* "If the group fails in its purposes and starts to break up,
its disintegration will be hastened by the increasing antagonisms
and mutual incriminations of the members. On the other hand,

the warmth of feeling between companions may be vastly heightened by their joint and successful confrontation of a dangerous environment." [88] Only part of the conclusions presented in *The Human Group* are borne out in *Social Behavior*. The earlier work posited that lack of success would breed in-group antagonisms; the latter work concludes that at least among groups in competition with each other "both reward and deprivation" or both success and failure is associated with increased within-group choice.

Since those aspects of activity which are singled out as sentiments are a constant theme in both of Homans' major works, especially the item of social approval, the summary here falls far short of being comprehensive. Sentiment will be encountered again as norms, rank, power, and sanctions are considered. However, enough has been presented to show that Homans' two major works are indeed companion volumes, and that the conclusions drawn from *The Human Group*, although not always substantiated, are generally shown to be sound by the different approach used in *Social Behavior* which explains behavior not considered in the earlier work. It is regrettable that in the present presentation the rich and humanly interesting research sources must be forgone, in the interests of brevity, to be represented only by hypotheses and propositions. Their sacrifice will be rectified to some degree as the research situations are used to illustrate Homans' treatment of the processual aspects of sentiment.

Tension management as process. Homans rarely writes of tensions *per se,* and does not use the term "tension management." As might be expected from one to whom sentiments have remained a central concern for many years, he nonetheless supplies the reader with considerable evidence that certain combinations of social factors are inevitably stressful and that there are fairly uniform ways to which men resort in order to reduce the stress. The tension reducing or managing devices he talks about are not what he would consider *societal* mechanisms. He avoids being identified with a position as functional as that. Never a complete functionalist, his change toward a non-functionalist position has been gradual. For example, in *The Human Group* he acknowledges that "theories of 'functionalism' . . . have something to teach us." [89] In that work he expresses the belief that functionalism presents some inherent problems, despite which "functional relations—and dysfunctional ones too—not only emerge but cannot help emerging . . . In the small group at least, they tend to produce a positive surplus, a margin of safety in the qualities the group needs for survival, and that this surplus may be used, not simply to maintain the existing adaptation of the group to its environment but to achieve a new and better adaptation." [90]   The functional relations Homans mentions here, are not by any means limited to tension managing functions, although Homans, in *The Human Group* concurs with Malinowski that men suffering from uncertainty are given confidence by the performance of a rite; that men suffering from fear experience bodily changes demanding action which can be fulfilled by ritualistic participation; that men suffering from worry are subject to paralyzing inertia which can be halted by their physical participation in the ritual.[91]

Appropriate to the *elementary* kind of social behavior that is the subject of his second major work, Homans tries to pin-point the components of interaction that yield reward and profit on the one hand, and on the other, those that are punishing or costly. Avoidance is one of the often used means of managing a situation which is potentially stressful: "punishment is a reason for avoiding and fearing the punisher." [92]   The leader of a group, for example, because he can punish as well as reward, is usually relatively isolated; "his followers are apt to keep out of his way." [93]   Although avoidance takes care of the tensions for the followers it poses the emotional problem of loneliness for the leader who consequently "will seek occasional escape in the society of men with whom he can relax and be at ease. In the nature of the case, the only such society open to him is the society of his equals. . . . Because leaders in any single group are few in number, a leader is apt to find his social equals in the leaders of other groups." [94] What Homans describes as " 'an attitude toward others which may best be described as emotional or psychological distance' " [95] is a commonly used device for reducing strain.

Also bearing upon tension management is the condition which Homans terms status congruence. "We shall say that a condition of *status congruence* is realized when all of the stimuli a man presents rank better or higher than the corresponding stimuli presented by another man—or when, of course, all of the stimuli presented by the two men rank as equal." [96]   Status incongruence emits conflicting signals to the would-be interactor who is confused about whether he should emit activity appropriate to the stimuli signifying high rank or that signifying low rank, both of which are exhibited by the status incongruent. Consequently, individuals may seek to avoid an incongruent person, or to limit their social interaction with him.

Whatever the cause of embarrassment or confusion, the joke is frequently used to manage the tensions. "A familiar example is the behavior of men at some kinds of reunions. They are supposed to be old pals together, yet they may not have seen one another for years or indeed ever have been very friendly at Yale. On such occasions, exaggerated back-slapping and shouts of the 'you out of prison, you old hoss-thief?' order can be—amazing as it may seem—appropriate." [97]

The person with a relatively high degree of status congruence may occasionally wish to emit activity which is generally considered to be incongruent with his status. Such is the case of the machinists, who as higher ranking workers than the operators, often loaned the latter their tools and gave them help, but who seldom borrowed from the other machinists or asked them for help; "when they did so [they] tried to disguise their behavior. They pretended it was not help they wanted but only a chance to compare notes, to discuss with a fellow expert technical problems of interest to both." [98] Some subterfuges which make status incongruence less obvious and therefore less painful take the form of rather institutionalized accommodations. Such is the case of the high ranking cook who must be told by the low ranking waitresses what the customer wants. At this point the waitress in effect controls what the cook does:

Perhaps as a result of a process of unconscious adaptation, waitresses often give their orders to the cooks through a small window or over a high barrier, where the two can see one another with difficulty if at all, and the consequent impersonality seems to take some of the curse off the incongruence: one cannot, so to speak, feel incongruent with a mere voice. [99]

Communication of sentiment as process. Activity, for Homans, incorporates the concept of communication: this "mutual dependence of sentiment and activity [comes very close to expressing communication of sentiment]. . . . any emotional attitude we take toward someone tends, like any other drive, to get itself expressed in activity, which may in turn arouse sentiment in the person to whom it is addressed, and so lead to reciprocal activity." [100] The activity may take many forms, and the dynamics of the external-internal systems are of the very stuff of sentiment communication. Whereas in *Social Behavior* some social exchange is definitionally sentiment communication because it consists of exchanged activities and some activities are sentiments, *The Human Group* is more discriminating in this respect. Each of the five studies of social behavior examined in *The Human Group* abounds in evidence of this process. Excerpts from two of them will suffice for present purposes. Among the Tikopia:

In all the great occasions of life . . . the mother's brother acts as an older friend [to the child] . . . and helps him over the rough places . . . When a man needs someone to hold his hand, the mother's brother is always ready . . . One may use his personal name, touch him, tell him lewd jokes, and talk to him about anything under the sun . . . It should be clear by now that a mother's brother is a practical and emotional necessity to a Tikopia man.[101]

Less idyllic sentiment communication than that of the Tikopia can be an emotional necessity too:

Maxmanian . . . was the most disliked person in the room. . . . He had trouble at first catching on to the use of his test set and thus slowed up the men whose work he inspected. They were irritated and did nothing to help him out. Instead they made fun of him, arranged their work so that he could not possibly keep up, and when he was not looking adjusted his test set so that it would not work. Finally he could stand it no longer. [He complained to the Personnel Division.] The news got back to the men that Maxmanian had "squealed." They were furious; cooperation broke down completely, and Maxmanian had to be transferred out of the room.[102]

ACHIEVING

End, goal, or objective as an element. Homans' parsimonious use of concepts and the conceptual simplicity afforded thereby can never be correctly interpreted as "not needing" or "not taking into account" the many social phenomena which most social analysts find necessary for an adequate explanation of social interaction. His use of the concept end or goal is illustrative of a number of such concepts which sometimes are specified but often are implicit, and which are only occasionally separated analytically from the broad terms which he designates as elements, descriptive terms, or variables. In so far as goals are not included in the givens, Homans prefers to treat goals as part of the behavior which is to be explained, by assuming that goal achievement is a reward which one's activities get from another person, another group, or the environment. The only difference for him between a goal and any "other rewards" is in the length of the chain of activities that are rewarded by the attainment of a goal. Attention is given to those activities which are goal-attaining (those for which "rewards" are anticipated) only as a part of activities, sentiments or upon occasion values. The basic hypotheses are constructed in terms of these broad concepts. Modifications are made only as those exceptions arise which seem to be occasioned by the non-discrete character of the broad terms. The basic hypotheses and propositions state the most general relations of sentiment or activity to a given variable. Only as goals, as a special class of sentiments (or activities), bear a unique relation to the variable which is to be explained, have modifications in terms of goal been made in the general statement of relations. A group goal in Homans' view is not a universal phenomenon of group behavior: some groups have "a task to accomplish in common—a condition that certainly does not hold for all human groups." [103] But this is not to deny that under some circumstances commitment to a group goal is one of the determinants of behavior, as it is with the leader who gives instructions, "particularly instructions that, if obeyed, coordinate . . . activities toward the attainment of some group goal." [104]

Some of the continuities from *The Human Group* to *Social Behavior* represent subtle changes. Both works tend to pay more attention to individual motivation or self-interest than to group objectives. In *The Human Group,* Homans explores how self-interest becomes transmuted into group motive; his position there is summed up by Mayo whom he quotes:

If a number of individuals work together to achieve a common purpose, a harmony of interests will develop among them to which individual self-interest will be subordinated. This is a very different doctrine from the claim that individual self-interest is the solitary human motive.[105]

Ten years later he observes "I now think this a truism. If they have a common purpose they have a harmony of interest to begin with." [106]

If the only purpose of the present chapter were to present Homans' basic theses in a sufficiently condensed form to give the reader a respectable over-all view of his works (a purpose which perhaps could be better served by his own condensations),[107] not much more would have to be said about the concept end. Since, however, the immediate purpose includes also the comparative function of examining what this analyst thinks about goal, whether specified or unspecified, in order to afford a contrast to what other analysts think about the same subject, it is necessary here to try to point out Homans' frequent *connotations* of goal, even though for the purposes of his analysis, the component may be included in the givens, and require neither specification nor special treatment.

The connotation of goal and the implied means-end schema in Homans' use of the word "value" is apparent as he describes "economic man":

We have tried to show how . . . our propositions and corollaries are wholly compatible with those of elementary economics. Indeed we are out to rehabilitate the "economic man." The trouble with him was not that he was economic, that he used his resources to some advantage, but that he was antisocial and materialistic, interested only in money and material goods and ready to sacrifice even his old mother to get them. What was wrong with him were his values: he was only allowed a limited range of values; but the new economic man is not so limited. He may have any values whatever, from altruism to hedonism, but so long as he does not utterly squander his resources in achieving these values, his behavior is still economic. . . . The new economic man is plain man.[108]

Connoted goal is similarly a component of "rational" or long-run behavioral determinants which in Homans' view is characteristic of a small number of calculating individuals, those few whose behavior is seriously addressed to the question: "Given that you value the attainment of certain ends, how could you have acted so as to attain them more effectively?" [109] But it appears to be no less a factor for that far greater number whose behavior is motivated by short-run considerations, those for whom "A bird in the hand is worth two in the bush"

[which] is by no means always an unintelligent policy. And so far as the pursuit of rationality entails study, forethought, and calculation, and such things hurt, as they often do, the pursuit of rationality is itself irrational unless their costs are reckoned in the balance. The costs of rationality may make rationality irrational.[110]

In one of the cases reported by Homans, the *professional* engineers collected the *same reward* as the *organizational* engineers but earned lower profits than the latter group, because the professionals had greater costs in terms of their investments of time, money, and study expended in university training, costs which must be "reckoned in the balance." Although Homans explains the lack of satisfaction on the part of the professional engineers "as a problem of social certitude" and does not use the term goal (or the term norm) in this connection, the present authors would have explained it through reference group theory. Through their referents the professionals had acquired different goals (and norms) than the organizationals and the goals of the former were less attainable (and their norms were more subject to violation) under the work conditions described than was the case for the organizationals. For instance the professionals' goal (a term not mentioned by Homans here) of contributing to knowledge through independent scientific research, as set by such reference groups as research engineers, was denied them by their job which consisted of running routine tests. The *organizational* engineers, in contrast, had no such investments, they identified themselves with business and a company career, and their goal, as set by their own reference groups, was quite congruent with the running of the routine tests. Goal, of course, is not mentioned by Homans as entering into this situation. As a prelude to it, he says:

Suppose two men are doing the same job, and objectively they are getting about the same reward for doing it. One of them values this kind of reward highly, while the other does not do so. No doubt the latter would be satisfied with the amount of reward he does get, if only he wanted that kind. Instead he sets a high value on a different kind of reward, which the job is not giving him much of.[111]

It is hard to conceive of investment, value, or reward in this instance as very significant without the *meaning* of goal whether or not it is called by that name. Their pertinence to goal as it is commonly conceived is suggested by the terms Homans uses in this connection—terms such as "satisfaction quantity" which he equates to "what psychologists call . . . *level of aspiration.*" [112] As Person emits activity which is reinforced by valuable activity from Other, Person is rewarded; as he is progressively rewarded his *satisfaction quantity* may change.[113] This and related phenomena are examined under the processual aspect of goal immediately following.

Goal attaining and concomitant "latent" activity as process. Homans says: "I always think of an activity getting a reward, instead of an activity attaining a goal. I think . . . [my statement] is more general." [114] This remark can serve as a key to the question he poses: "Suppose a man is performing more or less regularly a particular kind of activity; what circumstances make it more or less likely that he will say he is satisfied with the reward he gets from the activity?" [115] (In terms of the PAS Model under what conditions will he interpret his own activities as goal achieving and/or satisfying?) One circumstance which contributes to the likelihood that he will consider himself satisfied is the realization of distributive justice—i.e. that his profit is directly proportional to his investments (age, sex, seniority, skill, etc.).[116] Homans adds another contributing circumstance. Following Morse, he quotes as follows: "The greater the amount the individual gets, the greater his satisfaction and, at the same time, the more the individual still desires, the less his satisfaction." [117] Here recognition is being given to the varying satiation points of different individuals; what would be goal achievement for one would be but a half-way point for another. Whereas the satiation point of the pigeon eating grain or the man eating steak is relatively easy to establish, "when we are talking about pay, or variety, or autonomy, or promotion, it is by no means so clear what we might mean by satiation." [118] It is not enough in dealing with such items to talk of "a quantity of reward that . . . would satiate a man. [This must be modified to] 'quantity of reward that is in line with his investments according to the rule of distributive justice.' Then the amount the individual still desires of any particular reward is the amount by which the reward he has gotten falls short of this quantity, which we shall call the *satisfaction quantity*." [119] As a man's seniority, skill, and other investments increase, so may his "satisfaction quantity" change. If his rewards have not kept pace with his aspirational level (if, in terms of the PAS Model, his achievements have not kept pace with his goals), he is still unsatisfied. Satisfaction is by no means correlated with production (goal achieving activity in terms of the PAS Model), for often the more satisfied man is less productive than the less satisfied. The closer he is to satiation the less willing is he to do more work for the same reward. But this is not always true; a man's satisfaction and the frequency with which he emits an activity might vary together, as is often true when emitted activity aimed at a final accomplishment is scarcely rewarded at all until just before the result is obtained when all the rewards come at once. "Suppose, for instance, that soldiers have been fighting a battle all day, and at dusk the enemy is just beginning to give way. Then they will put on a last big push, and their elation will mount rapidly as they get sight of victory." [120]

This last excerpt is remindful of the constant thesis in *The Human Group* that successful interaction in the external system produces the positive sentiments which compose the internal system. Although the theme is almost absent from *Social Behavior* it appears as in the case of the soldiers just cited and again in Homans' introduction to his last chapter of *Social Behavior*.

According to my lights, a last chapter should resemble a primitive orgy after harvest. The work may have come to an end, but the worker cannot let go all at once. He is still full of energy that will fester if it cannot find an outlet. Accordingly he is allowed a time of license, when he may say all sorts of things he would think twice before saying in more sober moments, when he is no longer bound by logic and evidence but free to speculate about what he has done.[121]

The linkage of successful goal achievement in the external system to the abundance of sentiment in the internal system has proven useful to many sociologists and is regarded by many as one of Homans' most insightful contributions. Despite its relative neglect in his second major work, a picture of Homans' total works would indeed be incomplete without it. In *The Human Group* he concludes that conditions which combine to facilitate goal achievement "tend to produce a positive surplus, a margin of safety in the qualities the group needs for survival, and . . . this surplus may be used, not simply to maintain the existing adaptation of the group to its environment but to achieve a new and better adaptation. . . . Society does not just survive; in surviving it creates conditions that, under favorable circumstances, allow it to survive at a new level." [122] The possibilities for organic growth are among the most important "latent functions" of goal achievement, and for Homans, at least in the period around 1950 when *The Human Group* appeared, the surplus of goal achievement represented by such components as "morale, leadership, control, extension of the range of social contract," [123] is an important part of social evolution.

Both in the elemental and processual aspects of end or goal, considerable attention has been given to establishing what seems to be Homans' position not only in regard to ends, but to other components not often singled out for special attention, of which ends is illustrative. By and large what many others have designated as ends and goal attaining activities to be studied through the use of the means-ends schema Homans subsumes under the categories, activities and rewards. He does so because most of the time, the relations he observes between his variables and all kinds of activities and all kinds of rewards is true also of ends and goal achieving. When that special class of activities commonly identified as goal achievement appears among empirical data as bearing a different relation to the variables than do other classes of activities Homans identifies them and modifies his general hypothesis accordingly. The following excerpt from his writings, appearing as it does in a publication less widely disseminated than either of Homans' major works, is included to show how ends, or any number of other "x, y, and z factors" may occasionally be summoned to explain results not predicted by the most general statement of a proposition. The excerpt appears in a publication by William F. Whyte [124] in which the latter explores certain discussion groups of the National Training Laboratory at Bethel, Maine. As interaction among the group increased, so did hostility to the point that hatred and similar sentiments were openly expressed and some members were so upset that they resorted to psychiatric care. Whyte wrote to Homans suggesting that his observed groups offer evidence that the basic formulation of the correlation between liking and interaction as it appears in *The Human Group* is "by itself . . . not adequate." [125] (*Social Behavior* had not yet appeared at the time of this incident). Homans replied in part as follows:

I am inclined to agree with you that a better formulation might be "the more frequently persons interact with one another the stronger their sentiments toward one another are apt to be." My formulation is, in fact, a special case of a more general hypothesis. Suppose we say, and I am formulating the hypothesis very crudely, that the degree of liking of persons for one another varies with the frequency of their interaction and also with other, unspecified variables, x, y, and z. My statement is that, supposing x, y, and z constant but interaction free to vary, *then* an increase of interaction tends to increase favorable sentiments (up to some limit). Conversely, taking sentiment as the independent variable this time, a decrease in favorable sentiments will bring about a decrease in interaction (withdrawal). . . . There are probably plenty of such factors x, y, and z, and you mention one of them. I have had in mind one that sounds very much like yours, which might be stated like this: in a group that is not accomplishing its goals, increased or constant interaction makes for a decreased amount of sentiments of liking.[126]

The reader is asked to keep in mind the "plenty of such factors x, y, and z" as other elements and processes (in terms of the PAS Model) might seem on the surface to be relatively neglected in Homans' hands in his emphasis upon the most general relations possible between his broad concepts.

NORMING, STANDARDIZING, AND PATTERNING

Norm as an element. In *The Human Group* Homans makes clear that norms are not behavior but ideas: what people think behavior ought to be. A norm specifies the kind of behavior which ought to prevail under given circumstances and which is punishable if not followed.[127] His view of norm in *Social Behavior* remains essentially the same: "A *norm* is a statement made by some members of a group that a particular kind or quantity of behavior is one they find it valuable for the actual behavior of themselves, and others whom they specify, to conform to." [128] Homans' most frequently used example of a norm, and one which occurs in both of his major works, is the output norm in an industrial group. However, his main interest in norms lies neither in determining why certain groups adopt certain norms, nor in conformity itself, but rather in explaining why conforming behavior is valued. Relating value to activities and interaction is one of the basic jobs that *Social Behavior* attempts to do, a subject which will be examined here under *Evaluation*.

Evaluation as a process. The continuity and development of Homans' thought in the decade between his two major sociological works is illustrated by comparing his norm-value treatment as it appears in the earlier work with his usage in *Social Behavior*. In the earlier work [129] Homans views a norm as a limited idea of what is desirable and a value as an unlimited idea of what is desirable. An output standard is limited to a particular situation and is thus a norm which in the course of a day's work could be measured for degree of member conformity. Pay, however, is a value because "sentimentally speaking, one cannot get too much pay." [130] Normative evaluation, for Homans, then, could not be applied to pay in the same way as it is to an output standard. Nor could it be so applied to such "factors as education, seniority, ethnicity, autonomy" all of which are values of which it is impossible to have too much.[131] In *Social Behavior*, the terms "generalized" and "specific" have respectively replaced the terms "unlimited" and "limited." "Whereas we call the value put on social approval or on money a generalized reward, a norm remains specific to a particular situation: a different industrial group might value conformity to a different norm." [132]

Value and quantity are the two variables in accordance with which all activity and interaction is explained. Of the two, value requires the greater definition and attention in order that its meaning be precise enough for use in propositions. By itself, it is not unambiguous; it has at least two generally accepted meanings both of which signify considerations important to the social scientist. "There is the mathematical sense of value, the value of the variable X is 10. Then there is the other meaning of the word which is simply something which is rewarding." [133] Homans considered using the economists' word "utility" for this latter meaning of value but rejected it on the grounds that it connotes something useful, whereas a non-useful or even harmful activity (such as smoking cigarettes) may nevertheless be valuable to some individuals. Of the ten pages in *Social Behavior* devoted to clarifications of the term value the definition and the most salient precautions about its use will be given here, some of which may overlap slightly the introductory statements about values.

A man emits a unit of activity, however that unit be defined, and this unit is reinforced or punished by one or more units of activity he receives from anther man or by something he receives from the non-human environment: he may give another man help and receive approval, or he may bait his hook and catch a fish. The *value* of the unit he receives may be positive or negative; it is the degree of reinforcement or punishment he gets from that unit.[134]

From the point of view of Person, his own behavior may be the subject of evaluation because as he acts in certain ways he wins for himself or loses valuable rewards. Or Other's behavior may be the subject of evaluation by Person, because it is Other's behavior which rewards Person. Definitionally, it is only the second situation which signifies value: "It is always something one receives from another man or the environment that varies in value." [135] The measurement of value is a process of evaluative comparison: "Does a man find a particular kind of reward more valuable on one occasion than on another? And, on the same occasion, does he find a reward of one kind more valuable than one of another?" [136]

The clue to prediction of what a particular individual will tend to hold valuable under specific conditions including his present circumstances is to be found only in his past; a few generalizations about what certain men with certain backgrounds will probably evaluate highly may be made, but never with absolute precision. A generally similar past will make it more probable that men sharing that past will place a similar evaluation on items of behavior. It is rarely possible to know the whole past of any individual, however, so there is always the possibility for the mistaken prediction of what a man will find valuable.

. . . sometimes it may be hard indeed to explain why his present values are what they are. A taste for duck may look easy enough; a taste for duty does not even look easy. Nor, thank God, is it, as we shall see, the business of this book to explain. All we assert here is that a man's past is where we must look for enlightenment; the past offers in principle the information we need to assess values independently of the amount of activity a man puts out to get these values at present.[137]

An increasing differentiation of experienced pasts and of tastes transmitted from generation to generation may be expected as one's focus moves from all mankind to cultures to subcultures. It is only as particular groups of people are viewed that the norms which the group shares become evident, and that the values attached to conformity to the norms become observable. When finally the lone individual is viewed, he will exhibit a set of values which in some respects is unique, although obviously his values resemble those of members of the groups of which he is a part. Homans is not interested in establishing why a man's values are as they are, only in explaining why he behaves as he does in realizing his values, whatever they may be.[138] His choice will depend on which of two (or more) rewards he finds more valuable (the "deprivation or value" proposition), and which of the two rewards he is more likely in fact to get (the "success" proposition).

Different but complementary values held by two individuals facilitate exchange between them (as between Person and Other, the one valuing help more than approval and the other valuing approval more than help).[139]

All we argue here is that if two or more men are similar in the values they hold—if this fact is given—then we are in a position to predict that they will probably reward each other and come to like each other. Even if the similarity in values is not given us directly, but we do at least know that the men have similar backgrounds, we can make the same prediction with a high probability of being correct.[140]

Among those activities valued highly as reported by Homans is similarity in expressed opinion. Group members direct much activity in the research cases cited toward "the member whose behavior most needs changing, that is, to the man who has so far failed to yield to the influence they have brought to bear on him." [141] When persuasion fails, the nonconforming member is evaluated negatively by the group and will attract to himself the least of the directed activity. From the general propositions can be derived the following proposition: "Men will put out much activity to get a valuable reward, but if the reward is not forthcoming, the amount of activity will fall off," [142] a proposition substantiated by the research findings reported by Homans.

A number of circumstances contribute to a norm's being conformed to, so that sheer conformity may reflect a composite of evaluative choices.

Some members of a group conform for the norm's sake, that is, for the external reward, such as protection from management, that conformity gets them; and some for the approval's sake, but both will come to say that they do it for the norm's.[143]

Another factor is whether the potential nonconformist can find any support among the group for his position. "Savages, who seldom have another tribe than their own that they can join, are great conformers." [144] But let the nonconformers find only one other member who breaks the same rule, and the nonconforming position will be considerably strengthened: "a companion in misery is still a companion." [145]

It must be by now clear that "value" and the evaluative process, in Homans' schema, are by no means limited in its applicability to norms. The derived propositions which are to follow, are pertinent to normative evaluations, but their explanatory power covers a much wider range of elementary social behavior. They are stated with the usual qualification of "other things being equal."

The more valuable . . . to Person the activity (or sentiment) he gets or expects to get from Other, the more valuable to Other the activity (or sentiment) Person gives to him. And the more valuable to Person the activity he gets or expects to get from Other, the more often he emits activity that gets him, or he expects will get him, that reward. But as the expectation goes unrealized and his activity goes unrewarded by Other, Person emits the activity less and less often.

Since the cost of Person's activity is the value of the reward that he would have gotten by another activity, forgone in emitting the first, the presence of alternative activities open to Person tends to increase the cost to him of any one of them. The less his current profit from his behavior—the less, that is, the excess of value over cost—the more apt he is to change his behavior; and he changes it so as to increase his profit.

The alternatives open to Person may be not only different activities but different Others who may reward them; and the more heterogeneous these Others, the more likely it is that some of them will do so. As between different Others, Person tends to emit more activity to . . . that Other in exchange with whom he gets the greater profit.

When the similarity of his own activity with that of another is valuable to him—a condition that does not always obtain, but does obtain for the similarity of opinions—and when some people have actually failed, or will probably fail, to change their activity so as to make it like his own, Person will interact more often with Other, the more similar Other's activity is to his own.[146]

DIVIDING THE FUNCTIONS

Status-role incorporating both element and process. Neither of Homans' two major sociological works uses the terms status and role as analytical concepts. "We do not directly observe *status* and *role*," [147] he says in *The Human Group*. In *Social Behavior* he specifies that the subject matter of that book, elementary social behavior is "to be distinguished from obedience to the norms that a society has inherited from its past . . . [such as, for example,] certain unwritten rules or norms about how a physician ought to behave toward his patients and toward other physicians. It has inherited what sociologists call the physician's *role*." [148] In the same work he says "What we mean when we say a man has a role is that a certain kind of behavior has become established as congruent with his status in other respects." [149] It is chiefly in connection with status congruence and distributive justice that he deals with the many examples of division of labor and differentiated occupational role which appear in empirical studies cited by Homans in support of his deductive conclusions in *Social Behavior*. The bundlers and the cashiers of the super-markets, the ledger-clerks and the cash posters, the machinists and the assemblers all contribute to the readers' understanding of the derived propositions which they usually support, and their presence indicates that among Homans' "givens" is the bald fact of a high degree of division of labor.

Those status-roles with which Homans deals (although, of

course never by that name) outside of the cases by which he tests his propositions, are such categories as leader, follower, cooperator and competitor. In connection with the latter two, Homans expands somewhat on the idea of status-role (as that term is used in the PAS Model).

Two men reward each other, and thus cooperate with each other, when each provides the other with a service that he could not do for himself at all or could not do at such low cost. Sometimes the services the two men provide are similar, as when both put their weight into moving a rock neither could move alone. But often the services are different, which means that each man becomes a specialist as far as their cooperation is concerned. Thus in our example, Other became, in effect, a specialist in giving help and Person a specialist in giving approval. Competition, at least under the conditions we are interested in here, is much less likely to promote specialization and the division of labor.[150]

The basic condition which leads to similarities or differences of function centers in the reward. If both are after the same reward which can be obtained by only one kind of activity competitors become similar rather than different.

A really far-flung and well-developed system of job specialization requires a complex organization which for the most part lies outside the province of *Social Behavior*. The definitional requirement for relatively immediate reward, *now,* as specified in *elementary* social behavior precludes for the most part a consideration in that book [151] of those deferred rewards which specialization of activity generally promises. But even within that class of behavior which is strictly elementary, some specialization is found. "A man who shuts up and lets others talk is differentiating his behavior from that of the others. He is none the less a specialist for the fact that his specialization is keeping still." [152] In this cooperative activity, his partner does the talking.

Of the two forms of interaction, competition and cooperation, which is more desirable in elementary social behavior? Is it actually "better" for all group members to specialize on a portion of the task, and to cooperate by pooling their efforts, than it is for all group members to be doing the same task in competition with one another? The experimental evidence supplied by Homans suggests that the cooperative group finished their job of solving a logical puzzle sooner than did the group whose members were competing with each other. But Homans points out that unless they finished their job five times quicker than the competing members cooperative effort would be an inefficient use of man power. The competing arrangement would allow some of the five people to be taken off the puzzle solving job and be put to work elsewhere.[153] To "examine each case on its merits" as Homans suggests, is of course, to be evaluative, a frame of reference which permeates all of the explained elementary social behavior. The following propositions, for example, which are those most pertinent to cooperation and competition, are necessarily concerned with value. In contrast to the by now familiar example of Person and Other who get respectively more help and more approval by working together than either could by working separately is the situation of competition.

[Competition] means . . . that each emits activity that, so far as it is rewarded tends by that fact to deny reward to the other. The activity, if reinforced, withdraws reinforcement from the other. . . . The competition . . . may be interesting enough in itself to provide rewards that outweigh the costs of losing . . . competition . . . always raises the question of distributive justice.[154]

If the winner has won "fair and square," the loser's natural hostility will be much diminished. Nevertheless: "Even in games, the threat of hostilities is always present and may even add to the excitement. In short, the proposition that loss in competition tends to rouse anger remains true, though its truth is sometimes masked by stronger forces." [155] The effects of competition upon sentiment as it is evidenced upon in-group choice (when the competition is between groups rather than between individuals) has already been considered above under *sentiment as an element.* To preserve the logic of the immediate organization of this chapter, it must be remarked, however, that certainly the evidence presented for groups in competition poses no pertinencies for status-role or for division of labor, except as the artificially created groups of the experiment were predestined by the leaders to be "winners" or "losers." Indeed, it is Homans' argument that it is only under circumstances of cooperation that true specialization can flourish. Competition between groups, and cooperation between them as well, has an influence on the structure of groups which will be treated under *Evaluation as a process in ranking.*

RANKING

Rank as an element. In *The Human Group* Homans views rank and conformity as direct correlates: ". . . *the higher the rank of a person within a group, the more nearly his activities conform to the norms of the group."* [156] This position has been modified in *Social Behavior.* In that work conformity is seen as far too common a product to command a very high price: "If there are plenty of potential conformers, no actual conformer receives from the others a very high degree of approval—at least not on that account alone—though he is certainly not rejected." [157] The fact of differential rank and the reasons it takes the form it does is derived from "the stimuli proposition." *Status* becomes Homans' word for what is expressed in the present book as rank. "Social approval is an actual reward, but any activity (or sentiment) may be a stimulus as well as a reward, and we shall use *status* to refer to the stimuli a man presents to other men (and to himself). In other words, we shall use *status* to refer to what men perceive about one of their fellows." [158] Not only does status include *esteem* which is the expressed social approval a man receives from other members of his group, but "anything else about him, like the kind of clothes he wears or the kind of house he lives in, provided that these stimuli are recognized and discriminated by other men." [159] The stimuli must also be reducible to a rank order. Homans gives the name *status factors* to the many kinds of stimuli which *en toto* comprise an individual's rank or status: "by way of illustration let us say that among the status factors of two women are their pay, their seniority, the responsibility of their jobs, and the worry they incur in doing these jobs." [160] If *all* these items are ranked higher for one woman than for the other, both possess status congruence. To have all the status factors about an individual congruent may in itself be a reward just as to have some of the factors incongruent may be a cost to the incongruent individual. How much of a cost or how much of a reward incongruence and congruence may be is dependent, Homans suggests, upon the status factors which constitute the individual's rank.

If he [the Person who seeks help] is already established by his other
status factors as inferior to the other, his asking for help will cost him
little, for it is congruent with his inferiority in other respects. But if he
is already established as the other's equal, then his going to the other
for help will be incongruent with his equality and so cost him much.
He will be demeaning himself and putting his over-all status in jeopardy in the eyes of his fellows. We would therefore expect that men's
equals would ask them for help less often than their inferiors would.
By the same token, thrusting help upon a man who thinks he is your
peer is an act of hostility to him, and your generosity is apt to earn
you resentment and not gratitude.[161]

Thus far, only the status factors which make for congruence
or incongruence of an individual have been considered. Homans
touches upon the theme that groups, too, are congruent in different degrees. For group congruence to obtain for a task-oriented
group those who hold a subordinate position within the group
should work "for someone the characteristics of whose regular job
and social background are congruent, and superior to . . . [the
subordinate's] in other respects besides the superiority of . . . [the
job at hand within the group.]" [162] There ideally, however, should
not be so much difference between the statuses of the subordinate
and the superior that interaction is difficult.

Homans suggests that once differences in status have become
established among members, these very differences generate
further differences in their ranking.[163] A member of the upper
class, established in a position in which many are below him but
none above him, *can* gain by initiating innovative behavior. His
high rank will be augmented by a good guess about some new and
untried activity. He also stands to lose by a bad guess, but since
slavish conformity is not expected of him, the cost is not great
and he can well afford whatever cost accrues to him for his innovation. Members of the lower class, entrenched in a position
which receives few rewards in any case, have nothing much to
lose by deviant behavior, and they stand to gain whatever reward
the innovative behavior promises to bring them in accordance
with their personal sense of values. A member of the middle class,
however, "needs more to bring him up and less to bring him
down" [164] than does the member of the upper class. The possible
gains offered by nonconformity are usually more than offset by

the serious risk of loss. Conformity cannot hurt him and it may help him. Thus, quite apart from differential abilities—more or less energy, more or less intelligence, or other factors—high, middle or low class represents a vantage point from which behavior strategic to that position can be explained or predicted. If however, the rank order of individuals is not already fairly well established, the low status man who still has hopes of improving his status, will tend not toward nonconformity, but toward conformity or over conformity. The high status man in a fluid situation will similarly be willing to take fewer risks.

Evaluation as a process in ranking. As was shown above under the category *knowing*, Homans acknowledges that men perceive differences in the stimuli they encounter (such as the stimuli which have come to represent differential statuses) and they act in accordance with the principles embodied in Proposition 1. The status revealing stimuli carry the message "high rank" "low rank" "incongruent status" and so on, and he gives a great many examples of high and low status-stimuli.

There is one item which is a factor of status in which he is especially interested, and that is esteem. "We define *esteem* as follows: the greater the total reward in expressed social approval a man receives from other members of his group, the higher is the esteem in which they hold him." [165] The derivations concerning esteem are deduced from the "deprivation or value" proposition. "First, the higher a man's esteem, the more valuable the activities he gives to other members of his group. And second, the higher a man's esteem, the fewer are the members that are held in esteem equal to his; for so far as his esteem depends on his providing rare activities, the number of other members that offer such activities must be few." [166] Those individuals thus achieve high esteem who provide activities which are both *scarce:* "the number of members that demand it must be large in proportion to the number that can supply it," and *valued in themselves:* "for many members to find the same service valuable, many members must, for any number of possible reasons, share the same values." [167] The deprivation or value proposition and the success proposition are used as another derived proposition takes form: "The greater . . . the value of an activity to those receiving it, and the larger the number of members of a group who find it valuable to receive compared with the number who provide it—the more fully the activity possesses both these properties, the greater will be the social approval the man providing it is apt to get from every member he gives it to, and the larger the number of such members is apt to be." [168]

The applicability of these propositions does not necessarily extend to the more public positions in the society at large the status of which reflects position which may be historically entrenched and transmitted by inheritance, and thus bear little relation to scarcity and value of contributions. "In elementary social behavior [however] there is no unearned income, and it is this contrast that makes us so often dissatisfied with the status and wealth accorded to some public figures." [169]

The rare and valuable activity which wins for its emitter a relatively high esteem may be just one kind of activity; the individual may be quite ordinary in other activities which he emits. Despite this logical possibility, Homans reports that research findings [170] tend to show that an over-chosen (high ranking) individual tends to be considered valuable on all or nearly all measurements. He speculates that either the quality which was being ranked may have been a generalized ability rather than a special ability, or that the "halo-effect," the tendency to generalize to many aspects of behavior a judgment initially made in respect to only one aspect of behavior, may have been operative.[171] Or the results may have been connected with status congruence, or with a kindred concept, distributive justice, which has been mentioned above but which deserves additional attention as a factor in evaluation as related to rank.

It will be remembered that the condition of distributive justice prevails to the extent that a man's rewards, costs, and investments are proportional. The reward of high esteem requires then, that evaluative judgments be made on costs and investments before the proportional amount of esteem can be imputed to an individual. The story of how Cermak came to be "lunch boy" for a clique in an industrial plant is a study of distributive justice in respect to that reward which is rank. The task of being lunch boy was not a very valuable service consisting as it did of picking up food and drink from the plant restaurant for the other clique members. Before Cermak became a member of the clique another member had reluctantly done the job, but as soon as Cermak became solderman (a lower ranking position than that of wireman) for the wiremen and was accepted into their clique Cermak became "lunch boy."

Why was it appropriate that he should do so? He was a member of the "worse" clique; he was a solderman, and soldermen held the lowest job-status in the room; of the soldermen he was the least senior and the last to come into the group. Accordingly the group assigned him the least rewarding activity at its disposal: his menial job was in line with the other features of his status . . . it was hardly Cermak's fault in any immediate sense of the word that he was a solderman of low seniority, the last man to enter the group, and assigned to the selector wiremen. These were what we have called elsewhere his background characteristics determined by the events of his past history. But they had the same effect as if they had been his own fault. Inasmuch as the other members of the group had more pay, seniority, skill, etc. than he, they were "better" than he was, they held higher status in the larger society, and so they did not, but he did, deserve the menial job. No doubt when he should have served his time as lunch boy and acquired, again with time, higher pay, seniority, and skill, and when someone should have come into the room with less of these background characteristics than he, then he would be able to shove the lunch-boy job off on the newcomer.[172]

Allocation of status-roles as process. The lunch-boy story could as well illustrate the basis on which Cermak was assigned his status-role. The *job* had been evaluated by the wiremen, as had the man. In *The Human Group* Homans introduces a process (which like a number of other concepts he uses, stems from Pareto) he calls *circulation* and by it he means "The process by which able persons are brought to positions of responsibility in a society." [173] As society and systems become large and communications become poor, a split may grow up between leaders and the led, and the able men may not circulate to the most important posts of the larger units. In the small group the leader circulates to the position of authority. The reason for his doing so is attributed, in *The Human Group*, to the leader's close conformity with group norms; but in more recent writings a more important factor which explains the emergence of leadership is the rarity and value of his contributions, a subject which requires additional treatment under the subject of *Power as an element.*

CONTROLLING

Power as an element. Homans views power not as a basic element but as "subsidiary because it simply refers to the fact that a relatively few members can and do reward and punish others to a high degree." In *The Human Group* Homans' position was that the member conforming most closely to norms tends to have the highest rank and ". . . rank depends on . . . authority, and . . . authority on . . . rank." [174] With the altered position in respect to rank in *Social Behavior,* in which rarity and value of emitted behavior become the most important rank determinants, Homans' view of authority is accordingly modified. To understand Homans' use of authority it is necessary first to understand what he means by influence: "how one man . . . manages to change, or fails to change, the behavior of others." [175] A number of the substantiating studies cited by Homans suggest that influence was perceptible as individuals changed their activities at the suggestion of others from whom in return they received "liking." In short, activity was being exchanged for "liking." [176] Homans' explanation is derived from proposition 1, the "stimuli proposition": "the investigator's statement that a girl would find her fellow members congenial constituted a stimulus similar to those under which, in the past, a girl had found that compliance with a request was rewarded with social approval. She might expect that if she complied approval would be forthcoming, and so she was likely to comply." [177] The exchange is also consistent with the theory of distributive justice by which people who receive much should also give much. Unrewarded individuals in the same experimental situation, i.e. those who were led to believe that they would not get much liking, not only were not influenced to emit the suggested activity; in some cases they emitted the opposite kind of activity. "Revenge is a form of justice." [178] The would-be influencer as well as the individual who is being persuaded responded to the similarity of the stimuli situation: "The more closely the stimulus presented by the experimenter resembled stimuli of the past under which efforts to persuade another man had been rewarded with success, the more likely was the subject on the present occasion to emit efforts at persuasion." [179]

Whether or not a person yields to influence, however, depends not only upon the reward immediately forthcoming (which in the above cases was social approval) but also upon the cost exacted by the changed behavior. Homans posits three different kinds of reward for changing opinions or failing to do so: social approval, agreement for its own sake apart from any social approval it may yield, and personal integrity achieved by adherance to one's own convictions. The profit to the individual who changes his opinion can be measured only by deducting from his reward the cost of foregoing the possible rewards from alternative courses of action. Thus the reward of the individual who changes his opinion in return for social approval can be measured only by deducing what the exchange may have cost him in terms of personal integrity. The evidence suggests to Homans "that the less their profit, the more likely people are to change their behavior, and to change it so as to increase their profit." [180]

Deviants in a heterogeneous group tend to be more resistant to pressures than those in a homogeneous group, apparently because an individual with deviant opinions in a heterogeneous group is more apt to find a partner to share his opinions. "The heterogeneity of the members is one of the conditions in which any one member of a group is apt to find that others are alternative sources of reward." [181] In a homogeneous group, the deviate finds himself in "cognitive dissonance," a condition which it is valuable to escape from. Yielding to group influence in such a group reduces the painful "cognitive dissonance" as well as adding to the reward of social approval from group members. [182]

The uninfluenced individual who withstands group pressures and remains a deviant forgoes the rewards available to those who capitulate to group influence, but presumably collects the reward of personal integrity which to him is more valuable than the values forgone. As the nonconforming group member, he at first receives a disproportionately large share of the activities emitted by others —everyone tries to persuade him to change his mind. As he persists in his nonconforming behavior, the emitted activities toward him drop off; the group has given him up as unswervable. Thereafter he receives a disproportionately small share of the activities emitted by others; less social approval is given him and he may be the object of hostility. The quantity or "success" proposition combined with the "deprivation or value" proposition is seen to be operative. "The more valuable . . . to Person the activity (or sentiment) he gets or expects to get from Other, the more valuable to Other the activity (or sentiment) Person gives to him. And the more valuable to Person the activity he gets or expects to get from Other, the more often he emits activity that gets him, or he expects will get him, that reward. But as the expectation goes unrealized and his activity goes unrewarded by Other, Person emits the activity less and less often." [183]

The process of influence is omnipresent since men are always under influence, but it is particularly noticeable at the beginning of exchanges between individuals.[184] As each member in time settles down to the kind of behavior which is for him profitable and has given up those activities which under the circumstances are profit-less, the group is relatively stabilized and for a time is in a state of practical equilibrium,[185] a condition which will be examined more fully under the section *Social Change.*

The term authority for Homans is but an extension of the concept influence. In keeping with *elementary* social behavior Homans proposes to disregard the authority of office or status-role (which in PAS Model *is* authority) and concentrate upon that pattern of influence which emerges when one man often and regularly influences several other men at a time. Authority is defined in terms of influence: "the larger the number of other members a single member is regularly able to influence, the higher is his authority in the group." [186] Homans' interest in this pattern of influence which he calls authority is addressed to two questions: "How does a man earn authority? and, What effects does his authority have on the behavior of people he has authority over?" [187]

The answer to the first question goes back to esteem which individuals are given only as the activities they emit are considered by the other group members to be rare and valuable in themselves. As men acquire esteem they by the same token are acknowledged as able to give rewards—it is their rewarding behavior which wins for them the esteem in the first place. They may also withhold their rare and valuable services, and by so doing they punish. "A man's authority finally rests on his ability to reward and punish." [188]

Another part of the answer to the question "How does a man earn authority?" lies in the degree to which he has been influenced by the group, for it is only by being influenced by the group that patterned influence in the form of authority over the group can emerge.[189] In the first instance of exchange between Person and Other, for example, Other did concur with Person's request for help, that is, he was influenced by Person, before he rendered him aid. Some other individual, equally gifted, who may have denied help to Person (or had refused to be influenced by his request for aid) could not have become the authority figure precisely because he had not been influenced in the first place. This position is the same as is taken in *The Human Group* in which the authority figure is frequently seen as the leader whom the followers allow to occupy a controlling position to which the group itself in a sense has elevated him.

The leader's dependence upon the group over which he exerts his influence is pertinent to the second question: What effects does his authority have on the behavior of people he has authority over? Men obey orders only to the extent that they believe that obedience will be rewarding. A leader is therefore vulnerable each time he issues an order or suggestion; if obedience is not rewarding, the probabilities of future obedience are reduced and the likelihood of the leader's being deposed and replaced is greater. The reward that each group member gets from obedience comes not alone from the leader; it comes from other group members as well. The deviant who does not want to obey orders will be subjected to the pressures of influence from the group members as well as to the punishments at the disposal of the leader. The cohesive group, with its large number of members conforming to group norms, tends to respond positively to an order because "an order is very like a norm—a norm is only a standing order—and both name an activity that some members find valuable for themselves and others to emit." [190] The followers' relations with each other are therefore a determinant of obedience to authority just as the leader's relations with his followers are a determinant. The leader's chief instrument for fostering good feeling among the followers is the wielding of distributive justice. Situations correctly perceived by the leader and coordinated action directed by him lead to a string of successes for the leader which evoke future obedience which may be almost blind. His orders may come to be obeyed almost without regard for what the orders themselves may be.[191] As the leader provides the followers with the services they cannot so easily provide for themselves, he puts them in debt to him. A successful group effort gives the leader "liquid capital or call money" which he does in fact collect the next time he asks the followers to obey his orders. Unlike the "operators" who manipulate rewards in order to place others in their debt which is collectable at some future time, the leader wants fewer things of others than others want of him. "Accordingly a leader who values his position will not use the fact that he once did the follower a good turn as an argument for compliance with an order." [192]

As was seen above under *tension management,* leaders often do not enjoy a high degree of liking. Sentiments of followers toward leaders are at best ambivalent for a number of reasons: the followers must at times forgo other rewards in order to obey the leader; their rewards and punishments are in his hands. The best the leader can do is to try to maintain a surplus of positive sentiments over negative ones. Being on an equal footing with his followers in respect to social familiarity introduces an incongruent factor which places his own authority in jeopardy. "Since the success of the group in attaining its goals depends, among other things, on his authority, and since the maintenance of his authority depends in part on his aloofness, this aloofness, provided he can keep up his esteem at the same time, contributes to the effectiveness of his group." [193]

Decision making and its initiation into action as process. Homans' treatment of influence and authority emphasizes process. In fact, much of what appears above as power in its elemental form is, from Homans' point of view, process. It is, for example, the *process* of influence which is defined and explained. From the moment when Person has asked Other for help, Other consciously or unconsciously weighs the rewards and costs, gives help, and to that extent *decides.* For our immediate purposes discussion will be limited to those kinds of decisions which the group expects from their leader once he is in an undisputed position of authority, how those decisions are augmented, and how they are initiated into action. In *The Human Group* observations on the leader's behavior cover a wide range but a few are particularly pertinent to decision making and initiation into action. Among these are:

When a choice about the next move to make lies before a group, the members will expect the leader to consult them, but they certainly expect him to take action. . . . The leader, whatever his rank, with whom the decision rests must in fact decide.[194]

Whenever the leader originates interaction by giving an order, and he does not transmit that order to the lieutenant, he is, by that very fact, doing injury to the latter's rank. . . . If the leader will need in the future to transmit orders through the lieutenant, he has, by undermining the latter's authority, undermined his own. . . . The leader must not "jump the line." [195]

In *Social Behavior,* Homans frequently reiterates that the esteem basic to the leader's position comes to him because of his valued and rare services performed for the group. These may be many and varied but one such service, at least, is made very specific:

If, indeed, we agree that a man earns esteem and hence authority by providing services that others find both rare and valuable, the leader has provided the rarest and most valuable of all services: he has decided what the others are to do, and decided correctly, when the correct, that is, the rewarding, decision was not at all obvious. . . . [When faced with an ambiguous situation, the leader] will endanger his authority just as much by not deciding at all as he will be deciding incorrectly.[196]

The low ranking member of a group may have a good idea; but, if he suggests it, it is likely to be greeted with disdain and he will be regarded as being presumptuous to suggest from his lowly position what group action should be. In order to initiate it into action, "He had better take it to the established leader instead, and clear it with him. If the leader then takes up the suggestion and puts it out as coming from him, the others are apt to obey. Thus leaders get credit for more good ideas than their own abilities deserve." [197]

The kind of decisions a leader must make, the orientations to task completion which he must keep uppermost in mind, and the

resultant ambivalences toward him as a person, are of course as
varied as the situations in which groups find themselves. An example of one leader in the act of articulating his authority is given
by Homans as he reviews the Bales study [198] which identifies and
contrasts the instrumental or task leader with the popular leader.

First and always we must remember that the investigators gave each
group a definite task to accomplish: it was to reach by discussion some
solution to a set problem. The top initiator tended to be the leader of
the group in the sense that he was most occupied with directing it to
its goal and supplying it with ideas for a solution. . . . And as leader
he necessarily had to evaluate and criticize the contributions of others
and even, deliberately or in effect, to choke them off in the middle of
speeches that were not pertinent to a solution. In so doing he inevitably and to some extent punished the others, depriving them of
rewards in freedom and approval they might otherwise have enjoyed.[199]

Although the top initiator was generally conceded to be the
leader, a second study by Bales [200] sought to establish a relation
between interaction initiated and interaction received. The findings reveal that leaders who talk more than they were talked to
were disliked more than were those leaders who were talked to
more than they talked. "Now we may guess that a leader who
talked more than he was talked to was one who spent a particularly large part of his time bossing the group around, telling the
members how they ought to think and act, doing, that is, the sort
of thing most apt to be immediately punishing to the members,
however effective it might have been in accomplishing the group
task." [201] Such a leader could be expected to arouse more hostility
in his followers than the leader who was talked to much more
than he talked. The latter may be apt "to be more encouraging
to his followers' ideas, more willing to allow them free expression,
and so more rewarding to them." [202]

The exercising of authority which will incur for the followers
the highest costs is the authority exercised in coordinating the
groups' activities. Coordination, by its nature, prevents some people from doing what they want to do when they want to do it.[203]
The leader who leads, as in the case of many informal groups,
without having to make and carry out coordinative decisions,

without having to exercise authority over a full range of activities, generates much less hostility than the leader who must do these things. However, "Even though you coordinate the activities of others and so make them incur heavy costs, you may nevertheless recover the esteem you have put in jeopardy, provided that by exercise of your authority you can accomplish a result highly valuable to them . . . [For example] an officer who has brought his men successfully through a situation of great danger, and so has accomplished a result highly valuable to them, is apt to win something as close to adoration as we are likely to see this side of Paradise." [204]

As must by now be apparent, Homans' interest in power and in its articulating processes, decision making and initiation into action, is abundantly represented in his works, but always in terms of reward and punishment, of profit and cost. (Particularly is this true of that portion of his works presented in *Social Behavior*). Indeed, all of the above treated social components, organized around the PAS Model but representing Homans' interpretation, have been cast in the sanctioning terms of reward and punishment. The following section then, may at least summarize the special meanings Homans imputes to those terms and remind the reader of the main uses for which those terms have been employed.

SANCTIONING

Sanction as an element. The system of sanctions which is the core of *Social Behavior* has its genesis in *The Human Group* in which the genuineness of a norm is tested by the degree to which conformity is rewarded and nonconformity punished. "A norm in this sense is what some sociologists call a sanction pattern." [205] In that work Homans warns that whether sentiments are evoked by punishment or reward is difficult to distinguish; nearly all that is apparent is the continuance or discontinuance of the sanctioned behavior from which the observer can deduce that the behavior has changed in response to sanctions.[206] It is to this latter task of deducing, (or explaining) probable behavior as that behavior is a response to rewards and punishments that *Social Behavior* is addressed. Consequently, the theoretical framework upon which that work is based was summarized in the introduction of this chapter. There, the reader will recall, were the propositions from behavioral psychology upon which Homans based his work; there, too, the extrapolations from animal to human behavior from which his basic five propositions emerged. A review of these by the reader would better serve present purposes than would a recapitulation here of the same material. Homans' own summation of the material he draws from will suffice: ". . . the heart of the psychology used here is not a stimulus and a response but an operant and a reinforcer (an actitvity and a reward)." [207] His own pithy language can best establish his sequence from animal to human behavior.

[The psychologist] can only wait until the pigeon pecks the target spontaneously and then reinforce the peck. Not until then does the psychologist . . . begin to get some control over the pigeon's behavior. That the same is true of fresh humans, every mother knows. You can put the baby on the pot but you can't make him perform—at least not then and there. You can only wait until the blessed event occurs and then reward him—with coos of approval or, better still, by taking him off the pot. Although people are well aware of such dramatic cases, they find it hard to believe that all human behavior, no matter how subtle, is shaped by the differential reinforcement of quite simple actions produced the first time as if by chance.[208]

Keeping in mind that the term, reinforcers, is another name for rewards, the reader will recall that the forgoing parts of this chapter have referred to punishments as well as to rewards, to *aversive conditions* or negative reinforcers, as well as to positive reinforcers. These always receive less attention, however, than do the rewards. The reason for the secondary position of punishment is found in the observed behavior as elicited by both forms of sanctions.

The extinction of, the failure ever to reinforce, a particular activity leads to

. . . a permanent fall in the strength of the activity. Satiation leads to a temporary fall in strength until, for instance, the pigeon is hungry again. And the punishment of an activity once found reinforcing leads also to an ephemeral fall in its strength: after the punishment has been removed, the activity soon returns to its original probability of emission.[209]

Under these circumstances, the expectation that punishment will stop a particular kind of undesirable behavior will be fulfilled only if "we are in a position to punish the activity every time it appears." [210] More important as a reason for the secondary position of punishment as a sanction is its propensity to terminate interaction. While the exchange of rewards leads to continued interaction, "the exchange of punishments tends toward instability and the eventual failure of interaction in escape and avoidance: the pain experienced comes to outweigh the pleasure of revenge . . . the exchange of rewards takes a larger share in social behavior than the exchange of punishments, if only because the latter, when at all damaging, puts an end to social behavior." [211] The activity evoked by reward, furthermore, is fairly predictable: reinforcement of a specific activity brings forth more of that same activity. Not so with the activity evoked by punishment; "the threat of punishment renders more probable *any* behavior that avoids the punishment." [212]

Application of sanctions. In *The Human Group* Homans sees the very essence of a normative order inhering in a system of sanctions. Two examples taken from the field study of the Bank Wiring Observation Room are illustrative.

If a man did turn out more than was thought proper, or if he worked too fast, he was exposed to a merciless ridicule. He was called a "rate-buster" or a "speed king," but at the same time a man who turned out too little was a "chiseler." [213]

In a game called "binging"

. . . a man walked up to another man and hit him as hard as he could on the upper arm—"binged" him—, the other then had the right to retaliate with another such blow, the object being to see who could hit the harder. But binging was also used as a penalty. A man who was thought to be working either too fast or too slow might be binged.[214]

A number of the rules of behavior of the leader, which appear in *The Human Group*, deal with the application of sanctions. The leader is more concerned with creating the conditions under which the group disciplines itself than he is with inflicting punishment.[215] However, when the leader wishes to reward a follower, or when he finds it necessary to punish, he ideally avoids either blaming or praising in public. The leader's appraisal of the situation might not concur with the group's appraisal. Public praise or public blame embarrasses or humiliates the recipient and also places the leader's position in jeopardy, since the group rank-and-file might think that neither is deserved and so have a lowered regard for the leader.

In *Social Behavior* the very fact of interaction is by definition a sanctioning experience: ". . . when an activity (or sentiment) emitted by one man is rewarded (or punished) by an activity emited by another *man*, regardless of the kinds of activity each emits, we say that the two have *interacted*." [216] As was described above under *Power as an element*, particularly in that section dealing with influence, attempts to change behavior revolved around manipulations of reward and punishment. "The propositions that describe the final situation are the following. Person interacts more often with Other, the more valuable Other's actual activity (or sentiment) is to him, and the more often Other emits that activity. And since he may give sentiment in return for Other's activity, the higher is the degree of social approval he gives to Other." [217]

The giving or withholding of social approval is the most common application of sanction treated by Homans. As such it becomes a generalized medium of exchange. "[Just as] money is used to reinforce, to reward, a . . . [wide variety of activities and is thus spoken of] as a *generalized reinforcer*, [so too is social approval]: one can reinforce a wide variety of human activities by providing social approval and similar sentiments in return." [218] This idea of a medium of exchange by which interaction is facilitated introduces the propositions from elementary economics which, along with the propositions from behavioral psychology, form the basis for Homans' propositions concerning elementary social behavior. For present purposes those from elementary economics will be examined under the general category *facilitating*.

FACILITATING

Facility as an element. The economic background from which emerged proposition 5 was touched upon in the introduction to the present chapter. It is only as Homans sees human activities as goods entering into exchange that they deserve to be treated as facilities. In establishing the similarity between the principles of elementary economics and those of elementary social behavior Homans argues that they "Both deal with the exchange of rewarding goods." [219] He is well aware that the parallel is not a perfect one. The following dissimilarities are specified. Elementary economics generally deals with physical goods. In an economic exchange a number of objects—"several dozen apples, say for a dollar" [220]—can be exchanged at one time. Social exchange, in contrast because the goods are activities, can be exchanged only a unit at a time. Physical goods, like apples or a ton of steel, generally remains what it is unless effort is expended to change it into something else. Social goods, like the emission of approval, can shift much more easily. The money-price in economics also provides a measure of the goods' value that is independent of the value of other goods available for exchange, a condition not true of social exchanges. Economics also can cast its money-goods exchange in terms of a hypothetical perfect market in which any single buyer or seller has a negligible effect. "Our market, if we may call it that, is far from perfect: the behavior of each party has a marked effect on the rate of exchange of activities between them . . . and the economic market is 'impersonal' in a way ours can never be." [221] Despite these differences, the similarities are sufficient in Homans' opinion, to provide a basis for extrapolations from economic to social exchange. One marked similarity is in the laws of supply and demand:

"the higher the price of a commodity, the more of it a supplier will sell. This is equivalent to—we dare not say identical with—our proposition: the more valuable the reward gotten by an activity, the more often a man will emit it. For in the Law of Supply the price of the commodity is the reward obtained by selling it. In the same way the Law of Demand—the higher the price of a commodity, the less of it a consumer will buy—is equivalent to our proposition: the higher the cost incurred by an activity, the less often a man will emit it. For the Law of Demand the price of the commodity is the alternative reward a buyer forgoes when he spends his money on the commodity instead of spending it on something else or holding it for a fall in prices. [222]

Utilization of facilities as process. Each unit of activity emitted may be reduced to the by now familiar formula: Profit =

Value — Cost. However, the ultimate effects of the exchange between the interacting parties must include a consideration of the long run exchanges which in the case of Person and Other in the office, continue intermittently throughout the day and for many days to come. To take into account the degrees of satiation which come to an individual from an accummulation of rewards "we must consider not just his profit per unit-activity but his total profit over a period of time from the alternative activities open to him: the varying profit per unit times the number of units of each activity, which can if necessary be measured in time." [223]

As Person receives successive units of help from Other, he needs help less, and as Other receives successive units of social approval from Person the less rewarding they become. The cost to each increases too with each successively emitted unit of activity. Other finally gets to the point where doing his own work would be more rewarding than helping Person. Person finally gets to the point where further confessions of need for help are too punishing. For a time interaction ceases and "each distributes his time among alternative activities in such a way that he achieves a greater total profit than he would have achieved by some other distribution." [224] The problem of measuring this total profit is admittedly difficult. Homans suggests that as the men are faced with the necessity of distributing their facilities day after day, they may learn something about what kind of distribution brings them increased rewards; that each may achieve a greater total reward on later days than he did on earlier ones. Unlike the economist who posits conditions under which economic exchanges can maximize their utility, the sociologist does not have tools for measurement of social exchanges precise enough to discover whether a man maximizes his utility or reward. "Both would do so if each was ready to break off their exchange at just the same moment, but this is unlikely to happen often. The reward each gets is to some extent at the mercy of the behavior of the other, and Person may, for instance, want more help at a time when Other is beginning to find giving help distinctly burdensome. All we can usefully say is this: the two men will spend an amount of time together that gives each some reward but not necessarily the greatest conceivable reward." [225]

Both men also expect from the exchange that distributive justice will prevail—that is that there will be a fair distribution of rewards and costs. As men learn to utilize their facilities advantageously, they learn to achieve a tolerable level of distributive justice. "They learn to avoid activities that get them into unjust exchanges; they learn to emit activities that are rewarded by the attainment of justice, and by the same token to forgo these activities becomes a cost to them." [226] At the risk of a bit of repetition, attention is drawn to the excerpt quoted above which describes distributive justice. (*See citation 50 above*). A review of that concept will show that the expectations of cost and value of the emitted activity of both Person and Other are premised upon proportional costs and rewards, and upon proportional investments and profits.

Examples of investments cited by Homans are seniority, longevity of group membership, and skill, all of which describe conditions which change over a period of time, and others which do not: "to be a Negro or a woman, as compared with being white or a man, are investments that in some groups never change in value yet are always weighed in the scales of distributive justice." [227] Among the rewards which may accrue to investments are pay, autonomy, variety, and opportunity for social life. (And of course, what is a reward from the point of view of its recipient is a cost from the point of view of the other party to the interaction, in the cases cited, frequently to "management.") Among the costs are some of rewards' opposites—close supervision, monotony, and relative isolation. And profit, of course will represent the value minus cost equation. Distributive justice as a condition toward which individuals tend to strive as they utilize their facilities (or weigh their costs aganst rewards and investments against profits in a comparative manner) "is a curious mixture of equality within inequality." [228] The man who gets a $50 return from a $1000 investment is "equal" in one sense to the man who gets a $5 return from a $100 investment since both realize the same proportionality of income. At the same time they are unequal since their returns are certainly not the same.[229] An impressive number of research studies examined by Homans yield data which indicate that "men are alike in holding the notion of proportionality between investment and profit" [230] and that they will go to great efforts to establish a balance which they think of as just. The difficulty in establishing a condition which for every participant would represent for him a satisfactory utilization of his facilities is that men differ in their evaluation of different investments, rewards and costs. "Only perhaps for rather brief times and for rather small groups are men fully agreed not only on what the rule of distributive justice is but also on what particular investments, rewards, and costs should fairly be placed in the scales and at what weights." [231] Since there is no completely just society, "The open secret of human exchange is to give the other man behavior that is more valuable to him than it is costly to you and to get from him behavior that is more valuable to you than it is costly to him." [232] The definition of interaction as used in *Social Behavior* is so short that it can be repeated: "when an activity (or sentiment) emitted by one man is rewarded (or punished) by an activity emitted by another *man*, regardless of the kinds of activity each emits, we say that the two have interacted." [233] The emphases upon the word "man" is Homans' way of insuring that the reader will not confuse rewarded activities "like fishing" which are rewarded by the non-human environment with interaction. In *Social Behavior* Homans indicates that his use of the word "interaction" is roughly limited to occasions when nothing very specific about the emitted behavior is required; when he wishes to indicate "that the behavior, whatever it may be otherwise, is at least social." [234] The use of the term interaction in *Social Behavior* is essentially the same as its use in *The Human Group* where it was sometimes used as synonymous with communication.

COMPREHENSIVE OR MASTER PROCESSES

Communication. In *The Human Group* Homans considered using the term communication but rejected it because it generally conveys verbal behavior which is insufficient for his purposes. The word communication may connote the content of the message, or the process of transmission, or "the sheer fact, aside from content or process of transmission, that one person has communicated with another." [235] Only the last of the three meanings represents Homans' interest for which he chose the term interaction. "Our word for 'participating together' is *interaction*." [236]

In *The Human Group* the pattern of interaction is likened to a pyramid and again to a web. In the pyramid simile the leader is at the top, and all the channels flow to and from him, representing "scalar" interaction, or that which takes place between individuals of different rank. In the web simile, the leader is at the center, and all the radii from the center bisect a number of ever broadening concentric circles from the inner circle to the outer edge. The channels of communication thus represented can portray not only the "scalar" interaction between individuals of different rank represented by the radii channels, but also "lateral" interaction between persons of similar rank represented by each concentric circle.[237] The distance between the initiator and recipient affects the efficiency of the interaction; the greater the distance or "the longer the channel of communication" the less effective the interaction is likely to be, a factor which contributes to difficulties of communication in large organizations.[238]

The variability of interaction according to its value and its frequency was explored above under sentiment. A few of the elaborations which were not touched upon before are of immediate concern to the communication process. Members of a group who receive much interaction can be expected to give much interaction. Although the number of emissions is seldom exactly equal, nevertheless "most interactions between men take the form of talking. If I talk to you, you will find it hard not to talk back, and so the interactions each of us gives to the other will tend toward something like equality."[239] The origination of interaction tends to come from the man lower in esteem:

"after some break in their interaction, the man who is the more likely to emit the first activity in a new series is the one who finds the other's activity the more valuable. In the language of common sense, the man who needs the other's services the more is the man more likely to make the first move, and if necessary to go over to the other's place and ask him for his services, as Person asks Other for help.[240]

Homans reviews and summarizes *Social Behavior* by applying the various propositions developed in that work to "A Summary Group" which is one of the two described by Peter Blau in his book *The Dynamics of Bureaucracy*,[241] and which also provides the "Person-Other" distinction used throughout *Social Be-*

havior. Homans' own resumé as it appears in his final chapter sums up much of importance on the process of communication:

We have here further evidence of the complex interplay of two tendencies we have encountered again and again in this book: a tendency for a man to interact with his superiors in status, and a tendency for him to interact with his equals. A man establishes superior status by providing superior services for others. By the same token, accepting the superior services becomes a cost to a man, since he thereby recognizes his inferiority. Sooner or later he will turn to others who can provide him with services that no doubt reward him less but that also cost him less in inferiority. In the nature of the case, these others can only be his equals . . . A secondary development then builds on this primary one . . . By interacting with his fellows a man can then provide evidence for himself and for them that he is at least their equal. Still better, if he can get his superior to interact with him he may do something to raise his apparent status.[242]

Boundary maintenance. The imaginary line which Homans draws around the group under analysis and which identifies the group and separates it from all outside the line constitutes a boundary which, as Homans amply demonstrates, is maintained by the group. The high degree of conformity to norms exacted from the newcomer to the group, the retaliatory behavior exhibited to other groups as by work-terms in the Bank Wiring Observation Room and by the Norton's, the suspicious or unfriendly behavior of the Tikopia child to a non-community child are but a few of the many examples cited by Homans in *The Human Group* of preservation of group identity. "A group rent by backbiting factions will still join enthusiastically in presenting an unbroken front toward 'foreigners.' As in a healthy democracy, the conflicts may be loud but superficial, the unity silent but profound." [243] An idea suggested by Homans is that each subgroup may under certain circumstances maintain different boundaries, separate from one another but all confined within one common boundary. "An hypothesis worth considering is that, in these circumstances, *the activities of a subgroup may become increasingly differentiated from those of other subgroups up to some limit imposed by the controls of the larger group to which all the subgroups belong.*" [244] This theme is relatively unimportant in *Social Behavior,* as one would expect in a work in which everything external to the focal elementary social behavior is regarded as a given. Although the emphasis in that work is rarely if ever upon groups maintaining their boundaries, it occasionally crops up in an incidental way. Thus his examination of competition between groups, as explored above under sentiment, confirms that as hostility increases between the members of rival groups, previous intergroup friendships are likely to suffer and in-group choice is likely to increase in both the winning and the losing group.[245]

Concepts pertinent to boundary maintenance which were used occasionally in *The Human Group* but which since have been rejected because they are difficult to define operationally, are integration, disintegration and solidarity. Acceptable to Homans is the term *cohesiveness* which can be operationally defined in terms of intra-group rewards. The term is attributed to the Festinger Group whose research activities are frequently cited by Homans. Their definition of cohesiveness is as follows: " 'This property of groups, the attraction it has for its members, or the forces which are exerted on the members to stay in the group, has been called cohesiveness.' " [246] In Homans' own terms "cohesiveness refers to the *values* of the different kinds of rewards available to members of the group: the more valuable to a group's members are the activities (or sentiments) they receive from other members or from the environment, the more cohesive it is." [247]

Systemic linkage. The term systemic linkage, like the term boundary maintenance, is not used in either of Homans' major works. The idea for which it stands, however is used occasionally in *The Human Group* but only infrequently in *Social Behavior* the subject matter of which does not require the concept for the explanations attempted. The cases upon which *The Human Group* is based reveal several instances of systemic linkage which usually is accomplished through the activities of the group leaders. An industrial subgroup, for example, failed to get the kind of wire they needed through ordinary company channels, but succeeded through the efforts of Taylor, the group's informal leader, who "went out to the department and in a short time came back accompanied by the trucker, who had a whole truckload of wire." [248] Systemic linkage carried out by the group leader with groups external to his own is implied in the analysis of a street

corner gang as "[leaders] received more [money] precisely because they were leaders, because, for instance, they would deliver
the votes of the group in a political campaign." [249] Why the leaders were the instruments of systemic linkage is explained in *Social
Behavior*. There the aloof authority figure is pictured as escaping
from his own group occasionally so that he can relax and be at
ease in the company of his equals: "people who have nothing to
ask of him . . . and people whom he in turn has no leave to command." [250] Because his social equals are generally to be found
among leaders of other groups, the persons of high status in any
one group are regularly observed to have more "outside" contacts
than are people of low status.

The more highly specialized a group's activities, the more its
need for the products of other groups, and the more important
systemic linkage becomes. The ultimate of the kind of systemic
linkage occasioned by cooperative specialization is reached in
centralization, for which Homans sees no alternative.

Civilization means centralization. It means that men and women will
be related to one another in increasingly large organizations, and that
these organizations will be brought more and more under the influence
of the central directing body of the society, the government.[251]

Whether centralization is accomplished by relatively autonomous
controls, separate but linked, or by a unified control, the result is
the same. "The complexity of organization does not end with the
appearance of the hierarchy of leadership. In big concerns several different hierarchies arise and intersect one another. The
pyramid, from being two-dimensional, becomes three- and multi-
dimensional, with several different chains of interaction between
the followers and the upper leaders." [252] As centralization proceeds with its infinity of systemic linkages, society itself is "becoming a dust heap of individuals without links to one another." [253]
This appraisal from *The Human Group* is repeated in *Social Behavior* in the last chapter of which Homans allows himself the
license of departing from *elementary* social behavior. As a society
becomes increasingly differentiated "The length and roundabout-
ness of the chain of transactions mean that the innovations link a
larger number of people together than were linked hitherto. . .
But the innovations imply increased specialization, and as the

number of people tied together increases, the richness of any particular tie is apt to decrease." [254] *Social Behavior* is thus less pessimistic than *The Human Group* in not stating that individuals are without ties or links.

Social control. Social control is given explicit treatment by Homans in both of his major works. Since relatively fewer of the findings from *The Human Group* have been reported in this chapter, emphasis here will be made on social control as it is treated in that work, although a summary case will be given to recall Homans' attention to the subject in *Social Behavior*. The two treatments differ somewhat in language but very little in essential meaning. In *The Human Group* social control is defined as ". . . the process by which, if a man departs from his existing degree of obedience to a norm, his behavior is brought back toward that degree, or would be brought back if he did depart." [255]

A failure in social control based on the Hilltown case in *The Human Group* illustrates the conditions under which a breach of norms brought with it no punishment. Social interaction for the offender did not decrease, being already at a low point for all members; his loss of respect from neighbors did not occur, for they scarcely knew him; his social rank did not decline, for social ranking was not well established.[256] "The relationships between the elements of behavior were such as to lead, in time, toward the condition Durkheim called *anomie,* a lack of contact between the members of a group, and a loss of control by the group over individual behavior." [257] Whether the conditions in Hilltown would in time lead to *anomie* would largely be determined by whether the organizations which currently absorb the activities of Hilltowners, such as the big out-of-town industries at which many Hilltowners work, actually developed the characteristics conducive to social control which Hilltown once had. That an appreciable degree of social control is exercised in bureaucratic situations is suggested by the Blau study which constitutes Homans' summary chapter in *Social Behavior*.

For this particular group, the norms which represented high values numbered among them not completing more than eight investigative cases a month, and not reporting to their supervisors that firms which they investigated, had offered them bribes. The agents did their best to discourage offers of bribes from the business men whom they investigated, yet once the offer was made, the agent had a lever by which he might persuade the firm to comply with the law without resorting to legal action. Once a proffered bribe was officially reported, however, the agent lost his lever and made the company all the more likely to take the battle to court.[258] One member of the group flagrantly violated both the monthly caseload norm and the bribery report norm, and against him the group used a number of punishing sanctions. Since he continued in his nonconforming behavior, the group finally ostracized him.

Cutting off interaction with a member and thus depriving him of any social reward whatever is the most severe punishment a group can inflict on him; in fact he ceases to be a member. But once a man has stood that, he can, so to speak, stand anything; and the group has lost control of him, for it has left him with nothing more to lose. Certainly the department had pretty well lost control of this agent.[259]

Ultimately, a group exerts control by agreeing upon rewards which the members find valuable, and by withdrawing or threatening to withdraw these from any member whose behavior fails to reward the group. The low status member, who is not given much by way of reward in any event, has not much to lose by deviant behavior, for there is nothing left to withdraw from him. However, the high status member also, but for a different reason, is also not fully under the control of the group. He who has so much status that he can well afford to risk a little by a deviant stand is in his way exempt from group control. It is thus the conforming group of middle status which is most subject to the controls at the disposal of the group.[260]

Socialization. In Homans' *Social Behavior* he makes clear from the outset that he is not dealing with the process of socialization.

We say that the pigeon has learned to peck the target, but we need not dwell on the learning. Once the behavior has been learned a psychologist like Skinner is no longer interested in how it was learned, and "learning theory," as it is sometimes called, is a misleading name for his field of research. Instead he is interested in what variables thereafter determine changes in the rate of emission of operant behavior. The same thing will be true of us in this book: we shall be less interested in how men learn what they do than in what they do after they have learned it, and this is a big limitation on what we have to say.[261]

No such limitation was placed on Homans' analyses in *The Human Group*, and it is to that work that reference must be made to discover Homans' view on this subject. There he sees the adult individual displaying characteristics which result from the training and experiences of childhood. The training is carried on in groups of which the family is the most important. The modern urban family is at a disadvantage in this respect.

As the family disintegrates, and the transition from family to neighborhood group becomes more difficult, the personalities trained in these groups are apt to have an impaired capacity for maintaining a steady state under stress. . . . The feedback, which was once favorable, may become vicious.[262]

Homans' idea of favorable opportunity for socialization demands that society be organized in such a manner that the family has a fairly stable relationship to the neighborhood and community.

Homans' discussion of what he calls the social contract theory of Hobbes and the social mold theory of Durkheim deals in large measure with socialization. In a reconciliation of the two theories, the combination of inheritance and environment is emphasized.

The social contract theory, which holds that social behavior results from the characteristics of individuals, and the social mold theory, which holds that individual behavior results from the characteristics of society, are both correct, both incomplete, and complementary to one another.[263]

Homans treats the process as an aspect of his element sentiment, "Every group teaches its members to have sentiments it then proceeds to satisfy . . . The society breeds its own character-type, its basic personality." [264]

Institutionalization. Homans' view on institutionalization as expressed in *The Human Group* and in *Social Behavior* are similar, although his terminology in the two works is quite different. In *The Human Group*, he considers using the term "institution," but rejects it because of its ambiguity.

Is religion an institution, or is the church one? For us, who shy away from *institution* just because it is ambiguous, religion is a certain kind of activity, while the church is a specialized organization, a department, so to speak, of a society. Religious activities may be, but are not always, carried out by a specialized organization . . ." [265]

In that work the process of institutionalization is tacit and not directly dealt with.

Norms do not materialize out of nothing; they emerge from on going activities . . . Men bring their norms to a group; they work out new norms through their experience in the group; they take the old norms, confirmed or weakened, and the new ones, as developed, to the other groups they are members of. If the norms take hold there, a general tradition, the same in many groups, may grow up. [266]

What Homans calls *mode of standardization* comes closest in *The Human Group* to paralleling the concept of institutionalization. Stemming from the general hypothesis, "*The more frequently persons interact with one another, the more alike in some respects both their activities and their sentiments tend to become*," he observes that there will be a growing "awareness of the 'right' activities and sentiments . . . and [the] ability to imitate." [267] In *Social Behavior* Homans follows C. I. Barnard in using the term "authentication" to convey what seems to be the same meaning which is imputed to the term institutionalization by many sociologists, [268] and in much the same way in which Max Weber uses the term routinization. "Esteem plays in informal authority the part that official authentication of an officer's position plays in formal authority . . ." [269]

Homans' concern in *Social Behavior* does not lie to any large extent with the kind of social circumstances in which institutionalization is important; in fact, the *institutional* is precisely the kind of social behavior which is ruled out for the most part by his selection of *elementary* social behavior as subject matter, an area which he calls subinstitutional:

Since sociologists often call things like roles and their attendant sanctions *institutions*, and behavior so far as it conforms to roles *institutionalized* behavior, elementary social behavior might be called *subinstitutional*. But remember always that the institutional framework of elementary social behavior is never rigid, and that some elementary social behavior, pursued long enough by enough people, breaks through the existing institutions and replaces them. Probably there is no institution that was not in its germ elementary social behavior.[270]

At the subinstitutional or elementary level of behavior, some people will share ideas of what constitutes rewarding behavior—crying and weeping at the death of a loved one, for example. For these people, the crying and weeping constitute a *primary* reward; they do it because the behavior itself is rewarding to them. Others may not get any reward at all from crying and weeping, but they cry and weep nevertheless, in order not to seem heartless in the eyes of those for whom crying seems the "natural" way to behave. These people get only a *secondary* reward out of crying and weeping; they behave in this manner primarily because they have learned that this is the expected thing for them to do, and that if they did not, they would be punished by the withdrawal of social approval.

Once a number of people have cried a number of times at a number of deaths, they begin to make a norm of it—to say that it is the thing one does or ought to do—and the verbal statement of a rule is the first step in the making of an institution . . . And the first thing you know, the formal expression of grief at a bereavement has become an institution, taught to younger members of the society as part of their manners.[271]

A great number of institutions persist at any one time, many of them because they still represent the elementary social behavior which was their genesis, and because a considerable number of people receive primary rewards from their observation. If an institution exists, however, which no longer is yielding primary rewards, if the rules it embodies are observed merely for appearance, sooner or later it will vanish. Some institutions represent the adaptations which individuals have made as their activities have become specialized and they have thus increased their dependency on others' activities. For self-preservation "They must go by the rule, work by the book, which also means that institutional behavior tends to become impersonal." [272] If the personal and individual rewards are not sufficiently assured by the institutionalized rules and regulations, subinstitutional behavior will mount in pressure against the institutional constraints.

Informal activity directed toward improving institutional short-comings may itself become institutionalized. "Of course the new institution, once formed, may in time run into the same trouble with elementary social behavior as the old one did earlier." [273]

Social change. Social change is clearly effected as sub-institutional behavior modifies or replaces what previously has been institutionalized behavior. The conflict between the institutions and subinstitutions may upon occasion never be solved at all. The new forms of behavior which would resolve the conflict may not appear, either because they are not invented or because no one is willing to risk the social capital to experiment with them.

The result is a society of people to some extent apathetic, of institutions to some extent "frozen" in an unnatural equilibrium—unnatural in the sense that out of the elements lying around here and there something better might conceivably have been made.[274]

In contrast to this "unnatural equilibrium" is what Homans in *Social Behavior* designates as "practical equilibrium." When changes are regular and recurrent so that no new kind of change seems to occur,

the behavior of the group is in practical equilibrium in the sense that one day's work is much like another's. . . . Practical equilibrium, then, is not a state toward which all creation moves; it is rather a state that behavior, no doubt temporarily and precariously, sometimes achieves. It is not something we assume; it is something that within the limits of our methods we observe.[275]

These regular and recurring changes (the going out to lunch and coming back again, the finishing of one job and the starting of another, and so on), are of course accompanied by other changes "if only because the members of the group are growing older by the minute." Unless such changes are observable, however, by Homans' definition, the behavior of the group members is said to be in practical equilibrium.[276]

It is important to establish what Homans means by practical equilibrium because in his earlier work *The Human Group* he uses equilibrium more extensively and somewhat differently. Whether his later avoidance of a word he initially used is because of the arguments its interpretations have caused ("the almost mystical arguments that have encrusted the . . . word")[277] or because he has repudiated some of his formerly held views, a disservice would be performed by omitting from the present chapter what he had to say about equilibrium theory in *The Human Group*. In *The Human Group* Homans explores the idea that a social system is in equilibrium when a fairly stable relation is maintained between activities, interaction, sentiment and norms, the elements (as he saw them then) of social behavior. (The idea of *system*, incorporating dependencies and mutualities of systemic parts is a constant theme of *The Human Group*, but one to which little attention is paid in *Social Behavior*.) As small changes are introduced the equilibrium is maintained by compensations which take place among the mutually dependent elements. Sometimes the small changes come about through environmental conditions, sometimes they are induced as by the leader of a group which is striving to attain a group goal. Such a leader will not only redirect the group activities if these threaten to become non-goal directed; he also will manipulate the relationships so that the basic societal elements—activities, interaction, sentiments and norms will reinforce goal attainment and tend to minimize social changes not directly goal-centered. Such an equilibrium in which a degree of change is being sought by pursuit of a goal, and in which the amount of dislocation and inconvenience attending that pursuit is being minimized, is called by Homans a moving equilibrium.

Equilibrium thus becomes a "bridge to the study of social change." [278] It becomes Homans' purpose to explore how the equilibrium can be maintained so that social disintegration, a form of social change which occurred in Hilltown, and social conflict, a form of social change which occurred in The Electrical Equipment Company can be avoided. For in both of these instances the changes were accompanied by painful disequilibrium; as the value (in the mathematical sense) of any one of the elements was changed, equilibrating compensations in the dependent elements did not occur rapidly enough to keep the system in equilibrium. Homans poses the question: what conditions determine that such a change in elemental values will occur? One obvious answer is a change in the environment; improved transportation, wider markets, and the rise of industry, for example were environmental changes for Hilltown. An inevitable change in the internal system, residual as it is to the external, follows the environmental change.

Homans tentatively suggests in *The Human Group* that the rise of civilizations is marked by the surplus issuing from the external-internal systems and that their demise follows a shortage of the product. In the tradition of Toynbee, he traces this pattern throughout the rise and fall of Egypt and Mesopotamia, of classical India and China, and of Greco-Roman civilization. Supporting his argument by evidence from psychiatry he shows that a generation or two of individuals isolated by virtue of scant meaningful social contacts rear children who have a lowered social capacity.

The cycle is vicious; loss of group membership in one generation may make men less capable of group membership in the next. The civilization that, by its very process of growth, shatters small group life will leave men and women lonely and unhappy.[279]

Despite the signs of decay in Western civilization, there are a few healthy signs too. One such is that the paraphenalia of democratic governmental and legal institutions tend to maintain the values of the small group. For

at the level of the small group, society has always been able to cohere. We infer, therefore, that if civilization is to stand, it must maintain, in the relation between the groups that make up society and the central direction of society, some of the features of the small group itself.[280]

This last excerpt is almost echoed in *Social Behavior.*

In informal groups it is hard for government *not* to be carried on with the consent of the governed. Democracy aims at re-establishing this elementary value in a much more complicated institutional setting. It is an institution designed to make good the human deficiencies of other institutions.[281]

There is much in Homans' second major work, especially in his last chapter, to suggest that social change which he had expressed in terms of equilibrium in *The Human Group* can be expressed in terms of institutionalization and subinstitutionalization with less controversy, since the latter terms seem at the moment to be more acceptable and less inflammatory than the old term "equilibrium." This is not to say that equilibrium and institutionalization are equated in any sense, nor that institutionalized behavior and its constant pressures from subinstitutionalized behavior is the sole referent in *Social Behavior* by which social change is considered. He tells the critic who might object to the "horrid profit-seeking implications," [282] of the propositions in *Social Behavior*:

[to] ask himself . . . whether he and mankind have ever been able to advance any explanation why men change or fail to change their behavior other than that, in their circumstances, they would be better off doing something else, or that they are doing well enough already. On reflection he will find that neither he nor mankind has ever been able to offer another—the thing is a truism.[283]

And as has been hinted above, changes are induced under some circumstances much more rapidly than under others. Since competitors, out after the same reward, tend to engage in similar activities in order to get the reward, their activities tend toward similarity. Conditions conducive to cooperation, however, may contribute to the rise of differences, and hence, change.[284]

CONDITIONS OF SOCIAL ACTION

Time. Time as a condition of social action enters Homans' analyses in many ways. Thus the difference between distributive justice and status congruence is cast in temporal terms.

Distributive justice is a matter of the relation between what a man gets in the way of reward and what he incurs in the way of cost, *here and now;* status congruence is a matter of the impression he makes on, the stimuli he presents to, other men, which may affect their *future* behavior toward him and therefore the *future* reward he gets from them.[285]

Homans' focus in *Social Behavior* is on the relatively immediate rewards promised by a given activity, an emphasis which leads to the nonconsideration of the rational with its implied "calculation for the long run." [286] Again, time is a measuring rod of activity. The pigeon's emitted activity can be counted by the number of his pecks; man's emitted activity can better be quantified by the amount of time any one unit of activity consumes. Less easily conveyed are those considerations of time which condition social change, institutionalization, and equilibrium, but to think of any one of those processes—or to think of process itself, is to recognize time as a condition. The numerous allusions above to the temporal element, and many left unmentioned, clearly establish Homans' sensitivity to this condition of social behavior.

Territoriality. In *The Human Group* among the men of the Bank Wiring Observation room, "sheer geographical position . . . had something to do with the organization of work and even with the appearance of cliques." [287] Proximity conditioned the interaction of the Norton Street Gang too. Members of the gang came from families who had lived for a long time in the Norton Street neighborhood and all but two of the gang's members still lived in Cornerville. "To this extent, the environment had thrown them together until their interaction had become habitual." [288] The Tikopia followed a pattern of interaction within their households which was severely restricted by territorial considerations.

In *Social Behavior* Homans lists among the conditions he designates as "givens," those "features of the physical or functional proximity of men to one another that makes them likely to enter into exchange." [289] Thus he cites a housing study in which the geographic location affects the quantity of activity given by one person to another. Nearness need not be confined to sheer physical proximity. The people whose apartments were at the bottom of stairs, for example, made more social exchanges by virtue of their physical position than others, for someone coming down the stairs would have ample opportunity to meet the people living at the foot. People living in the center of a floor were also exposed to more social exchanges than people living at either end. He points out that "Functional proximity between two persons is naturally not limited to staircases. People who work on the same piece of equipment or on different stages of the same job, so that one passes work on to the other, are particularly likely to interact and hence, other things equal, to become friends." [290]

Not only is the frequency of social exchange between individuals affected by their proximity to each other but conformity and nonconformity tends to vary as proximity varies. The housing study cited by Homans demonstrates that deviates (in respect to opinions on matters of common concern to the group) were especially likely to come from those few corner buildings which, unlike all the others which faced each other around courts, faced away from the courts and opened out to the street. The findings in the two works are very similar in respect to territoriality, and this is not surprising, since what was the given of physical proximity in the latter work was part of the environmental given in the earlier work.[291]

Size. In *The Human Group* size is another of the "given" factors along with age, sex and time.[292] Relative size is basic to such propositions as *"An increase in the size of a group and in the specialization of activity will tend to increase the number of positions in the chain of interaction between the top leader and the ordinary member."* [293] It was increase in the size of the operation which led to maladjustments in the Electrical Equipment Company, one of the five case studies basic to *The Human Group.* In *Social Behavior* size of group is definitionally indicated in the book's subject matter: "Here the social behavior is elementary in the sense that the two men are in face-to-face contact, and each is rewarding the other directly and immediately: each is enabled to do his work better here and now." [294] He plots the differences in interaction patterns when absolute size is changed by the smallest possible amount: the advent of Third Man to the previously paired Person and Other. At the other extreme, especially in *The Human Group,* it is the size of inevitable centralization which Homans views as dangerous for civilization's survival. Only if the *small* group can be preserved within the Gargantuan structures can the internal system (or elementary social behavior in the terms of *Social Behavior*) be preserved.

Bibliographical Key [*]

CSS—George C. Homans, "A Conceptual Scheme for the Study of Social Organization," *American Sociological Review,* Vol. 12, No. 1, February, 1947, pp. 13-26.

EV—George C. Homans, *English Villagers of the 13th Century,* (Cambridge: Harvard University Press, 1941).

HG—George C. Homans, *The Human Group* (New York: Harcourt, Brace and Co., 1950).

MPSW—A. Zaleznik, C. R. Christensen and F. J. Roethlisberger, *The Motivation, Productivity, and Satisfaction of Workers: A Prediction Study* (Boston: Harvard University, Division of Research, Graduate School of Busi-

[*] For a more complete bibliography see the notes which follow and the bibliographical appendix at the end of the volume.

ness Administration, 1958). From this publication a "section [which] has been written in large part from notes prepared by George C. Homans for one of the prediction meetings (January 25, 1955)" is cited.

PASS—Henry W. Riecken and George C. Homans, "Psychological Aspects of Social Structure," in Gardner Lindzey (ed.), *Handbook of Social Psychology* (Cambridge: Addison-Wesley, 1954), pp. 786-832.

SACW—George C. Homans, "Status Among Clerical Workers," *Human Organization*, Vol. 12, No. 1, Spring, 1953, pp. 5-10.

SB—George C. Homans, *Social Behavior: Its Elementary Forms* (New York: Harcourt, Brace and World, Inc., 1961).

SBAE—George C. Homans, "Social Behavior as Exchange," *The American Journal of Sociology*, Vol. LXIII, No. 6, May, 1958, pp. 597-606.

SW—George C. Homans, "'The Small Warship," *American Sociological Review*, Vol. 11, No. 3, June, 1946, pp. 294-300.

NOTES

1. George Caspar Homans, *Social Behavior: Its Elementary Forms* (New York: Harcourt, Brace and World, Inc., 1961), p. 1. Hereafter cited as SB.
2. *Ibid.*, p. 11.   3. *Ibid.*, p. 10.
4. SB, *op. cit.*   5. *Ibid.*, p. 11.
6. George C. Homans, *The Human Group* (Harcourt, Brace and Co., 1950). Hereafter cited as HG.
7. *Ibid.*, p. 6.   8. SB, p. 8.
9. *Ibid.*, pp. 2-3.
10. The concepts appearing in *The Human Group* are usually called elements in that work (Chapter 2); referring back to them in *Social Behavior* they are designated as classes (p. 8), variables (p. 9), and descriptive terms (p. 35).
11. SB, pp. 8-9.   12. *Ibid.*, p. 12.
13. *Ibid.*   14. *Ibid.*, p. 15.
15. *Ibid.*, p. 9.
16. *Ibid.*, p. 10. Homans acknowledges particular reliance for his interpretation of philosophical explanation upon R. B. Braithwaite, *Scientific Explanation* (Cambridge, England, 1953).
17. *Ibid.*, pp. 9-10. Such deductions predict as well as explain; for a discussion of this and related topics see R. B. Braithwaite, *op. cit.* Homans himself notes that "it should be clear that the process of prediction runs parallel to the process of explanation." SB, p. 222.
18. An earlier version of this present chapter referred to the "subordination" of the external-internal theme in *Social Behavior*, to which Homans objected: "I don't think it's subordinated; it's less pretentious than it used to be, but it's still in there." From recorded interview, April, 1960.
19. HG, p. 90.   20. *Ibid.*, p. 88.
21. *Ibid.*, p. 133.   22. *Ibid.*, p. 90.
23. Integration is a term Homans no longer uses because "It seems to me that it's a variable that's very hard to define operationally." From recorded interview, April, 1960.
24. HG, pp. 275-6.   25. *Ibid.*, pp. 359-60.
26. *Ibid.*, p. 231.   27. *Ibid.*, p. 231.

28. *Ibid.*, p. 208.

29. HG, p. 86, SB, p. 231, recorded interview, April, 1960.

30. SB, p. 18.   31. *Ibid.*, pp. 21-2.

32. *Ibid.*, p. 25.   33. *Ibid.*, p. 28.

34. Peter Blau, *The Dynamics of Bureaucracy* (Chicago: University of Chicago Press, 1955).

35. SB, p. 35.   36. *Ibid.*, p. 38.

37. *Ibid.*, p. 40.   38. *Ibid.*, p. 42.

39. *Ibid.*, p. 44.   40. *Ibid.*, p. 49.

41. *Ibid.*, p. 53.   42. *Ibid.*, p. 54.

43. *Ibid.*, p. 55.   44. *Ibid.*

45. *Ibid.*, p. 75.   46. *Ibid.*, pp. 58-9

47. *Ibid.*, pp. 61, 63.   48. *Ibid.*, p. 69.

49. Homans attributes the notion of distributive justice to Aristotle (SB, p. 245); he emphasizes that he is not its originator any more than he is of the first four propositions taken from behavioral psychology: "All I have done is to apply them to a situation where the thing that is doing the rewarding is another person." Recorded interview, April, 1960.

50. SB, p. 75.   51. *Ibid.*, pp. 52-3.

52. *Ibid.*, p. 53.   53. *Ibid.*, p. 81.

54. *Ibid.*   55. *Ibid.*, p. 82.

56. *Ibid.*, p. 89.   57. *Ibid.*, pp. 85-90.

58. *Ibid.*, pp. 115-6.

59. Robert K. Merton, "Introduction," to HG, p. xix.

60. HG, p. 2.   61. SB, p. 16.

62. HG, p. 13.   63. *Ibid.*, p. 38.

64. *Ibid.*, p. 39.   65. *Ibid.*, p. 40.

66. *Ibid.*, p. 42.   67. SB, p. 34.

68. *Ibid.*, p. 32.   69. *Ibid.*, p. 55.

70. HG, p. 112.   71. *Ibid.*, p. 116.

72. *Ibid.*   73. SB, p. 186.

74. *Ibid.*, p. 187.   75. *Ibid.*, p. 181.

76. *Ibid.*, p. 182.   77. *Ibid.*

78. *Ibid.*, p. 186.   79. *Ibid.*

80. *Ibid.*, p. 187.   81. *Ibid.*, p. 187.

82. HG, p. 113.   83. SB, p. 144.

84. *Ibid.*   85. *Ibid.*

86. *Ibid.*   87. *Ibid.*

88. HG, p. 117.   89. *Ibid.*, p. 268.

90. *Ibid.*, pp. 271-272.   91. *Ibid.*, pp. 322-3.

92. SB, p. 300.   93. *Ibid.*, p. 311.

94. *Ibid.*   95. *Ibid.*, p. 313.

96. *Ibid.*, p. 248.   97. *Ibid.*, p. 254.

98. *Ibid.*, p. 253.   99. *Ibid.*, p. 253.

100. HG, p. 262.   101. *Ibid.*, p. 218.

102. *Ibid.*, p. 74-5   103. SB, p. 193.

104. *Ibid.*, p. 314.

105. E. Mayo, *The Political Problems of Industrial Civilization*, p. 21 as quoted in HG, p. 96.

106. From notes made by Homans on an earlier version of the present manuscript. For a more general and favorable evaluation of the work of his

friend and former teacher see George C. Homans, "Some Corrections to 'The Perspectives of Elton Mayo' by Reinhard Bendix and Lloyd H. Fisher" in Amitai Etzioni, ed. *Complex Organizations,* (New York: Holt, Rinehart and Winston, 1961).

107. George C. Homans, "A Conceptual Scheme for the Study of Social Organization," *American Sociological Review,* Vol. 12, No. 1 (February, 1947), pp. 13-26 and George C. Homans, "Social Behavior as Exchange," *The American Journal of Sociology,* Vol. LXIII, No. 6 (May, 1958), pp. 597-606.

108. SB, pp. 79-80.   109. *Ibid.,* p. 81.

110. *Ibid.,* p. 82.   111. *Ibid.,* p. 271.

112. *Ibid.,* p. 275.   113. *Ibid.*

114. From notes made by Homans on an earlier version of the present manuscript.

115. SB, p. 267.   116. *Ibid.,* p. 264.

117. N. Morse, *Satisfactions in The White-Collar Job* (Ann Arbor, Michigan, 1953) p. 28 as quoted in *Ibid.,* p. 267.

118. SB, p. 275.   119. *Ibid.,* pp. 274-5.

120. *Ibid.,* p. 281.   121. *Ibid.,* p. 378.

122. HG, pp. 271-2.

123. *Ibid.,* p. 272. As a *goal* of highest priority for society at large Homans specifies the attainment of industrial harmony in which Management and Labor "work together actively . . . to increase the human development and satisfactions of persons in the plant. [He argues that] increases in real wages, . . . leveling of material rewards . . . decrease in pressure for production, or . . . the elimination of hierarchical authority [what he calls] the external determinants of workers' behavior [are] . . . ones that, in the long run, under capitalism, socialism, or totalitarianism, we shall be least able to change. . . . You will have to convince [the worker] . . . to cooperate . . . that the system he lives under is a just system . . . [You must work] on the internal environment of the plant. . . ." In this article in this sense he uses the concept goal frequently. George C. Homans, "Industrial Harmony as a Goal," in. Arthur Kornhauser, Robert Dubin and Arthur M. Ross eds. *Industrial Conflict,* (New York: McGraw-Hill, 1954) Ch. 4.

124. William Foote Whyte, *Leadership and Group Participation* (Ithaca, N. Y.: New York State School of Industrial and Labor Relations, Cornell University Bulletin No. 24, May, 1953). For a more detailed account of one of the discussion groups included in the Whyte study see Charles P. Loomis and Zona Kemp Loomis, "Sociometry in Community Organization: A Case of Failure in the Achievement of Goal," *Sociometry and the Science of Man,* Vol. XVIII, No. 4, (December, 1955), pp. 302-326.

125. William Foote Whyte, *op. cit.,* p. 28.

126. *Ibid.,* p. 29.   127. HG, p. 123.

128. SB, p. 116.

129. In addition to *The Human Group,* pp. 127-8, see also A. Zaleznik, C. R. Christensen and F. J. Roethlisberger, *The Motivation, Productivity, and Satisfaction of Workers: A Prediction Study;* with the assistance and collaboration of George C. Homans (Boston: Harvard University, Division of Research, Graduate School of Business Administration, 1958), pp. 43-4. This last citation refers to a "section [which] has been written in large part

from notes prepared by George C. Homans for one of the prediction meetings (January 25, 1955)." *Ibid.*, fn., p. 43. Hereafter cited as MPSW.

130. MPSW, p. 44.
131. *Ibid.*
132. SB, p. 46.
133. Recorded interview, April, 1960.
134. SB, pp. 39-40.
135. *Ibid.*, p. 40.
136. *Ibid.*, p. 42.
137. *Ibid.*, p. 45.
138. *Ibid.*, pp. 42-9.
139. *Ibid.*, p. 214.
140. *Ibid.*, p. 215.
141. *Ibid.*, p. 112.
142. *Ibid.*
143. *Ibid.*, p. 129.
144. *Ibid.*, p. 118.

145. *Ibid.*, p. 129. For a convergence with Becker concerning "companions in misery" see fn. 244, Ch. 2.

146. *Ibid.*, pp. 110-11
147. *Ibid.*, p. 351.
148. *Ibid.*, p. 5.
149. *Ibid.*, p. 351.
150. SB, p. 135.

151. Only in the last chapter in which he considers that his case is established and that he no longer must write with the constraints observed in the major part of the work, does Homans consider aspects of social behavior not purely "elementary."

152. SB, pp. 136-7.
153. *Ibid.*, pp. 137-8.
154. *Ibid.*, p. 131.
155. *Ibid.*, p. 132.
156. HG, p. 141.
157. SB, p. 147.
158. *Ibid.*, p. 149.
159. *Ibid.*
160. *Ibid.*, p. 248.
161. *Ibid.*, pp. 251-252.
162. *Ibid.*, p. 258.
163. *Ibid.*, See Chapter Sixteen.
164. *Ibid.*, p. 353.
165. *Ibid.*, p. 149.
166. *Ibid.*, p. 53.
167. *Ibid.*, p. 147.
168. *Ibid.*, p. 149.
169. *Ibid.*, p. 152.
170. *Ibid.*, pp. 153-160.
171. *Ibid.*, p. 160.
172. HG, p. 236.

173. From notes made by Homans on an earlier version of present chapter; also, HG, p. 460.

174. HG, p. 267.
175. SB, p. 83.
176. *Ibid.*, p. 89.
177. *Ibid.*, p. 90.
178. *Ibid.*
179. *Ibid.*, p. 93.
180. *Ibid.*, p. 99.
181. *Ibid.*, p. 102.
182. *Ibid.*, p. 104.
183. *Ibid.*, p. 110.
184. *Ibid.*, p. 84.
185. *Ibid.*, p. 99.
186. *Ibid.*, p. 286.
187. *Ibid.*, p. 283.
188. *Ibid.*, p. 292.
189. *Ibid.*, p. 286.
190. *Ibid*, p. 295.
191. *Ibid.*, p. 296.
192. *Ibid.*, p. 299.
193. *Ibid.*, p. 315.
194. HG, pp. 428-429.
195. *Ibid.*, p. 430.
196. SB, pp. 296-297.
197. *Ibid.*, p. 297.

198. R. F. Bales, "The Equilibrium Problem in Small Groups," in Talcott Parsons, R. F. Bales, and E. A. Shils, *Working Papers in the Theory of Action* (Glencoe, Illinois: 1953), pp. 111-61; as cited in SB, p. 302.

199. SB, p. 305.

200. R. F. Bales, "Task Status and Likeability as a Function of Talking and Listening in Decision-Making Groups," in L. D. White, ed., *The State of the Social Sciences* (Chicago, 1956), pp. 148-61; as cited in SB, p. 306.

201. SB, p. 306.   202. *Ibid.*
203. *Ibid.*, p. 308.   204. *Ibid.*, p. 310.
205. HG, p. 123.   206. *Ibid.*, pp. 285-286.
207. SB, p. 22.
208. *Ibid.*, pp. 18-19. "Every small action of a man is sanctioned. It is one of the fundamentals of all human behavior." From Homans' notes on previous version of present manuscript.
209. *Ibid.*, p. 26.   210. *Ibid.*
211. *Ibid.*, p. 57.   212. *Ibid.*, p. 58.
213. HG, p. 60.   214. *Ibid.*, pp. 60-61.
215. *Ibid.*, p. 235.   216. SB, p. 35.
217. *Ibid.*, p. 111.   218. *Ibid.*, pp. 34-35.
219. *Ibid.*, p. 68.   220. *Ibid.*
221. *Ibid.*, p. 69.   222. *Ibid.*
223. *Ibid.*, p. 70.   224. *Ibid.*, p. 71.
225. *Ibid.*, p. 72.   226. *Ibid.*, pp. 232-233.
227. *Ibid.*, p. 236.   228. *Ibid.*, p. 244.
229. *Ibid.*   230. *Ibid.*, p. 246.
231. *Ibid.*, p. 247.   232. *Ibid.*, p. 62.
233. *Ibid.*, p. 35.   234. *Ibid.*
235. HG, p. 37.   236. *Ibid.*, p. 84.
237. *Ibid.*, p. 105.   238. *Ibid.*, p. 461.
239. SB, p. 192.   240. *Ibid.*, p. 201.
241. Peter Blau, *op. cit.*, pp. 99-248, as cited in SB, p. 359.
242. SB, p. 370.   243. HG, p. 134.
244. *Ibid.*, p. 136.   245. SB, p. 144.
246. K. W. Back, "The Exertion of Influence Through Social Communication," in L. Festinger, K. W. Back. S. Schachter, H. H. Kelley, and J. Thibaut, *Theory and Experiment in Social Communication,* (Ann Arbor; 1950), pp. 21-36 as cited in SB, p. 88.
247. SB, p. 88-89.
248. Fritz Jules Roethlisberger and William John Dickson, *Management and the Worker,* (Cambridge, Mass.: Harvard University Press, 1939), pp. 464-465, as cited in HG, p. 78.
249. HG, p. 294.   250. SB, p. 311.
251. HG, p. 466.   252. *Ibid.*, p. 106.
253. *Ibid.*, p. 457.   254. SB, p. 388.
255. HG, p. 301.
256. *Ibid.*, p. 366. In the realm of industrial relations Homans makes the following judgment: "I have come to the conclusion that no single non-material factor is more responsible for employee dissatisfaction within a factory than sheer confusion and disorganization." "Industrial Harmony as a Goal," *op. cit.*, p. 49.
257. *Ibid.*, p. 367.   258. SB, pp. 374-375.
259. *Ibid.*, p. 375.   260. *Ibid.*, p. 376.
261. *Ibid.*, p. 19.   262. HG, p. 280.
263. *Ibid.*, p. 330.   264. *Ibid.*, pp. 331 and 332.
265. *Ibid.*, p. 269.   266. *Ibid.*, p. 127.
267. *Ibid.*, p. 120.
268. See, for example, the sections on institutionalization in the chapters

of the present volume which analyze the works of Davis, Merton, Parsons and Williams.

269. SB, p. 293.

270. *Ibid.*, pp. 5-6.

271. *Ibid.*, p. 381.

272. *Ibid.*, p. 388.

273. *Ibid.*, p. 395.

274. *Ibid.*, p. 396.

275. *Ibid.*, pp. 113-114.

276. *Ibid.*, p. 113.

277. *Ibid.*

278. HG, p. 449.

279. *Ibid.*, p. 457.

280. *Ibid.*, p. 468.

281. SB, p. 395.

282. *Ibid.*, p. 79.

283. *Ibid.*

284. *Ibid.*, p. 135; the reader may find these observations related in an interesting way to what Talcott Parsons calls segmentation and differentiation. See in addition SB, pp. 385-389.

285. *Ibid.*, p. 250, italics added.

286. *Ibid.*, p. 181.

287. HG, pp. 88-89.

288. *Ibid.*, p. 173.

289. SB, p. 208.

290. *Ibid.*, p. 213.

291. HG, p. 231.

292. *Ibid.*, p. 231.

293. *Ibid.*, p. 406.

294. SB, p. 4.

CHAPTER 5

ROBERT K. MERTON AS A STRUCTURAL ANALYST*

Merton's major work, *Social Theory and Social Structure*,[1] is made up of papers which were not originally intended as consecutive chapters. The unity they achieve despite their consequent lack of "natural progression" attests to the consistency of viewpoint which marks not only this major work but the many miscellaneous works which have come from this seminal scholar. Merton identifies as the unifying principle in this volume his perspective relative to two sociological concerns: the first, "the concern with the interplay of social theory and social research," the second, "the concern with progressively codifying both substantive theory and the procedures of sociological analysis, most particularly of qualitative analysis."[2] The "central orientation" of Merton's writing is functional analysis which guides inquiry and analysis of data by setting forth explicitly the consequences of these data for the larger structures of theory to which they are related.[3]

These "larger structures of theory" culminate the practicing of strict scientific method which Merton describes and analyzes. The scientist hypothesizes that relations exist between selected phenomena in the empirical world; he delineates his field of observation in conceptual terms. He prescribes what phenomena are going to be observed by his selection of concepts which thereupon represent variables he suspects bear relations to each other.

* This chapter was prepared with the assistance of Robert G. Holloway as junior author.

The logically interrelated concepts combined into propositions suggested by his observations constitute a theory.[4] It therefore behooves him to observe three tasks of conceptual analysis: "to make explicit the character of data subsumed under his concept, to maximize the likelihood of the comparability, in significant respects, of data which are to be included in a research, and to institute observable indices of the social data with which empirical research is concerned."[5] The initial guideline of investigation is but a beginning to a well-developed and tenable theory. Merton sees increasingly refined theory developing through "successive approximations" by which the initial conceptualizations are re-cast, reconceptualized and respecified:

A set of ideas serves, for a time, as a more or less useful guide for the investigation of an array of problems. As inquiry proceeds along these lines, it uncovers a gap in the theory: the set of ideas is found to be not discriminating enough to deal with aspects of phenomena to which it should in principle apply. In some cases, it is proposed to fill the gap by further differentiation of concepts and propositions that are consistent with the earlier theory, which is regarded as demonstrably incomplete rather than fundamentally mistaken. In other cases, the new conceptions put in question some of the assumptions underlying the earlier theory which is then replaced rather than revised.[6]

More than many other theorists, Merton emphasizes that a mature science requires continuity and cumulation of inquiry. To that end he recommends "formal methodological re-analysis" of previous investigations, a task to which he upon occasion addresses himself in an attempt to uncover implications not fully developed or sometimes not even suspected in the original analysis.[7] The "serendipity component of research" is linked to theory development through "the fairly common experience of observing an *unanticipated, anomolous, and strategic* datum which becomes the occasion for developing a new theory or for extending an existing theory."[8]

Broad global concepts such as social system, social institution, social milieux, and values are seldom the center of the analyses to which he directs his attention; they are generally accorded less specificity than are those concepts which occupy the center of a given analysis. In his view, the precise definition of concept and

strict adherence to it are outweighed in importance by careful
attention to conceptual parsimony (as in the development of the
paradigm) which employs "the minimum set of concepts with
which the sociologist must operate in order to carry through an
adequate functional analysis. . . ." [9]

Throughout his works Merton seeks to formulate theoretically
significant, yet empirically testable hypotheses of sociological importance. Problem finding must occur, generally, before scientific
solutions may be examined.[10] Thus, certain strategic phenomena
and construction of theory to explain them are high in "problem
density"—reference groups perhaps serve as one excellent example of such endeavour at the "middle range" of theory. Although
acknowledging that there is no substitute for "comprehensive
schematic analyses" whether these be from general theory or
other frames of reference,[11] he believes that a more efficient allocation of sociological resources is represented by attention to
"*theories of the middle range:* theories intermediate to the minor
working hypotheses evolved in abundance during the day-by-day
routines of research, and the all-inclusive speculations comprising
a master conceptual scheme from which it is hoped to derive a
very large number of empirically observed uniformities of social
behavior." [12] Such theories might for example, emerge from hypotheses about class dynamics, the pressures arising from conflicting group interests, the workings of power and influence in
communities, and so on.[13] Here lies the greatest promise in Merton's view, "*provided that,* underlying this modest search for social uniformities, there is an enduring and pervasive concern with
consolidating the special theories into a more general set of concepts and mutually consistent propositions." [14]

His own "enduring and pervasive concern" for such consolidation is reflected in the attention he devotes to higher level generalizations such as "social structures" and "cultural structures,"
each developed from more modest inquiry for social uniformities.
Merton views the *social structure* as being comprised of "the patterned arrangements of role-sets, status-sets, and status-sequences," all of which represent less general concepts growing
out of his own "middle-range" investigations. Analytically distinct from the social structure is the *cultural structure* comprised
of *goals* which provide the "aspirational frame of reference" for

the variously located status-occupants of the system; of *institutional norms* which control the "means" or "acceptable modes of reaching out for these goals"; [15] and of values which include patterns of belief and attitudes.[16] Elaboration of both constructs appears below in the appropriate sections of the analysis in terms of the PAS Model.

Propositions emerging from fragmented research are highly amenable to consolidation into general theory if the research site [17] is chosen for its strategic importance. What constitutes a strategic research site is determined not by its "socially ascribed importance" nor by the idiosyncratic interest it holds for the investigator, but rather by its implications for scientific significance. Just as the geneticist has no intrinsic interest in the fruitfly, but nevertheless devotes attention to it because it provides insights into genetic transmission, so the sociologist may not be intrinsically interested in the immigrant, the stranger, small groups, voting decisions, or bureaucratic organization. "They may be chosen, instead, because they strategically exhibit such problems as those of marginal men, reference group behavior, the social process of conformity, patterned sources of nonconformity, the social determination of aggregated individual decisions, and the like." [18] For the most fruitful research, the types of concrete situations chosen for investigation must be capable of yielding generalizations which transcend the verities of the specific situation. As an illustrative case Merton poses the query: "How does a social structure produce new cultural norms prescribing behavior that was previously an unprescribed resultant of that structure?" [19] Strategic research sites which might yield a generalizable answer could probably be found among *various* groups similarly situated in the social structure, as in specified segments of the professions, workers, and delinquent gangs. Here a search would be made for uniformities of norm formation observable in all the selected groups. Merton's own research in bureaucratic organizations was based on the premise that such a site would be strategic for the uncovering of regulatory mechanisms, since "the interconnections of structure and mechanisms are more readily observable [there] than in less highly organized social systems." [20] Similarly, the housing project provides a "laboratory for the study of social and psychological processes" in the primary group, for analysis of the

emergence of small cohesive groupings, patterns of social interaction, interpersonal influence, the "ecology" of the dwelling unit,
resident morale, the consequences of diverse managerial policies,
privacy, resident turnover, race, class and ethnic attitudes and
relations. More important, it provides "checks upon' the many
ecological findings of sociologists which have been almost invariably based on crescive, unplanned areas." [21] Analysis of "strategic" data exhibiting high "problem density" at the "middle
range" of theory, it would seem, might move sociological inquiry
toward a path analogous to the important (though theoretically
provisional) physical science model of the "crucial experiment." [22]

Although Merton sets forth a provisional list of group-properties (see Addendum at the end of this chapter), its scope is
again "middle range." He is not concerned with specifying the
functional requirements of social systems *en toto,* nor with an
elaboration of all its elements or processes. The advantages thus
gained in maneuverability of conceptualization have been pur-
chased at the price of certain ambiguities, especially of the more
global terms such as social system, cultural values, cultural structure, and institutions. Medical schools and hospitals, for example,
as forms of bureaucracy, are variously called social systems, institutions, and organizations. These subsystems and others form the
"larger social system," the society.[23] At times the terms society
and social organization are made equivalent terms, both preferred
to social system.[24] The term "institution" may mean an organization such as a hospital or it may be the product of institutionalized
cultural and normative structures: "Like other social institutions,
the institution of science has its characteristic values, norms and
organization." [25] The concept "value" is probably the most frequently used term in Merton's writings, but it too is not defined
specifically. Such vagaries, however, can be easily over-empha-
sized. "Instructive ambiguity," Merton points out, may be sal-
utary. Ambiguities often pose temporary obstacles to effective
communication, understanding and research; and as such, provide
points for extension of theory by colleagues and students. Many
of these will be readily identified as Merton's works are juxtaposed
against the concepts of the PAS Model.

KNOWING

The dynamic interplay of beliefs and knowledge and the processes of reality testing has already been identified as one of the integrative components which give unity to otherwise miscellaneous writings of Merton. Although some of his most outstanding contributions are made in his analysis of knowledge and its validation, the cognitive aspect is not always a discrete category for Merton who often does not separate evaluative and expressive activity from it. Of the monographic contributions presented in *Social Theory and Social Structure* nine are primarily concerned with aspects of cognition. In addition to the selective representations appearing here as part of the element *Belief* (knowledge) or as part of the process, *Cognitive Mapping and Validation* the following chapters contain much pertinent material:

Chapter II, "The Bearing of Sociological Theory on Empirical Research"
Chapter III, "The Bearing of Empirical Research on Sociological Theory"
Chapter XI, "The Self-Fulfilling Prophecy"
Chapter XII, "The Sociology of Knowledge"
Chapter XIII, "Karl Mannheim and the Sociology of Knowledge"
Chapter XV, "Science and the Social Order"
Chapter XVI, "Science and Democratic Social Structure"
Chapter XVIII, "Puritanism, Pietism and Science"
Chapter XIX, "Science and Economy of 17th Century England"

Belief (knowledge) as an element. The term belief, as it is typically used by Merton, includes not only the beliefs which represent cognitive aspects of behavior but also what is elsewhere identified as sentiment and norm.[26] However, the term knowledge, is frequently used in much the same sense as the term belief (limited to cognition).[27] In Merton's view neither term represents a conceptual tool in the manner in which for him "cultural goal," "institutional norm," or "role-set" are tools. The proper content of the element knowledge is suggested by Merton's criticism of Mannheim's inclusive range which treated among other items, empirical fact, epistemological postulates, moral norms, etc. as knowledge. "Had he attended to the familiar distinction between the referential and emotive functions of language, for example, such a miscellany would scarcely have remained undifferentiated." [28] To recognize differentiations is not to neglect reciprocities, however.

The observability of norms is too important a variable to be left to an aside . . . In principle, all other kinds of social deviation and conformity are variously affected by the degree to which members of a group have access to knowledge about pertinent values and norms.[29]

The cognitive element of behavior is recognized by Merton in many of his miscellaneous writings. It appears, for example, in his discussion of studies of radio and film propaganda, in his treatment of the function of authority in groups, and in his works on collective behavior. From among the many cases in these and other works which illustrate the cognitive element, the following are typical. There is the expert on x-rays who sought to share with his audience his own competent knowledge, but who failed to recognize the cognitive beliefs his audience already possessed concerning quackery in the field of x-ray. He consequently "neglected to integrate the problem [of how to avoid quacks] into the experience-world of his audience" and produced the boomerang effect of creating general anxiety about the use of x-rays.[30] The cognitive element is equally apparent here:

The same audiences which set up defenses against fervent appeals to patriotic sentiments show a readiness to accept the implications of another type of propaganda which we may tentatively call *technological propaganda* or *the propaganda of facts. . . . The fact, not the propagandist, speaks.*[31]

The importance of the cognitive element in the functioning of a bureaucracy is illustrated by the recognition that those in authority must have greater knowledge of the norms than other members of their organization. "Otherwise, orders issued by authority will often and unwittingly violate these norms and cumulatively reduce the effective authority of those who issue them." [32] It is with the processual aspects of cognition rather than with the elemental aspects, however, that Merton's chief interest lies.

Cognitive mapping and validation as process. The dynamic interplay of knowledge and the processes of reality testing are handled in detail by Merton.

It is my central thesis that empirical research goes far beyond the passive role of verifying and testing theory: it does more than confirm or refute hypotheses. Research plays an active role; it performs at least four major functions which help shape the development of theory. It *initiates,* it *reformulates,* it *deflects,* and it *clarifies* theory.[33]

Here the empirical is seen as playing the active role. In other analyses experiential reality is seen to be relatively passive, being molded and formed by the active theory, even when that theory is false. This situation, appropriately labelled "the self-fulfilling prophecy," occurs when "a *false* definition of the situation [evokes] a new behavior which makes the originally false conception come *true.*"[34] For the social scientist attempting to test theory and/or investigate an empirical datum this inexorable mutuality and affectability of concept-experience poses a problem.

The self-fulfilling prediction and the suicidal prediction hold double interest for the social scientist. They represent not only patterns which he wishes to investigate in the behavior of others, but also patterns which create acute and very special methodological problems in his own research. . . . [The] social scientist everlastingly faces the possibility that his prediction will enter into the situation. . . . This characteristic of predictions is peculiar to human affairs.[35]

Not peculiar to human affairs, but applicable to all scientific experiment is the

. . . *logical structure* of experiment . . . [which] does not differ in physics, or chemistry or psychology. . . Nor do the near-substitutes for experiment—controlled observation, comparative study and the method of "discerning" differ in their *logical structure* in anthropology, sociology or biology.[36]

Processes pass for validation which in truth accomplish nothing of the sort. *Post factum* explanations are among those which, although not entirely avoided by Merton and other accomplished sociologists, are nonetheless logically condemned by him.

The logical fallacy underlying the *post factum* explanation rests in the fact that there is available a variety of crude hypotheses, each with some measure of confirmation but designed to account for quite contradictory sets of affairs. The method of *post factum* explanation does not lend itself to nullifiability, if only because it is so completely flexible.[37]

It is for this reason that "explanations" of a *post factum* nature do not feed back to test and reformulate and clarify theory. Their deficiencies lead Merton to place "stress on empirically-oriented sociological theory as an ongoing *development.* . . ." [38]

Merton also recognizes the pedestrian process by which conceptualization, verbalization, and ideas are being checked against experience, by everyone, everyday; and in reverse there "runs the basic theme of the unwitting determination of ideas by the substrata; the emphasis on the distinction between the real and the illusory. . . . The ideological analyst does not so much create a following as he speaks for a following to whom his analyses 'make sense,' *i.e.*, conform to their previously unanalyzed experience." [39]

An elaboration of this theme occurs as Merton expands on Whorf's idea that in cognitive mapping "response is not to the physical but to the conceptualized situations." In the case reported, workmen were cautious about smoking around drums of gasoline which were filled with liquid, but careless about smoking near the "empty" drums. In reality, the former were not so likely to explode as the unfeared "empty" cans which were filled with explosive vapor, a physical fact over-ridden in the workmen's minds by their conceptualization evoked by the word "empty." Here Merton's optimistic note concerning the possibility of "breaking out" of terminology embedded in language, contrary to what "Whorf tended to imply in this theory of linguistic behaviorism" is well taken.

Men are not permanently imprisoned in the framework of the (often inherited) concepts they use; they can not only break out of this framework but can create a new one, better suited to the needs of the occasion. . . . During these sometimes prolonged periods of lag, misapplied concepts do their damage. [40]

A variation of the theme of response to the conceptualized situation is provided by an example taken from one of Merton's medical studies. The medical student, not yet a doctor, but possessing more medical knowledge than the layman, develops the image of himself as a doctor as he is called upon in a small way to render medical aid to the extent of his ability. Families to whom he is assigned in a quasi-physician role present him with definite medical problems. ". . . it is when these problems are not unduly great, when students find that the requirements of the assigned tasks do not outrun their still quite limited knowledge and skills, that they are most likely to develop this self-image." [41]

Although the establishment of the conditions conducive to the development of science may not in itself be a property of cognitive mapping and validation, Merton's work on the determination of the scientific climate increases the understanding of the process under discussion.

. . . the emerging connections between science and religion were indirect and unintended. . . . [The] reformers were not enthusiastic about science. . . . Nevertheless, the religious ethic which stemmed from Calvin promoted a state of mind and a value-orientation which invited the pursuit of natural science. . . . It appears that once a value-orientation of this kind becomes established, it develops some degree of functional autonomy, so that the predilection for science could remain long after it has cut away from its original theological moorings. [42]

The points of difference between institutionalized science and institutionalized religion are so manifest that in Merton's opinion, it is all too easy to lose sight of "the less visible, indirect and perhaps more significant relationship between the two." [43]

FEELING

Of the monographs presented in *Social Theory and Social Structure* two chapters in particular contribute to aspects of what is here categorized under Feeling. They are Chapters 6 and 7 which deal with bureaucracy. Also pertinent are many of the observations about anomie, in Chapters 4 and 5. Neither should Merton's medical studies be overlooked in respect to the affective component.

Sentiment as an element. In Merton's conceptual scheme, meaning is composed both of cognition and sentiment. One of the five types of data specified by Merton as requirements or *desiderata* for effective functional analysis consists of the " 'meanings' (or cognitive and affective significance) of the activity or pattern for members of the group." [44] Merton's own observations on many investigative fronts abound in data which document the emotive aspect of meaning of the situation for the actors. So diverse are his contributions in this respect that in the interests of orderly presentation they will be treated here under two headings —the cultural and social structures as suggested by his own typology of adaptive responses to *anomie*. Although the typology was developed in quite a different connection, its concern with *strain* suggests that the emotive meanings of situations to the actor can well be categorized: those associated with "the cultural structure —'the normative pattern'—and the social structure—patterned attachments to other people or alienation from them." [45]

Merton deals widely with those sentiments which attend commitment to goals, to values, and to the established way of doing things (the cultural components). He pays corresponding attention to the injured sentiments devolving from unrealized ambitions, flaunted values, and cultural changes which are harbingers of new norms. A few examples will suffice. For the U.S. case, the culturally prescribed success goals, relatively easy to achieve by the upper middle and upper classes, have been internalized and *affectively* assimilated by an appreciable minority of the lower social strata and an even larger proportion of the lower middle class whose opportunities for successful goal achievement are considerably smaller than obtains for actors in the upper classes. Individuals in the lower social strata consequently suffer disproportionate anxieties which are passed on to their children in the form of pressures to conform and pressures to succeed, which training leads the children in turn "to carry a heavy burden of anxiety." [46] Also culturally associated is the sentiment designated by Merton as that of "moral indignation." This sentiment attends the flaunting of cherished norms, even though the indignant actors are not directly affected in any way by the normative breach.[47] Sentiments become attached also to the established way of doing things; they are often sufficiently strong to withstand and oppose the introduction of newer and perhaps more appropriate methods. Merton notes this development of what he calls "vested sentiments" in his observations of medical schools,[48] although of course, the phenomenon can be found in all stable organizations. Devotion to the traditional method is matched by fear of the new. "It has been observed that an environment of uncertainty, fear, and hostility may be skillfully created by quickening the pace of unpresaged changes in technology." [49]

As with sentiments associated with the cultural plane, Merton deals widely with those pertaining to the social plane where the positive sentiments are displayed in patterned attachments and the negative sentiments in patterned alienations in respect to other people. Being patterned, the attachments and alienations are of course no less normative than are the phenomena just considered which were labelled cultural and normative. The difference lies in the context of patterned *interaction* which for Merton demarks the social plane from the cultural plane. For example, the *culturally structured* reaction of "moral indignation" which is felt by large numbers of people upon the occasion of some normative offense committed by someone unknown to them, may be upsetting but it requires no change in the behavior or in the role definition of the indignant actors. The *socially structured* reaction of those people who share with the transgressor a patterned relationship requires much more adjustment. Each person must, in light of the transgression, redefine the relationship and repattern his own behavior to the deviant accordingly. The illustrative samples of socially structured sentiments will be limited to pertinent selections from works developed in connection with the reference group theory and from Merton's analyses of bureaucracies.

Support and security come from having "an established niche" in some organization; disturbance and anxiety usually are associated with the lack of structured relations. Most transitional stages—induction into the army or leaving high school to enter college, for example, are marked by a weakening or severing of old group ties and the establishment of new ones. Uncertainties and anxieties are common to this transitional stage but less severe for the newly-forming group made up totally of newcomers who are all experiencing the same problem (as a group of college freshmen for example), than for the single individual who is severed from an old established group and must seek attachment to a new group (the lone mid-semester transfer, for example). If the conditions of severance from the old group are not alienative, an intensification of sentiment toward the old ties may prevail for the individual until assimilation into the new group has occurred; "his old friends, his former teachers, his old school are imbued with disproportionately great affect." [50] Sizable numbers of initiates to a new group, all disproportionately loyal to old groups, might seriously impair the integration of the recipient group. Merton suggests that the replacement depots, "those army stations through which [soldiers] . . . filtered from their training outfits to some depleted combat outfit in need of personnel" [51] in effect loosened the soldier from affective involvement with previous army group ties "thus making him more amenable to ready absorption into his combat outfit." [52] As a parallel, Merton cites the incentives of hunger, acute anxiety and insecurity used during the 19th century to motivate people to work. Not mentioned by Merton is the equally applicable contemporary parallel of the planned disruption and violence and consequent destruction of expectancy patterns with accompanying anxiety as it is conscientiously used by communists in creating a felt need for order and solidarity.[53]

If the severance of old group ties has come about by alienation, it is no more easily relinquished, although the lingering affective attitude will of course be negative.

It can be provisionally assumed that membership in a group which has involved deep-seated attachments and sentiments cannot be easily abandoned without psychological residue. . . . The group remains pertinent precisely because they are alienated or estranged from it; it is therefore likely to be a negative reference group.[54]

It is likely that the alienated member will be extreme both in his attachment to his new group and in his alienation from the old, toward which he very possibly may bear "dependent hostility." There is also a likelihood that his extreme repudiation of the alienated group will be reciprocated by its members who will regard the former member with much more hostility and bitterness than they will an individual who has never been a member of the group.

Sentiment is also associated with the assimilating of new members into a group. An outstanding example is provided by the spectacle of out-marriage: "the greater the degree of group solidarity, the more marked the sentiment adverse to marriage with people outside the group. . . . Outmarriage *means* either losing one's group-member to another group or incorporation into one's own group of persons who have not been thoroughly socialized in the values, sentiments, and practices of the in-group." [55]

Great as is the need for personal interaction and meaningful affective ties, the normative constraints on interaction in the bureaucracy have become institutionalized in the form of *affective neutrality*.

. . . the substitution of personal for impersonal treatment within the structure [of a bureaucracy] is met with widespread disapproval and is characterized by such epithets as graft, favoritism, nepotism, applepolishing, etc. These epithets are clearly manifestations of injured sentiments. The function of such virtually automatic resentment can be clearly seen in terms of the requirements of bureaucratic structure.[56]

Tension management and communication of sentiment as process. Every illustration of sentiment given above is for Merton but a half-told story; its relation to social process in terms of testable propositions which determine its function or dysfunction is the other half. The hypothesized function may be social control, or perhaps boundary maintenance; the hypothesized dysfunction may be obstruction of needed social change or again overconformity at the expense of sufficient flexibility; but often it is tension management and communication of sentiment, the subject to which the present section is addressed.

The tension managing function of some of the above noted sentiments is fairly obvious. The group to whom solidarity, cohesion, and homogeneity is important, for example, would obviously be exposed to strains for which it would not be prepared were it to lose many of its members to out-groups or were it freely to incorporate out-group members into its own numbers. The strong sentiments against out-group marriage clearly reduces the probability of the group's being subjected to such tensions. (They are equally clearly boundary maintaining mechanisms.)

In contrast, the bureaucratic structure gives primacy to speed, efficiency, and other instrumental considerations. Sentiments must be channeled toward discipline in accordance with the operational rules devised to insure maximal returns on input rather than toward the affective relationships of workers in the bureaucracy. The bureaucratic structure "approaches the complete elimination of personalized relationships and nonrational considerations (hostility, anxiety, affectual involvements, etc.)."[57] Only by such affective neutrality can the rules be applied on a universal basis to all individuals or situations which are similarly categorized, without regard to individual differences and without the need for specific instructions and decisions. The tensions of particularistic treatment and of the uncertainties which might be expected to stem from particularism are thereby avoided.[58]

Misdirected affective neutrality can cultivate rather than reduce tensions for the bureaucrat, as for example, in the case when the client is rendered impersonal treatment. The expectancy pattern of the client is violated and he may retaliate by "reach[ing] across the counter and shaking one of them by the collar" or by becoming the client of another organization.[59]

The rules, devised as purely instrumental means to the end of efficient production, may be easily confused in the minds of some as being themselves somewhat sacred. They may come to be regarded as ends in themselves toward which misplaced sentiment is directed. Over-concern with regulations, timidity, conservatism and technicism are among the attitudes Merton perceives as stemming from over-commitment to norms which moderately observed, would both further the goal and reduce the tensions.

Although the cultivation of affective neutrality within the bureaucracy is indispensable for relations which are categorically determined, affectivity is equally indispensable to other organizations, such as political parties, and is equally capable under particularistic conditions, of managing tensions.

In our prevailingly impersonal society, the machine, through its local agents, fulfills the important social *function of humanizing and personalizing all manner of assistance* to those in need. Foodbaskets and jobs, legal and extra-legal advice, setting to rights minor scrapes with the law, helping the bright poor boy to a political scholarship in a local college, looking after the bereaved—the whole range of crises when a feller needs a friend . . . it is important to note not only that aid *is* provided but *the manner in which it is provided.*[60]

To examine Merton's contributions to an understanding of the process of sentiment communication it is necessary to become acquainted with his concept of "visibility," the "name for the extent to which the structure of a social organization provides occasion to those variously located in that structure to perceive the norms obtaining in the organization and the character of role-performance by those manning the organization." [61] The concept has implications for communication generally, and hence for communication of sentiment also. Although acknowledging that neither empirical inquiry nor theoretical formulations have sufficiently been devoted to the problem of how individuals acquire their information about groups other than their own which serve as evaluative and comparative frames of reference (that they *do* so do is the crux of the reference group theory) Merton tentatively postulates that the *norms and values* of non-membership groups are perhaps more visible and thus communicable, than is the actual behavior within them. If this should be borne out, the non-member, seeing the official norms and taking them at face value, would be seduced into unqualified idealization of positive reference groups and unqualified condemnation of the negative reference groups whose official norms represent something totally alien to the outsider's values. Likewise, since he should be in a position to know well the actual activities of his own group, he would minimize the importance of the official norms of his own group, knowing that actual behavior would amount only to a rough approximation of the values represented by the official norms. Different social structures display distinct differentials in visibility. Yet "the attitudes, opinions, sentiments, and expectations of organized groups and of unorganized masses" [62] must somehow be communicated to those occupying positions of authority. The pressure group, as an example of an organized group, has received a large amount of attention relative to the fairly unexplored "*unorganized* interests, sentiments, and orientations. It is partly the expressive behavior, partly the instrumental behavior, of large and often unorganized collectivities and the patterned procedures for making this visible to the holders of power which are still poorly understood and require further study." [63] Some of the social procedures used historically or currently to make non-membership collective sentiments visible to those who would or should know them range from Napoleonic police spies to modern opinion polls and the "functional equivalent of a continuing plebiscite, partial and not binding in force" represented by the tons of mail sent by the unorganized masses to those who hold positions of authority.

On a quite different level of analysis Merton examines the communication of that sentiment which the ethnic in-group expresses toward the ethnic out-group. Definitionally, sentiment is non-rational, and non-rational indeed is the "moral alchemy" by which the "in-group readily transmutes virtue into vice and vice into virtue, as the occasion may demand." [64] This process may be institutionalized rather than rationally calculated. The Trobriand Islanders serve as an example of the former where "the right activity [sexual success] by the wrong people [the rank and file] becomes a thing of contempt, not of honor." [65] It is only by the chiefs' uninhibited expression of resentment at what they (the in-group in this case) would consider too much ambition or too much success on the part of the lower-ranking Trobriander that they retain their power and their claims to special privilege. The hostile sentiments freely expressed toward the ethnic minorities in the United States, Merton sees as overwhelmingly dysfunctional and amenable to remedy only by supplanting certain institutions in the society (unspecified) with deliberate institutional controls. "And it is only with the rejection of social fatalism implied in the notion of unchangeable human nature that the tragic circle of fear, social disaster, and reinforced fear can be broken down." [66]

Among the fears which are reinforced in this expressively hostile cycle, are the fears of unfulfillable aspiration. What various groups regard as "too much ambition" or "too much success," and under what circumstances the disadvantaged are enjoined to be ambitious but disenjoined from being successful is part of the subject of goals and goal-attaining to which Merton devotes much attention.

ACHIEVING

Of the monographs comprising *Social Theory and Social Structure*, Chapters 4 and 5 which are devoted to a consideration of *anomie*, and Chapters 6 and 7 which are devoted to bureaucratic considerations, make the greatest contributions to what is treated here as ends, objectives or goals and the process of goal achieving and concommitant latent activities.

End, goal, or objective as an element. Merton uses the three terms—end, goal, and objective—interchangeably; also his terms motivation and values sometimes come close to suggesting the same meaning. The usage which is most common by far, however, is the term goal.

. . . culturally defined goals, purposes and interests [are] held out as legitimate objectives for all or for diversely located members of the society. The goals are more or less integrated—the degree is a question of empirical fact—and roughly ordered in some hierarchy of value. Involving various degrees of sentiment and significance, the prevailing goals comprise a frame of aspirational reference. They are the things "worth striving for." They are a basic, though not the exclusive, component of what Linton has called "designs for group living." And though some, not all, of these cultural goals are directly related to the biological drives of man, they are not determined by them.[67]

Intimately bound to goals are those regulatory norms which prescribe, permit or proscribe the acceptable modes of reaching these goals. The two components merge in empirical situations but are seen by Merton as analytically separate, a view which permits their separate examination in the present analysis although their interdependencies will require occasional simultaneous reference to both components as each in turn is the subject of analysis.

Important characteristics of a society may be found in the balance of emphases placed variously on the goals and on the institutionally prescribed means of achieving the goals. When the goals are held to be so important that they must be pursued by almost any means, opportunism and unprincipled expediency become characteristics of the social group so oriented. At the opposite extreme, when the goal may be lost sight of because of preoccupation with the institutionally prescribed means of goal achievement which become "self-contained practices, lacking further objectives,"[68] ritualism becomes characteristic of the social group so oriented. Both extremes are polar types of malintegrated cultures. Most societies fall somewhere between the two extremes by maintaining "a rough balance between emphases upon cultural goals and institutionalized practices, and these constitute the integrated and relatively stable though changing, societies."[69]

Of the two extreme types Merton pays particular attention to the one which emphasizes goals at the expense of institutionalized norms, taking contemporary American culture as an illustrative case which "appears to approximate the polar type in which great emphasis upon certain success-goals occurs without equivalent emphasis upon institutional means." [70] There are many success goals which comprise frames of aspirational reference in the American culture, but for illustrative purposes upon which hinges his analysis of the concept goal, Merton has chosen accumulated wealth or money, as an item which "has been consecrated as a value in itself." [71] The success goal symbolized by money is insatiable; i.e. there is no stable resting point at which its ultimate fulfillment is thought to be realized. "An observer of a community in which annual salaries in six figures are not uncommon [Hollywood], reports the anguished words of one victim of the American Dream: 'In this town, I'm snubbed socially because I only get a thousand a week. That hurts.' " [72]

Alternative career patterns such as intellectual and artistic achievement which may not net large monetary rewards but which command a certain amount of prestige may be substituted as legitimate objectives. And of course, broad classes of subgroups define objectives pertinent to the given group, but these are socially structured and auxiliary to the more general success-achievement goal specified in the cultural pattern. Thus originality for the scientist, effective persuasion for the propagandist, maximum utility of resources for the industrialist may be specific goals subsumed under the broad cultural mandate of the goal to succeed in the accumulation of wealth.

Wealth as a goal is by no means confined to America; the component which makes the situation in America different from most other cases is the accompanying attitude held out as a legitimate objective that top-notch success is the proper aspiration for *everyone*, "irrespective of his initial lot or station in life." [73] Although the exhortation to climb up the economic ladder is actually defined somewhat differently for the different social strata so that the identical standards of achievement are not expected of everyone, the cultural orientations hold that all should strive to go upward. The assimilation of the cultural emphasis and its transmutation into personal goals does not, however, occur in the same proportion for different social strata. Opportunities for realization of the goal prevail decreasingly from upper to lower classes.

Merton tentatively concludes on the basis of research focused on the assimilation of cultural goal by class that the percentage frequency of commitment to the cultural goal for any social class may decrease as opportunity for its fulfillment decreases. However, the absolute number committed to the success-goal and the intensity of commitment to the goal he recognizes as other important variables which require investigation before the *effects* of the over-all degree of commitment can be known.

Goal attaining and concomitant "latent" activity as process. Goal attaining activity must perforce be viewed as an articulation of the socially structured *specific* goals of the individual's status-roles or of the collective bundle of status-roles which comprise group enterprise. Thus the scientist, or the bureaucrat, or the physician or the propagandist directs his activities to goals appropriate to the function specified by his status-role, goals which, of course are generally auxiliary to the broader culturally specified goals of "things worth striving for." Neither individuals nor groups are uniformly clear about what their goal is. The effectiveness of activities performed in the pursuit of goals can most easily be measured in those situations in which the goal is unequivocally specific. Activities which are functional from the view point of groups committed to a particular goal are not necessarily functional from the view point of groups committed to other goals or from the view point of the total society. Accordingly, Merton avoids the "postulate of functional unity." His own works, which are always oriented to a *functional* analysis, meticulously observe the dictum, "The theoretic framework of functional analysis must expressly require that there be *specification* of the *units* for which a given social or cultural item is functional. It must expressly allow for a given item having diverse consequences, functional and dysfunctional, for individuals, for subgroups, and for the more inclusive social structure and culture." [74] The "given item" which may be functional or dysfunctional is by no means limited to activities directed toward goal achievement. Beliefs, sentiments, actual behavioral norms, status-roles, and many other items prove upon Merton's analysis to possess functional (or dysfunctional) qualities for specified units. In fact, there is no more pervasive point of view in all of Merton's writings than that provided by his postulates of functional analysis. In this chapter the functional framework is examined at this point under goal attaining activity for two reasons. First, goal attaining activity more than most other processes incorporates the articulation of many of the interdependent components here recognized as elements. Second, goal attaining activity offers a prime locus for an examination of a working distinction between what Merton specifies as "manifest function" and "latent function."

Merton views *manifest functions* as "those objective consequences contributing to the adjustment or adaptation of the system which are intended and recognized by participants"; *latent functions* as ". . . those which are neither intended nor recognized," dysfunctions as ". . . those observed consequences which lessen the adaptation or adjustment of the system." He also notes the "empirical possibility of nonfunctional consequences, which are simply irrelevant to the system under consideration." [75] As *consequences* they are not primarily concerned with the actual activities by which the subjectively conceived goal is fulfilled but rather with the state of the entity (individual or group) as a result of having pursued certain courses of action, or of having entertained certain beliefs and sentiments, or of having subscribed to certain norms. (In this respect, manifest function must be distinguished from "goal-attaining activity" as conceptualized in the PAS Model in that the former focuses on the consequences, the latter on the process leading to that consequence. Similarly, latent function must be distinguished from "latent activity," the former, focusing on unintended or unanticipated consequences, the latter on auxiliary activity which unsuspectingly is directed at goal achievement.)

Manifest functions as perceived by Merton will be given relatively little treatment here, precisely because the consequences they attest to, are in truth, manifest, as exemplified by the ideal type of bureaucratic organization: "A formal, rationally organized social structure involves clearly defined patterns of activity in which, ideally, every series of actions is functionally related to the purposes of the organization." [76] In actual operation, the bureaucratic organization like all others, from the point of view of the observer, displays patterns of activity which yield unanticipated consequences. Merton is particularly insightful in recognizing these latent functions and identifying them as being functional, dysfunctional, or occasionally non-functional.

A well-known illustration is Merton's analysis (after Max Weber) of the relations between Puritanism and Pietism and the development of science. Merton joins the ranks of "practically all the scholars who have made intensive studies of the matter [and] are agreed that most of the numerous sects comprising ascetic Protestantism provided a value-orientation encouraging work in science." [77] For him "it was the *unintended and largely unforeseen consequences* of the religious ethic formulated by the great Reformist leaders which progressively developed into a system of values favorable to the pursuit of science." [78] Thus, although such leaders as Luther, Calvin and Melanchton opposed certain scientific developments, the beliefs, ends and norms of the systems they espoused performed the latent function of furthering these same developments.

Perhaps the most directly effective element of the Protestant ethic for the sanction of natural science was that which held that the study of nature enables a fuller appreciation of His works and thus leads us to admire the Power, Wisdom, and Goodness of God manifested in His creation.[79]

Perhaps equally well-known is his description of the function of the political boss and machine in its relation with "big business." Illegal activities such as particularistic "protection" of vice, maneuvered by the political machine would be generally held to be dysfunctional from the point of view of society at large; in Merton's analysis they become latently functional for numerous segments of that society. "The distinctive function of the political machine for their criminal, vice and racket clientele is to enable them to operate in satisfying the economic demands of a large market without due interference from the government." [80] At the same time that this function is performed for the illegitimate business, it is latently performed for the legitimate business which may be as averse to public scrutiny and control as is the racketeer. The boss of the political machine serves the business community well, providing linkage and representation for it in government circles which are sometimes alienated.[81] For the poor, the machine provides *Gemeinschaft*-like access to welfare relief and service, and to many it provides the opportunity to be upward mobile, all unanticipated or latent functions of the political machine.

Some of the legion latent functions or dysfunctions of social or cultural items noted by Merton have already been treated in preceding sections. The replacement depots described in the reconceptualization of *The American Soldier* and referred to above under sentiment, may, in Merton's view, have performed the latent function of

. . . loosen[ing] the soldier's previous army group ties, thus making him more amenable to ready absorption into his combat outfit. In much the same way that the sandhog adjusts to normal atmospheric pressure at the end of a day's work under water by going through decompression chambers, so the soldier is *"de-grouped"* by passing through replacement depots.[82]

Other examples of latent functions (or dysfunctions) will incidentally occur as this chapter unfolds. The reader's attention is directed to such forthcoming examples as the "often unanticipated and unregarded" consequences of modifications in the network of social relations ushered in by new productive processes and equipment (treated in this chapter under utilization of facilities); or, the "unexpected response" of the viewers of propaganda films who, instead of experiencing revulsion at Nazi unconcern for common human decencies, concluded that the Nazis were very efficient (treated in this chapter under communication). This preview may sensitize the reader to Merton's predominantly functional viewpoint as well as to his ingenuity in discerning latencies of function.

NORMING, STANDARDIZING OR PATTERNING

Although norms are treated in all of Merton's writings, particular consideration is given them in the following monographs of *Social Theory and Social Structure:* Chapters 4 and 5, dealing with social structure and anomie, and Chapters 6 and 7, dealing with bureaucratic structures.

Norm as an element. Just as a fairly clear and consistent meaning of *goal* emerges from Merton's use of diverse terms, so the intent of meaning in regard to norms is established although the terms used may be "acceptable modes," "disallowed procedures," "value-laden sentiments," "standardized practices," "institutional means," "institutionalized norms" and perhaps others such as regulatory norms as opposed to technical or efficiency norms. The culturally structured norm "defines, regulates and controls the acceptable modes of reaching out for . . . [the culturally defined] goals." [83] In a stable (although changing) and relatively integrated society, individuals receive satisfactions from goal achievement, but equally, from observing the "institutionally canalized modes of striving to attain them." [84] In such a society, the product of the achieved goal is no more important than the process by which it is obtained; the outcome of the activities are of equal consequence with the activities themselves. Thus, on a cultural level, the normative or regulatory order is viewed by Merton primarily as a *means*—means which are culturally prescribed, preferential, permissive or proscribed. On the social level, where individuals in interaction behave more or less in accordance with their various role requirements, the behavior is by no means a replica of the behavior culturally defined as *expected.* Actual behavior makes many concessions to conditions attending particular situations, conditions which in the eyes of the actor provide extenuating circumstances which modify his strict adherence to the institutionalized norms. The patent fact of nonobservance of norms on the part of all individuals some of the time and of some individuals much of the time, does not vitiate in the least the general societal recognition that there *are* expected modes of behavior which serve as guides to actual behavior.

Norms are central to at least three of the twenty-six components which Merton designates as provisional group properties (see items 16, 17 and 18 in addendum at end of chapter). In this and the following paragraphs the norm centered group properties are designated by the italicized quotations. The *"character of social relations obtaining in the group"* are expressed in sociological literature by the terms primary and secondary, in-group and out-group, *Gemeinschaft* and *Gesellschaft,* formal and informal. A step beyond these dichotomous or polar concepts which definitionally recognize the opposites among possible patterns of social relationships is Parsons' pattern variables which in Merton's view "serve to characterize distinctively concrete social relationships prevailing in a group." [85]

Normative also is the *"degree of expected conformity to norms of group: toleration of deviant behavior and institutionalized departures from the strict definition of group norms."* [86] Strict adherence to norms is exacted by some; the connotations of the term "bureaucracy" when used in the derogatory sense usually signify strict rule adherence at the expense of flexibility. Merton's own analysis of bureaucracy clearly utilizes this group property as well as the property described in the above paragraph. The character of social relations in a bureaucracy are overwhelmingly secondary, *Gesellschaft*-like and formal. Merton sees the tendency to over-conformity in observing the bureaucratic rules as being dysfunctional for the structure, and in time, as having the effect of changing the original nature of the bureaucratic norms.

The process may be briefly recapitulated. (1) An effective bureaucracy demands reliability of response and strict devotion to regulations. (2) Such devotion to the rules leads to their transformation into absolutes; they are no longer conceived as relative to a set of purposes. (3) This interferes with ready adaptation under special conditions not clearly envisaged by those who drew up the general rules. (4) Thus, the very elements which conduce toward efficiency in general produce inefficiency in specific instances. Full realization of the inadequacy is seldom attained by members of the group who have not divorced themselves from the meanings which the rules have for them. These rules in time become symbolic in cast, rather than strictly utilitarian.[87]

Some groups, on the other hand, permit a wide range of departure from norms "as, for example, in groups which pride themselves on making large allowance for individuality and creativity." [88] What Merton develops in another connection would seem to be pertinent here: the element of the risk which the innovator invariably faces is present precisely because the permissible limits of departure from norm observation is not specified. The white collar criminal, like the robber baron who preceded him, may find himself lauded for having achieved a goal or spurned for having trespassed by using proscribed methods. Merton uses Veblen's words to describe the dilemma: "It is not easy in any given case—indeed it is at times impossible until the courts have spoken—to say whether it is an instance of praiseworthy salesmanship or a penitentiary offense." [89]

Many evasions of the norms are individualistic and private, but to the extent that the evasions are made in response to constraints or requirements which a sizeable number of affected individuals feel to be inappropriate, the evasions themselves become patterned, a condition appropriately labelled by Merton as "institutionalized evasion of institutional rules." [90] Institutionalized evasions may develop as new situations require an adaptive behavior which conflicts with long standing norms to which the group is deeply committed. The old norms are ostensibly retained while departures from them become progressively accepted—that is, the evasions become institutionalized. Or it also can happen that the newly imposed institutional demands are superficially obeyed, but in fact evaded while the slowly changing norms of the old situation continue to dominate actual behavior.

The third norm-centered group property has to do with *"the system of normative controls,"* which are exhibited by different groups. Some exercise control principally "through expressly formulated rules (law); through less definitely formulated but definitely patterned [rules] . . . reinforced by sentiment and supporting moral doctrine (mores); and through routinized, often habitual but less strongly affective, expectations (folkways)." [91] A nice contrast between the mores of science and those of business is provided by Merton's respective examinations of the scientist as he performs in a democratic social structure and of the intellectual as he performs in a bureaucracy. The norms of science as seen by Merton are four: universalism, communism (in the sense that the substantive findings of science are a product of social collaboration and are assigned to the community, constituting a common heritage from which the discoverer's equity is limited or removed), disinterestedness, and organized scepticism. These "comprise the ethos of modern science." [92] In his own peer group the scientist is permitted little freedom for deviancy from group norms; "the activities of scientists are subject to rigorous policing, to a degree perhaps unparalleled in any other field of activity." [93] Each piece of activity in which he engages is non-secret and supposedly totally visible, and subjected to the scrutiny of his fellow-scientists whose concern lies not so much in the results as the methods. "The translation of the norm of disinterestedness into practice is effectively supported by the ultimate accountability of scientists to their compeers."[94] The intellectual, often steeped in scientific tradition, who essays to serve in a bureaucracy becomes exposed to a very different normative structure. The policy maker whom he is supposed to help may choose to define the exact field of investigation in which the intellectual is to concentrate. The value orientations of the bureaucracy may countenance only particularistic approaches to some matters. The findings are often not made immediately available to the scientific world but are kept secret in the interests of competitive advantage. The bureaucracy is by no means disinterested in the implications of the result of the scientist's activities although it is not preoccupied with his method. The cultivated scepticism entertained by the intellectual is antithetical to the bureaucracy. These differences are among the chief reasons identified by Merton which explain why intellectuals in the bureaucracy either lose their original orientation and become technicians, or are in constant conflicts with the policy makers of the bureaucracy and leave it in order to retain their scientific orientation.

The basic norms of science, functional though they be for the fruitful performance of scientific activity, do pose problems for the scientist. Since he forfeits property rights in his contributions which become "communal" or "societal" property, his only equity in his achievement is in the recognition accorded him for originality and priority. He may quite understandably have an urge to be "first"—to be known as the originator but this motivation is in conflict with the norms of disinterestedness and humility which are also required of the scientist. "The institutional values of modesty and humility are apparently not always enough to counteract both the institutional emphasis upon originality and the actual workings of the system of allocating rewards."[95] The case of the scientist provides an example of what Merton has come to call "socially patterned ambivalence."[96]

A basic thesis of Merton's and central to his study of anomie is that although norms which govern conduct are found in every society, "societies do differ in the degree to which the folkways, mores and institutional controls are effectively integrated with the goals which stand high in the hierarchy of cultural values."[97] Not only do societies differ in this respect, but groups within societies do not maintain equally constant balances between norms and goals.

Merton's treatment of *anomie* as a phenomenon of "the middle range" brings into focus the distinctions noted above between social and cultural structures as he conceptualizes them. It also brings to light an "instructive ambiguity" in the original use of the concept "institutionalized means." [98] Although Merton uses the term norm in the sense in which it is employed in the PAS Model, the concept "institutionalized means" as originally employed seems to straddle cultural and social structures in that it appears to include norms, facilities and their utilization, and patterns of interaction. Nevertheless, as developed by Merton and extended by Parsons the focal interest in the anomie paradigm involves discriminatory evaluation of ends and norms and is consequently treated here under the process of evaluation.

Evaluation as a process. Merton views both goals and norms as culturally determined values, empirically interrelated but analytically distinct. As such they provide points of reference by which adaptation to the "culture-bearing society" is made by individuals occupying different positions in the social structure. Upon these points of reference is based Merton's well-known typology of modes of individual adaptation. Figure 1 presents the typology. "Institutionalized means," it will be remembered, roughly equates with norms but possesses the additional attributes noted above.

Conformity represents adaptation in which both the ends and norms are positively evaluated and relatively balanced. It is the mode of adaptation for most people in a given society in whatever position they occupy. Their very commitment both to ends and to norms constitute the chief components of the *stable* society. "It is, in fact, only because behavior is typically oriented toward the basic values of the society that we may speak of a human aggregate as comprising a society." [99] Merton's basic thesis, however, is that by focusing, not on the conforming, the "normal" and the stable, but on deviancies to this behavior, basic stresses in the social structure will be revealed. He sees the various kinds of deviancy from conformity, not mainly as individual quirks, nor mainly as psychological predispositions to deviancy, but as uni-

FIGURE 1 *

A TYPOLOGY OF MODES OF INDIVIDUAL ADAPTATION

Modes of Adaptation	Cultural Goals	Institutionalized Means
I. Conformity	Acceptance	Acceptance
II. Innovation	Acceptance	Rejection
III. Ritualism	Rejection	Acceptance
IV. Retreatism	Rejection	Rejection
V. Rebellion	Rejection of prevailing ends and substitution of new ones	Rejection of prevailing norms and substitution of new ones

* Adapted from: Robert K. Merton, *Social Theory and Social Structure* (Glencoe, Ill.: The Free Press, 1957), p. 140. Application of the typology to any specific group must always be made with society as the reference point. Take as an example the Old Order Amish whose social structure has been examined elsewhere.** If the social system represented by the Old Order Amish is taken as a reference point, the mode of adaptation is extremely conforming, possessing very little of Modes II-V. If the social system represented by the American Society is taken as a reference point, however, the Amish emerge as non-conformists of Mode V persuasion; they have rejected both the cultural goals and the norms of the larger society and supplanted both with other goals and other norms.

** Charles P. Loomis, *Social Systems: Essays on Their Persistence and Change* (Princeton: D. Van Nostrand and Co., 1960), Essay #5.

form adaptations to the similar social situations in which various classes of individuals find themselves. He therefore devotes relatively little attention to conformity as a mode of adaptation, but concentrates instead on the other four modes.

Innovation, or the rejecting of institutionalized norms at the same time that a high evaluation is placed upon the culturally prescribed goals, is that mode of adaptation which tends to be used by a sizable minority of individuals who share a lack of realistic opportunities for achievement of the goal by institutionally sanctioned means. The accumulation of wealth as a success goal is the illustrative case used by Merton to demonstrate his thesis, although he is careful to specify that there are many others. Rejection of institutionalized norms may lead to "white collar" crime in upper classes and various forms of delinquency, crime and racketeering in the lower classes.[100] These substitutions of proscribed norms, classifiable generally under forms of crime or delinquency, are by no means the only innovative adaptations to which individuals resort. Nor does Merton believe that all deviation from the dominant group norms is dysfunctional. A certain amount of innovation may in time form the basis for new institutionalized patterns which are better equipped than the old to provide an adaptive base in the winning of cherished goals: "some . . . cultural heroes have been regarded as heroic precisely because they have had the courage and the vision to depart from norms then obtaining in the group." [101] Whether functional or dysfunctional for the given society there is a certain amount of dynamism in the innovative situation.

A mounting frequency of deviant but "successful" behavior tends to lessen and, as an extreme potentiality, to eliminate the legitimacy of the institutional norms for others in the system. The process thus enlarges the extent of anomie within the system so that others, who did not respond in the form of deviant behavior to the relatively slight anomie which first obtained, come to do so as anomie spreads and is intensified.[102]

Ritualism is a mode of adaptation by which the cultural goals are rejected and the institutional norms accepted. Individuals situated in the lower classes may be more prone to adapt by innovation, whereas the lower-middle class tends toward ritualism. The adaptation is "a *private* escape from the dangers and frustrations which seem to them inherent in the competition for major cultural goals by abandoning these goals and clinging all the more closely to the safe routines and the institutional norms." [103] The ritualist is generally the over-conformist who cannot tolerate ambiguity. Merton concurs with Blau's interpretation that the ritualist slavishly follows the rules not because of over-identification with them so much as " 'from lack of security in important social relationships in the organization.' It is, in short, when the structure of the situation does not allay the status-anxiety and anxiety over the capacity to measure up to institutionalized expectations that individuals in these organizations respond with over-compliance." [104] Although culturally prescribed goals are replaced by goals more possible to achieve, conformity, for the sake of conformity, becomes a central value.

Retreatism is "a privatized rather than a collective mode of adaptation" of the socially disinherited.[105] Originally associated in Merton's view chiefly with such social derelicts as "psychotics, autists, pariahs, outcasts, vagrants, vagabonds, tramps, chronic drunkards and drug addicts," he later came to include in this type of adaptive behavior, a typical response by many of those who had suffered an abrupt break in the familiar normative framework and established social relations of their lives. Such disruptions as were described in the Durkheimian terms of "the anomie of prosperity" and "the anomie of depression" are typical situations to which this adaptation may be made. Enforced retirement or sudden widowhood is each an example of a situational genesis of this mode of adaptation manifested by a "nostalgia for the past and apathy in the present." [106] Because of its private nature its incidence often is not recorded in social statistics. Yet its prevalence is attested to by psychiatrists, theologians, novelists and other social commentators. Merton suggests that there is some merit in investigating its incidence in relation to such well known social phenomena as political and organizational apathy. At any rate, this failure to evaluate anything highly enough to extend effort toward either realization of a goal or observance of the norms, whether called torpor, cynicism, disenchantment, or what not, is a form of deviancy.

Rebellion, as a type of adaptation, "presupposes alienation from reigning goals and standards" and expenditure of effort to "bring into being a new . . . greatly modified social structure." [107] Merton carefully distinguishes rebellion from what he calls *ressentiment* (after Max Scheler) which asserts that the unattainable objective is after all, not nearly as desirable as it is given credit for being, much in the manner of the fox who concludes that the unobtainable grapes are sour. Rebellion "involves a genuine transvaluation, where the direct or vicarious experience of frustration leads to full denunciation of previously prized values. . . ." [108] Two factors contribute to the adaptation by rebellion. One is the pressure for achievement coupled with restrictions of opportunity, particularly in the lower classes in the American case. The other is ambivalent or conflicting norms resulting from an admixture of open class and caste norms in the society.

These latter four types of adaptation then, innovation, ritualism, retreatism and rebellion, are individual evaluations of various aspects of the goal-norm complex. Considered in relation to society as a whole they are atypical, though occurring with sufficient frequency that they are recognizable as patterns of evaluative behavior for significant numbers of individuals. Explicitly, for Merton, they are adaptive modes of role behavior the identification of which adds to the understanding of *anomie* as that phenomenon was noted by Durkheim. In response to various critiques [109] of his analysis, Merton makes clear that conformity is modal for all groups and to the degree that deviant adaptation occurs, it is a subsidiary pattern sufficiently established as such by being subscribed to by any sizable minority. Further, he emphasizes that the theory in its concern for isolating the *origins* of the strains in the social structure makes no claim that the nonconforming adaptations are "rationally calculated and utilitarian"; on the contrary, since they arise out of pressure and frustration, a degree of irrationality might be expected. Whereas Merton's work on *anomie* deals with the evaluative process and concentrates on the evaluative results, his work on reference groups considers more systematically the dynamics of the evaluative process by which those results come into being. [110]

As a recapitulation of the functions of reference groups, Merton restates his own views thus: "They are said to provide 'a frame of reference for self-evaluation and attitude-formation'; there is said to be a need for 'systematic study of the processes of value-assimilation as part of reference group behavior'; there is a short comment 'on the reference group contexts of attitudes, perceptions and judgments.'" [111] In the pursuit of a methodical examination of these primarily evaluative functions of reference groups, two major types of reference groups are distinguished: the normative type which sets and maintains standards for the individual, and the comparison type which provides a frame of comparison relative to which the individual evaluates himself and others. This distinction is similar to the evaluative distinctions in terms of the PAS Model where evaluation, which articulates *norms* with things other than actors, is distinguished from the evaluation which results in *rank* for actors. For the purposes at hand in this presentation, therefore, the functions of the normative type of reference group will receive emphasis. The comparative type which provides a "context for evaluating the relative position of oneself and others" [112] is more appropriately handled in terms of the PAS Model as a part of the evaluation of actors, a process in which the element *rank* is articulated with other system elements and processes.

Reference groups of the normative type comprise "a source of values assimilated by designated individuals (who may or may not be members of the group)." [113] Reference groups of the normative type may be "membership groups" or "non-membership groups." Individuals who comprise a membership group are not equally members. Degrees of membership vary by such factors as rate of interaction due to spatial considerations, rate of interaction due to special interests which induce distinctive social relations among a subgroup of the total membership group, and sentiments and values peculiar to subgroups. The common norms and values which can be distinguished as those subscribed to by the membership at large, are thus variously assimilated by members depending upon their degree of membership in the group.

Individuals who are not members of a group may nonetheless in varying degrees, assimilate the values of groups to which they do not belong. "Other attributes of non-membership being equal . . . non-members eligible for membership will presumably be more likely to adopt the norms of the group as a positive frame of reference [than will non-members who are ineligible for membership]." [114] Non-members also differ in respect to their *attitudes* toward membership; they may aspire to become members, or be indifferent to membership, or be negative toward affiliation. Those who aspire to become members may be expected to show a relatively high degree of assimilation of the values and norms which are associated with the group in question. (By the same token, these same individuals tend to exhibit a relatively low degree of assimilation of the values and norms associated with the groups of which they actually are members.) "Anticipatory socialization" is the term coined by Merton to designate the commitment of individuals to values and norms which are characteristic of groups to which they as yet do not belong but to which they aspire. The social climber is an obvious example which comes to mind. If he is not in fact eligible to membership in the group to which he aspires, he becomes marginal, belonging in no full sense either to the group whose norms and values he has repudiated or to the group which is not willing to accept him. Those who are indifferent to membership in a particular group are "entirely outside its orbit." If the membership group seeks to extend itself toward completion by enfolding in its ranks all eligibles, it will actively seek out from these "indifferents" those who in fact are eligible. To the degree that the members succeed, some of the "indifferents" will assimilate the norms and values of the group and become members. They are potential members, even though at a given time they are "indifferents." The third class of non-members is negatively oriented to the group in question. The individual who rejects the group even though he be eligible for inclusion in it "symbolizes the relative dubiety of its norms and values which are not accepted by those to whom they should in principle apply." [115] For him, as well as for the non-eligible negatively oriented individual, the membership group in question becomes a "negative reference group."

The values symbolized by various groups may either be attenuated or strengthened by extensive membership. Various elites, for example, would attenuate their symbolic values by extending membership opportunities to broad segments of the population. They are therefore designated as "closed groups" whose norms are the more valuable even to non-members by virtue of their inaccessibility. Political parties in totalitarian societies where party membership is synonymous with an elite, thus typically restrict the size of the group. In contrast, "open groups" stand to strengthen the values by which they are symbolized by relatively unrestricted membership. Political parties in democratic societies, industrial unions, and certain religious bodies are examples cited by Merton as groups which by the device of extensive and relatively inclusive membership can expect to increase the assimilation of values symbolized by their group.

Based upon these various forms of value-engendering groups, Merton addresses himself to the problem of determining "whether reference group behavior differs as one or another of these broad types of social formations is taken as a frame of reference . . . [and of determining] how the structure of the society makes for the selection of others with whom individuals are in actual association as the reference group, and how, in the absence of such direct association, it makes for the selection of reference groups among collectivities or social categories." [116]

Merton concurs in the widely held thesis that "reference

groups operate as such in conjunction with distinct kinds of evaluation and behavior . . . some groups presumably take on pertinence for a wide variety of behaviors and others for only a
few." [117] Among types of individuals and groups which provide
to others the normative and comparative frames of reference for
evaluation, there are those which operate as *single* sources of
orientation and there are those which operate as *multiple* orientation sources. From the perspective of those who adopt one
or another group or individual as orientation sources, some of
the adopted orientations are of segmental rather than of total
relevance to the adopting individual's values. Reference groups
are important in some instances as symbols of ultimate values; in
others their importance lies in their contribution to concensus
concerning the relative importance of various roles or spheres of
behavior.[118] Merton interprets the selection of each type of reference group as hinging upon the immediate social situation: "a
reference orientation toward this pervasive type of norm, relating
ultimate values to specific situations of social interaction, serves
as a mechanism of social control, under conditions of impending
or actual disorganization, *within* subsystems of a society rather
than under conditions of potential conflict *between* different subsystems. The second type of norm tends to be called into play
when diverse and conflicting definitions of the social situation by
different groups present the individual with a choice between
conflicting roles." [119]

An essential part of the dynamics of adopting or rejecting the
values central to a reference group is in the correct perception of
what constitutes those values in actuality. The failure of a non-
member of a reference group to distinguish between the actual
patterns of behavior within a group and that group's formally expressed norms and values may lead him to an idealization of, or
a condemnation of the supposed values of the group. *Visibility*
and *observability* of norms is a necessary condition to their being
realistically adopted by others. The convert's frequently rigid
conformity (above and beyond the conformity of long-established
members of the group) to the official statement of group norms,
stems in Merton's opinion, not primarily from his desire to insure
acceptance into the group, but rather from "want of having had
first-hand knowledge of the nuances of allowable and patterned

departures from the norms . . . [which] the long-established members of the group . . . have acquired . . . in the course of their socialization." [120] Reference groups may be sources both of positive and negative value orientations because their norms are not sufficiently visible to the potential adopter to be realistically appraised. The adopter may have converse blind spots concerning the values of his own membership groups, because as he has become socialized to the ways of the group, he is more aware of actual behavior than of the formally declared values. Thus, the various patterns of conformity and deviance which are central to the evaluations implicit in the modes of adaptation developed in Merton's earlier work, are continuous threads of evaluative significance in his later works which utilize the reference group theory.

DIVIDING THE FUNCTIONS

Status-role incorporating both element and process. Consistent with Merton's belief that science advances by cumulation, he builds upon the work of others by choosing from sociological literature concepts of status and role which fit his needs. He turns to Linton for definitions of status and role:

> By status Linton meant a position in a social system occupied by designated individuals; by role, the behavioral enacting of the patterned expectations attributed to that position. Status and role, in these terms, are concepts serving to connect the culturally defined expectations with the patterned behavior and relationships which comprise social structure.[121]

With free acknowledgements to Newcomb,[122] Gross [123] and others who have extended the concept, he accepts the idea that each position has "multiple-roles" associated with it, and then differentiates from it the concepts of "role-set," "status-set," "role-sequence" and "status-sequence." The examples used by Merton to communicate his concepts will serve the present purpose better than secondary descriptions.

> . . . [By] role-set . . . I mean that complement of role relationships which persons have by virtue of occupying a particular social status . . . [The] status of public school teacher has its distinctive role-set, relating the teacher to his pupils, to colleagues, the school principal

and superintendent, the Board of Education, and, on frequent occasion, to local patriotic organizations, to professional organizations of teachers, Parent-Teachers Associations, and the like.[124]

The sum of various role-sets comprises the "status-set": ". . . the complement of social statuses simultaneously occupied by each of a plurality of individuals." [125] Thus, a status-set might consist of the statuses male, teacher, Protestant, Democrat, etc., each with its array of related roles. Further, status-sets are the linking structural units between institutions and the subsystems of a society. The concept of "role-performance" is used to refer to the behavior of the status-occupant as it is assessed or appraised by the members of his role-set. Figure 2 presents schematically not

FIGURE 2

Schematic Diagram of Merton's
Social Structure Elements

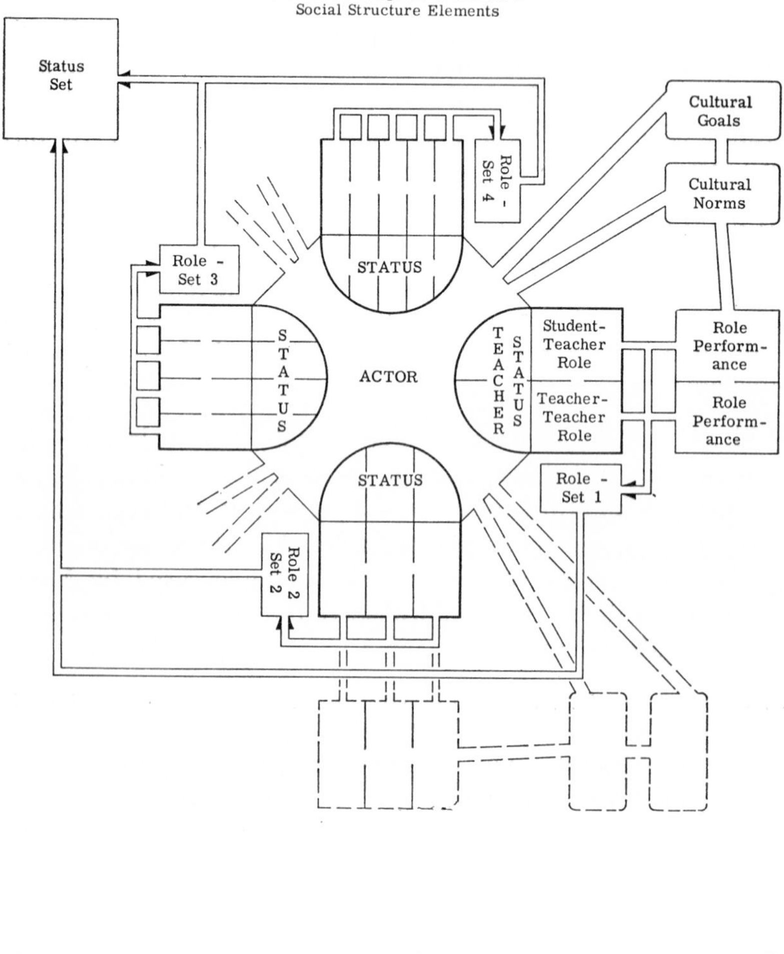

only the cultural goals and norms which up to this point have comprised a considerable part of the chapter, but relates them to the immediate consideration of status-role. In it the actor is represented by the central octagon. He is shown as occupying several statuses in the social structure. (The number of such statuses is schematically represented as four for the purposes of simplicity, although in a highly differentiated society the number could be expected to be much higher). Each status represented by the Norman window-like sketches, is related to an array of social roles represented by the broken-lined "panes" of the Norman windows, the sum of which comprises the "role-set" depicted by the rectangles. The combined role sets converge in status-set which appears as a square in the upper left hand corner.

All the elements so presented are static, in that their reference is to social phenomena at a particular time; they are as Figure 2's designation indicates, structural elements. To provide for the processual or dynamic aspect of functional analysis Merton introduces the concept "status-sequence" which refers to the successive statuses which an actor occupies in the course of time, provided that the succession is patterned, as for example the "statuses successively occupied by a medical student, intern, resident, and independent medical practitioner." [126] Similarly, role-sequence refers to the succession of role-performances [127] of an actor with a specific status, as for example, the reoccuring interaction between teacher and student interspersed regularly by reoccuring interaction between teacher and other teachers.[128] Both status-sequence and role sequence are schematically presented in Figure 3.

Roles which inevitably incur interaction with specified others lead their incumbents naturally to greater or lesser amounts of involvement with role incumbents differentially situated in the social structure with respect to status. This relationship is compounded for all statuses of the "set." As a result the potential for conflicting goals and norms is great. Since "this appears to be the major structural basis for potential disturbance of a stable role-set" [129] Merton turns his attention to identifying the social mechanisms responsible for a "reasonable degree of articulation among the roles in role-sets," and those mechanisms which fail to produce or retain order.[130] He identifies six such mechanisms.

FIGURE 3

Role-Sequence and Status-Sequence

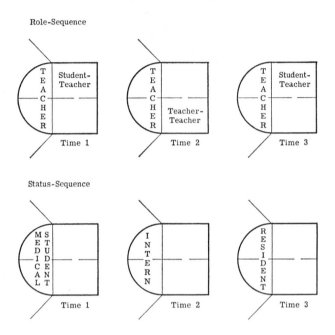

1. *The mechanisms of differing intensity of role-involvement among those in the role-set.* For example, the teacher must articulate her role to parents as well as to members of patriotic organizations. The expectations of each group may differ, but the teacher may meet the parents' expectations more fully than those of the patriotic organizations because the parents are more vitally concerned with the teacher's evaluations and controls than are the members of the patriotic organizations whose concern is relatively marginal.

2. *The mechanism of differences in the power of those involved in a role-set.* To the degree that a status-occupant, e.g. a teacher, is beset by conflicting expectations on the part of those with differential power, she may deliberately or unwittingly, be a party to coalitions of power whereby the will of the most powerful is offset by the combined wills of the less powerful. Other balances of power may obtain "as the child who succeeds in having his father's decision offset his mother's contrasting decision."

3. *The mechanism of insulating role-activities from observability by members of the role-set.* Since the frequency and intensity of interaction of members of the role-set is different for each status-occupant,

the extent of observability of role-performance by role-partners is directly related to differentials in competing pressures on the status-occupant. Certain statuses prescribe norms which contribute toward insulation. Thus, "the norm which holds that what is said in the classrooms of universities is privileged" protects the college teacher. Similarly, the norms of medical ethics may protect both doctor and patient.

4..*The mechanism making for observability by members of the role-set of their conflicting demands upon the occupants of a social status.* Thus, if two or more members of a role-set make conflicting demands upon an actor, communication of these conflicting demands to members of the role-set may free the actor in the focal position from the conflict since they in turn may become aware of the conflicting nature of the demands.

5. *The mechanism of social support by others in similar social statuses with similar difficulties of coping with an unintegrated role-set.* Thus, librarians scattered throughout the United States, by presenting a united front through the American Library Association and with the help of the American Book Publishers' Council, protect their libraries and operations from local would-be censors.

6. *Abridging the role-set: disruption of role-relationships.* Under certain conditions, as in friendship, a relationship may be broken off.[131]

Chief among the problems of status-set articulation is the complexity of the status-set and differentials in flexibility toward new status assumptions which may require value orientations in conflict with those old statuses to which the actor has already been socialized.[132] Certain mechanisms mitigate the conflict of status-set inconsistencies; among them are status-sequence, "empathy," consensus in evaluation of conflicting status-obligations and the process of self-selection of successive statuses. Concerning this last mentioned mechanism Merton notes that:

In terms of the value-orientations already developed, people reject certain statuses which they could achieve, because they find them repugnant, and select other prospective statuses, because they find them congenial . . . those reared as Christian Scientists and committed to this faith do not ordinarily become physicians. . . . These two successive statuses . . . do not occur with any frequency as a result of the process of self-selection.[133]

Merton cites the example observed by Max Weber, in which ascetic Protestants entered capitalistic businesses. The "empathy"

between the two statuses led to increasingly compatible definitions of social roles. The frequency of incompatible social roles
tends to be negatively correlated with the degree of societal integration. "Type-cases are numerous and familiar; the Catholic
Communist . . . the marginal man . . . the professional woman." [134]
The strain resulting from the incompatibilities of simultaneously
held multiple roles is to be distinguished from that which is imposed by conflicting expectations of the single role. Already mentioned in the latter respect is the status-role of scientist which
demands that discovery of knowledge be made known to other
scientists, that the reward for originality be reaped, while humility and the negation of self interest is exacted.

Most of the status-roles dealt with by Merton are the familiar
and easily identified ones such as teacher, soldier, scientist, physician, nurse, engineer or politician. He draws attention in addition,
to "the growing subdivision of work tasks" creating "numberless
new occupations for which, as Roethlisberger has observed, 'there
exist no occupational names that have any social significance outside of the particular industry, factory or even department in many
cases.' The splintering of work tasks involves *loss of public identity of the job*," [135] a condition which inevitably has consequences
for the social rank of the affected individuals.

RANKING

Among those monographs rich in contributions to the concepts
here dealt with under Ranking those devoted to reference group
theory perhaps come most immediately to mind. Others noteworthy in this respect are *Social Structure and Anomie, The Role
of the Intellectual in Bureaucracy, Bureaucratic Structure and
Personality,* and in a general way *The Sociology of Knowledge.*

Rank as an element. Although the terms differentiation and
status are somewhat suggestive of rank, Merton's distinction between the terms is unequivocal:

. . . social differentiation is often identified with social stratification,
partly, perhaps, as a result of the tendency for differentiated statuses
to be variously evaluated (and thereby ranked) by members of the
society. But as the concept of the division of labor reminds us there
can be much or little differentiation of status on the *same* plane of

stratification: jobs differentiated in terms of function, for example, may be similarly ranked.[136]

His works are concerned much less with the more statistical aspect of rank expressed in "shape and height of stratification" than with formulations of *relative social standing*, a concept equivalent to rank and used extensively in his works on *anomie.* The differential opportunities of achievement, an accompaniment of differential rank, is basic to the reasons behind the modes of adaptation examined above. Explicitly, rank is identified as one of the group properties identified by Merton. (See Addendum below).

Relative social standing of groups: Just as individuals are socially ranked in terms of prestige and access to opportunity for culturally valued returns, so with groups. Sociologists take it for granted that occupational statuses are evaluatively ranked and that occupants of these statuses tend to be correspondingly ranked. But we are somewhat more capricious in our research practice when it comes to incorporating systematic data on the relative rank of groups and organizations.[137]

Rank is an implicit component of another group property.

Degree of visibility or observability within the group: This property refers to the extent to which the norms and the role-performances within a group are readily open to observation by others (status-inferiors, peers, and status-superiors). It is a more extended idea than that which American sociologists have long described as "social visibility," meaning by this the degree to which the status-identity (especially of class, caste, race and ethnicity) of individuals are readily visible.[138]

No further purpose would be served by reiterating that for Merton, differential rank does exist as a component of the social structure. His greater interest in the subject lies in the processes by which rank evaluations take place and the consequent allocation of actors to similarly ranked status-roles.

Evaluation of actors and allocation of status-roles. Of immediate interest here is that type of reference group which Merton calls the *comparison type* which provides evaluative standards by which the individual evaluates himself and others on a comparative basis. The relativity of comparative standards provided by different reference groups is succinctly told in a half-century old citation from DuBois which Merton uses: "A white Philadelphian with $1,500 a year can call himself poor and live simply. A Negro with $1,500 a year ranks with the richest of his race and must usually spend more in proportion than his white neighbor in rent, dress and entertainment." [139] Both the "poor" white and the "rich" Negro in this case were obviously using different frames of reference than was the earlier reported "poor" man in Hollywood who complained of being snubbed because he only earned a thousand dollars a week!

Merton is well aware that sociological investigations are replete with appraisals, judgments, and evaluations which by their very nature are essentially comparative, as suggested by "varying terminologies such as promotion, assimilation (and acculturation), class strivings (and over-conformity), socialization, social deviation, renegadism, or again, relative deprivation, role conflict, cross-pressures, and false consciousness." [140] His reference group theory takes stock of these, but "aims to systematize the determinants and consequences of these processes of evaluation and self-appraisal in which the individual takes the values or standards of other individuals and groups as a comparative frame of reference." [141] It should be noted that although this section of the present chapter is devoted to the *evaluation of actors,* use of Merton's reference group theory requires that the *initial* evaluation is imputed *to* the reference group(s) *by* the actor as he is motivated to membership or non-membership, or to positive or negative attitudes toward it. It is only secondarily, by the understanding provided by the theory of the forces which affect his selection of reference group and of the patterns of his selection, that the evaluation *of* the actor (especially his rank evaluation in line with present purposes) is revealed. Finally, since both norm type and comparison type of reference group function is frequently represented by the identical reference group, the analysis of the norm type of reference group appearing above under evaluation is in many essentials applicable here. Repetitions will be avoided, however, and only those parts of Merton's presentation which are particularly applicable to rank considerations will be treated here.

Membership and non-membership in various reference groups

as well as positive and negative attitudes about them have various implications for the rank of an individual as well as for that of a group. A group's rank in terms of its power and influence is to some extent a function of its "completeness," a term borrowed by Merton from Simmel. Completeness is not to be confused with size; it simply refers to the inclusion as members of all who are eligible. Eligible non-members of course reduce a group's completeness. High group rank is more often associated with the completed closed group than the completed open group. Examples not taken from Merton, but which may be illustrative may be found in the open group of a labor organization whose power and influence is extended by the inclusion of all eligible members, but whose rank is in some ways low because of the inclusiveness of its membership. On the other hand, a closed group such as the Daughters of the American Revolution or a closed collectivity such as Pulitzer prize winners in some sense suffers an indignity of rank when membership is offered to those who are deemed eligible but who are motivated not to belong.

To Merton relative social standing (or rank) includes, but is not solely composed of, the relative value accorded occupational statuses or the hierarchically designated levels of position. This is exemplified by his re-study of *The American Soldier* in which he finds that although the institutional definition of a soldier's rank is precise as are his rights and duties befitting his institutional rank, the soldier perceived himself and others in relation to an array of reference groups much broader than that provided by his prescribed niche in the army. This is schematically presented in *Figure 4* which shows the many orientations of soldiers as revealed by excerpts from the original study of *The American Soldier*. The selection of the excerpts is based upon the use of the concept "relative deprivation" or the kindred concept, relative status.

Merton's concept of anticipatory socialization is introduced in connection with his reexamination of data included in *The American Soldier*. General acceptance of army life and military mores was the exception rather than the rule among these soldiers. Those individuals who conformed most nearly to the institutional norms of the army (and thereby conformed least to the norms of the immediate primary group composed of other en-

FIGURE 4

ATTRIBUTES OF INDIVIDUALS, SOCIAL CATEGORIES AND GROUPS TAKEN AS A
FRAME OF COMPARATIVE REFERENCE BY INDIVIDUALS *

In sustained so-cial relations with individual	Same Status	Different Social Status		
		Higher	Lower	Unranked
Yes—(member-ship- or in-group)	#1 married friends #2 non high school acquaintances #6 friends at same educational level	#5 offi-cers	#8, 9 Ne-gro civil-ians in South	#3 friends #7 acquaint-ances
	▲	▲	▲	▲
ORIENTATIONS OF INDIVIDUAL TO				
	▼	▼	▼	▼
No—(non-mem-bership or out-group)	#4 soldiers in U. S. or in active combat #6 soldiers of equal longevity #7 other captains	#5 offi-cers	#8, 9 Ne-gro civil-ians in South	

* The numbers refer to the appropriate excerpts *Social Theory and Social Struc-ture,* p. 228-9, which are here being provisionally classified.
SOURCE: Robert K. Merton, *Social Theory and Social Structure* (Glencoe, Ill.: The Free Press, 1957), p. 232.

listed men in their outfits) were in the parlance of their peers bucking for promotion. The actual incidence of promotions among those actors who were oriented to the army was higher (nineteen per cent) than among those oriented to their immediate membership group (twelve per cent). Merton concludes on the basis of theoretical implications which here can only be summar-ized that "For the individual who adopts the values of a group to which he aspires but does not belong, this orientation may serve the twin functions of aiding his rise into that group and of easing his adjustment after he has become part of it." [142]

Anticipatory orientation on the part of non-members to mem-bership in closed groups is a potential rank-increasing device in societies having high rates of social mobility.

In an open system, the positive orientation to non-membership groups will more often be rewarded by subsequent inclusion in the group; in a closed system, it will more often lead to frustrated aims and marginal status . . . open systems [thus] encourage a high rate and closed systems a low rate of positive reference to non-membership groups.[143]

Even in the open system, in terms of an individual's past history of class status, there are "significant differences of reference group behavior between those who are downwardly mobile, upwardly mobile or stationary in their class position." [144] Merton's examination of sociological works other than his own lends support to his thesis that non-membership group orientation tends to accompany realistic chances for social mobility.[145] Non-American examples not only reinforce his position but help somewhat to remove cultural bias. A sample of immigrants to Israel, for example, were found to select reference groups largely on their capacity to " 'confer some prestige in terms of the institutional structure of the society,' " [146] whereas in traditional and relatively socially immobile France there was little evidence of orientation to non-membership groups.[147] The definition of the system of stratification, then, is an important determinant in the selection or non-selection of comparison reference groups outside the strata to which an individual belongs. If the rigid stratification system is thought of as right and legitimate there will tend to be little cross-class comparison. If it is "under wide dispute" and hence not fully legitimized, cross-class comparisons may be expected. This accounts in Merton's mind, for the fact that dissatisfaction is often more frequently expressed by those who apparently are "better off" than by those who are apparently severely disadvantaged. The following oft-quoted statement from Merton presents a wide range of situations in which the dynamics of reference group comparisons and evaluations are obviously a prelude to social mobility.

An Army private bucking for promotion may only in a narrow and theoretically superficial sense be regarded as engaging in behavior different from that of an immigrant assimilating the values of a native group, or of a lower-middle-class individual conforming to his conception of upper-middle-class patterns of behavior, or of a boy in a slum area orienting himself to the values of a settlement house worker rather than the values of the street corner gang, or of a Bennington student abandoning the conservative beliefs of her parents to adopt the more liberal ideas of her college associates, or of a lower-class Catholic departing from the pattern of his in-group by casting a Republican vote, or of an eighteenth century French aristocrat aligning himself with a revolutionary group of the time.[148]

As to the problem of allocation of status-roles, Merton emphasizes that a "process of self-selection—both social and psychological—operates to reduce the prospects of random assortments of statuses." [149] The non-randomness of personnel recruitment, observable in connection with social science, has general applicability: "The higher the social standing of a discipline the more likely it will recruit able talents, the greater the measure of its financial support and the greater its actual accomplishments." [150] The same process which enables the organization to be selective in staff recruitment enables the individual to avoid the assumption of inconsistent status-roles; the self-elected hobo does not have to be an achievement-oriented striver; the "bureaucratic virtuoso" is rarely the upward mobile climber or the rebel.

In the organization of the bureaucratic prototype, role allocations are ideally made on the basis of examinations, technical qualifications and other formalized, impersonal procedures. Evaluations and promotions are made on the same basis.[151] (That the ideal bureaucratic behavior is not always operative is shown, as reported above, by the promotion policies in the army which is surely a bureaucratic organization. Merton reports: "Since the decision of the commanding officer regarding promotions was by no means based upon objective tests of capacity or performance by enlisted men, there was much occasion for interpersonal relations and sentiments to play their part in affecting this decision.")[152] The self-selection factor which prompts some kinds of individuals (the bureaucratic personality) to find work in bureaucracies, and which conversely, prompts some kinds of individuals (the intellectuals who are unwilling to be converted into "technicians") to get out of the bureaucracy once they stray into it, is also at work in other status-role allocations. Following Max Weber's lead, Merton finds for instance that pursuits which lead to empirical scientific endeavor recruit a disproportionately large number of pietistic Puritans. Status-sequences are equally important in allocation of status-role.

Presumably, there will be distinct shifts in reference individuals and role models as people move through sequences of statuses during their life cycle. This would again imply that much of such selection is not idiosyncratic but is patterned by structurally determined and statistically frequent career sequences, actual, anticipated or desired.[153]

CONTROLLING

The concepts treated under controlling, i.e., power, decision making, and initiation of action receive relatively less attention from Merton than those concepts heretofore considered in this chapter. Chapter 10, *Patterns of Influence* and the chapters devoted to bureaucracies, as well as reference group theory, are the richest sources for this material.

Power as an element. Merton follows Weber's concept of power as "the observed and predictable capacity for imposing one's will in a social action, even against the resistance of others taking part in that action." [154] Groups possess *"relative power,"* defined as the "varying capacity of a group to enforce its collective decisions upon (a) its members and (b) its social environment." [155] For Merton, power is not an "element" in the sense in which it is conceived as such in terms of the PAS Model. Rather it is a resultant of other group properties, the complexities of which Merton claims not to have fully explored. Despite this modest disclaimer, he is responsible for a sizable output of theoretical work on authority as well as a whole monograph [156] which is devoted to influence.

Merton defines authority as "the power of control which derives from an acknowledged status, inheres in the office and not in the particular person who performs the official role." [157] In the tradition of most modern sociologists, he views the prescribed and formalized relations which generally obtain in the bureaucratic organization as being integrated with the distribution of authority, and as performing the function of minimizing friction by restricting on-the-job contacts to an interactive pattern which is defined by the rules of the organization. His unique contributions to the understanding of the authority component emerge, however, from his analysis of reference group behavior as it is related to the social structure. Of the group properties believed to be most promising for further development of the reference group theory, the property of visibility or observability has an important, if not prime, place. It is in its elaboration that the chief connections are made between reference group theory and the authority component. (See the Addendum below.)

For Merton, the authority vested in an office is without hope of being effective if the agent administering it is not intimately cognizant of the norms operating within the group. Orders which violate the norms of the group in any essential way will be flouted or evaded. Although the authority figure must anticipate the normative reaction of the group which receives his orders and limit the exercise of his authority accordingly, it is also true that he is in a position to modify the norms within limits, to a greater degree than is true of his subordinates.[158] For Merton, it is a functional requirement for effective operation that the authority figure have adequate knowledge of group norms as well as a knowledge of individual role-performances. There are social mechanisms by which such knowledge is supplied to the authority figure and these Merton identifies.

1. *Differentials in communication.* Merton follows Homans in placing the authority figure at a nexus of two-way communication: " 'The higher a man's social rank, the larger will be the number of persons that originate interaction for him, either directly or through intermediaries.' And 'The higher a man's social rank, the larger the number of persons for whom he originates interaction, either directly or through intermediaries.' " [159] The authority figure is thus relatively advantaged in keeping abreast of group norms and group behavior. In fact, "Effective organization requires that those in authority be located at junctures in the network of communication where they are regularly apprised of the norms actually obtaining in the group." [160] Full visibility is itself limited, however, by the norms of the group. Authorities who exceed the normative limits by knowing too much of what is going on in the group generate hostility and institutionalized evasions of the rules of the organization. The excessive knowledge of the "organizational martinets" is dysfunctional. Merton suggests that "for various social structures, [there may well be] some *functionally optimum degree of visibility.*" [161]

2. *Differentials in motivation.* The authority figure seeks more information about the behavior of the group than does the rank and file member, because he is held accountable for its success. A kind of inquisitiveness is part of his job. Because he is accountable, subordi-

nates "clear" with the authority figure on any matters which are not routine, an acknowledgement of authority which prevails in informal as well as formal groups.

3. *Obstacles to visibility.* There are countervailing mechanisms at work which reduce visibility by authorities below the point which would obtain were only mechanisms 1 and 2 operative. The top levels of authority cannot observe all that needs to be known; lower echelons of authority also possess higher access to communication than the rank and file and are more highly motivated than *their* subordinates to keep informed (although less so than authorities above them). The authority of the intermediate levels would be threatened were there not obstacles to visibility which necessitates the flow of information through the lower and intermediate levels of authority to the top authority. Coupled with the isolation of top level authority by which interaction is restricted to near-equals, the filtering effect of information which reaches the high levels of authority usually results in a tolerable degree of visibility at that level.

4. *Social selection of personality types suited to maintain visibility.* Focusing his attention on the importance of the actors, Merton is interested in the extent to which *specific* personality attributes can be shown to be required for effective exercise of authority. Much of the literature on "leadership" he eschews as banal and unsuited to his purpose; much more that may have merit he has not examined and collated. What he does provisionally submit as a start in the right direction are personality characteristics identified by Shils [162] as functional requirements for effective exercise of authority. For present purposes, these need not be examined here.

Merton's contributions to the analysis of influence (as distinct from power) occur chiefly in his own study of influentials [163] in which he distinguishes between the *local* man of influence and the *cosmopolitan* man of influence, both of whom exert their influence in the community which he studied. Of immediate interest for the purposes of this section is his definition of "interpersonal influence [which] refers to the direct interaction of persons in so far as this affects the *future* behavior or attitude of participants (such that this differs from what it would have been in the absence of interaction)." [164] As such it describes an "*asymmetrical social relation*" which although not precluding reciprocal influence, usually tends toward a degree of influence which is stronger upon one of the actors than it is on the other. Further,

Merton concludes that "although they may be variously correlated, interpersonal influence, social class, prestige and power
do *not* coincide." [165] People high in power, such as a political
boss, may be low in prestige (or rank in terms of the PAS Model),
people high in prestige or rank may have little power, some members of the upper-middle-class may have great wealth but less
direct influence upon decisions of associates than more humble
people: "... *positions in the class, power, and prestige hierarchies contribute to the potential for interpersonal influence, but do
not determine the extent to which influence actually occurs.*" [166]

Decision making and initiation of action as processes. Decision making is viewed by Merton as a process which is the particular responsibility of those in authoritative positions. In view
of the strong normative content with which he vests authority
it is not surprising that his inquiries concerning decision making
should hinge upon the question of "how the social structure provides for those in authoritative positions to become informed
about the state of public opinion." [167] It behooves the "authoritative strata" to identify the values, norms, interests, and behavior
of those in other strata, just as the latter seek also to let the
authoritative strata know their minds. In the organization of
well-defined hierarchies or in the informal group with its efficient
channels of informal communication this inter-strata exchange
takes place subject to the mechanisms of visibility reviewed
above.

Important decisions are made by other authoritative strata,
however, in situations possessing neither hierarchical arrangements nor informal communication channels to an effective degree. Those responsible for decision making on the national or
state levels, in the case of America, are examples. Besides the
opinion poll, of importance here is the constituent's practice of
communicating by letter and telegram his reactions to issues
which are about to be decided. When such communications arrive *en masse* their sheer number may obscure rather than increase observability; nonetheless it serves as an imperfect index
of public sentiment, and "... this kind of observability provides
for *direct* communication with topmost authority without undermining the authority of intermediates." [168] Few decisions are un-
affected by any sizable showing of public support or the lack of it.

SANCTIONING

Sanction as an element. Like power, the concept sanction is generally treated by Merton as an aspect of norms. Unlike power, the concept sanction is not accorded a specific place in Merton's list of group properties. His references to sanctions are nonetheless sufficiently frequent to warrant a short treatment here.

The equilibrium between commitment to goal and commitment to institutionalized norms "is maintained so long as *satisfactions* accrue to individuals conforming to both cultural constraints." [169] The rewards to be reaped by the individual who strives toward success must lie in part in the sheer fact of participation whether or not all of his efforts are crowned by success. If the source of reward shifts solely to the successful outcome of competition, the unrewarded individual will in time work for a change in the institutionalized norms. "The sacrifices occasionally . . . entailed by conformity to institutional norms must be compensated by socialized rewards. The distribution of statuses through competition must be so organized that positive incentives for adherence to status obligations are provided *for every position* within the distributive order." [170] The promise of reward for the maintenance of culturally approved goals is an intrinsic part of American culture. There is also a correlative emphasis upon "the penalizing of those who draw in their ambitions. . . . The cultural manifesto is clear: one must not quit, must not cease striving, must not lessen his goals, for 'not failure, but low aim is crime.'" [171]

On less general levels of abstraction, Merton occasionally points out the rewards and punishments which obtain for certain types of organizations. Admittedly, the satisfactions or rewards which come from participation itself are somewhat strained as division of labor creates occupations which have no social significance outside of the department in which they are carried on. "What distinguishes the pride in work of a doughnut sugarer from that of a doughnut pumper, who successfully injects jelly into fried doughnuts with a jelly pump? To the outside world, these esoteric specializations are all of a piece and, consequently, for the outside world there must be other marks of status and significant work activity that count." [172]

The bureaucrat is expected devotedly to perform his official duties unmoved by extraneous pressures. For dutifully fulfilling this expectation he is rewarded by "security of tenure, pensions, incremental salaries and regularized procedures for promotion." [173] The scientist is expected to fulfill quite different expectations. "These imperatives, transmitted by precept and example and reenforced by sanctions are in varying degrees internalized by the scientist, thus fashioning his scientific conscience. . . ." [174] Deviation from the scientific ethos brings almost certain discovery and arouses moral indignation.

Application of sanctions as process. The point at which sanctions are actually applied is determined of course by the latitude allowed the deviant, an allowance which varies from group to group (i.e., patterned and even "institutionalized evasions"). Not only are sanctions invoked in different groups in response to different degrees of deviance, but the vehicles of sanction application vary widely. "At the one extreme, the delimited and officially promulgated norms are enforced by agents assigned this role; at the other the norms are enforced by the 'spontaneous' yet socially patterned responses of other members of the group, even though they have not been allocated specific roles for this purpose." [175]

On a less general level Merton provides an assortment of examples pertinent to the application of sanctions. Quoting Sutherland, he comments on the well documented prevalence of "white-collar criminality" among business men, most of whom have not been prosecuted either because their crimes were not detected or, "if detected, because of 'the status of the business man, the trend away from punishment, and the relatively unorganized resentment of the public against white-collar criminals.'" [176] Of a quite different order is the vilification which appears spontaneously and "primarily in affective terms of sentiment" by members of a group from which an erstwhile member seeks disinvolvement. In terms of reference group theory, group sanctions are directed against the member who is orienting himself to what at the time is a non-membership group for the deviant individual. "For since he is progressively seceding from the group and being penalized by it, he is the less likely to experience rewards for adherence to the group's norms." [177]

Merton cites as illustrative some of the data in *The American Soldier*. There it is reported that those few who are turning from group norms to official norms and are displaying a too zealous discharge of army mores are characterized by the sanctioning epithets of "brown-nosing, bucking for promotion, and sucking up." [178] Excerpts from the diary of an enlisted man are cited by Merton. They show affectively applied group sanctions as well as attempts at boundary maintenance:

[The over-zealous "defector" says] "But you're *supposed* to [work over there]. The lieutenant said you were supposed to." —this evokes group hostility expressed in epithets and ridicule—"Everybody is making sucking, kissing noises at K and S now. . . . Ostracism was visible, but mild . . . few were friendly toward them . . . occasions arose where people avoided their company . . . W, S and K sucked all afternoon; hung around lieutenants and asked bright questions." [179]

In a slightly different vein, Merton reports that sanctions are levelled against those who are overly devoted to membership group norms, those for whom Merton thinks the term "prig" is applicable.

a prig of low rank may be tolerated, if not liked, but a prig of high rank, standing to gain disproportionately by his insistence upon the letter of the norms will be twice condemned and hated; once because he does not temper the norm to the exigencies of the situation, and in this he is like others who fail to recognize that norms are only guidelines, and twice, because he profits by making a virtue of strict conformity. Only when he plainly loses by unqualified conformity to the norms he would enforce upon himself and others, is the man of established rank reluctantly and ambivalently admired. He is then defined as a man of principle, rather than a self-serving prig.[180]

The sanctions of disapproval are equally levelled at those who violate norms by under-conformity, as witnessed by the case of the scientist who does not observe the expectation that he communicate his findings fully and openly.

Layman though he is, Aldous Huxley's comment on Cavendish is illuminating in this connection: "Our admiration of his genius is tempered by a certain disapproval; we feel that such a man is selfish and anti-social." The epithets are particularly instructive for they imply the violation of a definite institutional imperative. Even though it serves no ulterior motive, the suppression of scientific discovery is condemned.[181]

The threat of negative sanctions can at times be as effective as their actual application. The sanctioning component as well as aspects of the power component are revealed in exchanges between management and organized labor.

Technology has been employed not only for the production of goods but also for the management of workmen. It has, in fact, been repeatedly defined as a weapon for subduing the worker by promising to displace him unless he accepts proffered terms of employment.[182]

Sanctions are invoked whether increased mechanization vs. high-priced labor is viewed as "the self-contained workings of the market" or as the nineteenth century doctrine: "when capital enlists science into her service the refractory hand of labor will always be taught docility." [183] For whatever rationale is elicited for the displacement of labor by machine, the result is sanctioning. "It is not only the sentiments of workers which are affected by technological change. It is not only their social ties and their status—it is also their incomes, their job chances, and their economic interests." [184] Such threats, as sanctions, may not work. "Quite conceivably it may be found that the exercise of naked power no more produces a stable structure of social relations in industry than in other spheres of human behavior." [185]

FACILITATING

Facility as an element. The concept of facility is clearly a minor one for Merton, although he is by no means unmindful of it. References to facilities which appear sporadically throughout his various monographs would seem to serve no real function here which cannot be served better by quoting a paragraph which sums up his contributions in this respect.

With increasing bureaucratization, it becomes plain to all who would see that man is to a very important degree controlled by his social relations to the instruments of production. This can no longer seem only a tenet of Marxism, but a stubborn fact to be acknowledged by all, quite apart from their ideological persuasion. Bureaucratization makes readily visible what was previously dim and obscure. More and more people discover that to work, they must be employed. For to work, one most have tools and equipment. And the tools and equipment are increasingly available only in bureaucracies, private or public. Consequently, one must be employed by the bureaucracies in order to have access to tools in order to work in order to live. It is in this sense that bureaucratization entails separation of individuals from the instruments of production, as in modern capitalistic enterprise or in state communistic enterprise (of the midcentury variety), just as in the post-feudal army, bureaucratization entailed complete separation from the instruments of destruction. Typically, the worker no longer owns his tools nor the soldier, his weapons. And in this special sense, more and more people become workers, either blue collar or white collar or stiff shirt. So develops, for example, the new type of scientific worker, as the scientist is "separated" from his technical equipment—after all, the physicist does not ordinarily own his cyclotron. To work at his research, he must be employed by a bureaucracy with laboratory resources.[186]

As is so often the case with Merton, he is less interested in establishing the fact of existence of a particular component (facilities in this case) than he is in delving into the complexities of social relationships associated with that component. Although he uses no such term as utilization of facilities, a short 1947 article entitled *The Machine, The Worker and the Engineer* [187] is devoted largely to examining the processes of social interaction as these are changed by machine utilization.

Utilization of facilities. For most people technological advance has become synonymous with progress and both tend to be regarded as an unadulterated good. There can be no question that in its wake comes about an increased capacity to produce goods, but against this desirable consequence must be weighed some of the social repercussions of technological change. Among the modifications of social relations regarded by Merton as consequential are "size and composition of the work team; the range, character, and frequency of contact with associates and supervisors, the status of the worker in the organization, the extent of physical mobility available to him . . ." [188] all of which affect employee satisfaction but which are often unanticipated and unregarded. The introduction of improved technologies, especially at *tempos* which preclude the possibility of gradual adjustment, may improve the competitive position of the firm at the expense of creating an environment of uncertainty, fear and hostility for the workers. The psychological investment which skilled workers have in the plying of their skills as well as the statuses which are theirs by virtue of their skills is wiped out by the *"enforced obsolescence of skills"* which comes with the utilization of labor-saving technology. Jobs whose meanings are known to only a few hold negligible rewards for their performer. These are but a few of the manifestations that

The interdependence of the industrial structure, tightened by applications of science to industry, infects the decisions of large industrial firms with the public interest. In consequence, government comes increasingly to regulate and to supervise these decisions, at least at the margins where they plainly affect the larger community.[189]

Technological facilities, especially new applications of science, are not merely methods of production; the consequences of their utilization are inescapably social. Whatever the engineers' specialties,

. . . so long as they are concerned with the design, construction, or operation of the equipments and processes of production, they are confronted with social and political implications of their position in our society . . . within our economic and social structure each technological contribution meshes into a cumulative pattern of effects, some of which none has desired and all have brought about.[190]

Scientists share with engineers what Merton has called an "ethical sense of limited responsibilities." [191] Both disclaim responsibility for having anything to say about how the discoveries made on the frontiers of knowledge (in the case of the scientist) or the processes of production (in the case of the engineer) are eventually utilized. Merton concurs with John Dewey that "we have to include consequences impartially; . . . It is willful folly to fasten upon some single end or consequence which is liked, and permit the view of that to blot from perception all other undesired and undesirable consequences." [192] Merton cites the TVA experience as a pioneering example of collaboration between engineers, or others oriented chiefly to the facilities of production, and social scientists oriented to the social structures and processes affected by the utilization of those facilities. In effect his proposal is for the extended utilization of social science to the end that general welfare be promoted by the most efficacious utilization of facilities of all kinds. "Just as men for centuries neglected the problem of soil erosion, in part because they were unaware that erosion constituted a significant problem, so they are still neglecting the social erosion ascribable to present methods of introducing rapid technological changes." [193]

COMPREHENSIVE OR MASTER PROCESSES

Communication. Both the communication of sentiment and the frequent references in the foregoing pages to the communication component contained in the group property of *"degree of visibility or observability"* have abundantly established the comprehensiveness of communication as a process in Merton's theoretical works. These need not be reiterated here, but some attention can be given at this point to Merton's investigations of radio and film propaganda. Propaganda as a form of communication is defined as "all sets of symbols which influence opinion, belief or action on issues regarded by the community as controversial." [194] The production of propaganda is intended, of course, to elicit an anticipated response. To the extent that it elicits, instead, the unexpected response it is failing in its purpose. Episodes in a propaganda film chosen to show the ruthlessness of the Nazi fails in its purposes if the episodes are interpreted as an example of Nazi efficiency. The reasons for failure of a given piece of propaganda to elicit the anticipated response are sought by the communications analyst. The following case is illustrative. A pamphlet designed to marshall the sentiments of American Negroes in the fight against Nazism chose two themes by which the message was to be conveyed: Negroes in the United States, despite continued discrimination, had made great strides in achieving individual success and in making social contributions; Hitler was quite clear about his contempt for Negroes so that if he were to be the victor, all Negro gains would be lost. The pamphlet itself was made up of one main article and of a large assortment of pictures, the article concentrating on the potential Negro losses under Hitler, the pictures concentrating on the bettered conditions of the Negro in the United States. Together they might be expected to elecit the desired effect. The propensity for "readers" to look at pictures whether they read the article or not, and this particularly marked tendency among Negroes of a generally lower educational level, caused the pictured theme of Negro achievements in the United States to get across, but the article's theme of the dangers of a Hitler victory to be lost. Propaganda analysis, then, is devoted to isolating the key themes and symbols by a process of content analysis. A more precise forecast of response to propaganda than would otherwise be the case, is the aim as well as an improved propaganda output.

Merton distinguishes between the propaganda of sentiment and the propaganda of "facts." Informational communication about complex events can be facilitated by propaganda techniques. *"The concrete incident, rich in circumstantial detail, serves as a prototype or model which helps orient people toward a part of the world in which they live. It has orientation-value."* [195] Merton suggests that the need for morale-builders is not outlived, that common values and common attitudes still need to be established and maintained. Effective communication which does not run counter to events is important in this process because "it can serve to root both policy and action in the understandings of the people." [196]

Boundary maintenance. Although not used as a concept, Merton's interest in social cohesion makes the phenomenon of boundary maintenance an important one. One of the "group-properties" is *"Types and degrees of social cohesion."* Three types are identified, of which the last is especially important in connection with boundary maintenance:

a) Culturally induced social cohesion: resulting from common norms and values internalized by members of the group;
b) Organizationally induced social cohesion: resulting from realization of personal and group goals through the interdependent activities of others in the group;
c) Social cohesion induced by the structural context; resulting, for example, from the contrasts of in-groups and out-groups, conflicts with other groups, and the like.[197]

A second group property is similarly pertinent: *"The potential of fission or unity of a group,"* a property which describes processes remindful of systemic linkage and boundary maintenance as those concepts are employed in the PAS Model. In this connection Merton's position on the error of functional unity seems to be pertinent. Whether the boundary that is being maintained is that of family, of community, of religious group, or whatever, the overweening commitment to the particular group in question means under-commitment to groups of societal importance which compete for the loyalty of the family members, community members, religious group members, as the case may be. Thus, the integrating force of any one example of boundary maintenance must be interpreted from a clearly specified reference point. The boundaries maintained by religious groups, functional though they be for that particular group, may be societally dysfunctional as witnessed by "the entire history of religious wars, of the Inquisition (which drove a wedge into society after society), of internecine conflicts among religious groups." [198]

What Merton has to say about the boundaries between professional fields is applicable to other activities. Further, like the concepts, unity and fission, this consideration underscores the relationship between what is here called boundary maintenance and systemic linkage. In Merton's view the only part of a profession that is firmly fixed is "a hard core of activities and functions that are uniquely the special competence of one profession," [199] such as surgery for the surgeon, trial supervision for the judge, absolution granting for the priest. Much else lies in a "zone of ambiguity," a zone over which conflicts arise between adjacent occupations. Redefinition and transfer of professional functions come about through "(1) the growth of knowledge underlying each profession; (2) the changing social definitions of human problems and of the skills needed to cope with them; (3) newly emerging demands and expectations of the clientele served by the professions, and (4) the competitive interplay between the professions themselves." [200] Resistance to the transfer of duties to adjacent professions will not be uniform. Low ranked duties will be gladly turned over; highly prized duties will, upon transfer, be regarded as a "virtual amputation" and will be the subject of many boundary maintaining disputes before the transfer is accomplished. "One thing alone seems reasonably clear: if this unceasing process of transfer of functions in the zone of ambiguity is to benefit society, there must be enduring liaisons between adjacent professions and occupations." [201]

Systemic linkage. Such "enduring liaisons" are but one evidence of Merton's attention to the process which in terms of the PAS Model is called systemic linkage, a term not specifically used by Merton. In expanding his idea that once differentiation has occurred some form of linkage must follow, he draws a parallel between the United Nations which "provides a forum for the expression of conflicting interests and values" and interprofessional councils which provide for "the public review of issues among adjacent professions." [202] The fact of systemic linkage by whatever name is too well documented in the above pages to bear repetition here. Merton's concepts of role-set and status-set, of closed or open groups, of membership and non-membership groups, and of subgroup and encompassing group all attest in their elaborations to the assumption of group interconnectedness. Attention will therefore be limited at this point to representative examples of the linking process.

Often the process is planned, rational and *Gesellschaft*-like. Both the United Nations and the interprofessional council mentioned above are examples of systemic linkage which requires a sort of planned diplomacy by which compromises in the name of peace, or efficiency or co-existence are effected. "With all their limitations, diplomats are as necessary to interprofessional relations as they are to international relations." [203] Similar in that it is planned and rational (and perhaps possessing no less need for diplomacy) are those communication hubs in the bureaucratic hierarchy whereby the upper echelons of authority are effectively linked with the rank and file as was reported above in connection with power. Of a different order are those rationally conceived redefinitions which move groups from the closed to open category. The bi-racial housing project, for example, supplanting the idea of the closed segregated community, becomes a vehicle for systemic linkage, as does the redefinition of union membership eligibility when re-cast to include Negroes as potential members.

Other examples of systemic linkage are less planned, more informal and *Gemeinschaft*-like in nature. One such example is provided by the linkages effected by the political machine.

The machine welds its link with ordinary men and women by elaborate networks of personal relations. Politics is transformed into personal ties. . . . Holding the strings of diverse governmental divisions, bureaus and agencies in his competent hands, the Boss rationalizes the relations between public and private business. He serves as the business community's ambassador in the otherwise alien (and sometimes unfriendly) realm of government. . . . Since the machine serves both the businessman and the criminal man, the two seemingly antipodal groups intersect.[204]

The cosmopolitan influential serves as a systemic linkage mechanism too. Although he belongs to the community upon which he informally exerts his influence, he is in another sense a member of a non-geographic community of the better-informed, the less judgmental, the more tolerant. Merton concurs with Riesman that

Cosmopolitans who take on positions of formal leadership in the community . . . may be obliged to become middlemen of tolerance, as they are caught between the upper millstone of the tolerant élite and the nether one of the intolerant majority, and thus become shaped into being less tolerant than their former associates and more so than their constituency." [205]

Institutionalization. The concept of institutionalization as used by Merton is important not only because expected behavior is thereby defined, but also because as a process it bridges the cultural and social planes. This latter function must be understood before its relation to predictable behavior can be clear. At no point in Merton's writings is the subject of institutionalization systematically dealt with, but the composite impression created by frequent allusions to the process and to its results justifies the following analysis which is supported by interviews with the author in which printed works were generously supplemented with lecture and manuscript material on the subject.

Merton conceptualizes a three-fold breakdown, initially represented by the familiar two-category division of the social and the cultural. The first may be represented by a social system and its subsystems which may for example be a society and its parts, in which socially patterned interaction takes place between individuals occupying structured roles and statuses. The second division, culture, he sees as possessing a content which is the resultant of man's activity represented in value objects (which in a sense are artifacts) which can be transmitted from generation to generation and diffused. A special class of such transmitted cultural items which constitutes the third division are those cultural items which define the social structure: the norms which define statuses, the norms which define roles, the norms which define relative positions.

Any such cultural value, a goal for example, holds significance for very widespread, although perhaps unevenly spread, populations. The success value, or money value in the American culture, is an example of a cultural goal often used by Merton. To the degree that it is shared by sizable numbers of people as a basis for interaction it becomes an *institutionalized* goal and as such becomes part of the social structure. The very fact that numerous individuals address their relations to others in terms of a shared goal demonstrates its institutionalization. Some individuals will have so internalized the goal that its pursuit is an integral and unquestioned part of life's meaning. Others who have not internalized the goal may pursue it none the less, for reasons of expediency. The goal's institutionalized state is attested to by the very distinction of attitudes toward it. Even those who have not internalized it may recognize it and pattern their relations to others in terms of it.

Similarly, norms have a cultural base; on the cultural plane they formulate types of behavior which widespread populations find significant as definitions of the behavior that ought to be. To the degree that they become definitions of *expected* behavior in social interaction they are *institutionalized* as part of the social structure. The very fact that numerous individuals accept as reasonable and right the expectation that behavior be conducted in compliance with the normative definition constitutes its institutionalization. Some individuals will have accepted it as expected behavior because they have internalized it; the attitude of others may be acceptance for expedient reasons only. Their very acceptance despite their somewhat negative attitude toward it substantiates its institutionalization. The sequence from cultural formulation or definition to institutionalized expectation moves next to actual behavior which often may be a departure from expectations. However, the very recognition of unexpected be-

havior as being deviant again testifies to the degree of institutionalization which has been accorded a norm in a given system or
subsystem.

Another cluster of culturally based norms defines the social
structure in terms of roles, statuses, and relative position. These
too become *institutionalized* as legitimate "rights, perquisites, and
obligations" appropriate to the differential positions involved in
social interaction. The basic theme of Merton's treatment of
anomie hinges upon opportunities and situations which are institutionalized as being differential as these are juxtaposed by the
affected individuals against goals and norms which are institutionalized as being uniform or nearly uniform.

The process of institutionalization itself comes about partly in
response to the resultant stresses. Dysfunctional as are the stresses
for the then existing social system, such mechanisms of adaptation as institutionalized evasion and innovation "may result in the
formation of new institutionalized patterns of behavior which are
more adaptive than the old in making for realization of primary
goals." [206] The concept of institutionalization as an on-going process by which non-conforming behavior, to the degree that it is
adaptively superior, gradually supplants the old institutions to be
in turn institutionalized as conforming behavior is a key process
responsible for social change.

Socialization. Merton's definition of socialization is in the current sociological tradition.

. . . the technical term socialization designates the processes by which
people selectively acquire the values and attitudes, the interest, skills,
and knowledge—in short, the culture—current in the groups of which
they are, or seek to become, a member. It refers to the learning of
social roles.[207]

Merton sees the family as "a major transmission belt for the diffusion of cultural standards to the oncoming generation." [208] Since
each family has relatively unlimited access only to that part of the
culture relegated to its own social stratum, the child is accordingly
socialized to the cultural goals and norms characteristic of a narrow range of the total society. He incorporates social patterns
and attributes not only by direct training and disciplining but also
by exposure to social prototypes. Merton believes that "*children*

*detect and incorporate cultural uniformities even when these re-
main implicit and have not been reduced to rules.*" [209] He cites
as corroborative evidence the persistent language errors of children which show children's sensitivities to uniformities. Terms
such as "mouses," "moneys," "falled," "runned," "singed," and so
forth, in Merton's opinion indicate a detection of certain speech
uniformities which have not been taught. Merton tentatively in-
fers that the child "is also busily engaged in *detecting and acting
upon the implicit paradigms of cultural evaluation, and categorization of people and things, and the formation of estimable goals*
as well as assimilating the explicit cultural orientation set forth
in an endless stream of commands, explanations and exhortations
by parents." [210]

It is typical of Merton that, starting with the generally subscribed to idea of socialization, he has enlarged and expanded it
to include what he has termed "anticipatory socialization," to
which mention was made above under evaluation. On the basis
of the application of reference group theory to the data of *The
American Soldier* Merton proffers hypotheses concerning anticipatory socialization, or orientation to the values of a non-membership group. Anticipatory socialization may serve the function of
aiding the individual's rise into the non-membership group; it
may also serve the function of easing his adjustment to the group
after he has in fact become a member. He posits conditions under
which such functions may obtain, the chief one being that the
total social structure be a relatively open-class structure. He
further suggests that the social structure renders support to the
phenomenon of anticipatory socialization by providing status-
sequences. Although it may not be known which specific individuals in lower hierarchical statuses will move on to the upper
hierarchical statuses, the inevitability of status-sequence for some
individuals is a structurally provided mechanism for anticipatory
socialization. Merton's original work on *The American Soldier* led
him to postulate that although anticipatory socialization may be
functional for the *individual* in an open social system it apparently
is dysfunctional for the solidarity of the group which he is re-
nouncing, his old membership group. Consistent with his later
relating of anticipatory socialization to status-sequence, he concurs with the suggestion of the present authors [211] that some

groups profit by the "upstairs" move of their successful members, a transfer of membership which may provide the original group with a particularly effective systemic linkage with high levels of authority.

It is wise to emphasize that Merton's hypotheses about anticipatory socialization as it relates to the individual and to the social structure are conjectural and tentative. He specifies a number of problems which must be explored before more definitive statements concerning them can be made. An arresting problem in this connection revolves around the degree of conscious aspiration represented by anticipatory socialization. Does the individual orient himself to the higher ranking group simply because the values of that group seem to him to be superior, with no conscious thought of aspiring to membership? Or does he deliberately adopt the non-membership group values on the chance that he will be accepted into it? [212] Although Merton does not specify the probable structural impacts which would accompany the prevalence of either possibility it would seem that wide-spread orientation to a higher ranking group without thought of personal membership might in time visibly obscure class distinctions. It also suggests that although the army (as portrayed in *The American Soldier*) is a strategic research site for the development of initial hypotheses and for a limited amount of testing of their validity (certainly many of Merton's insightful "hunches" stem from this source), it is equally true that the involuntary nature and relatively short duration of army "membership" requires that hypotheses developed on the basis of army behavior be tested in more stable groups. This Merton foresaw even at the time of developing his reference group theory on the basis of army life. Other investigations by him have served to extend and refine those initial impressions; the socialization of the student physician is a case in point.

As the adult medical student is socialized to the status-role of physician Merton perceives two broad categories of factors which contribute to the process: "direct learning through didactic teaching of one kind or another, and indirect learning, in which attitudes, values, and behavior patterns are acquired as by-products of contact with instructors and peers, with patients, and with members of the health team." [213] It is the latter "less conspicu-

ous and more easily neglected processes of indirect learning"
toward which Merton directs primary attention. He finds that
medical students acquire the attitudes and value components of
the physician's role not only (and perhaps not as enduringly)
from formalized instruction but also from sustained relationship
with the medical staff, fellow student physicians and patients.
The many influences leading to the finished product of practicing
physician ranging from early role models to medical school philosophies containing built-in areas of uncertainty to which students
must adjust, deserve first-hand examination for an understanding
of a remarkably broad sociological view of the process of socialization.

Social control. Social control as a process is intimately bound
to norms and sanctions. Its operation is implicit throughout all of
Merton's work, although it is rarely treated *per se.* A glance at its
implicit treatment in the preceding pages will recall the controls
evoked in the form of moral indignation—the outraged sentiments
against deviation from norms experienced by those not immediately engaged in interaction with the offending individual and
therefore defined as cultural.

Were it not for this reservoir of moral indignation, the mechanisms of
social control would be severely limited in their operation. They
would be confined only to the action of people who are *directly* disadvantaged by nonconformist and deviant behavior . . . [In fact] moral
indignation and disinterested opposition to nonconformity and deviant
behavior serve to lend greater strength to the mechanisms of social
control . . .[214]

Also the importance of the property of visibility in the process
of social control will be recalled, especially as authority figures
are responsible for controls over role performance and other
normative requirements on the part of subordinates. In Merton's
view such social control cannot function unless the actual (not
the assumed) norms of the group and the actual (not the assumed) role performance of its members are visible in a maximally
efficient degree to the authority figures. The structural nature of
social control as seen by Merton is expressed in this typical excerpt:

For operating social structures must somehow manage to organize these sets and sequences of statuses and roles so that an appreciable degree of social order obtains, sufficient to enable most of the people most of the time to go about their business of social life without having to improvise adjustments anew in each newly confronted situation.[215]

CONDITIONS OF SOCIAL ACTION

Territoriality. Territoriality, as a condition of social action, is not treated at any great length by Merton. However, there are two studies in particular in which territoriality emerges as a condition which affects the outcome. The different territorial orientations largely accounts for the difference in the pattern of influence exerted by the cosmopolitan influential from that exercised by the local influential. While the area of impact in both cases is almost exclusively the community of which both are members, the content of the influence reflects the territorial range which is of greatest significance to the two types of influentials. The localite's interests are primarily confined to the community, but the cosmopolitan "is oriented significantly to the world outside . . . and regards himself as an integral part of that world." [216] Territoriality plays no less a part in friendship patterns; not only physical propinquity but the spatial orientations of the buildings in which people live determines to a marked degree the selection of friends.

Clearly, quite apart from other factors, sheer propinquity played a major part in determining the patterns of personal association. Upon examining the location of friends of people living in each zone, we noticed the curious fact that one spatial pattern of friendship was consistently related to residence [orientations] . . . 74 per cent [of the friendships reported] involves cases in which *both* the informant and his friend live in street-oriented dwellings.[217]

Accordingly, Merton specifies what is here called territoriality as one of the group properties which he provisionally lists:

Ecological structure of the group: This refers primarily to the one ecological variable of the spatial distribution of the members of a group. . . . It is evident that groups differ in this respect: the members may be spatially adjacent and highly concentrated or widely separated and thinly dispersed. Recent studies of this property uniformly show that the extent of spatial and functional propinquity affects the formation of social relations, the types of social control, and the degree of involvement of members with the group. It is presumably related also to the observability of role-performance.[218]

Size of group. Merton specifies two group properties which are devoted to this concept, the *absolute* size of a group, or of its component parts, and the *relative* size of a group, or of its component parts. He emphasizes that the two properties must be explicitly distinguished from each other. The failure to make such a distinction can seriously affect the interpretation of statistical data. One such example is reported by Merton as he deals with Hyman's re-analysis of data in terms of the *anomie* paradigm. Essentially, Hyman's position hinges upon his findings that a successively smaller proportion of individuals are committed to cultural goals as each descending status level is examined. The inadequacy of the position, in Merton's view, lies in Hyman's failure to stipulate the absolute size of each status contingent. Since the absolute number of the upper class is small, a very high proportion of goal commitment by that group could in fact represent a very small number so committed. Since the absolute number of the lower class is large, a relatively small proportion of commitment to goals by that group could in fact represent a fairly large group so committed. In this case, *"it is not the relative proportions of the several social classes adopting the cultural goal of success that matter, but their absolute numbers."* [219] Neither absolute number nor relative number means much by itself as a condition of social action; both must be placed in the perspective provided by the conjunction of the two group properties.

This is to say, that groups or organizations of the same relative size will function differently depending upon their absolute size, and correlatively, groups of the same absolute size will function differently depending upon their size relative to other groups in the social environment.[220]

Time. In view of the contemporary accent on social change and the disposition on the part of some to stake off as a latter day event the attention currently devoted to the subject, it is instructive to note the early attention devoted thereto by Merton and to be sensitized to its pervasive presence in his works. In his earliest use of functional analysis [221] his recognition of time as a condition of social action merely reinforced an already long-standing interest in social change reflected in the socio-historical studies which constitute his first writings. Merton has remained the functional analyst and as such is irrevocably committed to a study of the dynamics of social change no less than to the stabilities of social structures. Merton takes the position that functional analysis, like any other theoretical orientation poses *intrinsic* ideological commitment neither to "the glorification of the existing state of things" nor to its debasement. As a theoretical orientation it is neither conservative nor radical although diametrically opposed ideological implications have been imputed to it. His attack on the position of those who would infuse a framework of systematic inquiry with extraneous ideological orientations deserves a more careful scrutiny than can be given here. Those excerpts most pertinent to the immediate subject of time and change may encourage the reader to pursue the original in its entirety.

This more exacting form of functional analysis includes, not only a study of the *functions* of existing social structures, but also a study of their *dysfunctions* for diversely situated individuals, subgroups or social strata, and the more inclusive society. It provisionally assumes, as we shall see, that when *the net balance of the aggregate of consequences* of an existing social structure is clearly dysfunctional, there develops a strong and insistent pressure for change.

By focusing on dysfunctions as well as on functions, this mode of analysis can assess not only the bases of social stability but the potential sources of social change. To the extent that functional analysis focuses wholly on functional consequences, it leans toward an ultra-conservative ideology; to the extent that it focuses wholly on dysfunctional consequences, it leans toward an ultra-radical utopia. "In its essence," it is neither one nor the other.

As we survey the course of history, it seems reasonably clear that all major social structures have in due course been cumulatively modified or abruptly terminated. In either event, they have not been eternally fixed and unyielding to change. But, at a given moment of observation, any such social structure may be tolerably well accommodated both to the subjective values of many or most of the population, and to the objective conditions with which it is confronted. To recognize this is to be true to the facts, not faithful to a preestablished ideology. And by the same token, when the structure is observed to be out of joint with the wants of the people or with the equally solid conditions of action, this too must be recognized. Who dares do all that, may become a functional analyst, who dares do less is none.[222]

Merton deals with directed change as well as that inexorable and unplanned change which occurs with the passage of time. The former in the hands of the "social engineer" is doomed to failure in Merton's opinion unless the concepts of manifest and latent functions or their equivalents are taken into account. His most telling analysis is in connection with illegitimate enterprises which the social engineer may be tempted to "outlaw." So long as the illegitimate activity is regarded by any sizable number as performing a function, any attempt at political reform is typically shortlived and ineffectual. *"To seek social change, without due recognition of the manifest and latent functions performed by the social organization undergoing change, is to indulge in social ritual rather than social engineering."* [223]

As a source of social change, Merton regards as of prime importance the strains and tensions between the cultural expectations and the social realities. The modes of nonconforming adaptation frequently referred to in the above pages are in reality non-modal alternatives employed by the minority, which may in time supplant the conforming adaptations, and are likely to do so to the degree that they are functionally superior for greater numbers of the population than presently employed behavior patterns. Once having made the point that functionalism (or dysfunctionalism) and social change are inextricably bound, Merton is too good a craftsman to reiterate his thesis constantly. He credits his reader's ability to see that change no less than stability is the essence of shifting membership groups, of bureaucracies whose regulations come to signify meanings not originally intended, of institutionalized means of counteracting minority group inequities, and of innumerable other social phenomena which possess stable as well as changing structural components in an inevitably changing world.

ADDENDUM

Merton's "Provisional Group-Properties" as Related to Elements and Processes. This listing of Merton's "group properties" [224] (appearing below in quotation) is set forth here in relation to the concepts of the PAS Model (appearing in italics) in order to provide a consolidated and succinct comparison for reference purposes.

1. "Clarity or vagueness of social definitions of membership in the group." *Boundaries* as related to both *Boundary Maintenance* and *Systemic Linkage*.

2. "Degree of engagement of members in the group." The element of *Sentiment* articulated through the process of *Communication of Sentiment* and the element of *Norm* articulated by the process of *Evaluation*.

3. "Actual duration of membership in the group." The condition of *Time*.

4. "Expected duration of membership in the group." The element of *Status-role* (as member) and the process of *Allocation of Status-roles*, i.e., memberships; and the element of *Belief (knowledge)*.

5. "Actual duration of the group." (*Same as 3 above.*)

6. "Expected duration of the group." (*Same as 4 above.*)

7. "Absolute size of a group or of component parts of a group." The condition, *Size*. Size to the extent that it is controlled is omitted from elements and conditions. As a group property it is more concrete than are elements to which it is related, such as power.

8. "Relative size of a group, or of component parts of a group." (*Same as 7.*)

9. "Open or closed character of a group." *Boundary and Boundary Maintenance;* in some respects *Status-roles* and *Allocation of Status-roles*.

10. "'Completeness': ratio of actual to potential members." (*Same as 9.*)

11. "Degree of social differentiation." Element of *Rank* and *Evaluation as a Process in Ranking*.

12. "Shape and height of stratification." (*Same as 11.*)

13. "Types and degrees of social cohesion." Merton specifies three types: a) "culturally induced social cohesion: resulting from common norms and values internalized by members of the group." The element *Norm*, as indicated in the discussion above is a sponge or global term which through the process of evaluation and "application of sentiment" may be attached to any item. It

may include *Ends, Beliefs* to which commitment is given, *Status-roles, Facilities,* in fact all the elements. b) "Organizationally induced social cohesion: resulting from realization of personal and group goals through the interdependent activities of others in the group." Consensus with respect to *Ends* and *Goal Attainment.* c) "Social cohesion induced by the structural context: resulting, for example, from contrasts of in-groups and out-groups, conflicts with other groups, and the like." Consensus with respect to *Boundary Maintenance.*

14. "The potential of fission or unity of a group." *Boundaries* and the processes of *Systemic Linkage* and *Boundary Maintenance.*

15. "Extent of social interaction within the group." *Goal Attainment* and *'Latent' Activity as Process.* All the other elemental processes are involved here.

16. "Character of the social relations obtaining in the group. This property has traditionally been . . . the major one distinguishing various types of groups . . . primary and secondary groups, in-group and out-group, *Gemeinschaft* and *Gesellschaft,* formal and informal group, etc. It is in connection with this property, also, that Parsons has developed his well-known system of pattern variables." The element *Norm* and the process of *Evaluation* provide the closest, albeit imperfect, parallel here.

17. "Degree of expected conformity to norms of group: toleration of deviant behavior and institutionalized departures from strict definition of group-norms." The element of *Norm* articulated by the process of *Evaluation;* the element, *Sanction* and the process *Application* of *Sanctions.*

18. "The system of normative controls." The process of *Social Control* as mediated through *Norms, Sanctions* and *Sentiment.*

19. "Degree of visibility or observability within the group." The process of *Communication.*

20. "Ecological structure of the group." The condition of *Territoriality,* in so far as space is not controlled by the pertinent system.

21. "Autonomy or dependence of the group." *Boundaries* and *Boundary Maintenance* as related to *Systemic Linkage* and *Power.*

22. "Degree of stability of the group." *Boundary Maintenance.*

23. "Degree of stability of the structural context of the group." (*Same as 22.*)

24. "Modes of maintaining stability of the group, and of the structural context." (*Same as 22.*)

25. "Relative social standing of groups." The group as used in this sense is an actor. Social standing is covered by the element, *Rank.*

26. "Relative power of groups." The element, *Power.*

BIBLIOGRAPHICAL KEY *

FSP—Paul F. Lazarsfeld and Robert K. Merton, "Friendship as Social Process: A Substantive and Methodological Analysis," in Morroe Berger, Theodore Abel, and Charles H. Page, eds., *Freedom and Control in Modern Society* (New York: D. Van Nostrand Co., Inc., 1954).

PF—Robert K. Merton, "Introduction: Notes on Problem-Finding in Sociology," in Robert K. Merton, Leonard Broom, Leonard S. Cottrell, Jr., eds., *Sociology Today: Problems and Prospects* (New York: Basic Books, Inc., 1959).

PSD—Robert K. Merton, "Priorities in Scientific Discovery: A Chapter in the Sociology of Science," *American Sociological Review*, Vol. 22, December, 1957.

RS—Robert K. Merton, "The Role-Set: Problems in Sociological Theory," *The British Journal of Sociology*, Vol. 8, June, 1957.

SCDOS—Robert K. Merton, "Social Conformity, Deviation and Opportunity Structures," *American Sociological Review*, Vol. 24, April, 1959.

SP—Robert K. Merton, George G. Reader, and Patricia L. Kendall, *The Student-Physician: Introductory Studies in the Sociology of Medical Education* (Cambridge, Mass.: Harvard University Press, 1957).

SPH—Robert K. Merton, "The Social Psychology of Housing," in a symposium on *Current Trends in Social Psychology* (Pittsburgh: University of Pittsburgh Press, 1948).

SSME—Robert K. Merton, Samuel Bloom and Natalie Rogoff, "Studies in the Sociology of Medical Education," *Journal of Medical Education*, Vol. 31, August, 1956.

STSS—Robert K. Merton, *Social Theory and Social Structure* (Glencoe, Ill.: The Free Press, 1957, rev. and enlarged ed.).

NOTES

1. Robert K. Merton, *Social Theory and Social Structure* (Glencoe, Ill.: The Free Press, 1957, rev. and enlarged ed.). Hereafter referred to as STSS.
2. *Ibid.,* p. 3.   3. *Ibid.,* pp. 46-47.
4. *Ibid.,* p. 89.

* For a more extensive bibliography including unabbreviated items see the notes which follow and the bibliographical appendix at the end of the volume.

5. *Ibid.,* pp. 89-93. In this connection it is observed as a truism that "if concepts are selected such that no relationships between them obtain, the research will be sterile." It must be assumed that this statement is not to be taken literally. What is no doubt meant is that the concepts should be related in the paradigm or in the mind of the investigator. At another point in his works it is observed that failure to report negative findings leads to various biases and much is made of discoveries resulting when the original formulation reveals no relationships.

6. Robert K. Merton, "Social Conformity, Deviation and Opportunity Structures," *American Sociological Review,* Vol. 24, No. 2, April, 1959, p. 177. Hereafter referred to as SCDOS.

7. See, for example, Robert K. Merton and Paul F. Lazarsfeld, eds., *The American Soldier* (Glencoe, Ill.: The Free Press, 1950), pp. 40-106; Robert K. Merton, "Introduction: Notes on Problem-Finding in Sociology," in Robert K. Merton, Leonard Broom, Leonard S. Cottrell, Jr., eds., *Sociology Today: Problems and Prospects* (New York: Basic Books, Inc., 1959), pp. ix-xxxiv (hereafter referred to as PF); and Paul F. Lazarsfeld and Robert K. Merton, "Friendship as Social Process: A Substantive and Methodological Analysis," in Morroe Berger, Theodore Abel, and Charles H. Page, eds., *Freedom and Control in Modern Society* (New York: D. Van Nostrand Co., Inc., 1954) Chapter II (hereafter referred to as FSP).

8. STSS, p. 104 ff. See also Bernard Barber and Renée C. Fox, "The Case of the Floppy-eared Rabbits: An Instance of Serendipity Gained and Serendipity Lost," *The American Journal of Sociology,* Vol. 64, No. 2, September, 1958, pp. 128-136.

9. STSS, p. 55. Merton's 11-point paradigm for functional analysis remains the classic in the field. The investigator's descriptive protocol is summarized as follows: "1) location of participants in the pattern within the social structure—differential participation; 2) consideration of alternative modes of behavior excluded by emphasis on the observed pattern (i.e., attention not only to what occurs but also to what is neglected by virtue of the existing pattern); 3) the emotive and cognitive meanings attached by participants to the pattern; 4) a distinction between the motivations for participating in the pattern and the objective behavior involved in the pattern; 5) regularities of behavior not recognized by participants but which are nonetheless associated with the central pattern of behavior." STSS, p. 60. Merton's interest in the development of taxonomies and typologies tends to be limited by their utility in leading to propositions about behavior, an issue which is at the core of his exchange with Dubin. SCDOS, p. 186.

10. PF, pp. ix-xxxiv.

11. Robert K. Merton, "The Role-Set: Problems in Sociological Theory," *The British Journal of Sociology,* Vol. 8, June, 1957, p. 108. Hereafter referred to as RS.

12. STSS, pp. 5-6.

13. Robert K. Merton, "Discussion of Talcott Parsons' 'The Position of Sociological Theory'," *American Sociological Review,* Vol. 13, No. 2, April, 1948, p. 166. See virtually the same statement in STSS, p. 9.

14. STSS, p. 10.   15. *Ibid.,* pp. 132-133.

16. Robert K. Merton, George G. Reader and Patricia L. Kendall, *The Student-Physician: Introductory Studies in the Sociology of Medical Educa-*

tion (Cambridge, Mass.: Harvard University Press, 1957), p. 57 (hereafter referred to as SP). See also STSS, p. 162.

17. "Site is used here in a somewhat special sense which includes the idea of 'research target'."

18. Robert K. Merton, "Social Conflict Over Styles of Sociological Work," paper presented at the Fourth World Congress of Sociology, September, 1959, Stresa, Italy. For further discussion of strategic empirical data see: Merton, PF, pp. xxiii, xxix, xxx. For a brief list of examples of utilization of strategic research sites for examining theoretical problems, see PF, pp. xxvi and xxix; also STSS, pp. 124-125.

19. PF, p. xxiv.   20. STSS, p. 124.

21. Robert K. Merton, "The Social Psychology of Housing," in a symposium on *Current Trends in Social Psychology* (Pittsburgh: University of Pittsburgh Press, 1948), p. 23 ff. Hereafter referred to as SPH.

22. For a discussion of crucial experiments see Irving M. Copi, *Introduction to Logic* (New York: The Macmillan Co., 1953), pp. 417-425.

23. The strongest statement in favor of functional analysis of social systems is made in a favorable appraisal of data available in *The American Soldier,* one of the few places where the term social system is used repeatedly. STSS, Chapter VIII.

24. SP, p. 42. See also SP, p. 39, p. 44, p. 77.

25. Robert K. Merton, "Priorities in Scientific Discovery: A Chapter in the Sociology of Science," *American Sociological Review,* Vol. 22, No. 6, December, 1957, p. 659. Hereafter referred to as PSD.

26. Charles P. Loomis, *Social Systems: Essays on Their Persistence and Change* (Princeton, New Jersey: D. Van Nostrand Company, 1960), pp. 11-13.

27. See, for example, SP, p. 41, p. 49. In an early article Merton criticizes M. Levy-Bruhl for assuming that primitives lack rationality, and on the basis of findings of Rivers, Malinowski and Goldenweiser concludes "that every primitive community is in possession of a considerable store of knowledge, based on experience and fashioned by reason." Quoted in Robert K. Merton, "Recent French Sociology," *Social Forces,* Vol. 12, No. 4, May, 1934, p. 543, from B. Malinowski, "Magic, Science, and Religion," in Joseph Needham, ed., *Science, Religion and Reality* (New York: Macmillan and Co., 1925), p. 28.

28. STSS, p. 497.   29. SCDOS, p. 185.

30. STSS, p. 518.   31. *Ibid.,* p. 525.

32. *Ibid.,* p. 340.   33. *Ibid.,* p. 103.

34. *Ibid.,* p. 423.   35. *Ibid.,* p. 129.

36. *Ibid.,* p. 48.

37. *Ibid.,* p. 94. This condemnation is directed toward *post factum* "explanations," not *post factum* derived propositions "to be confirmed by *new* observations." Some of Merton's most brilliant analysis, such as those based upon *The American Soldier* may by his own definition be called *post factum* interpretations. See his interpretation of Nathan Glazer's use of the term, STSS, p. 230, fn. 3.

38. STSS, p. 230, fn. 3.   39. *Ibid.,* pp. 458-459.

40. *Ibid.,* p. 92.

41. Robert K. Merton, Samuel Bloom and Natalie Rogoff, "Studies in the

Sociology of Medical Education," *Journal of Medical Education*, Vol. 31, No. 8, August, 1956, p. 563. Hereafter referred to as SSME.

42. STSS, pp. 605-606.

43. *Ibid.*   44. *Ibid.*, p. 58.

45. *Ibid.*, p. 164.   46. STSS, p. 151.

47. PSD, p. 639; SCDOS, pp. 178-179.

48. SP, p. 6.   49. STSS, p. 564.

50. *Ibid.*, p. 273.   51. *Ibid.*, p. 272.

52. *Ibid.*, p. 274.

53. Charles P. Loomis, *op. cit.*, Essay 3; also, Charles P. Loomis, "Tentative Types of Directed Social Change Involving Systemic Linkage," *Rural Sociology*, Vol. 24, No. 4, December 1959, p. 383 ff.

54. STSS, p. 294.

55. *Ibid.*, p. 59. Stated so categorically, this seems to need qualification in light of Merton's important insight that Sumner's claim for "inner-cohesion and outer-hostility" needs reexamination. STSS, p. 298.

56. *Ibid.*, p. 204.   57. *Ibid.*, p. 196.

58. Affective neutrality serves the latent function of maintaining the essential bureaucratic structure. Tension management breaks down when particularistic treatment of co-workers is substituted for universalistic treatment—a structurally internal source of conflict.

59. *Ibid.*, p. 203, fn. 20, as quoted by Merton from E. W. Bakke, *The Unemployed Man: A Social Study* (New York: E. P. Dutton and Co., Inc., 1934), pp. 79-80.

60. *Ibid.*, p. 74.   61. *Ibid.*, p. 350.

62. *Ibid.*, p. 353.   63. *Ibid.*, p. 354.

64. *Ibid.*, p. 428.   65. *Ibid.*, p. 429.

66. *Ibid.*, p. 436.   67. *Ibid.*, pp. 132-133.

68. *Ibid.*, p. 134.   69. *Ibid.*

70. *Ibid.*, p. 136.   71. *Ibid.*

72. *Ibid.*, as quoted by Merton from Leo G. Rosten, *Hollywood: The Movie Colony, The Movie Makers* (New York: Harcourt, Brace and Co., 1941), p. 40.

73. STSS, p. 167.   74. *Ibid.*, p. 30.

75. *Ibid.*, p. 51.   76. *Ibid.*, p. 195.

77. *Ibid.*, p. 596.   78. *Ibid.*, p. 597.

79. *Ibid.*, p. 580.   80. *Ibid.*, p. 80.

81. *Ibid.*, pp. 73-76.   82. *Ibid.*, p. 274.

83. *Ibid.*, p. 133.   84. *Ibid.*, p. 134.

85. *Ibid.*, p. 317.   86. *Ibid.*

87. *Ibid.*, p. 200.   88. *Ibid.*, p. 317.

89. *Ibid.*, p. 141.

90. *Ibid.*, p. 318. This concept is used extensively by Robin M. Williams, Jr., and many others who give Merton credit for its origination.

91. *Ibid.*, p. 319.   92. *Ibid.*, p. 553.

93. *Ibid.*, p. 559.   94. *Ibid.*

95. PSD, p. 649.

96. "I think that every social role can be analyzed into ambivalences and that there are always conflicting demands, not conflicting roles but within a single role, potential conflicting demands." Tape-recorded interview, (December 11, 1959), p. 14 of transcript.

97. STSS, p. 134.

98. *Ibid.*, pp. 133-135; 140-141. Merton suggests that the very ambiguities of some statements may be instructive in themselves. What seemed to him to be ambiguities in Dubin's typology, upon pursuance revealed a distinction between attitudinal and behavioral conformity to norms, SCDOS, pp. 178-180. In the opinion of the present authors, certain ambiguities in Merton's works are similarly instructive; his concept of "institutionalized means" would seem to provide an example. The fusion of norm, facility, and other elements and processes was more common among writers, including those of the present volume who used the "means-ends schema" in the late thirties and forties, than it is now.

99. STSS, p. 141.

100. *Ibid.*, pp. 176-184. Merton is consistently concerned with identifying absolute as well as relative proportions as a necessary adjunct to systematic analysis. See p. 174. Unfortunately, the authors did not have access to Merton's paper on deviant behavior until after this manuscript went to press. See Robert K. Merton, "Social Problems and Sociological Theory," in Robert K. Merton and Robert A. Nisbet, eds., *Contemporary Social Problems: An Introduction to the Sociology of Deviant Behavior and Social Disorganization* (New York: Harcourt, Brace and World, Inc., 1961), pp. 697-737. In addition to an extended treatment of "institutionalized evasions of institutionalized rules," (pp. 729-731), and the differentiation between social disorganization—inadequate role-sets or conformity to roles which are in conflict, and deviant behavior—deviation from role norms (pp. 718-723), in this paper Merton distinguishes between two forms of deviant behavior—nonconforming and aberrant. The actor in the former publicly dissents from the norms, challenges their legitimacy, attempts to change them, is recognized as having disinterested purposes in so doing, and appeals to ultimate values rather than particular societal norms. These criteria, Merton maintains, are characteristic of "rebellion" in the *anomie* typology, whereas "innovation, ritualism and retreatism . . . comprise forms of aberrant behavior." (pp. 723-729, esp. fn. 24.)

101. *Ibid.*, p. 183. 102. *Ibid.*, p. 180

103. *Ibid.*, p. 151. 104. *Ibid.*, p. 185.

105. *Ibid.*, p. 155. 106. *Ibid.*, p. 189.

107. *Ibid.*, p. 155. 108. *Ibid.*, p. 156.

109. See, for example, STSS, p. 170, fn. 21; *Ibid.*, p. 178, fn. 30.

110. *Ibid.*, p. 239. 111. *Ibid.*, p. 283.

112. *Ibid.*, p. 284. 113. *Ibid.*, pp. 283-284.

114. *Ibid.*, p. 289. 115. *Ibid.*, p. 291.

116. *Ibid.*, p. 300. 117. *Ibid.*, p. 326.

118. *Ibid.*, pp. 330-331. 119. Ibid., p. 331.

120. *Ibid.*, p. 352. 121. *Ibid.*, p. 368.

122. Theodore M. Newcomb, *Social Psychology* (New York: Dryden Press, 1950), pp. 285-286.

123. Neal Gross, *et al.*, *Explorations in Role Analysis: Studies of the School Superintendency Role* (New York: John Wiley & Sons, Inc., 1958), Chapter IV. Here it is stated "for another set of concepts that embrace somewhat theoretically similar ideas see Robert K. Merton, *Social Theory and Social Structure*," p. 69, fn. 26. Merton on his part writes, "Theoretically

compatible ideas have also been developed by Neal Gross, in his forthcoming study of school executives." STSS, p. 369, fn. 115.

124. STSS, p. 369.   125. PF, p. xviii.

126. STSS, p. 370.

127. *Ibid.*, pp. 368-384; also pp. 320-322.

128. This definition of role-sequence is constructed from Merton's formulations on sequences of role-adaptations such as shifts from *conformity* to *ritualism* (STSS, p. 188) and sequence of role-sets (STSS, p. 371). Since the role-set refers to a single status it would follow that role-sequence must also.

129. STSS, pp. 370-371.   130. *Ibid.*, p. 371.

131. *Ibid.*, pp. 371-379.   132. *Ibid.*, p. 381.

133. *Ibid.*, p. 383.

134. *Ibid.*, p. 116. Among the status-roles given special interpretation in STSS are the following: the bureaucratic virtuoso, p. 199; the precinct captain as compared with the lady bountiful and the bureaucratic social worker, pp. 74-78; the cultural hero, p. 183; middle men of tolerance, p. 405; nonconformists as versus the criminal, p. 360 ff; group deserters and estranged ex-members such as renegades, traitors, etc., p. 296; social scientists, p. 207; citizen, p. 569; engineer, p. 568 ff; prig, pp. 352-353.

135. *Ibid.*, p. 564.

136. *Ibid.*, p. 315. Merton also lists a wide array of "terms for generic social position." "In ways not too clearly understood, these several hierarchies of stratification are inter-related. But we cannot *assume* that they are identical." STSS, pp. 417-418.

137. STSS, p. 323.   138. *Ibid.*, p. 319.

139. *Ibid.*, p. 276, fn. 51, as quoted in Merton, from W. E. B. DuBois, *The Philadelphia Negro* (Publication of the University of Pennsylvania Series in Economy and Public Law, No. 14, 1899) as quoted by E. F. Frazier, *The Negro in the United States* (New York: Macmillan and Co., 1949, p. 299, fn. 43.)

140. *Ibid.*, p. 279.   141. *Ibid.*, p. 234.

142. *Ibid.*, p. 265.   143. *Ibid.*, p. 293.

144. *Ibid.*, p. 294.   145. *Ibid.*, p. 305.

146. *Ibid.*, p. 305, fn. 38.   147. *Ibid.*, pp. 305-306, fn. 40.

148. *Ibid.*, p. 278.   149. *Ibid.*, p. 383.

150. Robert K. Merton, "The Role of Applied Social Science in the Formation of Policy: A Research Memorandum," *Philosophy of Science*, Vol. 16, No. 3, July, 1949, pp. 161-181.

151. STSS, p. 196.   152. *Ibid.*, p. 263.

153. *Ibid.*, p. 303.   154. *Ibid.*, p. 372.

155. *Ibid.*, p. 324.   156. *Ibid.*, Chapter X, "Patterns of Influence."

157. *Ibid.*, p. 195.   158. *Ibid.*, pp. 339-340.

159. *Ibid.*, p. 342, as quoted in Merton from George C. Homans, *The Human Group* (New York: Harcourt, Brace and Co., 1950), p. 182.

160. *Ibid.*, p. 342.   161. *Ibid.*, p. 344.

162. E. A. Shils, "Authoritarianism: 'right' and 'left,' " in Richard Christie and Marie Jahoda, eds., *Studies in the Scope and Method of The Authoritarian Personality* (Glencoe, Ill.: The Free Press, 1954), pp. 24-49; and also summarized in Merton, *Ibid.*, p. 349.

163. *Ibid.*, Chapter X, "Patterns of Influence."

164. *Ibid.*, p. 415.   165. *Ibid.*, p. 419.
166. *Ibid.*   167. *Ibid.*, p. 353.
168. *Ibid.*, p. 357.   169. *Ibid.*, p. 134, italics added.
170. *Ibid.*, p. 134.   171. *Ibid.*, pp. 138-139.
172. *Ibid.*, p. 564.   173. *Ibid.*, p. 196.
174. *Ibid.*, p. 551.   175. *Ibid.*, p. 319.
176. As quoted in Merton, *Ibid.*, p. 144; see fn. 15 for references.
177. *Ibid.*, p. 270.   178. *Ibid.*
179. *Ibid.*, pp. 270-271.   180. *Ibid.*, p. 353.
181. *Ibid.*, p. 557.   182. *Ibid.*, p. 565.
183. As quoted in Merton, *Ibid.*   184. *Ibid.*, p. 572.
185. *Ibid.*, p. 565.   186. *Ibid.*, pp. 196-197.
187. *Ibid.*, Chapter XVII.   188. *Ibid.*, p. 563.
189. *Ibid.*, p. 566.   190. *Ibid.*, p. 568.
191. *Ibid.*
192. As quoted in Merton, *Ibid.*, p. 569.
193. *Ibid.*, p. 570.   194. *Ibid.*, p. 509.
195. *Ibid.*, p. 525.   196. *Ibid.*, p. 528.
197. *Ibid.*, p. 316.   198. *Ibid.*, p. 29.
199. Robert K. Merton, "Issues in the Growth of a Profession," a keynote address presented at the 41st Convention of the American Nurses' Association, Atlantic City, New Jersey, June, 1958, p. 8.
200. *Ibid.*, p. 9.   201. *Ibid.*
202. *Ibid.*   203. *Ibid.*
204. STSS, pp. 74-76 and p. 82.
205. *Ibid.*, pp. 405-406. These observations are based upon Samuel A. Stouffer's study, *Communism, Conformity and Civil Liberties* (New York: Doubleday & Company, 1955), and reported in "Orbits of Tolerance, Interviewers, and Elites," *Public Opinion Quarterly*, Vol. 20, No. 1, Spring, 1956, pp. 49-73. Riesman, on the basis of the Stouffer study which finds tolerance positively correlated with education but with greater differential between classes, hypothesizes "that the college graduate in the South is . . . quite sharply cut off from the rest of the community. . . ." As quoted in STSS, p. 406.
206. *Ibid.*, p. 182.   207. SP, p. 287.
208. STSS, p. 158.   209. *Ibid.*
210. *Ibid.*   211. As recorded in taped interview.
212. STSS, p. 268.   213. SP, p. 41.
214. STSS, p. 362.   215. *Ibid.*, p. 370.
216. *Ibid.*, p. 393.   217. SPH, pp. 44-47.
218. STSS, p. 322.   219. *Ibid.*, p. 174.
220. *Ibid.*, p. 313.
221. A 1937 paper is pertinent with respect both to functional analysis and to the concept of time as a condition of social action: "Social Time: a Methodological and Functional Analysis" (with Pitirim A. Sorokin), *The American Journal of Sociology*, Vol. 42, No. 5, March, 1937, pp. 615-629.
222. STSS, pp. 40-41. As the reader who turns to the original work will see, Merton here is demonstrating that theoretical concepts themselves show no necessary propensity for one or another ideological interpretation. Even the theoretical underpinnings of dialectical materialism as propounded by Marx do not necessarily lead to "Marxist" interpretation, a circumstance

which led to Marx's paradoxical remark *"je ne suis pas un marxiste."* Merton's
terminology which expresses the neutral logic of the functionalist's position
purposely paraphrases Marxian terminology which expresses the neutral logic
of *his* position. The purposes of comparison are well served. The excerpts
quoted in the present text are out of context and thus may require this explanation for a style which is clearly not one generally employed by Merton.
Additional work on Marxian analysis undertaken for quite a different purpose is found in Chapter XII of STSS.

 223. STSS, p. 81. 224. *Ibid.*, pp. 310-326.

CHAPTER 6

TALCOTT PARSONS'
SOCIAL THEORY*

No doubt the leading exponent of the concept "social system" is Talcott Parsons. Despite wide usage of the concept by other sociologists,[1] its development by Parsons on many levels of abstraction and its application by him to a wide range of human interaction not only gives him undisputed primacy in its use but also has provided a basis for an extensive secondary literature. This in turn has broadened the usage of the concept, "social system."

This chapter is an attempt to analyze Parsons' conceptualization of the social system. As with the other chapters appearing in this volume, the analysis will be carried out in terms of the PAS Model the details of which appear in Chapter 1 and elsewhere.[2] Such an analysis, however, must be preceded by an over-all view of Parsons' work which, taken *in toto* through more than two decades, is marked by a high degree of integration and inviolate unity. Nonetheless, its subtleties, complexities, and refinements, its frequent preoccupation with the border lines which sociology shares with other disciplines—such as psychology, economics, political science, and anthropology—and the continuously developmental stages of his works variously representing different levels of analyses have led to the charge (unfounded in the view of the present authors) that his theory is discontinuous and even contradictory through time.[3] The essential unity and remarkable

* This chapter was prepared with the assistance of Robert C. Bealer as junior author.

consistency of his conceptualized social system, although amenable to analysis by the PAS Model, cannot be communicated adequately without an attempt at a panoramic view of the whole together with a statement of his general theory. The developmental aspect of his works therefore demands examination.

In his first book, *The Structure of Social Action*,[4] Parsons, following Max Weber, saw the unit act as focal. The ordered nature of the unit act sprang from a moral, integrative value structure, non-logical in basis of commitment, in one sense an external coercive force, not unlike what Durkheim called "constraint," somewhat "above" the individual, and in another an immanent force springing from the subjective internalization of evaluative criteria in means-ends relationships.[5] What he termed the "voluntaristic" theory of action focused on an actor in relation to his situation. The problem of order posed by this first work demanded further elaboration which appeared a decade and a half later in *The Social System*.[6] In this work order remained the central theme, but emphasis had shifted from the unit act to institutional patterns, the ultimate referent being society as *the* social system, interpenetrated by the personality and cultural systems, with all other social systems constituting subsystems or parts of subsystems. Here the unit act diminishes in importance because the level of analysis has shifted from the individual actor to collectivities of individuals.

The emphasis in each work is appropriate to the phenomena under examination. For example, in *The Structure* an essential distinction was made between logical and non-logical action. The normative implications of the latter served as the touchstone from which Parsons attacks earlier theoretical interpretations of human conduct—instinct schools, simple behaviorism, monistic determinants of all hues, but most particularly the "simple-minded" rationalism of certain economic theories. In contrast, the logical non-logical distinction, while not repudiated, is used relatively little in *The Social System* where it appears only as an aspect of the cleavage between instrumental and expressive behavior. The relativity of any and all social attributes is consistent with Parsons' view of "system" itself. "The distinction between unit and system is, of course, relative. What is a unit in terms of one point of reference may always be treated as system from another; this view of macroscopic-miscroscopic relations is fundamental to our whole treatment of action." [7] Unlike some of his critics [8] who insist upon a constant vantage point, i.e. either the individual or the group, from which reality must be viewed, Parsons finds "reality" within certain limits, in both perspectives.

Sequentially, his early interest in economic institutions led to inquiries into the border lines shared by economics and sociology, and this in turn to a search for a sociological counterpart to the generalized theoretical economic system. Suspected defects in the conceptualization of motivation theory in economics prompted a study of medical practice which ideally is not governed by economic self interest. This pursuit led not only to hypotheses focused on motivation but to explorations of the boundaries shared by psychology, sociology, and cultural anthropology. [9] Viewed separately, any one work of Parsons might be heavily microscopic, e.g. the ego or superego viewed as units or subsystems of the personality system; or it might be macroscopic, as in the case when the chief referent is society.

Varied as have been the segments of man's social action which at any one time received Parsons' attention, a point of invariance has been his thought on theory *per se.*

There is, more often implicit than explicit, a deep-rooted view [in sociology] that the progress of scientific knowledge consists essentially in the cumulative piling up of "discoveries" of "fact." . . . . Theory, according to this view, would consist only in generalization from known facts, in the sense of what general statements the known body of fact would justify. . . . Against the view just roughly sketched may be set another, namely, that scientific "theory"—most generally defined as a body of logically interrelated *"general concepts"* of empirical reference —is not only a dependent but an independent variable. . . . Concepts correspond not to concrete phenomena, but to elements in them which are analytically separable from other elements. There is no implication that the value of any one such element, or even of all those included in one logically coherent system, is completely descriptive of any particular concrete thing or event. [10]

This does not mean for Parsons that the general concepts of theory are simply fictional and totally arbitrary. Rather, in some sense they " 'grasp' aspects of the objective external world." [11] One test for the validity of "general concepts" is their fruitfulness in analy-

sis at variant levels of focus. The varying levels of analysis used
by Parsons is entirely consistent with his expectations that a sound
theory can be applied to innumerable cross-cuts of social phenomena.

In line with Parsons' view of theory as being logically interrelated general concepts constituting an independent variable,
the main attributes of that theory must be established independently of the analytical results of its application. Obviously the
minutiae of the theory cannot be included nor can all its stages
of development be indicated. One basis of inclusion will be
recency, for since the theoretical framework has progressed by
accretion rather more than by discretion and discard, most salient
concepts will be thus represented. The second basis of inclusion
will be primacy of orientation to the social system as a sociological
construct, although the essential "interpenetration" of the social
system by the personality and cultural (and to some extent and
more recently the biological) systems as conceived by Parsons
renders this separation one of mere focus or emphasis.

General action theory and the place of the social system. Parsons postulates a general theory of system applicable to different
components of social relations. The social system is one such
component to which general systemic theory is deemed applicable, but equally analyzable by the general systemic theory are the
personality system, the cultural system, and the biological system.[12] At least two units are required to constitute any given system, with the units thought of as analyzable in their own right as
systems or as parts of systems at higher levels of organization and
abstraction.[13] Whatever the focal unit—a cell, a status-role, an
individual, a collectivity, or any other unit—its external systemic
relation is to other units which from the point of view of the focal
unit represent components of a *situation*. The focal unit is designated as the *actor* (which by Parsons' definition is not confined
to the concrete individual). The actor bears a relation to objects
in a situation which may be nonsocial (physical objects or cultural resources) or social (individual actors and collectivities).
The systemic relationship is one of action. The analysis of action
then, is essentially the examination of the actor and situation as
units in a system.

Parsons views all four components of organization—the cultural, social, psychological, and biological—as being analytically separable and not mutually reducible, each possessing unique and emergent properties which make its distinction fruitful. At the same time there is a high level of interrelatedness and interpenetration among the components or systems, a circumstance which is basic to a fundamental working assumption: that the different systems should be derivable from a *common* set of postulates; that the empirical constants displaying the same fundamental variables in all four systems should constitute the basis for sub-theories; that within the general framework different classes of systems must be differentiated and related.[14] Parsons, although emphasizing social system in the tradition of sociology, is always eminently concerned with the *general* theory of action without which, in his opinion, important boundaries of the social system with the other three systems remain unexplored.

As a key to an understanding of much which is to follow a summary of the basic characteristics of and/or interdependencies between these systems are given here, shorn of all the explanatory detail which accompanies their presentation later, beginning with the category "knowing" in the PAS Model analysis.

The actor's orientation to the situation is *motivational* and *value orientational*.

The motivational orientation supplies the energy; it is "simply an urge to 'get something.' "[15]

It is cognitive, cathectic and evaluative, each of which corresponds respectively to beliefs, sentiments and morals.

The value orientation supplies norms or standards for action. Internalized, they are need-dispositions within actors; institutionalized in the social system they contribute to integration; abstracted from the concrete situation, they are cultural value-standards.[16] Their modes are cognitive or standards of reality; appreciative, or standards of "immediate gratificatory significance"; and moral, or standards by which the consequences of action for personality integration and social system integration are assessed.

These two classifications of "actor orientations" Parsons considers to be independent variables. The differentiation of "need" primacy from "norms" or "standard" primacy, neither of which can be inferred from the other, Parsons believes to be crucial to culture-personality theory. Their integration he sees as "the core phenomenon of the dynamics of social systems." [17] Action itself is instrumental, expressive and/or moral. (After 1959 the term consummatory has been used for the non-instrumental aspects of action.)

Instrumental action is goal-directed, with the cognitive mode of motivation primary.

Expressive action is itself a goal; the need disposition is acted out in terms of expressive symbolism.

Moral action is ego-integrative for the personality system and collectivity integrative for the social system.

This greatly compressed and consequently inadequate recognition of the immensely complex and global dimensions of Parsons' undertaking may serve as a reminder that general theory—not the unit act, or the concrete individual, or collectivities, or cultures, but all these and more—are here being treated.

Organization and control are exhibited by one ordering of levels of the four systems. The psychological system organizes and controls the organism (in its behavioral aspects); the social system organizes and controls the psychological system and the cultural system performs similarly in respect to the social system. By an opposite ordering of the levels, sets of conditions are provided. Social systems provide a set of conditions basic to the cultural systems, psychological systems a set of conditions on which the social systems depend, and the organism provides the conditions underlying the psychological system. [18] There are characteristic interchanges among the four systems. The organism, for example, provides the personality system with inputs of motivational energy part of which is fed back to the organism in the form of control that increases the performance potential of the organism. Between the psychological and cultural systems a mutually integrative interchange takes place in which the psychological system is provided with legitimation by cultural components by which its functioning is made subject to normative patterns. Culture is provided with a "motivational commitment" by the psychological system which transcends an understanding of the norm to become a total internalization of it, so that the norm becomes a part of an internal regulatory mechanism which is part of the personality system itself.[19]

The ordering of the four systems—the organism, the psychological system, the social system, and the cultural system—somewhat parallels an ordering of the units of the social system, each successive level of which provides a control to the level of phenomena immediately below it.

A social system . . . may be analyzed on four levels of generality so far as its units are concerned: 1) Individuals in roles are organized to form what we call 2) collectivities. Both roles and collectivities, however, are subject to ordering and control by 3) norms which are differentiated according to the functions of these units and to their situations, and by 4) values which define the desirable kind of system of relations.[20]

Somewhat the same ordering, except that it is reversed, is established among the units of the social system as degree of differentiation is considered. At the least differentiated level of a society as a social system, values may be viewed as "modes of normative orientation of action . . . which define the main directions of action."[21] Institutions such as property and authority fall at the next level on the undifferentiated-differentiated continuum and at the next level come collectivities, followed by roles. A collectivity is defined as "a concrete system of interacting human individuals, of persons in roles."[22] For Parsons, the social system "consists in a plurality of individual actors interacting with each other in a situation which has at least a physical or environmental aspect, actors who are motivated in terms of a tendency to the 'optimization of gratification' and whose relations to their situations, including each other, is defined and mediated in terms of a system of culturally structured and shared symbols."[23] It is not made up of "the *total* action of concrete persons and collectivities, but only their actions in specific roles."[24]

The central point of articulation between the social and personality systems is the status-role which also provides the channel through which the cultural system in the form of value orientation enters action. Culture is transmitted, learned, and shared. It enters both the personality and social system through the norm or value orientation standards as they become applicable within the status-roles.[25] Although various dimensions are specified for systemic analysis including levels at which respectively, values, norms, collectivities, and roles have priority and are increasingly stressed in *The Social System,* the status-role receives major emphasis. As Parsons puts it:

> . . . the fundamental *common sector* of personalities and social systems consists in the value-patterns which define role-expectations. The motivational structures thus organized are units *both* of personality as a system and of the social system in which the actor participates; they are need-dispositions of the personality and they are role expectations of the social system. . . . This fundamental relationship between need-dispositions of the personality, role-expectations of the social system and internalized-institutionalized value-patterns of the culture, is the fundamental nodal point of the *organization* of systems of action.[26]

At the same time that Parsons uses society as the model for the social system, he frequently uses examples focusing on the genetic ego-alter relations in such dyads as the doctor and patient. He recognizes that "a committee, a work group, or even a family clearly do not constitute in the usual sense, societies. But equally clearly they are for the purposes of sociological theory, social systems." [27] Nonetheless, society alone furnishes the long term endurance requisite to a social system model. Society endures beyond the life span of individuals through recruitment by biological reproduction and socialization of progeny. Further, it possesses the requisites for giving and maintaining order to interaction despite inherent centrifugal tendencies arising from age and sex differences, limited resources of time, talent and territoriality and the implied problems of power, commitments and related phenomena of pattern maintenance, and value integration.[28] The subtle fusion of empirical and analytical elements in Parsons' handling of the social system generally is underlined when he concludes on this note: "It is not essential to the concept of a society that it should not be in any way empirically interdependent with other societies, but only that it should contain all the structural and functional fundamentals of an independently subsisting system." [29]

Parsons does not intend that his sociological analysis be merely nominal.[30] He believes that the only ultimate justification for his general theory of action as well as that specifically of the social system is its empirical relevance. [31] Of particular interest to him, therefore, are what he has noted as "empirical clusterings of the structural components of social systems": 1) kinship systems, 2) instrumental achievement structures and stratification, 3) territoriality, force and the integration of the power system, and 4) religion and value-integration. Their universal occurrences convince him that there exist "certain functional exigencies without which we cannot account for the fact that the known range of actual social structures is only a fraction of those which would result from a random assortment of the permutations and combinations of their structural components." [32] The relation of these "empirical clusterings" to the more recent "four phases and fundamental problems of exigency" of any social system will be apparent.[33]

Phases and fundamental problems of social systems. Two basic dichotomies underlie Parsons' delineation of four categories of activity which are variously related to social systems as phases, problems, and functional imperatives. He subscribes to the view that the action generated within any given social system is in part directed toward its *external* situation and in part toward its *internal* situation, the proportions varying with the type of system. The external-internal dichotomy is one axis. Consistent with his earlier means-ends formulations, he also sees some activity as *instrumental* in that its product represents the means to a goal and not the goal itself, whereas other activity is *consummatory* in that the product *per se* of the activity (or the activity itself) represents goal attainment. The instrumental-consummatory dichotomy is the second axis, which upon intersection with the external-internal axis describes four general areas of activity as revealed in Figure 1. The activity occurring in each social system is directed in part to all four categories described by Figure 1, although its emphasis in one of the four categories justifies its classification as *primarily* of one type or another. Thus the family falls into the L cell above but nevertheless exhibits all four patterns: ". . . the differentiation of familial roles by generation is a special case of the external-internal differentiation in its hierarchical version, with the parental generation performing the 'external' roles; differentiation by

FIGURE 1

	INSTRUMENTAL	CONSUMMATORY	
A			G
EXTERNAL	Adaptive Function (or Phase)	Goal-Attainment Function (or Phase)	
INTERNAL	Pattern-Mainte-nance and Ten-sion Management Function (or Phase)*	Integrative Function (or Phase)	
L			I

* Originally called "Latent-Receptive Meaning Integration," etc., hence the "L." See Figure 8.

sex is a special case of the instrumental consummatory line of differentiation . . . the masculine role performs . . . primarily instrumental functions . . . the feminine . . . primarily [the] consummatory." [34]

The important subsystems of the larger modern society are differentiated by their assumption of activity predominantly devoted to one of the four categories. The execution of such activity is its functional imperative, its specialized role legitimatized societally by cultural evaluations. The economic producer, or in more comprehensive abstract terms, the economy, belongs to cell A in Figure 1. Representing "a rather drastic revision of [a] previous conception" [35] is the placing of the polity in cell G. Organizations oriented to the generation and allocation of power fall here and would, in Parsons' view, include most organs of government, much of banking, and the corporate aspect of organizations. Those subsystems are predominantly integrative whose functional imperative is the marshalling of agreement out of potential or actual conflict, such as is done by political parties and "interest groups"; also primarily integrative are those subsystems whose functional imperative is the institutionalizing of norms such as is done by the courts. Hospitals and most health agencies fall here, for although they are not concerned with activity which adjusts conflicts in the same sense as those just specified, they presumably motivate the individuals whom they serve to the fulfillment of

institutionalized expectations, i.e. to act in accordance with the
expectations specified by the sick status-role and to reassume eventually the status-role of the healthy. The I cell of Figure 1 would
be represented by these groups. Churches, schools, research activities, the arts, and kinship groups perform primarily a pattern
maintenance, or a tension management function, and would consequently be designated as belonging to the L cell of Figure 1.[36]
Each of the four categories possess distinctive functional problems
or dimensions of social structure and process and hence give rise
to differentiated organizations: "a good organization for the physical production of goods at the technical level would inevitably
be a bad one for the educational process." [37]

The concrete formal organization, whatever its functional imperative, exhibits differentiated activity levels separated from each
other by observable breaking points, each level responsible to the
organization for its own functional imperative in much the same
way that the organization as a subsystem is responsible to society
for a given function. As such, each organizational level—from the
primary technical, to the managerial, to the institutional—predominantly faces one of the four functional "problems" unique
(within the organization) to that organizational level and articulated by primary reference to status-role, norms, and values, an
elaboration of which appears below in appropriate sections of the
PAS Model analysis.

A more concrete presentation of these theoretical considerations appears as Parsons poses the picture of an economic organization which faces the *adaptive* exigencies of procurement of the
factors of production: land, labor, capital, and "organization" in
the sense that Alfred Marshall used the term. Labor and capital
are the most fluid of these factors. The recruitment of labor, most
often by contract, and the mobilization of capital are therefore
the chief adaptive problems of a going concern. The requirements
of money funds in a society such as the United States are overwhelmingly the most important and are not limited to organizations of a business nature.

Having procured the fluid resources through the *adaptive* process, the organization is now faced with the necessity for providing
"a set of mechanisms by which these resources can be brought
to bear on the actual process of goal-implementation in a changing

situation." [38] These "operative *goal-attainment* mechanisms" prove to be decisions emerging from the decision-making process executed at various organizational levels, but always a function of the power vested at that level. There are policy decisions, allocative decisions, operative decisions, and coordinative decisions. This last, while obviously contributing to goal attainment, clearly affects the state of internal integration also.

The central focus of the integrative subsystems of a society is illustrated by Figure 1a. The subparadigm at the bottom of Figure 1a illustrates the structural components (capital letters A, G, I and L) and the functional aspects (lower case letters a, g, and i). Integration results from boundary interchanges not only among various subsystems, as in Figure 1a, but also by interchange among subsystems on other dimensions. [39] Thus a given subsystem of a society—for example a business firm, a university, or an army—may be differentiated into the primary technical or work level on through managerial, institutional, and societal levels. Interchanges and systemic linkage of these components and levels one to another and to society as well as to other subsystems in society is required for efficient organizational operation.

With differentiation in a given previously undifferentiated society, particularly if change is in the direction of modern democratic industrialized societies, boundary exchanges become increasingly important for systems falling in the I cell of Figure 1. Likewise the roles of systems in the A cell become increasingly important. [40]

The very pattern maintenance which gives subsystems their cohesion can be a centrifugal force which jeopardizes cohesion of social systems at higher levels. If, for example, an actor were oriented *completely* to his family, his commitment to his occupational status-role would suffer, a fact important for the "integrative problem" of a system. If he were oriented *completely* to his occupational status-role his commitment to his citizen status-role would suffer. The "problem" of integration, then, for a given social system becomes one of extending and maintaining the range of solidarity to a point of inclusiveness more or less commensurate with the boundaries of the given social system. Loyalty, coordination, cooperation, efficiency, motivation are all terms used by Parsons in connection with internal integration.

There is for Parsons, another point of view from which the

FIGURE 1a

Boundary Interchanges Between the Primary Sub-Systems of a Society [*]

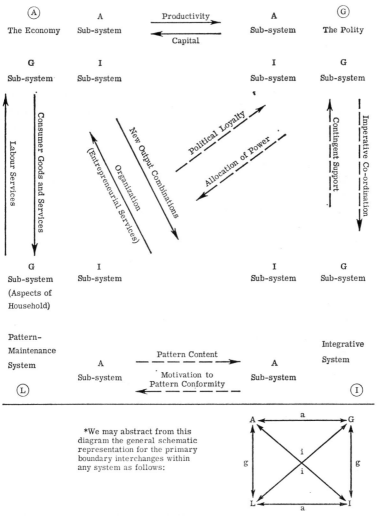

SOURCE: Talcott Parsons and Neil J. Smelser, *Economy and Society*, op. cit., p. 68. It may be noted that Figures 2-7 are different from Figure 1a in that they carry sub-L cells. Since Figure 1a stresses function as well as structure "the 'special' boundary of the latency subsystem at any given level is a *cultural* rather than an interaction boundary," and therefore the L does not appear in the subsystems of the various quadrants. E & S p. 69. In another connection Parsons notes that "there is a pattern-maintenance subsystem *below* the adaptive subsystem in the hierarchy of control of any system of action and another *above* the integrative sub-system. . . ." PVR. p. 471. In Figure 1a, as the firm is related to the household the L is *below*, in Figure 7 it is above.

problem of integration becomes important; it refers to the situation external to the organization.

> The problem concerns . . . the compatibility of the institutional patterns under which the organization operates with those of other organizations and social units, as related to the integrative exigencies of the society as a whole (or of subsystems wider than the organization in question) . . . For example, if a given firm hires and fires on a certain basis, will other firms in the same industry be allowed to follow this precedent? Or if the security officers in the Department of Defense follow a given procedure in dealing with alleged security risks, can the same procedure be tolerated in the State Department? If the two sets of procedures are in conflict, can the two organizations continue to differ or must they be subjected to a common set of principles? [41]

Parsons notes three complexes of integrative patterns: the contract, institutionalization of authority, and universalistically defined rules or norms all of which transcend any particular organization and are therefore integrative on the societal level.

Designated as a phase or problem, the pattern maintenance and tension management cell of the paradigm represented by Figure 1 is, relative to the other three cells, not as well developed, although various subsystems which belong in this cell—notably kinship, religious, and educational systems—have been accorded considerable attention. Its elaboration like the others treated in the organizational analysis just completed, will appear in the PAS Model analysis. Its eventual development by Parsons will no doubt clarify some of the dilemmas which can easily arise as pattern-maintenance and integration, particularly its internal aspects, are probed.[42]

If the organization under analysis were not predominantly adaptive—i.e. if it were primarily goal-attaining as the governmental agency; if it were primarily integrative, as a court; or if it were primarily pattern maintaining, as a school—the exigencies it would encounter and the circumstances governing their solution would vary in many details from the production organization just outlined. To high-light this difference Parsons gives considerable attention to military and academic organizations. Some of these differences will emerge under the PAS Model analysis, but enough has been presented here to acquaint the reader with the saliencies of phase theory. Other details of phase theory will inevitably be treated as pattern variables are examined.

The pattern variables. Parsons' first attempts to discriminate types of social structure followed the lead from Toennies' distinction of *Gemeinschaft* and *Gesellschaft* and from Max Weber's refinements thereof. Gradually he became convinced that although a given structure might clearly exhibit attributes suggestive of one polar type it often possessed other attributes not necessarily represented by that same polar type. As an example he noted that "Marshall was right in interpreting increasing economic rationality as an inherent tendency of human action" [43] but wrong in thinking that it is associated only with a specific type of social organization, such as free enterprise which is *Gesellschaft*-like, and that it cannot be made compatible with another type of social organization, such as traditionalism or the Indian caste system, which is *Gemeinschaft*-like. As Parsons undertook to examine occupational structures he was led to the same conclusion. The professional status-role, that of physician for example, belonged wholly to neither type. The physician's relations to his patient is *Gesellschaft*-like insofar as it includes the application of the principles of medical science; nonetheless, "by virtue of the canon that the 'welfare of the patient' should come ahead of the self-interest of the doctor, this was clearly one of *Gemeinschaft*." [44] As a result of such observations, "Gradually it became clear that this dichotomy [*Gemeinschaft-Gesselschaft*] concealed a number of independently variable distinctions." [45] He consequently sought to isolate these variables with the result that he came to see all of action or "changes of state" as directional, toward one or the other alternatives of the following five dichotomies termed by Parsons the pattern variables:

Affectivity	vs.	Affective neutrality
Diffusion	vs.	Specificity
Particularism	vs.	Universalism
Quality	vs.	Performance
Collectivity-orientation	vs.	Self-orientation

An actor confronting a situation sees its meaning in terms of one or more of these five categories each of which presents two alternative interpretations. His subsequent action is taken in accordance with his interpretation(s); the necessities for choice are termed the dilemmas of action. The choice of any one alternative over another is one of preference or primacy,[46] not of exclusive and unvarying rigidity, and the choice becomes patterned only after repeated choices in one direction or another. Further, the pattern variables yield only "first approximations" in comparative analysis.[47]

Stated in the most general terms, "the pattern variables constitute categories for the orderly description and comparative analysis of the 'structure' of systems of action as systems." [48] They may be applied at four analytical levels. On the concrete level of empirical action they exist as five discrete choices which the actor must explicitly or implicitly make before he can act. On the collectivity level they constitute aspects of role definition or of role expectation whereby roles are characteristically specified in terms of one side or the other of the dilemmas denoted by the pattern variables. On the cultural level they represent aspects of value-standards. Finally, insofar as an actor as personality is committed to a value-standard (the boundary exchange between culture system and personality system will be recalled here whereby occurs a legitimation-motivation complex of exchange) such an actor will habitually choose the horn of the dilemma specified by adherence to that standard.

Affectivity vs. *affective neutrality* is the gratification-discipline dilemma. This dilemma is posed because on the one hand no action system can be organized or integrated unless members renounce some gratifications. On the other hand no actor can live without some gratifications. In an organized action system the most direct path to gratification is through expressive orientations. Subscribing to such an orientation represents affectivity. Eschewing such a path for instrumental, evaluative, or moral considerations means renunciation of gratification, i.e. discipline. Such an orientation represents affective neutrality.

Diffuseness vs. *specificity* is the dilemma of defining the relation borne by object to actor as indefinitely wide in scope, infinitely broad in involvement, morally obligating, and significant in pluralistic situations, (diffuseness); or specifically limited in scope and involvement, (specificity). Thus at one horn of the dilemma (namely, that of diffuseness) the "burden of proof" is on anyone who would claim that the actor in a given role has the moral right to limit responsibilities to the object; at the other horn of the dilemma (namely, that of specificity) the burden of proof is on anyone suggesting that the actor has obligations which transcend the established limitations of responsibility institutionalized in the role.

Particularism vs. *universalism* poses cathectic standards against cognitive standards. If among a class of objects which possess the same relative attribute(s) pertinent to the situation, a sub-class is singled out to stand in some special and individual inclusive relationship to the actor (kinsman and neighbor are mentioned), the choice is particularistic and implies the primacy of cathectic standards. Completely generalized evaluative dimensions applied impartially by an actor to a class of objects possessing the same relative attribute(s) is universalistic and implies the primacy of cognitive standards.

Quality vs. *performance* (formerly designated as ascription vs. achievement) is the dilemma of according primary treatment to an object on the basis of what it *is* in itself (quality) or what it *does* and the quality of its performance.

Collectivity-orientation vs. *self-orientation* is the collective-interest vs. private interest dilemma. Subscription to values commonly held by a collectivity and conformity with the value pattern because such a course is a "good thing" in itself and because of obligation and responsibility to the referent action systems are ingredients of a collectivity orientation. If such subscription is made for private instrumental advantages or because of fear of reprisal, it is not collectivity orientation but self orientation, as is also the case with active dissent and deviation from commonly held values.

Parsons sees four of the sets of pattern variables as being paired. The first two sets above, affectivity vs. neutrality and diffuseness vs. specificity, constitute *attitudinal pairs* which focus on the actor and are termed "the orientation set." The second two sets above, particularism vs. universalism and quality vs. performance, constitute the "object-categorization pairs" which focus on the object and "formulate[s] the fact that members of a collectivity are objects to each other in the sense that *their relative locations in a system* always transcend the involvement of any particular personality in that system." [49] These pairs constitute the "modality set." To be logically complete the list of pattern variables, Parsons feels, should provide a sixth dilemma to pair with this fifth, unmatched pattern variable. Although unformulated as yet in any detail, he predicts its development as dealing with the dilemma of "short-run and long-run interests or values." [50] After 1959 this was supplied by the instrumental-consummatory axis of Figure 1. The collectivity-orientation vs. self-orientation pattern variable which as employed with the other four pattern variables "was an unduly restricted formulation" [51] becomes the external-internal axis of Figure 1.

Although the inadequacies of typologies accounted for the formulation of the pattern variables, it became apparent to Parsons as he applied the latter to a wide range of analytical problems that they bore a basic relation to the four functional problems of systems, a resumé of which immediately preceded this present treatment of pattern variables. He consequently undertook to clarify that relation. [52]

The pattern variables as related to the four system problems. In substance, Parsons proposes to find out what systemic structures are suggested if every possible logically stable combination of the pattern variables is proposed and how the results fit with the system problem schema which was developed on the external-internal axis (which represents the dimension originally contained in the pattern variable, self-orientation vs. collectivity orientation) and instrumental-consummatory axis. He starts with the orientation set: the affectivity vs. neutrality pair and the specificity vs. diffuseness pair of pattern variables in which the actor is the focus. The interest of the actor in his object may be one which he has no desire to change; its interest is one of consummation. Or the object may be of interest to the actor because he needs it as an instrument for some more ultimate object relationship; its interest in that case is instrumental. The orientation may be toward the environment in which case differentiations must be made among objects of the environment for specific, meaningful qualities. Or the orientation might be toward internal needs of the acting system; under these circumstances the objects are more diffuse. The crossing of these four attitudinal variables, then, yield logically a block which would look like this:

FIGURE 2 *

| INSTRUMENTAL | CONSUMMATORY |

S p e c i f i c i t y	Orientation to Objects	
	Neutrality	*Affectivity*
	INTEREST IN INSTRUMENTAL UTILIZATION	CONSUMMATORY NEEDS
D i f f u s e n e s s	NEEDS FOR COMMITMENT	NEEDS FOR AFFILIATION

L

* NOTE: The attitudinal components as developed earlier in SS for the quadrants designated as A, G, I, L in PVR were respectively as follows: Approval, receptiveness-responsiveness, love, and esteem. See below under sentiments.

The types of orientation of actors to objects obtained by crossing the two sets of attitudinal or orientation variables in terms of the instrumental-consummatory axis and the internal-external axis (here represented by the internal-external aspects of diffuseness-specificity) are compatible with the system problem of pattern-maintenance and tension management; hence it is designated as the L cell, (Figure 2) or latent expressive, a term sometimes used for the pattern maintenance-tension management nexus.

Continuing with the modality set, the same procedure is applied to the four variables of particularism-universalism and performance-quality, with the result as described by Figure 3.

FIGURE 3

P e r f o r m a n c e	Modalities of Objects	G
	Universalistic	*Particularistic*
	OBJECTS OF UTILITY	OBJECTS OF CATHEXIS
Q u a l i t y	OBJECTS OF "GENERALIZED RESPECT"	OBJECTS OF IDENTIFICATION

The explanations given for these cells reveal not only pertinencies of two of the pattern variables but also the light touch which Parsons upon occasion uses to advantage. A man in love, for example, "may, like some other gentlemen, prefer blondes, but he is not in love with the category, but with one particular blonde. . . . A man sufficiently in love with blondeness as such, who therefore pursues any blonde, cannot establish a very stable love relationship with a particular woman. That there is an important 'matching' between consummatory bases of interest and particularistic meaning of objects is clear. . . ." [53] An object defined in universalistic terms (all blondes for example) may be said to be an object of utility in that it possesses potentialities needed to bring about consummatory states of the acting system. The internal-external axis here is represented by the quality-performance variables. If the interest in the objects is in terms of what they "are" rather than how they perform, "The internal reference of the acting system matches with interest in the qualities of objects rather than their performances, since these are presumptively more independent of direct situational exigencies." [54] Objects which are both particularistic and meaningful for what they are rather than for what they do, are designated as objects of identification. The objects of "generalized respect" when occurring in a social context are similar to the type "Durkheim speaks of as generating attitudes of 'moral authority.'" [55] The characteristics displayed by the types of object orientation obtained by crossing the two sets of modality variables are compatible with the system problem of goal-attaining and hence is designated as the G-cell.

Parsons considers that the two cells thus far described, each with its four compartments, contain the elementary components of action—that is actor and situation respectively—but that *interaction* as the organizational stuff of systems cannot be adequately analyzed until interrelations of a plurality of elementary actor-object units is made explicit. To be applicable to interaction between actor and object it becomes necessary to designate those variables of the orientation set which could combine stably with selected variables of the modality set; they were consequently regrouped to "establish connections across the attitude-object line." [56] The pairing of affectivity and performance was the first. Parsons contends that affectivity or "the release of an impulse into actual overt behavior" [57] is the actor focus of *performance* which as an object "represents the actor in the process of acting." [58] This relation across the motivational-situational axis becomes the prototype of other attitude-object combinations: affective-neutrality-quality (ascription), specificity-universalism, diffuseness and particularism.

In viewing possible actor-object interaction combinations as system organizing, Parsons distinguishes two functions for the system as a whole which must be accomplished by that organization of component parts. These are the modes of *internal integration* of the system, and secondly "the mechanisms by which the system as a whole is adapted to the environment within which it operates." [59] These two functions clearly match the system problems of integration and adaptation respectively. Parsons conceives the problem then, as so arranging the respective attitude-object variables that the resulting combinations maximize the integrative function in one case and the adaptive function in the other. He postulates that in the case of internal organization, the

function of the object for the needs of the actor must be matched
with the functional meaning with which the object is categorized.
In operational terms, this involves matching the modality or object variable of a particularly placed cell, e.g. universalism, with
the orientation or attitudinal variable of a similarly placed cell,
e.g. specificity in order to maximize the external attributes of both
actor and object, a process completed by matching affectivity as
an attitudinal variable with performance as an object variable.
The internally important attributes of both actor and object are
similarly maximized by the pairing of quality and neutrality and
of particularism with diffuseness. On this basis the combinations
for the integrative function are made as Figure 4 shows.

FIGURE 4

	Integrative standard *for* orientation	
E	Univ	Perf
x	Spec	Aff
t		
e		
r	ADAPTATION	GOAL ATTAINMENT
n		
a		
l		
I	Qual	Part
n	Neut	Diff
t		
e		
r	PATTERN	INTEGRATION
n	MAINTENANCE	
a		
l		
	Instrumental	*Consummatory*

I

The function represented by the I or integrative cell (all of Figure
4) for the system as a whole is that of stabilizing. Stabilization
cannot occur simply by one set of actor-object relations. Rather,
each "problem" that is faced by the system as a whole requires
for a stable answer its own combination of variable adjustment.
Thus the adaptive problem of the system as a whole requires, in-

sofar as stability is attached to that problem, a characteristic set of actor-object relations. For the adaptive problem, objects must be regarded universalistically and interest in the objects must be confined to specific relevant characteristics. Universalism and specificity thus become also descriptive of a category of norms specifically applicable to the problems of stability of adaptation. And so with the problems of goal attaining, pattern maintenance, and integration itself, characteristic actor-object relations are necessary for the stability of those respective functions and are achievable by the application of norms categorized in terms of the appropriate pattern variables. Parsons suggests that such an analysis transcends description by providing a base for theorems. A theoretical proposition based on the present analysis is a system of action exposed to "plural functional exigencies" and requiring a differentiation of its total normative culture relative to these functional exigencies; "action oriented to the four different standards must be appropriately balanced, if the system is to remain stable." [60]

There remains the problem of so arranging the respective attitude-object variables that the adaptive function of the system will be maximized. The function represented by the A(daptation) cell for the system as a whole is to symbolize and categorize the significance of objects external to the system but possessing present or potential interest for the system. Parsons defines the boundary between those objects which are constituents of the system and those which are part of its environment by the test of particularism; those categorized as possessing a particularistic interest for the system by this definition belong to the system. "Adaptive mechanisms, then, must be conceived as ways of categorizing the meanings of objects universalistically, that is, independently of their actual or potential inclusion in a given system." [61] The mechanisms are symbolic media—language, empirical knowledge, money, and so on—capable of conveying meanings which may be internal to the system, whether or not the objects themselves remain external. The pattern variable combinations which, for Parsons, maximally symbolize and categorize the significance of external objects, are accordingly laid out as in Figure 5.

FIGURE 5

A		
E x t e r n a l	Adaptive exigencies represented by 'symbolic' meaning *of* objects	
	Perf Neut	Part Spec
	COGNITIVE SYMBOLIZATION	EXPRESSIVE SYMBOLIZATION
I n t e r n a l	Univ Diff	Qual Aff
	EXISTENTIAL INTERPRETATION	MORAL-EVALUATIVE CATEGORIZATION
	Instrumental	*Consummatory*

In order to "understand" cognitively the significance of symbols of *adaptive* significance it is necessary to state them in terms
of what they "do" (performance) and to orient them independently of their gratification potentialities (affective neutrality).
Maximal objective understanding thus comes about through cognitive symbolization. Symbols of goal-attaining significance must
have as their focus their meaning for specific motivation (specificity) and their potential appropriateness to the meanings
which defines the system of action (particularism). "This we call
'expressive symbolization,'" [62] the generalization of particularistic
meanings to a universalistic level of significance. Norms that are
external to the system are revealed as significant (the integrative
function is the focus here) only as they are treated as "aspects of
an objectively 'given' state of affairs" [63] (quality) and as the actor
feels emotionally committed to them (affectivity). This is the
moral-evaluative categorization. The sources of normative authority are symbolized and categorized by a combination of universalistic objects (possessing properties not dependent on its inclusion
in the system) with a diffuse actor interest "so that the meaning

in question cannot be treated as contingent on the fluctuating relations between the orienting actor and the environment." [64] This is called "existential interpretation." Figure 5 may be considered as symbolizing the cultural system "organized about patterns of the *meaning* of objects and the 'expression' of these meanings through symbols and signs" [65] and viewed as categories of process. (Column 3, Figure 5).

The pairing of variables in the adaptive cell follows exactly the same pattern as that used in the integrative cell except that the opposite attitudinal or "orientation" partner is combined with a given object or modility partner. This was called the "auxiliary" combination in *The Working Papers* portrayed in parenthesis in Figure 8. Whereas the I(ntegration) cell maximizes the external and the internal, the A(daptation) cell appropriately maximizes the mixtures of these.

The original presentation of all four cells was given in one diagram as shown in Figure 6 which is merely a composite of their above presentation, here given separately to facilitate simplification in this necessarily attenuated version. All sixteen sub-cells have been further rearranged by Parsons. (Figure 7). When the L(atent), I(ntegrative), G(oal-attaining) and A(daptation) sub-cells are arranged horizontally in descending levels or rows, and the L(atent), I(ntegrative), A(daptation) and G(oal-attaining) sub-cells are arranged vertically in columns from left to right a sixteen cell composition is achieved which demonstrates three major considerations of the perspective of the system as a whole. Each descending cell on the vertical axis represents a control over the cells below it; each ascending cell represents a set of conditions imposed on the cells above it. From left to right, each successive cell represents in respect to successive cells "implementation vis-a-vis environment"; from right to left "environmental stimulation." The two left-hand columns represent structural categories, the two right hand columns, categories of process. The significance of this arrangement and the theoretical propositions it supports should be pursued in the original by the serious student of Parsons who will also watch with interest to discover whether Pattern Variables Revisited, the article containing this presentation, portends a permanent and continuous relation between them and their author after some years of absence,

FIGURE 6
(COMBINATION OF FIGURES 2, 3, 4, 5)
THE COMPONENTS OF ACTION SYSTEMS

(Adaptation)   (Goal-Attainment)
INSTRUMENTAL   *CONSUMMATORY*

A   G

	External			P e r f o r m a n c e		
	Adaptive exigencies represented by 'Symbolic' Meanings *of* Objects				Modalities *of* Objects	
E x t e r n a l	E x t e r n a l	→ Perf ↓ Neut	→ Part ↓ Spec		*Universalistic*	*Particularistic*
		COGNITIVE SYMBOLI-ZATION	EXPRESSIVE SYMBOLI-ZATION		OBJECTS OF UTILITY	OBJECTS OF CATHEXIS
	Internal	→ Univ ↓ Diff	→ Qual ↓ Aff	Q u a l i t y	OBJECTS OF "GENERAL-IZED RESPECT"	OBJECTS OF IDENTIFI-CATION
		EXISTEN-TIAL INTERPRE-TATION *Instrumental*	MORAL-EVALUA-TIVE CATEGORI-ZATION *Consum-matory*			

	Specificity	Orientations *to* Objects			Integrative Standards *for* Orientation	
I N T E R N A L	Specificity	*Neutrality*	*Affectivity*	E x t e r n a l	↑ Univ ← Spec	↑ Perf ← Aff
		INTEREST IN INSTRU-MENTAL UTILIZA-TION	CONSUM-MATORY NEEDS		ADAPTA-TION	GOAL-ATTAIN-MENT
	Diffuseness			I n t e r n a l	↑ Qual ← Neut	↑ Part ← Diff
		NEEDS FOR COMMIT-MENT	NEEDS FOR AFFILIA-TION		PATTERN-MAINTE-NANCE *Instrumental*	INTEGRA-TION *Consum-matory*

L   I

(Pattern-Maintenance)   (Integration)
SOURCE: PVR p. 470.

FIGURE 7

STRUCTURAL CATEGORIES		CATEGORIES OF PROCESS	
Units of Orientation to Objects (L) (Properties of Actors)	Integrative Standards (I)	Symbolic Representations of External Objects (A)	Internal Meanings of Objects (G) (Inputs-Outputs)

Direction of Control →

Direction of Limiting Conditions

	L	Neut Diff NORMA- TIVE COMMIT- MENTS	Qual Neut Ground-of- meaning Anchorage PATTERN- MAINTE- NANCE	Diff Univ EXISTEN- TIAL INTERPRE- TATION	Univ Qual "RESPECT"	Outputs to environment
	I	Aff Diff AFFILIA- TIONS	Manifold of evaluative selections Part Diff INTEGRA- TION Allocative selection	Aff Qual MORAL- EVALUA- TION	Part Qual IDENTIFI- CATION	Responsible Action
	G	Aff Diff CONSUM- MATORY NEEDS	Range of action-choice Perf Aff GOAL (attainment) SELEC- TION	Spec Part EXPRES- SIVE SYMBOLI- ZATION	Perf Part CATHEXIS	Expressive Action
	A	Neut Spec INSTRU- MENTAL CAPACI- TIES	Empirical cognitive field Univ Spec ADAPTA- TION Means- Selection	Neut Perf COGNI- TIVE SYMBOLI- ZATION	Perf Univ UTILITY	Instrumental Action

Direction of Implementation vis-a-vis Environment———————→
←———————Direction of Environmental "Stimulation"

SOURCE: PVR p. 476.

or whether he happened to be in their vicinity and "just dropped in." The article explains that the convergence of pattern variables with Bales' functional problems of systems "opened up such a fertile range of possibilities that for several years my main attention has been given to their [functional problems] exploration rather than to direct concern with the scheme [the pattern variables] out of which it grew." [66]

This completes the over-all view of certain aspects of Parsons' work which among his voluminous contributions are perhaps the most distinctive. Juxtaposition of its parts against the elements and processes of social systems as conceptualized in the PAS Model * will reveal details not heretofore considered in this chapter, and where appropriate, comparisons with the conceptualizations of the PAS Model will be made. The components of the Parsonian theory will further be examined, particularly as they apply to the modern medical profession in the United States as in the manner of Parsons' *The Social System.*

KNOWING

Belief (knowledge) as an element. Belief systems are for Parsons one of the initial classifications of a cultural pattern, its basic position in that pattern equalled only as conceived in *The Social System,* by two other systems, the expressive and the value-oriented.[67] Beliefs were there classed on two axes. The first differentiates empirical and non-empirical beliefs; on this axis they are respectively amenable or not amenable to scientific validation. The second axis differentiates existential belief (the "pure type," that of simply knowing) from evaluative belief (in which the

---

* As indicated in Chapter I the present volume is organized by means of a conceptual scheme which borrows liberally from the writings of the various theorists whose works are herein treated. The reader should not assume, however, that the analyses in terms of the PAS Model of the various theorists in any case yields a presentation that is organizationally similar to the original theorist's presentation. In the present chapter, for example, Parsons' influence on the PAS Model will be easily detected at the same time that the model itself differs substantially from the central core of his conceptual scheme, the nature of his extensive contributions and the direction of their development. While Parsons' many helpful suggestions issuing from his readings of two preliminary drafts of this chapter have improved the interpretation, it must be emphasized that no one category of the PAS Model presents that aspect of his material as he himself has presented it in his works. The analyses in terms of the PAS Model categories *en toto* represent not so much a replica in miniature of the original works as they do an analytical codification by which, it is hoped, comparisons can be facilitated.

cognitive, the cathectic and evaluative are fused). An intersecting of the axes yields a four cell table, each cell representing a type of belief designated by Parsons as the scientific, the philosophical, the ideological and the religious.[68]

It should be noted here that the differentiation of beliefs which appeared in *The Social System*, (empirical-nonempirical and existential-evaluative) includes Parsons' most exhaustive treatment of belief and cognition. The present treatment is therefore to a considerable extent based on that work. Parsons' later attention to system problems identifies the adaptive problem as primarily cognitive (See Figure 5) and implies but never specifies many parallels to his earlier paradigm, which he considers in some respects inadequate.

More recently Parsons has "come back to the knowing subject-object dichotomy"[69] (Figures 2 and 3). "The knowing subject and the object known as a special case of the internal-external distinction."[70] He thus stresses "the meanings of *objects* oriented *to*, on the one hand, which is the external aspect of a cultural system, and the meanings or *orientations by* actors on the other hand, which is the internal aspect."[71] In line with this thinking the integrative standards (Column 2, Figure 7), and symbolic representations of external objects, (Column 3, Figure 7) are important.

I would like to suggest four basic structural components (i.e. units) of cultural systems: 1) patterns of empirical existential ideas, defining the conceptual schemes in which empirical objects are "cognized"; 2) patterns of expressive symbolization defining the "forms" and "styles" in which objects are cathected and symbolically represented, or through which they acquire and express emotional meaning; 3) patterns of evaluation, or the patterns through which objects are evaluated as better or worse than each other, and 4) patterns of the grounding of meaning, or the modes of orientation in and to the world in which the "major premises" of all other components of culture are grounded.[72]

Differentiation of the cognitive aspect of culture from other components and the cultural from the social aspects has been the focus of various writings,[73] and may be illustrated by Figure 5, in which cognitive symbolization (A cell) provides the substance for science, and existential interpretation (L cell) provides the "grounding of meaning." As examples of the cultural components of action as they are articulated into the social system (first in terms of values, then respectively of norms, collectivities and roles), cognitive symbolization (A cell of Figure 5) furnishes the chief cultural component of universities; the existential interpretation (L cell of Figure 5) the chief component of religious collectivities; and the two components may fuse in various subsystems of "political religions" such as communism. In Parsons' thinking interrelations of rewards and penalties as articulated in expressive symbolism (G cell of Figure 5), patterned evaluation (I cell of Figure 5) and existential interpretation (L cell of Figure 5) must be noted and differentiated one from another and from cognitive symbolization (A cell of Figure 5) if the state of knowledge of a given system at a specific time is to be understood. Likewise the contribution of interaction as it transpires in the social system producing various selective and distorting pressures in relation to its values, norms, collectivities and roles must be understood. In short the cultural and social factors which influence systems of knowledge and belief must be analyzed.

All four types of beliefs—the scientific, the philosophical, the ideological, and the religious—are invariably fused in empirical action. Ideological beliefs are commonly held by members of a collectivity and deal with evaluative ideas of the goals, nature, and integration of the collectivity; the scientific and philosophical classifications possess a cognitive primacy and are concerned with aspects of reality testing. Every social system possesses beliefs which comprise "reality" for its members. "Without a relatively high development of . . . ['empirical lore'] we could not speak of a human society at all." [74] But in addition to the existential belief of pure cognition there enters the question of the belief's meaning in terms of the actors' interests. They ask "what of it" and answer by meshing the particular bit of cognition with evaluative, expressive and moral considerations. Thus ideological beliefs include scientific beliefs plus other components and religious beliefs include philosophical beliefs plus other components. Parsons sees a symmetry in the transition into the non-empirical which occurs on the existential and on the evaluative levels. "In both cases the transition to the evaluative category means a change in the 'stake' the actor has in the belief system, it means the transition from acceptance to commitment." [75] Since all four types are fused in empirical action, one type is not generally more important than another, although any one type may be seen to have primacy in accordance with the predominant functional exigency of a given social system.

Perhaps from the original impetus of the influences of Weber and Durkheim, Parsons has made significant contributions to the body of knowledge about religious beliefs which will here be summarized. Subscribing to and defending the Durkheimian distinction between sacred and secular, religious beliefs for Parsons focus on the supernatural. [76] They are non-empirical, evaluative, and concerned with meanings and moral problems of human action, involving man's relation to man, collectivities, and his universe. As commitments to action, they impose upon the actor a degree of *moral* obligation which defines responsibilities not only to the supernatural but to society as well. A degree of "moral irrationality" in human action is unavoidable; a consistent pattern of value orientations internalized as part of the personality and institutionalized in the social system is bound to encounter situations and circumstances in earthly existence which makes its complete realization impossible. [77] Adjustment to such earthly inconsistencies is facilitated by mechanisms provided by various religious beliefs. Discrepancies in effort and reward may be tempered by the "after life" belief in heaven and hell as is typical of Catholic Christianity. Or the impact of earthly inequities can be reduced by rejecting the institutionalized order and making the winning of salvation of primary importance, a mechanism typical of earlier Catholicism, earlier Lutheranism, and various sects. Another possibility is that of improving the institutionalized order to the end that society itself will gradually approach perfection. Western "progressive" religious belief fits this type.

Parsons questions the position of Troeltsch who considered that Christian values would provide the framework for the societal value system as emergent from a single Established Church (as in the versions of mediaeval Catholicism, Lutheranism, and Calvinism). Parsons argues that in American society there has evolved an institutionalized Christianity which fosters the traditions of the Christian Society not by a unified established church, but by diversificaton. Building the Kingdom of God on Earth in the Weberian tradition, has proceeded by commitment to essentially unchanged values—those of "ascetic Protestantism"—but by implementations consistent with the changes in society's structure. The "Kingdom" is no longer thought of as exclusively governed by religious considerations, "there is an autonomous secular sphere of the 'good society' which . . . may still be interpreted as 'God's work.'"[78] Thus, "instrumental activism" common to Calvinism is still a value; but "universalizing the essential conditions of effective performance through equalization of civil rights and of access to education and health,"[79] might be regarded as a secular goal within the religious tradition. Secularization within the religious tradition has essentially paralleled the proliferated differentiations characteristic of American society. "The keynote of it is the personal intimacy and privacy of the individual's faith and relation to his conception of Divinity,"[80] a kind of relation to which secular authority in religious matters is repugnant, as is the idea that *any* human authority has any kind of monopolistic access to religious goods.

Theological preoccupations are thus not a prime requisite for religious genuineness, and although denominational pluralism is completely consistent with and the result of departure from a belief system institutionalized as *the* religious system of a society, the "main trend is toward greater integration of these various elements in a viable system."[81] Such a belief system, most differentiated and *ipso facto* most intra-tolerant in the United States, is increasingly prevalent in societies which are increasingly differentiated. "Now, every important European state (except Spain) has at least some important degree of religious toleration and in a few, like France, formal separation of Church and State has been put through."[82] This stands in contrast to the USSR in which the "dialectic" becomes to the Marxists what "providence" has been for the Christians and both are sacred religious entities.[83] In the communistic countries the integration of societies does not provide for belief pluralism. On the contrary, beliefs are not a private matter and the subsystems differentiated by functional imperatives are not permitted pluralistic interpretations. In fact the polity and the integrative collectivities such as the party tend to fuse and control the beliefs of other spheres.

Cognitive mapping and validation as process. Parsons views these processes as primarily processes of symbolization, with each of the four types of beliefs possessing a characteristic symbolic process involving different combinations of the pattern variables (Figure 5). Even though the objects so symbolized might be external to it, the symbolized *meanings* of the environmental object-world are internal to the system. Experience is never "raw." "Raw experience is itself an abstraction of an element of knowledge." [84] Put somewhat differently, "the thing 'out there' depends on symbolization. I think we should probably infer that on pre-symbolic levels, objects simply do not exist as entities independent of the relation of observations. It is only through special symbolic elaboration that this 'out there' can exist at all, apart from an observer." [85] The manner in which reality is validated thus depends on some already established conceptualization, some "intermediate symbolism," which is "believed in" without observable proof. The need for symbols to give body to and to validate beliefs is underscored by an interesting analogue: "believing that God is 'an old man with a long white beard,'" in the non-empirical realm is not unlike "believing that an electron is a spherical solid particle of 'matter,' that is, a little round ball," in the empirical realm.[86] Both make it possible to have a concrete image for what one believes.

Since all four methods of symbolic representation are fused in empirical action it is not surprising that there are great variations among societies in the primary choice by which cognitive mapping takes place. Although no system can exist, Parsons maintains, which completely disregards truth as developed by reality testing (whether by the sophisticated canons of science or by the more elementary methods of "proto-science"), commitments to other symbolic representations greatly influence the prevalence of the scientific approach. Commitment to and vested interests in idealogical and religious beliefs, urgency of immediate instrumental action, and the motivationally gratifying practice of magic are among the factors mentioned by Parsons as being inhibiting to scientific development. "Knowledge does not 'apply itself,' no matter how advantageous to the society the results may . . . appear." [87] To influence action it must be incorporated into the social system through the "mechanisms of institutionalization of roles . . . [and] the requisite combinations of motivational and cultural elements." [88]

Even under the favorable conditions provided by a cultural milieu in which scientific validation has primacy and in which the status-role of scientist is fully institutionalized there are sufficient commitments to differently symbolized beliefs to make scientific knowledge less than automatically accepted. The status-role of scientist requires the acceptance of validated findings and the rejection of disvalidated findings. The findings often require the rejection or rearrangement of beliefs to which the larger society is committed. The status-role of scientist, therefore, and particularly of the social scientist, can thrive only in a liberal pattern of freedom of thought,[89] an exceptional condition which permits ideological controversy between scientific and ideological levels, and one not afforded by either traditionalism or authoritarianism.

Without an institutionalized value orientation consistent with the cultural tradition a collectivity would possess no integration—would in fact, not be a collectivity. Commitment to a value orientation, built into membership status-roles is thus a prerequisite of all social systems. Ideological beliefs are thus basic: ". . . there must be a set of beliefs, subscription to which is in some sense an obligation of collectivity membership roles, where the cognitive conviction of truth and the 'moral' conviction of rightness are merged." [90] The ideological beliefs "rationalize" choices in accordance with the pattern variable dilemmas as recounted above. For example, the choice between technical competence and kinship or friendship solidarity when only one may be chosen must invoke the ideological position, which provides "reasons why one direction of choice rather than its alternative should be selected, why it is right and proper that this should be so." [91] Cognitive mapping and validation is consequently effected. Thus Parsons, following Max Weber, agrees with Merton that "ascetic Protestantism" contributed to the growth of science in the Western world.[92]

Demands for internal pattern consistency and maintenance (although never fully realized) maximize the likelihood that societies exhibiting certain value orientations favor certain types of belief systems and the kinds of symbolization by which they are represented. Thus, a firmly institutionalized belief in supernatural compensation goes with an ascriptive emphasis in the institutionalized value system. Similarly, when the supernatural element is explicit, as in Calvinism as noted by Max Weber, the belief may be in the divine mission of man for the establishment of the Kingdom of God on Earth. Predestination tended, in this case, to push salvation as a goal into a less important position. Demonstrating the badge of membership in the appointed company of saints "who share the responsibility for implementing the Divine will" [93] became of utmost importance. Predestination thus formed a belief which affected the goal-directedness of the social order, in this case, orienting it to this world rather than to salvation in another world. Within the realm of religion, then, the type of validation which "makes sense" to individuals depends upon what the nature of the supernatural order itself is believed to be, a determining factor also, for the type of action to be pursued.

Religious action may be *ritualistic* if the goal is non-empirical, or *magical* if the goal is empirical. It may be *supplicative* if the supernatural is conceived to be a decision-making actor and can take the direct role of alter, or it may be *contemplative,* if supernatural influence is conceived to operate on the actor's own state of mind when it is properly receptive, as exemplified by "mystical" religions such as Buddhism and Taoism. This latter type of religious technique and belief, is closely related to those which may specify articulation by such acts as mortification of the flesh and asceticism which are intended to induce a more receptive state by removing the influence of the personality and the corporal body.

Some religious belief systems, such as those of radical salvation, have their chief locus in transcendental values and goals but paradoxically enlist worldly interests in the motivation of religious conformity. The institutionalized church acquires power in a worldly as well as spiritual sense. The inconsistencies of such cognitive mapping lead Parsons to the conclusion that under such circumstances it is unlikely that the "religious orientation itself will remain entirely unchanged for long." [94]

As with the other theorists whose works are treated in this volume, Parsons illuminates by his own scientific theories, the role of the scientist and the kind of cognitive mapping and validation articulated by that role. His first important theoretical monograph, *The Structure of Social Action,* not only examined the cognitive mappings of Alfred Marshall, Pareto, Durkheim, and Max Weber but showed that their separate works displayed a remarkable convergence in a "single coherent body of theory . . . the 'theory of social action,' " [95] even though each had started from diverse bases and was concerned with different empirical problems. Parsons' explorations into the factors contributing to the convergence inevitably led to the development of his own epistemological position.

. . . it is maintained that at least some of the general concepts of science are not fictional but adequately "grasp" aspects of the objective external world. This is true of the concepts . . . called analytical elements. . . . These concepts correspond, not to concrete phenomena, but to elements in them which are analytically separable from other elements. There is no implication that the value of any one such element, or even of all those included in one logically coherent system, is completely descriptive of any particular concrete thing or event.[96]

If the analyses of the separate investigators are correct, i.e. valid, at some level of generality the analytic elements emerging from one investigation will coincide with those emerging from another analysis, equally correct and valid. Indeed, the lack of convergence when both analyses had been generalized to a given level, would impute unreliability to one, or the other or both of the analyses which preceded the conflicting generalizations. This is essentially Parsons' contention,[97] which bears importantly on his own subsequent theorizations. His inclusion of the cultural, social, psychological and biological systems (the latter called "behavioral organisms") in one general theory rests upon this earlier idea of the inevitable convergence in cognitive mapping of present-day specialties.

Once one has learned to avoid reifying analytical systems and has understood that plural analytical systems are involved in the same concrete phenomena, there need be nothing mystical about what is meant by mind (i.e., a psychological system) as *analytically distinguished* from organism or body.[98]

Noting that "science and ideology can be only analytically distinguished from each other; [and that] in its development social science differentiates out from ideology as it emerges from the same roots in common sense," [99] Parsons undertakes to analyze knowledge through highlighting cultural and social system categories. He employs two paradigms representing "levels at which problems of meaning" are developed, one called "Relating Values to the Other Cultural Components," and the other called "Relating Values to Non-cultural Components." [100] Although a belief system in any society can only be understood in terms of the interrelatedness of its four components, (Figure 5) he notes that "evaluation and . . . expressive symbolization—are so different . . . [from empirical science and the grounding of meaning] that it is of dubious utility to include values and expressive symbols at all as forms of 'knowledge.' " [101]

In the most general sense "what is evaluated as a good society" is the key consideration for cultural systems and the "grounding of meaning" (L cell of Figure 5) is supplied by the religious system or becomes a prominent component in ideological systems which act as "political religions." "It is in the *relation* between institutionalized values and empirical concepts of the evaluating social systems that the problem of ideology arises" [102] providing evaluations of the status-quo in such a manner that actors of a given society are classified as radicals, conservatives, etc.

The second paradigm permits consideration of beliefs on the social system level with primary emphasis on values, norms, collectivities and roles. Thus belief systems may be influenced by "malintegration of the value structure itself," as in the case of an immigrant minority system. Conflicting norms and expectancy patterns may be reflected in the belief systems. Goals of collectives and actors may differ as when firms strive for profits which are not the motives of members. "Strain is not itself an explanation of ideological patterns, but a generalized label for the kind of factors to look for in working out an explanation." [103] "Only through an analysis of both social and cultural systems and their interpenetration and interdependence . . . can an adequate sociology of knowledge be worked out." [104]

Many of Parsons' explicit positions with respect to theory must, in the summarizing nature of this present volume, remain implicit. However, because of the technique used here of juxtaposition against the PAS Model, his discussion of models is relevant, especially since to some theorists, exactitude in model use and designation is a requisite of theoretical sophistication. Parsons claims no clear set of views on the utility and role of models, acknowledging that to him:

The most general sense of the term model seems to be that of an "ideal type" of structure or process, arrived at by hypothetical reasoning from theoretical premises, which is then used, through comparison with empirical data, to analyze such data. In this meaning, model seems to be almost identical with theoretical scheme. And, if it is theory, and of course, good theory, I am in favor of it.[105]

He recognizes in the use of models the danger of the fallacy of misplaced concreteness. The temptation is to preserve intact the conceptualized model by imputing unproven randomness to variations which may properly belong in the internal structure of the model. This of course, is a form of model reification. "The important point is that every model must be conceived to have a *theoretically* ordered context; it is a product of the special abstraction of part of a range of theoretical relationships for specific purposes and must never be 'reified.'"[106] He notes that "there are many possible types of models appropriate for use and stresses that it is exceedingly important to be highly pragmatic . . . and to try out a variety of devices."[107]

While appropriately sympathetic with and supportive of the vast amount of "applied" research done on levels capable of being stated in fairly specific "equations," Parsons' work on the whole is overwhelmingly preoccupied with levels of relationships to which the application of "'equations' are still too specific . . . [and which, at this stage are amenable only to] cruder and more elementary procedures, especially relatively formalized classifications."[108]

For these classificatory purposes, the fundamental starting point is the "fourfold table," namely, the simple cross classification of what in some sense are the "polar" or widely separated values of two variables. The general justification of using the logic of this procedure is related to the extremely wide usefulness of *binary* discriminations; the binomial theorem in mathematics, the "bit" theory in communication theory; various trends in symbolic logic, and substantively, empirical evidence such as the predominance of division into two in the biological process of cell division.[109]

The "formalized classifications" of which he speaks, however, are by no means as crude as he would indicate, and there is an inescapable impression created by his works in their entirety that he is in quest of the equation which will prove to be the keystone to all of social science. The zest with which he responds to the stimulation of others' ideas and the rapidity with which the salient features of these are incorporated into the snow-balling of his work reveals the scientist's quest for knowledge no matter where it may lead. At the same time his commitment to the ideological position of the larger society is attested to by the simultaneous attention given to such "social problems" as ethnic relations, economically under-developed countries and inequities of education and health opportunities.

Beliefs and medical practices. Moral irrationality, potential in all action, and based in conflicting commitments, is exemplified in doctor-patient relations. Many American doctors believe the doctor-patient relation to be *Gemeinschaft*-like, its essential nature jeopardized by outside control. Its preservation remains an ideal supported by heavy belief commitment despite its actual atrophy by virtue of medical specialization and other broader societal factors which render the ideal unrealistic.

Religious beliefs, too, render health and medical practices less than maximally rational, as the belief that high mortality is God's will, which either *can* not or *should* not be tampered with.[110] Magic, as a type of religious action with an empirical healing goal would of course be overtly taboo as a medical practice in modern societies. Nonetheless, Parsons makes a good case for the parallel between primitive magic and the "optimistic bias" which attends the application of scientific medicine in cases where the cure is uncertain and subject to considerable unpredictability. In fact, "The world over the rational approach to health through applied science is . . . the exception rather than the rule, and in our society there is, even today, a very large volume of 'superstition' and other non-or irrational beliefs and practices in the health field." [111]

Beliefs about death similarly have an influence on health practices. In America, for instance, beliefs about the sacredness of the cadaver require that ordinary attitudes be substituted by others more compatible with rationally prescribed practices such as autopsy, and dissection. Dissecting of the first cadaver in the training of each medical student usually requires a type of ritual or initiatory rite which serves as a legitimizing recognition that the earlier attitudes toward the dead, fostered in the home and community are being supplanted. Apparent here is a merging of belief with *sentiment,* a subject to which attention is now turned.

FEELING

Sentiment as an element. Parsons states without qualification that "the prototype of the expressive symbol, within the context of interaction, is the *symbolic act."* [112] He then characteristically treats objects in relation to the actor as subject. For Parsons, then, sentiments are "culturally organized cathectic and/or evaluative modes or patterns of orientation toward particular objects or classes of objects." [113]

The patterned cathectic orientations of ego (actor or subject) to object are attitudinal and designated by Parsons as types of attachment describable in pattern variable terms: 1) approval, with primacy of neutrality and specificity; 2) receptiveness-responsiveness, with primacy of affectivity and specificity; 3) love, with primacy of affectivity and diffuseness; and 4) esteem, with primacy of neutrality and diffuseness.[114] (These correspond to the cell designated as Figure 2 above which portrays the orientation of actors to objects and comprises the pattern-maintenance segment of action systems. Despite the latter's focus upon "system problem," an area which had not been developed by Parsons at the time of the writing of *The Social System* upon which this present treatment of sentiment is based, the parallel between the earlier formulation and the later broader generalization is clear.)

The objects toward which the attitudes are directed must also be characterized by some ordering of allocation (or reward) since no expressive mutuality between actor and object could prevail if the latter could not fulfill the attitudinal expectancies of the actor. Object types relative to the attitudes of ego or actor just summarized, are also describable in pattern variable terms. The primarily affective attitude on the part of the actor tends to be associated with *particularism* on the part of the object, whereby particularization is imparted to 1) the legitimate content of affective symbolism, 2) the legitimate objects of attachment, and 3) the expressive interests and obligations thus assumed. Affective attitudes which occur within limits in a predominantly neutral setting—e.g. an occupational social system—tends to be associated, in the United States at least, with a limited particularism which shades into *universalism* on the part of the object. Expressive orientations of affectivity toward such objects are not permitted to be particularistically exclusive but must be manifested relatively impartially to all associates. Object types also differ from each other in degree of access to expressively symbolic cultural objects *(quality* or *ascription)* and in tasteful utilization of the cultural objects which are at their disposal *(performance).* The cathectic object types described in pattern variable terms correspond to the cell designated above as Figure 3, which, like the other cells in that series of Figures, was developed as a system problem, this particular one representing goal-attaining. Despite somewhat different terminology used in the earlier development of expressive symbolism, the parallel between it and the later formulation is clear.

Any one of the four basic attitude types may be expressed or symbolized by any symbolic entity: an act, a quality of personality or of the organism, a physical object, or a cultural pattern.[115] The affective and diffuse love relation, e.g., would involve all four symbolic entities either in the erotic aspect of the relation or in the wide range of associated behavior. The mutual expectancies of any such relation demand that both gratificatory significance and symbolic significance prevail both for ego and alter (actor and subject). The same situation is true for cases in which primacy of affective neutrality prevails as in approval or esteem. A student who may entertain sentiments of approval toward his teacher in the *particularistic* sense of limiting his interest to the latter's technical competence is justified in an expectancy that the teacher extend toward him respect for his ability and appreciation for his class performances. "Here, though in another context the actions may be of primarily instrumental significance, they also have an aspect of expressive symbols." [116] When the symbolic reference is directed toward the supernatural, religious symbolism results.

Sentiments are learned or acquired and thus culturally structured. This means that both actor and object view each symbolic entity in terms of internalized normative standards. They exercise appreciative and evaluative judgments toward their own specific actions, expectations and reciprocal attitudes in terms of the common cultural patterns which define the situation, which in the case of sentiment, is related chiefly to cathectic interests. Those cathected acts and objects which become singled out as expressive symbols tend to become institutionalized, or stabilized on a cultural basis.[117] In this respect sentiment is seen by Parsons to be primarily a "relational possession"; actor can either give or withhold a favorable response or attitude from alter contingent on alter's behavior in a variety of respects. The mutually oriented expectations of actor and object are institutionally defined, legitimized expectation on the part of one, entitling him to a particular type of attitude on the part of the other. "The conditions on which alter may legitimately change his attitude toward ego are institutionally defined just as are the conditions on which he may legitimately dispose of a physical object in his possession." [118] The normative-evaluative emphases so apparent here, reiterates the mutualities of common values and common sentiments supportive of the culture pattern.

Conformity with the relevant expectation is treated as a "good thing" relatively independently of any specific instrumental "advantage" to be gained from such conformity . . . this attachment to common values, while it may fit the immediate gratificational needs of the actors always has also a "moral" aspect in that to some degree this conformity defines the "responsibilities" of the actor in the . . . social action system in which he participates.[119]

This integration of common value patterns with internalized need dispositions of the constituent actors in a social system stabilizes the social system through the approximate but never perfect coincidence of private and collective interests.[120] That the two never coincide completely is one source of tension in personality systems which in turn influences the stability of social systems.

Tension management as process. The concept, tension management, is used by Parsons in much the same way as it is used in the PAS Model. Basic to its use in both instances is recognition of the incompatibility of the simultaneous pursuance of maximal instrumental activity and maximal consummatory or expressive activity. Parsons expresses that incompatibility thus:

> In instrumental activity the actor manipulates objects and relations seen as "causes" in order to obtain certain "effects" . . . in this context, where the goal is not yet attained and where one must deal with objects in a "realistic" way it is necessary to inhibit affective or emotional reactions to the objects in order to avoid being drawn off toward other goals, to avoid making inappropriate choices . . . and to avoid premature relaxation of instrumental efforts. Hence the attitude tends to be marked by a certain inhibition or *neutrality* with affect to some extent held neutral.[121]

In a great number of potentially stressful situations, the actors do not consciously evoke the necessary affectively neutral attitude, but do so through custom or habit because cultural definitions of the situation prescribe the expectation of a neutral attitude. "Conformity with the relevant expectations is treated as a 'good thing'" by which the responsibilities of the actor to the social system in which he participates is specified. The diffuse friendliness among male occupational associates in the United States, which avoids unlimited particularistic attachments while still preserving a degree of affectivity is one such example. Similarly, Parsons observes that norms which provide an affective-particularistic and overwhelmingly *Gemeinschaft*-like nature to the sex act in certain institutionalized situations such as marriage may place primacy on the communication of sentiments between partners through symbolic acts and meanings whereas in the *Gesellschaft*-like context of prostitution, the primacy may be placed upon norms which require affective-neutrality and may be considered as tension managing.

The social structuring of paired expectancy patterns such as husband-wife or doctor-patient similarly effects tension management. Role definitions of task leaders—such as of foremen or of doctors—and many other comparable status-roles, specify affective neutrality as the primary attitudinal type for interaction with subordinates, patients and others with whom affective relations would be stressful and dysfunctional. "The definition of a role in terms of affective neutrality excludes any expressive interest from primacy in the orientation structure and gives the primacy either to instrumental or to moral considerations." [122] Within a collectivity what Bales calls the instrumental leader who keeps the group moving toward its goal generates tensions within the system which generally are reduced by the expressive leader who promotes solidary sentiments by being the "funnyman," or the conciliator.[123] Within the society at large Parsons hypothesizes that labor unions perform a similar integrative and pattern-maintenance function "by protecting the workers' interests through bargaining and by symbolizing his anxieties and other sentiments and reinforcing his self respect and confidence. . . . This occurs largely through *non-economic* mechanisms of the type involved in rituals, political campaigns and therapy." [124]

Rituals are another societal device which reduces emotional tensions by providing a situation in which wishes and strains can be "acted out" symbolically.[125] The uncertainties of uncontrollable and unpredictable situations are likewise reduced by resort to magic. On a different level, certain groups within a social system are subjected to tensions peculiar to that group. Lower classes in an achievement-oriented society, may be unable to move higher, in which case gambling may serve a tension-managing function. Youth in America are subjected to tensions unique to their age group which may be eased by a youth culture. The norms which require tact in interpersonal relations or those which permit or foster anonymity are tension managing mechanisms along with the more obvious phenomena such as the church confessional or the provision in many organizations for opportunities to "blow off steam," by the encouragement to members to let their views be known.[126] The attaining of a goal, by definition, permits the lessening to some degree of the discipline characteristic of the actual working toward the goal and hence reduces tensions. However, strictly speaking, tension management refers to those procedures and mechanisms for maintaining discipline while the goal is being sought. Although the nuclear family of industrialized societies in Parsons' thinking has as one of its "primary societal functions . . . the psychological or personality tension-management of its adult members" [127] on the PAS Model it is one of the central arenas for the communication of sentiment.

Communication of sentiment as process. Expressive symbolism tends to be organized relative to reciprocal attitudes which focus on cathectic interests. By the time a basic attitude type is symbolized by an entity, i.e., an act, a quality of personality or of the organism, a physical object, or a cultural pattern, it is already a part of process. Overture and response, in short, interaction, can thereafter take place in terms of expressive symbolization, which, as Figure 7 shows, is one of the categories of process.

From this point of view the concrete expressive symbols which are part of the process of interaction serve a threefold function . . . 1) they aid in communication between the interacting parties, in this case the communication of cathectic "meanings"; 2) they organize the interaction process through normative regulation, through imposing appreciative standards on it; and 3) they serve as direct objects for the gratification of the relevant need-dispositions.[128]

In this section the primary concern is with the first part of the threefold function: the communicative process by which the expressive symbols are "signs to alter of what ego's attitudes toward him are." [129]

The interactive relationships of actor(s) and object(s) and the reciprocal roles of the parties, the basic units of a social system, themselves become endowed with expressive symbolism. As the interactive relationship is established "there is a process of selection of appropriate symbolization of the relevant attitudes from among the possibilities available in the situation." [130] Parsons illustrates his thesis here by two sustained examples. If the "relevant attitude" is one of love, with primacy of affectivity-diffuseness, appropriate symbolization will involve the imputing of symbolic meanings to erotic acts, to qualities of personality or of the organism, to physical objects, or to a cultural pattern. If the relationship is defined as a *love* relationship, erotic acts in American society, for example, require such conditions as privacy, appropriate dress, the proper setting, and affectionate non-erotic acts such as speech, exchange of gifts, sharing of activities and so on, all of which carry their symbolism by which sentiment is communicated. If the "relevant attitude" is one of approval with primacy of affective neutrality and specificity and verging on esteem with primacy on affective neutrality and diffuseness as in the student-teacher relationship referred to above, appropriate symbolization will involve the imputing of symbolic meanings (evaluative, rather than cathectic) to the teacher's technical competence and to the student's performance. Beyond this, lectures, seminars, research techniques and other acts will be drawn into the complex and will be appropriately symbolized as will such things as the organizational setting, the teacher's role in it, premises, buildings etc. Should the relevant attitude shift from approval to esteem, more diffuse characteristics will be symbolized and communicate admiration. "In that case there is very likely to be a cathexis of a variety of aspects of the teacher's general style of life, his tastes in clothing or in literature or hobbies, a predisposition to think well of his wife and many other things." [131]

As roles become proliferated by societal differentiation, the role itself becomes endowed with expressive symbolism; certain symbolic significances come to be associated with specialized roles,[132] some of which are more responsible than others for the communication of sentiment. Leadership roles fall in this class. Besides the British monarch, which is the "stock example," Parsons cites the toastmaster and the elder statesman whose instrumental functions in a given social system may be quite negligible, but whose expressive and integrative functions as sentiment communicators are considerable. Further, the value-sentiments which pervade a social system are projected upon the leader. The leader becomes their symbol and "loyalty to these values, to the collectivity, and to the leader in his role become indistinguishable." [133] As a result, only the chief of state can perform certain symbolic acts,[134] i.e. can effectively communicate the collective attitudes or sentiments. In a similar manner not specified by Parsons, and on a lower level of organization, a social object can get his cue about what the actor's attitude toward him is by identifying the hierarchical role of the incumbent designated to interact with him. He would be correct in assuming that he was attitudinally central if he were given the "red carpet" treatment by the top executives of the collectivity (which is actor in this case) but incorrect in such an assumption if his interaction was confined to an exchange with a minor figure of the collectivity. Roles characteristic of the family may be projected to fill need-dispositions. Thus fraternities and sororities may have "house mothers," never "house fathers." The Roman Catholic Church, emulating family status-roles of father, mother, brother and sister, comprises a symbolic family in which the lay-Catholic may be symbolized as a child.

Such role symbolism presupposes that certain roles express by their symbolism attitudes characteristic of the wider society of which collectivities are a part. There are symbols other than those attached to roles which may essentially represent the solidarity of particular collectivities. Parsons considers family observances, as for example, Thanksgiving and Christmas as illustrative of this type, where the interaction is predominantly "familial expressionalism" although religious and cultural connotations are also present. In contrast are the collectively moral expressions of solidarity articulated in collective rituals and marked by solemnity in the manner of the religious ritual as described by Durkheim. Here Parsons distinguishes, however, between that collectively moral communication of sentiment which by religious symbolism expresses the solidarity of the main institutionalized collectivities (the core type of relgious ritual as described by Durkheim) and that "religious symbolism which serves as an institutionalized channel for the adjustment of emotional strains" [135] resulting from discrepancies between institutionalized expectations and human experience, especially those resulting in the disruption of social relations. This latter type was emphasized by Malinowski, "the type case being the funeral ceremonial,"[136] and although it is expressive, it is more especially tension managing. Other symbolism manifesting collective solidarity is evaluative in emphasis but not religious in that it is not directed to the supernatural, such as Fourth of July celebrations and university Commencement ceremonies.

New symbols of sentiment communication are brought into being by the creative artist whom Parsons views as being "a direct parallel to the . . . scientist and philosopher" [137] who creates beliefs. Despite the "individualism" of the creative artist, he is concerned with communicating, and thus his expressive symbolism is not private (if it were he would be a schizophrenic) but cultural. Although primarily interested in expression, the creative artist must possess and give attention to technical competence and this aspect of his work is instrumental and comparable to techniques in other fields. The "performing" artist, in contrast, specializes in the skilled implementation of expressive symbolism but does not himself create the symbols. He, like the creative artist, communicates by expressive symbols, "supplies a want or meets a need in his public, and on the expressive level he receives 'appreciation' and admiration in return." [138] His role is institutionalized on much the same basis as other institutionalized roles.

Sentiments and medical practice. The physician-patient relation is collectivity-oriented forming a *Gemeinschaft*-like "community of fate" in that the welfare of the patient must come ahead of the self-interest of the doctor. [139] It is different, however, from the *Gemeinschaft*-like relationship such as between parent and child because the physician's relation to the patient must be characterized by affective-neutrality in order that he may avoid emotional or sentimental involvement with the patient. Thus near relatives are typically avoided as patients and some physicians do not like to take patients through successive difficult sicknesses because of involvement of sentiments resulting from having "shared the fight." In professional dealings with friends physicians usually prefer that the setting be the affectively neutral one provided by the office. Some tensions and sentiments obstructive to the medical arts are never completely overcome. The strain due to uncertainty and incurability of some cases lead, in Parsons' view, to what Pareto calls the "need to manifest sentiments by external acts." [140] Overactivity in operating and prescribing drugs are often a result of this need.

ACHIEVING

End, goal or objective as an element. The means-end schema was the chief tool of analysis in Parsons' earliest work, *The Structure of Social Action,* in which the concept end was, of course, focal. Since 1951 the term "end" is rarely used in his work but "goal" is widely employed. [141]

We conceive action to be oriented to the attainment of goals, and hence to involve selective processes relative to goals. Seen in their relations to goals, then, all the components of systems of action and of the situations in which action takes place, are subject to the process of evaluation, as desirable, or undesirable as useful or useless, as gratifying or noxious.[142]

Various terminologies: goal-orientedness as a system of relations,[143] the goal state as a maximal stabilizing relation between the system of reference and situational objects,[144] and goal-directedness as a fundamental property of action systems,[145] are used as interpretations of goal, and of course bear witness to the basic position of goal in Parsonian theory.

Important for the concept goal are the more recent works in which Parsons has spelled out in some detail the distinguishing features of the type of social system "to which the term 'bureaucracy' is most often applied"; its defining characteristic in his view is in the *"primacy of orientation to the attainment of a specific goal"* with attainment of goal defined as "a *relation* between a system (in this case a social system) and the relevant parts of the external situation in which it acts or operates." [146] *Relationship* is emphasized definitionally because of the functional interdependencies of modern societies, a condition by which the goal state of many collectivities inevitably suffers a deprivation by faulty goal perception or attainment on the part of one or a few collectivities. The goal product (output) of one social system is a resource (input) for another. Parsons gives examples of three different types of organizations: the economic organization, the goal of which is to produce goods, the government agency, the goal of which is to produce regulatory decisions, and the university, the goal of which is to produce trained capacity. A clarifying illustration might be constructed from these three examples to demonstrate why the goal of any one is primarily relational.

The output of trained capacity as a goal of a university would include the "production" of trained engineers. If the goal were improperly conceived (and/or implemented) the faulty or non-available product would constitute a deprivation to an economic organization for which well-trained engineers is an input (resource). Likewise, the output of reliable products as a goal of an economic organization would include the production of some goods destined for university use. If the goal were improperly conceived (and/or implemented) the faulty or non-available product would constitute a deprivation to the university for which

well-constructed buildings and safe, well-designed research equipment is an input. Both might be subjected to deprivation if the
output of regulatory measures as a goal of a government agency
were improperly conceived (and/or implemented) resulting in
faulty or non-availiable controls and standards. "What from the
point of view of the organization in question is its specified goal
is, from the point of view of the larger system of which it is a
differentiated part or subsystem, a specialized or differentiated
function. This relationship is the primary link between an organization and the larger system of which it is a part. . . ." [147] Unless
the organization is to be a deviant, its value system must be harmonious with the value system of the larger society of which it is
a part and from which it procures its legitimized and identified
goal. In turn, the organization, besides fulfilling its privately conceived narrower goals, fulfills an obligation to the larger society
by commitment to the societal goal for which purpose it is legitimately "in business." This means that part of the goal-structure
of a business firm might be its money return (which is a condition
of its continued existence in a market economy) but its *primary*
organization goal must be the fulfillment of the functions required of it by the larger society, or production. [148] The relational
focus of goal for the economic organization is thus an adaptive
focus, the goal itself fluctuating as external conditions fluctuate.
For this kind of organization Figure 5 describes major goal considerations.

What Parsons so carefully spells out for the bureaucratic organization is at least partially applicable to the non-bureaucratic
social system. Although the family, the social club, the pair of
friends, each case viewed as a social system, would presumably
have a much less specific goal than the bureaucratic organization,
the goals and sub-goals that each does possess (except in the case
of deviancy) are consistent with the value-system of the larger
society. The consequences of the relation that each establishes
with larger social entities in terms both of what they get from the
higher level entities and what they give back, make an immediate
difference at those higher levels with which they are directly connected and an ultimate difference to the general society. Most of
the interaction between family members, club members, and a pair
of friends however, is not primarily adaptive to external conditions

but rather to the immediate conditions within the group; the inter-action itself constitutes the goal which is still, of course, relational, but pattern-maintaining rather than adaptive, and subject chiefly to the variables described by Figure 2. Similar generalizations with appropriate modifications can be made for other social systems whose functional imperatives specify a type of goal. "The same basic classification can be used for goal types which has been used earlier in dealing with the functions of a social system. Thus, we may speak of adaptive goals, implementive goals, integrative goals, and pattern-maintenance goals." [149]

Goal attaining and concommitant "latent" activity as process. As with the concept goal, that of goal attaining is most elaborated by Parsons with respect to the bureaucratic organizations. In contrast to goal identification and legitimation in respect to these organizations, goal attaining is the actual producing of that "iden-tifiable something which can be utilized in some way by another system." [150] As summarized above, Parsons views this process as being chiefly a function of power manifested by decision making at the policy level, the allocative level, the operative or technical level, and finally through a coordination of levels. Depending upon whether the goals are principally adaptive, implementive, integrative or pattern-maintaining (they are never wholly of one type) the goal attaining process is marked by characteristic power articulations. Parsons analyzes three illustrative cases, here sum-marized. The business firm, with its adaptive goal in mind, con-centrates power among those status-roles (usually called top management) responsible for adaptation to the external situation. External relations remain in the hands of top management, but managerial and technical jobs are delegated. The military organi-zation, with its goal of technical effectiveness and maximization of power in its field in mind, is the most authoritarian type of or-ganization found on a large scale in U. S. society. Legitimation focuses on authorization from a higher source, and once a com-manding officer's position is legitimized, his standards of effective-ness are not subjected to comparisons such as those which prevail on the market. He has powers of decision and coercion with no institutionalized right to quit on the part of his subordinates. "This pattern clearly derives from the overwhelming importance of effective coordinated action in dangerous emergency situa-

tions," [151] coordination presumably being enhanced by the reduction of "top management" incumbents to the one sole figure of
the commanding officer. Decision making in the military as well
as in the business organization, however, is increasingly modified
by dependencies on technical professional services, the trained
capacities of which lead to an inevitable degree of decentraliza-
tion.

This condition is central to goal attaining in the university
organization, with its goal of pattern maintenance by socialization
and of creative modification of cultural tradition in mind. The
university is typically not a "line" organization but a balance of
responsibility, in which the faculty as technical professionals have
heavy obligations for specifying what constitutes "trained capacity" and how it can be achieved, in fields much too diverse and
technical for effective decision making solely on the part of the
administrative staff. The latter of course would be responsible
for that part of the goal which is adaptive to situations external
to the university. Similar generalizations, with appropriate modifications, might be made for those social systems such as the
family, and some churches which are pattern-maintaining but
non-bureaucratic. Whether the diffuse responsibilities for goal
attaining were attributable to technical specialization or to other
capacities specified by the pattern which is being maintained, it
is more likely that democratic norms of power articulation for
goal attainment would prevail in social systems of this type than
in those of either the adaptive or implementive type. The important thing, from Parsons' point of view, is that the work gets
done, or the group moves on its way toward the fulfillment of its
goal precisely because the power invested in the group and generated by the group is used at the points most strategic for attainment of the main goal. "Mastery" of this type as "performance
process" has as its "basic paradigm . . . the means-end schema.
[In Figures 6 & 8] the directionality of such process is clockwise
relative to the goal-focus, from A to G." [152]

Parsons believes that generally only within limited ranges and
to a limited extent are the consequences or ends which the sociologist takes as significant and central, those which are explicitly
intended by the actor, individual or collective.[153] He provides
many insights by which "latent" concommitant activity is actually

seen to be operative. The mother whose objective is the socialization of her child, or the psychotherapist whose objective is the rehabilitating of his patient seldom sees the diffuse and affective relations characteristic of the permissive and supportive phases of child-rearing or therapy as acts which provide the leverage for "denial of reciprocity" and "manipulation of rewards," which are processes overtly recognized as socializing or rehabilitating. The woman teacher, in the lower grades whose objective is to teach her pupils, seldom sees her "tenderness and solicitude" (unbecoming to a man teacher) as a needed mother surrogate function but only as an adjunct to rapport with her pupils, desirable for the maximal learning experience.

Beginning with his analysis of the Weberian theory of social change and his account of the origin of modern rational bureaucracy, a "latent" component symbolized as the "Archimedian place to stand" has influenced Parsons' thinking. In this connection he refers to a statement Archimedes is reputed to have made: "Give me a place to stand and I will move the world." By analogy the Protestant belief in the transcendental God and conception of salvation provided "a place to stand"; i.e., "the *ascetic* aspect of its ethic ... [which was] its driving force ..." [154] The worldliness of such ethics as the Confucian denied their adherents "a place to stand" in the use of the Archimedian lever. In passing to the next section on medical practice an interesting parallel may be mentioned. Noting that "a friend [or a father] does not have a 'place to stand' outside certain reciprocities" he calls attention to certain latent activity:

Psychotherapy to the militantly antipsychiatric organic physician is like theory to the militantly antitheoretical empirical scientist. In both cases he practices it whether he knows it or wants to or not.[155]

The role of the physician which among other features requires its incumbent under varying conditions to deny reciprocity to the patient provides the Archimedian place to stand. A professional change agent may likewise be provided similar features.[156]

End or goal and medical practice. In describing the status-role of the sick person and patient as a deviant one, Parsons emphasizes the importance of the patient's accepting the goal of "trying to get well." The physician has the goal of facilitating the patient's recovery to the best of his ability. There may be "secondary gains" such as neurotic deviancy available to the patient when he is sick. Whether the patient is well or sick these "secondary gains" are generally "latent" in that they are unconscious.

"To give impetus to the patient's desire to re-achieve wellness" [157] requires that consideration be given to these.

Well-chosen, well-balanced exercise of the supportive *and* the disciplinary components of the therapeutic process . . . [are necessary to overcome the] . . . well-known phenomenon of secondary gain; a possible consequence of the transference relationship of patient and physician [158] [may occur as when the] wife-mother [for example] might "choose" the sick role as an institutionalized way out of her heavy "human relations management" responsibilities in the family.[159]

NORMING, STANDARDIZING, PATTERNING

Norm as an element. Beginning in 1937 with *The Structure of Social Action* "normative orientation . . . [a quality] fundamental to the schema of action" [160] has remained a central focus in Parsons' writings. In *The Structure* the concept, norm, constituted an integral part of the unit act. It was defined as:

a verbal description of the concrete course of action . . . regarded as desirable [and] held to manifest or otherwise involve a sentiment attributable to one or more actors that something is an end in itself . . .[161]

The differentiation of the norms of *Gemeinschaft*-like and *Gesellschaft*-like situations in 1937 foreshadowed the pattern variables [162] as well as the modes or patterns of value orientation and normative cultural standards which in *The Social System* and *Toward a General Theory of Action* supplanted in large measure the concept norm. Although the suggestion that Parsons "does not define 'norm' or any substitute for it" [163] in *The Social System* is scarcely correct, it does accent the changed emphasis given the term. More recently, as noted above, the concepts value, norm, collective, and role have entered the center of the arena of analysis of normative orientation. As Parsons uses the terms they are related as follows:

Norms can be legitimized by values, but not vice versa. . . . A collectivity stands at a still lower level in the hierarchy of normative control of behavior [and] role . . . the primary point of direct articulation between the personality of the individual and the structure of the social system [is lowest].[164]

To relate "normative orientation" of the more recent Parsonian schema to the concepts, norming, norm, and evaluation of the PAS Model it may be helpful to see the concepts, value, norm, collective, and role as Parsons uses these concepts in relation to the other components of his theory. If these latter terms are arranged to represent the social system as the terms of Figure 5 and column 3 in Figure 7 are sometimes used to represent the cultural system,[165] value falls in the L cell; norm in the I cell; collective in the G cell and role in the A cell.[166] In the treatment of values Parsons considers it necessary to differentiate this dimension which on Figure 7 is called direction of control from that which distinguishes "the value component from cognitive (existential) beliefs, patterns of motivational commitment (these are close to Durkheim's 'sentiments'), and patterns of legitimation of collective action."[167] (See, for instance, top two rows of Figure 7.)[168]

According to Parsons' conceptualization, norms are intimately connected with the boundary exchanges between the cultural system, the personality system and the social system. On the cultural level there are value patterns and on the personality level there are gratification-deprivation complexes which are somewhat balanced by modes of motivation. The actor, motivated to maximize his gratifications and minimize his deprivations, does so in accordance with *value-orientations,* derived from the cultural value pattern and internalized by the process of socialization, to become a part of personality itself. An exchange provides *legitimation* emanating from the cultural system in return for *commitment* emanating from the personality system which thereafter exhibits need-dispositions to observe the rules which are the content of value-orientations. "Thus culture includes a set of *standards.* An individual's value orientation is his commitment to these standards."[169] Upon interaction with other actors who similarly have acquired a set of value-orientations to which they are committed, the standards are institutionalized through mutual expectancies of status-roles and thereby become *norms* of action, or attributes of the social system.

Cognitive, expressive, and moral standards are the three functional categories of value orientation. Both cognitive and expressive components attend every act and must therefore be synthesized in some manner by evaluative standards if the system is to persist. The moral reference is basic to integration and to the "definition of the patterns of mutual rights and obligations, and of the standards governing them in . . . [the actor's] interaction with others" and hence is "that aspect of value-orientation which is of greatest direct importance to the sociologist." [170]

Given this all-too-brief summary of the concept norm, it is now possible to take a fresh look at belief and sentiment and to comment on the normative content imputed to them by the logical necessity of Parsons' schema. The normative element is always present in the cognitive symbol system, "since observation of the conventions and standards of the language and belief system is a condition of communication." [171] Although the most developed empirical knowledge at a given time is based on scientific beliefs validated by scientific authority the prevailing ideology serves many interests other than pure cognition. The norms of scientific validation will not prevail if interests other than the quest for knowledge are sufficiently compelling and if the norms governing the other interests are thought to be repudiated by science. Then, for Parsons, although the universalistic methodological canons of science must serve logically as the "major point of reference for the analysis of belief systems in general," [172] for philosophical and religious beliefs the standards are particularistic to the system from which they evolve. For example very broad areas of expressive behavior and symbolism are attached to an equally wide range of norms or standards which include such diverse items as "canons of 'good taste' " to proprieties in the sex act. Many expressive norms, thus, are difficult indeed to separate from moral norms. They are considered to be cathectic or expressive norms if they provide rules for acting out expressive interests and hence direct gratification, and are not easily subjected to universalistic considerations.

A backward look may also be cast at the pattern variables as they are used in connection with the concept "norm." "The pattern variables are the categories for the description of value-orientations which . . . are in various forms integral to all three systems," [173] (namely, personality, social and cultural systems). Consequently, a choice of either horn of a pattern variable dilemma is in effect a normative choice. In this light the wide and varying applications made by Parsons of the pattern variables, which upon occasion has excited the reaction that they were being made to do tasks that were too many and too big,[174] become not only justifiable but not at all contrary to the general practice of imputing a normative component to all human behavior. Their extensive use by Parsons between 1951 and 1959 also explains in part the relative infrequency of the term "norm" in his writings during this period, an infrequency which in no way diminishes the importance of the concept as a structural element. As noted above, more recently, the part norm has played in the set of concepts including value, norm, collective and role as focal terms for social system analysis has been great.

Evaluation as a process. For Parsons "values held in common constitute the primary reference point for analysis of a social system as an empirical system." [175] This is, of course, because:

The primary focus of articulation between the social system and the cultural system is the institutionalization of patterns of evaluation from the cultural system into the social system to constitute its topmost controlling component.[176]

Several forms and levels of evaluation have been delineated. These include evaluation of systems in terms of 1) components of meaning as object (somewhat but not specifically in terms of Figure 3), including, a) level of control, and b) order of precedence or importance of meanings of objects of cathexis, and 2) the meaning in mode of orientation or "disposition" of the acting system (again somewhat but not specifically in terms of Figure 2). This latter "cultural evaluation" as discussed from the vantage point of mode of orientation is specified as, a) evaluation of costs as related to production and utilization; b) evaluation of desirability and undesirability of action-goals; c) evaluation of the systems themselves; and finally d) the grounds of the orientation of meaning themselves, including "world views" or definitions of those conditions of human life which underlie orientations to more particular problems (again suggested by but not exactly specified as following the categories of Figure 5). This latter category is arranged in a "hierarchy" from lowest to highest on the basis of evaluation of: 1) performance and achievement or evaluation of "work" in Weber's sense; 2) source of authority as for example from Divine Will; 3) nature of "order" in the universe in general; 4) "the problems of meaning [including] the major premises in which nonempirical components of the total belief system of a culture are grounded." [177]

There is thus, in this as in the other three cases, a four-step hierarchy of levels of ultimacy in the grounding of meaning which we have characterized as the meaning of performance, of authority for performance, of the order on which such authority is grounded, and finally, of the ultimate grounding which transcends all others, including the legitimizing order.[178]

In terms of typologies of evaluation: (See Figure 5)

Where the cognitive meanings of objects as such have primacy over the other components we will speak of *belief* systems. Where the cathectic meanings of objects have primacy we will speak of *expressive* symbol systems and where the evaluative aspects of orientation have primacy we will speak of *value-patterns*. Finally we might speak of systems of 'existential meaning' where the grounds of meaning-orientation have primacy over the other components of cultural orientation in general.[179]

The modes of motivational orientations as presented in *The Social System* are actually descriptive categories each of which designates a possible constellation of motives which an actor might exhibit in relation to a situation; he may want to know or believe (the cognitive mode); he may want to appreciate, express, or gratify (the appreciative mode); or he may want to do what is morally right (the moral mode). Most typically, his motivations would be a complex of all three modes, and he must distinguish, test, sort and select what motivations will improve his gratification-deprivation balance. The modes of value-orientation are also descriptive categories each of which designates a possible constellation of standards which, because they are internalized in the personality system he is disposed to obey.[180] These categories of standards are also descriptive of the cognitive (or what the actor has internalized as truth), of the appreciative (or what the actor has internalized as appropriate expressive activity), and of the moral (or what the actor has internalized as "right"). The actor thus has various wishes to gratify which he is disposed (or permits himself) to fulfill only according to certain standards. Assessing the alternatives and their ramified consequences in relation to the situation and making a choice among them is called *evaluation*. Parsons is particularly interested in the case in which the situational object is another actor who, of course, is also bringing to the situation a complex of motivations, value-orientations, and expectations of the future state of affairs.

How either actor will choose to act will be contingent upon how he thinks the other actor will choose to act. This is the "double contingency" [181] which always implies the rejection of certain alternatives of action and the selection of others, or *evaluation*. The expectations of neither actor will be fulfilled if one is observing norms (institutionalized value-orientations) which are markedly different from those of the other. Repeated unfulfillment would satisfy neither, of course, and future voluntary interaction between these two actors would be minimal. Stability of interaction, then, requires "that the particular acts of evaluation on both sides should be oriented to common standards." [182] When this situation widely prevails action has pattern, the system has order.

Cognitive and expressive norms attend every act but each category describes "what ought to be" in connection with fairly identifiable kinds of activity. Their presence together in every act means that a synthesis of them or a balance between them must constantly be made. They thus themselves become the object of evaluation made in terms of moral standards, the latter kind of value-orientation (or norm when institutionalized) thus being more general than either the cognitive or expressive.

Pattern variables were above classified on the basis of actor-orientation *to* objects and the modalities *of* objects. They are also partially classifiable on the basis of primacy to modes of value orientation and are central to the analysis of evaluation. Choice on the affectivity-affective neutrality dilemma determines whether or not cathexis is going to take place at all. Universalism-particularism concerns the relative primacy of cognitive standards or cathectic standards. Self-orientation vs. collectivity orientation (which as noted above after 1959 serves in the external vs. internal dimension of Figure 1) is the least used of the pairs in connection with evaluation. It distinguishes whether the actor will be subject to "those positively defining obligations of membership in superordinate collectivities . . . [or] those merely setting the limits of permissible action relative to the superordinate collectivity." [183] As such it is the uniquely specifiable referent for moral norms and, in the strictest terms, can not be applied except to this type. A moral issue is invoked only if the dilemmas of action relate to the solidarity or integrity of an interaction system when the preservation of that solidarity or integrity is itself a value.[184] In fact one of the tests of the actual existence of a collectivity is whether an actor's choice of self-interest over collective interest is viewed by participant members as a violation of responsibilities to the system.

Symbols of solidarity are part of the cultural tradition and internalized sentiments by which they are manifested usually require no conscious articulation on the part of the actors. Should some subgroups (such as scientists) come to regard as valid some beliefs (cognitive symbolization in Figure 5) which are not consonant with that merging "of cognition, cathexis and evaluation . . . in . . . a common matrix" [185] and especially if these new beliefs threaten integration, sanctions may be evoked against their holders. Charismatic leaders likewise evoke moral modes of value orientation and in the earlier stages of their leadership are themselves symbols of beliefs and sentiments which are not generally institutionalized in the social system. The belief-sentiment-morality complex which they represent is finally either evaluated negatively in which case it becomes extinct, or it is evaluated so highly by such a large part of the membership of the relevant social system that it may be made sacred. Later, charisma may be routinized, the evaluation is passed into the social structure, and is pronounced legitimate. "Legitimacy is thus the *institutional* application or embodiment of charisma." [186]

The process of evalution may focus on any concrete part of the social system, and endow it with sanctified beliefs and sentiments. It is true that obedience to norms, even from a sense of moral obligation, certainly involves cognitive elements. The content of the norm and its consequences for conduct must be intellectually understood . . . But the attitude of respect is something in addition to this cognitive element, distinguishable from it . . . As far as intrinsic properties are concerned, anything may be sacred. Anything *is* sacred as long as people believe it is; it is their belief which makes it sacred.[187]

In every society this fundamental attitude of respect is directed toward some entities as well as toward moral obligations. Beliefs concerning these entities produce the "sacred character" of things of religious significance in Durkheim's sense. "By virtue of their sacredness these entities are assimilated to moral norms, and sharply distinguished from instrumental facilities toward which a very different attitude is held." [188] There is then a close relation between the sentiment appropriate to sacredness and beliefs in supernatural beings. "The supernatural order thus gives cognitive meaning to the moral-evaluative sentiments and norms of an action system, not in the sense that either the sentiments or the cognitive beliefs have causal priority but that they tend to be integrated with one another, and that this integration is importantly related to the stabilization of the system." [189]

Norms and evaluation and medical practice. The American value system is characterized by Parsons as "one of *instrumental activism*" [190] in which the society or any part of it may be used instrumentally in attaining or producing "worth while" things and not elevated to "an end in itself." Those social systems which promote capacity to achieve (such as health and education) are highly evaluated, accent is upon youth because of its achievement potential and there is a "denial" or devaluation of death because it terminates effective achievement. In contrast "Indian society seems to involve almost a glorification of death as that for which life is really lived" and accords health a lower evaluation, placing emphasis instead upon the after life symbolized by Nirvana and by ritual purity. "The neglect of health as Westerners understand it in India (until very recently) is too well-known to need emphasizing." [191]

In Western medical practice the high evaluation placed upon the collective interests of doctor and patient as a "community of fate" requires that norms supporting that value be observed by each. The patient is restricted from "shopping around" for medical advice; if not satisfied with physician A he cannot consult physician B independently unless he terminates his relation with A. The physician cannot advertise or bargain over fees nor refuse patients on grounds of credit risks.

DIVIDING THE FUNCTIONS

Status-role as a unit incorporating both element and process. The structure of social systems, for Parsons, is essentially the structured relations between actors in interaction. The position that a particular actor occupies in that structure is his status; [192] in a structured or patterned system of parts it is *his part* which also is an object of orientation for other actors in the given social system. When he acts in this status he is said to be acting out a *role*.[193] A particular role, from the point of view of the actor "is a sector of the total orientation system . . . organized about expectations in relation to a particular interaction context, that is integrated with a particular set of value-standards which govern interaction with one or more alters in the appropriate complementary roles." [194]

If ego and alter in interaction with each other interacted simply as two personalities, the total interaction of all the egos and alters would be as diverse as are all the personalities and quite without pattern. Any social system can be maintained, however, only by a fulfillment of its functional prerequisites which is effected by roles. In this sense roles constitute the necessary division of effort requisite to any social system. "There is the same order of relationship between roles and functions relative to the system in social systems, as there is between organs and functions in the organism." [195] Thus, instead of unlimited diversity of action, there is complementarity of action effected through role-expectations which become institutionalized. Of strategic structural significance in the social system is the institution which is "a complex of institutionalized role integrates . . . or status-relationships. There are no roles without corresponding statuses and vice versa." [196] Marriage and parenthood, for example, as a complex of patterned elements in role-expectations, applies to a tremendous number of collectivities. Parsons believes that "with all the variation of kinship terminology, there is no known system where . . .

four roles, namely mother, father, brother, sister and conversely, self, spouse, son, daughter, are not discriminated from each other. . . . Frequently incumbents of these roles are classified together with other kin . . . but there is no known system which fails to discriminate the four cardinal roles in the nuclear family . . ." [197]

Roles differ in the degree of institutionalization they possess; those which are fully institutionalized "are fully congruous with the prevailing culture patterns and are organized around expectations of conformity with morally sanctioned patterns of value-orientations shared by the members of the collectivity in which the role functions." [198] The actor (who will be the incumbent of a number of status-roles) also possesses value orientations which have been internalized as part of his personality. It follows then, that the pattern variables which describe alternatives of value-orientation can be applied to the analysis of role orientation. At the level of system analysis discussed in *The Social System,* the attitudinal variables of affectivity-neutrality and specificity-diffuseness are considered as "the major axes of the organization of action with reference to the needs of personality," while the object modality variables of universalism-particularism and ascription-achievement (quality-performance) "have primacy for analysis of the variability of social systems as structures." [199] Since the status-role is the linking mechanism between personality and social system, status definition and the actual process of role enactment exhibits these variables in various combinations.

An analysis in terms of the pattern variables constitutes only the "fundamental starting point for a classification of possible types of social structure," and hence complementary role definitions, since such an analysis is based only on the element of value-orientation without accounting for the rest of the components of the social system. But as a starting point, a provisional classification of generalized types of social system in structural terms and the character of the role-complementarity thereby indicated is made by Parsons. First he specifies kinship systems with their functions of status-ascription, socialization and regulation of erotic relations. (Why these *are* the functions of the kinship group, since all conceivably could be accomplished by other social arrangements, is another story.) [200] In spite of the many variations of kinship groups themselves, they all possess these functional imperatives, and roles within them are always functionally diffuse, particularistic, collectivity-oriented, and also affective to the extent that instrumental action does not have primacy.[201] The second empirical clustering of structural components is the "instrumental achievement structures and stratification," responsible for instrumental needs and the distribution of facilities and rewards. In the Western type of occupational role structure the instrumental organization is marked by universalism, specificity and affective neutrality.

Within the instrumental organization roles are oriented to performance and to collectivity orientation, both having axes which discriminate between various intra-organization roles as demanding "more skill" or "less skill" on the performance axis and "greater responsibility," or "less responsibility" for collectivity orientation. Access to facilities and rewards, or stratification, is thus intimately connected with role definition itself.[202] In a rough way kinship groupings represent the attributes imputed to those systems primarily at the lower level of the L (pattern maintenance) type and the instrumental achievement structures of the second category, those represented by the A(daptive) type (Figure 1). The characteristics of each are expanded in Figures 2 and 5, respectively and represent later theoretical developmnet than the empirical groupings here being discussed in relation to complementary role expectations. The third and fourth empirical groupings as designated by Parsons in *The Social System* were not elaborated there by pattern variables or articulating roles. Since they obviously suggest the work which was to come later in the form of the G(oal) cell (the earlier designation was "territoriality, force and the integration of the power system) and in the form of the I(ntegration) cell (the earlier designation was religion and value integration)[203] the Figures 3 and 4 no doubt represent pattern variables applicable to these empirical groupings. This continuity of theoretical development is a prime example of what was in the very early part of this chapter referred to as "the inviolate unity" of Parsonian theory.

This ideal typing of empirical clusterings, organized by ideal typing of status-roles and "manned" by incumbents ideally typifying need-dispositions perfectly congruent with the requisite value-orientations constitutes, as Parsons points out, only "the fundamental starting point." Concrete social systems are never purely of one type. They are differentially institutionalized, different role complementarities within a social system may possess elements of value-orientation incongruencies, and finally the actor himself (or the role incumbent) has not internalized all value-orientations equally nor can he possibly possess equal motivational commitment to all the roles he is called upon to play. Thus, no normative pattern is fully integrated and role expectations will therefore be marked by some degree of failure. "It is this circumstance which makes the problem of conformity and deviance a major axis of the analysis of social systems." [204] Deviance toward one interacting partner may be compliance with another, so that deviance must always be referred to the specific system or subsystem to which it applies.[205] "Deviance is a motivated tendency for an actor to behave in contravention of one or more institutionalized normative patterns." [206] It has important implications for the process of socialization, and more especially, for the process of social control and hence will be treated more fully under those considerations. The subject of status-role, however, would be incomplete were the conformity-deviance components to be omitted.

Parsons posits an activity-passivity axis and a set of orientations, the one to alter as a person and the other to the normative pattern integrating interaction. Across this four celled paradigm cuts the alienative need-disposition (disavowal of expectations) and the conformative need-disposition (compliance with expectations). Eight type-situations with characteristic status-roles are hereby described. Parsons' schema converges with and extends Robert Merton's well known paradigm on "Social Structure and Anomie." [207] Most "normal" status roles would fall at an equilibrated point with reference to norms, and personalities would be active and conforming. Each of the other logical possibilities has its characteristic empirical types. The hobo and the Bohemian, exemplify "retreat" on the Merton paradigm; on the Parsons paradigm they would fall at the intersection of passivity, alienation, with focus on norms rather than on objects. In the "submissive" type would come the "sick" status-role at the intersection of passivity and compulsive acquiescence. Exotic religious sects such as the Jehovah's Witnesses would fall here also, though, as

Parsons notes, "they also usually involve elements of active de-
fiance here and there, but very likely as a secondary phenomena." [208]

Status-roles and medical practice. The status-role of the sick
person, in terms of the pattern variables, is not ascribed but "negatively achieved." It is inherently universalistic in that it is based
upon objective criteria and is functionally specific revolving about
specific "complaints." It is affectively neutral in orientation in
that "the expected behavior, 'trying to get well,' is focused on an
objective problem not on the cathectic significance of persons or
orientations to an emotionally disturbing problem though this
may be instrumentally and otherwise involved." [209] Vis-a-vis the
physician, the patient assumes the obligation to cooperate and do
his part. Incumbents of the sick role are "entitled" to that role to
the degree that four criteria are applicable to their condition:
Disturbance of capacity to perform tasks and/or roles (with task
defined as more differentiated and more highly specified than
roles, one role constituting a plurality of tasks); [210] "exemption
from role-obligations, holding the patient not responsible for his
state, conditional legitimation of the state, and acceptance of the
need for help and of the obligation to cooperate with the source
of help." [211] Observations of these criteria legitimize the status-
role and regularize the steps toward recovery at the same time
that they prevent permanent claim to the role, avoiding thereby
a subculture of the sick. It is observed that increasing rates of
mental illness may not mean more social disorganization, but
rather, diversion into the role of the mentally ill from other status-
roles more dangerous to society.

The status-role of the physician is achievement oriented, universalistic, specific and affectively neutral. The physician in having an unusual degree of access to ordinarily "private" concerns
of the patient, such as his body and his private affairs, may be
accorded a parent-like status-role and the patient assume the
child-like status-role. There is only provisional reciprocity in this
respect, and the likelihood of a diffuse relationship such as lover
is thereby diminished. In therapy, particularly mental therapy,
the early permissive relations are later replaced by "support," followed by "denial of reciprocity" and finally "manipulation of
rewards" by the therapist.

RANKING

Rank as an element. Rank as a structural element of the social system is intimately related to status-role and to goal, and shares with the total structure of the system the common value-pattern aspect of its culture. With society as the referent social system, each subsystem possesses a legitimized primary function, the performance of which is its goal. The value-patterns specify that some of these functions are more basic than others in the total social system and hence are differentially ranked. The actor (in this case a subsystem such as a business firm, a church, a family) is "located" in the system by identifying the function assigned to him (it); this is his (its) status. When the relative value of that status, in comparison with other statuses in the system, is taken into account one aspect of rank is indicated. Among many actors all possessing the same legitimized function (all chemical manufacturers, for example, or all banks) some are judged in terms of the common value-pattern as performing their function (achieving their goal and playing their role) better than others. Another aspect of rank is thus indicated. With a given concrete subsystem as the referent social system, each concrete individual can similarly be "located" in the system by identifying the function assigned to him. One aspect of his rank will be indicated by the value imputed to his status; the function of the position of shipping clerk would rarely be valued as highly as the function of the position of general manager. Among a number of shipping clerk positions, some performances in light of relevant value judgments would be regarded as superior to others. Rank of a particular shipping clerk would thus be a composite of evaluative judgments rendered in terms of his positional status, on his role-performance, and also on the overall rank of the company for which he works. Rank designation must always be made with a specific system referent in mind. To make the presentation as simple as possible Parsons' most explicit treatment of the subject [212] specifies that the referent system is the social system and that the entities to which rank is being attributed are only one kind of unit, or the membership role in which each actor may be a collectivity or an individual human being.

Evaluation of actors and allocation of status-roles as process.

Parsons defines stratification as "the ranking of units in a social system in accordance with the standards of the common value system." [213] The term "units" is used advisedly because its general meaning of "membership" enables analysis of rank to be made on many different levels of inclusiveness. An individual who is a member of a twosome is a unit just as the largest corporation is a unit by virtue of being a member firm of society. Judgment of units is made in relation to unit properties which are either qualities, possessions or performance. This immediately suggests a parallel to expressive symbolism and the reward system as developed in *The Social System* of 1951 and treated above under the communication of sentiment. There it was seen that objects were differentially endowed with qualities, possessions and performance potentials which as expressive symbols had a pronounced effect upon their desirability for actors in a given situation. Once sensitized to this parallel, the reader will find many evidences of it in this section on rank which is based primarily on "A Revised Analytical Approach to the Theory of Social Stratification," which appeared in 1953, thirteen years after an earlier work on the subject. [214]

Qualities refer to those properties of a unit which may be ascribed to the unit as such independently of its relation to objects. A man's intelligence as expressed in an intelligence quotient is an example of quality. Performance is a process of change in the unit relative to other situation objects, as for example a grade on a test. [215] Possessions are valued situational objects under control of an actor and are transferable: transferable as facilities in instrumental action, and transferable as rewards in expressive action either as "objects of direct gratification or . . . symbolically associated with such objects." [216] Although possessions are viewed by Parsons as one of the properties of units in relation to which evaluations are made, possessions are primarily a function of power, and in instrumental action are facilities; their full treatment in this chapter is therefore more appropriate elsewhere, although the complex of power, possessions, facilities, rewards and sanctions should be considered as constituting a part of the stratification process, albeit not as central a part for Parsons as that held by quality and performance (the familiar ascription-achievement pair.)

The value-orientation of the system specifies the standards by which each unit will be measured in relation to its qualities, its performance and its possessions. Those standards can be reduced to four fundamental types which correspond to the by now familiar four dimensions of action systems represented by Figure 1. The *qualities* of individual units of a specified category win for each such unit a rank based upon the degree to which that unit displays *adaptive qualities* of technical competence, *goal-attaining qualities* of system goal commitment or legitimation of unit-goal commitment, *integrative qualities* of loyalty, and *pattern-maintenance qualities* of cultural value-commitment. The *performances* of individual units of a specified category win for each such unit a rank based upon the degree to which that unit observes *adaptive performance norms* of technical efficiency, *goal-attaining performance norms* of relational responsibility and regulative rules of the game, *integrative performance norms* showing solidarity, and *pattern-maintenance performance norms* of cultural responsibility. One of the four fundamental types will constitute the paramount value pattern of a system as a whole; the other three will constitute lesser and varying degrees of strategic significance. The rank of a given unit will reflect a weighting of qualities and performances in accordance with the strategic significance those qualities and performances hold for the system of which the unit is a part. For example, two units, one belonging to a predominantly adaptive system and one to a predominantly integrative system, might exhibit equal technical competence. Since this quality is of greater importance to the adaptive system than it is to the integrative system, the unit of the adaptive system is ranked higher in respect to this particular quality than is the unit from the integrative system in respect to this particular quality because for the latter it is of less consequence that the unit does possess this quality. The qualities and performance norms which are the standards of judgment can be expressed in pattern variable terms as on Figure 8, which also shows in pattern variable terms the sanction norms applicable to high or low measures of quality-performance (indicated on Figure 8 by italics and treated later under sanctions).

This abstract conceptual scheme used as a basis for the analysis of stratification may be made more concrete by examining

FIGURE 8

PHASES IN THE RELATIONSHIP OF A SYSTEM TO ITS SITUATION*

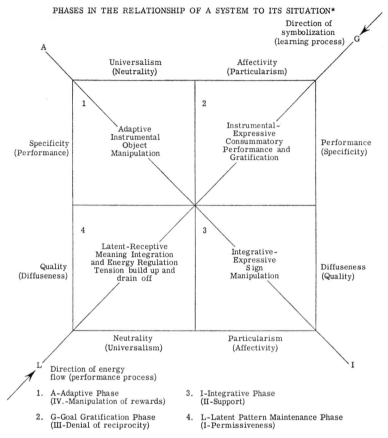

1. A-Adaptive Phase
   (IV.-Manipulation of rewards)

2. G-Goal Gratification Phase
   (III-Denial of reciprocity)

3. I-Integrative Phase
   (II-Support)

4. L-Latent Pattern Maintenance Phase
   (I-Permissiveness)

*The stages in task performance follow a clockwise sequence and are listed first;
i.e., I-A, 2-G, 3-I, 4-L. The stages in socialization and therapy follow a reverse
order. Source: WP, p. 182.

the American system of social stratification. Parsons sees American society as representing very nearly the ideal type of universalistic-achievement value system. Unit qualities and performances which have adaptive functions are thus primary. Lack of stress on a specific system-goal (in contrast to the situation in the USSR for example) couples emphasis on productive activity with an "'individualistic' slant." [217] Continued industrialization which has augmented the prominence of the corporation in comparison with the inherited family firm has made the processes of appointment and promotion increasingly important means of placing responsibility upon "professional career executives" resulting from "pressure to link executive responsibility with competence."[218] Increased world responsibility and unsettled international conditions are increasing the importance of government and other "noneconomic" sectors of society, although systems devoted to other functional imperatives such as the family, recreational, health and school systems tend to be outranked by systems which are centrally a part of the economy. Parsons sees for the United States three major types of collectivities which are related to stratification: the typically "bureaucratic" organizations such as business firms, schools, hospitals, and the like; collectivities of more diffuse function, including such associations as political units and churches for which there are many limitations on the degree of bureaucratization; and "diffuse solidarities," the most important being the local community, kinship, and ethnic groups.[219] The mainstreams of stratification are institutionalization of the occupational system and the kinship system,[220] followed closely by "ethnic belongingness" of which the most conspicuous example is the Negro, even in the North.

Although America is by no means a classless "society," its fluidity of mobility from one group to another as well as the indeterminate shadings between groups which make them nondiscrete, form a distinctive type among class societies.[221] "The best single index of the line between 'upper middle' class and the rest of the middle class is the *expectation* that children will have a college education."[222] The line between the middle and lower classes is more blurred in the United States than elsewhere. The disappearance of "sheer drudgery 'pick and shovel' work" and the rapid growth of white collar and service occupations has, contrary to Marxian predictions, reduced the relative size of the industrial labor force as the productivity of the economy increased.

In respect to allocation of status-roles the norm of universalism is again apparent in American society. "The focus of it is the universalistic definition of 'equality of opportunity' as applied both to individuals and to collectivities."[223] Parsons sees the high valuation placed on health and education as stemming directly from the disposition to universalize opportunity, for without good health and without training commensurate with the capacity of the individual, potentialities for productive achievement cannot be realized. "It is notable that these [health and education] are two fields where there is the strongest consensus that 'competitive' forces should not be permitted to operate unmodified, especially that access to health and to education should not be a simple function of ability to pay for them." [224]

The ideal of equality of opportunity is impossible of complete achievement because the family, a unit in which rank depends upon ascription, is so important in the allocation of rewards and the determination of life style for individual actors. The advantages of a highly placed family are enjoyed to some extent by the children whether in terms of performance they deserve it or not, just as the disadvantages of a low ranking family are borne by the children whether their performance deserves such a ranking. The ascription aspect of family membership despite the strong universalistic-achievement orientation of the United States, "is a basic limitation on the full implementation of our paramount value system. . . ." [225]

A further limiting feature is that "women, regardless of their performance capacities, tend to be relegated to a narrower range of functions than men, and excluded, at least relatively, from some of the highest prestige statuses." [226] The husband-father's occupational role, given the value orientation of the society, is by far the most important single adaptive role for the whole family system. No matter how crucial the intra-system role the mother plays —and it is increasingly important as the father is increasingly occupied elsewhere—a family role cannot compete equally in the attainment of rank with an occupational role given the societal value-orientation.

In contrast to most European countries where an individual's education is a mark of his quality, in the United States education primarily "serves as a path to future occupational status." [227] Although it no doubt bequeaths a rank in its own right, it is infinitely more important as a means of access to status-roles unavailable without a specified amount and kind of education.

During the frontier period of national development emphasis was upon physical prowess and endurance. Allocation of status-roles defined in such terms gave the great advantage to youth. More recently, "accumulated and organized knowledge, technical competence and sophisticated skills, capacity to plan and carry sustained responsibilities and balanced judgments" [228] have increasingly become components of status-role definition with the result that the allocation of older actors to status-roles of considerable rank has increased.

Rank and medical practice. The patient does not have the required knowledge to chose the most technically competent doctor, so he tends to choose a physician because of a recommendation of a friend who is an equally incompetent judge. Almost all patients tend to think that their doctor is the best in town or one of the best, a situation patently impossible. However, whether the physician enjoys a high rank or low in the eyes of his colleagues (and colleague ranking is of course unavailable to the patient) it is important that the patient rank him high since "therapeutic success is not possible unless the patient can be brought to trust his physician." [229] Physicians in general enjoy a high rank which is one of performance (achievement). Certain classes of physicians, such as surgeons, enjoy a higher than average physician rank which Parsons believes to be related to the value-system which favors activity over inactivity. The activity of surgery is interpreted as "something being done" in contrast to the waiting around of diagnostic work which is "inactive" and less valued.

CONTROLLING

Power as an element. Parsons defines power as "the generalized capacity of a social system to get things done in the interest of collective goals." [230] As such it is a generalized category of means directed with specific reference, not toward any one or a few of the separate goals which may be valued in a society (with society as the referent system) but to all of those goals collectively so that all can be realized in a balanced and integrated manner in the best interests of society. [231] It is represented, therefore, by the G(oal-attaining) cell on Figure 1 and is the particular province of the polity just as the A(daptive) cell is the particular province of the economy.

There must be sufficient power generated to mobilize societal resources for the attainment of collective goals and there must be allocation of power to various subsystems proportionate to the differential societal needs of the products of the subsystems. This interpretation of power reflects Parsons' subscription to the Hobbesian thesis that controlled power integrates societies (or that uncontrolled power is disintegrative), as well as his rejection of the Max Weber thesis [232] that the sum total of power can be expressed in the "zero-sum" concept: that power is the capacity of one unit in a system to gain its ends over the opposition of other units. The network of collectivities called government is the primary, but by no means the only, instrumentality with the functional imperative of producing and allocating power, and as such is the chief locus of "differential responsibility" or "leadership," which differs from non-political institutionalized responsibilties and leaderships to the degree that it is imbued with a public interest, or with *collective* goals.

Within areas categorized as prescribed, permitted and prohibited, subtypes of institutionalized leadership responsibility are institutionalized rights to *control,* directed to *private* spheres of interest and consisting of *specific* decisions; they are also institutionalized rights to *regulate,* directed to public spheres of interest and specifying acceptable limits. Both sub-types require that the objects of control or regulation concern matters bearing on the attainment of collective goals or the public interest. Authority is viewed by Parsons as an institution (somewhat parallel to the institutions of contract and property); as such it represents the institutionalized rights of leaders to expect support from the members of the collectivity as well as the rights to control and regulate within the institutional framework. Parsons hypothesizes that authority will be relatively more important as a function in societies which place high valuation on goal-attainment or system-integrative values. Since the United States, in his view, places the greatest emphasis upon the adaptive component (which includes business) and on pattern-maintaining systems (e.g. education, science, and family) the authority component here is and will be played down.[233]

When this generalized analytical scheme of authority and power is applied to subsystems of society, the whole structure ". . . is a differentiated hierarchy of permissions, prescriptions, and prohibitions such that the higher level prescribes the limits within which the lower and more differentiated ones may operate." [234] A business firm, for example, in respect to power and its *external* situation, is subject to the institutionalized norms of a superordinate system; it has been delegated a specific part of *public authority* by the laws of incorporation which define its status and its goal. It has been delegated certain *authorization* (in contrast to authority which is the institutionalized value-pattern) by which it can mobilize power to achieve its goals in compliance with the institutions of property and contract. The authorization of any particular collectivity permits a wide range of *internal* latitude within institutionalized limits; "it can create its own order, its own pattern of authority, rules of property and the like." [235] Power may be either diminished or enhanced by conformity with value standards.

If ego—the unit of reference—conforms relatively more fully than the others this may diminish ego's power relative to that of the others because he is less willing to exploit opportunities forbidden by the norms. On the other hand his own deviance, if it happens to mesh with that of others, may increase his power, because he is allowed to "get away with it" . . . Similarly, access to possessions is always to some degree . . . adventitious" from the point of view of value-standards of the system.[236]

Power as a component in a given social system shades directly into authority. "Authority . . . is full blown when [the institutionalized expectation of role] . . . comes to include the legitimation of 'coercive' sanctions." [237] Authority, like role, is evaluated and thus stratified; it is "always an aspect of a status in a collectivity; in so far as this is not the case but there is only realistic ability to control others [influence in terms of the PAS Model] we speak of power." [238] It is thus, the authority, or the "authorization" feature of the power-authority complex which is most in evidence as decisions are made and action initiated.

Decision making and initiation into action. Parsons' most specific use of the concept decision making occurs in his treatment of "bureaucratic" or formal organizations.[239] Central to Parsons' treatment of decision making in such an organization is his observation that what has so long been regarded as "line" authority or "chain of command" is in reality *not* one continuous chain by which orders referring to the same function are relegated to lower and lower levels of authority in lesser and lesser magnitudes. He suggests instead that there are distinct breaking points in the chain whereby levels are described at which decision making takes place, each level dealing with organizational problems which are interrelated but functionally separate. At whatever level the decisions are made, they are functions of the power vested at that level.

There are policy decisions which relatively directly commit the organization as a whole; they are relatively long range in point of time. The setting up or liquidating of an organization, decisions to merge or not to merge, decisions concerning the nature and quality of product are among the examples Parsons gives of alternatives of action faced at this level. Fiduciary and other kinds of boards and the highest level executives make such decisions. To do so they must be vested with unequivocal authorization, for the legitimized right to make the decision is as important as the content of the decision. The orientation of this level is chiefly external. The mobilizing of resources and the channels of distribution of the finished product are among the concerns of this level as are the relationships which involve the referent social system with "some 'organized superior' agency with which the organization articulates." [240] Decisions emanating from this level are designated as policy decisions and are primarily external, involving what on the PAS Model would be regarded as systemic linkage.

Secondly, there are allocative decisions by which the resources of personnel, finances, and facilities are distributed. These are the province of the managerial level. The managerial personnel who cannot themselves possess the many specialized capacities to supervise the many technical operations allocate personnel to departments, divisions, bureaus and other suborganizations where operative decisions are made. The allocation of personnel to these suborganization posts is in reality the allocation of responsibility—"the decision who should decide." [241] Managerial decisions also entail allocation of means (in terms of budget allocation) to each of the subdivisions by which the responsibilities may be carried out.

At the technical level there are operative decisions, exemplified by the teacher who makes decisions about the actual processes of teaching and conducting classes; the income tax functionary who processes the returns and makes decisions about handling recalcitrants; the line supervisor who makes workaday decisions about the processing of material. Whatever the type of organization, once the technical level of operation reaches a professionalized state (as a doctor in a hospital, a professor at a university, an engineer in an economic organization) "a crucial problem of organization appears." [242] The professional technician, although subordinate to the executive level, makes decisions independently of the executive. Within the area of his competency the professional's decisions are subject only to the veto power of the executive, but not subject to collaboration with the executive. The professional, like the executive, must stand or fall on the soundness of his own decisions.

A further class of decisions, but one less specifically attached to any one organizational level is designated by Parsons as coordination decisions which are designed to "bring the performance of subunits and individuals more closely into line with the requirements of the organization than would otherwise be the case." [243] Coordinative decisions are decisions designed to motivate workers to adequate performance and are implemented by sanctions and what Parsons terms "therapy."

Just as power for Parsons is not articulated by a continuous chain of lesser and lesser decision making, so initiation into action does not take place either in an ever-diminishing chain of command. Rather, he sees points at which each level articulates its decisions with the other levels. "School boards, boards of directors, or trustees and political superiors do not, in the nature of the case, simply tell the people at the next level down 'what to do,'" because each level exhibits competencies and responsibilities which are not simply delegated; as has been seen, they are competencies and responsibilities which are functionally different. The exchange referred to above between the higher level professional technician and the executive is one such example. Although ultimate decision lies in the hands of the executive, he must reach his decision by taking the word of the professional as an accurate appraisal of a given situation. Similarly, the board when it is properly oriented to functions of legitimation and community support or other external matters for the organization cannot know the internal matters of the organization except as they are communicated by the executive. The latter's actions are a far cry from simply carrying out the board's policies. There is an exchange which is vital to the work of each. Parsons summarizes his ideas about initiation into action (a term which he does not employ) by noting "a two-way interchange of inputs and outputs" between the levels he has designated. "What has to be 'contributed' from each side is qualitatively different. Either side is in a position, by withholding its important contribution, to interfere seriously with the functioning of the other and of the larger organization. Hence the *institutionalization* of these relations must typically take a form where the relative independence of each is protected." [244] This protection tends to focus on the lower hierarchical levels, since by the nature of the hierarchical structure itself these levels have less power and their functional contribution hence could be more easily overlooked or jeopardized.

Power and decision making and medical practice. Most pertinent here is Parsons' famous dictum on Weber's work on bureaucracy. Parsons takes issue with Weber for throwing "together two essentially different types . . . [of authority which] are analytically separate," in the office of the " 'bureaucratic' structure." These are authority based on technical competence and hierarchical rational-legal authority of office. Parsons holds that articulation of authority or power which stems from technical competence is not typically bureaucratic. The doctor's power over the patient is an example.

In private practice the physician does, to be sure, exercise a kind of authority, he issues . . . "orders" to his patients, and there is a rather high probability . . . that these orders will be followed. This authority rests . . . on the belief on the part of the patient that the physician . . . has knowledge and skill which the patient does not have, and cannot criticize in detail so that the patient must take his doctor's advice or orders "on authority."

It is true also that this position of authority is not a matter wholly of the individual impression made by the particular physician, but is institutionalized. Its possessor is socially categorized through such instrumentalities as formal training, the M. D. degree, a license to practice, etc. But the distinctive thing is that this institutionalization does not carry with it coercive powers and the physician does not occupy an office in Weber's sense. His getting his orders obeyed depends entirely on securing the voluntary consent of his patient to submit to them.[245]

SANCTIONING

Sanction as an element. For Parsons the concept "sanctions" is a part of the complementarity or double contingency nature of social interaction. The sanction aspect of interaction lies in the influence of a particular act on others. To the extent that influential acts become institutionalized expectations, the sanctions (either rewards or penalties) are those of authority. Ego in a position of authority has the institutionalized right to impose "coercive sanctions" upon alter's failure to fulfill ego's expectations. As was shown above in Figure 8 norms of quality and performance provide the standards of judgment by which alter's response is evaluated. There are corresponding standards or norms which define the accompanying appropriate type of sanction.[246] Thus on Figure 8, if performance is to be evaluated in an adaptive situation in terms of universalism and performance the correspondingly appropriate sanction norms are neutrality and specificity (the italicized variables on Figure 8). Corresponding sanction norms are indicated for each type of performance judgment. Sanction norms in non-pattern variable terms are specified for the adaptive, goal-attaining, integrative and pattern maintaining quality-performance situations; respectively these are approval-disapproval, conditional response-reward, diffuse acceptance, and esteem. Since each unit, although predominantly of one of the functional patterns, is a subsystem which displays to lesser degrees the remaining three functional patterns as well, there will be present all four types of sanctioning patterns to the degree that performances occur in respect to all four types.

Parsons sees social interaction as "a continual back-and-forth alteration between performances and 'sanctions,' "[247] every act being to some degree a reaction to the acts of other actors and containing within it a sanction aspect of reward or punishment. Power and rank are in part functions of the rewards and punishments at the disposal of a particular unit. Each unit, in addition to exhibiting quality and performance properties, is endowed with *possessions* to varying degrees. Those possessions which are categorized according to performance norms are facilities, but those categorized according to sanction norms are rewards. Neither are classes of concrete objects but rather categories of the significance of objects. Especially will those objects which possess expressive-integrative meanings be valued not only for the consummatory gratification they yield; they will be rewarding also to the degree that they represent a desired status symbol. The status-qualities which impute rank are extended and reinforced by reward posses-sions and to this degree the latter are instruments of rank and power.

No summary of sanctions can do justice to Parsons' treatment of them, embodied as they are in every "set of expectations rela-tive to the contingently probable reactions of others." [248] Espe-cially in the work *Economy and Society* is the concept emphasized. There, from the point of view of the functioning of the system the contribution of status-role is a performance, but that same contribution is a sanction when viewed from the point of refer-ence of the object toward whom it is directed.[249] Sanctions are used not only for the reward or punishment of past performance but as inducements toward future conformity. Although rewards receive more attention than punishments, Parsons acknowledges that "In the last analysis force is an infallible means of the pre-vention of any human action . . . ," [250] and is in agreement with Durkheim that punishment functions as a means of system inte-gration and pattern maintenance on the community itself.

The institutionalization of sanction systems is intimately tied up with the stability and order inherent in society. All institu-tionalized mechanisms for securing observance of institutional norms are supportive of the sanction system, many of them such as the institutionalizing of status-roles, and the legitimizing of authority appearing in other contexts above. Another such mecha-nism is law of which two essential functions are "the definition of the scope of jurisdiction, and the authorization and implementa-tion of sanctions. . . ." [251] Law enforcing agencies are not strictly a part of the legal system but represent rather a political function; they are nonetheless part of the sanctioning system. Other im-portant extra-legal processes perform sanctioning functions but are generally considered as mechanisms of social control.[252]

Application of sanctions as process. The actual application of sanctions is particularly significant for the processes of socialization and social change and hence will receive direct attention below with respect to these considerations. The application of sanctions as in psychotherapy, however, may well be given here. (Figure 8). The therapist so directs his part of the interactive process that early in the relationship with his patient affective and diffuse rewards mark stages of "permissiveness" and "support." The patient attachment which grows out of this relationship and the expectations developed during these stages may then be used as "leverages" in a later stage marked by "denial of reciprocity" and "manipulation of rewards" to bring about the desired adjustments which are the core of therapy. As will be seen, the process of socialization follows much the same pattern. On a broader scale somewhat the same affirmation and denial of rewards must take place in the larger framework of society. Parsons notes in this respect that "there is little hope of a formal sanction system operating effectively in most cases unless it is backed by . . . a system of moral sentiments [which] . . . on the whole favor the institutionalized pattern system so that alter is inclined spontaneously to react favorably to conformity and unfavorably to deviance on ego's part." [253] All sanctions are symbolic relations to some code and may be employed to illustrate the relation between cultural and social systems. "We may regard a social system as in a sense suspended in a kind of 'web' of cultural definitions." [254] "The functions of signs and symbols in the elementary processes of social interaction" [255] are not only crucial for the performer but for his role partner as well. "On no other assumption is the matching of sanction to performance and vice versa, which is the very essence of the integration of an interaction system, conceivable at all." [256] For Parsons there is a ritualistic component in all sanctioning which possesses a negative or punitive element. The sanction which is immediately directed against the offender is also directed toward all others who might be tempted to deviate.

Sanctions and the practice of medicine. Since the sick role is defined by Parsons as an institutionalized deviant one, the usual system of sanctions is temporarily suspended and replaced by certain obligations the most important of which is the obligation to want to get well. The sanction against malingering, although primarily informal, is oriented toward obviating this deviancy. The patient, released from normal sanctions and more than normally emotionally charged, may tend toward a less than normal universalistic orientation to the physician.

Through the mechanism of transference the patient, usually without knowing what he is doing, not only has certain resistances, but he actively attempts by projection to assimilate his physician to a pattern of particularistic personal relationship to himself. He attempts to elicit the reaction which is appropriate to his own need-dispositions.[257]

The recourse of the doctor must be to a manipulation of sanctions whereby the particularistic relationship may be avoided and his own technical competence for the relationship left unimpaired at the same time that his patient's confidence in him remains steadfast. The patient's need-disposition coupled with his own technical incompetence creates a peculiarly vulnerable position for him. That physicians do not often exploit that vulnerability is attributable chiefly to "informal mechanisms." The formal laws which specify penalties for malpractice and the disciplinary procedures of medical associations "quite definitely are not the principal mechanisms which operate to ensure the control of self-orientation tendencies." [258] The place of professional ethics in institutionalizing conformity is important here.

FACILITATING

Facility as an element. Parsons notes that technology "involves values, norms, collectivities and role-expectations; and, as part of the social structure it should be analyzed in these terms." [259] Among the properties accruing to each actor (whether a concrete individual or a collectivity) is that of possession. The reward-objects which are possessions of the actor are sanctions. The other category of possessions are facilities, which always have instrumental functions for the actor. They are an aspect of the performance potential of the actor and are categorized by the same norms which categorize performance (see the unitalicized pattern-variables on Figure 8). The actor's functional imperative in the total social system, i.e. adaptive, goal-attaining, integrative or boundary maintaining, will indicate the predominant importance of some facilities over others for his particular function. "A blast furnace has instrumental functions for a steel-manufacturing concern, but pews and priestly robes have instrumental functions as facilities for a church." [260] As a form of possession, facilities for Parsons are "*always* a right or a bundle of rights . . . It is never as such a physical object, but always consists in *rights in* or relative to physical, social, or cultural objects, rights of use or of control or of disposal." [261] The possession of a facility by any one actor presumes ideally and according to norms of a perfect marketing economy that the right to that facility has been allocated to him by society on the assumption that of all possible contenders for that right his performance has demonstrated that he can use it most effectively for the promotion of system goals. His possession of it therefore symbolizes a recognition of his technical efficiency as well as his commitment to an institutionalized role through which his contribution to system-function will be made. Thus the rank order of control of facilities should ideally duplicate the rank order of actors.

However, the equating of facility value is difficult if not impossible without a common denominator, a mechanism of generalization, by which the value of one facility is translateable into comparative values of other facilities. From the example above, this question could be posed as, "How many pews and priestly robes equal how many blast furnaces?" Money is the most common mechanism of generalization. In these terms, the amount of money an actor (individual or collectivity) is able to marshall is a simple index to his rank and to his command of facilities. It is important to remember here that his rank is dependent not only upon his performance but also upon the societal evaluation placed upon his function. Thus it is possible that a mediocre performer whose function is viewed as of the highest strategic importance might mobilize facilities of as great or greater generalized or money value than the superior performer whose function is valued less highly. Thus, in the case of American society characterized by Parsons as primarily universalistic and achievement oriented, and hence primarily an *adaptive* society, a business firm of average performance might be expected to possess the rights to more valuable facilities than the superior school which is pattern maintaining. Since all functional types are interdependent, however, the paucity of access to facilities on the part of the school (or any other non-adaptive collectivity) can not be permitted to sink below a certain level without serious reverberations on the

primarily adaptive collectivities. An equilibrium is therefore maintained which from the societal view point results in the utilization
of facilities in accordance with the value standards.

Utilization of facilities as process. In the distribution of possessions of both the facility and reward-object type, financial resources as *generalized* access to possessions and "reputation" as a
symbol of reward-object accumulation, are ideally allocated in a
universalistic-achievement oriented society in a "free" competitive
market process. "But equally in both cases, this fails to operate
fully automatically even under what are empirically the best conditions." [262] Modifying interventions must be introduced to even
the balance.

Thus government or private philanthropy channels funds into uses to
which, under competitive conditions they would not be put, such as
health care or higher education, thereby increasing both the facilities
and the rewards available to those working in those fields and the
beneficiaries of their work. Similarly a person prominent in a field
goes out of the way to praise the work of a younger less known person.
By enhancing his reputation he also shifts the balance of facilities and
rewards in the latter's favor. Essentially what seems to be going on is
a kind of continual series of comparative judgments which say in
effect, class A of roles is receiving too little, class B too much, and then
a shift from B to A takes place.[263]

Discrepancies of occupational income (and hence in the long run,
the manner of facility utilization) by no means coincide with evaluative differentiations of function. "It is easy to cite cases where
discrepancy is clear—as for instance that between the salary of a
high Federal Judge and what the incumbent would usually earn
in the private practice of law." [264] On the American scene Parsons
sees two adjusting mechanisms at work which tend to channel
facility utilization more nearly in the direction of societal value-
patterns than can be accomplished by the free market exchange.

One is the wide range of facilities which are used without
status implications. The many facilities utilized generally by the
"public" without respect to rank minimizes the impact of that
differential distribution of facilities which is not consonant with
the basic value-pattern. Among uses of facilities which Parsons
mentions as not involving rank are the access to travel facilities,

hotels, and restaurants; the general usage of standardized brands of cigarettes which sell for about the same price, the fact that "many very high status people drive Fords and Chevrolets, (and some not-so-high drive Cadillacs) . . . ," [265] or in the early sixties some from each class drove small cars.

The second mechanism which adjusts malfunctioning of the free-market distribution of facilities which ideally would distribute in direct proportion to the evaluation of the recipients, are those which have become institutionalized so that the lower income groups "make more," and the higher income groups "keep less." The labor movement seen in this light has increased facility utilization by a wide segment whose value to the total system is not properly represented by free-market distribution. On the other hand

high progressive taxation, both of incomes and estates, and changes in the structure of the economy, have "lopped off" the previous top stratum, where the symbols of conspicuous consumption were, in an earlier generation most lavishly displayed. A notable symbol of this is the recent fate of the Long Island estate of the J. P. Morgan family, which had to be sold at auction in default of payment of taxes. One wonders what Veblen would say were he writing today instead of at the height of the "gilded age." [266]

The collected tax monies are obviously spent on items which are very different from those which the same money would have bought had it remained in the hands of those from whom it is collected. This is another way to say that available facilities are being utilized differently. Parsons specifies two principles which govern tax money utilization: 1) the goal must be considered important enough and the organization devoted to it unable to maintain service on a "paying" basis; "e.g., the care of large numbers of persons from the lower income groups who (by current standards) need to be hospitalized for mental illnesses," or 2) "if the *ways* in which the services would be provided by private enterprise might jeopardize the public interest, e.g., the provision of military force for the national defense might conceivably be contracted out, but placing control of force to this degree in private hands would constitute too serious a threat to the political stability of the society." [267]

Upon the procurement of funds from whatever source, the farther removed from a market economy a collectivity is, the more attention its policy makers must give to the evaluative process which marks the utilization of facilities. The university board, for example, not only has the responsibility for the availability of facilities, but they must also be concerned with "the kind and amount of performance capacity which in the societal interest, *should* be made available for this [teaching and research] function and hence the price, financially speaking, which *should* be paid for this performance capacity . . . They cannot escape a responsibility for the *level* of faculty salaries as well as for the conservation of the university's necessarily limited funds." [268]

Facilities and medical practice. The concept of facilities, in one sense, is central to the whole structure of modern medicine. "Modern medical practice is organized about the application of scientific knowledge to the problems of illness and health, to the control of 'disease,' " [269] but, more significantly, there is a segregation of these facilities to the technically trained person which is not only sanctioned by informal beliefs but codified in law. As Parsons notes, however, this segregation of means is not complete. Home remedies, patent medicines, and the existence of cults in the health field deny a total concentration of facilities.

In viewing the situation of the physician, Parsons observes that the application of facilities in the medical role constitutes "a perfectly straight forward technological job." [270] However, increasingly there is recognized a second set of facilities usually wrapped up, in their process dimension, as "bed-side manner." The legitimation of these as facilities is, of course, related to psychosomatic medicine and the willingness to concede the etiology of illness beyond the physiological and biological level.

Parsons also observes that the acceptance and utilization of new techniques characteristically runs into "vested interests" and for a time will be slow in catching on, then swing to the opposite end of being "overused" before settling into "a well established place in the professional 'repertoire.' " [271] This dialectic resulting in the full recognition of facilities as *rights to means* is illustrated by the classic case of "the opposition of the French Academy of Medicine to Pasteur, and for some time the complete failure to appreciate the importance of his discoveries." [272]

COMPREHENSIVE OR MASTER PROCESSES

Communication. Structured interaction takes place in terms of signs and symbols the meanings of which have become abstracted from the particularity of situations. Since the situations of two actors are never identical, communication would be impossible without symbolic meanings which transcend particular situations. "When symbolic systems which can mediate communication have emerged we may speak of the beginnings of a 'culture' which becomes part of the action systems of the relevant actors." [273] A shared symbolic system which functions in interaction is designated by Parsons as a *"cultural tradition."* [274] "Even the most elementary communication is not possible without some degree of conformity to the 'conventions' of the symbolic system." [275] The essence of cognitive and expressive symbolizations are elaborated above, especially under the categories of knowing and feeling, respectively. Effective communication consists of an interchange between the interacting units in terms of commonly shared symbols of both the cognitive and expressive types, but typical interaction situations give primacy to one or the other type of symbolism. A superimposing of Figure 5 on Figure 4 will result in a matching of the latter's cells with the types of symbolic meaning which are primary for the given cell. Thus, for effective adaptation cognitive symbols are the most important media of communication; the common understanding of the meaning of money is an example often used by Parsons in this respect. Similarly, for goal-attainment, expressive symbols are the most important communication media; the symbols representing rank and power and those related to the distribution of facilities and rewards must convey commonly shared meanings if they are to serve as effective communication media in the process of goal-attainment.

The problem of communication is not exhausted by the symbols of the cognitive and of the expressive, but as was pointed out above, derives also from the ideational meaning of objects. The moral-evaluative meaning of objects, if different for interacting units, can skew effective communication. Parsons suggests, for example, that the ideological differences between the Western and the Communist powers as they are represented in the UN pose a communication impassé concerning what the UN in fact consists of.[276] Similarly, in the area of existential beliefs, common commitment to an erroneous belief is more facilitative of communication and integration than is the situation in which one party of the interaction has corrected his distorted belief while the second party persists in the distortion. Subscription to a *common* symbolic meaning is thus the *sine qua non* of effective communication.

Boundary maintenance.[277] A stable social system (or a social system which is relatively in equilibrium) is a boundary-maintaining system; i.e. *"relative to its environment* . . . it maintains certain constancies of pattern, whether this constancy be static or moving."[278] Varying processes are resorted to in the effort to "neutralize" sources of variability which if they went far enough would change the structure. The sources of variability may be within the system itself and as such would always reflect an imperfectly institutionalized structuring of the components of the system. Parsons identifies four conditions of stability, all of which are bolstered by various boundary maintaining devices as members of a social system attempt to neutralize countervailing conditions. First, there is the stability of the normative pattern itself; secondly, there is a "minimum level of commitment of acting units, i.e. of dispositions to perform in accordance with the relevant expectations—rather than to evade or violate them—and to apply the relevant sanctions, positive or negative, to other units in response to performance, evasion or violation."[279] Third, there is acceptance of a commonly understood "definition of the situation." Finally, there is the integration of the normative complex of the particular social system in question with that of the larger system of which it is a part. "Integrative mechanisms" (or boundary maintaining devices) are directed at keeping within limits compatible with the maintenance of the main structural patterns any endogenous variations of these four conditions of stability. In a typically stable system there are normatively patterned interchanges between the units comprising the system by which each unit furnishes outputs to other units and receives inputs from other units. "For stable interchange to go on there must . . . be flexibility for inputs and outputs to move, but there must also be ways of 'channeling' this process to keep its variability within limits." [280] These "ways of 'channeling'" are in terms of the PAS Model, the mechanisms of boundary maintenance.

The sources of variability, against which boundary maintaining devices will be marshalled, may also come from environmental factors outside the system. These exogenous influences include not only the patently external—such as other organisms, collectivities, societies—but those changes originating in the personalities of the members of the social system and those flowing in from the cultural system. These latter, less obviously "external" influences are treated by Parsons as being exogenous in accordance with his analytical distinction between the *social* system and the personality and cultural systems which interpenetrate it but which are analytically separate. As indicated above, from the societal point of view the "L" cell in Figure 6 has primacy in maintaining boundaries and managing tensions produced under such circumstances.

Consistent with his view that each social system represents a societal mandate for providing a type of service or goods, and hence possesses a function legitimized by the larger society, Parsons views as an important source of social change the increased capacity for levels of performance by new organizational devices which are not possible under old organizational arrangements. To maximize these *adaptive* exigencies for the society at large new *kinds* of units are legitimized with the functional imperative of performing a role previously performed by the "residual" unit left by the establishment of the new one. The boundaries of the "residual" unit are of course threatened. Its continued operation in the realm which is increasingly that of the new unit represents vested interest and an equivocal institutionalization.[281] The power at the disposal of the residual unit will in part determine how long the old boundaries can be maintained, e.g. how long it can continue to command facilities commensurate with the fulfillment of the functional imperative and to what extent it can maximize rewards for its members other than the reward of maximal goal attainment. In respect to this latter, the family-sized farm or the small independent business firm, for example, continues to do its old job (and maintain its old boundaries) not because its organization is as admirably adapted to goal attaining as the factory-farm or the large incorporated business firm, but because the rewards offered by a sense of responsibility, by being one's own boss, by maintaining a way of life, are thought to be greater than those to be gained by the forfeiting of these for a more rational or efficient goal attaining activity under a system with an entirely different structure.

Boundaries of whole classes of social systems (farms, families, schools, factories, hospitals, etc.) are affected less by *segmentation* by which additional units of the same type are proliferated in order to get done the societal job that needs doing, than by *differentiation* by which additional units of entirely new types are societally legitimized to carry on part of the work previously done by the members of the referent social systems.[282] As new boundaries are inevitably designated and institutionalized for both the emergent and the residual systems, boundary maintenance devices are increasingly supplemented and supplanted by coordinative or integrative devices, treated in terms of the PAS Model as systemic linkage.[283]

Systemic linkage. Parsons uses the terms "systematic linkage," "boundary exchanges," "system interdependencies," and simply "linkage" in approximately the same way in which "systemic linkage" is used in the PAS Model. By whatever name, the interrelatedness of the cultural, personality, and social systems, the linkages between the social systems which are designated as primarily adaptive, goal attaining, integrative, or pattern maintaining, the interdependencies of levels in bureaucratic structures, and many others, are so overwhelmingly evident in the body of this chapter that they need not be repeated here. Suffice it to remind the reader that the hierarchical nature of system for Parsons logically requires that any unit from society as one limiting case to the organism as another, may be analytically differentiated as a system at the same time that it comprises a unit of the higher level systems of which it is a part. Assuming then, that the fact of systemic linkage in Parsons' works is sufficiently established, this section will be devoted to a consideration of the less obvious mechanisms of systemic linkage as they apply to social systems which, relative to the attention given them by Parsons, are somewhat under represented in the foregoing parts of this chapter.

Basic to the idea of systemic linkage is the idea of boundary maintaining, differentiated systems, each of which not only "does what it does, but . . . does not do what the other does." [284] This specializing of function requires that there be a process of "interchanging inputs and outputs between units (subsystems) of the system on the one hand, and between the system, through the agency of its units, and its environment on the other." [285] The interchange between family and school may be used as an example. The family produces the children, provides them with an emotional mooring and contributes a degree of socialization. The school emancipates the child from the solely family-tied emotional attachment, contributes to his internalization of social values beyond what he can learn in his family, differentiates among the children in terms of achievement and the valuation of achievement, and sets the stage for allocation of adult status-roles. [286] The child himself is a link between the two social systems as are parent-teacher associations.

There is a certain amount of risk involved in a unit's devoting itself solely to a specialized commodity or other output. The family producing and partially socializing children risks the chance that the school will not perform its function. The schools risk the chance that collective families will not provide essential facilities. The husband-father may prefer poverty on a subsistence farm to the risks of uncertain or disadvantageous systemic linkage with an outside wage-paying production unit. That the production of imperative outputs and their orderly interchange will not be a random affair, the social systems at any one hierarchical level are systemically linked to social systems of a higher level. Some social systems such as the courts and the legal profession have as their main function the job of regularizing such linkages.

The focus of the legal system is to be found in the courts which are interstitial between political and nonpolitical systems in a sense parallel to that in which political parties are interstitial between government and the "public." The private legal profession is still another interstitial structure which is even less "political" than are the courts, mediating between the judicial processes and the interests of clients. [287]

There are many other institutionalized mechanisms which serve to effect systemic linkage by reducing the risks of unreciprocated expectation and thus motivating collectivities toward the performance of a differentiated function. The family and the school rely on a fundamental condition of common values, the chief one in this case for the United States being the shared valuation of achievement. The erstwhile farmer and the occupational social systems rely upon the institutions of contract, of money, and of labor market mechanisms such as competition between employers, collective bargaining among workers, and the controls exercised by public agencies. Many units in the underdeveloped areas of the world have not arrived at a point from which rapid change to an industrialized and differentiated system can be launched. "It is quite clear that no 'primitive' society (defined for example as non-literate) could develop a full-fledged industrial economy." [288]

Parsons identifies "support" and "legitimation" as requirements for differentiation of function and the subsequent systemic linkage which must occur between formerly undifferentiated units. Support refers to the climate of public opinion in the community most vitally affected by the differentiation of function.[289] Whether the differentiation concerns the employed mother, the care of the family's sick in hospitals, the education of the family's children in schools, the employment of the father outside the kinship unit, the consequent family linkages to other systems will be prevalent only to the extent that community opinion condones the differentiation. This is intimately connected with the problem of legitimation by which the basic pattern of organization of socially important functions is either justified or questioned. Both support and legitimation involve ideological beliefs.[290] Ideas about property and property holders may have to change so that responsibility as a virtue is imputed to others besides property holders. Ideas about the "public interest" and "private interest" of non-kinship organizations may have to change. To be legitimized they must be imputed with a degree of public interest. The role of government in legitimizing differentiated roles to social systems by the process of incorporation and in exercising other governmental controls, such as anti-monopolistic linkages in a capitalistic society, is itself an evidence of inter-level linkage as well as a force which tends to maintain intra-level linkages deemed publicly advantageous. It is this highest level of systemic linkages of which Parsons speaks in regard to underdeveloped countries:

Government must be sufficiently stable and also sufficiently *differenti-ated* from institutionalized structures in the society which are incom-patible with industrialization . . . to exert a strong leverage on the society to create more favorable new structures.[291]

Social control. The two master processes just considered, boundary maintenance and systemic linkage, deal with the same phenomena and are in a sense "paired" processes. The one about to be considered, social control and the following one, socialization also deal with the same phenomena and connote activities which reinforce each other. "The processes by which resistances to conformity with social expectations develop, and the mechanisms by which these tendencies are or tend to be counteracted in social systems," [292] are considered by Parsons to be respectively, deviance and social control. From the point of view of the individual actor, "A mechanism of social control . . . is a motivational process in one or more *individual* actors which tends to *counteract* a tendency to deviance from the fulfillment of role-expectations, in himself or in one or more alters. It is a re-equilibrating mechanism." [293]

Deviance for Parsons is analyzed primarily in terms of a vicious circle paradigm whereby the fundamental interaction model is upset, that is, as "a disturbance is introduced into the system . . . such . . . that what alter does leads to a frustration, in some important respects, of ego's expectation-system vis-a-vis alter." [294] This failure places a strain upon ego because his ex-pectations are part of his need disposition system either specifi-cally with alter as a cathected object particularistically, or as a manifestation of a more universalistic value object. When expec-tations are not met ego must resolve the strain; he must either inhibit the original need disposition through one of the psycho-logical defense mechanisms, transferring cathexis to a new object, or "renounce or seek to redefine the value-orientation pattern with which alter is no longer conforming." [295] In deviancy these pos-sible solutions on the motivational level are not made sufficiently by one or both of the generic parties. The types of deviant moti-vation structure and the characteristic structural analogue in terms of status-roles taken by these types were discussed above under "status-role." There, it will be remembered, the differentiations in terms of compulsive conformity, compulsive alienation, activity, and passivity were noted.

Parsons notes that the principles of socialization and social control of deviance pass through the same stages. This is the case since the control of deviance is essentially a resocialization process. Starting with the phase of "permissiveness" a basis for reassurance is established; the need for aggressiveness and deviant motivational need-dispositions is lessened. The next phase of "support" results in the toleration of natural reactions of frustration occasioned by the failure to meet expectations. However, it must be strictly limited to prevent the encouragement of a new "vicious circle." This is the "restriction or denial of reciprocity" phase. Finally with conditional manipulation of sanctions there is the phase called "manipulation-of-rewards" which is institutionalized in the value pattern and, in successful control, internalized by ego.[296] (See Figure 8).

Parsons takes as the prototype of all specific mechanisms of social control the four successful conditions of psychotherapy (just noted) but observes that "the most fundamental mechanisms of social control are to be found in the normal processes of interaction in an institutionally integrated social system," and "that without deliberate planning on anyones' part there have developed in our type of social system, and correspondingly in others, mechanisms which, within limits, are capable of forestalling and reversing the deep-lying tendencies for deviance to get into the vicious circle phase which puts it beyond the control of ordinary approval-disapproval and reward-punishment sanctions." [297]

The denial of reciprocity and manipulation of sanctions in an effort to induce alter to fulfill ego's expectations is done, as is shown by the italicized pattern variables appearing on Figure 8, in terms of affectivity, specificity, and neutrality. "Domination through love seems to be what happens in what is sometimes called 'maternal overprotection' . . . the 'authoritarian' father presumably dominates mainly through the affectively neutral sanctions." [298] The variables of specificity-diffuseness, likewise, are involved in the definition of the sanctions directed toward compulsive motivational behavior. Moreover, the two pairs of variables, affectivity-neutrality, and specificity-diffuseness are basic to the classification of types of attachment and consequently of modes of identification in the process of socialization itself.

Socialization. The process of socialization centers on the "complementarity of action." The core focus of the process of socialization lies in the "internalization of the culture of the society into which the child is born. The most important part of this culture . . . consists in the patterns of value . . ." [299] It is because "the *human* personality is not 'born' but must be 'made' through the socialization process that in the first instance families are necessary. They are 'factories' which produce human personalities." [300] Parsons, however, does not limit the process to infancy or to the family as the social structure for carrying it out. The specific status-role, "socializee," is posited and in interaction with others such as parents, teachers, bosses and colleagues the socialization process continues throughout life. Considerable attention is given to the levels of difficulty of internalizing principal value patterns in the socialization process, and the shifting models which the "socializee" as well as the "socializing agents" must internalize. For the child the affective orientations come first and are easiest to acquire. Affective neutrality is more difficult and must be motivated through diffuse-affective attachments. The universalistic orientations are most difficult. Societies differ in the priorities assigned to all of these types of adjustment and impose different strains in socialization. There exist instances of the "hierarchy of regression possibilities." Thus "emotional types" do not mature into affectively-neutral types, but retain throughout adulthood the affective orientation characteristic of childhood. In the socialization process the "socializee" may fail to identify with models and alienation may result.

In the permissive and support stages, identification attachments develop which make the "leverage" of the "denial of reciprocity" and "manipulation of rewards" effective in the socialization process. (Figure 8.) Parsons states the important theorem that "value-orientation patterns can *only* be internalized from outside through reciprocal attachments" or complementary role relationships.[301] Whereas in performance processes goals are *given*, in learning processes they must be redefined. Relative to the goal-focus, then, the directionality of such process is counterclockwise, from I to G in Figure 8.

In the context of American culture Parsons has indicated that the socialization process has a definite broad plan: "My thesis is that the socialization process goes through a series of stages, defined as learning to participate in the various levels of organizations. . . . The first of these takes place in the nuclear family, the second centers around the primary and secondary schools, and the third revolves around the college and the graduate and professional schools. . . ." [302]

Institutionalization. This is the process through which a plurality of relevant actors come to conform to value orientation standards. It is itself an "evaluative phenomenon." [303] Parsons notes that "a concrete action system is an integrated structure of action elements in relation to a situation. This means essentially integration of motivational and cultural or symbolic elements, brought together in a certain kind of ordered system." [304] This "integration" is the core of institutionalization. It can be viewed in terms of the double contingency present in interaction. For Parsons the individuals who ultimately form the units of action are assumed to be always seeking to maximize gratification; such gratification has to be "bound in." Institutionalized rewards and sanctions standardize the conforming behavior of both parties to the interaction and in a sense unify it with gratification. Although institutionalization is a matter of degree, its opposite is *anomie* in which the structured complementarity of the interaction process is absent and the normative order breaks down.[305]

The result of institutionalization is an institution definable as a complex of standardized role integrates or status-relationships which is of strategic structural significance for the social system. The institution is made up of a plurality of interdependent role patterns or components of them.

Institutions, or institutional patterns . . . are a principal aspect of what is, in a generalized sense, the social structure. They are *normative* patterns which define what are felt to be, in a given society, proper, legitimate, or expected modes of action or of social relationship. Among the various types of normative patterns which govern action there are two primary criteria which distinguish those of institutional significance. In the first place, they are patterns which are supported by common moral sentiments; conformity with them is not only a matter of expediency, but of moral duty. In the second place, they are not "utopian" patterns which, however highly desirable they may be regarded, are not lived up to except by a few, or by others in exceptional circumstances.[306]

Parsons classifies institutions into three types: relational, regulative, and cultural. Relational institutions are directly constitutive of the patterning of the interactive relationships in the social system through the definition of statuses and roles. Through the value standards these institutions constitute the structural core of the social system and are the primary mechanism of its stabilization. Regulative institutions prevent the "private" interests of the actor from deviating too much from the over-all interests of the collectivity. Their chief functions are the definition of appropriate goal orientations for the membership and the definition of appropriate means or other action procedures. The focus is on instrumental, expressive and moral interests. For example, the taboo is regulative. Cultural institutions furnish the content of value standards and consist of cognitive beliefs, expressive symbols and moral obligations. Commitment by members may, as in the case of loyalty, be strong on the one hand, or it may fall somewhat short of literal conformity, as in the case of the norms stipulated by the Sermon on the Mount. Parsons draws a careful distinction between the concepts of institution and collectivity. "A collectivity is a system of concretely interactive specific roles. An institution on the other hand is a complex of patterned elements in role-expectations which may apply to an indefinite number of collectivities. Conversely, a collectivity may be the focus of a whole series of institutions. Thus the institutions of marriage and of parenthood are both constitutive of a particular family as a collectivity." [307] The institution as a concept is a higher order unit than role. Thus, the "institution of property" may be associated with a plurality of interdependent role patterns.

Parsons accepts Max Weber's analysis of charismatic leadership in which, in Parsons' terms, "primacy of charisma means that the immediate expressive significance of the role takes precedence over its instrumental functions in the collective division of labor" and may be communicated by the norm "take no thought for the morrow." The routinization of charisma is the process by which the expressive orientation primary in the initial stages shifts to an instrumental orientation whereby the charismatic movement may be extended and continued. This routinization process is a process of institutionalization.[308] In somewhat oversimplified terms, the sacred quality of the leader moves into the office status-roles and symbol system through routinization or institutionalization. The symbol system, now stabilized on a cultural basis, is thus capable of being transmitted as an organized entity.[309]

CONDITIONS OF ACTION

Parsons sees the *situation,* or that part of interaction to which the actor responds, as being comprised of means and conditions, the conditions being those aspects "over which the actor has no control, that is which he cannot alter, or prevent from being altered, in conformity with his end." [310] Although concrete things in the situation are actually partly condition and partly means, and thus cannot be empirically distinct, for analytical purposes the distinction is a useful one. One of the analytically distinct conditions is territoriality.

Territoriality. Territoriality as a condition of action is seen by Parsons to be related chiefly to the power component. ". . . force must be territorially organized. It is not possible to have a variety of different jurisdictions commanding force within the same territory without definition of their limits." [311] The state, in which ultimate societal force usually resides, is territorially organized. The village, in contrast, unless it has very firmly established systemic linkages with the state, is relatively non-defensible, a condition which Parsons uses to explain the "striking fact that the Communist movement has had so much more success in peasant societies than in industrialized societies, which have a much firmer structure between the lowest level community unit and the paramount integration of the power system." [312] The importance of the actual physical boundaries of states, prisons, and many other collectivities inheres in the basis provided by those boundaries and what lies within them for keeping within bounds disruptive conflicts which inevitably become "struggles for power." [313]

In addition to the component which in *The Social System* was discussed under the heading, "Territoriality, force and the integration of the power system," but later in *Structure and Process in Modern Societies* designated as the third element of community, defined as "some process of decision-making where the ultimately relevant agency is held to have 'legitimate authority' under a system of normative order," [314] three other aspects of systemic territoriality are discussed. These are:

1) Residence [or] . . . the locational reference of persons in roles in which their status *as persons*, independently of the exigencies of more specified roles, is most salient. . . .[315] 2) The work or occupational reference . . . where *adaptive* functions are primarily at issue . . . [and] [316] 3) the communicative complex . . . [which] refers not to the boundaries of interactive systems but to the *processes* of interchange.[317]

Time. Time, like space, is partly a facility and partly a condition of action. "Time is *never* a manipulable variable; time is a frame of reference within which one can state and interpret the assumptions about and the consequences of the operations of manipulable variables." It is unalterable in the same sense that space as such inevitably exacts a price to transverse it. The primary "cost" in relation to time is that of change or attempt toward change in the social system. Indeed, the implication of change as a condition of time is perhaps the single most pivotal (and hence controversial) aspect of Parsons' social system treatment.

Parsons begins with the consideration that the actor is conscious of the fact that his own and his associates' life spans are limited. This being true as in the case of Max Weber's traditionalism the actor may consider that he has a vested interest in stability because change involves risk of losing irretrievable time required to get back to the accustomed level of gratification.[318] Stability as a concept is illustrated by the equilibrium of constant body temperatures of mammals and birds in varying environmental temperatures. Presumably extremly low or high body temperatures would signify "cost" in life span.

In an analysis of social change three dichotomies which are analytically distinct, two of which involve time as a condition, are specified. As noted above social analysis in general requires that the subject (Figure 2) and object (Figure 3) be specified. Then "there are two other dichotomies which are in the same class of indispensability, namely that between structure and process and that between stability and change." [319]

The reason for insistence on the importance of keeping the concepts of structure and process and of stability and change analytically distinct is not a predilection in favor of one or the other item in each pair, but in favor of *orderly procedure* in scientific analysis.[320] The specificities of significant change could not even be identified if there were no *relative* background of nonchange to relate them to.[321]

A crucial initial distinction for Parsons is between processes of change within a system and change of the total system as such, a distinction which later he came to designate as the difference between structure and process as distinguished from stability and change. The equilibrium assumption, Parsons argues, "enables one to discriminate two sets of forces in dynamic analysis; that is, from the point of view of their effects on the states of systems. We might call 'disturbing forces' those which make for change in the state, and 'equilibrating forces,' those which make for maintenance of state or restoration of disturbed state." [322] Furthermore, "structure, equilibrium, inertia, are all ways of saying essentially the same thing—that there are features of systems that we use as stable reference points for analyzing the relations of those features to less stable factors in the situation. I'm inclined to think that this is a general characteristic of the logic of science." [323] In structural-functional analysis the more stable pattern consistencies of existential data are "frozen" as structure and the question becomes one of asking how these constant aspects change or remain the same.

In conformity with the equilibrium model, Parsons notes the general resistance to social change derived from vested interests.[324] Because any behavior pattern is institutionalized in some degree there is implied role expectations for the relevant actors which are part of their gratification-deprivation make up. To have change, *ipso facto,* is to have broken expectations and hence resistance identified as vested interests.[325] On the other hand he sees the origins of change as plural. They may be physical (geographic environment, etc.), biological (shift in gene structure, sex ratio, etc.), in the belief system (for example, science with its built-in norms of "obsolescence"), in facilities (sheer technological change), or in the malalignment of one or more institutional complexes of the total system.[326]

The general procedural outline for the analysis of intra-system change then is to identify both the sources of change and the structure of vested interests, which essentially means adequate description of the system prior to change. As careful detail as possible of intermediate system "stabilities" or "what has changed into what and through what . . . stages" [327] should follow this. Overall is the guide of functional imperatives limiting the range of compatible structure and specifying differentiated functions with the result that new *kinds* of social systems are assigned functions which previously were performed by a less differentiated unit.

In these terms we can ask whether the change tends to violate . . . imperatives, to jeopardize the motivational needs of important groups in the population, to weaken the controls over important parts of the power system . . . [etc.] When any of these "problems" can be precisely identified and stated we can then proceed to analyze the processes of adaptation and adjustment which ensue from the introduction of a change.[328]

In sum, by jointly considering motivational processes and structural elements description of changes can be launched. Thus, for instance, knowledge of the "family role-system" is related to adolescent identification processes to predict conforming and nonconforming outcomes to the socialization sequence.[329] The processes of boundary maintenance and systemic linkage are intimately connected both with the condition of time and with social change, and hence the content of those sections are applicable here.

Size. Among the conditions of action Parsons accords size the least attention. His chief interest is in general theory and in this context size has not become a focus of attention. Thus he emphasizes, "There are continuities all the way from the two-person interaction to the United States of America as a social system," [330] and, "I think we can translate back and forth between large scale social system and small groups." [331] Perhaps not unrelated to this assumption is the fact that large parts of Parsons' analysis involve a generic two-party system though at the same time he considers society to be the only true bridging concept of potentially complete social systems. Technically, all less inclusive groups are considered subsystems.[332]

These considerations should not be taken to mean that Parsons assigns no significance to size. For instance, he notes "the scope of general participation in group-decision varies inversely with the size of the group . . . it is more difficult to implement the wide participation of 200 people than it is of five." [333] The allocation of roles faces a similar limit. "In the face-to-face group of ten or twelve, only that many different roles can be allocated to the members, but there are far more than 500 different kinds of roles in American society. This is a simple function of size." [334] Size as such, however, is not generally assigned causal necessity. Thus, Parsons has criticized Durkheim's explanation of increasing functional differentiation as a result of population increase.[335] On the other hand he has noted that "the primary group provides for some functional needs that are common to all human groups of whatever size." [336] Among these are "integration of the group" and "providing expressive leadership." These functional imperatives need to be met in any social system that persists. Although the specifics concerning how these needs must be met in groups of varying size are not clearly stipulated, variations of authority patterns for different units are considered. Authority in the family must have a different pattern than that in a military organization not only because the functions of these two collectivities differ. The family "is a small group with a necessarily limited level of structural differentiation. Hence, authority in it must be linked with the diffuse responsibility of the two adult members vis-a-vis their children. . . ." [337] With larger groups "it is theoretically possible . . . for all members effectively to bear equal responsibility . . . but, in general, and the more so the larger the system, there are fundamental factors making for inequality." [338]

BIBLIOGRAPHICAL KEY *

APT—Talcott Parsons, "An Approach to Psychological Theory in Terms of the Theory of Action," in Sigmund Koch, ed., *Psychology: A Science* (New York: McGraw-Hill, 1959), Vol. III.
ASK—Talcott Parsons, "An Approach to the Sociology of Knowledge,"

* See end of key.

manuscript of a paper read at the Fourth World Congress of Sociology at Milan, Italy, September, 1959.

ASR—Talcott Parsons, "Some Comments on the State of the General Theory of Action," *American Sociological Review*, Vol. 18, No. 6 (December, 1953).

CSS—Talcott Parsons, "Culture and the Social System," Part IV in Parsons, *et al.*, eds., *Theories of Society* (Glencoe, Ill.: The Free Press, forthcoming).

DCT—Talcott Parsons, "Durkheim's Contribution to the Theory of Integration of Social Systems," in Kurt H. Wolff, ed., *Emile Durkheim, 1858-1917* (Columbus, Ohio: The Ohio State University Press, 1960).

DHI—Talcott Parsons, "Definition of Health and Illness in the Light of American Values and Social Structure," in E. Gartly Jaco, ed., *Patients, Physicians and Illness* (Glencoe, Ill.: The Free Press, 1958).

E&S—Talcott Parsons and Neil J. Smelser, *Economy and Society* (Glencoe, Ill.: The Free Press, 1956).

ESSAYS—Talcott Parsons, *Essays in Sociological Theory* (Glencoe, Ill.: The Free Press, Revised Edition, 1954).

FSIP—Talcott Parsons and R. F. Bales, *Family, Socialization and Interaction Process* (Glencoe, Ill.: The Free Press, 1955).

GTIS—Talcott Parsons, "General Theory in Sociology," in Robert K. Merton, Leonard Broom, Leonard S. Cottrell, Jr., eds., *Sociology Today: Problems and Prospects* (New York: Basic Books, Inc., 1959).

IT—Talcott Parsons, "The Incest Taboo in Relation to Social Structure and the Socialization of the Child," *British Journal of Sociology*, Vol. 5, No. 2 (June, 1954).

PVR—Talcott Parsons, "Pattern Variables Revisited: A Response to Robert Dubin," *American Sociological Review*, Vol. 25, No. 4 (August, 1960).

RTSS—Talcott Parsons, "A Revised Analytical Approach to the Theory of Social Stratification," in Reinhard Bendix and Seymour Martin Lipset, eds., *Class, Status, and Power: A Reader in Social Stratification* (Glencoe, Ill.: The Free Press, 1953).

SC—Talcott Parsons, "Some Considerations on the Theory of Social Change," dittoed manuscript (to be published in *Rural Sociology*, Vol. 26, No. 3). Paper read Nov. 2, 1960 to the North Central Regional Rural Sociological Committee of the Farm Foundation, Chicago, Illinois.

SCSS—Talcott Parsons, "The School Class as a Social System: Some of Its Functions in American Society," *Harvard Educational Review*, Vol. 29, No. 4 (Fall, 1959).

SPMS—Talcott Parsons, *Structure and Process in Modern Societies* (Glencoe, Ill.: The Free Press, 1960).

SS—Talcott Parsons, *The Social System* (Glencoe, Ill.: The Free Press, 1951).

SSA—Talcott Parsons, *The Structure of Social Action* (Glencoe, Ill.: The Free Press, 1949, 2nd ed.).

TGTA—Talcott Parsons and Edward A. Shils, eds., *Toward A General Theory of Action* (Cambridge, Mass.: Harvard University Press, 1951).

THM—Talcott Parsons, "Toward a Health Maturity," *Journal of Health and Human Behavior*, Vol. 1, No. 3 (1960).

TUTHB—Roy P. Grinker, ed., *Toward a Unified Theory of Human Behavior* (New York: Basic Books, Inc., 1956).
WP—Talcott Parsons, R. F. Bales and E. A. Shils, *Working Papers in the Theory of Action* (Glencoe, Ill.: The Free Press, 1953).

* For a more complete bibliography see the notes which follow and the bibliographical appendix at the end of the volume.

NOTES

1. Of course the term, social system, appears in the writings of Comte, Spencer and other earlier theorists as well as many later writings. For a general treatment see Charles P. Loomis, *Social Systems: Essays on Their Persistance and Change* (Princeton, N. J.: D. Van Nostrand, 1960), Essay 1. Parsons mentions particularly Florian Znaniecki, *The Method of Sociology* (New York: Rinehart Co., 1934), Ch. 5.

2. Charles P. Loomis, *op. cit.*

3. Cf., for instance, Don Martindale, "Talcott Parsons' Theoretical Metamorphosis from Social Behaviorism to Macrofunctionalism," *Alpha Kappa Deltan*, Vol. 29, No. 1 (Winter, 1958), pp. 38-46.

4. Talcott Parsons, *The Structure of Social Action* (Glencoe, Ill.: The Free Press, 1949, 2nd ed.). Hereafter this is designated in the footnotes as SSA. The first book to appear was the important translation of Max Weber, *The Protestant Ethic and the Spirit of Capitalism.* (London and New York: Allen and Unwin and Scribners, 1930).

5. SSA, pp. 697 ff. Parsons' main thesis that the voluntaristic theory is a convergence stemming directly from the works of Marshall, Pareto, Durkheim and Weber is not significant here.

6. Talcott Parsons, *The Social System* (Glencoe, Ill.: The Free Press, 1951), pp. 45 and 36. (Hereafter designated as SS.)

7. Talcott Parsons, R. F. Bales and E. A. Shils, *Working Papers in the Theory of Action* (Glencoe, Ill.: The Free Press, 1953), p. 168. Hereafter designated as WP.

8. See, for example, fn. 3 *supra.*

9. Talcott Parsons, "An Approach to Psychological Theory in Terms of the Theory of Action," in Sigmund Koch, ed., *Psychology: A Science* (New York: McGraw-Hill, 1959), Vol. III, pp. 619-623. Hereafter designated as APT.

10. SSA, pp. 6 and 730. (Italics added by present authors.)

11. *Ibid.*, p. 730.

12. The biological system or "organism" was added after the other three were developed, APT, p. 613. Economic, political and other systems are for the most part analyzed in terms of the original three: the cultural, social and personality. "We conceive the conceptual scheme of the theory of action to be applicable over a range running all the way from the behavioral systems of elementary organisms to the most complex social and cultural systems, and on the human level, from the elementary learning processes of the infant to the processes of development of historical change in the most complex societies," WP, p. 172. See also SSA, pp. 618 ff. for an early statement for the necessity of developing a general theory.

13. This has been called "unitary isomorphism" by Alfred L. Baldwin, "The Parsonian Theory of Personality" in Max Black, ed., *The Social Theories of Talcott Parsons* (Englewood Cliffs, N. J.: Prentice-Hall, Inc., 1961).

14. APT, p. 165.   15. WP, p. 208.

16. Talcott Parsons and Edward A. Shils, eds., *Toward a General Theory of Action* (Cambridge, Mass.: Harvard University Press, 1951), p. 60. (Hereafter designated as TGTA.) The generic term "mode" as used with motivational and/or value-orientation in SS, TGTA, and other writings is also used in SSA. For example see SSA, p. 658.

17. SS, p. 42. "The clear recognition of the independent variability of these two basic modes or levels of orientation is at the very basis of a satisfactory theory in the field of 'culture and personality.' " Failure to understand this has led to an oscillation between "psychological determinism" and "cultural determinism," SS, pp. 14-5.

18. APT, p. 616.   19. *Ibid.*, pp. 656-7.

20. Talcott Parsons, "An Approach to the Sociology of Knowledge," manuscript of a paper read at the Fourth World Congress of Sociology at Milan, Italy, September, 1959, p. 3. Hereafter referred to as ASK. Parsons has demonstrated these may be entered in the left column of Figure 7 in text as follows: values at the intersection of the L column and L row; norms at L and I; collectivities at L and G; and role at L and A. Alpha Kappa Delta lecture at Michigan State University, 1959.

21. Talcott Parsons, *Structure and Process in Modern Societies* (Glencoe, Ill.: The Free Press, 1960), p. 171. Hereafter designated as SPMS. Among the additional dimensions which Parsons specifies are the following: 1) Specification of values, 2) Inclusiveness of membership, 3) Range of adaptibility and 4) Level of normative control. Notes on present manuscript in final draft.

22. *Ibid.*   23. SS, pp. 5-6.

24. Talcott Parsons and Neil J. Smelser, *Economy and Society* (Glencoe, Ill.: The Free Press, 1956), p. 21. Hereafter designated as E & S.

25. Cultural systems like social, personality, and biological systems are now considered by Parsons to be "action" systems. This means that the conceptualization of the cultural system as conceived in *The Social System* has changed. Originally for Parsons a cultural system such as a system of beliefs, mathematics or linguistics "does not 'function' except as a part of a concrete action system, it just 'is,' " SS, p. 17.

In another context, in delineating culture as outside action *per se* he writes, "The role of the cultural value patterns is analogous to those modern machines which approximate 'thinking' processes. The institutionalized value patterns are analogous to the basic 'programme' or set of instructions which are 'stored' in the machine's 'memory.' In response to more specific 'information' fed in, the machine performs a series of operations to arrive at particular results. But the programme pattern cannot be derived from the specific operational procedures or vice versa; they are analytically independent factors," E & S, pp. 69-70.

More recently he writes: "It would seem to follow from the general premises of action theory that, if the functions of culture are as essential as, in a variety of ways, they clearly seem to be, the important patterns of culture, i.e., complexes of meaning, could not be created and/or maintained as resources available for action primarily oriented to their creation and/or maintenance. . . . [Thus] a church . . . as a collectivity with cultural primacy . . . [is] in the first instance a cultural 'system of action' and secondarily a social system." Talcott Parsons, "Culture and the Social System," in Parsons, *et al.*, eds., *Theories of Society* (Glencoe, Ill.: The Free Press, Part Four 1961). Hereafter designated as CSS.

26. SS, p. 540. This was the formulation in *The Social System*. More recently, the four crucial concepts ranging from the most general to the most specific and the greatest "control" to the least are: values, norms, collectivities and status-roles.

27. Talcott Parsons, "Psychology and Sociology," in John Gillin, ed. *For A Science of Social Man* (New York: Macmillan Co., 1954), p. 70.

28. See SS, pp. 26-36, 151-80, esp. pp. 167-77 for a discussion of the functional and structural prerequisites of society. The work of some of Parsons' students is also important in this regard. To be particularly noted is D. F. Aberle, A. K. Cohen, A. K. Davis, M. J. Levy, Jr., and F. X. Sutton, "The Functional Prerequisites of a Society," *Ethics*, Vol. 9 (January, 1950), pp. 100-11 and Marion J. Levy, Jr., *The Structure of Society* (Princeton, N. J.: Princeton University Press, 1952), pp. 111-97.

29. SS, p. 19.

30. Parsons in *The Social System* does indicate that in strictest terms the conceptualization there offered is a treatise on nominal definition. See esp. pp. 536-7. This does not detract from his claim. See Nicholas S. Timasheff, *Sociological Theory*, rev. ed., (New York: Random House, 1957), p. 246. Timasheff considers Parsons' original view of social institutions nominalistic, but after the appearance of *The Social System* notes "but this apparently nominalistic view seems to have been modified . . . ," *Ibid.* Robert Bierstedt criticizes Parsons for what he calls the latter's use of nominalistic definitions and his "highly formal and indeed taxonomic approach to sociology." "Nominal and Real Definitions in Sociological Theory," in L. Gross, *Symposium of Sociological Theory*, (Evanston, Ill.: Row, Peterson and Co., 1959), p. 137. He goes on to challenge Parsons' statement in *Essays in Sociological Theory* (1954), p. 224 that "mathematics in physics *is* theory." The apparent difficulty here is failure to distinguish between the "logically necessary" and the "logically contingent" components of theory. See R. B. Braithwaite, *Scientific Explanation*, (New York: Harper Torch Book Edition, 1960).

31. SS, p. 19.   32. SS, pp. 153-67.

33. The "empirical clusterings of social structure" are related in the following manner to the four phases or problems of social systems as developed later: kinship and religious systems both fall in the L cell at different levels; the instrumental achievement structures of the economy fall in the A cell; the power component of "territoriality, force and the integration of the power system" falls in the G cell; stratification which was previously combined with instrumental achievement structures is placed in the I cell. From notes on the final draft of the present manuscript.

34. Talcott Parsons, "General Theory in Sociology," in Robert K. Merton, Leonard Broom, Leonard S. Cottrell, Jr., eds., *Sociology Today: Prob-*

lems and Prospects (New York: Basic Books, Inc., 1959), pp. 9-10. Hereafter designated as GTIS.

35. SPMS, p. 7.　36. *Ibid.*, p. 46.

37. *Ibid.*, p. 94.　38. *Ibid.*, p. 28.

39. Note here that boundary interchanges among subsystems of a larger social system parallels the idea of boundary exchange among systems (the cultural, social, psychological systems and the organism) as well as that among analytical units of a social system (values, norms, collectivities and individuals).

40. Talcott Parsons, "Durkheim's Contribution to the Theory of Integration of Social Systems," Kurt H. Wolff, ed., *Emile Durkheim, 1858-1917* (Columbus, Ohio: The Ohio State University Press, 1960), pp. 133 ff. Hereafter designated as DCT. Talcott Parsons, "Pattern Variable Revisited: A Response to Robert Dubin," *American Sociological Review*, Vol. 25, No. 4 (August, 1960), p. 479. Hereafter designated as PVR. It is interesting to note that in WP and in *Family, Socialization and Interaction Process* as Parsons' attention was focused on the "instrumental and the system integrative norms" the A cell was designated as *Gesellschaft*-like and the I cell as *Gemeinschaft*-like in Toennies' sense. As Parsons' interest in differentiation and change developed and as the four-fold approach of Figure 1 was elaborated, Durkheim's mechanical solidarity (usually considered as comparable to *Gemeinschaft*) is characterized by priority in the L and G cells of Figure 1. Organic solidarity (usually considered comparable to *Gesellschaft*) is characterized by emphasis on the I and A cells. See also Ferdinand Toennies, *Community and Society—Gemeinschaft und Gesellschaft,* translated and introduced by Charles P. Loomis (East Lansing, Michigan: Michigan State University Press, 1957), p. 277.

41. SPMS, pp. 35-6.

42. For example, Harry Johnson finds *ideologies* functioning in both cells and in some instances places religious leaders in the integrative and in others in the L cell, *Sociology* (New York: Harcourt, Brace, and Co., 1960), pp. 597, 241, 627. Also Johnson places medical care in the L cell whereas Parsons in more recent writings places it in the I cell.

43. SSA, p. 619.

44. E & S, p. 34. The forerunners of the pattern variable schema, although used earlier in the classroom, first appeared in print in 1939. Talcott Parsons, "The Professions and Social Structure," *Social Forces,* Vol. 17 (1939), pp. 457-467. Four pairs then appeared: disinterestedness vs. self-interest (later changed to self-orientation vs. collectivity orientation), rationality vs. traditionalism, functional specificity vs. functional diffuseness, universalism vs. particularism. By 1942 the pair, affective neutrality vs. affectivity, had been added. Later the rationality vs. traditionalism pair was withdrawn on the explanation that the distinction is "certainly not on the same level . . . [but] on a level antecedent to the pattern variables." TGTA, pp. 90-1. (Thus the instrumental-consummatory axis of Figure 1 seems imminent as it appeared in GTIS having been preceded by "types of evaluation action-orientation," instrumental, expressive and moral, as appearing in SS, pp. 58 ff. and "three classes of problems that must be solved by all role occupants," TGTA, pp. 297 ff.) Later the pair proposed by Linton as the distinction between ascription and achievement was added as the

fifth dichotomy. This was subsequently changed to the "quality-performance distinction" to make the distinction applicable to other than social system analysis, E & S, p. 35.

45. E & S, p. 33.   46. TGTA, pp. 78-9.

47. *Ibid.*, p. 79.

48. Talcott Parsons, "Some Comments on the State of the General Theory of Action," *American Sociological Review,* Vol. 18, No. 6 (December, 1953), p. 623. Hereafter designated as ASR.

49. *Ibid.*, p. 625.   50. *Ibid.*, p. 626.

51. PVR, p. 480.

52. He notes that "in my own earlier work I considered the pattern variables to be categories of social structure as such. It was one of the most important insights of the new work under review that they were in fact categories of systems of action in general . . . ," ASR, p. 627.

53. PVR, p. 472.   54. *Ibid.*

55. *Ibid.*, p. 473.   56. E & S, p. 36.

57. WP, p. 82 (italics omitted).

58. *Ibid.*, p. 83 (italics omitted). The great "rapidity following the initial 'breakthrough' " of the convergence between pattern variables and Bales' system problems is recorded in the *Working Papers.* The case for affectivity-performance as the prototype of relationships across the motivational-situational axis is graphically presented: "The affective case constitutes the permission to 'go ahead,' the 'green light' for positive overt action, while the 'neutral' case is the 'red light,' the signal to hold up and wait," WP, p. 82. Thus, affectivity is directly linked with performance, whereas neutrality does not mean indifference, but the lack of performance at the moment of cathexis, and hence tension. Denied gratification for the sake of some future state of affairs, whether it be denied sexual gratification, denied impulse to vent anger, or denied self-indulgence of any form thus moves to the neutrality-quality combination, whereas the sex act, the physical or any immediate gratification shows both affectivity and performance.

59. PVR, p. 473.   60. *Ibid.*, p. 481.

61. *Ibid.*, p. 475.   62. *Ibid.*

63. *Ibid.*   64. *Ibid.*

65. ASK, p. 3.   66. *Ibid.*, p. 468.

67. SS, p. 327.

68. An elaboration of this table and its interpretation appears in a companion volume of this present work: Charles P. Loomis, *Social Systems, op. cit.*, p. 173.

69. Recorded discussion, November, 1960.

70. CSS, p. 2.   71. CSS, p. 3.

72. ASK, p. 3.   73. CSS and ASK.

74. SS, p. 332.   75. *Ibid.*

76. *Ibid.*, pp. 368-9.   77. *Ibid.*, p. 370.

78. SPMS, pp. 311-12.   79. *Ibid.*, p. 311.

80. *Ibid.*, p. 312.   81. *Ibid.*, p. 321.

82. *Ibid.*, p. 297.   83. SS, p. 374.

84. SSA, p. 587.

85. Roy P. Grinker, ed., *Toward a Unified Theory of Human Behavior*

(New York: Basic Books, Inc., 1956), p. 188. Hereafter designated as TUTHB.

86. SS, p. 377.   87. *Ibid.*, p. 348.
88. *Ibid.*   89. SS, p. 358.
90. *Ibid.* p. 351.   91. *Ibid.*

92. *Ibid.*, p. 341. For a different point of view see Pitirim Sorokin, *Social and Cultural Dynamics* (New York: American Book Co., 1937), Vol. 2, pp. 152-3. Parsons treats the subject further in his review of Reinhard Bendix's *Max Weber, American Sociological Review,* Vol. 25 (October, 1960), pp. 750-1.

93. SS, p. 375.   94. *Ibid.*, p. 379.
95. SSA, p. v.   96. *Ibid.*, p. 730.

97. Within this position, Parsons implicitly notes the youth of the social sciences observing, "It is only recently, if now, that it has come to be no longer possible to say in social science circles that "it all depends on your conception of human nature,' " SS, p. 365.

98. APT, p. 651.

99. ASK, p. 20. In the social sciences epistemological problems pose special concern not present to the same degree in the physical sciences. For the sociologist "the object is both 'out there'—in Durkheim's sense an external object—and part of the observer himself, i.e., is internalized. There is doubtless a sense in which this is also true of physical objects, but it is somehow a remoter sense," *ibid.*, p. 14. He eschews the relativistic position sometimes attributed to Mannheim. On the contrary he assumes "a fundamental unity of human culture and of the condition of human orientation to the world . . . variability, but . . . not random variability," *ibid.*, p. 15. For Parsons "the system of empirical knowledge is considered to be the adaptive subsystem of a system of culture. [Figure 5.] Its basic standards . . . [are] institutionalized in *its* 'pattern maintenance' subsystem and thus relatively immune from influences emanating from other cultural subsystems." *Ibid.*, p. 15a.

100. *Ibid.*, pp. 5 ff.   101. *Ibid.*, p. 10.
102. *Ibid.*, p. 6.   103. *Ibid.*, p. 23.
104. *Ibid.*, p. 36.   105. APT, p. 695.
106. *Ibid.*, p. 696.   107. WP, p. 172.
108. APT, p. 701.

109. *Ibid.*, see also WP, pp. 172, 174. In further discussion Parsons notes that in "the learning of language . . . the child develops essentially from the personal pronouns and it is a process of differentiation of a binary system." From the distinction of "me" and "you" the concept of "we" develops then " 'they' or a 'non-we' because 'we' is meaningless if it's the universe." From taped discussion, November, 1960.

110. SS, p. 373.   111. *Ibid.*, p. 446.
112. *Ibid.*, p. 387.   113. *Ibid.*, p. 41.
114. *Ibid.*, pp. 389-94. 115. *Ibid.*, pp. 388-9.
116. *Ibid.*, p. 391.   117. *Ibid.*, pp. 393-4.
118. *Ibid.*, p. 415.   119. *Ibid.*, p. 41.

120. *Ibid.*, p. 42. As a corollary to this, it can be noted that Parsons agrees with Pareto when he observes that "where values are involved which are not facts which everyone must admit to be true or false . . . there is no

rational means of getting another to accept the end . . . the only recourse in such cases is an appeal to sentiments. Values are either accepted or rejected; they are not proved or disproved as facts are." SSA, p. 277.

121. WP, pp. 183-4.   122. SS, p. 81.
123. WP, pp. 249-50.   124. E & S, p. 149.
125. SS, p. 304.   126. *Ibid.*, pp. 304, 308, 317, 333, 378.

127. Talcott Parsons and Winston White, "The Link Between Character and Society," manuscript made available to the authors, p. 37. Prepared and since published in Seymour M. Lipset and Leo Lowenthal, eds. *Culture and Social Character—The Work of David Riesman Reviewed, Appraised and Criticized by his Contemporaries in Social Sciences* (Glencoe, Ill.: The Free Press, 1961).

128. SS, p. 386.   129. *Ibid.*, p. 387.
130. *Ibid.*, p. 393.   131. *Ibid.*, p. 392.
132. *Ibid.*, p. 399.   133. *Ibid.*, p. 400.
134. *Ibid.*, p. 401.   135. *Ibid.*, p. 397.
136. *Ibid.*   137. *Ibid.*, p. 408.
138. *Ibid.*, p. 409.   139. E & S, p. 34.
140. SS, p. 466.

141. This may well signal the increasing importance of psychology, particularly psychoanalytic thought on Parsons' work. At the same time, recent discussion with Parsons has indicated that "end" may again come into favored use on the belief that it is a more general term than goal and hence more congruent with his most recent theoretical emphasis. Taped discussion, November, 1960.

142. Talcott Parsons, "A Revised Analytical Approach to the Theory of Social Stratification," in Reinhard Bendix and Seymour Martin Lipset, eds., *Class, Status, and Power: A Reader in Social Stratification* (Glencoe, Ill.: The Free Press, 1953), p. 93. Hereafter designated as RTSS. See also fn. 212 below.

143. ASR, p. 622.   144. E & S, p. 17.
145. SS, p. 8.   146. SPMS, p. 17.
147. *Ibid.*, p. 19.   148. *Ibid.*, p. 47.
149. *Ibid.*, p. 45.   150. *Ibid.*, p. 17.
151. *Ibid.*, p. 53.   152. PVR, p. 482.
153. SS, p. 30.   154. SSA, pp. 549 and 573.
155. SS, p. 462. See also *ibid.*, p. 400.

156. E & S, pp. 257-258. See also Charles P. Loomis, "Tentative Types of Directed Change Involving Systemic Linkage," *Rural Sociology*, Vol. 24, No. 4 (December, 1959), pp. 383 ff.

157. Talcott Parsons and Renee Fox, "Illness, Therapy and the Modern Urban American Family," *The Journal of Social Issues*, Vol. 8, No. 4, p. 43.

158. *Ibid.*   159. *Ibid.*, pp. 34-5.
160. SSA, p. 76.   161. *Ibid.*, p. 75.
162. *Ibid.*, p. 690.

163. N. S. Timasheff, "The Basic Concepts of Sociology," *American Journal of Sociology*, Vol. 58, No. 2 (September, 1952), p. 181.

164. DCT, pp. 124-125. Here it is noted that "values, norms, collectivities, and roles are categories that are descriptive of the structural aspect of a social system only," *ibid.*, p. 125. Parsons observes in this article that the peasant and urban families of industrial societies are not "cognate units."

When mechanical (Parsons prefers the term "diffuse") solidarity exists as in peasant societies primacy is accorded the G and L cells of Figure 1. After differentiation and as organic solidarity supplants mechanical solidarity in Durkheim's terms, primacy is given to the A and I cells of Figure 1. Parsons notes that in socialistic and communistic societies organs of collective goal-attainment, represented by the G cell of Figure 1, may serve as the direct agencies of defining and enforcing integration or solidarity of this type, pro-ducing a near-fusion of mechanical and organic solidarity, *ibid.*, pp. 130-141.

165. As presented in the 1959 lecture to Alpha Kappa Delta at Michigan State University.

166. *Ibid.*   167. DCT, p. 126.

168. Charles P. Loomis, *Social Systems, op. cit.*, pp. 18 ff.

169. TGTA, p. 60.   170. SS, p. 14.

171. *Ibid.*, p. 328.   172. *Ibid.*, p. 376.

173. TGTA, p. 78.

174. See, for example, Brewster Smith, review, "Toward a General The-ory of Action," *Psychological Bulletin*, Vol. 49, No. 6 (November, 1952).

175. DCT, p. 122.

176. ASK, p. 4.   177. CSS, p. 12.

178. *Ibid.*, pp. 12-13.   179. *Ibid.*, p. 13.

180. Parsons notes, "We do not mean . . . to imply that a person's val-ues are entirely 'internalized culture' or mere adherence to rules and laws. The person makes creative modifications as he internalizes culture; but the novel aspect is not the cultural aspect," TGTA, fn. 21, p. 72.

181. A term for which he gives Robert R. Sears credit, TUTHB, pp. 55-6.

182. SS, p. 37.   183. ASR, p. 626.

184. SS, p. 97.   185. CSS, p. 12.

186. SSA, p. 669.   187. *Ibid.*, pp. 388, 415.

188. SS, pp. 368-9.   189. *Ibid.*, p. 369.

190. Talcott Parsons, "Toward a Healthy Maturity," *Journal of Health and Human Behavior*, Vol. 1, No. 3 (1960), p. 164. Hereafter designated as THM.

191. Talcott Parsons, "Definition of Health and Illness in the Light of American Values and Social Structure," in E. Gartly Jaco, ed., *Patients, Phy-sicians and Illness* (Glencoe, Ill.: The Free Press, 1958), p. 175. Hereafter designated as DHI.

192. TGTA, p. 40.   193. *Ibid.*

194. SS, pp. 38-9.   195. *Ibid.*, p. 115.

196. A review of the various meanings of role and status in sociology is given by Neal Gross, *et al.*, *Explorations in Role Analysis* (New York: John Wiley and Sons, 1958), in which work Parsons' not completely consistent usage of the terms is noted. See also SS, p. 39. In publications after *The Social System* institutions become complexes of norms. At the least differ-entiated level are values. "The second level is that of institutions . . . [such as property and authority]," SPMS, p. 171. Less differentiated still are col-lectivities and roles.

197. Talcott Parsons, "The Incest Taboo in Relation to Social Structure and the Socialization of the Child," *British Journal of Sociology*, Vol. 5, No. 2 (June, 1954), p. 116. Hereafter designated as IT.

198. TGTA, p. 23.

199. SS, pp. 105-6.

200. *Ibid.*, pp. 155 ff.

201. *Ibid.*, pp. 153-5.

202. *Ibid.*, pp. 157-9.

203. *Ibid.*, pp. 161, 163. See footnote 33 for the relationship between the empirical clusterings of *The Social System* and the later four phases and functional problems. The importance of law for the integrative function has received considerable attention.

204. *Ibid.*, p. 251.

205. *Ibid.* Since this statement in *The Social System* Parsons has come to distinguish creativity from deviance, designating them as "two modes of contravention," See APT, p. 677.

206. *Ibid.*, p. 250.

207. Robert K. Merton, *Social Theory and Social Structure* (Glencoe, Ill.: The Free Press, 1957, rev. ed.), pp. 131-60.

208. SS, p. 288.

209. *Ibid.*, p. 438.

210. DHI, p. 167.

211. *Ibid.*, p. 182.

212. RTSS. This represents a revision of Parsons' earlier paper, "An Analytical Approach to the Theory of Social Stratification," first published in the *American Journal of Sociology* (May, 1940) and later appearing in his *Essays in Sociological Theory* (Glencoe, Ill.: The Free Press, 1949). The 1954 revised edition of this latter work contains the revised stratification essay in the same form in which it appears in the citation noted in fn. 142 *supra*. The book of essays is hereafter designated as ESSAYS.

213. *Ibid.*, p. 93.

214. See fns. 142 and 212 *supra*.

215. RTSS, p. 95.

216. *Ibid.*

217. *Ibid.*, p. 112.

218. SPMS, p. 209.

219. RTSS, p. 115.

220. *Ibid.*, p. 118.

221. *Ibid.*, p. 122.

222. *Ibid.*, p. 124.

223. *Ibid.*, p. 113.

224. *Ibid.*

225. *Ibid.*, p. 117.

226. *Ibid.*

227. *Ibid.*, p. 120.

228. THM, p. 166.

229. SS, p. 465.

230. SPMS, p. 181 (italics omitted).

231. *Ibid.*, p. 182.

232. Others besides Max Weber, of course, have subscribed to the zero-sum concept. Among those mentioned by Parsons are H. D. Lasswell and C. Wright Mills, *ibid.*, pp. 182, 199-225.

233. RTSS, pp. 106 and 108; SPMS, Chapter VI.

234. SPMS, p. 194.

235. *Ibid.*

236. RTSS, p. 96.

237. *Ibid.*

238. *Ibid.*, p. 107.

239. SPMS, Chaps. I & II.

240. *Ibid.*, p. 63.

241. *Ibid.*, p. 33.

242. *Ibid.*, p. 66.

243. *Ibid.*, p. 34.

244. *Ibid.*, p. 69.

245. Max Weber, *The Theory of Social and Economic Organization*, tr. by A. M. Henderson and Talcott Parsons; ed. with an introduction by Talcott Parsons (New York: Oxford University Press, 1947), fn. p. 59.

246. RTSS, p. 99. See the section on Sanctions in Ch. 4 above for parallels with Homans.

247. *Ibid.*

248. SS, p. 38.

249. On this basis, a parallel is drawn between supply and demand in economics and performance and sanction in sociology.

250. SS, p. 277.
251. SPMS, p. 190.
252. *Ibid.*, p. 192.
253. SS, pp. 134-5.
254. CSS, p. 25.
255. *Ibid.*, p. 27.
256. *Ibid.*, p. 28.
257. SS, p. 460.
258. *Ibid.*, pp. 463-4.
259. DCT, p. 125.
260. RTSS, p. 103.
261. SS, p. 119.
262. RTSS, p. 109.
263. *Ibid.*
264. *Ibid.*, p. 122.
265. *Ibid.*
266. *Ibid.*, p. 123.
267. SPMS, p. 26.
268. *Ibid.*, p. 92.
269. SS, p. 432.
270. *Ibid.*, p. 447.
271. *Ibid.*, p. 468.
272. *Ibid.*, p. 433.
273. SS, p. 5.
274. *Ibid.*, p. 11.
275. *Ibid.*

276. Talcott Parsons, "Some Considerations on the Theory of Social Change," an address given Nov. 2, 1960, before the North Central Regional Rural Sociology Committee of the Farm Foundation, Chicago, Illinois (ditto). Hereafter designated SC. To be published in Rural Sociology, Vol. 26, No. 3.

277. For Parsons, systems either maintain their boundaries or they die. "A social system [which does not maintain boundaries] may cease to exist by the disappearance of its boundaries both vis-a-vis the member personalities and vis-a-vis other social systems," WP, p. 98.

278. SS, p. 482.
279. SC, p. 8.
280. *Ibid.*, p. 7.
281. SS, p. 492.

282. SPMS, p. 262 and SC.

283. Parsons notes that "There are good reasons for believing that there is an intimate connection between the overcoming of the excessive autonomy of the nuclear family and the possibility of a cultural level of social development. . . . One of the important consequences of the incest taboo is to enforce the mixing of family cultures. . . . There is an analogy here to the biological functions of sexual reproduction. If, therefore, I may hazard an extremely tentative hypothesis about socio-cultural origins, it would be that the earliest *society* had to be a multifamily unit which enforced an incest taboo." IT, p. 117. In Parsons' thinking, students in schools and universities and patients in hospitals constitute a kind of fusion of "customer" status-role to use a market analogy and "employee" to use an industrial example. In discussing the failure to differentiate such status-roles he notes that "the case of fusion includes not only the hospital and the school, but above all, the two great superordinate collectivity structures of historic societies, the state and the church which 'purvey' services only to their own members . . . kinship units are universally included in this type." Talcott Parsons, "The Mental Hospital as a Type of Organization," in Milton Greenblatt, Daniel J. Levinson and Richard H. Williams, eds. *The Patient and the Mental Hospital* (Glencoe, Ill.: The Free Press, 1957), pp. 115-116. See also Talcott Parsons, "The School Class as a Social System: Some of Its Functions in American Society," *Harvard Educational Review*, Vol. 29, No. 4 (Fall, 1959), p. 309. Hereafter designated as SCSS.

284. SC, p. 28.
285. *Ibid.*, p. 7.

286. *SCSS*, p. 309.   287. *SPMS*, p. 191.

288. *Ibid.*, p. 163.

289. Parsons points out that American dedication to free enterprise and advocacy of it for underdeveloped countries may be disfunctional. "A society . . . deeply oriented to . . . its own identity and internal solidarity will . . . be . . . concerned with problems in the *political* area . . . economic individualism is unlikely to have a strong ideological appeal in underdeveloped areas . . . [and] if pushed [may] 'backfire' . . .". *Ibid.*, p. 124. He emphasizes "technological" rather than "managerial" support and doubts that American "business men" render appropriate support.

290. In discussing change in "underdeveloped" countries Parsons observes that "Where the primary process of value change involves borrowing from a model external to the society, I suggest that ideology tends to serve functions analogous to those of religious movements in the case of internal value change." *Ibid.*, p. 141.

291. *Ibid.*, p. 156.   292. *SS*, p. 249.

293. *Ibid.*, p. 206.   294. *Ibid.*, p. 252.

295. *Ibid.*   296. *Ibid.*, pp. 299-301.

297. *Ibid.*, pp. 319-320.   298. *Ibid.*, p. 263.

299. *FSIP*, p. 17.   300. *Ibid.*, p. 16.

301. *SS*, p. 213.   302. *GTIS*, p. 30.

303. *SS*, p. 51.   304. *Ibid.*, p. 36.

305. *Ibid.*, p. 39.

306. *ESSAYS*, pp. 53-54. In respect to this definition of Parsons see Levy, *op. cit.*, who stresses two aspects of "indeterminacy" of institutionalization, the degree to which conformity is generally to be expected and the degree to which failure in conformity is met with moral indignation (which Parsons mentions in *ESSAYS* p. 60) of those involved or aware of the failure. He also comments on Parsons' use of institutions on other grounds. Cf., pp. 102 ff.

307. *SS*, pp. 39-40.   308. *Ibid.*, pp. 402-403.

309. *Ibid.*, p. 394.   310. *SSA*, p. 44.

311. *SS*, p. 162.   312. *Ibid.*, p. 163.

313. *Ibid.*, p. 162.   314. *SPMS*, p. 259.

315. *Ibid.*, p. 276.   316. *Ibid.*, p. 277.

317. *Ibid.*, pp. 278-9.

318. Notes on margin of revised manuscript of present chapter.

319. *SC*, p. 2.   320. *SC*, p. 4.

321. *SC*, p. 2.

322. Talcott Parsons, from the recorded text of an address before the Faculty Seminar on Parsonian Theory, Cornell University (Jan. 6, 1959), Mimeo, p. 5. In revised form this was printed in Talcott Parsons, "The Point of View of the Author," in Max Black, ed., *op. cit.* See also *SC*.

323. *Ibid.*   324. *SS*, pp. 491 ff.

325. At the same time Parsons feels the direction of change for social structure as a whole in the Weberian sense cannot lie at the level of gratification optimization. It can only account for change from one system state to another, *SS*, pp. 496-8. Directionality of change otherwise generally follows the Weberian model, see *SS*, pp. 498-503. Cf., *SSA*, pp. 566 ff.

326. *SS*, pp. 487-90.   327. *Ibid.*, p. 495.

328. *Ibid.*, pp. 495-6.   329. TUTHB, pp. 194-9.
330. *Ibid.*, p. 190.   331. *Ibid.*, p. 194.
332. *Ibid.*, p. 327 and SS, p. 19.
333. *Ibid.*, p. 194.   334. *Ibid.*, p. 192.
335. SSA, pp. 321 ff.   336. *TUTHB*, p. 192.
337. SPMS, p. 193.   338. *Ibid.*, pp. 183-184.

CHAPTER 7

PITIRIM A. SOROKIN AS HISTORICAL AND SYSTEMIC ANALYST*

One of the most prominent of the analysts and theoreticians of the social system is Pitirim A. Sorokin. Many of the essential elements of his approach to the social system were formulated at an early stage in his career and have been stated in a number of his works. They were set forth in a preliminary form in *Systems of Sociology* (published in Russian) in 1921. Since then they have been analyzed and published both in abbreviated or extended forms in *Social and Cultural Dynamics,* (especially in volumes one and four); *Sociocultural Causality, Space, Time;* and *Society, Culture and Personality: Their Structure and Dynamics.*[1]

Sorokin's conceptualization of the social system rests upon his analysis of the nature of the superorganic world, the area of study of the social sciences. This world "is equivalent to mind in all its clearly developed manifestations,"[2] and would embrace such things as language, religion, philosophy, science, the fine arts, law, ethics, and social organization. Found mainly in the interacting of human beings and in the products of such interaction, its rudi-

---

* This chapter was prepared with Reed H. Bradford as junior author. It differs from the other chapters of the present volume in that it was originally prepared for a *Festschrift* honoring Professor Sorokin and edited by Edward Tiryakian. The space restrictions for the manuscript in its original form were great and the consequent treatment of the many writings, the volume of which exceeds those of other writers here reviewed, was thereby made shorter than it otherwise would have been.

ments can be observed outside the human species in such phenomena as "reflexes and instincts; sensations, feelings, and emotions; traces of reproductive imagination; elementary association of images; and rudimentary ability to learn by experience." [3] Sociology, as one member of a team of disciplines that study the superorganic world, deals with those properties of that world which are repeated in time and space, both those common to all sociocultural phenomena (*general sociology*) and those common to a given class of sociocultural phenomena (all wars, all nations, all revolutions, all religions, etc., or *special sociologies.*)

He recognizes two main general sociologies: structural sociology which deals with the structure of social, cultural, and personality features of the superorganic; and dynamic sociology which investigates "(1) repeated *social processes* and change, together with the uniformities of the how and why; (2) repeated *cultural* processes and change; (3) the processes and changes of *personality* in its relationships with the social and cultural processes." [4]

Schematically, these very broad underpinnings upon which Sorokin's analysis of the social system rests, may be represented as follows:

I. Nature of superorganic world: mind in its clearly developed functions including language, religion, philosophy, science, fine arts, law, ethics, social organization, all observed chiefly among interacting human beings and in the products of that interaction.

II. Sociology: one of disciplines which study superorganic world; deals with those properties of that world which are repeated in time and space.

   A. Those properties common to all sociocultural phenomena (general sociology)

      1. Structural

         a. Social systems and congeries

         b. Cultural systems and congeries

         c. Personalities in their structural aspect, main types, and interrelations

      2. Dynamic: theory of the recurring

         a. Social processes and change

         b. Cultural processes and change

         c. Personality processes and change in their types, interrelationships, rhythms, trends, and causal factors

    B. Those properties common to a given class of sociocultural
       phenomena (special sociologies)
         1. Structure (generic aspects and relationships)
         2. Dynamic (repeated aspects and relationships)

The social system both in its structural and dynamic aspects, Sorokin defines thus:

> By social system is meant an *organized group* that possesses a set
> of enforced, obligatory law norms defining in detail the rights,
> duties, social position and functions, roles, and proper behavior of
> each and all its members towards one another, outsiders and the
> world at large; a set of prohibited actions-relations sanctioned by
> punishment; and a set of recommended non-obligatory norms of
> conduct. As a result of these norms, this organized group is a
> clearly differentiated and stratified body, each member of which
> is assigned a definite position in this differentiated and ranked sys-
> tem, with legal rules that determine a member's promotion and
> demotion. Such a group has a definite name and symbol of its
> individuality. It also has some funds and material means necessary
> for carrying on its functions and making possible the activities of
> its members.[5]

Sorokin intends the concepts "institution" and "social system" to
be examples of such organized social groups.[6] "An organized
group—be it family, or labor union, or state—is a social system. An
organized institution—be it the Roman Catholic or other church,
a university, a Supreme court, an army, and so on, is again a social system." [7]

    Of the cultural system, both in its structural and dynamic as-
pects, Sorokin writes:

[It is] a logically or aesthetically consistent system of meanings—such
as mathematics or physics, a philosophical system like Plato's or Kant's,
a religious credo, a law-code or ethical system, a masterpiece by Beethoven or Michelangelo, the epic of Homer, or Shakespeare's dramas,
all objectified by their vehicles and used and communicated by human
beings . . .[8]

From his definitions, the interdependence of social and cultural
phenomena becomes obvious; his constant use of the term "sociocultural" further testifies to this interdependence. The most
"generic" model of a given sociocultural phenomenon "is the

meaningful interaction of two or more human individuals," with interaction defined as "any event by which one party tangibly influences the overt action or the state of mind of the other." [9] Every process of meaningful human interaction is seen to comprise three basic components: "(1) thinking, acting, and reacting human beings as subjects of interaction; (2) meanings, values and norms for the sake of which the individuals interact, realizing and exchanging them in the course of the interaction; (3) overt actions and material phenomena as vehicles or conductors through which immaterial meanings, values, and norms are objectified and socialized." [10] In this analysis of human interaction can be found, of course, the interplay of the three systems isolated in the above schematized view of the superorganic world: "1) *personality* as the subject of interaction; (2) *society* as the totality of interacting personalities, with their sociocultural relationships and processes; and (3) *culture* as the totality of the meanings, values, and norms possessed by the interacting persons and the totality of the vehicles which objectify, socialize, and convey these meanings." [11] Amplifications of these three systems and their interplay will develop as the analysis of Sorokin's writings unfolds.

KNOWING

Sorokin's masterpiece, *Social and Cultural Dynamics*, categorizes systems as *sensate, ideational,* and *idealistic* with a residual category he calls *mixed.* The basic characteristic underlying the categorization is the kind of reality perceived as "true" by the members of the given sociocultural system. The element of belief (or knowledge) and its articulating process, cognitive mapping and validation are central to Sorokin's schema.

Belief (knowledge) as an element. ". . . At the basis of the Ideational or Idealistic or Sensate form of integrated culture lies, as its major premise, its system of truth and reality. It is this premise that, to use W. I. Thomas' term, 'defines the situation' for the rest of the related compartments of each of these forms of culture." [12] Among the sensate systems the "true reality and true value is sensory . . . beyond the reality and value perceived by our sense organs there is no other reality and no value." [13] Those which place prime emphasis upon a "*super-sensory, super-rational God,*" and believe "*the sensory reality and value . . . either a mere*

*illusion, or the least important, least real, sometimes even nega-
tive, reality and value"* [14] are called *ideational.* Those which integrate these two types are called *idealistic.* Combinations which
are not integrated are called *mixed.* Sorokin argues that all the
main systems of truth are contained in "truth of faith, of reason,
of the senses, plus some mixed forms." [15] Further, he theorizes
that what is perceived as truth, as science or as a criterion for truth
is a " 'function' of the sociocultural variable," [16] and that the particular form that truth assumes for its believers reveals itself in
every facet of activity of the sociocultural system.

Sorokin assembles an imposing array of evidence to support
his classification of cultures; his historical analysis, partly statistical and partly descriptive, is based upon art forms, documents,
ideologies, social forms and structures, social wars and revolutions
and many other indices. Whatever the index, Sorokin makes clear
that the item is but an indicator of the way in which reality is perceived in that system. Sorokin contends that evidence over a tremendous span of recorded time leads to the classifications of
epochs of Greek culture, for example, as variously ideational (from
the eighth until the end of the sixth century, B. C.), idealistic
(including the Golden Age of Athens), and sensate (including
the development and flowering of the Roman Empire). Similarly,
European culture is classified as idealistic during the 12th to 14th
centuries when the perception of a super-sensory, super-rational
kind of truth expressed itself in Gothic cathedrals, the works of
Dante and of St. Thomas Aquinas. The sensate culture which
followed has recently reached a climax and apparently a swing to
the ideational pole is in the offing.[17]

Indices indicating the strength of realism correlate positively
with those indicating the strength of the truth of faith (the ideational culture); those of nominalism with the truth of the senses
(the sensate culture); and, perhaps less closely, those representing
conceptualism with truth of reason (the idealistic culture). Sorokin not only arrays evidence which reveals the kind of reality
and truth held by different societies at different stages of history.
He frequently reveals his own set of beliefs concerning the age of
which he is a part; to the extent that his works are action-oriented
he appears to be the judge as well as the theoretician. Sorokin
the scientist and Sorokin the man, as revealed by his works, are

often inextricably blended. He believes, for example that the "exclusive empiricism" of the sensate culture is "stripping man and values of anything absolute, superempirical, divine and sacred; reducing them to mere 'electron-proton complex,' or 'complex of atoms,' or 'reflex-mechanism' . . . or mere 'stimulus-response relationship,' " resulting in "the current triumph of rude force in national and international human relationships. . . ." In one who believes that "all values are [being] relativized to such an extent that nothing absolute and sacred is left, and everything is ground into dust" [18] it should be no surprise to find an activist crusader. Nor is the preferential note in the following, unexpected: [For the Western medieval culture] "Its major principle or value was God, the true-reality value. . . . Its science was a mere handmaid of Christian religion. . . . The sensory world was considered a mere temporary 'city of man' in which a Christian was but a pilgrim aspiring to reach the eternal City of God and seeking to render himself worthy to enter it. . . ." [19]

Sorokin's arguments marshalled in evidence of his classifications of culture based upon kinds of belief are overwhelmingly persuasive. Only when they will be juxtaposed against those of other scholars whose works are as global in their embrace and as infinite in their historical sweep will they be given a thorough test. Sorokin himself cites as corroborative evidence many substudies, all a part of his analyses, but done by independent investigators who did not know about any other parts of the study. Illustrative of these is the computation of scientific discoveries by Robert Merton (based on Darmstaedter's work) and the computations of Lossky and Lapshin who systematically registered all the known or all the important known thinkers who are mentioned in histories of philosophy, epistemology, logic and science. Sorokin writes:

(Professors Lossky and Lapshin had no knowledge of my study, and Dr. Merton, who made the computation of the scientific discoveries, was unaware not only of my study but also of the computations made by Professors Lossky and Lapshin.) Under the circumstances, the agreement between the curve of the scientific discoveries and inventions . . . and the curve of the fluctuations of the influence of the system of truth of senses . . . is particularly strong evidence that the results obtained in both cases are neither incidental nor misleading.[20]

These and other sub-studies within Sorokin's monumental work show a high correlation between sensate empiricism and the production of inventions. Although this finding is almost incidental, ranking as it does, as only one of many other findings of the same order, the present authors believe that the relationship between inventiveness and the sensate culture may be a very important factor in the present deep concern for humanity which Sorokin manifests in his writings of recent years. The senior author remembers that a quarter of a century ago, long before nuclear weapons and before World War II, Sorokin several times challenged his audience somewhat as follows: "Suppose someone should discover a simple but terrific explosive which could easily destroy a considerable part of our planet . . . out of 1,800,000,000 human beings there certainly would be a few individuals who, being 'scientifically minded,' would have to test the explosive." World events and inventive progress since that time certainly would not have diminished his always keen appreciation of the possible ramifications of sensate empiricism unbridled by the super-sensory, and goaded by the urge to "find out."

Other analysts, using different terms and working within a different framework have theorized about the relationship between a culture's beliefs and the kind of culture it has become. Northrop, for example, attributes to the eastern cultures the primacy of "the aesthetic component" and to the west "the theoretic component"; the former, he claims, conceptualizes with its senses, the latter rationalizes and theorizes.[21] Weber saw the followers of Confucius as being empirically oriented.[22] Parsons by use of a double-axes paradigm distinguishes between empirical and nonempirical beliefs, and between existential and evaluative beliefs, the possible combinations of which presumably describe differentially classified cultures. On the surface, at least, none seem to be inconsistent with Sorokin's findings, although a convincing comparison would, of course, require thorough treatment. Most of the findings would tend to be in agreement with the Sorokinian statement of the different processes of validation and cognitive mapping that actors with different cultures employ to legitimize their brand of truth and reality.[23]

Cognitive mapping and validation as process. In sensate culture, validation of knowledge is mainly through "the reference to the testimony of the organs of senses . . . supplemented by the logical reasoning, especially in the form of mathematical reasoning" [24] which latter helps develop hypotheses to be rejected if sensory facts contradict them. Ideational truth is validated by reference to the Sacred Source or by revelation or inspiration.

Truth has different meanings in Ideational and Sensate culture mentalities. What is truth or science for one is often prejudice, ignorance, error, heresy, blasphemy, for the other . . . The first culture type builds its concepts, theories, arguments, evidence, mainly from the data supplied by the inner experience; the second, from the objects of external observation . . . 'Vomit thy (empirical) knowledge' and 'The wisdom of this world is foolishness with God': so an Ideationalist talks about the Sensate truth. And vice versa, 'superstition,' 'ignorance': so will an Epicurean express himself in regard to the Ideational truth." [25]

NORMING, STANDARDIZING, PATTERNING

Sorokin's conceptualization of the social system has been characterized as a combined *relationalism* and *normativism*.[26] Norms (or law-norms in Sorokin's terminology) cover so much in his analysis of interaction that their examination will yield to the reader some of the content that he might expect to find under such social-systemic elements as sanctions, status-role, sentiments, and ends. Because of the encompassing nature of Sorokin's law-norms they are presented at this point, next to his all-important consideration of the belief system. He writes:

The reasons for making law-norms the most important and most symptomatic criterion of organized structure (or unorganized state) of groups are: a) without law-norms as the attributive-imperative convictions neither the structure nor status, nor role, nor social differentiation and stratification can be defined clearly; b) the official and unofficial law-norms define more precisely more clearly and in the greatest details all the aspects of structure of the group, all the functions (role) and social position of each member of the group, their interrelations, their sentiments and sanctions—more precisely and better, than "expectations," "folkways and mores and vague and wrong approaches to definition of structure, social differentiation, status, sanctions, etc.[27]

Norm as an element. Sorokin examines organized interaction (group, institution, or social system) and concludes that its "central trait . . . is . . . the presence in it of law-norms as the conduct-regulating and behavior-controlling aspect of the component of meanings-values." [28]

Irrespective of their content, any norms of conduct (of doing, non-doing, toleration) that attribute a certain right (the object of right) to one party (the subject of right) and a certain duty (the object of duty) to another party (the subject of duty) are law-norms.[29]

The norms, then, are for Sorokin the determinant of (a) the rights and duties of the members, (b) the circumstances governing what "to do or not to do," (c) the roles and/or functions of each individual, (d) one's status, (e) official law and government, (f) the forms of interaction, whether they are obligatory, prohibited or recommended; (g) a system of differentiation and stratification of members, (h) an economic complex of vehicles to carry out the functions of the group, and (i) to some degree, as a result of the above factors, the symbols of identity of the group.

From these general broad definitions Sorokin proceeds to detail and refine law-norm characteristics, to sub-divide the class, and to distinguish between various functions, a schematic representation of which follows: [30]

Formal aspects of law norms:
  Imperative-attributive relationships between parties is established by law-norms.
    Law-norms ascribe to one party a duty (imperative) and to the other a right (attributive).
    A *defining part* and a *sanctioning part* compose each law-norm.
    The defining part indicates a definite obligatory form of conduct.
    The sanctioning part formulates the consequences of the violation of this form of conduct. The sanctioning part may assume various forms:
      Punishment, as in the case of incarceration for commission of a crime
      Compulsory realization of the demand as in foreclosure
      Voiding or nullification as in a situation where a contract is made under circumstances not allowed by the law norms.
  A fully developed law-norm indicates
    The subject of the right (that party entitled to whatever is specified in the law-norm, e.g. a creditor)

The subject of the duty (that party which must carry out the duty indicated by the law-norm, e.g. a debtor)

The object of the right (the totality of activities, doing, nondoing, nontolerating, of the subject of right, to which he is entitled by the law-norm)

The object of the duty (the totality of the actions of the subject of duty, required from him by the law-norm

Reference to the source of the law

Additional specifications of time, place, conditions, way of acting, etc.

Addressees of the law-activities (Third parties who are neither subject nor object).

Informal aspects of the law-norms: psychological characteristics

An "idea" or conception of the pattern of action prescribed by the law-norm

A normative motivation of the respective actions

Powerful emotional (affective and volitional) backing of the actions propelling us simultaneously to realize unhesitatingly our right and to fulfill unflinchingly our duty

Functional aspects of law-norms

Distributive: they distribute rights and duties including specific roles and functions, social values and burdens

Organizational: a function employed in the enforcement of law-convictions. When enforcement is compulsory, it requires the application of sanctions

Law-norms must be further classified on a different basis:

Official law (those law-norms which are obligatory for all members of a social system)

Unofficial law: confined to those areas of lesser importance in total group life

occupational

professional

religious

codes of decency

professional ethics

unofficial law-convictions of sub-groups and persons (relationships in informal organizations are regulated not by the official law but by the unofficial law-convictions of the persons involved.)

The most overwhelming quality of Sorokin's law-norm treatment, given here in only barest detail, is its all embraciveness. The law-norms become sponge-like, absorbing most of the structure of the social system. Sociologists consulting Sorokin for such usable and pragmatic elements as end, status-role, rank and power will find no such discrete abstractions here. Although most, if not all, would agree that all the commonly used systemic elements have a normative aspect few would agree that finer abstraction of these elements than is here given do not at once represent insightful analyses of social systems and provide a means of furthering perception and insight. Time after time in the pages to follow, as other elements and processes are explored, reference will have to be made to this law-norm section which for Sorokin subsumes most of the social system-in-analysis.

Four additional categories of norms recognized by Sorokin ought to be mentioned here; those he calls *moral, technical,* those of *"religion, mores, folkways, customs,"* and those of *etiquette and fashion.* Moral norms recommend but do not require a certain form of conduct and thus are imperative but not attributive. (A member of a social system has the duty (imperative) to perform the act regarded as moral by the system, but no other member has the right (attributive) to demand that he do his moral duty.) Technical norms are utilitarian and describe how something is to be done. They are "devoid of the imperative-attributive urge, having neither subjects nor objects of right and of duty. . . ."[31] The category of the norms of "religion, mores, folkways, customs" are made up of heterogeneous elements. Norms of etiquette and fashion, when not regarded as imperative-attributive, have nothing in common with law or moral norms. Because of the comprehensive nature of Sorokin's law-norms and other normative concepts its gradual elaboration will come about in this chapter as the systemic elements and processes are examined. The first to receive attention will be the evaluative process by which, in accordance with the general conceptualization of the PAS Model, norms move from their static structural quality to become activated in the on-going life within a social system.

Evaluation as a process. Sorokin enumerates nine "logical satellites" of his main culture mentalities: 1) Weltanschauung, 2) power and object of control, 3) activity, 4) self, 5) knowledge, 6) truth, its categories, criteria, and methods (of derivation), 7) moral values and systems, 8) aesthetic values and 9) social and practical values.[32] The process of evaluation (though frequently by some other terminology) is shown to be operative as quite different priorities are assigned to different value-items by his seven * types of culture, three of which are here schematized in relation to three of the "logical satellites."

TYPES OF CULTURE	KNOWING ** "Truth, its categories: criteria, and methods (of arriving at)	FEELING ** "Aesthetic values"	ACHIEVING ** "Social and practical values."
Ascetic Ideational	"Based on inner experience, 'mystic way,' concentrated meditation; intuition and 'revelation'; prophecy"	"Ideational" subservient to the main inner values, religious nonsensate"	"those which are lasting and lead to ultimate reality: only such persons are leaders; only such things and events are positive, all others are valueless, or of negative value, particularly wealth, earthly comfort, etc.: principle of sacrifice."
Active Sensate	"based on observation or measurement or experimentation with the exterior phenomena through exterior organs of senses, inductive logic."	"sensate, secular, created to increase joys and beauties of rich sensate life."	"everything that gives joy of life to self and partly to others: particularly wealth, comfort, etc.: prestige is based on the above; wealth, money, physical might become 'rights' and basis of all values; principle of sound egoism."
Idealistic	"Both (of above) equally emphasized (Scholasticism)"	"both equally emphasized"	"both equally emphasized; live and let live."

* Sorokin's seven types of culture are made up of combinations of the three basic types shown above under Knowing as, the ideational, the sensate, the idealistic.

** PAS Model categories. Sorokin's terms for his logical satellites are in italics.

When systems change from one mentality or cultural type to another, crises may prevail. According to Sorokin the modern world stands at such a period in passage out of the sensate type. Evaluation in this period is characterized as follows:

Being a member of many conflicting groups and strata, an individual receives from them opposing commands, norms, and values. He is placed in the position of a ball pushed and pulled in opposite directions. . . . His soul becomes parceled and divided into many mutually contradictory selves. He becomes a rudderless boat. . . . Amidst the jungle of contradictory norms and values, an individual lacks a consistent set of standards . . . The slightest biological or other stimulus is sufficient to induce him to violate his norms and standards. Such violations multiply. . . . Brute force and fraud raise their ugly heads as the supreme arbiters. . . .[33]

From his point of view, the only way in which inner conflict can be avoided is for the individual to belong to groups which have a "solidary" relationship to one another and "urge the individual to think, feel, and act in the same way." Thus he considers the rearrangement of social groups to be the paramount task of our time.

This can be done when *all groups and strata subordinate their values and standards to a set of universal values and of concordant norms of conduct.* The essence of such values and norms for interpersonal and intergroup relationships has been sublimely formulated in the Sermon on the Mount, in the Golden Rule. . . . If all groups and strata, no matter how diverse they may be, apply these norms in their ideology and their overt actions, . . . humanity will achieve real unity in diversity . . . and the individual will regain his integrity, happiness and peace of mind.[34]

FEELING

As noted above, the law-norms or attributive-imperative convictions are not merely ideas or images of the proper actions but they are experienced with, supported, and "powered" by the force of the intense emotions and feelings, like the emotion of indignation when our rights are violated or emotion of "guilt" when we fail to fulfill our duty, or emotion of satisfaction when a violation of law-norm is restored and "justice" is rendered.[35]

Sentiment as an element. One set of sentiment constellations in Sorokin's conceptualization is concomitant to the culture systems in which the sentiments flourish. Satisfaction of the ego self and expression of the ego are to be found in a sensate culture, just as self-sacrifice along with a pervasive reverence is found in the ideational culture. A recent Sorokin work [36] concerns itself entirely with sensate epochs in history which can be characterized by the phrase, "eat, drink and copulate for tomorrow we die." [37] It furnishes evidence that human interaction patterned after such sentiments is reflected in the art, literature, laws, and all the other culture-bearing institutions of the sensate groups under examination. Such treatment of sentiments is, of course, entirely culture-related.

In contrast, those sentiments which are common to all cultures constitute another classification in the Sorokinian scheme. Basic categories of this classification are (1) solidary (the type which exists when the aspirations, meanings-values, and overt actions of the parties concerned "concur and are mutually helpful for the realization of their objectives"); [38] (2) antagonistic (the type which exists when the aspirations or desires as well as the overt actions of the parties mutually hinder one another); and (3) mixed (a type which exists when the desires and overt behavior of the parties are partly antagonistic, partly solidary). [39] Both antagonisms and solidarities lend themselves, under Sorokin's treatment, to a number of qualifying attributes. He sees them as ranging:

in intensity:	antagonism can range "from a mere coldness between parties to the most intense hatred satiated only by the extermination of the enemy and by vilification of him even after death." [40] solidarity can range "from mere tolerance of a person to a joyful readiness to sacrifice everything for him." [41]
in extensity:	Solidarity can range from a small fragment of one's total life being involved in interaction (a shop-owner and customer, e.g.) or the interaction can involve nearly all the values and various facets of the lives of the parties involved—a Ruth-Naomi kind of relationship. Antagonism can range from the single incident of interaction marked by conflicting interests to "the unquenchable hatred of two mortal enemies that

hate everything the other approves and admires, all of whose values collide and conflict." [42]

in motivation: *Fundamental and conditioned motivation* propels the interactors toward an attitude of solidarity or antagonism which is "neither purposively planned, nor forseen in advance, nor do they have any preliminary motives of utility or advantage. They arise spontaneously as a result of certain characteristics of the other party . . ."[43]
Purposive solidarities or antagonisms come about by considerations of "utility and disutility, of advantage or disadvantage, of pleasure or pain." [44]

Sorokin indicates that solidary and antagonistic relationships exist not only in pure forms but also in various combinations of these forms. He designates three combinations that are particularly important:

1. *Familistic type.* As an "ideal" type, the familistic combination has the following characteristics as far as the solidary-antagonistic interaction pattern is concerned:

(a) predominantly solidary; (b) total or broad in extensity; (c) of high intensity; (d) durable; (e) direct; (f) mutual, or two-sided; (g) marked by the fundamental, normative, and purposive types of motivation, all working harmoniously with one another; (h) based upon a deep sense of the sociocultural oneness of the parties; (i) possessing leadership or government that is natural and spontaneous and truly paternalistic, with a leader who is merely a *primus inter pares.*[45]

Examples of this type include the relationship between real friends, or between a loving parent and child. Members help each other, not from any utilitarian standpoint, but from what Sorokin would call "a spontaneous organic impulse." [46] He agrees with Aristotle who observes that a real friend is "one who . . . does what is good (or what he believes to be good) for another for that other's sake, and one wishes his friend to . . . live for that friend's own sake" [47] and not because the friend is useful in the attainment of some other end. This kind of friendship involves a merging of selves into one unity. The relationship of this concept to that of informal law-norms is revealed in Sorokin's exposition that there is no necessity for an external setting forth of rights and duties or other specifications because they are transcended by the relationship of unselfish love, and because no domination-subordination pattern exists. Rather, there is the coexistence of love and "internal freedom of the individuals with the external appearance of its limitation." [48]

Sorokin chose the term "familistic" to designate this type of relation because it is most often met and found in its purest form in the family characterized by harmonious relations among the members thereof. It is similar to the kind of relationship developed by Confucius in setting forth his five fundamental relationships, by Le Play in his analysis of the patriarchal family, by Aristotle and Cicero in their concept of the "real" friend, by F. Toennies in his *Gemeinschaft* relationship and to some degree by Makarewicz, Kistiakowsky, and Max Scheler. [49]

2. *Mixed (contractual) type.* In this type of relationship solidarity is limited in extensity. It covers only a portion of the lives of the concerned parties. This portion is stated in specific terms. The duration of the solidarity is limited and although usually mutual, may sometimes be one-sided, giving one party an advantage and another a disadvantage. "In almost every contractual variety of mixed relationship the main motivation of solidarity is of the *purposive, implicitly egoistic, utilitarian type, often supplemented and moderated by the legal normative motivation.*" [50] In the solidary sector of the relationship there is no real merging into a "we" feeling, and outside the sector, there may be feelings of antagonism. Sorokin distinguishes several forms of the mixed type of interaction with self-descriptive names: 1) benevolent neutrality; 2) passive resistance-reluctant cooperation; 3) competitive cooperation; and 4) simultaneous love and hate.

3. *Compulsory type.* Antagonism is the basic characteristic of this type of relationship. On the intensity scale there may be variations from the one extreme of the most intense hatred to the other of some mild discomfort. Its extensity may be all-embracing. It can be either direct or indirect, temporary or permanent. "It may be rooted in the *fundamental, the normative, or the purposive type of motivation* or in a combination of all three." [51] An example of this kind of relationship is despotic governments which use brute force and fraud as their chief instruments to achieve goals.

Sorokin defines both a pseudo-contractual and pseudo-familistic kind of relationship. In the former, a person apparently enters into a contract of his own free will, but actually he is under duress. In the latter, one member of the relationship may assume good and sincere intentions toward the other, but in reality not be concerned with the other's welfare.

Despite the applicability of the above concepts to all of the main culture types Sorokin indicates that the kind of attitude held is in part related to the cultural supersystem. This intimation plus the tendency to incorporate into law-norms what the authors of the present work would abstract as "sentiment" is apparent in the following:

The immediate and most decisive factors of either solidarity or antagonism of the interacting parties are (a) the character of their law and ethical convictions; (b) the concordance or discordance of the law and moral convictions of each party with those of the others; (c) the degree to which these norms are consistently and adequately practiced by the overt actions and vehicles of the parties.[52]

Thus if the moral norms prescribe that one should love others and the law-norms are in essential agreement with the intent of these moral norms, then interaction "will be essentially solidary." Similarly, if there is concordance between the moral and law-norms and the conduct of the interacting parties conforms to these norms, the interaction will be solidary.

Just as Sorokin attributes either solidarity or antagonism to the total pattern of the prevailing law-norms, so he attributes the total pattern of the prevailing law-norms to the over-all pattern of the total society. *"The loving or hating, cooperative or competitive character and the concordance or discordance of the law and moral norms are determined largely by the social and cultural milieu in which the parties were born, reared, live, and act."* [53]

Writing of the informal or "psychological" aspect of law-norms, Sorokin clearly shows their heavy emotive content:

The very idea of performing an act of murder immediately arouses in us a negative normative motivation followed by a powerful emotional and volitional drive inhibiting such an action as "horrible" "awful," "repellent." This emotional repulsion is similar to that aroused by the idea of eating a meal made up of rotten earth-worms, rats, and vermin. This inner motivation, and not an apprehension of punishment, is the reason why these millions of people do not murder and kill . . . Thus the law-norms of all of us (no matter what may be their content) are not merely mental patterns of a certain form of conduct but *living convictions charged with all the emotional, affective, and volitional force that one possesses.*[54]

The appraisal of the emotional force as being such a strong one prepares the reader for the *process* aspect of emotion, which likewise, is embedded in Sorokin's law-norms.

Tension management as process. For Sorokin, the emotional tensions which demand action and interaction in order to be resolved or diminished, are chiefly clustered around the individual's rights and duties. The party or circumstance which opposes the realization of an individual's rights, invites "all the energy of these emotional, affective, and volitional forces" to mobilize to eliminate the opposition. Similarly, undischarged duty creates such tension that the strong emotional forces are finally unleashed in the fulfillment of that duty.[55] For Sorokin, the emotions thus become the cause of the tension in the first place, and the dynamics by which the tension is relieved in the second place.

When deeply ingrafted, law-norms represent one of the most powerful forces that control our conduct; they not only indicate in the minutest detail the course of action we must follow in millions of different interactions with thousands of different persons under the most varied conditions, but they effectively drive us to such a course through the emotional, affective and volitional forces behind them.[56]

Such normative and emotional motivation is differentiated by Sorokin from what he calls " 'the because of' type of motivation: blushing and mumbling because of embarrassment; reacting by insult because of preceding insult; becoming angry and shouting because of preceding irritation, and so on . . ." [57] Normative motivation differs from "because of" motivation by its self-sufficiency and by its definite pattern of compliance with some norm. In contrast to it, "because of" actions do not have any definite norm or pattern; they may assume any form depending on the nature of the preceding stimuli.

The degree to which tensions build up and demand management differs by culture type. The focus on the other-worldly in the ideational culture minimizes the buildup of tensions and maximizes their reduction or management. In the sensate culture, on the other hand, sooner or later man who makes the satisfaction of his senses the goal of his activities is driven toward anomie.

In the overripe stage of Sensate culture, man becomes so 'wild' that he can not—and does not want to—'tame himself.' . . . These call for 'the policeman of history' who imposes, first, a hard and purely physical coercion upon him, as the contemporary totalitarian policemen of history do . . . gradually . . . he is put into the strait-jacket of the Ideational culture.[58]

Although Sorokin seldom mentions rites of passage and other forms of tension management as such, they tend to be stronger and more ritualistic in the ideational culture and less so in the sensate.

Communication of sentiment as process. No other sociologist has as effectively demonstrated how painting, sculpture, music, and literature function as vehicles for expressive communication. Just as the inventiveness of a social system is directly related to that system's empirical orientation of sensory apprehension, so the appearance in art pieces of the qualities of nominalism, materialism and nudistic pieces is correlated with the empirically oriented sensate-directed system. Counts made of art pieces in recorded artistic epochs showing such qualities describe a curve which remarkably resembles the pattern of the rising and falling of sensate cultures.

Sensate art . . . moves entirely in the empirical world of the senses . . . Its aim is to afford a refined sensual enjoyment . . . For this reason it must be sensational, passionate, sensual, and incessantly new. It is marked by voluptuous nudity and concupiscence. It is divorced from religion, morals, and other values, and styles itself "art for art's sake" . . . *Its style is naturalistic, visual, even illusionistic, free from any supersensory symbolism.*[59]

It is in strong contrast to the art of the ideational periods in which the topics are mainly religious (God, His Kingdom, mysteries of salvation, redemption, saints, etc.). This art communicates the pious, ethereal and ascetic. It does not admit any sensualism, eroticism, satire, comedy, caricature or farce. "It is a communion of the human soul with itself and with God . . . *Its style is* and must be symbolic . . . The signs of the dove, anchor, and olive branch in the early Christian catacombs [are examples]." [60]

The law-norms once more determine the appropriate sentiment for the occasion as well as the appropriate means of communicating it. Sorokin's study of the objectivication of this communication through the expressive arts as well as through instrumental forms, even if stated in what some colleagues consider excessively evaluative terminology, will remain one of his lasting contributions to sociology and knowledge.

ACHIEVING

Although Sorokin disallows the use of the concept "end, goal, or objective" except for a small portion of systemic phenomena, many insightful analyses of his work gain their highest value through reading into the text some form of the "means-end" schema. His careful repudiation of many sociologists who have attempted to use the concept "end" leads one to suspect that among the other reasons for Sorokin's avoidance of the concept is his low evaluation of various schemes other than his own, which *do* use this concept. He specifies several reasons for his position:

1. If the terms "means-end" are used without further specifications, they may mean several different things; a) means-end of purposeful motivations and actions; b) cause and effect; c) temporally preceding and consequent actions; d) and several of Aristotle's six forms of causes. The result of such a general (loose) use is a vague hodge-podge covered by one term.
2. Such a use may lead to a wrong conclusion that there is only one-purposeful-motivation among all motivations and that all human actions have always goal (purposeful end) and respective means for reaching it.
3. It overlooks the real existence of vast classes of goalless actions without any end projected into the future, without any consciously thought out series of mean-actions . . . actions such as unconscious and reflexo-instinctive, as motivated by the normative and fundamental motivations and other actions.

   These three gross fallacies of the unrestricted and unspecified use of "means-end" schema are sufficient to make it utterly unscientific and wrong.

The only legitimate and correct use of this schema is on the class of purposeful actions and motivation.[61]

End, goal, or objective as an element. Sorokin's position on the use of means-ends as an essential element of interaction is preponderantly negative. He says: "Only with reference to purposeful phenomena is the schema applicable and helpful, and they constitute merely a small fraction of sociocultural phenomena."[62] To defend his position which holds that the means-ends concept of interaction is overworked and often fallacious Sorokin points out that an idea of a conscious future goal is a necessary condition of the means-ends concept; much of human action and interaction, however, (he points out) is nonpurposive.[63] He also maintains that what many investigators call "means-end" are actually cause and effect and therefore, not correctly related to goal. He further distinguishes between those purposive actions which are legitimately means-end actions and those he labels "because-of actions" as described in the section above under *tension management.* Conscious actions are not necessarily purposive; in fact they may be contrary to purpose as the alcoholic who despite his vow and purpose of abstinence cannot resist the temptation.

Yet to say that Sorokin built his entire conceptualization of the workings of the sociocultural system without providing ends for the actors and interactors is to overstate the case. Each epoch seems to have a destiny, an almost inevitable set or direction, in compatibility with which the individual actors in the epoch perform their actions. Sorokin writes:

If a given group possesses the right hereditary endowment, at the intersection of cultural streams, and enjoys good luck, *it tends to evolve great systems in those fields of culture in which it urgently needs them for its unity and for the continuity of its existence.*[64]

This is, of course, not a clear-cut statement that purposeful action is taken in response to perceived needs. Whatever implications of goal the statement might have are dispelled by Sorokin's response to such an interpretation:

This comes out as a result of all sorts of actions and motivations of the interacting members of a group plus out of the anonymous, collective forces of culture and social life of the preceding period, but not a re-sult of the purposive actions. As a result and evidence of this the crystallized integrated culture and social structure of a given epoch assumes forms and patterns hardly foreseen by almost any of the pur-posefully acting members of the group. These incessant "surprises of history" are due not only to Wundt's "heterogeny of purposes" of dif-ferent members, but to the operation of all their non-purposeful actions-reactions, plus to the mentioned anonymous forces of preceding socio-cultural life and environment.[65]

Although not imputed to end or goal as such, Sorokin attributes ingenious methods of maritime transportation to sea-shore and island dwellers, technological invention and advance to pastoral and agricultural peoples, industrial know-how to mechanical social systems; he also attributes an excellence in religious and moral invention to the Hindus and the Hebrews who otherwise would have lost their identity since strong political unity was denied them. Likewise a superiority in military and political organzation by some societies, according to him, may be in part due to their constant threat from invasion and extermination.

Goal attaining and concomitant "latent" activity as process. By implication, Sorokin establishes the way in which the individ-ual acquires the ends from the powerful influence of the social and cultural systems, and how the group becomes activated to-ward the realization of the goals. He postulates that the individ-ual has separate biological egos (nutrition ego, self-protection ego, sex-ego, etc.). Similarly, the indivdual has as many social egos as there are groups to which he belongs; also, the goals for which man strives are given to him by the groups to which he belongs.

Sorokin establishes three levels of integration of the culture possessed by individuals and groups: (a) *purely meaningful or ideological* (which leaves unintegrated his overt actions, reactions, and the vehicles involved); at this level, the individual either does not practice what he preaches or practices something opposite to his ideology; (b) *Double, meaningful behavior-integration;* (at this level most of what he practices is consistent with what he preaches, but has a few inconsistencies); (c) *Triple, meaning-ful-behavioral-vehicles integration* of the culture and personality of an individual when his ideological culture is integrated and all his actions, reactions, and the vehicles used consistently articulate

and practice his ideology.[66] Presumably the more completely integrated the individual or the individual group, the closer his (or
its) complete identity with his culture system, and the more likely
he (or it) will be a vehicle of the directional activities of the
system.

Only in part do they [the cultural system and the organized group]
coincide and overlap, namely, insofar as any organized group has a
set of meanings, values and norms as the *raison d'etre* of its existence;
and this set must be and usually is integrated in the bulk of its meanings, especially in its law-norms, and in the respective actions and
vehicles of the group enforced by it.[67]

Since among the culture systems, only "the ultimate supersystems
taken with all their sub-sub-sub . . . systems, covers the whole
realm," each individual deals with many different aspects of
reality, he incorporates within himself, not just one cultural system, but many. "Hence the individual's 'encyclopedism,' the
pluralism of his cultural systems and congeries." [68] Presumably,
only to the extent that the sub-sub-sub-systems articulate the
need, end, objective, or motivational force of the supersystem
would the individuals comprising the sub-systems be consciously
or unconsciously expressing by their interaction the driving, propelling, force of their supersystem.

DIVIDING THE FUNCTIONS

The "encyclopedism" and pluralism of the individual's cultural
systems cited above must certainly have alerted the reader to an
imminent treatment of "role." Sorokin is responsible for some of
the earliest and most penetrating insights relating to the concept
which in the present monograph is called status-role. He is likewise responsible for a strong denunciation of the whole idea.[69]

Status-role as element and process. Much of the personality
conflict of individuals, according to Sorokin, is due to conflicts,
imposed upon these selves or role incumbencies by various groups.

*If the groups of an individual are in conflict; if they urge him to con-
tradictory actions, duties, thoughts, convictions;* if, for instance the
state demands what is disapproved by the church or the family, *the
respective egos will be mutually antagonistic.* The individual will be
a house divided against himself, split by the inner conflicts.[70]

In the great work, *Social Mobility*, the concept status-role, particularly the structural aspects, is implicit throughout. There are many other places where the term might have been used.

Every individual is like an actor incessantly playing different roles in his life process. The difference between these and those of a theatrical actor lies in the fact that each role of our own self is real, played in life, unlike the make-believe roles of an actor . . . Thus *man is indeed a creature of several different empirical roles. Their difference manifests itself introspectively and behavioristically, in man's mentality as well as in his overt actions.*[71]

Like so many other concepts, that of status-role is somewhat obliterated because of the global nature of Sorokin's concept law-norm.

The law and moral norms of a group define precisely the conduct, the relationships, the possession, the advantages and burdens, the sayings and doings or functions and roles, social statuses and social positions of its members . . . Therefore the term 'social role' adds practically nothing to the more precisely defined term 'the totality of right and duties' except some pedagogical value of vividness.[72]

The performance of one's status-role (process) is unequivocally demanded by Sorokin's law-norm requirement of *rights* and *duties* of interacting individuals: the debtor, the creditor; the buyer, the seller; the leader, the led; all perform their role as they charge their rights and discharge their duties. In fact, role performance Sorokin sees as the very basis of social organization.

One hundred musicians in a hall, each playing his own instrument and his own piece of music, interact with one another but produce a phenomenon fundamentally different from the same hundred musicians in the same hall, united into one orchestra, with one conductor, with the clearly outlined rights and duties, functions, and roles of each member, playing together the same musical composition, according to the composer's score and conductor's guidance. The difference between these systems of interaction is enormous. In the first place we have an unorganized interaction; in the second, organized.[73]

Interspersed throughout Sorokin's works is similar evidence that the eschewal of the term "status-role" is based on organizational and semantic grounds rather than on the concept itself.

CONTROLLING

Power as an element. For Sorokin, power may be approached from two different standpoints: (1) from the internal standpoint, or the different status positions within a group; (2) from the external standpoint, or the factors producing "powerful" groups. Of the attainment of power *within* a group, Sorokin suggests that (1) innate physical and mental qualities of the individuals themselves, and (2) the environment, permitting some individuals to promote themselves and preventing others, are the responsible factors. Of the attainment of power *by* a group, he sees as important:

1) the size of the group: other things being equal, the bigger the group the more powerful it is likely to be [74]
2) The amount of scientific and technological knowledge, degree of development of philosophic, religious, economic systems, state of vitality and health: all positive attributes for the group to possess; the greater the possession, the more likely that the power held by the group will be greater.
3) The totality of the "vehicles" for influencing individuals possessed by the group; a group rich in means of tranportation, communication, land, money, means of production, etc. tends to be more powerful than one deficient in such things.
4) The solidarity of the group: a solidary group is more likely to have power than an antagonistic group.
5) The technical perfection of its "structural and functional organization" tends to determine group power (a subdivision of the second and third condition).

Sorokin maintains that in all of history, the groups which made an impact were those possessing to a greater degree than others the above mentioned characteristics.[75]

Sorokin further distinguishes between "unibonded" and "multibonded" groups. In the first instance there is one set of meanings-norms-values (with their vehicles) which make up the central value. Individuals in this group interact for the sake of the enjoyment and realization of this set of meanings-values-norms. In the second case, there are more than one set of meanings-values-norms —at least two or three. Thus classified, he lists those groups which have been the most powerful throughout history: [76]

I. Important Unibonded Groups (centered around the main values)
  A. Biosocial Characteristics
    1. Race
    2. Sex
    3. Age
  B. Sociocultural Characteristics
    4. Kinship
    5. Territorial proximity
    6. Language (nationality)
    7. The state
    8. Occupational
    9. Economic
    10. Religious
    11. Political
    12. Scientific, philosophical, aesthetic, educational, recreational, ethical, and other "ideological" values
    13. A nominal group of the elite; leaders, men of genius, and historical persons
II. Important Multibonded Groups (made by a combination of two or more unibonded values)
    1. Family
    2. Clan
    3. Tribe
    4. Nation
    5. Caste
    6. Social Order
    7. Social Class

As would be expected from Sorokin's blanket use of the law-norms, the basis of the power structure lies with these norms. He believes that if the law-norms are explicit in both their imperative and attributive functions and if there is an adequate system of sanctions provided, the power inherent in the governing positions can be effectively and efficiently carried out.

Decision making and its initiation into action as process. For Sorokin freedom is not the equivalent of (1) potential for decision making and (2) authority or influence in initiating action. Freedom must in his formula include "wishes" which are important in determining the "mentality of a culture"; that is, whether sensate, ideational or idealistic. Following is his formula for freedom:

$$\text{Freedom equals } \frac{\text{Sum of the Available Means of Possibilities of Gratification of Wishes}}{\text{Sum of Wishes}} \quad [77]$$

Thus there are two forms of freedom, and two ways to preserve it, or even to increase it: first, the individual may minimize his wishes until they equal or are less than the available means of their gratification; or he may increase the available sum of the means of their satisfaction. The first is the inner Ideational way of being free; the second is the external Sensate way to be free.[78]

Viewing the application of power as that which extracts the performance of duty, Sorokin distinguishes between its operation in the familistic and in the contractual or compulsory social systems. To an outsider, a mother's devotion to her duty may appear like "frightful" slavery or serfdom.

However, when one puts himself in the position of the familistic party, most of these 'limitations of freedom' of the individual are not such at all. The mother or the father does not feel [it] . . . the familistic relationship permits us to reconcile duty and discipline with freedom; sacrifice with liberty.[79]

The application of power in the compulsory type of social system is characterized by "the relationships of master and slave or serf; of the executioner and the executed; of the conqueror and the conquered; of the despotic government and the governed; of the extortionist and the victim; of the ravisher and the ravished . . ." [80]

RANKING

Stratification in a social system is inevitable, according to Sorokin, because of needs of the social system itself, because of physical and mental characteristics of human beings, and because of environmental factors. Sorokin discusses stratification in both its structural and dynamic aspects. The structural aspects will be considered first.

Rank as an element. Sorokin distinguishes between differentiation, which merely notes individual differences, and rank, which evaluates the differences so noted. He further distinguishes these from stratification which acknowledges that a group of individuals is similarly differentiated and that their differentiations are similarly evaluated. For Sorokin there are real and quasi-real stratifications. "The organized real strata" usually are defined by the official law of the group, "like the ranks of the pope-cardinal-archbishop-bishop hierarchy in the church group, like the full-associate-assistant professor-instructor grading in the university, and so on for other groups." [81] The "as if real and organized stratum" is made up of all of those individuals possessing the same position, "rights, duties, function, etc.—in the hierarchy of strata, and who therefore think, feel, and act similarly so far as such a similarity is imposed on them by the similarity of their stratum-positions." [82] However, since they are not organized they may not even be aware of their co-belonging to the same stratum.

There are unibonded strata and multibonded strata, both of which concepts are based upon the unibonded and multibonded groups as discussed above under *Power*. Unibonded sex groups, *men* and *women*, may become unibonded strata when they are differentially evaluated; unibonded racial groups, Caucasians and Negroes, may become unibonded strata when they are differentially evaluated; unibonded occupational groups, doctors and nurses, may become unibonded strata when they are differentially evaluated. A single characteristic is basic to the identity of the group and to the evaluation given the group. The multibonded groups, the Jukes family and the Lowell family, become multibonded strata when they are differentially evaluated. A bundle of characteristics is basic to the identity of the group and to the evaluation given to the group. The family, the clan and the tribe have distinctive characteristics among multibonded strata, as do the nation and caste. The nation is "a multibonded, solidary, organized, almost closed group made up of a coalescence of territorial, state, and language bonds,[83] whereas the caste is "a closed, solidary, organized or quasi-organized, multibonded group made up of racial, kinship, occupational, economic, territorial, religious, and language bonds . . . Furthermore, a given caste forms a definite stratum in the hierarchy of castes ranked by the religious law in the order of their superiority and inferiority." [84] The order or estate is defined as somewhat organized so far as the upper orders are concerned and quasi-organized or unorganized so far as the lower orders or "collectivities" are concerned. It is partly hereditary and more open than the caste. It might be called, from both a quantitative and qualitative standpoint, a diluted caste.[85]

So far as stratification is concerned, Sorokin is chiefly known for his often quoted and much used treatment of class. Definitions as used by some other social scientists are rejected, which for example, may note stratum in a vertical hierarchy but not specific differentiating characteristics; identify social class with one of the unibonded groups such as economic, occupational or racial; accord rank in accordance with the number of privileges and disfranchisements accruing to the various levels; or represent a stratum merely as a multibonded group. Sorokin assigns the following characteristics to social class:

It is (1) legally open, but actually semi-closed; (2) 'normal'; (3) solidary; (4) antagonistic to certain other groups (social classes) of the same general nature . . . (5) partly organized but mainly quasi-organized; (6) partly aware of its own unity and existence and partly not; (7) characteristic of the western society of the eighteenth, nineteenth, and twentieth centuries; (8) a multibonded group bound together by two unibonded ties, occupational and economic . . . and by one bond of social stratification in the sense of the totality of its essential rights and duties . . .[86]

The specific characteristic of a social class "is the coalescence of occupational and economic bonds plus the bond of belonging to the same basic stratum, whose properties are defined by the totality of its essential rights and duties, or by its privileges and disfranchisements, as compared with those of other classes. [Here the political bond is not eliminated but included in] the totality of rights and duties." [87] Although a similar position in respect to occupational, economic, and political status frequently distinguishes a totality of people as a distinct social class [88] there are exceptions which make it necessary to "talk separately of the economic, the occupational, and the political strata or classes." [89]

Sorokin treats social class and stratification in considerably greater detail than some of the other concepts which have come to be regarded as elemental in social structure. Nonetheless, their treatment is as solidly based in his law-norms as are some of the lesser expanded elements.

The specific characteristic of the social class is the coalescence of occupational and economic bonds plus the bond of belonging to the same basic stratum, whose properties are defined by the totality of its essential rights and duties, or by its privileges and disfranchisements, as compared with those of other classes. In this sense the social class differs fundamentally from all other groups (multibonded or unibonded.) [90]

The evaluative aspect of any group's "essential rights and duties" make this relationship to the law-norms more specific.

Evaluation of actors and allocation of status-roles. The system of stratification always has its evaluative aspects. At any given time in the history of a large sociocultural system, certain organizations such as the family, church, the military or an occupational grouping will be the "mechanism for testing, selecting and distributing" the individuals in the system. Such organizations will have certain criteria which determine who will attain to the positions with the highest status and who will be distributed to the remaining positions. The dynamics of social stratification is called by Sorokin vertical "social mobility." Social mobility is for him "any transition of an individual or social object or value—anything that has been created or modified by human activity—from one social position to another." [91] He recognizes two principal types: *horizontal,* or the transition of an individual or social object from one group to another which occupies the same level; and *vertical,* or the movement of an individual or social object from one social stratum to another.

A vast amount of data are examined by Sorokin to discover general propositions. These data bring him to state the following principles:

1. There has scarcely been any society whose strata were absolutely closed, or in which vertical mobility in its three forms—economic, political and occupational—was not present . . .
2. There has never existed a society in which vertical social mobility has been absolutely free and the transition from one social stratum to another has had no resistance . . .
3. The intensiveness, as well as the generality of the vertical social mobility, varies from society to society . . .
4. The intensiveness and the generality of the vertical mobility—the economic, the political and the occupational—fluctuate in the same society at different times . . .

5. In the field of vertical mobility, in its three fundamental forms, there seems to be no definite perpetual trend toward either an increase or a decrease of the intensiveness and generality of mobility. This is proposed as valid for the history of a country, for that of a large social body, and, finally, for the history of mankind.[92]

He also analyzes the "channels," "elevators," or "holes" which permit individuals to move up and down, or from one stratum to another. In the history of mankind he concludes that the family, army, church, school, political, economic and professional organizations have been the chief channels which permit individuals to move up and down the social ladder from stratum to stratum.

In times of insecurity for society or in times of war, the army is of crucial significance. Thus, it becomes possible for an individual born in the lower stratum to achieve the highest positions in the society and in this process the army plays the role of "Social Stairway" through which these high positions become available. The Church has also been of importance as a channel of vertical mobility. This was specifically true in Europe during the time the Catholic Church was the chief influence in the lives of the people. In periods of high industrialization and specialization, the school is of great significance as a social elevator. Positions demanding the highest skill and providing the greatest financial and status remuneration are available usually only to those who have successfully gone through an extensive period of training which the school provides. Political organizations perform the same function, especially in a democratic society. An unknown individual gets elected to a governmental position. This automatically raises his status and gives him a position of power and influence. Failure to be re-elected may mean the loss of such power and influence. Occupational and professional organizations are another such channel. Sorokin shows that important percentages of the permanent professional leaders in various countries were born in the laboring classes and subsequently reached the highest professional positions. Also economic, or wealth-making organizations are the vehicles by which the individual who amasses a fortune is propelled upward. Finally, family alliances by marriage are cited by Sorokin as a means by which individuals achieve either social promotion or degradation.

These same channels are also the " 'sieves' which test and sift, select and distribute the individuals within different social strata or positions." [93] Some of these such as the school and family have the function of testing for the general qualities of individuals, such as intelligence, health, and social characteristics. Some others, such as occupational organizations, test for the specific qualities of individuals necessary for successful performance of various functions in the society. Sorokin emphasizes the important role of the family as an organization which throughout history has been one of the chief bases for the social distribution of the members of the society. He states:

Other conditions being equal, in a society where the family is stable, marriage is sacred and durable; intermarriages between different social strata are few; the training and education of the children go on principally within the family; the number of other testing and selective agencies is small; and they receive the young generation for training only at a relatively late age; in such a society, the family, as a testing, selecting, and distributing agency plays an exclusively important role. In such a society, an inheritance of the father's position by the son is usual and natural. And contrariwise, in a society where the family is unstable, the marriage is easily dissolved; intermarriages between different strata are common; the education of the children after their early period goes on outside of the family, in other institutions; and their number is relatively numerous; in such a society the family as a testing and selecting agency plays a role far less important than in the first type of society.[94]

Sorokin cites among the many factors of vertical mobility, one which he terms demographic. This covers the phenomenon of lower replacement rates for the upper classes. Others cited are the dissimilarity of parents and children: children sometimes have greater or less intelligence than their parents as well as many other characteristics which differentiate them from their parents. Finally, radical changes in environment effect a change in status of a given individual. An artisan may have a high position in a handicraft society, but a relatively low position in a society of machine production. In some societies the mechanism for testing and selecting is performed inefficiently. This may mean an accumulation of gifted individuals in the lower strata of a given social system. In his book, *The Sociology of Revolution* this is discussed as an important factor in the violent upheavals of society.[95]

An extensive amount of horizontal mobility has also been exhibited in Western society. An increasing territorial circulation of individuals related, of course, to improved means of transportation contribute to this kind of social mobility.

Sorokin examines some of the effects of mobility on social systems. For one who has rather mistakenly been labelled a worshiper of the ideational, he enumerates an impressive list of positive influences he attributes to mobility, a trait more closely associated with the sensate than with the ideational culture. One must doubt that he deplores the sensate as much as has been claimed when one examines his list [96] of the effects of mobility. Among them: "behavior becomes more plastic and versatile"; "Increase of mobility tends to reduce narrow-mindedness and occupational and other idiosyncrasies"; "Mobility facilitates invention and discoveries"; "Mobility facilitates an increase of intellectual life"; "Mobility, under some conditions, facilitates a better and more adequate social distribution of individuals than in an immobile society"; and others. While it is true that there are others of a more negative nature: "Mobility tends to increase mental strain"; "Mobility diminishes intimacy and increases psychosocial isolation and loneliness of individuals"; "Mobility facilitates disintegration of morals" for example, the list obviously is the work of a thinker who objectively surveys and reports upon his data.

Societies differ greatly in the amount of mobility that prevails. Some societies are characterized by a great deal of mobility; attempts to up-grade one's rank are encouraged. In others where there is less mobility attempts to change one's rank may be penalized. Such sanctioning as accompanies changing of rank are only a small part of the total store of sanctions a social system employs. These will be treated next.

SANCTIONING

Sanctions as an element and application of sanctions as a process. Sorokin's concept of sanctions is imbedded in the nature of his law-norms: "In a fully formulated law-norm there are, first, its *defining* part, which indicates a definite obligatory form of conduct; second, the *sanctioning* part, which formulates the consequences of the violation of this form of conduct." [97] The various forms of punishment which the sanctioning part of the law-norm may assume have been treated above under a discussion of the law-norms.

Although a social system's body of official law is generally replete with fully formulated consequences attending the breaking of the law, Sorokin's position is that very few members of a social system conform with the law merely to avoid its sanctions. "For persons with strong law-convictions the very idea that they do not murder, do not steal, and do not take bribes, just because they are afraid of punishment or of losing some utilitarian advantage would appear insulting, and rightly so." [98] The law-norms, including their sanctioning parts, are then, what "everyone" believes ought to be done, and what should happen to anyone who believes and acts differently. Sorokin is careful to point out, however, that generally, "there is some discrepancy between . . . official law and the unofficial norms, of some of its members, though normally this discrepancy is not too great." [99] When a great number of unofficial norms are advocated by a great many members of a social system, either the official law in its defining part and in its sanctioning part change in an orderly way by due process of law; or one of two alternative results occur, each carrying with it a sort of mass-sanctioning action: (1) The official law is violently overthrown, and with it its government and its partisans in the form of a revolution; or (2) the unofficial law and its partisans are denounced in a bloody suppression, by the iron hand of the official government. Thus societal stability (represented by official law) and its proponents, and social change (represented by unofficial law) and its proponents incessantly mutually stimulate one another, and the application of sanctions does not loom as a causal factor in the obeying of the law-norms except when discrepancy between the two bodies of laws becomes very great. Otherwise, "The fear of punishment and the utilitarian advantages in law-conduct are necessary only for those who do not have strong law-convictions—persons such as the cynics, the demoralized, the criminals, the dishonest." [100]

FACILITATING

Facility as element and utilization of facilities as process. It
will be recalled that a facility, according to the PAS Model, is a
means used within the system to attain the system's ends. It will
also be recalled that Sorokin by and large—but not entirely—rejected the means-ends schema. It will be no surprise, therefore,
to find that that body of objects designated on the PAS Model
as facilities has no exact counterpart in Sorokin's scheme. "Vehicles" and "conductors," Sorokin's designation for those "funds and
material means necessary for carrying on [the] functions [of the
social system] and making possible the activities of its members" [101] enters the social system from his treatment of culture.
Most simply stated, immaterial meanings are objectified and
socialized into material vehicles. Whereas in terms of the PAS
Model, a facility is a means to an end, by Sorokin's conceptual
scheme, a vehicle is a conductor of meaning. Some idea of the
latitude of this concept (comprising as it does the cultural aspects
of the sociocultural system) may be had from its typology of
which the following [102] is only suggestive:

sound: (physical, e.g. noise) and (symbolic, e.g. spoken words, music)
light and color: mostly symbolic; written language, signs, insignia
pantomimic: mostly symbolic; gestures, postures, grimaces, etc.
thermal, mechanical, chemical and electrical: examples—central heat-
    ing, bombs, hot water bottles, blows, shots, caresses, surgical opera-
    tions, cooking, medicine, broadcasting
object: a dollar bill, a lock of hair, a wedding ring, an heirloom, a
    scepter

Of this last class Sorokin writes:

In thousands of forms object conductors function in social interaction
as physical and especially as symbolic conductors. As such they objectify a wide range of meanings and convey them to others, influencing their state of mind and their overt actions. In a sense the whole
of material culture—tools, utensils, machinery, weapons, cultivated
fields and gardens, roads, buildings, and entire cities—represent object conductors.[103]

It is abundantly clear that Sorokin's "vehicles" as transmitters and
objectifications of meaning is a much more comprehensive term

than facilities. Most of the symbolic vehicles discussed by Sorokin are actually phenomena which are treated here under communication. Some of them are phenomena which have already been treated above under communication of sentiment.

It is in the physical rather than in the symbolic aspect that the two concepts—vehicles and facilities impinge. As a vehicle the atomic bomb can thus be viewed as objectifying the pure meaning of defense; as a facility it can as justifiably be viewed as a means by which a specific act of defense (an end) can be accomplished. Sorokin in explanation of his "inseparable trinity," personality, society and culture gives this example:

> In the classroom the instructor and students are the *personalities;* the totality of these personalities, with the norms of their relationships, constitutes the *society of the classroom;* the scientific and other ideas which they possess and exchange, as well as the books, the blackboard, the furniture, the lamps, and the room itself, represent *the culture of this society.*[104]

In the Sorokinian schema the blackboard, furniture and lamps are of the same order as the scientific ideas and books as vehicles for conveying meaning (albeit the former are physical, the latter symbolic). The PAS Model would designate the books, the blackboard, the furniture, the lamps and the room itself as facilities which provide the means of learning (the end) of scientific and other ideas (knowledge) by exchange, reading, listening, observing (communication).

While the imperfect or uncontrolled use of facilities may bring some unexpected results not calculated in the process of utilization (lack of control of an automobile may result in a collision instead of a safe arrival) implicit in the facility concept is the idea of purposeful use and control of the facility by the members of the social system. Vehicles as conductors of meaning can similarly be used purposively and controlled consciously by their users. They have an additional attribute in the process of utilization, however. Sorokin claims, and quotes Durkheim and Simmel in support of his position [105] that once created, vehicles have the capacity to condition the behavior and mental states of members of social systems. For example, roads dictate the direction of movement; other objects predetermine the kind of dwelling. Sorokin calls this the retroactive influence of vehicles and attributes to its force such phenomena as status-role image creation and the fetishization of vehicles in which the substance of the conveyed meaning attaches to the vehicle of conveyance and causes it to become sacred.[106]

COMPREHENSIVE OR MASTER PROCESSES

Sorokin sets forth those social processes that he considers to be the legitimate domain of a "generalizing science," namely those "that are recurrent in the life of any group, past, present, and future," and not the "specific and unique processes of which the life of a given unique social group is made up." [107] General sociology therefore deals with a limited number of basic repeated processes the nature of which is suggested by a number of "how" and "why" approaches. These include how and why:

(1) Social groups originate (the passage from a state of isolation to one of interaction and contact)
(2) Groups organize
    (a) Official laws-norms emerge in the conduct of members, recommended, required, and prohibited relationships emerge
    (b) Intragroup and intergroup differentiation and stratification appear with the government and hierarchy of the respective ranks and authorities (Organization, institutionalization and adjustment processes)
(3) Social groups maintain their existence
(4) Groups change in such things as size, in stratified profile, in the proportion of contractual, familistic, and compulsory relationships, etc.
(5) Groups change now in an orderly and now in a revolutionary manner
(6) Groups disintegrate, die, and "resurrect." [108]

Communication. As was indicated above under *facilities,* Sorokin views all of culture as objectified or symbolized meaning and each such cultural object or symbol a "message carrier" which he calls a vehicle. The processes by which patterns of cultural transmission emerge and reoccur constitute his field of interest in communication.

Sorokin indicates that for any cultural phenomenon to be socialized, it must pass or be transmitted from person to person, from group to group, stratum to stratum.[109]

Any such passage or transmission of a cultural value gives a process of mobility (migration, circulation) of cultural phenomena . . . In this sense the processes of socialization and mobility of cultural processes are inseparable from each other.[110]

He therefore discusses both socialization and communication together. As with individuals, the mobility of cultural phenomena may be either horizontal or vertical, with a residual category of intermediary. It is horizontal when the "phenomenon passes from person to person, group to group, of the same or similar social stratum and position." It is vertical "when it passes from upper to lower and from lower to upper strata." It is intermediary "when the ranks and strata of the persons and groups remain undetermined or blurred." [111] Cultural phenomena move from the place where they were invented along the channels of communication, reaching other persons in contact with these channels. Sorokin used the self-evident proposition that "the more developed is the total system of communication between these points the more easily they move" to refute theories of diffusion of culture such as concentric spread. The "upper-middle-urban groups" having a more efficient system of communication than other groups, import or acquire the phenomena of another sociocultural system earlier. Cultural phenomena will pass from person to person or group to group without essential change if the culture of departure is similar to the culture of infiltration. If two sociocultural systems differ widely, much of the phenomena cannot pass from one group to the other.

Those cultural phenomena that satisfy the most basic needs of human beings are passed easiest and become most readily socialized. Such needs would include those related to food, drink, clothing, shelter and sex. Also such cultural values as "language, script, rudimentary arithmetic, practical lore, ethico-legal norms, and elements of the fine arts" are universal in their generic form.[112] Finally, Sorokin generalizes that "among the cultural values of the same kind, price, and cultural milieu, the more refined and complex the value, and the more special training is required for its use, the less widely it spreads, in comparison with less complex values." [113]

Sorokin also generalizes concerning the speed with which ideological, behavioral and material culture move. "Ideological culture moves faster and more easily than behavioral and material cultures of the same system or congeries . . . The ideological element tends to diffuse first, and more rapidly than behavioral and material aspects . . . Sometimes there is a considerable lag between the indoctrination of a meaning and its realization in behavior and material vehicles." [114]

Socialization. In Sorokin's conceptual scheme, this process would include all activities by which the main values of a group become part of the individual.

For instance, when the religious culture of the group is a set of animistic or totemic beliefs and practices, the individual's religious orientation will also be animistic and totemic. If his religious group is Christian or Buddhist, his religious ego will also be Christian or Buddhist. The same can be said of all the other aspects of the individual personality . . . Since the scientific, religious, ethical and other ideas, beliefs, and values are not biologically inherited, the individual acquires these mainly from the groups with which he interacts.[115]

Since this is done by the transmission of a culture-meaning, and since for Sorokin "meaning" is so all-encompassing (see Facilities above) his treatment of the subject of *communication* (or transmission object and symbol meanings) is essentially his treatment of *socialization*.

Boundary maintenance. It is in Sorokin's analysis of how a group maintains itself that those components which comprise boundary maintenance are found. Despite the omnipresent fact of internal and external factors of change, the groups maintain their identity by the following methods:

1. The group must retain the identity of its components of meanings, norms or values
2. It must maintain its set of vehicles
3. It must maintain its membership
4. It must maintain the meaningful-causal connections between these three components.

Each of these sub-processes necessary for group or boundary

maintenance contains many devices applicable to boundary maintenance. Only a few will be selected here as illustrative of the maintenance process. Important are:

"selectivity in adopting certain new elements that do not destroy its identity and in rejecting those elements that are totally uncongenial to it." [116]

Maintenance of the symbols and basic rites of the group, including its: name, symbolic signs and gestures, basic rites and ceremonies, specific persons or status-roles, relics and symbolic objects, all symbolic "conductors."

Persistence of meanings as represented in external factors: especially the visible, objective tangible vehicles: cities, buildings, churches, schools, factories, etc. (these would be examples of a large supersystem).

Devices for constant indoctrination of members.

Selectivity in admission of new members.

Affective aspects of inter-relations among members: factors making for morale, sympathy, loyalty, devotion.

Optimum size of membership, deviation from which adversely affects group identity and boundary maintenance.

Effective meaningful-causal bonds uniting the three components (1) meanings-values-norms (2) vehicles and (3) membership, into a structural and dynamic whole.

The inevitable internal change and the inexorable external pressures constantly demand of a group that it "preserve a vital minimum of its organization, solidarity and cultural integration" if it is to retain its identity as a group. The above itemization is but a sampling of the processes necessary for the task of boundary maintenance. Sorokin's total treatment [117] of group maintenance of identity and continuity includes some aspects of such processes as are here included under socialization. His whole treatment shows "how difficult the task is. No wonder, therefore, that, as we shall see, many groups are short-lived and that only a few survive for hundreds or thousands of years." [118]

Systemic linkage. For Sorokin interaction between groups like that between individuals may be solidary, antagonistic, neutral, or unrelated causally and meaningfully. The interacting groups in their solidary interrelationships are demonstrating the process of systemic linkage. Sorokin recognizes two types:

(a) *first, a subsystem within a larger system.* A precinct in a city is an administrative subgroup in the larger group of the city; the city itself is a subgroup in the larger group of the state, and the state is a subgroup in a still larger group of the United States. (b) A *second* form of solidary intergroup relationship is *co-ordination of two or more groups into a vaster federated unity.* Here none of the groups is a subsystem in the others; each is autonomous and remains so without domination or subordination. Assuming their relationship is solidary, the Federal Council of the Church is an example of this. None of the denominations of the Federal Council of the Churches of Christ is dominant or subordinated to another. Federation of states, labor unions, chambers of commerce, political parties (especially in the time of national emergency), of the church and the state, of United Nations, are further examples of the coordinated interrelationship of groups.[119]

Sorokin is also responsible for other analyses which are pertinent to systemic linkage. The cultural diffusion which takes place as meaning and object vehicles transmit cultural phenomena in the manner described under communication above is often concomitant to a systemic linkage on which the imports and exports of international trade is based. The unibonded totalitarian state group with its constellaton of state-dominated subgroups, a type of solidary group described above, is treated in some detail by Sorokin.

Sorokin specifically uses the term "link" and chain, although "systemic linkage" *per se* is not found among his works. The sequence of "conductors" necessary to get a telegram sent from the office of A to the office of B leads Sorokin to term the process a "chain of conductors" with human beings serving as necessary intermediate links.[120] It is but a step to proceed from the linking of vehicles as Sorokin has noted to the linking of systems as he has implied. Group-wise, the chain of relationships, as exemplified by a marriage, connects the families of the newly wed pair, and the connecting links are two human beings. The multibonded family system is indeed one of the world's most prevalent results of systemic linkage.

Institutionalization. As indicated above Sorokin intended that the word institution be regarded as synonymous with social system or organized group. It follows, then, that "systemization" or "organization" could also express what Sorokin means when he spells out the process by which institutions (social systems or organized groups) come into being. His specific "how" and "why" questions here are: Why and How Social Groups Become Organized (Process of Organization, Adaptation, and Accomodation).[121] In answer to the Why part of the question, Sorokin points out that durable interaction of individuals is bound to pass from an unorganized to an organized form in order to avoid incessant conflicts, and to assure some peace and order, some safety and security. *"The organization of a group is the indispensable condition of its survival and durability."* [122] The organization need not be just, fair, or equitable, but if it operates on a code of law-norms it is organized or institutionalized.

How the group becomes organized may happen by four principal methods:

(1) intentional or purposeful on the part of all the interacting individuals . . . the easiest, quickest and fairest mode of origin, the purposeful or contractual way is possible . . . only in groups of individuals whose norms, values, meanings, are congenial and similar to a considerable extent.

(2) fortuitous or spontaneous, a process of "natural crystallization" . . . the very purpose of creating an organization grows spontaneously . . . An interaction process, spontaneously initiated and spontaneously maturing, eventually engenders the purpose of formalizing and crystallizing an already roughly organized group.

(3) intentional on the part of some and fortuitous or even opposed in the case of others . . . deliberative coercion of parties imposing it upon other parties either antagonistic or indifferent to the organization in question.

(4) opposed by all the parties concerned . . . a marriage imposed upon both parties . . . contrary to the inclination of the parties is a case in point [as is the] . . . war prisoners coercively inducted into the German army and forced to fight the army of their own country.[123]

Sorokin maintains that if a social investigator has a fully adequate knowledge of law-norms and a clearly differentiated appreciation of other norms as related to law-norms, he will unerringly locate all the institutionalized characteristics: "law-norms in their fullest implications, contain all the other characteristics of organized groups or institutions." [124]

CONDITIONS OF SOCIAL ACTION

Territoriality. Sorokin was among the first of the modern social scientists to differentiate in social science terms between social and geographical space. Writing in *Social Mobility* he says:

To sum up: 1) social space is the universe of the human population; 2) man's social position is the totality of his relations toward all groups of a population and, within each of them toward its members; 3) location of a man's position in this social universe is obtained by ascertaining these relations; 4) the totality of such groups and the totality of the positions within each of them compose a system of social coordinates which permits us to define the social position of any man." [125]

Later in both the *Systematic Source Book in Rural Sociology* and in *Principles of Rural-Urban Sociology* Sorokin played an important part in counteracting what then "in many textbooks" was "a popular topic for discussion . . . 'the great isolation of rural people.'" Admitting "that rural people, especially on large open farms, have a less number of contacts than the urban," higher suicide rates among the latter were in part accounted for by "what we style as psycho-social isolation or loneliness or a low intensity of social bonds. Man may be amidst a crowd of thousands of people and yet he often feels quite isolated, a stranger to all other men, lonesome and untied . . . Community of tradition, feeling, belief, interest, and intimacy in the relationships are much greater in the rural than in the urban" society.[126]

In the now famous "definition of rural and urban worlds" in these earlier writings density of population was specified as a principle difference between the rural community and the non-rural. "As yet, it is not possible either for thousands of people to secure a means of subsistence from a few acres or to carry on the cultivation of land . . ." [127] In a discussion of the system of interaction in the rural as compared with the urban world the former was characterized as familistic and *Gemeinschaft*-like, the latter as contractual and *Gesellschaft*-like. In the former there is "comparative simplicity and sincerity of relations; 'man is interacted as a human person.' " In the latter "greater complexity, manifoldedness, superficiality, and standardized formality of relations" prevails. "Man is interacted as a 'number' and 'address.' " [128] Therefore, although people in the rural world may have fewer contacts and territorially be further apart much of the time than is true in the urban world, in terms of social space there is less "isolation" in rural than urban communities.

Size. Sorokin recognized that in terms of operation

there seems to be an optimum size of an organization of a given type in given circumstances. A great deviation from such an optimum size either in the direction of overgrowth or undergrowth, seems to be negatively correlated with the longevity of the institutions of the same kind.[129]

After patterns and fluctuations of the size of groups are discussed he concludes that

It is improbable that any of the groups could grow to such proportions as to swallow up all the groups of the same kind, the more so since virtually all social groups have a limited life span. Having reached their maximum possible size, sooner or later they decline in size, disintegrate, and eventually disappear.[130]

In the classical work on stratification, *Social Mobility,* size of social systems and their heterogeniety (in race, sex, health, age, psychologically, and socially) are specified as the key determinants of the pattern and level of stratification. Other things being equal "when both of these factors increase, the stratification tends to increase still more; and vice versa." [131]

In the above mentioned treatises on rural sociology it was observed that there is always a negative correlation between the size of community and percent of the population engaged in agriculture.[132] The continued urbanization of the rural worlds in east and west is predicted but it is stated that this

'urbanization' . . . *means only an approach of its characteristics to the characteristics of the urban world but does not mean a complete obliteration of all differences between them.* In order that such an obliteration become possible it is necessary for the urban and rural areas to have the same density of population, the same size of community, the same homogeneity or heterogeneity of population, the same occu-

pational milieu and nature of the occupation, and the same intensity and character of the interaction system.[133]

Social and cultural change. Social systems begin, as was discussed under the process of *Institutionalization;* they maintain themselves, as was seen under *Boundary maintenance.* They also change in the course of maintaining themselves. Basic to Sorokin's theory of change is the assumption that "all empirical phenomena—inorganic, organic, and sociocultural—are subject to change in the course of their empirical existence." [134] Immanent and external forces both make for change, but of the two Sorokin considers immanent change more important, and moreover, inevitable. The sociocultural system "cannot help changing, even if all its external conditions are constant." [135] The sociocultural system, comprised as it is of persons, social organization, and culture, *must* make immanent change in the following respects:

(1) People age and otherwise change
(2) The performance of any activity by its very performance creates change
(3) Meanings, values and norms, even when they attend a constant idea or subject, change
(4) The vehicles as conductors of meaning must adapt to the new meanings and therefore, change.

Sorokin, by giving primacy to immanent change does not reject external change; in fact he finds untenable, theories of change based exclusively on the one or the other source.

The endorsement of the immanent principle of change does not hinder a recognition of the role of the external forces in the change of the sociocultural system.[136]

There are the other sociocultural systems all of which are changing and through systemic linkage and other means, influencing one another. Likewise natural and other forces may bring about change such as destruction. However although

external conditions can crush the system or terminate an unfolding of its immanent destiny at one of the earliest phases of its development (its immanent life career), depriving it of a realization of its complete life career . . . they cannot fundamentally change the character and the quality of each phase of the development; nor can they, in many cases, reverse or fundamentally change the sequence of the phases of the immanent destiny of the system.[137]

Since a system must change, it follows that it will not endure unless it does change. Endurance, then (or maintenance or boundary maintenance as this phenomena has been called in the present writing) can be measured in immanent-external terms too, as a kind of concomitant to change:

Since the destiny or life career of any system is the result of the system's self-control and of the influence of the environmental forces, the relative share of each of these two factors in molding the system's career is not constant for all sociocultural systems. The share of the self-control of the system is the greater, the more perfectly the system is integrated and the more powerful it is.[138]

Having established the inevitability of change Sorokin explains the "why" of sociocultural rhythms and swings. The principle of limit is crucial in this. Both in his lectures and writing he has used many illustrations to explain this principle:

The more strongly I strike a piano key, the louder the resulting sound. Within a certain limit the loudness of the sound is a direct function of the force exerted in the stroke . . . beyond a certain limit the result will not be an increase in the volume of sound, but rather a broken piano . . .[139]

Sorokin concludes that

eternally linear sociocultural processes are . . . impossible . . . Since practically all the sociocultural systems have limited possibilities of variation of their essential forms, it follows that all the systems that continue to exist after all their possible forms are exhausted are bound to have recurrent rhythms. Hence, the inevitability of recurrence in the life process of such systems.

Other conditions being equal, the more limited the possibilities of variation of main forms, the more frequent, conspicuous, and graspable are the rhythms in the process of the system, and the simpler the rhythms from the standpoint of their phases . . . The valid conception is that of an 'incessant variation' of the main recurrent themes which contains in itself, as a part, all these conceptions, and as such is much richer than any of them.[140]

GLOSSARY

Antagonistic Interaction. It is antagonistic when the aspirations
   or desires as well as the overt actions of the parties mutually
   hinder one another.

Catalytic Action. Social actions that exert an influence merely
   through the known existence of the party or parties concerned.

Causal-Meaningful Unities. An example of this could be an as-
   sembled car, meaningfully created, with all parts depending
   mutually on one another, one part depending upon the whole
   and the whole depending upon the parts; the cathedral of Chartres; a railroad station with all the rail lines and hundreds of
   various machines and buildings and warehouses—all causally
   connected with one another and all created by the purposive
   activities of the groups the integrated part of the culture of all
   the organized groups: church, school, business firm, etc. found
   in an area.

Compulsory Relations. Characterized by overwhelming antagonism. An example of this type is found in a despotic government based upon force and fraud in which the interests of the
   few are served, but the many are oppressed in most ways.

Congeries. A conglomeration of norms, values, meanings without
   causal functional integration of a meaningful nature.

Cultural Mentality-Active Ideationalism. Identical with general
   ideationalism in its major premises, it seeks the realization of
   the needs and ends, not only through minimization of the carnal
   needs of individuals but also through the transformation of the
   sensate world and especially of the sociocultural world, in such
   a way as to reform it along the lines of the spiritual reality and
   of the ends chosen as the main value.

Cultural Mentality-Active Sensate. It seeks the consummation of
   its needs and ends mainly through the most "efficient" modification, adjustment, readjustment reconstruction, of the external
   milieu. The transformation of the inorganic, organic (technology, medicine, and the applied disciplines), and the sociocultural world, viewed mainly externally, is the method of this
   variety. The great executives of history, the great conquerors,
   builders of empire, are its incarnation.

Cultural Mentality-Ascetic Ideationalism. This seeks the consummation of the needs and ends through an excessive elimination and minimization of the carnal needs, supplemented by a complete detachment from the sensate world and even from one's self, viewing both as mere illusion, nonreal, nonexisting. The whole sensate milieu, and even the individual "self," are dissolved in the supersensate, ultimate reality.

Cultural Mentality-Cynical Sensate. (Cynical "Epicureans"). The civilization dominated by this type of mentality, in seeking to achieve the satisfaction of its needs, uses a specific technique of donning and doffing those ideational masks which promise the greatest returns in physical profit. This mentality is exemplified by all the Tartufes of the world, those who are accustomed to change their psychosocial "colors" and to readjust their values in order to run along with the stream.

Cultural Mentality-Idealistic Culture. This is the only form of the Mixed class which is—or at least appears to be—logically integrated. Quantitatively it represents a more or less balanced unification of ideational and sensate, with however, a predominance of the ideational elements. Qualitatively it synthesizes the premises of both types into one inwardly consistent and harmonious unity. For it reality is many-sided, with the aspects of everlasting Being and ever-changing Becoming of the spiritual and the material. Its needs and ends are both spiritual and material, with the material, however, subordinated to the spiritual. The methods of their realization involve both the modification of self and the transformation of the external sensate world.

Cultural Mentality-Passive Sensate. (Passive "Epicureans"). This is characterized by the attempt to fulfill physical needs and aims, neither through the inner modification of "self," nor through efficient reconstruction of the external world, but through a parasitic exploitation and utilization of the external reality as it is, viewed as the mere means for enjoying sensual pleasures. "Life is short"; "Carpe Diem"; "Wine, women, and song"; "Eat, drink, and be merry"—These are the mottoes of this mentality.

Cultural Mentality-Pseudo-Ideational. Another specific form of the Mixed type is the unintegrated, Pseudo-Ideational mentality. One might style it "subcultural" if the term culture were used to designate only a logically integrated system. This type has occupied a conspicuous place in the history of culture mentality. Its characteristics are as follows: The nature of reality is not clearly defined, but is felt largely as sensate. Here needs and ends are predominantly of a physical nature. They are only moderately satisfied, and the method of satisfaction is neither an active modification of the milieu to any appreciable degree, nor a free modification of self, nor a search for pleasure, nor successful hypocrisy. It is a dull and passive endurance of blows and privations, coming from the outside, as long as these can be borne physically. This minimization of spiritual and carnal needs is not freely sought, it is imposed by some external agency (vis absoluta).

Culture. The totality of the meanings, functions and norms processed by the inter-acting persons and the totality of the vehicles which objectify, socialize and convey these meanings.

Direct Causal-Functional Unities. For example, causal-functional dependence between the social anomie and movement of suicide; between depression (in certain conditions) and crimes against property; between war and the change in the rate of divorce or marriage; between a social emergency and growth of the government control and regulation. These unities, again, are given in any culture area in hundreds of different forms.

Familistic Form. Interaction would be predominantly solidary, broad in extensity, of high intensity, durable, direct, mutual, characterized by the "fundamental, normative, and purposive types of motivation, all working harmoniously with one another"; based on a profound sense of sociocultural oneness and possessed of a leadership that is natural, spontaneous and paternalistic.

Generalizing Science. The Science which studies phenomena that is repeated in time and space.

Generic Sociocultural Phenomenon. The most generic model of any sociocultural phenomenon is the meaningful interaction of two or more human individuals.

Horizontal Social Mobility. The transition of an individual or social object from one group to another which occupies the same level.

Indirect Causal-Functional Objects. An example of this would be cultural objects gathered together in a study, or cultural objects found on a person—his clothes, hat, letters, money, comb, handkerchief, pencil, cigarettes, and what not in the pockets of his coat. All these cultural objects (with the meanings, values, and norms they objectify) do not have a direct causal-functional interdependence with one another, nor do they logically or aesthetically demand one another; but each of these A, B, C . . . M being causally meaningfully united with the needs of an individual, the common factor X, are indirectly united with one another not only by the tie of spatial adjacency but also by that of indirect causal-functional relationships.

Individualizing Science. The Science which concentrates its attention upon the study of phenomena that is unique and unrepeated in time and space.

Interaction. Any event by which one party tangibly influences the overt actions or the state of mind of the other.

Mixed-Interaction. It is mixed when the desires and overt behavior of the parties are partly antagonistic, partly solidary.

Multibonded Social Group. A group whose members are united by two or three central systems of meanings-values-norms.

Pure Meaningful, Logico-Aesthetic Unities. These exist in the form of small and vast systems of meanings, values, and norms, objectified in the actions and vehicles of the individuals of a given area.

Spatially Contiguous and Mechanically Cohesive Unities. Example of this would be a box containing unassembled parts of a radio or automobile, or a scrap book with a page of Plato's Republic bound together with a recipe of how to make a mince pie and a picture of a movie star.

Spatially Contiguous and Perceptional Unities. These unities consist of two or more culture phenomena, united only by their spatial adjacency, for example, the Saturday Evening Post, a broken bottle of whisky, and a worn-out shoe lying side by side in a street or on a dump. These phenomena are total logico-aesthetic and causal strangers to each other. In thousands of forms such merely spatially adjacent cultural "bedfellows" are found in practically any culture area, from the smallest to the largest.

Social System. An organized group that possesses a set of enforced obligatory law-norms, defining in detail the rights, duties, social position, and functions, roles, and proper behavior of each and all its members towards one another, outsiders and the world at large; a set of prohibited actions-relations sanctioned by punishment; and a set of recommended non-obligatory norms of conduct.

Society. The totality of interacting personalities with their sociocultural relationships and processes.

Solidary Interaction. It is solidary if and when the aspirations (meanings-values) and overt actions of the parties concerned "concur and are mutually helpful for the realization of their objectives."

Subject of the right. This is the person or group entitled to whatever is stated in the law-norms.

Superorganic. The equivalent of the mind in all its clearly developed manifestations.

The Object of the Right. This includes all the activities (doing, nondoing, nontolerating) of the subject of right to which he is entitled by the law-norm.

The Object of the Duty. By this is meant all the actions of the subject of duty required from him by the law-norm.

The Subject of the Duty. This refers to the person (individual or collective) who is required to perform the duty indicated in the law-norm.

Unibonded Social Group. Members of the group are united in a social system by one basic tie—the central system of meanings-values-norms.

Vehicles or Conductors. Overt actions and material phenomena through which immaterial means, values, and norms are objectified and socialized.

Vertical Social Mobility. The movement of an individual or social object from one social stratum to another.

BIBLIOGRAPHICAL KEY *

COA—*Crisis of Our Age* (N. Y.: E. P. Dutton and Co., 1946).
F & F—*Fads and Foibles in Modern Sociology and Related Sciences* (Chicago: Henry Regnery Co., 1956).

* For a more complete bibliography see the notes which follow and the bibliographic appendix at the end of the volume.

PRUS—Pitirim A. Sorokin, and Carle C. Zimmerman, *Principles of Rural-Urban Sociology* (N. Y.: Holt and Company, c1929).

SCD—*Social and Cultural Dynamics* (N. Y.: American Book Co., 1937, 4 Vols.). See the next entry.

SCD—*Social and Cultural Dynamics: A Study of Change in Major Systems of Art, Truth, Ethics, Law and Social Relations* (Boston: Porter Sargent Publisher, 1957). It is this edition which is cited unless a volume number is given in which case it is the entry above.

SCP—*Society, Culture and Personality: Their Structure and Dynamics* (New York: Harper and Brothers, 1947).

SM—*Social Mobility* (N. Y.: Harper and Brothers, 1927).

SPAC—*Social Philosophies of an Age of Crisis* (Boston: The Beacon Press, 1951).

TASR—*The American Sex Revolution* (Boston: Porter Sargent, 1956).

TRH—*The Reconstruction of Humanity* (Boston: Beacon Press, 1948).

TSR—*The Sociology of Revolution* (Philadelphia: Lippincott, 1925).

NOTES

1. Although the above works give his sociological framework most completely and systematically, various aspects of it are discussed in other books of which a fairly complete list is given on the flyleaf of Pitirim A. Sorokin, *Fads and Foibles in Modern Sociology and Related Sciences* (Chicago: Henry Regnery Co., 1956). Hereafter referred to as F & F. See the bibliographic appendix at the end of the volume for a more complete listing.

2. Pitirim A. Sorokin, *Society, Culture and Personality: Their Structure and Dynamics* (New York: Harper and Brothers, 1947), p. 3. Hereafter referred to as SCP.

3. *Ibid.*, p. 4.   4. *Ibid.*, p. 367.

5. Pitirim A. Sorokin, *Social Philosophies of an Age of Crisis* (Boston: The Beacon Press, 1951), p. 202. Hereafter referred to as SPAC.

6. SCP, p. 70.

7. F & F, p. 267.   8. *Ibid.*, pp. 267-8.

9. SCP, p. 40.   10. *Ibid.*, pp. 41-2.

11. *Ibid.*, pp. 63-4. The relationship of culture in Sorokin's sense, to groups is expressed in the following: "A given cultural system does not localize and delimit itself within one group, but like an ocean current, washing many shores and islands, spreads over different groups, sometimes an enormous multitude of these." *Ibid.*, p. 336.

12. Pitirim A. Sorokin, *Social and Cultural Dynamics: A Study of Change in Major Systems of Art, Truth, Ethics, Law and Social Relations* (Boston: Porter Sargent Publisher, 1957), p. 679. Hereafter referred to as SCD. References are to the 1957 edition of this, Sorokin's major work *Ibid.* which is a one-volume condensation, unless a volume number accompanies the abbreviation SCD. If a volume number is used the reference is to the earlier edition: (New York: American Book Co., 1937, 4 Vols.).

13. SCP, p. 320. Although Sorokin does not use the concept "external system" as George Homans does it is obvious that sensate groups place priority on the external system. *Ibid.*, pp. 445-9.

14. *Ibid.*, p. 320. Ideational groups place highest priority on the internal system, *Ibid.*, pp. 445-9.

15. SCD, p. 657.   16. *Ibid.*, p. 231.

17. Nicholas S. Timasheff, *Sociological Theory: Its Nature and Growth* (Garden City, N. Y.: Doubleday and Co., 1955), p. 272.

18. SCD, p. 281.

19. Pitirim A. Sorokin, *Crisis of Our Age* (N. Y.: E. P. Dutton and Co., 1946), pp. 17-9. Hereafter referred to as COA.

20. SCD, p. 235.

21. F. S. C. Northrop, *The Meeting of East and West* (N. Y.: The Macmillan Co., 1947).

22. Max Weber, *The Religion of China—Confucianism and Taoism. Translated and edited by Hans H. Gerth* (Glencoe, Ill.: The Free Press, 1951), p. 155.

23. Robert K. Merton, and likewise Talcott Parsons and Max Weber find the Puritan ethic important in the production of science and scientists. Sorokin questions this. See SCD, Vol. II, pp. 150-2. He writes: "As a matter of fact at the present time there are hardly even few historians of this period and a few sociologists (who studied this problem) who support Max Weber's theory." From correspondence. Although religious factors are only a few among many involved, Merton's findings are *not successfully refuted by Sorokin and other critics.* See Robert K. Merton, *Social Theory and Social Structure* (Glencoe, Ill.: The Free Press, 1957), pp. 601 ff.

24. SCD, p. 229. Here "Methods of validation" are described. Validation for idealistic truth is mainly the scholastic method.

25. SCD, Vol. I, p. 91.

26. N. S. Timasheff, "The Basic Concepts of Sociology," *American Journal of Sociology*, Vol. 58, No. 2, (September, 1952), pp. 176-86. In reality Timasheff should have described Sorokin's system as including his third type, functionalism. Sorokin's *Social and Cultural Dynamcs* is perhaps the greatest undertaking in *functional* analysis.

27. Sorokin writes on the subject as follows: "As a matter of fact and logic, without law-norms all these terms are entirely meaningless or are something very vague and even wrong. E.g. 'expectation,' 'deviation' do not define at all the essential structural network of social relations of any group, nor do they have any meaning. A may expect from B $500 as a Christmas present. If, however, the existing law-norms do not entitle A and do not oblige B to such a present, B's conduct does not become criminal or socially deviant, nor A's expectations become lawful and enforceable. On the other hand, A may not expect any punishment for, say, actions like Charles Van-Doren's actions; and yet if the existing law-norms really prohibit this type of conduct, A is punished by several 'official and unofficial' sanctions. In brief, 'expectations,' 'mores,' 'folkways,' 'status,' 'role' and other terms prevelant among American sociologists in their attempts of strucural analysis are very poor tools and concepts. For this exact reason a greater part of structural-analytical works of these sociologists have not been fruitful and remained in the state of a jibberish collection of these terms giving no deep and real knowledge of the structures of the studied groups and of the psycho-social physiognomy (social, and cultural and personalistic) of their members. Finally, the law-norms give the shortest, most economical and unified way for

a study of structural (and dynamic) properties of any group and its members." Notes on the margins of the original draft of the manuscript for the present chapter.

28. SCP, p. 70.   29. *Ibid.*, p. 72.

30. Based upon SCP, pp. 70-92.

31. *Ibid.*, p. 84.   32. SCD, pp. 37-8.

33. Pitirim A. Sorokin, *The Reconstruction of Humanity* (Boston: Beacon Press, 1948), pp. 131-33. Hereafter referred to as TRH.

34. *Ibid.*, p. 125.   35. From correspondence.

36. Pitirim A. Sorokin, *The American Sex Revolution* (Boston: Porter Sargent, 1956). Hereafter referred to as TASR.

37. *Ibid.*, p. 90.   38. SCP, p. 93.

39. *Ibid.*   40. *Ibid.*, p. 96.

41. *Ibid.*   42. *Ibid.*

43. *Ibid.*, pp. 96-7.

44. SCP, p. 98. "It is to be noted that in Sorokin's Theory of Motivations, the purposeful motivation (an action deliberately undertaken for the sake of achievement of a goal in the future) is only one of several basic motivations. A great many actions are motivated not 'for the sake of purposeful realization of a goal, but because of certain factors of the past, without any idea of a realization of a future goal. [This is his reason for rejection] of the theories of 'means and end,' of 'goals and purposes' as the universal (characteristics and motivations) 'schemas' of *all* human actions." Notes on the margins of the original draft of the manuscript for the present chapter.

45. SCP, p. 99.   46. *Ibid.*, p. 100.

47. Aristotle, *The Nicomachean Ethics* (Everyman's Library Ed., Book IX), p. 1166a.

48. SCP, p. 101.   49. *Ibid.*, p. 102, footnote.

50. *Ibid.*, p. 103.   51. *Ibid.*, p. 106.

52. *Ibid.*, p. 121.   53. *Ibid.* p. 124.

54. *Ibid.*, p. 75.   55. *Ibid.*, p. 75.

56. *Ibid.*, p. 75.   57. *Ibid.*, p. 76.

58. *Ibid.*, p. 698.   59. COA, pp. 32-3.

60. *Ibid.*, p. 31.

61. From notes on the margins of the original draft of the manuscript for the present chapter.

62. SCP, p. 47.   63. *Ibid.*, pp. 44-5.

64. *Ibid.*, p. 551.

65. From notes on the margins of the original draft of the manuscript for the present chapter.

66. SCP, pp. 321-2.   67. *Ibid.*, p. 335.

68. *Ibid.*, p. 337.

69. It is apparent that in Sorokin's view consistency is not paramount and its violation inevitable when one's material includes cultures past, present, and future, and the full sweep of world history from the grandiose to the minute. The cause of the inconsistency noted above, however, may well have its explanation in the specific time and place of Harvard in the 1930's and '40's. The senior author prepared a paper which was read as an introduction to Sorokin who presented the address at the annual banquet of the

Michigan State University chapter of AKD in 1959. The introduction was designed to honor Sorokin in a humorous but realistic sort if way. As an aside it may be noted that this introduction was submitted to the editors of the proposed *Festschrift, Reminiscences of Sorokin*, before the manuscript for the present chapter was prepared. The introduction was rejected as being "too personal" and unscientific. Nevertheless it was truthful. In it the author, coming into Cambridge from a boyhood in the ranch country, sees Sorokin and his colleagues at Harvard as the master bronc stompers. He soon saw that the aspiring bronc buster student greenhorn like himself could not foretell what mounts Sorokin would be likely to use for training the greenhorns, nor what pieces of equipment would be recommended. What the colleagues were doing had an awful lot to do with the orneriness of the mount and the equipment permitted. If status-role were a piece of equipment highly prized by a colleague master-bronc buster, almost certainly Sorokin would demonstrate that it was possible to ride just as tough a mount without benefit of this piece of equipment. As to mounts, he might ride those others could not ride: societies, cultures and civilizations, but he could and did try his hand at the mounts of colleagues (small groups, etc.) Aspiring bronco tamers may have a mimeographed copy of *Reminiscences of Sorokin* through proving the seriousness of their interest. Callouses in the proper place is the only proof needed.

70. SCP, p. 351.   71. *Ibid.*, p. 348-9.
72. *Ibid.*, p. 89, footnote 16.   73. *Ibid.*, p. 70.
74. *Ibid.*, p. 169. For the summary index of power of a system see SCD, pp. 644 and 646.
75. *Ibid.*, pp. 169-70.   76. SCP, p. 173.
77. SCD, p. 488. Obviously this formula functions in evaluation as related to or preceding decision making and its initiation into action.
78. *Ibid.*   79. *Ibid.*, pp. 446-7.
80. *Ibid.*, pp. 449-50. Here wishes as related to means for their gratification has obvious means-ends implications as well as the power implications of the concept "freedom."
81. SCP, p. 277.   82. *Ibid.*
83. *Ibid.*, p. 254.   84. *Ibid.*, p. 256.
85. *Ibid.*, pp. 260-1.   86. *Ibid.*, p. 271.
87. *Ibid.*, p. 271-2.
88. Pitirim A. Sorokin, *Social Mobility* (N. Y.: Harper and Brothers, 1927), p. 18, footnote 2. Hereafter referred to as SM.
89. SM.   90. SCP, p. 272.
91. *Ibid.*, p. 73.   92. SM, pp. 139-60.
93. *Ibid.*, p. 183.
94. SM, p. 185 (this citation appears in the text in italics).
95. Pitirim A. Sorokin, *The Sociology of Revolution* (Philadelphia: Lippincott, 1925), pp. 405 ff. Hereafter referred to as TSR.
96. *Ibid.*, pp. 493-545.   97. SCP, p. 73.
98. *Ibid.*, p. 76.   99. *Ibid.*, p. 82.
100. *Ibid.*, p. 76.
101. Pitirim A. Sorokin, *Social Philosophies of an Age of Crisis* (Boston: The Beacon Press, 1951), p. 202. Hereafter referred to as SPAC.
102. SCP, pp. 53-6.   103. *Ibid.*, p. 56.

104. *Ibid.*, p. 63.   105. *Ibid.*, pp. 58-9.

106. *Ibid.*, p. 60. The process of evaluation as understood by Sorokin may be illustrated by his treatment of "fetishization of vehicles, and its retroactive influence." *Ibid.*, pp. 60 ff. See Facilitating, below. "A given biophysical object, functioning for a considerable length of time as a vehicle of a certain meaning, norm, or value, identifies itself with it to such an extent in the minds of the subjects of interaction that it tends to become a self-sufficient value in its own right. It is often transformed into a fetish loved or respected, feared or hated, for its own sake." Material objects such as a nation's flag, and non-material symbols such as words are discussed in this connection. *Ibid.* "The picture of a saint or a national hero becomes in time endowed with the virtues of the subject and is capable of arousing strong emotions *per se.*" *Ibid.*, p. 62.

107. *Ibid.*, p. 367.   108. *Ibid.*, pp. 367-8.

109. *Ibid.*, p. 564.   110. *Ibid.*

111. *Ibid.*   112. *Ibid.*, p. 575.

113. *Ibid.*

114. *Ibid.*, p. 580. This, of course, stands in contradiction to many theories of social change such as William Ogburn's and others. Sorokin challenges what he calls the "dichotomic" theories of change and especially those that maintain that "material" culture changes and spreads more rapidly than "non-material" culture.

115. *Ibid.*, p. 355.   116. *Ibid.*, p. 382.

117. *Ibid.*, pp. 380-414.   118. *Ibid.*, p. 389.

119. *Ibid.*, p. 177.   120. *Ibid.*, p. 57.

121. *Ibid.*, p. 371.   122. *Ibid.*

123. *Ibid.*, p. 371-6.   124. *Ibid.*, p. 88.

125. SM, p. 6.

126. Pitirim A. Sorokin and Carle C. Zimmerman, *Principles of Rural-Urban Sociology* (N. Y.: Holt and Company, c1929), pp. 176-7. Hereafter referred to as PRUS.

127. PRUS, p. 20. Other differentiating features as specified were 1) Occupational, 2) Environmental, 3) Sizes of Communities, 4) Homogeneity and heterogeneity, 5) Social mobility, 6) Direction of migration, 7) Social differentiation and stratification and 8) System of interaction.

128. *Ibid.*, p. 57.   129. SCP, p. 533.

130. *Ibid.*, p. 452.   131. SM, p. 85.

132. PRUS, p. 18.   133. *Ibid.*, p. 624.

134. SCD, p. 630.   135. *Ibid.*, p. 633.

136. *Ibid.*, p. 638.   137. *Ibid.*, p. 639.

138. *Ibid.*, p. 645-6.   139. *Ibid.*, p. 649.

140. *Ibid.*, p. 674-5.

CHAPTER 8

ROBIN M. WILLIAMS, JR., ANALYST OF SOCIAL INSTITUTIONS AND SYSTEMS[*]

The extensive sociological works of Robin M. Williams are consistently based upon systemic analysis; "It is in the central tradition of sociology as a discipline to think in terms of social systems, of interconnections and interdependencies among social structures, of complex repercussions among social processes."[1] In his major theoretical work, *American Society*,[2] he essays "to analyze America as a social system."[3] The same conceptualization is used in his treatise on intergroup relations in which he emphasizes that "to be most effective, research on approaches for reducing intergroup hostility must be oriented in terms of the total social system in which it operates."[4] Williams perceives as a source of fallacious and unrealistic analyses the failure to forsee the repercussions of particular acts taking place in context, in a larger system.[5] His use of the concept "system" is generic, and thus is not limited in applicability to those phenomena which are social. The generic meaning of system, signifying a "definite arrangement of parts having boundaries, unity or cohesion, resistance to external forces, and enduring through time,"[6] is commonly encountered in the physical sciences. In Williams' view it is applicable to many levels of human behavior: to personalities,

[*] This chapter was prepared with the assistance of Robert C. Bealer as junior author.

498

relationships, groups, associations, institutions, societies, cultures,[7] of which the last three receive by far the greatest amount of attention in *American Society*.

The broadest distinction that Williams makes in analyzing society is between culture and social organization—what he calls the "culture-society coin."[8] Culture embodies many things, but of overwhelming importance for the sociologist is that part of culture which is the normative structure or system of "blueprints for behavior."[9] Social organization, in contrast, is the actual incorporation of these cultural normative standards for behavior into relations between concrete individuals whereby the expectancies of each party to the interaction become predictable.[10] Williams limits his use of the term social structure to that social action, thought and feeling which is shared by many actors, repeated in many situations, related to other patterns of the same social entity and for these reasons manifests regularity and relatedness.[11]

For purposes of sociological analyses, culture is given a normative emphasis with three components initially distinguished: values, norms, and cognitive beliefs.[12] The first refers to standards of desirability phrased in terms of good-bad, pleasant-unpleasant, appropriate-inappropriate. Norms are seen as prescriptive or proscriptive elements indicating how actors should or should not act, think and feel in various kinds of situations. Cognitive elements refer to what exists in terms of entities, causes, and consequences.[13] Cultural values, norms, and cognitive beliefs as these relate to social organization comprise the core of Williams' conceptual scheme to which this section of the present chapter is but an introduction—an attempt to give a swift overview. Williams' concept of "institutions" which in the tradition of Parsons, Sorokin and others does not neglect the personality as a system, must also be summarily introduced before an elaboration of these and other concepts is undertaken in accordance with the basic plan of the present volume (and in terms of the PAS Model).

The sense of self-respect of each individual is intimately tied to the observance of some norms more than others just as is the individual's guilt, shame, and horror differentially related to violation of these same norms. Those norms which for him are "moral imperatives" are for that individual *institutional*. Wide consensus

among a group or society about the deservedness and justification
of severe penalties upon the violation of certain norms generally
indicates a state of group or societal institutionalization for the
norms so regarded. In operation, institutional norms tend to be
relatively permanent, enforced through definite social structures,
and mutually binding on the occupants of designated social positions.[14] Furthermore, institutional norms as behavioral injunctions
are not random but related to one another in definite patterns.
Those norms which group or cohere around relatively distinct and
socially important complexes of values are referred to as "institutions." [15] Those norms, for example, which have to do with the
social relations attendant upon sexual union, the birth of children,
and care of dependent children constitute the kinship institutions
of a society just as those which are concerned with the control of
some individuals by others constitute the political institutions of
a society.[16] The main conceptual framework of *American Society*
is provided by *institutions*, which also furnish the mode of organization for that volume. Functionally important value complexes
are in turn examined: the family, social strata, economic enterprises, political, educational and religious activities as these are
represented by congeries of institutions. The interrelations among
these institutions, some in mutual conflict and some in reciprocal
consistency and support, provide the key, along with the values
and beliefs of the society, to the degree of integration which it
possesses. Williams consistently maintains an analytical distinction (much as do Parsons and Merton) between the complex of
norms which composes a given institution (the cultural) and the
concrete social organizations themselves, such as families or political parties, etc., (the social) in which social relations are "mediated through the direct person-to-person interaction of individuals
occupying differentiated statuses [status-roles]." [17]

The cultural is analytically distinct from, but dually related to
the individual and the personality system. Institutions are meaningful to individuals as sets of norms by which they know what is
expected and required. Besides orienting the individual toward
coercive "facts of the external world" institutions also become internalized values which are incorporated into the very personality
itself in the form of "conscience, life goals, preferred subjective
states of various kinds." [18] The immediate presentation will not

be concerned at this point with the institutional variations and evasions which are found by Williams to exist even in highly integrated groups and societies. Here it *is* noted, however, that by no means all of social behavior is institutionalized. Outside those zones of great functional and moral importance which are characteristically highly institutionalized, there are countless situations in which individuals interact. In these latter situations cultural content is present but in them interaction lacks the morally imperative nature which is by definition required of an institution. As such interaction is repeated over time the actors come to take into account the actions of others, and patterns emerge. Williams uses as an example the stable expectancies which permit individuals to correctly anticipate that if each walks on the right side they will be able to pass, as in going around a corner in opposite directions, without teetering in indecision. Any one stable expectancy which gives interaction a pattern is called by Williams a *social relation.* The social system is comprised of "all those social relations or complexes of relations that are clearly guided by culturally stylized rights and obligations shared by the participants." [19] *Social organization* is the embodiment of cultural norms in concrete social relations whether the norms so embodied are of the institutional type or are no more than a statement of expectancy involving no deep moral commitment.

For very general purposes—such as that of locating in the larger social framework more particular types of social relations, social systems, or groups—Williams finds merit in the classical distinction between sacred and secular social structure. Among the several variants of the basic distinction [20] Williams chooses the terms community and association and/or *Gemeinschaft* and *Gesellschaft* to express his version of the ideal types which he infrequently employs. For less general levels of analysis he finds it preferable to utilize a distinction between formal and informal organization. The characteristics of formal organization immediately suggest the prototype of the bureaucratic structure: a high degree of repetitiveness in interaction between participants; the existence of specialized roles; highly rigid regulative norms; explicit sanctions for non-conformity to norms; explicit organizational norms; a high degree of impersonality or detachment (i.e. low emotional involvement) of persons in the structure; and finally, a strong emphasis on crystallized and strong deference patterns between incumbents of the hierarchically ordered positions.[21] Alongside the formal organization there always develops an informal organization by which patterned interaction between individuals emerges which is "different from and even [at times] counter to the formal patterns." [22] Other specific classificatory variables for social organization mentioned by Williams but not elaborated, such as size, duration, accessibility and complexity will be treated below at appropriate points in the main body of this chapter.

One additional concept, that of value, must be explored in this over-all introductory section although its detailed examination will appear below under *evaluation.* So pervasive is the concept, value, that a rudimentary understanding of the meaning imputed to it by Williams will be needed throughout the analysis of his works. Values are defined by Williams as *"modes of organizing conduct*—meaningful, affectively invested pattern principles that guide human action." [23] They are real determinants of behavior, acting as the criteria by which goals (and means) are chosen among alternatives. Even though selection may be deliberate or unconscious, every act (or failure to act) costs the individual the gains he would have received from other possible courses of behavior. Values and their hierarchical arrangements thus are observable as choices; [24] they provide a means of studying all human action in a way that culture in its strict normative sense can not.

Williams suggests a number of ways in which choice can be studied. These include: 1) direct observation of natural, spontaneous behavior involving preferences (e.g. budgetary allocations); 2) inferences from amount of attention or emphasis which may be derived from many sources (e.g. from literary themes or from "hot points" in arguments); 3) the testimony of respondents of what their values are, along with attention to the implicit premises behind the explicit statements; 4) observation of the reward-punishment systems of groups. Each of these defines an operational approach to value identification and are held to give reasonable, mutually consistent results.[25]

The empirical range of values may be thought of as a continuum; at one pole would be found those intense moral values internalized by the individual and institutionalized by society. Less compelling moral values would progressively follow at points of the continuum until simple norms of expediency or technical efficiency were reached at the second pole. Following Linton, Williams views all shared values as *cultural;* those values, which, in addition to being shared, are regarded as matters of collective welfare by an effective consensus are *social* values. The social values for a complex, differentiated society are never monolithic. Whatever stability such a culture may possess must be thought of as being achieved by "a dynamic process in which a delicately balanced system of values is maintained." [26] The delineation of such a value system is the major task of *American Society.* The substantive accumulation of data concerning the major societal institutions to which more than half the book is devoted contributes enormously to the accomplishment of that task. The same empirical data should dispel any notion that Williams is interested solely in theoretical considerations. If such an image has been evoked by the unavoidable leanings in that direction so far in this chapter, it can immediately be corrected by drawing attention to his thorough going interest in action research (particularly intergroup relations),[27] his long standing identification with rural sociology which typically has had a practical orientation, and his own stated position which stipulates that good theory always has sound practical implications, just as well conceived empirical research must also yield generalizations which have significance for theory.[28]

The mutualities of fact and theory are represented admirably in the value-configurations he attributes to American society. The process by which he arrived at their delineation will emerge as his work is juxtaposed to the PAS Model, as will the similarities between what are termed elements on the PAS Model and those aspects of action designated as major value-configurations by Williams. The corresponding items are listed in Figure 1. In addition to the identification of fifteen value configurations, he includes action elements relating to them. Consequently, Figure 1 includes each of Williams' value configurations categorized with both elements and structural-functional categories from the PAS Model.

FIGURE 1

Williams' Value and Belief Configurations *	PAS Model	
	Structural-Functional Categories	*Elements having primacy*
1) Science and secular rationality	Knowing	Belief (knowledge)
2) Nationalism-patriotism 3) Humanitarian mores	Feeling	Sentiment
4) Achievement and Success 5) Material comfort 6) Activity and work 7) Progress	Achieving	Ends
8) Efficiency and practicality 9) Moral orientation 10) External conformity	Norming	Norms
11) Racism and related group-superiority themes 12) Equality 13) Individual personality	Ranking	Rank
14) Freedom 15) Democracy	Controlling	Power

* The classification is made on the basis of Williams' general use of the concepts. As Winston White has demonstrated they may be classified on various "levels of generality" and location "in the situation in the social system." See fn. 86 below. In Parsonian terms their applicability to "society, institutions, collectives, roles, and specific performances of tasks within roles" may form the basis of classification. Below in the section on utilization of facilities more specific aspects of the "configurations" are considered in relation to objects as Williams himself demonstrates it.

The fifteen value orientations in turn yield still more general "dimensions" and the corresponding processes from the PAS Model are shown on Figure 2.

Whatever injustice has been done to the breadth and import of Williams' work by the inadequacies of this brief introductory over-all view will be mitigated somewhat as his analysis is juxtaposed to the framework of the PAS Model.

FIGURE 2

WILLIAMS' VALUE ORIENTATIONS	PAS MODEL PROCESSES
1) *Active mastery* rather than *passive acceptance*	Goal attaining and concomitant "latent" activity
2) Manipulative behavior rather than contemplative; interest is focused on *external* things and events	Goal attaining activity and utilization of facilities
3) Emphasis on change, flux and movement; the world view is *open;* central personality types are adaptive, accessible, outgoing and assimilative	Systemic linkage as opposed to boundary maintenance
4) *Rationalism* rather than *traditionalism*	Cognitive mapping and evaluation
5) *Orderliness* in all phases of existence	Evaluation; in mental activity, cognitive mapping
6) *Universalism* rather than *particularism*	Evaluation
7) *"Horizontal"* or non-authoritarian as opposed to "vertical" or superordinate-subordinate relations	Allocation of status-roles; decision making and initiation of action
8) Emphasis upon *individual personality* rather than group identity and responsibility	Status-role performance and evaluation of actors

KNOWING

Belief (knowledge) as an element. One of the components of culture in Williams' conceptual scheme is "cognitive belief." Beliefs refer simply to what exists or is supposed to exist. For practical convenience Williams designates three types of belief or knowledge: that which is held to be true because of scientific confirmation, possessing high levels of probability although falling short of "certainty"; that which is believed in through ignorance and error which is subject to scientific testing but shows up as fallacious when tested; and non-empirical beliefs, such as the existence of supernatural deities or the claimed superiority of particular societies, which are not subject to scientific testing.[30]

The cognitive element is pervasive in human behavior, appearing in some manner in every behavioral prescription or norm and in every value-orientation. Each act which is to any degree normative is cognitive in that it requires of the individual that he relate himself to other entities in a certain way. Existential (and therefore cognitive) elements, attend each evaluative act. As a result, institutions as organized enactments of norm complexes and value-orientations, cannot long outlive some cultural rationale which makes actions either just or inevitable.[31]

Although belief is for Williams an analytically distinct component of culture, he recognizes that empirically, knowledge is never distinctly separable from sentiment.

Men classify entities and events as sacred and profane, with many complicated intershadings between the two; the sacred is not necessarily a separate class of phenomena, but is part of a continuum ranging from the purely technological, through the conventional, aesthetic, and moral over to those orientations of high seriousness in which religion is to be found. Religion deals with "sacred things" that are objects of nonempirical ideas and of intense moral respect.[32]

The actor's orientation to the situation is influenced by his nonempirical as well as by his empirical beliefs. The religious aspects of a society must be grasped for an understanding of that society.[33] Religion is uniquely preoccupied with the problems of meaning and the concomitant emphasis upon the ultimate ends of conduct.[34] In the functional tradition, Williams examines the relation of religious belief to other social phenomena: inevitable death, limited control of nature, unjust rewards such as prosperity and fortune which occasionally come to the violator of moral standards. Individuals ask for meanings which help them to cope with problems of deep emotional significance; they search as well for some ultimate "why" for existence. More than many other analysts, however, he proceeds beyond these rather negative reasons for the existence of religious belief to emphasize that not only in times of crisis and ill-fortune but in the ups and downs of daily life, a positive value attached to living and a certainty of ultimate goodness are sustained for many individuals by their religious beliefs.[35] Whether a reaction to the tragic or a reinforcement of vital life forces, "In so far as religion represents a complex of ultimate value-orientations, it can never be a neutral factor in social integration. Every functioning society has, to an important degree, a *common* religion." [36]

Religious attitudes and moral attitudes are not identical. Some religious beliefs emphasize a mystical communion with a transcendental deity to the relative exclusion of ethical norms which prescribe man's relations to other men. Others, such as the Judaic-Christian religion comprise a fusion of religion and social morality. In either case, a man's religious belief bears some relation to his norms for social behavior. The Judaic-Christian belief, for example, initially held that all souls are equal before God. Equality of rights was not a part of the original notion, but equality before God lends support to the extended idea of the worth of the individual, humanitarian ideals and various philosophies of human equality.[37]

If one conceives of religious beliefs as ultimate for people committed to them, then differences in religious belief are not amenable to compromise or resolution.[38] Intrinsic religion must not be confused with churches or other organized religious groups which are often distinguishable on grounds other than a common belief in the nature of the ultimate. Science as a faith or set of beliefs (though not necessarily as the organized structure through which the beliefs are actualized) may be a religion to some in that it represents ultimate value. "The long history of the 'warfare of science and theology' " [39] attests to its high resistance to compromise. Beliefs about racial or ethnic or societal superiorities and inferiorities may or may not be religious beliefs, and beliefs held by organized religious bodies are variable in the degree to which they are intrinsically religious.

The products of applied empirical knowledge (i.e. the products of technology) are important in their own right, but not nearly so important in net impact on behavior as is the unique orientation to problems furnished by science as a mode of thought.[40] Williams endorses the observation of the physicist Henry Margenau that "Our culture has the outstanding property of striving to convert all experience into rational scientific knowledge." [41] The process of translating experience into systematic abstract concepts is one method by which cognitive mapping takes place.

Cognitive mapping and validation as process. There is, according to Williams, a "tendency in our culture to translate experience into systematic abstract concepts—to transform the fleeting, confused flow of immediate experience into standardized categories that permit, and in part create, prediction and control." [42] The standardized categories into which experiences are pigeon-holed may represent the generalizations of scientific thought arrived at only by "systematic diligence and honesty" and exacting the painful price of the renunciation of previously cherished beliefs. Or the standardized categories of experience, appropriately symbolized, may represent rationalizations by which validity is imputed to beliefs in accordance with the vested interests of the individual (or group). Williams' major work offers a wide array of examples of cognitive mapping, the relations which exist between ways of appraising reality and the value-orientations of the actors, and the compensations made in one set of beliefs when another equally compelling set of beliefs presents conflicts. Williams' strategy of analysis of belief, cognitive mapping and validation follows the same pattern he uses for value, sentiment, norm, and so on. By examining the belief constellations of six major American institutions and by noting the mutualities among them (and by following the same procedure for the other constituents of culture) he gradually amasses his evidence for the over-arching values of American society depicted on Figures 1 and 2. The immediate purposes of this section will be served by examining only a selected few of the many examples he gives of beliefs in process of formation, change, or confirmation.

How do parents in modern American society justify the succession of child-rearing beliefs which they sequentially practice as the fads of child training shift? Williams reminds the reader that unlike most young mothers throughout the experience of the human race, the young American mother of the mobile nuclear family is likely to face child-rearing armed only with inadequate memories of her own childhood and cut off from the stabilizing contacts with another generation of parents. "Both [parents] have absorbed something of the general ethos of respect for rationality, practicality, scientific methods, and thus they tend to seize upon the latest pronouncements of the presumed experts in order to gain some sense of dependability and security." [43] Here what are presumed to be scientific methods of validation are being used, although the users may not be sufficiently sophisticated in the disciplines of science to make adequate judgments about what scientific validation really is.

The kind of cognitive mapping which tends to conserve the status quo and the kind of validation which tends to justify the existing order is exemplified by data concerning the institutions attending stratification. Following Useem, Williams reports that "Persons in the locally recognized upper strata, as compared with persons from the levels of least prestige were . . . more likely to attribute high rank to personal excellence and to give quasi-biological explanations for the existence of low-status groupings." [44] According to national studies by The American Institute of Public Opinion, used by Williams, the individuals in the low-status groupings however, sized up their own comparative rating quite differently in response to identity with "lower class" as compared to identity with "working class." [45] The symbolic meaning of "lower class" and its importance for cognitive mapping is demonstrated by the avoidance of self identification with the "lower class" by all except eight per cent of respondents. The quite different symbolic meaning of "working class" and its importance in cognitive mapping is equally apparent as self identification with "working class" was accepted as valid by fifty-one per cent of respondents. At the introduction of the "working class" category into the study of self appraisal the middle class shrank from eighty-seven per cent to forty-three per cent. Concerning stratification in general, Williams concludes that "[There would seem to exist] a pervasive, meaningfully interconnected set of 'folk doctrines' that explain and justify the existing order. Into this category seem to fall—to take only a limited sample of items—belief in equality of opportunity and the correlated beliefs that tend to equate ability and reward, the popular prestige of economic success, and the whole complex that we call 'individual responsibility.'" [46]

Validation of presently held beliefs by simply ignoring some of the pertinent facts is indicated as Americans perceive differential power: ". . . there is a common tendency, perhaps especially in American thought, to slur over or minimize the great historical significance of coercive power. The facts of how the strong tend to behave toward the weak are bitter medicine for a people who believe in the "consent of the governed." [47] The same situation holds with respect to the judiciary. "In view of these [contradictory] facts, it is impressive that the courts, and especially the Supreme Court, are widely regarded as endowed with detachment and infallibility. And to the extent that this belief prevails the stability of the state is supported through faith in the continuing judiciary." [48]

In any case the thought process of individuals in situations are influenced by prejudgments arrived at in earlier experiences and which appear to be similar to those presently faced. These prejudgments are the essence of prejudice, an area of investigation to which Williams contributes substantially, especially as he undertakes to discover the basic reasons for inter-group hostilities and possible methods of their reduction. Prejudice, as one manifestation of the human ability to form general concepts, has characteristics which distinguish it from other manifestations of the ability to generalize: 1) the prejudgment of individuals involves negative attitudes violating norms or values of import which are given nominal cultural acceptance [49] and, 2) the basis of prejudgment is not formulated upon "functional position in the social order or real differences in values" but instead centers on "symbols such as skin color which have no intrinsic functional importance." [50] Essentially, then, prejudice involves an overgeneralized conception with attached affect. The overgeneralized conception is what is meant by the term "stereotype."

Williams suggests that the products of the initial process of classification by which the child identifies both self and others may represent "fundamental psychological dispositions" which would mean that prejudice may be "not a set of isolated attitudes but rather a functional part of a total personality system" [51]—the bold hypothesis of *The Authoritarian Personality*.[52] Various researches support the view that the rigid personality applies by rote standardized modes of action and belief to variant nonrelated conditions to which the standardized modes are inapplicable. Some situations offer more alternative paths to action and hence require that more effort be devoted to cognitive mapping than others if the outcome is to be in line with the most general norms. It is in such situations that personality determinants may play the greatest part in determining action—situations, for example, which are not clearly defined by prior social norms, and situations defined as calling for behavior which is functionally diffuse, particularistic, and affective.[53] The more structured the situation and the more instrumental the behavior deemed appropriate to the situation, the more important social determinants become in its interpretation. Although neither personality nor social factors can be precisely related to the prejudiced appraisal of a situation, Williams argues that stereotypes and prejudices can be broken more effectively by changing the attitudes of groups than of isolated individuals.[54] Whatever the process of apprehending reality, "it must be always kept in mind that these themes, values, and systems of belief *do not operate as single and separate units* but *are in continually shifting and recombining configurations* marked by very complex interpenetration, conflict, and reformulation." [55]

FEELING

Sentiment as an element. Whether or not Williams can be said to single out sentiment as a separate conceptual tool becomes an academic question in light of his frequent use of sentiment as a variable of human behavior.[56] Furthermore his basic task in *American Society* of isolating the commonly held values from among the seeming welter of variously held attitudes, beliefs, and ideas insures that the affective component will be frequently encountered. It is in connection with a definition of value that the most outright acknowledgement for the need of the concept sentiment is encountered:

What are experienced by individuals as values have these qualities: (1) They have a conceptual element—they are more than pure sensations, emotions, reflexes, or so-called needs. Values are abstractions drawn from the flux of the individual's immediate experience. (2) They are affectively charged: they represent actual or potential emotional mobilization.[57]

The importance of the component, sentiment, is nicely illuminated by the inclusion of "tension" in the very title of his now classic 1947 monograph,[58] and by such succinct passages as: "Instru-

mental behavior is expressive behavior 'in harness,' and we well
know which comes first in any life history." [59] "Love of country"
is noted as a sentiment which is particularly strong in the United
States. As reflected in public opinion polls, by the low percentage
of citizens who wish to live outside the country, only Australians
appear to exceed Americans in the intensity of this sentiment.[60]

An enumeration of the kinds of sentiments—the loyalties, hostilities, affinities, conflicts and so on, which play their part in social
interaction as analyzed by Williams is not necessary for present
purposes which can be better served by elaborating instead on
the process by which potential tension is averted and actual tension is reduced. To do so will, *ipso facto*, identify to a degree the
elemental components of sentiments involved in the tensions. The
same dual purpose will also be accomplished by treatment of
communication of sentiment.

*Tension management and communication of sentiment as proc-
esses.* Each of the institutional patterns examined by Williams
exhibits abundant examples of conditions which create tension as
well as compensating features which are interpreted as reducing
strain. Only a selective representation of these can be dealt with
here. Many of these reinforce Williams' position as a functional
analyst. Of the various explanations of the universality of the
incest taboo Williams selects as the most promising the function
of the taboo in preventing potentially disruptive sexual conflicts
within the kinship group. Besides minimizing intra-family sexual
conflicts in America he sees the taboo as performing the additional
function of making the society "more diffuse and mobile by a marriage system tending to establish kinship relations cross-cutting
segmentary local groups." [61] An American pattern of considering
the husband-wife pair as a unit and thus as social equals in many
respects prevents a serious strain upon the marriage bond. "It is
not a trivial matter of 'mere convention' or 'manners' that in the
typical middle-class, urban community, if either spouse is invited
to a mixed 'social' gathering, the other spouse must be likewise
invited." [62] . . . The solidarity engendered by being identified as a
unit and by sharing common experiences is of paramount importance in a kinship system of dispersed, multilineal nature built
around the marriage bond.[63]

The clashes of interest between various economic groupings

in America have been frequent enough, but few conflicts have been genuine *class* conflicts. Williams seeks to locate the points of strain between the different strata and then discover what "alleviating factors or 'compensations'" he assumes must be operative in view of the relative lack of violent class struggle. Among the countervailing forces which help to manage inter-class tensions are nominally equal legal and political rights even though these are imperfectly institutionalized, the accessibility of public facilities and services, and the prevalence of equalitarian symbols and behavior patterns. The latter, Williams suspects, may be of much greater importance than might appear at first glance. He argues that the prevalence of "democratic" manners

. . . minimizes demands for deference and thereby makes it possible to an important degree for less privileged members of the society to avoid continual reminders of status differences in contexts where intense emotions might otherwise be aroused. It is our hypothesis, therefore, that equalitarian symbols and behavior patterns are not inconsequential "illusions" that simply "mask the real class struggle" but rather that they have a tangible cushioning effect upon interpersonal relations between persons of different station in the stratification scale.[64]

There is an insulation of classes by which visiting patterns, friendship groups and marriages are more or less confined within a given class thereby providing "buffers and barriers to relationships that contain the possibility of serious conflict." [65] At the same time impersonal activities of a functionally specific nature and often representing common interests unrelated to class distinctions, provide opportunities for contact on neutral grounds. Finally, the apparently growing emphasis upon "fortuitous success: the 'lucky break,' the '$64 question,' the unexpected opportunity, the inspired idea, the winning number . . . [is significant in] that it decisively sunders reward from achievement and personal excellence . . . if success and failure are thought to depend upon essentially accidental factors, neither the individual nor the social system itself can be perceived as the source of deprivation and malaise." [66]

Williams notes that the affective neutrality so widely attributed to industrial bureaucracies as a means of channeling sentiment is not unlike that which prevails in schools where the norms of impartiality, formal equality and a degree of social distance have tension reducing significance. By the minimization of personal attractions and antipathies, conditions disruptive to learning are controlled and the vulnerability of the teacher on matters outside his realm of authority is reduced.[67]

As was seen above, religious institutions are in part concerned with providing assurances for those features of life which are inherently tension producing and affectively loaded. "The fires of religion glow most intensely in the blast of collective terror, deprivation, and social disorganization." [68] Dogma, theology, the intermediate symbolism of death ceremonies, the Catholic confessional and ritual absolution plus similar other specific techniques and arrangements represent tension managing mechanisms. The degree to which different religious persuasions provide for the release of affect bears an instructive corollary with the apparent needs for such release by the communicants:

. . . the most prosperous, stable, and secure groupings tend to be characterized by formalistic religious practices and lack of overt fervor. Seriously deprived, frustrated, or oppressed groups, having no major realistic control of their situation, tend to produce sects and cults with a proliferation of emotional religious observances, especially if there is a free religious structure. The formal patterns of a universally established church can strongly inhibit and channelize such religious activity, born of desperation and alienation.[69]

Williams turns his attention from tensions and their management within any one institutional constellation in the American scene to those which emerge as the relative isolation of diverse subcultures are inevitably linked and as interinstitutional conflicts exert disruptive influences upon those individuals who subscribe to plural institutional patterns.

. . . what were at first *conflicts between the standards of different groups* tend to become *intrapersonality conflicts* for the individual. It is in part through this specific dynamic mechanism that a "strain for consistency" is set up in the total culture.[70]

In those many instances where consistency of the individual's incorporated ethics and his social realities is not established, the torn individual "may resolve the conflict by developing a militant reform mentality or becoming 'cynical'—we often suspect that the self-styled cynic is a highly moral person who is reacting to loss of faith in the efficacy of his code. Often ideals are insulated from action or restricted to limited groups and narrowly circumscribed situations." [71]

What Williams labels "cultural fictions" become helpful mechanisms. He concurs with Woodward's suggestion that formality, protocol, and conventionalization are at their peak when the maintenance of interaction is important, when the ties between the participants are few and weak, and when severe conflict of interests or values is the substance of the interaction. "Examples include diplomatic convention, military courtesy, much of etiquette, academic decorum, judicial procedures," [72] all of which may be termed not hypocrisy but functional deviousness.

Related to formality and protocol, but of a somewhat different order, are those tension-producing items which are resolved by withdrawing them from general social circulation as is expressed in such maxims as "never argue about religion or politics." Such controversial matters are reserved for discussion among intimately known and like-minded people, although Williams notes that this implies that "agreement on procedure has dominated over disagreement on other values." [73]

Other strains may develop as value emphases are changed even if the values themselves do not change, leaving some individuals dedicated to the earlier normative patterns. The increased amount of leisure time, the greater number of creature comforts and the wider availability of services may be enjoyed fully only by those who have relinquished somewhat the high evaluation of asceticism and have modified the future-time orientation of the Puritan ethos. Those who have not modified their evaluations of the goodness of work and their ideals of present sacrifice for future reward will tend to have guilt and ambivalence about leisure and comfort. [74]

Other tensions wrought by change arise from the transition from a *Gemeinschaft*-like to a *Gesellschaft*-like society with its dissolution of older patterns of group interaction and its impoverishment of stable, reoccurring interaction patterns. "Group membership in a Rotary club may seem radically different from membership in the American rural neighborhood of a half-century ago, but the loss of the latter has been a tangible factor in the growth of the former." [75] Williams sees the familistic and com-

munal symbols and creeds of a plethora of associations in the
United States as designedly contrasting to the functionally specific
and affectively neutral relations so prevalent in many of the major
institutional relations. A sense of community and a feeling of belongingness is to some extent provided by the wide array of organizations which Americans join in large numbers.

Williams notes a well-defined pattern of "withdrawal, alienation, entrance, and assimilation" as individuals are confronted
with vertical occupational mobility, or with transitions of residential mobility.

The very casualness, specificity, and impersonality of public contacts,
we may suggest, tends to insulate individuals from many conceivably
traumatic consequences of unpredictability and misplaced expectations. Rigidity or flexibility, stability or change, predictability or its
lack—these are, after all, *relative* notions. The most important fact,
within quite wide limits, may not be the absolute amount of instability
or change, but the range of the expectable zone of variation. In so far
as individuals in our society have been prepared to discount a marked
degree of change and variation, their reduced expectations of performance and stability permit acceptance and support of a society of
"becoming" rather than "being." [76]

For research investigators in the field of intergroup relations
as well as for many social workers the monograph, *The Reduction
of Intergroup Tensions* is considered as more or less a handbook
for reduction of potential tension as well as tension management.
Likewise, the article reviewing studies on "Racial and Cultural
Relations" reports findings of importance for investigators and
workers in the field. Much of the content of the two works is
particularly pertinent to this present section, but much of it quite
understandably overlaps the treatment of the same subject as it
appears in *American Society.* They are called to the attention of
those for whom the subject has particular interest for the many
additional ideas which are either omitted in the present treatment
or at best, only touched upon. For example, Williams posits an
inverse relation between amount of hostility and the number and
adequacy of "harmless outlets" for aggression which do not violate
the major norms of the social system. In the United States such
outlets as competitive sports, swearing, joking, some uses of alco-

hol, drama and pageantry are indicated as falling in this class.[77]

Hostile and prejudiced groups under some circumstances are reinforced in their attitudes by criticisms of their prejudice. When strong prejudice is present in a group which is highly self-conscious, and strongly bound together, outside criticism of its prejudice is likely to strengthen the prejudice, which by virtue of the attack becomes a symbol of in-group membership and solidarity.[78] Exposure to the group toward which hostility is expressed, however, tends to modify the stereotyped attitude.

Even in discordant or "prejudiced" interaction which, for any cause, is continued over a considerable span of time, the participants mutually come to have increased concern for one another: the relationship grows in salience and importance . . . affective attitudes will become increasingly differentiated, complex, and organized; that is, cognitive, cathectic, and evaluative orientations become richer, more dense, more elaborately structured . . . processes . . . [that] tend to modify or dissolve previously held rigid and affectively gross stereotypes.[79]

ACHIEVING

End, goal, or objective as an element. Williams occasionally analyzes social behavior in terms of the means-ends schema; none the less the relatively infrequent usage perhaps reflects the many reservations he has about the clarity of its meaning and the precision with which goal as a concept, is helpful in distinguishing for him what he wants to know. The greatest danger of ambiguity in Williams' view, lies in the possible blurring of meaning of the terms goal and value. When value is used, as it often is, to signify some object of regard, some item which in itself is thought of highly, it comes close to meaning what is better conveyed by the word goal. Williams specifies that value refers to the *criteria* by which goals are chosen, the *standards* of judgment by which the object or the item is bequeathed the regard in which it is held. Once understood, it is immediately apparent why the concept goal is of limited utility for his purposes.

What these standards are is not immediately given to us by knowing the goals men seek, the ideologies they profess, or the gross preferences they exhibit in conduct. To know that a man seeks, say money or success tells us next to nothing about the *criteria* in terms of which these goals are judged worthwhile.[80]

The distinction between an evaluated object (in some ways similar to goal) and the criteria by which value is imputed to the object appears in both editions of *American Society* but it is one of the few points which has been greatly elaborated in the second edition, from which the conclusion may be drawn that the expanded treatment [81] represents Williams' most recent thinking on what he regards as an important distinction. The second edition, however, which reduces the ambiguities by definitional and expository precision, continues in a number of instances to carry *usages* by which the word value would seem from the context to mean not the criteria and standards which it is definitionally supposed to mean but the object itself which is held in high regard. For example, he identifies such items as wealth, power, work, efficiency as interests which "may become values in themselves (but) it is convenient to consider them primarily as instrumental to the achievement of other values." [82] At another point almost the same list of items, in this case wealth, power, and prestige are referred to forthrightly as goals: "Emphasis [may be placed] on the goals of wealth, power, and prestige. . . ." [83] It is this latter use which is consistent with the expanded exposition of the second edition, and consistent too with Williams' intent in regard to the value-goal complex.[84] Williams concurs [85] with a judgment made by Winston White [86] that the value configurations of Figure 1 and the value orientations of Figure 2 represent varying levels of abstraction within each set and that not all of the set in Figure 1 may be subsumed under the categories of Figure 2. Some of the categories such as manipulative behavior and universalism of Figure 2 represent dominant values of *American Society,* whereas other categories refer to more specific ends, or other elements. Thus "achievement, activity, humanitarian mores and efficiency are concerned with valuation of individuals in roles or in performance of tasks." [87] As such these categories represent various elements in the PAS Model, and they have been arranged in Figure 1 in terms of the primacy of the context within which Williams uses them in his writing. In terms of the present section achievement and success, material comfort, and activity and work seem to require that they be related to a goal of some sort.

Williams supplies definitions for the value-goal concepts as they are applied on the one hand to separate individuals who comprise a group, and on the other to the collectivity:

"group value" is an ambiguous term that may refer either to (a) a *shared* goal, as when "getting ahead" (as individuals) represents a value-complex held in common throughout the group, or (b) a desired state *for* the group taken collectively (as military security may be so regarded). A "group goal" we may define as a future state of affairs intended to be reached by group (collective) action. ("Intended" means either explicitly stated, or inferred, by an observer.) Thus a group goal is *not* necessarily identical, or even congruent, with the values, motives, or goals of individual members considered distributively.[88]

Despite these operational difficulties, Williams frequently uses the concept, goal or end. "*Some* human behavior, at least, is purposive: people can and do state their goals in advance and can then be observed to act as if they were in fact pursuing those ends. Objects, events, experience are desired and sought out, or are eschewed or avoided." [89] One of the central characteristics of associational (or *Gesellschaft*-like) relations is the relative ease by which the goal can be isolated and separated sharply from the norm (and other elements of the PAS Model). "In communal relations, on the contrary, the main emphasis is upon the relation itself and the personalities and other values directly activated in it." [90] Williams finds it useful to distinguish between short-run and long-run goals, and typically, seeks to identify the broader value implicit in the distinction. To the degree that practicality is valued—and in the American society "the practical man is the good man, an embodiment of a major value" [91]—the adjustments made tend to be short range, the goals sought to be those immediately attainable, the problems solved those pertaining to a given situation. Practicality with its emphasis upon immediate short term goals presupposes other values: "For instance, it typically assumes the worth of the basic social order within which action occurs." [92] Besides defining the nature of the immediate ends practicality is one of the guiding criteria for arranging ends into a hierarchy of value. If action were to be directed toward a single value or end, logically all other considerations except the achievement of that end become irrelevant such as exemplified by the

fanatic, the hedonist, or "the monomaniacal economic man." [93]
Such single-purposed activity is not the result when practicality
has been the guiding principle in arranging priorities. There occurs instead a "rational weighting of values in a pluralistic framework . . ." [94]

Obviously, the institutional complexes which yield the most
clear-cut ends are those which are *Gesellschaft*-like or associational in type of interaction. Williams' discussion of kinship institutions, for example, relies upon the concept goal a good deal
less than his discussion of economic institutions. He sees as one
of the social mechanisms controlling economic activity the "influence of *common cultural goals,* which may be collective aims
such as military victory, or distributive goals such as profit making." [95]

The rise of the corporation in *American Society* and changes
through the years concerning the privileges and responsibilities
of that legal entity emerge from Williams' treatment of it as a
societal device specifically invented to further the national goal
of production; although the distributive goal of a given business
corporation is profit-making: "it must meet the test of rational
capital accounting or go out of business." [96] Technical apparatus
and materials, human labor, and "organization" are the means
"whereby the efforts of large numbers of persons are integrated
toward corporate objectives." [97] The large number of persons
whose efforts are so integrated do not normally include, however,
wage workers and "salaried officialdom" who are motivated only
indirectly by profits.

The separation of ownership from control shows that the "profit motive" is not a *motive* at all but an institutional goal; it is not a psychological state but a social condition. The fully developed corporate
form today is likely to be manned by people with goals and incentives
not so different from those of the personnel of nonprofit organizations.
This fact is not envisaged in the traditional theories of property and
economic incentives, and neither the law nor popular thought has yet
come to terms with its implications. [98]

In contrast to the economic institutions with instrumental means
sharply differentiated from ends is the most prominent of the
political institutions, the *state.*

It seems impossible to gain any clear notion of what the state might usefully mean by considering only the ends to which it is devoted. There is hardly any human interest that some political association that we would be forced to recognize as a state has not undertaken to further; hardly a collective activity for which some state at some time has not taken responsibility.[99]

Whether the political activity be that of the state or of any other organization Williams sees political conflict, real or potential, as arising directly out of the pursuit by a large number of human beings of goals which by their nature can only be realized by a few. "Even if the goals or ends of individuals are compatible, there is still the possibility of conflict over the means used. Above all, other human individuals are always potential means for the attainment of any one person's goals,"[100] and thus is the concept of power, which is the very stuff of politics, related to ends. In a heterogeneous society such as that of the United States, consensus upon common ends is very difficult to achieve. A number of factors combine in the American case to produce effective agreement on broad procedural questions in politics, so that political method may represent a consensus even when ends are nonconsensual. Political method, specifically the essence of political democracy has acquired "the status of ends" in its own right.[101] While it is important, in order to understand the political institutions, generally to identify the various pressure and interest groups and be aware of their goals—a subject about which Williams tells a great deal in a small space—it is also well to be aware that some representatives in the national government at least some of the time place general welfare ends before territorial ends [102] and that some pressure groups take broader view of goal than the immediate self-interest of those they represent.[103]

In American schools as in politics there is no unequivocal end to which all schools are dedicated. Education, whether in the American scene or elsewhere, is variously undertaken to preserve a static culture, to produce and maintain a ruling class, to develop a liberal elite, to instill religious principles, to produce technological and vocational skills, and to inculcate humanistic traits.[104] There is no agreement from school district to school district concerning the emphases given to these goals and their derivatives, but given the frontier background of America and its business civilization, certain specific educational products taken as end types, are *not* indicated: for example, the scholar (except possibly for the religious leader), and the gentleman (in the classic tradition).[105]

Some of the goals of religious institutions were necessarily implied in the foregoing sections on beliefs and sentiment. It must be enough to indicate here that the conception of religion as an ultimate end is often reversed by pragmatic Americans who frequently interpret religion as a means to an end, to the end for example, of "morality, peace and order, and worldly success." [106]

Before passing to goal attaining activity as process it may be noted that Williams in his early studies of minority group relations considered the determination of group goals as first order business. Observing that a gain in status or rank on the part of one group may be at the expense of short run harmony he observes: "Research on the control of intergroup tensions requires as a first step an analysis of the underlying *goals* . . . upon which action is predicated." [107]

Goal attaining and concomitant "latent" activity as process. Williams raises the question whether "success" (usually an accumulation of money or prestige) constitutes goal-attaining in the popular mind, or whether goal-attainment demands that a level of achievement (i.e. accomplishment) by normatively acceptable methods be demonstrated. If emphasis is on success the norms for its evaluation are applied to the rewards. If emphasis is upon achievement the norms for evaluation are applied to the action with emphasis on conformity with norms for goal attaining. Williams concludes that although in the United States, the successful person is often regarded as the goal-attaining person even though there be no correlation between success and moral virtue

. . . yet the success pattern is still linked to achievement, achievement is still associated with work, and work is still invested with an almost organic complex of ethical values. Thus, success is still not a primary criterion of value in its own right, but rather a derivative reward *for* active, instrumental performance.[108]

Should, however, the importance of "getting yours" by whatever means possible become the paramount way of goal achievement, most effective normative regulation is thereby negated and (as in Merton's paradigm for anomie) the pressures toward deviation are immediately apparent.[109] There is a long standing expectation in America that virtue will be rewarded and similarly, that effort will end in achievement. Those who do not achieve goals are very likely to be charged, therefore, with lack of virtue or lack of effort, or both, while those who do achieve "find it expedient to justify their position in the name of 'service' and 'steward-ship.'"[110]

Although it would indeed be difficult to establish that everyone who achieves is either overly-virtuous or industrious, "achievement is difficult to index." With few traditional, hereditary symbols of accomplishment, the symbols of business achievement are very often applied quite generally; "there is a strong tendency to use money as a symbol of success."[111]

The patterns of activity which are pursued toward the attainment of the goal are too diverse and detailed to be recounted from Williams' explorations of the various institutions which provide the basis of his study. Also the goal attaining activities of both economic and political institutions have a strong power component which can more appropriately be treated under that subject below. However, some of his perceptions concerning latent functions (whether or not they involve latent goal-directed activities) are worthy of note, for they provide evidence concerning activities supposedly directed toward the fulfillment of a goal characteristic of one set of institutions while actually contributing toward the goal-fulfillment characteristic of a different set of institutional groupings.

The manifest goal of building codes is to protect public health, safety and convenience. In actual operation, some state and municipal codes minimize competition and protect favored positions among contractors and craft unions. Likewise, sanitary regulations, inspection requirements, and safety provisions turn out with noteworthy frequency to be means of co-ordinating economic action or centralizing control. For example, the requirement that milk be pasteurized led quite directly to the growth of giant milk distributing firms, primarily because large capital is required for effective operation of pasteurizing plants.[112]

Or, in the quite different field of educational institutions:

Much of what the school teaches is incidental to its explicit aims and goals. Perhaps few schools explicitly "indoctrinate for conformity" although "character development" and "education for citizenship" frequently are pseudonyms for instruction that in fact, if not in intent, produces generalized acquiescence to established authority and convention. But any education must educate for conformity to *something* —a point that certain educational theorists in the United States seem never to have admitted.[113]

In an association of complex and interdependent parts each part may typically be working toward the achievement of rather particularized goals the sum total of which adds up to an over-arching goal which is seldom aimed at by many of the smaller units which comprise the whole. Williams cites the example of the university, an important part of which is comprised of administrators whose goal achieving activities might variously be represented by increasing the size of the student body, by improving the financial resources or by winning athletic contests. The university's manifest aim—the transmission and creation of knowledge is not automatically brought closer to achievement by budget increases which do, however, make it possible to procure better faculty and better research facilities. As students are better trained a body of alumni is formed for whom high academic standards are the criteria by which university prestige is judged. Williams notes that:

A general principle is here illustrated: participants in systems of social action can contribute to achievement of the goals of the system without necessarily or even typically consciously working toward those goals. Indeed, the accomplishment of such goals appears to depend upon the mobilization of a variety of particularized goals that are seldom identical with the manifest ends of the total system.[114]

A glance at Figures 1 and 2 in light of this discussion, both at end as an element and at goal attaining as process, will reveal that goal in either its elemental or processual form is not strictly limited to the corresponding items as shown on the Figures. As Winston White observes some items such as freedom and individual personality assume plurality of goals whereas moral orientation assumes commitment to ends and other elements of systems.[115] Williams gives some attention to the idea that new goals are to a degree generated out of the fulfillment of previously held ends. Thus, "at least in Western societies, the objective opportunity to secure material comforts elicits, in the long run, a desire for them." [116] What at first were incidental outcomes of goal achieving can in turn become manifest motives and thus represent changes in value structure. The fiercely religious Calvinistic grandfather can find the ownership of his company in the hands of his devoutly a-religious and comfort oriented grandson.

NORMING, STANDARDIZING, AND PATTERNING

Norm as an element. For Williams "A norm is a standard (not necessarily explicit) of the course that action *should* follow, not a description of action that actually occurs." [117] Among the areas governed by norms is the definition of allowed and disallowed goals and the means of reaching the goals. From among the normative zones so demarked, values indicate a basis for preference within the zone by furnishing criteria to the individual or to the group by which the more desirable or less desirable may be chosen. Thus a wide range of goals may be normatively approved as worthy of striving for, but values determine the actual choice among them. Cultural norms vary tremendously in emphasis from such moral imperatives as "thou shalt not kill" to technical norms such as how to cook an egg.[118] Norms may vary by universality of acceptance as valid guides to action, universality of application in a given population, the mode of enforcement, the explicitness of the norm, the specificity of the injunction, and the rigidity or flexibility of exact conformity.[119]

Institutional norms, or those which are felt to be moral imperatives and are thus closely identified with the individual's sense of self-respect, may be illustrated by the widely accepted prohibitions against murder, treason, cannibalism and rape. Some norms may be institutional for certain sectors of the society and not for society as a whole. Therefore, if society is the referent, it is necessary to specify the degree of consensus with which sanctions are accepted in supporting an institutional norm. The tendency for institutional norms to cluster around functionally imperative societal activities has already been mentioned both in the introductory section of this chapter as well as in the elements and processes thus far examined. In operation, institutional norms tend to be relatively permanent, enforced through definite social structures, and mutually binding on the occupants of designated social positions.[120]

Even in highly integrated groups norms are not uniformly actualized in behavior. Moral norms are characteristically of a generalized nature, whereas the situations which are the context for social behavior are specific. Translation of the moral injunction is required and this is subject to personal variability. There are differences in perception and interpretation of a given situation as to whether it is covered by a certain type of moral directive. In many instances nominally accepted norms are too stringent for full conformity.[121] Finally, in any pluralistic society there are different subcultures with incompatible moral demands. The process by which norms are actually articulated in social behavior is treated here under evaluation.

Evaluation as a process. What is termed evaluation as a process on the PAS Model denotes only some aspects of what by Williams' broader term is designated as value. It is therefore appropriate, at the risk of some repetition, to explore more fully than heretofore, the concept of evaluation as a derivative of value which latter, of course, is Williams' dominant theme.

At times Williams distinguishes between norms and values, as, for instance, in setting out the components of culture.[122] More often they are merged just as in many places ends are merged with values. In the last analysis, however, values are the broader element for Williams since "the initial location of value [is] in *a relation of a person to an object of interest.*" [123] Of the qualities characteristic of values which have already been considered in this chapter (the cognitive, the affective, and the criteria-bearing) it is the latter which must be given primacy in any consideration of evaluation. It has already been shown that within variously demarked zones, norms exist from which individuals select their goals, their means, their ways of interacting with others in empirical situations. The process of choice by which some goals are selected over others as being more desirable, by which some means are acknowledged to be both effective and appropriate while others are deemed perhaps effective but inappropriate, by which some kinds of interpersonal relations are judged more satisfying than others demands that criteria be applied. Williams has suggested a number of ways by which choice can be studied, ways which appeared in the introduction of this chapter but which may be reviewed here as being based upon: 1) direct observation; 2) inferences from amount of attention and emphasis; 3) testimony of respondents; and 4) observation of sanctions application. As he applies these methods to the American scene a bewildering array of choices are seen to occur even within any one constellation of institutions. Neither family members nor business men, nor individuals of a given social stratum, nor religious communicants nor educators universally apply the same criteria in the same way to the situations with which they are faced. Some values more than others, however, exhibit persisting importance through time; some more than others are extensive in terms of the number of people who adhere to them as well as the number of situations in which they are evoked; some more than others are intensively sought (and severe sanctions imposed upon those who do not seek them); and some more than others were found to represent the modes of choice found in the study of prestigeful cultural heroes.[124] The dominant values thus extracted from the almost endless currents and cross-currents of choice-making appear in Figures 1 and 2. Hence, all are in some sense evaluative, but a few have greater evaluative primacy in terms of choice between normative directives which is the essence of the evaluations being considered here. "Value-belief clusterings" of special pertinence here are what Williams calls moral orientations, external conformity, and efficiency-practicality. Such themes as equality, freedom, democracy, and racism-group superiority are clearly evaluative on a normative basis too, but to the extent that they emphasize power and/or rank they can be most appropriately considered under those sections below.

Moral orientation is the most general evaluative criterion. It refers, for Williams, to a particular kind of ethical quality in the total cultural outlook. It is the tendency to test conduct against systematic ethical principles which transcend expediency or immediate utility. It does not mean mere conformity to specific prescriptions although the evaluative outcome is to assign terms of good and bad, right or wrong on action. The important quality is that there be an ethical baseline for the action at all. In a word, "Americans tend to 'see the world in moral terms.'"[125]

Efficiency for Williams refers to the combination of "activity and substantive rationality, focusing upon a choice of the most effective means for a given end." [126] It posits universalistic standards by which performance, work, and task may be judged. Practicality, in addition to its relation to goals—especially short-term goals as described above, bears a relation to the application of the norm of efficiency. Furthermore, in the American case the practical excludes any dominant interests in primarily intellectual or aesthetic or historical interests; asceticism or philosophies of withdrawal or deep pessimism have not had great influence on American culture.[127] Practicality also implies possible tendencies toward the dissipation of ultimate values in favor of immediate adaptability to current interests and satisfactions. In this sense, practicality as a value theme is opposed to the moral orientation theme except to the extent that externality, universalism, and active mastery form a moral complex themselves.

The value theme of external conformity is particularly difficult to disentangle as a value simply because society presupposes some degree of conformity to exist as a fact. At the same time, especially in highly differentiated social organizations, the need of integration to attain goals may force external conformity in a way that is not strictly within the domain of value but is, to the individual, a part of the conditions of action. Because of other values, external conformity may be manifest but not as a value in and of itself as, for example, in the case of the socially mobile person who may adhere to standards overtly only for the sake of its aiding his "climb." Williams recognizes these possibilities stating "conformity can be treated as a value only in so far as *sheer adherence to group patterns* is actually divorced from the content and implications of those patterns." [128] American "individualism" might be taken by some as invalidating this theme in the United States. However, Williams holds that the United States as an active, democratic society limits tolerance of individual nonconformity to technological and economic innovation.[129] American individualism has not meant the autonomous individual set up in rebellion against his social groups. Williams argues that, indeed external conformity dovetails nicely into the integrative needs of the society. " 'The looser the package, the tighter must be the string'—if the package is to be held together at all . . . the very heterogeneity of American culture tends to produce a stress upon external conformity." [130]

It is not a simple matter to discern what behavior is actually nonconforming except in that model, occasionally posited by Williams, of the nonexistent *perfectly integrated society* [131] in which the norms of the culture and the patterned expectations of social organization are one and the same, both universally internalized and without variation in execution. Here the "incessant effort and active social evaluation," [132] by which normative consensus and individual conformity is maintained in the empirical world would be unnecessary. How and why are they different—*this idealized conforming society* from any patterned social structure known to man? First, there is an incomplete uniformity which is intrinsic in the very nature of the norms. *Some* unevenness and variation of evaluative choice is to be attributed to the nature of the normative order itself and should not be confused with evasion, deviation, or violation.

All cultures have numerous alternatives and flexibilities in their effective norms . . . It is not always simple to determine whether one is observing *evasion* of a norm actually expected to guide real behavior or simply an *alternative norm,* widely accepted or acquiesced in, although of lower cultural value than the ideal but nominal standards. . . . [Furthermore] there are "ideal" norms, and then there are "latent" (covert and unrecognized) norms, shading over into *sub rosa* practices and countermores patterns. In addition there is differentiation of norms by age, sex, class and so on. It is important not to mistake differentiation or permissable variation for evasion or violation.[133]

In the actual world of events actors are singled out both because they over-conform as "fanatics" [134] or under-conform as delinquents. Likewise, there may be a different "private" and "public" evaluation of the same action. Williams is intrigued particularly by what he calls "large-scale patterned evasion of nominally dominant norms." [135] In its simplest and barest form such a situation involves public affirmation of a norm or sets of norms but covert acceptance of widespread violation and adherence to somewhat opposed norms. For Williams the situation is a generic one in which two (or more) functionally important but opposed conditions are juxtaposed; it illustrates his point that cultural norms are never completely integrated nor even integratable; that individual evaluative choices, while they may be patterned, can never be wholly consistent. Among others, Williams notes as examples of evasion patterns in American society: nepotism, racial discrimination, and the use of other particularistic criteria vs. promotion by technical competence; such practices as fee-splitting among doctors and ambulance-chasing among lawyers vs. professional codes; some advertising, financial transactions and the whole range of rationalized behavior where "business is business" is the tone vs. ethical concepts of truth; "void" divorces, "alimony rackets" and actual court practice in general vs. legal rules governing divorce; the speakeasy-bootleg complex prior to repeal of the 18th Amendment vs. prohibition.[136] Contranormative behavior, obviously, is crucial in handling change and will be discussed again below under that heading.

This section can be closed by noting the distinction Williams draws between distributive and nondistributive values. The latter like those of religious devotion or group pride are participated in rather than divided up. Enjoyment by one person in the value complex does not diminish another's participation in the same. The distributive values are divisible. What is available to one person is, by that very act, denied to others. Williams notes that everywhere and always men want or need things that are not available in unlimited quantities. In its broadest sense this evaluative problem is the basic one of the economic institution; i.e., the allocation of scarce means to alternative ends.[137] Williams concludes that:

The whole economic order, looked at sociologically, is a network of norms and expectancies—a web of "promises" as to the course that economic action will take, or is supposed to take. . . . These norms are varied in object, content, and mode of influence or enforcement; they include statutory laws, common law, court decisions and interpretation, governmental regulations and policies, business codes, union rules, diffuse "customs," "trade practices," and many other varieties of normative standards that taken together make up a regulative framework without which a complex economic system is simply unthinkable.[138]

This complexity of the societal control mechanisms shows not only the wide range from which a few choices must be made but also, clearly indicates the deep interpenetration of all institutional patterns and, hence, values as systems.

DIVIDING THE FUNCTIONS

Status-role incorporating both element and process. One of the noteworthy differences between the first and second editions of *American Society* is that the latter singles out the concepts of role and status whereby culture and social organization is linked.

> The entire set of statuses of a society constitutes a kind of map which identifies labeled positions and shows the complex relationships among them. Along with every status goes a set of norms which defines the expected and approved behavior for the occupant of the status . . . Statuses and roles tend to occur in organized sets, not just as isolated units.[139]

Although the institutionalized *statuses,* the established positions, are culturally defined in terms of rights and obligations which are recognized and enforced as interaction occurs between role incumbents and are subject to common evaluation, to the individual the organization appears "as a set of *roles,* partly corresponding to the statuses and partly a matter of incipient, latent, or noninstitutionalized regularities in individual conduct." [140]

In the theoretically limiting case of the completely undifferentiated society, institutional interrelationships would be readily apparent since, here the various institutional functions would refer simply to different aspects of each individual's behavior. Hence, such relationships would be but intrapersonality adjustments. However, in every known society some specialization appears. "Whenever specialization appears, relations between institutions become relations of groups, organizations, or social categories *mediated through the direct person-to-person interaction of individuals occupying differentiated statuses.*" [141] Although intrapersonality adjustments between possibly conflicting ideas, beliefs, values, and norms relating ego to alter would continue, the new element "is the direct interrelation of specialized roles, representing partly autonomous normative systems." [142] The relationships of specialized roles may then be extended through a number of mediated or linked institutions—as when a priest or minister intercedes with a judge on behalf of a juvenile delinquent to have the latter referred to his school teacher who in turn deals with the family.[143]

As the various clusters of institutional norms are activated by distinct social organizations, each representing a functionally important activity, distinct statuses occupied by specialized personnel tend to emerge. The common lay proclivity to equate the social organization with the institution upon which it is based, under these circumstances is not too far amiss. The separateness of social organizations usually means that the individual occupies plural statuses and multiple group memberships. The outcome is role segmentation, the various expectancies of which may sometimes be in conflict and sometimes may be consistent and reinforcing. By looking at a few selections drawn from Williams' treatment of the various institutions, some breadth and concreteness may be added to Williams' basic idea that the connecting link between the culturally defined institutional norms and the operating social organization as a going concern is in the status-role, and more specifically in the individual who simultaneously occupies a number of the status-roles of widely varying institutional constellations.

If, in the American family there exists, as Willliams suspects there might, broad tendencies toward permissiveness and toward an idealization of childhood, how are these tendencies reflected in the various family status-roles? Although the child is subjected to multiple social authorities, in the relatively isolated nuclear family he relates himself to very few persons for his emotional needs—chiefly his mother and father. The parents' role thus becomes dual; they must thwart him as they exercise authority over him, but they must also meet his needs for security and affection in a singularly intense way. The mother's role to which is entrusted the early socialization of the child, looms larger in respect to the child by virtue of the heavy demands of the occupational world upon the father. The expectation that the child love as well as obey and respect his parents further enhances the importance of the mother. The mother who detects that she is the *only* person to whom the child can turn for support can understandably interpret her role as one which should reduce his frustrations as much as possible and she may accent the permissive rather than the denying functions which her role calls for.[144] The elders of the family typically may have such insignificant status-roles that some may scarcely possess any role at all. Cultural emphasis upon youth, action, strength and competition results in "a certain social isolation and loss of firm, institutionalized status and esteem for aged parents." [145]

Entirely unlike the diffuse family status-roles are those of the bureaucratic social organization where functional specificity attends a bewildering array of specializations. Williams identifies six fairly distinct categories of status-roles to which parallels are found in nonindustrial as well as in industrial organizations of large size: (1) executives or top managers; (2) technical specialists; (3) junior line-supervisors ("middle management"); (4) secretarial and clerical workers; (5) first line-supervisors (foremen, etc.); (6) shop and bench workers. The expectations and obligations of functionally specific status-roles are circumscribed by well-defined regulations: "the military officer can give orders legitimately only to his subordinates in the service, the policeman's reach is explicitly limited and circumscribed, the judge is not empowered to detect and prosecute as well as render judgment." [146] Despite the specificity of definition, however, there is often a wide difference in interpretation of role definition. Role incumbency is much more than an automatic performance.

Some status-roles more than others lend themselves to role interpretation by the incumbent. One such status-role which definitionally "is an *office*, not a position solely of personal leadership, nor of authority not bounded by constitutional rules" [147] is the presidency of the United States. Despite the written Constitution and the impact of legal forms which tend toward traditionalism, "In the presidency more clearly than elsewhere in the federal structure, we can see the impact of great forces focused through the personalities who have filled the office in crucial periods: Washington, Lincoln, Wilson, F. D. Roosevelt . . . Some of the actions of F. D. Roosevelt may have stamped him in some quarters as a 'dictator,' but any analytical comparison will quickly show how very far the New Deal presidency was from the rule of a Hitler or a Peron, especially in its responsibility to a prior body of laws, and the fact that it was limited by the judiciary and legislative branches." [148]

A given status-role not only defines the rights and obligations of its incumbent; it also relates him to a definite complex of reciprocal statuses and roles. Thus, the teacher, by the fact that he is a teacher, is unavoidably in relation to the incumbents of such status-roles as student, parent, school administrator, board member and so on. Some of the reciprocal statuses produce inevitable strains making for boundary maintenance, especially as such status-roles are collectivized into polarized organizations such as labor and management.[149]

Some status-roles are particularly subject to public scrutiny and concern. "Since society is so largely equivalent to consensus, those who deal with values and beliefs as part of their occupational role—ministers, judges, writers, some artists, social scientists, teachers—touch upon the sensitive fringes of the bases of social order. In part for this reason, persons who deal with the beliefs and values that the community feels basic to its existence are the object of special surveillance and concern."[150] Few incumbents of such status-roles may limit their duty as it is perceived by the public, to the meritorious performance of the segmented job. Their private lives as represented in other status-roles they may hold will tend to fall under the same surveillance for possible clues as to what beliefs and values they really hold and are therefore likely to transmit while on the job.

Quite different is the situation for those incumbents of status roles between which the necessity for precise and rapid co-ordination is great. Corresponding tendencies "toward explicit regulation, hierarchy, and impersonality"[151] will likewise tend to be great. Incumbents of status-roles in specialized associations will tend toward a "marked compartmentalization of social activities —in particular, a radical separation of occupational activity from other life areas."[152] Among the consequences of a high degree of regulation and definition of operating procedures are the interchangeability of personnel and an atmosphere of affective neutrality. While the tension managing functions of the latter cannot be denied, impersonality can also fail to meet the expectations of those at the fringes of the organization, the citizen, client or newcomer. The reciprocities of these status-roles, then, are sometimes in conflict with those of the associational structure which are being enacted in full accordance with the expectations of the association.[153]

The increased elaboration of the division of labor in formally organized groups gives rise to greater differential interests, rewards, status-ranking and control. This forces greater interdependence of individuals and groups. Williams hypothesizes that the heightened interdependence leads to greater recognition of and a higher value upon the preservation of the existing order of relationships among the participants of the organization. In one direction this leads toward formalization of relationships which can function in tension management. At the same time in terms of evaluation, Williams hypothesizes that the more the process of maintaining the organization is valued as a process, (or in the PAS Model terms, the higher the value placed upon boundary maintenance) the greater will be the formality in communication, including face-to-face interaction. Hence, the greater the emphasis on boundary maintenance in large-scale organization, the greater the bureaucratic requirement for affective neutrality of status-role incumbents.[154]

Formalization or conventionalization of interpersonal relationships and hence explication of status-roles is favored also by the fact that as the size of the organization becomes larger its lines of communication tend to become longer. Such formalization creates "expressive-emotional" difficulties. The greater these difficulties produced by the rise of what Toennies call the *Gesellschaft*-like features of organization the greater the tendency to form informal subgroupings or cliques. Williams, like Homans, sees in this a further tendency toward status-role differentiations with inherent inclinations toward conflict. For, on the one hand, roles are crystallized with orientation to what Homans (in the *Human Group*) called the external system demands on the technical and executive direction of goal attainment, and on the other hand, roles are pointed toward internal demands or integrative and solidarity functions. Thus, Williams following Bales, recognizes that "high participation and specialization in the technical and executive directions . . . tends to provoke hostility." [155]

Status-role is utilized by Williams in his intergroup work also. In this regard he draws the line of meaning he wishes to give to part of the concept. Although it is commonly held that there is a "status" of Negro (or other minority group individual), Williams prefers to speak of "Negro" as a "category" because "Negro" does not "designate the same kind of complex of reciprocal rights and duties as appear in family, occupation, and certain other highly institutionalized systems." [156]

Williams hypothesizes that if interaction is to be maintained the need for clearly defined role expectations increases directly with the heterogeneity of beliefs and values of the participants and if such a heterogeneous collectivity continues operation this "need" will be experienced by the actors in the form of ambivalence, confusion, frustration, and conflict.[157] One way to clarify heterogeneity is through high formalization of status-role definitions as is characteristically seen in formal organizations. It was noted previously that formal contacts, which are the easier to initiate, are also the less likely to change stereotypes. One of the reasons for this failure is that such relations often involve super-subordinate interaction. In this Williams proposes that sentiments of the status-role performers will be ambivalent and the amount of interaction will be restricted to the minimum necessary to discharge the specific functions and will tend to be characterized by a high degree of "etiquette" and formal conventions. But, Williams argues, contact must be intense enough to result in *personal* likes and dislikes vis-a-vis an other if stereotypes are to be broken up. His "dictum" for effective prejudice reduction to: "Personalize, personalize, personalize" [158] tends to be defeated at the outset in the interaction of formal structure.

Many students of ethnic and race relations, including Williams, have noted that the status-role is very important in ranking and stratification and these in turn are related to various cleavages. Consideration of some of these relations will be made in the analysis of the next element, rank.

RANKING

Rank as an element. For Williams, stratification refers to the existence of a rank order predicated upon a commonly accepted basis or set of criteria for evaluation. All *social organizations*—churches, armies, factories, schools, and so on—manifest some rank order which Williams designates as "segmental stratification." Class or caste stratification, on the other hand, refers to rank in "the broader *institutional systems* of a society," and derives in part from the weighted summary of the segmental stratification positions individuals or groups hold.

Class stratification is seen essentially as a scale of objective rights and responsibilities which is correlated to a scale of invidious reward and deference.[159] High rank is usually associated with rights such as those of access to wealth, health facilities, income, power and authority which are symbolized by forms of deference such as honorific titles, tones of voice in address, ritualized salutations, and acquiescence in material advantages. Certain immunities also often are a part of the rights associated with high rank. Social class refers to an aggregate of individuals who occupy generally similar positions in the rank system of a society.

Williams makes clear that any system of ranking represents a complex of differentially evaluated components—economic, political, social. By far the easiest component to single out as a rank determinant is the occupational; it is both identifiable and subject to a relatively high degree of consensus concerning the prestige attached to different occupational levels.[160] Other determinants of rank can to some extent be derived from occupation. The non-occupational criteria may be less identifiable or less agreed upon as measures of rank once they are identified. In American society occupations which call for manual labor and unskilled personal service are ranked lowest. As occupations call for increased skill and authority over others their rank order tends to ascend. Williams also sees "size of income derived" [161] as a criterion for prestige ranking but notes that income is far from an infallible index to prestige of occupation: "Many prestigeful occupations do not pay particularly well. A general with a moderate income may have vastly more authority than a wealthy stockmarket operator. History is full of impoverished aristocrats, as well as of the new wealth that does not yet command high prestige." [162]

Stratification as it is manifested in the United States is documented by Williams in a remarkably compact but comprehensive treatment of which only the major points can be touched on here. He notes the "marked differentials in the distribution of scarce values" [163] as represented by incomes. Few incomes are modal, most falling considerably above or below average, with attendant great differences in total life-situation. Income distribution has greatly changed since the end of the Second World War as has occupational distribution. The low prestige jobs have decreased in proportion, while those thought to be more desirable and of higher rank have correspondingly expanded. The old status symbols which were purchaseable such as clothing, automobiles and recreational patterns decreasingly convey class differentiation. Although wealth is probably the most universal, generalized, and most easily recognized mark of occupational success, its correlation with prestige, like that of income, is far from perfect. There are a few social effects of stratification which are more dependable indicators of class than wealth. Participation in formally organized associations, the amount of formal education and the mortality and morbidity rates are mentioned. Certain immunities and privileges in the dispensation of justice also signify rank.[164] Attitudinal differences on a large number of socio-political issues likewise indicate variations in rank.

Williams makes little or no attempt to separate out those aspects of rank which in terms of the PAS Model are elemental or structural. What has been reported above has been gleaned from his excellent chapter on stratification which for the most part merges the processes of evaluation of actors and allocation of status-roles with rank as an elemental component of social systems. His specifications for analyzing a ranking system illustrate this tendency. He warns that any rank order can have meaning only by specifying the referent social system, but believes that *any* ranking system can be analyzed in terms of the following:

a. the distribution of objective privileges;
b. rankings by members of the society (prestige and esteem);
c. the criteria of rank, whether personal qualities or achievements, family membership, possessions, authority, or power;
d. the symbols of rank, e.g. style of life, clothing, housing, organizational membership, etc.
e. the ease or difficulty and frequency of changes in rank position;
f. the solidarity among individuals or groups sharing a similar position in the system:
   (1) interaction patterns;
   (2) similarity or dissimilarity of beliefs, attitudes, values;
   (3) consciousness of stratification position shared with others;
   (4) concerted action as a collectivity—for instance, "class warfare."[165]

A number of considerations included in these items have already been examined. Prestige for example, was seen above to attend, among other things, the occupational position. How the individual performs within his position is similarly evaluated with the result that he is imputed an amount of esteem. In this respect Williams' terminology follows Kingsley Davis (see Chapter 3 of this volume.) This and other evaluative judgments will here be examined in the section immediately to follow.

Evaluation as a process in ranking. The identification of an individual with a particular occupation imputes to him a rank associated with the occupation. *Within* a specific occupation the performances and contributions of individuals vary, and as these are differently evaluated, differential esteem is accorded them. Many occupational performances can be adequately judged only by others in the same occupation, but evaluation by peers is correlated only loosely with broader reputation in the total community. Following Parsons' early publication in stratification, Williams identifies six classes of criteria which may affect the sum total of an individual's rank: birth and kinship affiliation, possessions or wealth and income, authority, power, personal qualities and personal achievements.[166] The first four of these are extrinsic based upon what a person has, the last two are intrinsic, based upon what a person is. Extrinsic criteria allow an extended scale of ranking and hence are typically more important than the intrinsic criteria in the evaluations which yield social stratification.[167] Although the valuation of the status-role held by an individual is separate from the incumbent, in practice the prestige of the office tends to be transferred to the incumbent.

The minister receives deference because of his institutional function; only gross failure or misconduct can prevent any individual in such a position from receiving at least a minimum of institutionalized deference. Similarly, respect is required for the symbols of legitimized authority, regardless of the intrinsic qualities of a particular officer.[168]

In the same manner, a status-role generally accepted to be of low functional importance in the social system, e.g., that of servant, is imputed a prestige which is reflected in its incumbent's total rank. No matter how good the servant, i.e. in whatever high esteem he may be held, he ordinarily has little prestige.

Despite the actual practice of applying extrinsic criteria in rank evaluation, Americans are dedicated to the idea that intrinsic criteria—those which evaluate the personal qualities and the personal achievements of an individual—are the important standards of judgment. This is related to the "reigning conception" of equality which obviously is not supported by what a person has (extrinsic criteria) and must therefore look for support in the intrinsic criteria of what a person *is*. The persistent idea of equality despite a ranking system which denies that men are equal tends to modify sharply drawn evaluations and is itself based on a number of evaluative beliefs and practices. A specifically religious conception of equality (the equality of souls before God, the divine nature within every person, and so on), and a secularization of the same idea—" 'a man's a man for all that' "—contributes to the equality doctrine. This sense of equality of condition which Williams relates as the value theme of individual personality has as its core the belief that each person is "something of intrinsic worth, not valued simply as a member of a group nor as a means to some ulterior end." [169] This finds its expression primarily in the extraordinary informality, directness and lack of rank consciousness in interpersonal contacts, and in the de-emphasis placed upon authoritarian and hierarchical relationships even in those social organizations based on these principles. Subordination to a superior does not extend beyond the office. In this way the equality theme and the individual personality theme combine to constitute something of a floor below which the person as such cannot be degraded or devalued.

A second type of equality for Americans is found in the formal rights and obligations ideally extended to all, such as the right to vote, the obligation to perform military service, the right to public education and the obligation to pay taxes. A third type of equality—access to social and economic rewards—is clearly dominated by and subordinated to the principles of economic freedom and individual achievement. Equality of opportunity rather than equality of condition is the evaluative principle which applies here. So strong is the principle that a man should be rewarded in relation to his individual achievement that Williams considers it "quite striking that one of the earliest and most widespread reactions to Marxism, as popularly understood, was to select precisely the idea of 'equal distribution of wealth' as the target of censure and moral outrage." [170]

There are, notwithstanding, inherent tendencies which mitigate against a purely achievement based evaluation of rank. The identification of personal achievement is necessarily local and a matter of first hand experience. In order to generalize the rankings based on achievement, symbols of achievement are required to convey the evaluative judgments which have been made on the informal level of local first-hand experience. To the extent that these symbols can be usurped and made ascriptive a purely achievement based ranking system does not prevail. The common and pervasive ascription of worth and privilege on the basis of birth as in the case of inherited wealth or as in the case of race constitutes a "counter-current" of evaluation, which in its logical implications denies much of the previous value themes discussed, that is, rationality, progress, equality, freedom, democracy and so on. The tension between the achievement and ascriptive valuations is particularly focused in status-role allocation. [171]

Allocation of status-roles. Allocation of status-role can be handled at two levels of generality paralleling Williams' distinction between segmental stratification and social stratification. The latter will be considered first. At once the simplest and yet most far reaching outcome of evaluation is the constancy in allocation of occupational status-roles even in so called open-class systems. For instance, Williams notes that even in the United States there is a high degree of occupational inheritance in the sense that, "in the majority of cases the sons enter the occupation of the father in a greater proportion than any other . . . each of the occupations is recruited principally from the sons of the fathers who have such an occupation." [172] Similarly, occupational inter-level movement when it does occur is typically by steps rather than by great jumps. Again, most Americans marry within their own class. Williams' comments on this show not only how classes as objective phenomena are precipitated and, derivatively, how status-roles in stratification can be allocated but also demonstrates that causal sequences are many times "reciprocal, mutual, and circular." [173]

Since marriages create families and children initially absorb the culture of their parents, and since the *initial* status of the child *must* be that of his parents, class endogamy necessarily generates forces tending toward the emergence of recognizable status groupings from aggregates of objectively like-circumstanced persons. It is in this way that the apparently discrete facts of occupation, income, residence, visiting, intermarriage, and child training are woven into the pattern from which definite status groupings can emerge.[174]

Access to education, differential participation in social organizations, immunity to prosecution by law, incidence of sickness, even death and life itself with the possible attached status-roles of father, or bereaved wife, and so on are to an appreciable degree functions of economic position and of rank more generally. What is true, of course, for the open class system is only multiplied in caste and estate type systems.

Williams' distinction between segmental and societal or class stratification is carefully interrelated when he turns to his applied interests in intergroup work.

Ethnic and racial factors help fix the ranking of individuals; class distinctions stratify ethnic groupings internally. But individuals may belong to the same stratum and be divided by ethnic or racial lines, and stratification occurs where no ethnic or racial distinctions exist. The two systems thus crisscross while remaining analytically separate.[175]

He speculates as a result that ethnic conflicts may prevent focalization of class conflicts while interclass struggle may direct a given "charge" of hostility away from ethnic targets.[176] In any case, the fact that the American does place great emphasis upon status mobility coupled with the fact that prestige is a distributive value means that there is an endemic increment of frustrated goal attainment which needs outlet.

This process of status-role allocation in the United States, Williams contends, is most marked in its ascriptive bent in smaller communities and in areas of static or declining economic activity. On the other hand, industrial or commercial expansion affords the possibility of rapid occupational shifts and concomitant geographic mobility which jointly cut through the rigidity factors of kinship affiliation and established group memberships. "The very fact that economic relations in the larger centers tend to become impersonal and narrowly specific in nature frees the individual from the lineal transmission of established status and permits him to compete for placement." [177] It is quite clear for Williams that in any given social organization the allocation of status-roles will be in accordance with the particular values central to the group. In instrumentally directed organizations universalistic criteria tend to be used while the converse is the tendency in non-instrumentally oriented units or in the tension management structures within instrumentally oriented groups.

CONTROLLING

Power as an element. Power is defined as "the probability of the effective control of an individual or other social unit by another, regardless of the former's wishes." [178] In the broadest Hobbesian sense, power suffuses all human interaction. That is, other human beings are always potential means for the attainment of one's goals. Therefore control of others is always a technically effective way of advancing personal interests that may be contrary to the interests of those controlled. Hence, there is a demand for power.

Williams sees power ranging from "illegitimate" coercion or brute force outside social sanctions to authority which is the legitimized rights to control others. Authority is predicated upon value consensus in the relevant social organization but it can not exist effectively without the backing of coercive power—American values to the contrary, force or the potential of force always must lay behind authority. The converse is also true; force can not maintain itself unaided by value consensus. While power takes many specific forms Williams argues that these can be reduced to two broad, fundamental ways of controlling: 1) the situation within which people must act can be changed either by altering the actual conditions of action or by altering the actors' perception of the situation, and through sanction manipulations; and 2) the individual's attitudes and values may be appealed to or changed by persuasion and propaganda.[179]

In Williams' view, political institutions

. . . are the complexes of norms regulating the acquisition and exercise of power by some individuals over others within a given territory, through social structures claiming a monopoly of ultimate authority

. . . [and] Government is the legitimate power-holding *group;* the state is the *structure* by which the group's activity is defined and regulated.[180]

Of course, the exercise of socially validated authority occurs in all groups and organizations and because of this neither the state nor government is coexistensive with society although in the completely centralized totalitarian regime such a claim may be made and quite nearly realized. The political is always only one aspect of social control and social consensus. Social authorities such as the family and church, and the values these represent always compete to some degree with the state for power. For this reason Williams maintains that it is fruitful analytically to consider the state as the reflection of the ever shifting balance of power among diverse interests and groups. Indeed, the regulation of conflicting and divergent loyalties of the variant groups that comprise a nation as a territorial unit is often the prime function of the state. This function along with the establishment of procedures for acquiring and using power is made the more imperative in complex, industrial nations like the United States where secularization and high internal differentiation on the one hand, attenuate the basis for control and consensus but, on the other hand, make the need more imperative. Williams indicates that the main areas of state coercion are police power, particularly the sanction of organized force *within* the society, taxing powers and the monopoly of facilities to carry on external armed warfare.

Williams asserts that the form the state may take follows a differentiation of authority in general, namely, the polarity of status of office vs. that of the person irrespective of office. Thus constitutional states, as an example of the first type, have a body of fundamental rules and regulations by which those who govern are themselves governed. That is, the rulers are bound to a legitimate order of established laws, precedents and custom which they are considered to have no right to violate. This has been the case in America where the authority of power holders has tended, under government by law to be functionally specific and explicitly defined.[181] The polar opposite of constitutionalism is rule by the charismatic leader to whom is imputed (by his followers) absolute authority which resides solely in the magical effervescence of the person *qua* person who rules. Just as it is true that no charismatic leader can completely divorce himself from the traditions of past rules of officiating power and be successful, it is also true that charisma in some small measure probably is invested in all power aspects of a situation since rarely is a status reacted to solely as a status. Even the Army with its strenuous stress on the authority of office can not make all second lieutenants "the same." [182]

"The relation of the individual to the state demonstrates the distinctive nature of the political monopoly of power . . . [the individual] can resign from citizenship only at the cost of resigning from the whole society at the same time." [183] In the American case, however, popular tradition has emphasized the rights of individual citizens as over against the state. The value themes of democracy and freedom are cogent in this vein. Freedom for Williams refers most generally to the legitimate claim of the individual to a wide plane of moral autonomy in decision making.[184] Specifically Williams notes in America a tendency to stress rights over duties and a deep aversion to accept without question established authority, particularly personal authority.[185] Democracy is simply the multiple nexus of more specific beliefs and primary values—freedom, equality, humanitarianism—which are precipitated in the polity. For Williams the "theme of democracy" is "an agreement upon *procedure* in distributing power and in settling conflicts," [186] particularly the reservation of certain "inalienable rights" for the individual as unalterable by majority rule.

Power is intimately associated with rank in Williams' thought. As seen above, legitimized power is one basis for ranking in stratification systems. At the same time, an individual or group may use non-sanctioned coercion to gain or maintain station even though such methods may be contrary to many of the major institutionalized norms and values nominally accepted in the society. Sheer force (concealed or open) may be used in legitimizing station; it must be available to use in the stabilization of any social order. This follows from the distributive nature of power.

Since power is intimately associated with rank it is not surprising to find extensive treatment of the power component in connection with the economic institutions which in America command an extremely high rank. Williams devotes much attention to the mechanisms of control which ideally and actually are exercised over organizations of production as well as by and between such organizations. The self-regulation of economic activity in the tradition of the most abstract models of a *laissez faire* economy is a far cry from actual economic practice in a society such as the United States which values highly the idea of competition basic to *laissez faire* theory. A regulative frame-work consisting of "statutory laws, common law, court decisions and interpretations, governmental regulations and policies, business codes, union rules, diffuse 'customs,' 'trade practices,' and many other[s]" [187] constitutes specific institutional structures which display strong power components. Not to be underestimated too, is the expansion of what Williams terms administrative or organizational coordination enforced by a definite and identifiable social organization such as factory, corporation or trade association. In contrast to an earlier period when volume of production, time and place of production and sale, type and quality of commodity, and allocation of productive resources were determined by a large number of small producers acting independently, in contemporary America one "single corporate organization will control a large number of subsidiary units through an elaborate administrative network." [188] The concentration of economic control augmented by such devices as interlocking participation, common sources of financing, trade associations, interest groupings, cartels, and so forth is a sharp contrast to "the quasi-mythical portrait of an economy of individualistic competitive production." [189] Of fourteen features singled out by Williams as constituting the sociologically significant features of the American economic system at least six deal essentially with power. [190] The summation of power concentration as it has developed in industry and a counter-development in organized labor can only be hinted at here as one of the most arresting accounts of a pervasive institution. Williams concludes:

The confrontation of large corporation and organized workers is a central fact of our economic system that is utterly alien to the ideology of an atomistic, free enterprise system. None of the traditional concepts—"private property," capital, labor, enterprise, individualism—has its old meaning . . . Yet for the foreseeable future the corporation and the union will occupy the center of the stage—unless the third member of the cast, government, takes over the full play. [191]

Although available patterns of governmental power for the future are often cast in the "rightest" terms of fascism, the "leftist" terms of communism or the middle of the road terms of "liberal capitalism," Williams is of the opinion that both extreme right and left power concentrations with their unavoidable totalitarianism "are so alien to the American needs and traditions that one must rationally doubt that they necessarily represent the 'wave of the future.'" [192] Nevertheless, as long as large numbers of people are increasingly encompassed into "highly organized power units focused upon the advancement of partly disparate economic interests," increased governmental regulation is inevitable. Only as the issues "can be subjected to reason, discussion, research, negotiation, and disciplined interplay of power within a morality that cuts across class-bounded moralities" [193] can a middle road be traversed. ". . . we can see how thin is the line between 'economic' and 'political' activities and how questions of power unavoidably confront us at every turn." [194]

Decision making and its initiation into action. Much of Williams' analysis of the political institutions is a detailed picture of the ideal and real patterning of decision making mechanisms and their interrelated execution at levels, in the American case, beginning with officially designated organizations of government, such as the courts and executive agencies, through the political party and outward to the individual and the pressure or interest groups and back through the repercussion and influence these place on the political party and government. Williams emphasizes MacIver's characterization of the societal decision making function as "the *web* of government." [195] The shifting nexus of decision making is nicely given in the American case by the observation that:

The "impersonal majesty of the law" must be filtered through lawyers, juries, judges, administrators. The practical meaning of a constitutional precept, statutory enactment, or common-law doctrine is never simply given, but is always determined by interpretation. [196]

The courts then not only discover what the law is but also make and change it. The same is true as administration applies edicts and policy directives. Williams traces tendencies toward: "(1) the delegation of legislative powers to executive agencies; (2) an increased proportion of legislation initiated and influenced by executive agencies; (3) the increased role of governmental administrative agencies and their employees as 'pressure groups'; (4) a diminished influence and prestige of legislative bodies. The separation of powers is, more and more clearly, a creed rather than a specific operating principle." [197] The interplay which precedes decision making may be seen, for example, in the operations of the main standing committees of Congress. Not only do they decide what will and will not be brought to a vote, but their decisions also influence executive action. "For the key officials of governmental agencies affected by a particular committee—military affairs, for instance—will be in frequent liaison with that body and will inevitably both influence and be influenced by it." [198]

Despite the diffuseness of the decision making process suggested by the above line of thought, Williams notes a tendency in the American polity toward a centralization of that function. "In governmental bodies the growth in volume, scope, and complexity of activities creates a . . . transformation in which *residual power* gravitates to the *active* and *continuing* control centers of the executive agencies." [199] For Williams this is but an instance of the wider phenomena of centralized control in formal organization when rapid action is imperative, a phenomenon which occurs particularly in the face of sensed threat to values as a whole by external groups.[200] Centralization is also the mark of the totalitarian state. However, even in the most monolithic dictatorships Williams notes conflicts of interests, schisms and disagreement which may be all the more crucial because of their very concealment.[201] Centralization does not undo the problems of power nor render decision making a unitary event.

The implications of centralized power on decision making are not confined to the state. The corporate system of business brings together numerous bits of wealth under a single management just as the factory system brought large numbers of workers under unified control and direction. The corporation leads in its extreme to the paradox that the more widely diffused in stock ownership, the more probable is it that effective control of business wealth will be concentrated.[202] It is thus democratic in ownership though not in control. Furthermore, Williams also points out that the very nature of economic activity tends to generate strong centrifugal forces which would break through social regulation.

Modern developments have made it increasingly plain that control is the central problem for economics as well as for politics, and that the distinction between economic power and political power can become hazy indeed.[203]

Perhaps the most immediate outcome of this fact is Williams' recognition that "as the size and power of organizational units increase, *the consequences of decisions increasingly outrun the limits of the unit in which they originate.*" [204] Thus, whether they like it or not the decision making consequences of such organizations as corporations and labor unions are increasingly freighted with public interests in the widest meaning of the term.

Of course, this phenomenon can be used in deliberate intent as was true in terms of the Supreme Court decisions on desegregation. In this respect Williams notes that power in the institutional setting of the polity has not received great attention in the hands of American researchers interested in intergroup relations although by definition race and ethnic groupings as "minorities" receive that categorization vis-a-vis some dominant grouping. He suggests that the power, policy, and tactical outcomes of organized interest groups are perhaps more important than the folkways and individual dimensions of personal prejudice in controlling behavior in situational contexts. The "decisions at a distance," which the former represent, in such concrete cases as "Little Rock," *apartheid*, or the official abolition of segregation in the Army, are generically categorical, that is, involve the perceptual processes of simplification, clarification, and levelling. Socially the correlates are abstract generality, universal administrative applicability, and concrete definiteness of classification.[205] As a result, he hypothesizes that they are more effective.[206]

Decision making for Williams is neither confined to instrumental behavior nor restricted to formal or hierarchical relations. The informal organizations which emerge within the formal structure also exhibit power loci and decision making processes which, in operation obtain a vacillating balance with the decisions of the formal organizations much as the internal and external pattern demands are in continuous oscillation. Some decision making is carried on by bodies of members who are approximate equals (such as the elected bodies of the House or Senate) and ideally

reach their decisions by discussion, negotiation, and various informal agreements.[207] Actually there is, even here, a tendency
toward power differentials which are reflected in decision making.
Here, as in the American family where the equalitarian pattern
is the ideal mode of organization, "equality is only relative or
comparative. There is not exact equality and certainly not identity of rights and duties. . . . Family organization must have an
elaborate division of labor and differentiation of authority among
the various members so long as any coherent group exists at all." [208]

SANCTIONING

Sanction as an element. Williams believes that "It may be
taken as an *identifying criterion* that no organized group exists
without a viable system of positive and negative sanctions that
both index and help to maintain regularized patterns of behavior." [209] In the perfectly integrated society there would be no
need for sanctions, since there everyone would want to do what
he had to do. In the real world, however, individuals often do
not feel like doing what is expected of them. Others to whom
conformity is important induce the expected behavior by rewards
such as wealth, power, social esteem and prestige. They punish
nonconforming behavior by penalties which may range from physical punishment and socially disgraceful death through degrees
of ostracism and condemnation to relatively mild penalties such
as minor deprivations, ridicule and disapproval.[210] Although Williams is fully aware that sanctioning may result from sanctions
which are not consciously directed at persuading the other to
conform—the disapproving word from a cherished person, for example—and that both reward and punishment may be self-inflicted
by the clear or guilty conscience, he says that "For any *practical
purposes of exposition and explanation,* I would still like to focus
on those kinds of behavior in which there is a fairly clear intention to reward or deprive or punish." [211]

Despite Williams' preferential use of reward (or punishment)
as a specific intent at social control the value theme dominant in
American Society injects the sanctioning idea into situations
in which clear intention is somewhat blurred. The tendency in
American culture, for example, to identify standards of personal
excellence with competitive occupational achievement and to

mete out rewards accordingly poses the problem of distinguishing between success and achievement. The valued accomplishments which ideally comprise achievement can easily be confused with success which lays the emphasis not upon the accomplishments of an individual but upon the rewards which have already come to him. When success itself is considered an adequate basis for reward, without much thought to what accomplishments or attributes of the individual led to the reward, what means were used to arrive at the accomplishments and whether sustained accomplishments merit further reward, a system of rewarding is generated by which a person continues to be rewarded simply because he already has been accorded a disproportionate share of scarce prestige, esteem, wealth, power, authority, rights, and privileges. Citing a study of biographical subjects whose lives would presumably show on what basis they were singled out for a degree of mass adulation or interest, he reports the finding that:

"It is neither a world of 'doers' nor a world of 'doing' . . . Instead of the 'givers' we are faced with the 'takers.'" Although the biographies approved in general of 'doing things,' success seems to be treated as something that merely happens—an accidental, lucky event—not a rational outcome of integrated effort.[212]

Despite such a tendency to reward individuals by thinking highly of them because they have succeeded in taking more than their fellows, Williams still is inclined to believe that success is for the most part based upon achievement, achievement is associated with work, and that work still represents a value. "Thus, success is still not a primary criterion of value in its own right, but rather a derivative reward *for* active, instrumental performance."[213] Blurred also is the idea of money or wealth, which like success, is variously regarded as a reward and as a criterion for ranking. If the prestige of an occupation (and hence, to some extent the prestige of the individual in that occupation) "seems to follow roughly . . . the size of the income derived"[214] the reward of prestige would seem to be accorded to an individual because he made money. Thus again, the possession of one reward would seem to be the basis for the according of another.

Even when the sanctioning system is relatively explicit as in the bureaucracy which imposes sanctions designed to encourage such bureaucratic attributes as accuracy, caution, punctuality, and so on, the observation of bureaucratic norms is frequently no guarantee that the highest rewards will go to the greatest conformist. "The corporation may develop informal groups which act like 'political machines' in rewarding members and excluding outsiders. At the logical extreme, membership in a particular informal group becomes a prerequisite for advancement." [215]

Williams suggests that a reexamination is in order for the goal-activity-reward complex of corporate business. The segmentation of corporate ownership and the separation of ownership from goal-achieving activities makes the assumption dubious that the profit incentive is a prime force for the wage workers and "salaried officialdom" who do the work of the corporation. As was touched upon above under end as an element, "Profit-making is a second-order control, so to speak, and may very little 'motivate' those actually operating the business . . . the 'profit motive' is not a *motive* at all but an institutional goal; it is not a psychological state but a social condition. The fully developed corporate form today is likely to be manned by people with goals and incentives not so different from those of the personnel of nonprofit organizations." [216]

Application of sanctions as process. "The *offer of advantage* or the *threat of disadvantage* to bring about desired action from others," [217] is among the ways that some men control others. Williams contrasts the enforcement of norms as it occurs in *Gemeinschaft*-like social organizations, for instance small towns, and in the large highly differentiated communities with *Gesellschaft*-like structures. In the former, norms are enforced primarily by the diffuse pressure of the total community with nearly every member of the community acting to penalize violations. In the latter, clearly designated and publicly acknowledged functionaries such as the policeman, the military officer, the teacher, the boss, assume a relatively well-defined role in relation to the violator and in part supplant the diffuse sanctioning mechanisms of the communal society. Remembering that in American society norms themselves are conceived as zones within which there can be considerable variation of interpretation and explicitness, it can be anticipated that there will be latitude in the process of sanction application even by those whose specialty it is.

. . . a policeman is supposedly an impartial instrument for law-enforce-ment. However, quite aside from criminal connivance, the policeman usually has a wide range of discretion in when, how, and upon whom he will visit sanctions. He may show "favoritism"—or he may show kindness, take intentions and extenuating circumstances into account.[218]

A great deal of latitude may be expected in the diffuse sanctioning process which is characteristic of those many areas of American life not easily subject to institutional controls. Here the interplay of personalities exercise an important control. Those sanctions which spring from frequency of interaction are of general interest in themselves, but of particular interest is interaction between in-group and out-group members. Proceeding from the frequently replicated findings that in intergroup relations frequency of in-teraction with out-group members is closely associated with favor-able attitude toward persons of such social groupings, Williams casts his argument in sanctioning terms:

To the extent that the reward-punishment ratio in the interaction is actuarially positive, the mechanism of *reinforcement* will operate. To the extent that one actor develops positive feelings for the other, the likelihood increases that he will reward the alter. The more alter is rewarded the more likely it is that he will reward ego . . . The "be-nign cycle" will be further facilitated to the extent that *complementary interests* and *"symbiotic" emotional needs* are found to be served by the interaction. It is through the cumulative interplay of these proc-esses, that mutually gratifying relationships of solidarity emerge.[219]

Of course, as Williams points out, this account of sanctioning does not consider the potentiality of nonconformity and deviancy. The "benign cycle" may become instead a vicious cycle, in which the counter-posing processes of broken expectations culminate in mis-understanding, alienation, and interpersonal conflict.

Should nonconformity to norms become so widespread as to represent institutionalized evasion "there is . . . a strong resistance to wholesale punishment . . . Hence, the situation is handled by: (a) public affirmation of the norm; (b) covert acceptance of widespread violation and evasion; (c) periodic token or 'ritual-istic' punishment, and/or punishment of those whose arrears un-avoidably become public." [220] Ritualistic punishment as exemplified by periodic "round-up days" during prohibition when mass arrests were made or by the widely dramatized recurrent raids on commercialized vice such as on prostitution is seen by Williams as "a ceremonial affirmation tending to assimilate or obscure the covert pattern of evasion." [221] It is in sharp contrast to the highly disapproved practice of bribing policeman or judges which practice is culturally registered as a law violation. An interesting case of what Williams calls counter-institutional patterns is provided by the punishment occasionally meted out to those individuals who fulfill the moral codes too thoroughly. "Sometimes these heroic individuals are regarded as 'saints'; but they are also regarded, in certain circumstances, as 'fanatics,' 'trouble-makers,' 'subversive.' [222]

FACILITATING

Facility as an element. What is termed facilities in the PAS Model is variously treated by Williams as ends, norms or "culturally approved means," [223] by utility, resource or facility. By whatever name, the importance of technology, especially transportation, instruments of mass communication and the apparatus of mass production in factories and farms is set out as part of the structure which has taken shape in American society and, in turn, has been a factor in shaping the society.[224] Thus, besides pointing out that "The functioning of the contemporary United States as a social system is greatly dependent upon the remarkable set of facilities for transportation and communication" he notes that facilities representing material comfort come sometimes "very close to a terminal goal at the level of hedonistic gratification." [225]

While the above observations point to the physical items that may be facilities or, sometimes, ends, Williams is also concerned with the essential nature of facilities. "Property consists, first, not of *things,* but of *rights;* it is not a concrete object of reference, but a socially recognized claim. The essence of property is *an institutionalized right of persons or other social units to scarce values.*" [226] In the United States the emphasis on active mastery and secular rationality has meant the basic compatibility and translation of much property to the realm of facilities; a translation that is generally the case in instrumentally oriented social systems.

In this respect Williams' usage of property is close to that of facilities in the PAS Model.

Utilization of facilities as process. The uses to which the resources of a society are put are subject to the directive influence of common cultural goals. Such collective aims as military victory would obviously indicate a kind of utilization which would be different from a multi-purpose distributive goal such as profit making. "At one time the economy may concentrate upon refrigerators and fashionable clothing; then, within a few months, the national resources are turned toward production of tanks and guns." [227] Even more glaringly different utilization of facilities is represented as comparisons are made between one culture and another or between historical epochs within the same culture. "The productive 'surplus' remaining after subsistence needs have been met may be invested in tools and factories—but it may be, and has been, used to construct magnificent cathedrals, or used up in conspicuous consumption as part of a culturally stylized game of prestige." [228] Because every society has limited resources, the uses to which they are put reveals what is considered important by that society.

Williams develops the theme of facility utilization by two approaches—1) the productive process as affected by intrinsic economic conditions or by a given mode of economic organization; and 2) the criss-crossing of interests and values as these are reflected by facility utilization. For the immediate purposes of this chapter a few examples will be given which will be little more than illustrative of the first approach and considerable attention will be given the second approach which lies at the heart of the value identification theme of *American Society.*

The diversion of resources into varied consumer products is not a simple response to societal need or consumer tastes, for these very needs and tastes are themselves nurtured and developed from technological innovations and the creation of new products. To a considerable extent the creation of the product *develops* the "need" rather than responding to a need.[229] The economic organization also to a considerable extent exerts influence, relatively independently of consumer need or societal requirements, on the use to which the facilities of technological knowledge and invention is put.

Buying and suppressing an improved patent in order to protect the investment already made on the basis of an older patent; making applications for patents in order to delay a competitive improvement; continuing and ingenious litigations against inventions seen as threats . . . all these devices enable dominant concerns or groups of concerns to maintain favorable positions.[230]

The same effect is accomplished by other machinations such as the exercise of strategic control over critical materials, techniques or personnel. Obviously, the kind of controls exercised over the economic organizations themselves has an effect upon the utilization of facilities, and much provocative material is provided by Williams to force a redefinition of the competitive economic structure which most Americans presume they have.

In every economy, however, there are some goods and services which cannot be chosen by individuals in the market; these are public goods and services, the benefits of which are not subject to division into separable individual returns. Highways and streets, community sanitation, parks, control of pollution of the air, fire protection, and military defense are examples . . . Imagine the consequences of competitive bidding for the services of fire-fighting companies.[231]

For a consideration of the much wider range of goods and services which are on the market and of the productive apparatus from which they spring it is imperative to seek answers to the questions *"what* control, by *whom,* for *what . . ."* [232] It is to the last of these questions, *production for what,* that Williams turns his attention in his quest for an identification of American values. As was shown above, there are other ways too by which values can be established—by observation of the regularity of choices in recurrent situations, by testimony and by the degree of sentiment with which certain attitudes and positions are attacked or defended. For present purposes of examining the process by which facilities are utilized, however, emphasis will be placed upon what Williams calls indirect evidence which yields data on choices.

. . . in a society with a highly developed money economy, much can be learned about the patterns of general values from the patterns of money expenditure, since money is a particular measure of economic "value"—that is, of value in exchange. The study of family budgets, general patterns of consumer expenditure, public expenditures, the flow of the national income, and so on, is subject to interpretation in these terms.[233]

It is proposed that for the immediate purpose of presenting the array of these indirect evidences as gathered by Williams, each of his American values be considered along with the supporting evidence that it *is* a value, to the extent that the evidence consists of facility utilization.

THE USE OF RESOURCES AS RELATED TO MAJOR VALUE ORIENTATIONS

Achievement and success. After all physical needs have been met and nearly all conceivable means for the satisfaction of desires have been won, wealth is still the object of great striving. Diverse occupations and the secondary and segmental knowledge individuals have of each other make it difficult to identify *bona fida* achievement by performance on any wide scale; acquisition of goods or money is utilized widely as a recognizable symbol of achievement. Williams concurs with Santayana's insight: "It is the symbol and measure he (the American) has at hand for success, intelligence, and power; but as to money, itself he makes, loses, spends and gives it away with a very light heart." [234] Bigness and quantity also represent an expressive utility which again is noted by Santayana: "Respect for quantity is accordingly more than the childish joy and wonder at bigness; it is the fisherman's joy in a big haul, the good uses of which he can take for granted." [235]

Activity and work. Full utilization of facilities is indicated by the ideal type which seeks to dominate the world of nature, to subdue and exploit the physical world around him and which is reinforced by the value that work is an end in itself representing a convergence of self-interest, social recognition and ethical precepts which become true matters of conscience. Full utilization of facilities can not be made unless the performance potential of all individuals is maintained at full capacity. Development and wide accessibility of health and educational facilities are often approved on these grounds.[236]

Humanitarian mores. "The enormous range of relatively disinterested humanitarian activities in America—the commonplace

Community Chest, the 'service club' activities, the public welfare agencies, the numerous private philanthropies, and so on—stands in striking contrast to the treatment meted out to 'the poor' and the 'sturdy beggars' in many other parts of Western society within the past two centuries." [237] The use of facilities in fulfilling this humanitarian propensity sometimes clashes with the concept of rugged individualism, and it may also be used to justify economic inequalities.

Efficiency and practicality. Methods of technological achievement abet maximal facility utilization, but also come to be valued for their own sake. "In economic activities and other fields that have acquired considerable autonomy apart from the ultimate-value systems of the society, the stress upon efficiency is a complex derivation from the values attached to action, to material comfort, and perhaps especially, to mastery over nature and disorder." [238]

Progress. Evolving from the conception that progress meant the unfolding of man's capacities for reason and goodness and from the later conception that progress was somehow connected with "the survival of the fittest," in the American scene it became more and more restricted to economic and technological realms, to a complex and expanding industrial order. "Progress could now become a slogan to defend the course of technological innovation and economic rationalization and concentration. If small entrepreneurs, farmers, or urban workers felt economic distress, their condition could be considered a regrettable but necessary and temporary by-product of the triumphant march of progress." [239]

Material comfort. Facilities are increasingly used in America to gratify the senses.[240] Utilization of facilities which in the first instance represent luxury, freedom from drudgery and novel automation in a short time come to be regarded as expected, accepted, and "normal" rights which will not be relinquished easily even in the face of great social emergency.[241]

Equality. If economic reasons were solely considered, there would be nothing to prevent an individual who had nothing else to exchange from selling himself as a slave. Such possible economic utilizations of the person are restricted by the illegality of slavery, indentured servitude, imprisonment for debt and by the corresponding legalities of such procedures as bankruptcy proceedings. Although the principles of economic freedom and individual achievement have dominated principles of equality in so far as the latter is measured by the substantive equality of economic rewards, some concessions to substantive equality are made as in the graduated income tax. When facilities are distributed unequally, resentment is minimized where control of facilities is regarded as necessary for performance of valued functions, as in the case of the capable business executive or military leader.[242]

Freedom. The American concept of freedom requires that controls be exercised by a diffuse cultural structure rather than by a definite social organization. "A foreclosed mortgage has been culturally defined in a radically different way from governmental confiscation of the same property." [243] The Soviet conception of freedom is based a good deal more on the idea of facility utilization than is the American conception of freedom. "Broadly speaking, the Soviet conception of freedom emphasizes security in the sense of rights to employment, medical care, economic support, education, and cultural participation *within* an accepted framework set by the neo-Marxist state." [244]

External conformity. The American society, organized around the economic enterprise and characterized by individual competition and upward mobility exacts a stringent discipline over patterns of consumption and over the uses of time and resources. Conformity in these respects is derived from equality of opportunity and from success striving. The sanctioned innovations may be found in technological and economic experimentation, not in consumption patterns and in individualistic time and resource use.[245]

Science and secular rationality. Since science is a discipline, the important question is: a discipline for what? "Science is disciplined, rational, functional, active . . . it is congruent with the 'means' emphasis of the culture. . . ." [246] In its applied form it is a tool for the control of nature. It represents "order, control, and calculability—the passion of an engineering civilization." [247]

Nationalism-patriotism. This value may be expressed in isolationism as it was during the historical period when economic exploration, development and utilization was confined to the still undeveloped and unwon continent. It may also be expressed in expansionism which began to show up in a somewhat chauvinistic way as the area encompassed by the nation had been explored and exploited. To the degree that expansionism fosters intense nationalistic conflict it inevitably affects the use to which facilities are put, as for example, in the maintenance of a large military establishment. "The modern state in time of war must by its own terms of existence have centralized control of production; it must regulate consumption—there is actually no more infallible prescription for the destruction of laissez faire, the free market, and the individual entrepreneur."[248]

Democracy. The use of resources as related to democracy is subsumed here under freedom, equality, humanitarianism and other values.

Individual personality. The personality that is the object of high value in this tradition is of intrinsic worth, and not to be used as a means to an ulterior end. Militaristic activities and an overwhelming stress upon profit making in organized economic enterprises are in conflict with this value, and although calculating, impersonal uses of other individuals is inevitable to a degree, the tendency to use people as facilities is held in check by the above mentioned legal measures which proscribe slavery, peonage, and imprisonment for debt and which provide for bankruptcy proceedings.[249]

Racism and related group-superiority themes. To the extent that these themes are extant, they contraindicate the values of progress, equality, democracy, freedom, humanitarianism, individual achievement, and the central values of personality.[250]

Conclusions. Williams identifies sub-classes which specify a conjunction of values with the utilization of facilities. The category of "gratifications" is exemplified chiefly by the discussion above under material comfort. The category of "*instrumental interests* or means-values" is revealed in the above sections which deal in various ways with wealth, power, and work efficiency.[251]

COMPREHENSIVE OR MASTER PROCESSES

Communication. This process is taken so much for granted in Williams' work that it is never indexed under this or related headings. Williams does not make an analysis of generic communication but rather incorporates its exposition into the specific substantive area under his investigation. Thus, in his presidential address to the American Sociological Association one of his main focuses is upon "miniature theories" of group relations and of formal organization.

Broadly Williams implies that any explanation of prejudice which does not involve the mechanisms of belief transfer and sentiment exchange is not sound. Prejudice is learned.[252] Thus one of the most fundamental relationships found in intergroup research is that the frequency of interaction with members of an out-group is closely associated with favorable attitudes and lack of prejudice. In turn, the opportunities for contact are importantly determined by the age, sex, and related categorizations of social structure, which indicate acceptable lines of communication.[253] In this regard the discussions above both of cognitive mapping and communicaton of sentiment should be recalled. Similarly Williams' stress on the inevitable emergence of informal organization with lines of communication outside the official structure in the analysis of large scale organizations was discussed above.

Williams in *American Society* sees the United States as uniquely equipped with the facilities for mass communication.[254] As a result, coupled with cultural pluralism, Williams suggests that the often noted "flatness" of American public discourse is attributable to a search for noncontroversial conversation pieces which, at the experienced level of the individual, reduces personal anxiety and conflict and, at the societal level, produces tendencies toward integration. In other words, the areas of "blocked" communication signal conflicts which can remain nondisabling only to the extent that they are kept from overt crystallization.[255] Complementing this phenomenon is the role of common symbols in the American culture. Williams hypothesizes that:

... the most important symbols of national unity have so little specific ideological content that they create a common allegiance by being all things to all men ... within wide limits, it is precisely the amorphous, protean, and unstructured nature of the most inclusive societal symbols that gives them their enormously powerful capacity for *defining as common* that which, from other points of view, is different or even incompatible.[256]

The role of communication is the integrating of interaction, a function which is further served by the next master process.

Boundary maintenance. The phenomena involved in this concept are important for Williams particularly in his treatment of societal integration and certain aspects of prejudice. The process is implied in his definition of system which is conceived as "a definite arrangement of parts having boundaries, unity of cohesion, resistance to external forces, and enduring through time." [257] Boundary maintenance as it occurs in the United States is evidenced particularly by the great proliferation of discrete groups and secondary associations, and is exemplified most sharply in prejudice.

Within the invisible walls of the collectivity, the expression of out-group "prejudice" provides a legitimized mode for the management of otherwise disruptive or uncomfortable intra-group aggressions, supplies a common universe of discourse, reinforces a sense of belonging, and serves as a set of credentials of membership.[258]

These integrative tendencies of group membership are among the most obstructive elements in reducing prejudice and serve to divide society. Group rivalry or competition is a factor in evoking strongly hostile feelings between groups or collectivities at the same time that it is an integrative force within the competing groups. The socio-cultural diversity of the United States makes it a near-pure type of the most difficult case of societal integration.

For Williams societal integration cannot be accounted for by biological and physical factors, nor can it be explained by "social contract" theories nor by the concept of society as a congery of power systems. The sociological explanation of integration must be sought in the shared common culture. "This is a hard-won insight in the history of thought about society and its importance must be given every possible emphasis." [259] This is not the entire picture, however. Willams singles out five factors which contribute to the cohesion and boundary maintenance of American society.[260]

First there is a necessary interdependence for the attaining of individual goals, especially as there is an elaborate division of labor. Second, the sense of external threat reduces the potency of the internal boundaries which separate groups and tends to create during the period of emergency a high degree of societal solidarity. Third, there is an important measure of unity in diversity. Overlapping identities and multigroup memberships serve an integrative function. Williams hypothesizes that "a society riven by many minor cleavages is in less danger of open mass conflict than a society with only one or a few cleavages." [261]

The fourth factor of cohesion—common value orientation—does not mean agreement upon all details or norms regulating specific behavior patterns. Underlying the great diversity is a belief of consensus upon the ultimate or basic principles supplying the generalized meanings for conduct. [262] Finally, Williams notes that for the "common interest" base of solidarity to function in the complex society there must be structural arrangements and techniques of action that articulate interdependence and block conflict. These he calls "mechanisms of cohesion." In American society mass communication is one such element which operates to give standardized information and common value stimuli. Another mechanism is a more universal phenomena.

To participate in groups that provide regularized expectations seems to be a necessary condition for the organization of personalities as unitary systems . . . group participation necessarily means a process of reciprocal control among individuals . . . individuals give up a considerable degree of autonomy and renounce many nonconforming tendencies in seeking group membership. [263]

This, of course, refers to primary group structure. The complex organization that is American society in total involves numerous smaller groups linked by step communication, pyramidal representation and chains of authority into end products of vast complexity. The pattern of growth and articulation is that involved in such familiar cases as say moving from the plant local to the national union or the local ward political unit through the city machine to state and finally national political parties. With this proliferation of large scale organization Williams feels that cohesion in such a society is in part a strictly technical problem, of knowledge and techniques for handling problems of intergroup and interorganizational relations. [264]

As larger and larger systems of organization have spread across our society, the roles of the nodal control-points and centers of communication have become increasingly . . . invested with a public interest. . . . At the levels at which separate systems of interaction, imbued with different values and interests come into contact, coordination is achieved (if at all) through processes of negotiation, compromise, and so on.[265]

Cohesion and boundary maintenance for society is partly dependent upon sheer techniques for successful compromise and negotiation. The final mechanism of importance to Williams is the isolaton and/or insulation of groups and statuses from one another. In the American case this ranges from the primarily important role of preferential association to categorical exclusion as witnessed in racial caste-like relations in parts of the South. Williams sees that if groups differ widely in their values and interests, a mutually accepted insulation is a mechanism for at least the temporary avoidance of overt friction.[266] At the same time this mechanism can be both cure and disease. Continued isolation often leads to value dissonance and therefore strikes ultimately at the heart of the boundary maintaining aspects of society.

Systemic linkage. As was true with boundary maintenance, this term as such does not appear in Williams' work but the idea is obviously present. Among the propositions that Williams accepts as fundamental to sociology generally are: 1) that institutions and groups can be meaningfully handled as systems and 2) such systems are not autonomous but have multiple interconnections—"the total society is constituted by various subsystems and their reciprocal linkages." [267] By linkage Williams means, a) interdependence of parts of the total system so that what occurs in one part of society can ramify widely to all aspects of the system whether that ramification is direct or not; or b) a more limited process of direct linkages between systems in the PAS Model sense. Much of Williams' analysis tends toward the first meaning, for instance, the interrelations of institutions in *American Society* as exemplified by the interconnections of kinship with the occupational, political and stratification systems and of the economic with the political systems.[268] The more limited idea of systemic linkage in the PAS Model sense is exemplified by instances in which status-role provides the linking mechanism.

. . . institutions are linked together in the expectations and values of individuals who are institutionally committed to deal with other role specialists. The study of institutions and their interrelations already has gained greatly in precision and predictive value by moving beyond the macroscopic approach to the specific investigations of *status-role problems* and *group structures*. In this way it is possible to bring out specific mechanisms of structural interrelation as well as to explore the dynamic processes of institutional change.[269]

The actualities of interdependence embodied in the first meaning, to some degree influence the specific contexts for the second meaning of systemic linkage. Thus, in American society there is little emphasis on family continuity. This fact is directly compatible with the competitive, economically oriented and secularly rational culture. At the same time that the isolated conjugal family deemphasizes the importance of systemic linkage it tends to maintain equal linkages to both husband's and wife's families of orientation. American economic activity has its distinctive kind of systemic linkage too. Williams enumerates seven mechanisms by which corporations are linked together: 1) interlocking directorates; 2) intercorporate stockholding; 3) concentrated stock ownership by individuals or groups in several corporations; 4) common servicing by large financial organizations; investment blocks; 5) trade and business associations; 6) legal and contractual controls (utilized to co-ordinate sub-contractors, retail outlets, patent controls, etc. etc.); 7) informal or tacit agreements and understandings.[270]

In a society marked by relatively great differentiation of function "*different individuals* and *different organizations* are the prime carriers of the various sets of norms which otherwise would be partial systems of the same personalities or overlapping roles in a relatively undifferentiated community."[270a] The effects of differentiation are expressed most vividly for Williams in respect to intergroup relations. He feels that a significant part of such contacts in urbanized societies takes the form of mediating linkage between collectivities as such rather than as a net of diffuse personal interactions. The mediating links are given as individuals act out roles as formal or informal representatives of various segments of society. Furthermore, unless otherwise constrained, *intergroup* relations tend to occur between persons with high status in their respective groups. Linkage between groups if it occurs, tends to be "at the top."[270b]

Socialization. Several factors combine to lend to the process of socialization a universally prominent place: the non-transmission of culture by biological inheritance, the consequent need that the cultural heritage be renewed for each generation, and the plasticity and long period of dependency of the human young. In a real sense the young constitute "barbarians" who must be taught the multitude of relevant skills, cognitive patterns, values, sentiments, and norms if the culture is to have continuity.[271] The institutions of a society are perpetuated in their necessary personality correlates by means of socialization.[272]

The process is never ending. Williams sees socialization varying from explicit instruction with specialized personnel responsible and operating in a special organization, as is true of education in highly differentiated societies, to the highly informal indoctrination among family, peers, and other primary type groups which occurs in all societies. "*Everywhere*, the child absorbs an enormous and complex range of cultural materials as a more or less unplanned, informal by-product of growing up in a family and community." [273] The converse is also true. Even in the less differentiated societies there are definite institutionalized and systematic patterns of instruction and indoctrination, taking such forms as initiation rites and inculcation to secret societies. Thus the socialization process is basically comprised of thousands of specific, concrete experiences with various persons in specific contexts.[274]

As long as man can learn he is susceptible to socialization. With diverse, multiple attachments coupled with the unlearning which attends much of learning, it cannot be expected that socialization as a process is unitary. Williams' substantive studies turn up evidence of inconsistent socializing experiences and these are assumed to produce "strains" which are conducive to social change.[275]

Social Control. As the process which either decreases deviance or makes it compatible within the functioning of a social system, social control has been anticipated primarily under the discussions of the elements norms, sanction, power, and sentiments. As a result only certain aspects and relevant points not made explicit in these prior discussions will be considered in the present section.

"The mechanism whereby a status system (or, more generally,

a social order) is maintained and perpetuated is that of the cultural patterning of attitudes (affects) in the direction of conformity with the going system of positions and by the establishment of emotional reactions against violations of the appropriate patterns." [276] In one direction this statement pinpoints the motivational aspect of social control and the non-rational bases of integration and control. The importance of the communication of sentiment in conforming behavior was reviewed above but less attention was given to other considerations related to motivation. It has been noted previously that Williams' major work, *American Society*, is expressedly and primarily a structural analysis of the normative order and pointedly does not try to give extended treatment to the "culture-and-personality" problem,[277] although this does not mean that the perspective of the motivated actor is neglected. Like Weber, Williams is concerned with this perspective and like Weber does not wish simply to psychologize his sociological interests.

The mechanisms of integration previously discussed take on added meaning for social control because, in one sense, boundaries of social systems necessarily imply minimal levels of adequate social control.[278] Williams finds social tension and struggle arising from two broad types of situations: 1) that in which there are differences in interest centered around scarce and divisible values but with ultimate convictions in common and 2) that in which ultimate values (the religious and moral) are at variance. Where the participants in a social aggregate hold ultimate convictions in common, there is a basis for control capable of overriding otherwise disruptive conflicts.[279] The second condition can bring on the most unholy spectacle—the holy war. In less severe form controls may be of the type designated as "cultural fictions." The phenomena handled by "cultural fiction" are two:

A cultural fiction exists whenever there is a cultural description, explanation, or normative prescription that is both *generally accepted as a norm* and is *typically followed* in conduct but is at the same time markedly at variance with the subjective conceptions or inclinations of participants in the pattern, or with certain objective scientific knowledges.[280]

Williams notes that when, on other grounds it is important

that interaction occur but there are few and relatively weak positive ties between the participants, and the interaction involves severe conflicts of values or interests then fictions in the mode of formality, conventionalization, protocol and stylized interaction will be maximized.[281] Examples of such "fictional" relations include diplomatic convention, judicial procedures, and military courtesy. Culturally ascribed meaning here is often in direct opposition to the privately held meanings actually involved and power is, necessarily, a crucial aspect and often barely veiled as the sanction for conformity.

Short of this limiting case of social control Williams summarizes the process by seeing that the general conditions fostering a high degree of conformity among institutional norms are, basically, those conditions that allow conformity to produce conformity.[282] With a high degree of consensus on the standards of conduct,

Behavior is incessantly and subtly corrected by the responses of others; firmly interdependent expectations are integrated into mutually supporting self-other patterns. Incipient nonconformity is subject to immediate and unanimous attempts at control, and overt nonconformity occasions reaffirmation of the threatened norms through disapproval and the imposition of sanctions.[283]

Institutionalization. For Williams institutionalization grows out of interaction: "As persons interact, mutual expectations and concerns arise, and as interaction continues over time, more-or-less definite *patterns* emerge." [284] The centrality of such patterned behavior and order in the form of shared cultural and institutional norms cannot be overstated for Williams. At the same time it has been noted continually that the institutionalized norms of social conduct never fully define concrete action. Patterned interaction varies along a continuum, from the point at which behavior is defined and set by a definite system of institutional norms to the limiting cases in which interaction transpires without mutually shared codes of conduct.[285] However, Williams sees interaction, considered as empirical phenomena, as tending to gravitate toward the first pole. The amplification of this tendency was made primarily under the element norm and in the introductory overview where institution was discussed. Already discussed but worthy of recall is the noteworthy contribution which Williams has made to the understanding of institutionalization as represented in those "secondary institutions" which he also calls "patterned evasion." [286]

CONDITIONS OF SOCIAL ACTION

Territoriality. For Williams sheer contiguity is always of prime importance in the problems of power and conflict. That is, social groups necessarily occupy geographical territory whose control is important. Furthermore, conflict, particularly the most destructive type of physical violence, must occur in a definite place.[287] On the other hand, with respect to intergroup relations, he observes that even in the presence of quite marked prejudices, the likelihood of social interaction is increased when the functional proximity of individuals in space is greater.[288] It was shown above that increased interaction tends to reduce prejudice. Of course, the relationship does not always hold. "Sheer physical proximity does permit interaction through which a common life can be developed, but there are too many instances of social conflict between, or estrangement of, geographically adjacent or intermingled populations for us to expect that proximity will *necessarily* increase the likelihood of integration." [289] Williams posits a corollary proposition which involves space and size: that dispersing minorities not as communities but as individuals and small groups in a wide area and at variant statuses in social structure tends to diffuse and reduce hostility to them.[290]

In his analysis of American society Williams finds territoriality particularly significant in the historic development of the society and its culture and in some degree important yet today.[291] The significance of the frontier as expounded by Frederick Jackson Turner is accepted and the idea or perception by the early settlers of the United States of having apparently unlimited land in contrast to their tight, localistic, and feudally-tinged homelands is deemed vital.[292] Williams argues that in agrarian societies the total structure of relations is closely connected with the scope of land resources and the territorial conditions under which utilization occurs. In this sense, unlike many sociologists in America he is willing to assert that for the United States, "In our correct recognition of the diminished contrast between city and country, we cannot assume that no important differences remain." [293]

Size. At a number of points in the foregoing discussions size as a condition of action has been implied. Williams frequently observes that what Toennies would call *Gesellschaft*-like features of institutional and social structure are associated with largeness. The converse tendency of large-scale formal structures to "break down" into informal, smaller scale units has also been noted in regard to communication and management of tension. In handling social control Williams observes that, irrespective of the size of society or social organization from the *observer's perspective,* effective normative integration and, derivatively, control *subjectively* is contingent upon the behavioral regularities encountered (or not) in the "relatively small circle of other persons" that is the meaningful interactive environment of most persons. In this vein, Williams' analysis is quite compatible with Homans who observes that large scale organizations throughout history tend to be formed from "building blocks" more or less the same size.[294] The number of actors capable of supervision *directly* by one status-role authority in *reciprocal relations* seems to have physical limits.

Time. As a condition of action time is given little direct attention by Williams. Within the focus of *American Society* the potential to "compress" time by rapid communication is seen as an important aspect to understanding the culture. Similarly, the recognition that time can (and must to some degree) function as a condition of action obviously underlies the a-historical propensity attributed to the American—an imputation which in Williams' view does not emphasize sufficiently the future orientation of the society. Williams' most recent analysis of the oscillation of external and internal system requirements of systems also points to time as a condition and leads directly to the last consideration of this chapter, namely social change.

Social Change. Like most structural-functional analysts, Williams argues that before change can be understood it is necessary to see what it is that changes, something which can only be done against an established structural bench mark.[295] Social and cultural change as a potential field of study should according to Williams, receive more attention than it has. Rather than developing a full blown theory of change himself, his work in this regard is perhaps best interpreted as a series of notes toward a theory of change.

Williams distinguishes between social and cultural change. The latter refers to "changes in systems of ideas of various kinds, in beliefs, in values and norms; included also in this category are changes in the technical apparatus used for dealing with the physical world." [296] Social change refers to shifts in the concrete interaction modes of person-to-person contacts. In both, what Williams calls "social motion" or eventfulness is not equated with change. Change occurs only when:

there is a shift in pattern—when new relationships emerge, new standards and goals become shared. It is not necessarily social change if an individual meets a situation new to him nor if individuals vary in their behavior in given types of situations—only when the difference is shared and endures long enough to be recognizable as a new structure can we say that the culture or the society has changed.[297]

The model social system with such perfect integration that its basic normative patterns would not change over long periods and which at any time would find social interaction manifesting only slight and rare deviation from norms would, according to Williams, require a small population, with stable birth and death rates, adjusted to a stable physical environment and isolated from other cultures. Obviously every modern society has important structural aspects and strains which move them away from this model state.[298]

Williams asserts that at least six "most general" factors contribute causally to social change. First, changes in the physical environment or biological nature such as climate shifts or genetic mutation can be important but are vigorously denied as *the* factor as these were used in earlier reductionistic theories. The five remaining factors contributing to change are: 1) the character and frequency of intercultural contact as examplified in conquests, invasions, migrations, or trade relations; 2) the complexities in the cultural and social structure and their relations as seen in the differentiation and contact of subcultures and status-roles; 3) the relative emphasis on traditionalism and innovation, sacred or secular interests, and related values; 4) the unanticipated or "latent" changes of purposive social action as when an unintended war transpires or secularization results from a religious creed; 5) the "idiosyncratic and creative variations in individual behavior arising both from various difficulties in conformity to norms and from certain sources of indeterminancy and spontaneity in the social development of the individual human being." [299] Three facts in this regard stand out for Williams; first, in largest part socio-cultural changes are derived from internal processes of social systems; [300] second, men's ideas and values are real causal variables; [301] and, third, social monofactorial explanations are inadequate. [302]

The last point needs further attention and its consideration will lead back to the first two. Williams argues that to refute monofactorial theories, does not necessarily lead to advocacy of indiscriminate eclecticism, or the easy evasion of the problem of causation through a multiple factor model which is unable to specify relative degrees of importance to the factors. [303] However, this situation is not explicitly met by Williams. Weights are never clearly assigned by him to his factors. Given his plural basis for change and granting that internal social system processes are crucial the difficulty of the task is implied when he observes that, "the central or leading institution(s) varies from society to society in a given period, and from one period to another in a given society. Further, there may not in fact be any one clearly dominant institutional system." [304] Thus, following Weber and Parsons, the Protestant ethic with its prophetic and worldly asceticism he considers as a strong influence in the development of capitalism, but, in turning to the American case Williams feels that the actions of the major churches as collectivities appear to have been mainly shaped by external pressures rather than by the immanent development of religious value-orientations. In a word the churches have usually trailed rather than led social change. [305] In related fashion, Williams finds the Ogburn "culture lag" theory, that technological change leads and other changes follow, is in large part valid for the American case but that the role of technology for social change is minor in other societies where a value system such as that which exists in the United States is not present. Williams succinctly characterizes Americans as holding a belief in rapid change; a belief accompanied by national pride making it almost unpatriotic to question this article of faith too closely.[306] As a result, technological change has taken on "special causal significance." [307]

Although Williams does not carefully specify the relative importance of the various factors which produce change in America, the development of his more general theoretical discussions has anticipated repeatedly one highly important aspect.

. . . much of the dynamism of the social system seems attributable to a continuing tension between ideal norms and situational realities . . . What we [as concrete actors] directly experience is always a variant of the patterns discernible by external scientific abstraction, and each of us has countless occasions for idiosyncratic interpretation of norms. The most complete description of institutional norms would still not tell us exactly how to act in specific situations. It is therefore not a source of wonder that there is variation, evasion, and complex change in institutions . . . Culture and society are always changing, and the first tiny breaches of normative structure are to be carefully watched in any attempt to comprehend the sources of social change.[308]

Williams' theory of change then emphasizes his major analytical distinction between culture on the one hand with its focus on the normative aspect, and social organization on the other hand. The degree of conformity as manifest in actual human interaction then becomes the crucial consideration.[309]

Focusing on the relative indeterminacy of any interaction situation as crucial in change does not mean for Williams that change is simply a matter of "drift." The social nexus of motivation was discussed above under patterned evasion in relation to the element norm. "It does bear repeating that drastic concerted action to transform a social system seems usually to come from *powerful* groupings that feel their *legitimate aspirations systematically blocked* or their vested positions drastically threatened." [310] Assuming then that power is important, the emphasis on indeterminacy does underline a basic dictum for Williams; "specific norms and values must be empirically traced through specific social roles and social groups," [311] before change can be really appreciated and prime movers specified. In this context his observation that "cultural diffusion and social change are initially absorbed by the least structured portions of institutional systems" [312] can be more accurately qualified and result in greater predictive specificity.

BIBLIOGRAPHICAL KEY *

AS—Robin M. Williams, Jr., *American Society* (New York: Alfred A. Knopf, 2nd ed., rev., 1960).

AS (1st)—Same as above, 1st edition, 1951.

CCSS—Robin M. Williams, Jr., "Continuity and Change in Sociological Study," *American Sociological Review*, Vol. 23 (December, 1958).

Comment—Robin M. Williams, Jr., comments on the paper by Allison Davis, "American Status Systems and the Socialization of the Child," *American Sociological Review*, Vol. 6 (August, 1941).

RCR—Robin M. Williams, Jr., "Racial and Cultural Relations," in Joseph B. Gittler, ed., *Review of Sociology: Analysis of a Decade* (New York: John Wiley and Sons, 1957).

RIT—Robin M. Williams, Jr., *The Reduction of Intergroup Tensions: A Survey of Research on Problems of Ethnic, Racial, and Religious Group Relations* (New York: Social Science Research Council, 1947).

RSCS—Robin M. Williams, Jr., "Rural Sociology in a Changing Society: Future Problems and Prospects," paper presented to the North-Central Rural Sociology Committee, November 11, 1959 at Chicago, Illinois; in *Rural Sociology in a Changing Society* (Columbus, Ohio: Ag. Ext. Service, 1960, mimeo.).

RVOIC—Robin M. Williams, Jr., "Religion, Value-Orientations, and Intergroup Conflict," *Journal of Social Issues*, Vol. 12, no. 3 (1956).

SOSR—Robin M. Williams, Jr., "Some Observations on Sociological Research in Government during World War II," *American Sociological Review*, Vol. 11 (October, 1946).

ST—Robin M. Williams, Jr. and Margaret W. Ryan, eds., *Schools in Transition* (Chapel Hill: University of North Carolina Press, 1954).

STTP—Robin M. Williams, Jr., "The Sociological Theory of Talcott Parsons: An Expository Review," paper prepared for the Faculty Seminar on Parsonian Theory, Cornell University, Fall, 1958 (mimeo.).

VMEUS—Robin M. Williams, Jr., "Values and Modern Education in the United States," a paper prepared for *Values in American Society: A Symposium* (University of Notre Dame, March 23-24, 1959).

NOTES

1. Robin M. Williams, Jr., "Rural Sociology in a Changing Society: Future Problems and Prospects," paper presented to the North-Central Rural Sociology Committee, November 11, 1959 at Chicago, Illinois, contained in *Rural Sociology in a Changing Society* (Columbus, Ohio: Ag. Ext. Service, 1960, mimeo.) p. 4. Hereafter designated as RSCS.

* For a more complete bibliography see the notes which follow as well as the bibliography which appears at the end of the volume.

2. Robin M. Williams, Jr., *American Society* (New York: Alfred A. Knopf, 2nd ed., rev., 1960). Hereafter designated as AS. Citation will occasionally be made to the 1st ed., 1951, designated as AS (1st).

3. AS (1st), p. 6.

4. See, e.g., Robin Williams, Jr., *The Reduction of Intergroup Tensions: A Survey of Research on Problems of Ethnic, Racial, and Religious Group Relations* (New York: Social Science Research Council, 1947) p. 47. Italics removed. Hereafter designated as RIT.

5. AS, p. 5.

6. *Ibid.*, p. 512.   7. *Ibid.*

8. *Ibid.*, p. 471.   9. *Ibid.*, p. 23.

10. *Ibid.*, p. 37. Cf. Marion J. Levy, Jr., *The Structure of Society* (Princeton: Princeton Univ. Press, 1952) pp. 145 ff. and Marion J. Levy, Jr., "Some Questions about 'The Concepts of Culture and of Social System,'" *American Sociological Review*, Vol. 24 (April, 1959) pp. 297 ff.

11. AS, pp. 20-21. Williams defines structure in general as a "relatively fixed relationship between elements, parts or entities." *Ibid.*, p. 20.

12. *Ibid.*, pp. 23-4.

13. *Ibid.*, (1st), p. 23. In the second edition Williams sets out knowledge, beliefs and technology as aspects under this category. Their meaning, however, is not changed. *Knowledge* refers to those aspects "reliably certified as true of the empirical world" by scientific canons; *beliefs*, involve propositions inherently "untestable by science" (e.g., the existence of heaven or hell) or those not yet rigorously tested but capable of test by science; *technology*, concerns the application of knowledge and beliefs to transform events in the existential world. Cf, AS, pp. 23-4.

14. AS, p. 31.   15. *Ibid.*

16. *Ibid.*, pp. 31-2.

17. *Ibid.*, p. 516. Italics removed.

18. *Ibid.*, p. 398.

19. Ibid., (1st), p. 445. The term social system is not used in the revised edition of *American Society* although the same distinction is made. Social relation is used to cover both levels of organization. Cf, AS, pp. 473-4.

20. AS, p. 477. Cf. also the preface by C. P. Loomis and John C. McKinney to F. Toennies, *Community and Society*, tr. and ed. by C. P. Loomis (East Lansing: Michigan State University Press, 1957) pp. 12-29.

21. *Ibid.*, p. 486.

22. *Ibid.*, pp. 483-4. In some respects the informal organization depicted by Williams but never specifically defined, resembles the subinstitutional elementary social behavior as portrayed by Homans in *Social Behavior*. See Chapter 4 of present volume.

23. *Ibid.*, (1st), p. 375.

24. The distinction between values as objects of choice and the criteria in terms of which choices of objects are made is emphasized in the revised edition of *American Society* and the important point made that values, as standards of the desirable, are "not immediately given to us by knowing the goals men seek." AS, p. 401.

25. AS, pp. 403-7.   26. *Ibid.*, p. 399.

27. See fn. 4 *supra*. See also Robin M. Williams, Jr., "Review of Cur-

rent Research in Rural Sociology," *Rural Sociology,* Vol. 11 (June, 1946) p. 109. Hereafter designated as CR.

28. The need for complementary research emphases is treated in the following: Robin M. Williams, Jr., "Some Observations on Sociological Research in Government during World War II," *American Sociological Review,* vol. 11 (October, 1946) pp. 573-7. Hereafter designated as SOSR. The same theme occurs in Robin M. Williams, Jr., "The Sociological Theory of Talcott Parsons: An Expository Review," paper prepared for the Faculty Seminar on Parsonian Theory, Cornell University, Fall, 1958, (mimeo.) Cf. particularly pp. 36-43. Hereafter designated as STTP. Here he sees as the most serious limit in Parsons' works the paucity of suggestions for operational meaning and for validations of hypotheses. Williams acknowledges that in his own work he has tried to see what could be done empirically with a minimal conceptual scheme. RSCS, p. 7. Since the above was written STTP has been published in Max Black, ed. *The Social Theories of Talcott Parsons,* (Englewood Cliffs, N. J.: Prentice-Hall, Inc., 1961).

29. AS, p. 469.

30. *Ibid.,* p. 23. Williams designates these distinctions as purely heuristic, "utilized because of practical convenience and claiming no 'ultimate validity.'" *Ibid.,* fn. 6. *See also,* RIT, pp. 25-6.

31. AS, p. 148.   32. *Ibid.,* p. 324.

33. *Ibid.,* p. 323.   34. *Ibid.,* p. 326.

35. *Ibid.,* p. 328.   36. *Ibid.,* p. 332.

37. *Ibid.,* p. 329.

38. Robin M. Williams, Jr., "Religion, Value-Orientations, and Intergroup Conflict," *Journal of Social Issues,* Vol. 12, No. 3 (1956) p. 13. Hereafter designated as RVOIC.

39. AS, p. 455.   40. *Ibid.,* p. 455.

41. Henry Margenau, "Western Culture and Scientific Method," in L. Bryson, L. Finkelstein, and P. M. MacIver, eds., *Conflicts of Power in Modern Culture,* Seventh Symposium on the Conference on Science, Philosophy and Religion (New York: Harpers, 1948), p. 16; as cited in AS, p. 454.

42. AS, p. 455.   43. *Ibid.,* p. 72.

44. *Ibid.,* pp. 113-4.   45. *Ibid.,* pp. 132-3.

46. *Ibid.,* p. 148.   47. *Ibid.,* p. 220.

48. *Ibid.,* pp. 242-3.   49. RIT, p. 37.

50. *Ibid.,* p. 36.

51. Robin M. Williams, Jr., "Racial and Cultural Relations," in Joseph B. Gittler, ed., *Review of Sociology: Analysis of a Decade* (N. Y.: John Wiley & Sons, 1957), p. 432. Hereafter designated as RCR.

52. T. W. Adorno, et. al., *The Authoritarian Personality* (New York: Harper and Brothers, 1950).

53. RCR, p. 435.

54. Cf. Robert F. Bales, "Social Therapy for a Social Disorder: Compulsive Drinking," *Journal of Social Issues,* Vol. 1, No. 3 (1945) pp. 14-22.

55. AS, p. 468.

56. Williams notes that "if one goes through [American Society] . . . he'll see a continual drumbeat of recognition of the affective dimension." Asked why he did not use sentiment or some comparable concept as a tool of analysis he replied that at the time he "was struggling . . . for independ-

ence from psychology . . . very much interested in linking [sociology] with psychology but trying to establish the possibility of talking analytically about social phenomena without introducing psychologcal intervening variables except when one wanted to and not being forced to do it. This is the gap in the treatment." From tape recorded interview, April, 1960.

57. AS, p. 400. Values have additional attributes including a relation to goal which is treated under end, goal or objective as an element.

58. RIT, *passim.*

59. Robin M. Williams, Jr., "Continuity and Change in Sociological Study," *American Sociological Review,* Vol. 23 (December, 1958) p. 628. Hereafter designated as CCSS. For a somewhat opposite view on the part of George Homans see fn. 20 Ch. 4 and related text.

60. AS, pp. 458-9.   61. *Ibid.,* p. 43.

62. *Ibid.,* p. 60.   63. *Ibid.*

64. *Ibid.,* pp. 145-6.   65. *Ibid.,* p. 147.

66. *Ibid.,* pp. 148-9.   67. *Ibid.,* p. 288.

68. *Ibid.,* p. 330.   69. *Ibid.,* pp. 334-5.

70. *Ibid.,* p. 376.   71. *Ibid.,* p. 425.

72. *Ibid.,* p. 393.   73. *Ibid.,* p. 454, fn. 3.

74. *Ibid.,* p. 436.   75. *Ibid.,* p. 498.

76. *Ibid.,* p. 510.

77. RIT, p. 57. For an early use of the concept "fund of good will" see *Ibid.,* p. 37. Williams writes "As best I can remember I was using the notion of 'fund of good will,' in teaching at Cornell in the Spring of 1946." From correspondence.

78. *Ibid.,* p. 63.   79. CCSS, p. 627.

80. AS, p. 401.

81. Compare AS, pp. 399-409 with AS (1st), pp. 374-82.

82. AS, pp. 468-469.   83. *Ibid.,* p. 378.

84. As specified in tape-recorded interview concerning earlier version of present chapter, April, 1960.

85. Tape recorded discussion, April, 1960.

86. Winston White, "Some Comments on Williams' Discussion of American Values," unpublished manuscript.

87. *Ibid.,* p. 18.   88. AS, p. 409, fn. 2.

89. *Ibid.,* p. 401.   90. *Ibid.,* p. 479.

91. *Ibid.,* p. 429.   92. *Ibid.,* p. 430.

93. *Ibid.,* p. 431.   94. *Ibid.*

95. *Ibid.,* pp. 158-9.   96. *Ibid.,* p. 191.

97. *Ibid.*   98. *Ibid.,* p. 200.

99. *Ibid.,* p. 217.   100. *Ibid.,* p. 218.

101. *Ibid.,* p. 220.   102. *Ibid.,* p. 261.

103. *Ibid.,* p. 272.   104. *Ibid.,* p. 320.

105. *Ibid.,* p. 321.   106. *Ibid.,* p. 362.

107. RIT, p. 10.   108. AS, p. 419.

109. *Ibid.,* p. 378.   110. *Ibid.,* p. 420.

111. *Ibid.,* p. 421.   112. *Ibid.,* p. 173.

113. *Ibid.,* p. 311.   114. *Ibid.,* p. 319, fn. 5.

115. Winston White, *op. cit.*

116. AS, p. 435.   117. *Ibid.,* p. 372.

118. Cf. Richard T. Morris, "A Typology of Norms," *American Sociological Review*, Vol. 21 (October, 1956) pp. 610-3. This work attempts to systematize norms partly from the lead offered by AS (1st). In turn, Williams generally follows the Morris work.

119. AS, pp. 26-30. 120. *Ibid.*, p. 31.

121. *Ibid.*, p. 33.

122. *Ibid.*, p. 24, pp. 397-399.

123. *Ibid.*, p. 408. Italics added.

124. *Ibid.*, pp. 409-410.

125. *Ibid.*, p. 424. 126. *Ibid.*, p. 428.

127. *Ibid.*, p. 430. 128. *Ibid.*, p. 452.

129. *Ibid.*, p. 451. 130. *Ibid.*, p. 453.

131. "I seem to use it [the completely integrated society] as a home base to come back and touch once in a while." From taped interview, April, 1960.

132. AS, p. 378.

133. *Ibid.*, p. 379. Material rearranged.

134. Williams makes the interesting observation that: "An organized religious body, dependent upon and integrated within the social structure can deal more easily with passive conformity than with extreme piety . . . For example, the Roman Catholic Church devised various monastic orders in which the drastically spiritual elements could be insulated from the steady operation of the ordinary religious community." AS, pp. 330-1.

135. *Ibid.*, p. 381. See fn. 286 below for credit to Merton.

136. See *Ibid.*, pp. 381-91.

137. *Ibid.*, p. 151.

138. *Ibid.*, pp. 153 and 158.

139. *Ibid.*, pp. 35-6. 140. *Ibid.*, p. 507.

141. *Ibid.*, p. 516. 142. *Ibid.*, pp. 516-7.

143. *Ibid.*, p. 517. 144. *Ibid.*, pp. 68-70.

145. *Ibid.*, p. 74. 146. *Ibid.*, p. 230.

147. *Ibid.*, p. 237. 148. *Ibid.*, pp. 236, 238.

149. *Ibid.*, p. 518. 150. *Ibid.*, p. 304.

151. *Ibid.*, p. 487. 152. *Ibid.*, p. 490.

153. *Ibid.*, pp. 503-4. 154. CCSS, pp. 627-8.

155. *Ibid.*, p. 628, fn. 22. Credit is given to Robert Bales for the observation.

156. AS, p. 552. 157. RCR, p. 445.

158. RIT, p. 66. 159. AS, p. 90.

160. *Ibid.*, p. 94. 161. *Ibid.*, p. 93.

162. *Ibid.*, p. 98. 163. *Ibid.*, p. 101.

164. *Ibid.*, pp. 104-5. 165. *Ibid.*, p. 92.

166. *Ibid.*, p. 96. 167. *Ibid.*, pp. 96-7.

168. *Ibid.*, p. 97. 169. *Ibid.*, p. 463.

170. *Ibid.*, p. 443. 171. *Ibid.*, pp. 466-7.

172. AS (1st), p. 106. The quotation is credited to P. A. Sorokin, *Social Mobility* (New York: Harpers, 1927) pp. 401-4. More current data reviewed by Williams leads to essentially the same conclusion. Cf. AS, pp. 117-24.

173. CCSS, p. 625.

174. AS, pp. 128-29.   175. *Ibid.*, pp. 125-6, fn. 5.
176. RIT, p. 58.   177. AS, p. 114.
178. *Ibid.*, p. 216.   179. *Ibid.*, pp. 215-6.
180. *Ibid.*, p. 217. Williams has noted that " 'social group' is one of those treacherous terms with an apparently simple common-sense connotation that conceals multiple unclarities." *Ibid.*, p. 474. He reserves the term "for those interacting aggregates of persons in which the participants regard themselves, for certain purposes, as a unit of solidarity possessing shared interests, values or behavior patterns that set them off from other groups." *Ibid.*, pp. 474-475.
181. *Ibid.*, pp. 229-30.   182. *Ibid.*, pp. 238-9.
183. *Ibid.*, p. 253.   184. *Ibid.*, p. 449.
185. *Ibid.*, p. 446.   186. *Ibid.*, p. 461.
187. *Ibid.*, p. 158.   188. *Ibid.*, p. 160.
189. *Ibid.*, p. 161.   190. *Ibid.*, pp. 163-4.
191. *Ibid.*, p. 207.   192. *Ibid.*, pp. 207-8.
193. *Ibid.*, p. 214.   194. *Ibid.*
195. *Ibid.*, pp. 217 ff. See also Robin M. Williams, Jr. and Margaret W. Ryan, eds., *Schools in Transition* (Chapel Hill: University of North Carolina Press, 1954). Here Williams offers a large number of specific case studies of decision making functions at the community level with respect to desegregating schools. This book will be referred to hereafter as ST.
196. AS, p. 230.   197. *Ibid.*, p. 233.
198. *Ibid.*, p. 234.   199. *Ibid.*, p. 233.
200. *Ibid.*, p. 488.   201. *Ibid.*, p. 276.
202. That this is the case is amply shown for American society and Western nations generally, cf., *Ibid.*, pp. 183 ff. In this regard Williams makes the highly provocative observation that: "The structure of power in the large economic organization is already somewhat similar to that of a 'socialistic' order." *Ibid.*, p. 277.
203. *Ibid.*, p. 278.   204. *Ibid.*, p. 506.
205. CCSS, p. 626.
206. Cf., RCR, p. 439; ST, pp. 233 ff.
207. AS, p. 246.   208. *Ibid.*, p. 59.
209. *Ibid.*, p. 475. Italics added.
210. *Ibid.*, p. 29.
211. Taped interview, April 16, 1960.
212. AS, p. 435.   213. *Ibid.*, p. 419.
214. *Ibid.*, p. 93.   215. *Ibid.*, p. 198.
216. *Ibid.*, p. 200.   217. *Ibid.*, p. 216.
218. *Ibid.*, p. 387.   219. CCSS, p. 626.
220. AS, p. 381.   221. *Ibid.*, p. 385.
222. *Ibid.*, p. 380.   223. *Ibid.*, p. 378.
224. *Ibid.*, pp. 10-3.   225. *Ibid.*, pp. 12 and 434.
226. AS, pp. 187-8.   227. *Ibid.*, p. 159.
228. *Ibid.*   229. *Ibid.*, p. 178.
230. *Ibid.*, p. 174.   231. *Ibid.*, p. 180.
232. *Ibid.*, p. 189.   233. *Ibid.*, p. 404.
234. *Ibid.*, p. 420.   235. *Ibid.*, p. 421.
236. *Ibid.*, p. 423.   237. *Ibid.*, p. 427.

238. *Ibid.*, p. 429.   239. *Ibid.*, p. 433.

240. *Ibid.*, p. 434. Winston White challenges the evidence supporting the judgment "we are going soft," calling it an ideological judgment. He points to the function of material comfort in "tension-release." *Op. cit.*, p. 12.

241. AS, p. 435.   242. *Ibid.*, p. 443.
243. *Ibid.*, p. 447.   244. *Ibid.*, pp. 446-7.
245. *Ibid.*, p. 453.   246. *Ibid.*, pp. 455-6.
247. *Ibid.*, p. 455.   248. *Ibid.*, p. 460.
249. *Ibid.*, p. 464.   250. *Ibid.*, pp. 467-8.
251. *Ibid.*, p. 468.   252. RIT, p. 52.
253. CCSS, p. 626.   254. AS, p. 13.
255. *Ibid.*, p. 558.   256. *Ibid.*, p. 559.
257. *Ibid.*, p. 512.   258. CCSS, p. 625.
259. AS, p. 546.   260. *Ibid.*, p. 547.
261. RIT, p. 59.   262. AS, p. 558.
263. *Ibid.*, p. 553.   264. *Ibid.*, p. 555.
265. *Ibid.*, pp. 554-5.   266. *Ibid.*, p. 551.
267. *Ibid.*, p. 512.   268. *Ibid.*, pp. 520-38.
269. *Ibid.*, p. 539.   270. *Ibid.*, p. 169.
270a. *Ibid.* p. 519.   270b. RCR, p. 451.
271. AS, p. 282.

272. Robin M. Williams, Jr., Comments on the paper by Allison Davis, "American Status Systems and the Socialization of the Child," *American Sociological Review*, Vol. 6 (August, 1941), p. 355. Hereafter designated as Comment.

273. AS, p. 283, Italics added.

274. *Ibid.*, p. 25.   275. *Ibid.*, pp. 57-85.
276. Comment, p. 355.   277. Cf., AS (1st), pp. 32-3.

278. Williams observes that the experience individual "sees society as consisting largely of the regularities he encounters in the behavior of a relatively small circle of other persons. To the degree that regularity disappears in that circle, the individual is in a normless situation, no matter how firm and consistent normative regulation may be elsewhere in the society." AS, pp. 561-2.

279. *Ibid.*, p. 368.   280. *Ibid.*, p. 391.
281. *Ibid.*, p. 393.   282. *Ibid.*, p. 376.
283. *Ibid.*   284. *Ibid.*, p. 472.
285. *Ibid.*, p. 473.

286. Williams acknowledges that the impetus to these ideas was given by Robert K. Merton but that a large part of the analysis was worked out independently. In similar fashion, Parsons had an important influence on Williams' general sense of problems and variables but again independent development occurred. Indeed, the first edition of *American Society* was published a few months before Parsons' *The Social System*.

287. AS, p. 218.   288. RCR, p. 438.

289. AS, p. 543. Italics added. Williams notes that when on occasion students in his classes overemphasize the importance of contiguity in reducing hostilities he may be able to instill more balanced judgment by a question such as "Why do people get divorces?" From taped discussion, April, 1960.

290. RIT, p. 76.

291. Robin M. Williams, Jr., "Values and Modern Education in the United States," a paper prepared for *Values in American Society: A Symposium* (Univ. of Notre Dame, March 23-24, 1959), p. 7. Hereafter designated as VMEUS.

292. AS, p. 10.

293. Robin M. Williams, Jr., "Unity and Diversity in Modern America," *Social Forces,* vol. 36 (October, 1957) p. 2.

294. George Homans, *The Human Group* (New York: Harcourt, Brace, 1950) p. 103.

295. AS, p. 567. 296. *Ibid.,* pp. 567-8.

297. *Ibid.,* p. 567. 298. *Ibid.,* p. 374.

299. *Ibid.,* p. 570. 300. *Ibid.,* pp. 570-1.

301. *Ibid.,* p. 569.

302. *Ibid.,* pp. 513 and 568-9.

303. *Ibid.,* p. 569.

304. *Ibid.,* p. 513. Italics removed.

305. *Ibid.,* pp. 365-6. 306. VMEUS, p. 7.

307. AS, p. 571 fn. 1. Cf., also Wilbert E. Moore, "Sociology of Economic Organization," in Georges Gurvitch and Wilbert E. Moore, eds., *Twentieth Century Sociology* (New York: Philosophical Library, 1945) pp. 438-65, esp. pp. 459-62.

308. AS, pp. 387 fn. 1. 391, 390.

309. Williams' emphasis on the relative indeterminancy (subjectively) of culture for an actor facing social interaction has been subjected to empirical test in his recent studies of intergroup relations in unpatterned situations, where what constitutes appropriate behavior is not clearly indicated for the actor. For instance the treatment thought appropriate to accord Negro patrons in a tavern never before frequented because of discrimination but sensitized to recent legal rulings on such practices was examined. While perhaps this research focuses on extreme cases of indeterminacy, it is nonetheless highly instructive. See Melvin L. Kohn and Robin M. Williams, Jr., "Situational Patterning in Intergroup Relations," *American Sociological Review,* Vol. 21 (April, 1956) pp. 164-74.

310. AS, p. 549. 311. *Ibid.,* p. 515.

312. *Ibid.,* p. 513.

CHAPTER 9

SOCIAL CHANGE AND
ITS CONCEPTUALIZATION

Within the life span of many now living, nations once weak in industrial and war potential have developed sufficient power to threaten the independence of all others. The world's most powerful nations have acquired their power relatively recently through rapid industrialization, urbanization, bureaucratization and other developments. Such changes have deep significance not only for those whose way of life has been radically altered but also for that two thirds of the world's population now contending with "a self-perpetuating vicious circle of poverty, disease, hunger, ignorance, and lack of technological skills and capital to improve their lot."[1] The social and economic development of the under-industrialized areas has been the subject of a whole recent literature[2] as has been for a longer period the stresses and adjustments of the swiftly altering industrial societies. As noted in the companion volume, *Social Systems*,[3] the changes incurred by industrialization and sometimes characterized as movement from *Gemeinschaft* to *Gesellschaft*[4] have always been of interest to sociologists. As Sorokin notes,[5] this theme has been a major preoccupation of philosophers and scholars through the ages. The theme is central to Durkheim's mechanical and organic solidarity, to Cooley's primary and non-primary groups, to Max Weber's *Vergemeinschaftung* and *Vergesellschaftung*, to Redfield's folk and urban societies; it is not unrelated to what some writers have discussed as social and cultural evolution.[6] The writers whose works are represented in the present volume are no exception; none has neglected social change.

The present chapter will deal with what appears to be their most important contributions to this important subject. No attempt will be made to present a complete treatment of the pertinent contributions of each author. Rather, the aim will be to present the salient features of change as it is treated by each writer in such a manner as to extract some general and common considerations of social change as well as to call attention to certain specific similarities and differences among the authors. Within this general plan consideration will be given to 1) problems of conceptualization and 2) analysis and explanation of change. The reader who has read the preceding chapters will recall reoccuring conceptualizations. The differentiation between cultural and social phenomena, for example, has been frequently encountered and often in the context of actual or potential social change. Likewise, functionalism is variously used and vowed and disavowed in relation to change. Some writers have emphasized structure over process while others have done the reverse. As these conceptualizations become the working tools applied to sociological analysis they assume an empirical quality as Gouldner points out when he sees in the social and cultural distinction "two strategic *empirical* generalizations . . . [which] might be formulated as follows: (a) some human behavior is *normatively* oriented, being shaped by values, symbols, signs, etc.; (b) most human beings live in groups at any given time in their life cycles, and their behaviour is influenced by their *interaction* with others."[7]

Some material in the present chapter will inevitably be reconsiderations of what has previously been presented under such headings as systemic linkage, boundary maintenance, time, social change, and others. Other material has not heretofore appeared in this volume. Occasional use will also be made in the present chapter of excerpts from tape recorded interviews which were held with each of the sociologists whose works are represented in this volume. The excerpts have been judiciously chosen so that clarification of debatable points in written works might be presented as well as more recently developed ideas and fresh, spontaneous elucidations. Since the interviews were long, many of them lasting from six to eight hours, and completely unrehearsed, it is remarkable that the oral style of each interviewee comes through as only a little less polished than the written style which has become familiar through the many quotations in the preceding pages. It is hoped that the reader's appreciation of the theorists will be enhanced as was the authors', by the inclusion of this otherwise unavailable material. The order will be the reverse of the alphabetical order used previously, and comparisons of procedures and contributions will be found throughout.

ROBIN M. WILLIAMS, JR.

Problems of cognitive mapping—conceptualization. Williams' conceptualizations seem to the present writers to be based upon two points of view which strongly parallel the two empirical generalizations mentioned above. On the one hand he was heavily influenced by Parsons, Sorokin, Merton and others who lay heavy emphasis upon the cultural and normative. On the other hand, the actual behavior of individuals in interaction with each other is similarly stressed, an emphasis which has been reinforced by his professional beginnings in rural sociology, by the practical aspects of the task represented by *The Reduction of Intergroup Tensions,* by his participation in the effort which produced *The American Soldier* and by other similar endeavors. Although he places no small value upon the development of theory *per se,* in his own professional activity he has always tried to stick close to the empirical.

You call me an empiricist; the way it is presented here I regard as a compliment . . . My early background in agricultural economics and then in rural sociology working with Horace Hamilton at North Carolina State, and then working with people like Harold Hoffsommer, T. J. Woofter and Rupert Vance and so on, and being continually immersed in field work and struggling with the data at first hand, are experiences I would never have lost and never will . . . I find it constitutionally impossible to cope with just a conceptual scheme as a conceptual scheme . . . That's just an additional footnote.[8]

Heinrich Hertz, the physicist, observed the importance of "internal pictures or symbols of external objects [by means of which] we can quickly derive . . . as by means of models, the consequence which in the external world would only occur in the course of a long period of time." [9] Williams upon occasion employs such "internal pictures":

In studying our own society, no one can avoid seeing that structure in the sociocultural world is the changing fixity of a continuous process, like the contours of a whirlpool in a rapidly moving stream.[10]

The analogy is made more specific as he continues in the same vein:

Every particle of [a whirlpool] is changing every instant and yet the pattern stays the same. In a similar way families are changing every minute and yet one can in a meaningful way speak of the family system which, as in the Chinese case, endures for centuries . . . What you study when you're studying change, it seems to me, at least at the level at which sociology deals, is a change in some kind of pattern . . . At one point one sees a certain sort of form and twenty-five years later one sees a different form . . . The analysis of change would [explain] how you get from T-1 to T-25.[11]

The idea of change is also conveyed by another set of symbols.

I have used [the following] way of describing values: If one takes a sheet of paper and puts iron filings on top of it and then takes a magnet and runs it underneath the paper so that it doesn't appear, other people can't see the magnet. One can nevertheless be reasonably sure the magnet is there from the way in which the iron filings move and pull themselves on the surface of the paper . . . One can infer the presence of values from the patterning of discrete opinions and bits of behavior in the same way . . . [For example] looking at the pattern made by . . . responses [on our Scale of Faith in People] one finds that this is a construct which allows you to make sense out of discrete pieces of behavior which otherwise don't have any other connections.[12]

This "mental picture" shows Williams' propensity to treat values, which he recognizes as an analytically distinct category, in close conjunction with the actual behavior which he is analyzing. Winston White's criticism of Williams' work is directed at this "unwillingness to 'disembody' values as a function separate from the concrete situations in which they are applied" [13] a feature of his work which is distinctly different from the analytical separateness maintained by such writers as White and Parsons. To Williams the difference is explainable in the level of abstraction or the point of reference adopted by the analyst. Whereas Parsons or White, at a sufficiently high level of abstraction may be impressed by the very broad themes which can be observed at that level,

I, on the other hand, turn around and look at the things from a little closer range or vantage point; what stands out for me is precisely a great deal of specific variation and change . . . The common element is there but only as a kind of background which is necessary for inter-action to occur in the first place. But once the interaction can occur because there is enough sharing, most of the actual determination of behavior from that basepoint on becomes a matter of much greater specificity and doesn't require this kind of sharing of values . . . [Some of our community studies such as the one in Eugene, Oregon, reveal friendships in which individuals] share astonishingly little and yet they are able to form continuing, durable and apparently satisfying relation-ships with one another.[14]

Such a position is reminiscent of Homans' dictum: "If they have a common purpose they have a harmony of interest to begin with." [15]

Using the analogy of the magnet, iron filings, and paper, Wil-liams sees in American society at any one instant many sub-pat-terns some of which are quite distinct. As the values change (or as the magnet moves) the major patterns change also. However, "underneath the external flux . . . there are substantial common themes and basic cultural axioms." [16] Whether or not the differ-ence in what is perceived by Williams as contrasted with Parsons is actually a difference of perspective, as Williams suspects, there is no doubt that the pattern as seen by Parsons tends to be all of a piece in contrast to the multi-configurations as seen by Williams.

Another construct to which Williams refers several times in *American Society* is that of the perfectly integrated society which he uses as a sort of "home base to come back and touch once in a while. . . . Here's the image of what a perfectly integrated society will be. . . . Let's look at what is going on. How does it differ [from the imperfectly integrated real-life society]? It always does differ so one then looks for what could cause the differences." [17] Among the specifications of the perfectly integrated society as noted by Williams are a small population, stable birth and death rates, a stable physical milieu and an isolated position. In such a society people would find it a pleasure to "do their duty" and spontaneous approval would be given to all who did so. Social control would be no problem since everyone would want to do what he had to do.[18]

We may set up the model of a social system in which institutions are not embodied in clearly defined associations or groups, but are merely norm complexes to which the behavior of all members of the society is oriented. In such a case, institutions would be cultural facts, not differentiated social structures within the society . . . However, this model of a society with unspecialized institutions does not exist—even at a tribal level, societies exhibit considerable specialization of institutions.[19]

The perfectly integrated society is indeed a fiction for Williams; confronted with a choice in emphasis between the normatively indicated and the actually exhibited behavior he tends to choose the latter. The emphasis Williams places on interaction is emphasized in his "miniature theory of formal organization." Some salient features of this may be repeated because of their significance for social change:

Let us begin by noting an empirical tendency for larger size of . . . [formal organizations] to lead to greater specialization of function . . . increased differentiation of interests, of status-ranking, of rewards, and of control . . . The high degree of interdependence . . . tends in turn to lead to a recognition [for need] of preserving the existing order of relationships, in whole or in part [in which case] differentiation will lead to increased *formality* in communication . . . [as a] means of controlling tension. . . .

The larger the size of the organization . . . the longer its lines of communication. The greater the specialization . . . the more complex . . . the communicative network. Both . . . lead directly to formality . . . One consequence of formality is to create difficulties of expressive-emotional communication, including the "corrective feedback" of feelings . . . so omnipresent in informal social relations . . . [and] the greater will be the tendencies to form informal subgroupings. . . . The more varied and changing are the problematic situations arising . . . the greater will be the part played by such *ad hoc* informal communication.

Still a third set of sequences can be discerned. Given . . . large size, differentiation, clashing interests, extended and complex channels of interaction, and formalization, we know empirically that there will be marked tendencies toward centralization of control and development of a hierarchy of influence and authority [resulting in further] . . . blockages and distortions of expressive, as contrasted with instrumental, communication . . . By two routes two sets of processes reinforce one another. The oscillation [between the formal-centralized and the informal-local] will not be random but will constitute necessary movements in the accomplishment of organization goals.[20]

Either convergence with Homans or influence by him is indicated in the obviously external-internal aspects of organization as represented by the above. Both writers are similar too, in the heavy stress they place upon the importance of validating generalizations and conceptualizations by experience. Williams resembles Becker and Sorokin in his avoidance of the particularizing emphases of historical accounts and his insistence upon generalizations from the particular.

Social change as a *historic* process is irreversible and concretely unique . . . In the attempt to establish any type of predictive generalization, the diffuse historic reality must be analyzed into repeatable categories that can be related as variables.[21]

Analyses and explanation of change. Technological factors (and what on the PAS Model is called the utilization of facilities) are important in Williams' view of the process of change. Unlike churches which have usually followed rather than led social change,[22] he sees economic activity as breaking through social regulation by the strong centrifugal tendencies which by its nature it generates.[23] To a considerable extent, the importance of technology in social change is a condition of the American society which is Williams' focus.

In American society, the valid element in [the "culture lag" theories] is found in the fact that the culture has been characterized by a value system that made it possible for economic and technological activities to change rapidly and hence to take on special causal significance. In other societies and in other times, the role of technology in social change is definitely minor.[24]

Williams' empirically oriented and systemic treatment of social change is most adequately exemplified in his writings on ethnic

relations which can be represented here by illustrative documenta-
tion. His extensive specifications concerning strategic research
and action areas in the field of ethnic relations suggests to him
that *"to be most effective, research on approaches for reducing
intergroup hostility must be* oriented in terms of the total social
system in which it operates."[25] From his own work and from
other sources Williams garners four general postulates of social
science which have significance for social change:

1. The principles of multiple causation of social events and of the
   interdependence of variables in a system. [Thus, the single instance of group hostility can be shown to have many causes].
2. The theorem of cumulation in social change. [From Myrdal's
   An American Dilemma, the principle of the "vicious circle" resulting from a social system in unstable equilibrium is assumed];
   a relatively slight change in a given direction tends to set off a
   chain of events . . . [although re-equilibration may also result].
3. The principle of limits in social change. [This principle, to be
   treated in the present volume in the discussion of Sorokin's
   works, is in some respects antithetical to the preceding item].
4. The principle of indirection in guided action aimed at planned
   social change. [This often applies when] direct attempts to
   change attitudes, or behavior patterns tend to be perceived by
   the recipients as attacks.[26]

The generality of these four postulates and the wide sources from
which they were drawn will be substantiated as they will be encountered in this chapter in one form or another in the works of
the other authors.

The systemic nature of change as viewed by Williams is documented by the mutualities which are particularly evident as one
element of the total situation is subjected to change. For example,
when a change of *feeling* about an ethnic group occurs a change
of belief will also occur. As between feeling and belief, however,
feeling is apparently the more basic element so far as ethnic relations are concerned for a change in belief can occur with no corresponding change in feelings.[27] Convergences with all the
authors treated in this volume are suggested by what Williams has
to say about territoriality and sentiment. The respects in which
the works of Homans and Parsons, and to a lesser extent, Merton
are strikingly brought to mind by the following excerpt should

not obscure the similarity of idea expressed in quite different ways by Becker, Davis and Sorokin.

As an actuarial matter, the evidence shows that (other things being equal) propinquity increases the frequency of interaction . . . The more alter is rewarded the more likely it is that he will reward ego . . . The "benign cycle" will be further facilitated to the extent that *complementary interests* and *"symbiotic" emotional needs are found to be served by the interaction* . . . [Although many exceptions may be noted] intimate and long-continued intergroup contacts tend to modify or dissolve previously held rigid and affectively gross stereotypes.[28]

The systemic linkage of diverse ethnic groups provided by "intimate and long-continued intergroup contacts" need not be the only kind of linkage capable of effecting change. Like Merton, Williams sees the formal decision emanating from a source of institutionalized power as an effective change agent.

Some of the most decisive intergroup processes are those involving contact between representatives of formally organized groups . . . involving decisions (whether unilateral or joint) about relations between collectivities . . . not just . . . individuals . . . [Examples are to be found in the] phenomena of the decisions leading to a "Little Rock" the . . . *Apartheid,* the perpetuation of segregation in publicly-supported housing, the abolition of official segregation in the armed services.[29]

PITIRIM A. SOROKIN

Problems of cognitive mapping—conceptualization. Sorokin advocates what he calls the "integralist" conception of truth which is not identical with sensate, ideational or idealistic truth, but embraces all of them.[30] The truth revealed by any of the epochal truth systems is correct but incomplete: "each of the systems of truth, within its legitimate field of competency, gives us genuine cognition of the respective aspects of reality."[31] Such a position poses communication problems of the first order not to mention other difficulties of a logical nature. How can findings based upon "the truth of faith" be communicated to sensate man, including any analyst who is of a sensate epoch? These colossal problems of communication together with the consideration that Sorokin is not writing in his mother tongue, in the present authors' view, invite the variation, not to say dilemmas which are common among scholars who attempt to interpret him.

Whether or not Sorokin's form of cognitive mapping is truly an integration of the three epochal types, the integration of the social and the cultural in his works is seldom questioned; [32] the two empirical generalizations mentioned in the first part of the present chapter pose little difficulty as Sorokin's works are considered.

Merton notes that although Sorokin justifies the "truth of faith" and maintains that intuition plays an important part in scientific discovery, he himself when applying criteria or norms of validation "accepts the facts and rejects the intuition." [33] He not only affirms the validity of "sensate truth" but notes that "a minimal real knowledge of physical, biological, and social phenomena is a condition of survival for a man or a group even for a period of a few weeks." [34] The level of abstraction of Sorokin's conceptualizations has progressively risen from those lower levels appropriate to his earlier less generalized interests such as *Sociology of Revolution* (1925), *Social Mobility* (1926) and *Principles of Rural-Urban Sociology* which he wrote with Carle C. Zimmerman in 1929. His conceptualizations of that period are similar in level of abstraction to those employed by Williams, Davis and Merton. His master work of a decade later, *Social and Cultural Dynamics* (1937-1941) required concepts cast at a considerably higher level of abstraction. His own conceptualizations as they varied with the subject to which he was addressing his efforts exemplified his admonition to his students: "let the kind and size of fish you want to catch determine the kind and size of net." Classroom use of such terms as Epicurean and Stoic adaptation were eventually supplanted by the famous triumverate, sensate, ideational and idealistic cultural types, which were employed both as ideal types and classificatory terms in the differentiation of meaning, value, normative attributes and other distinctions.

Some of the contradictions which have been noted in Sorokin's writings are more apparent than real; they frequently stem from differences in observation points and the described vistas noted from these points. Thus, when Sorokin is considering the sweep of history through thousands of years he can justifiably disclaim linear trends which seem to him from this vantage point to be

*"such only from a half-fictitious standpoint; and their linearity is
so pale and undetermined that it amounts only to a mere shadow
linearity."* [35] Yet, within a shorter span of time, linear developments may be noted. As Wilbert E. Moore has pointed out, Sorokin has posited a long term "growth of human knowledge and
inventions, population and differentiation and integration including the division of labor in the course of time." [36] The linearity
or illusion thereof is for Sorokin the short time perspective, not
the "universal view of social life, Oriental as well as Western,
ancient as well as modern." [37] Few writers and critics have the
competence in historical analysis and knowledge, even through
the perception of *one* form of truth, to interpret the vast spans of
human existence which Sorokin attempts to interpret. To attempt
what Sorokin calls the integralist point of view substantially com-
plicates such endeavors.

Analyses and explanation of change. Whether Sorokin focuses
attention upon social or cultural systems or personalities he finds
not stability but eternal fluctuation. Changes due to both immanent and external factors in all systems are for him inevitable.

The Principle of Immanent Change. The first principle which
explains why no social or cultural system is for any minute period
of time static is the principle of immanent change. Of the present
epoch he writes:

The capitalist system bears within itself the seeds of its own destruction. Hegel and Marx were correct in predicting its immanent, or
"dialectical," self-destruction . . . the contemporary sensate . . . system
. . . [whether capitalistic, Marxian, communistic or other form] is
rapidly crumbling under our very eyes.[38]

Although immanent change lies at the base of all fluctuations, the
rhythm of birth, oscilation and final death of all systems it aided
by "facilitating external factors." [39]

The Principle of Limits. The second great principle which
explains why sociocultural phenomena are always in a state of
fluctuation is the principle of limits. This principle has three
manifestations: 1) Limits in causal-functional relationship of interdependent variables; 2) Limits in linear direction of sociocultural change; and 3) Limited possibilities of basic variations of
systems. The limits in causal-functional relationships are sup-

ported by evidence from various sciences, both natural and social. Once it is granted that such limits always exist "precise causal formula demand . . . the specification of limits within which it is valid." [40] Thus in terms of the PAS Model if systems with high boundary maintenance are found to restrict systemic linkage with outside systems, the formula expressing such a relationship, Sorokin states, must specify at what point on the continuum of boundary maintenance its increase is no longer associated by decreased systemic linkage. Or if increasing evaluation of rational knowledge is found to be associated with decreasing evaluation of the law-norms and with reduced primacy of an ideational orientation, the limits within which this relationship holds must be specified. Other mutually dependent elements might similarly be used to show that changes in one are accompanied by changes in the other up to a point, and that point must be specified—the often noted informal organization with its up-surge of sentiment communication which up to a point increases as centralization of power in large-scale social systems increases, for example, or between members of different rank levels, the formality which increases up to a point as stratification is increased. Failure to specify such limits on the part of many sociologists leads Sorokin with his colossal view of time and region to classify their findings with *Fads and Foibles*.

The possibility of linear trends which, as shown above, may be impressive for the short-run, are ruled out for any long-run consideration.

When immobility persists too long, social systems generate forces working for differentiation. . . . Too much sensate freedom, laissez faire, or mobility generates forces within a system that tend to limit these factors and to reverse the trend . . . Too much restraint, governmental regimentation, or immobility elicits the opposite reaction in favor of more freedom, less governmental control, and greater mobility.[41]

The Limited Possibilities for the Variation of Systems. Whether on the dimensions which Sorokin stresses or on other dimensions this is another reason for eternal fluctuations of a nonlinear type:

Whatever classification of the basic types of *economic organization* is adopted, these rarely exceed six or eight in number . . . Similarly, the cardinal types of the *family* and *marriage* do not exceed ten . . . The chief types of *political regimes* and the *forms of government* [are limited to five or six] . . . No different is the situation with respect to the basic forms of *religion, language and writing, ethics and law, philosophy, or the fine arts.* The same is true of technological *systems.*[42]

The limited number of dimensions upon which systems may vary, whether these relate to systems of meaning, value and norms, form of expression of sentiment, tension management, purpose or end, sanctions or facilities and related processes in the PAS Model, provide both logical and empirical grounds for specifying that, *"The less numerous are the immanent possibilities of change of a system, the more is the rhythmical character of its processes."* [43]

Sequence and Prime Movers in Change. Unlike the Marxist position, or the position of many others which is often labelled "materialistic," Sorokin believes that meaning, value and norm components change before other components do, and this he holds to be true whatever stage the fluctuation is leaving or approaching.

In a qualitative change of a system its component of meaning, values, and norms—its ideology—tends to change [and spread] first while its component of behavioral and material vehicles, including technique, tends to lag in the change . . . Before a different airplane or gun or spade or any variation of a particular gadget is built, there is a prior variation of the controlling ideas. It is the conceived ideology that chooses its vehicles and not the vehicles that determine the ideology.[44]

Among the so-called non-material items of culture, there are two —the cognitive and the evaluative—which are prime movers: "Before the law-norms are changed on the books, and in the application within material culture, they first had to be changed in the minds of the lawmakers and in the ideological convictions of the population." [45] In maintaining that "Thought is the most dynamic form of reality" [46] Sorokin opposes Marx, Ogburn, Veblen, Mac Iver and others who make actual interaction and material or "civilizational" traits more important in change than the ideological. Williams' position in this respect tends toward middle ground as he holds that in a technological culture technological changes in themselves may be prime movers, but that in different kinds of culture this would not be true. For all the uniformity Sorokin sees in a series of changes with ideology *always* leading the series, in his view there is no such uniformity in which institutional subsystem will lead: "*No generalization can be made as to the order of change among subsystems. It is unlikely that any subsystem uniformly leads or lags.*" [47]

The above stated assumptions and convictions lead Sorokin to consider as fallacious the doctrine that " 'means and instruments of production' determine the change in religion and other 'ideological' systems of law, ethics, fine arts, and humanities." [48] He likewise criticizes Max Weber whom he maintains, stressed "the interdependence of all the systems, giv[ing] causal precedence to religion and its resultant *Wirtschaftsethik.*" [49]

Notwithstanding the emphasis given to the above considerations of change, all of which are predominantly immanent, Sorokin contributes to the idea of external change chiefly as he treats power. Any political or governmental system, whether it be a theocracy, a totalitarian secular state, or some other form, which articulates power may force change on weaker systems. Those social systems which do not have power are vulnerable to control and hence exposed to change factors at the hands of the more powerful nations.

Sorokin views his own analyses of change as differing from other well known analyses such as those of Danilevsky, Toynbee, and Spengler in that his deal with causal-meaningful systems while the others deal with congeries. This differentiation hinges upon the concept of integration, an attribute not possessed sufficiently by these congeries or so-called civilizations to constitute the province of sociological study but belonging rather to "historians and [students from] . . . other individualizing sciences." [50]

Sorokin specifies four basic types of integration [51] of sociocultural systems. First, there is integration by "spatial or mechanical adjacency (congeries)." These are compared to "a dump in which are fragments of a great variety of objects." [52] The second is integration through "indirect association through a common external factor," exemplified by the climatic conditions of Northern Russia during his own childhood where the use of *vodka*, houses of heavy timber, skis, winter folk entertainment in the evening, felt boots, large stoves, and so on was a common response to a common external factor. The third form of integration is causal or functional

which is exemplified by the relation of parts of a functioning automobile to one another. Relationships and parts in systems possessing this type of integration have "*tangible, noticeable, testifiable,
direct interdependence (mutual or one-sided) of the variables or
parts upon one another and upon the whole system.*" [53] The
fourth type of integration is the logico-meaningful integration
which "is integration in its supreme form." [54] It is illustrated by
"the inner consistency and supreme integration of the Cathedral
of Chartres, or the Gregorian chant, or the musical compositions
of Bach or Mozart or Beethoven . . . tragedies of Shakespeare,
or the sculpture of Phidias, or the pictures of Duerer . . ." [55] What
it is not is illustrated by a "highly developed ascetic-monastic
life and materialistic Sensate philosophy" side by side in the same
cultural conglomeration, or by the "strictest caste system and the
equalitarian idealogy shared by all castes" [56] in the same cultural
area. Sorokin labels those systems which possess the kinds of integration represented by types three and four as "meaningful-
causal systems and supersystems" and contends that they change
in togetherness, whereas congeries do not. Both causal integration and logico-meaningful integration are necessary for a change
in togetherness to occur: "purely causal unities change in togetherness, if they are close unities, but this togetherness is purely
causal, very different from the meaningful-causal togetherness.
The total cultures that are little integrated [such as the "civilizations" of Danilevsky, Spengler and Toynbee] change mainly in
the way of congeries." [57]

Sorokin more than any of the writers treated in the present
volume, stresses change and process in and among systems. In
terms of the PAS Model, the structural elements upon which he
places greatest stress are norm (law-norm), belief (meaning),
rank (stratification), power, facility (vehicle), and sentiments.
Those receiving the least stress are ends, status-role and sanction,
which are absorbed by the global concept law-norm. His use of
the concept which in terms of the PAS Model is expressed by
boundary maintenance is displayed in his distinction between
organized and solidary interaction [58] as shown in Chapter 7 of the
present volume. The distinction has important implications for
social change. Organized interaction is seen as a quality of the
system which specifies effective cooperation on the part of mem-

bers of systems such as orchestras or even concentration camps, while solidary interaction is that in which "aspirations (meanings-values) and overt actions of the interacting parties concur and are mutually helpful for the realization of their objectives." [59]

Another differentiation implicated in change is the alteration which results from variation and that which results from system substitution.[60] Early Christianity changed to Orthodox Catholic and Protestant faiths by the former process but when early Christian groups and individuals accepted atheism, Buddhism and Confucianism they changed by the latter process, that is by substitution. Various changes within a capitalistic economy may result from the linkage of systems, but for Sorokin a change to Communism is a change by substitution. Both forms, that is, change by variation and change by substitution may result from systemic linkage. In the case of substitution one system for various reasons ceases to exist and is superordinated by others.

Sorokin's treatment of change cannot be compared with the works of any other sociologist either in terms of the vastness of the phenomena analyzed or by the conceptualization employed. Only when others having equal knowledge of the phenomena and comparable tools of analysis have attempted replications will the validity of his results be tested.

TALCOTT PARSONS

Cognitive mapping—conceptualization. Parsons has been criticized by a number of sociologists for alleged failure to develop a theory of change and for the use of concepts in his basic system of analysis which in their opinion inhibit the development of such a theory. The focus of these criticisms is for the most part directed at Parsons' assumption of predictable regularities of interaction in groups by means of a construct called the social system which in the critics' opinion possesses change resistant properties. They point for example, to the fundamental paradigm of social interaction which includes the assumption "that stably established interaction process . . . as, one in equilibrium, tends to continue unchanged." [61] He has likewise been criticized for concentrating attention on the social system to the neglect of inter-system relations,[62] and to the neglect of changes due to "sudden shifts in the definition of a situation . . . [or to those changes due to] a 'creeping' kind of transformation which may, at some point . . . lead to a cumulative neglect . . . which can suddenly become a focus of disorganization." [63] Such crisis developments are suggested by the theory of limits as set forth by Pareto and Sorokin.

As Parsons' treatment of change is analyzed below the reasons will emerge why such criticisms in the opinion of the present authors seem exaggerated, especially as assessments are made of Parsons' publications from 1960 on. However, since Parsons has been charged with emphasizing structure at the expense of process his use of these concepts as related to change may be briefly reviewed here.

There are certain irreducible distinctions which must be made for the ordering of empirical knowledge . . . [In addition to] the distinction . . . between knowing subject and object known . . . two other dichotomies . . . are in the same class of indispensability, namely that between structure and process and that between stability and change. . . . The reason for insistence on the importance of keeping . . . [these concepts] analytically distinct is not a predilection in favor of one or the other item in each pair, but in favor of *orderly procedure* in scientific analysis. [64]

At another point in the same paper Parsons comments that

It is impossible to study everything at once. . . . The specificities of significant change could not even be identified if there were no relative background of non-change to relate to. [65]

Such pointed remarks concerning cognitive mapping and their relation to change will now be followed by considering the development of Parsons' treatment of change and his thinking on that subject beginning with *The Social System*. In line with the distinction made at the first of the present chapter between what was called the *normatively* oriented vs. influence from *interaction per se*, Parsons throughout his professional career has stressed the former; through the actor in quest of ends in *The Structure of Social Action* (1937); through motivational and value orientation as reflected in reciprocal expectation between actor and object in the pattern variables in *The Social System* (1951); through his differentiation of system levels ranging from the "most controlling" value level, to the lesser controlling levels of norms and collectivities, to the least controlling level of status-roles in *Structure and Process in Modern Societies* (1960); and finally, through his "activation" of culture as a functioning component in *An Approach to the Sociology of Knowledge* (1960) which is especially important in the "grounding of meaning."

Various constructs and analogies which Parsons has upon occasion used also shed light on his cognitive moorings. The following greatly abbreviated excerpt is used to elucidate the schema of *The Structure of Social Action* (1937):

This conceptual scheme . . . may be employed on two different levels . . . the "concrete" and the "analytical." On the concrete level . . . for instance, a student may have as his immediate end the writing of a paper on a given subject . . . this visualized product, perhaps being "handed in" is the concrete end . . . For the purposes of explanation a further step in abstraction [beyond the step of arranging data in a certain order] is generally necessary . . . Thus, to use the previous example, in the process of action leading to the writing of a paper for a course, various aspects of the concrete end cannot be attributed to the agency of the student, such as the fact that there are available given books in the library, and other conditions relevant to the act. An end, then in the analytical sense must be defined as the *difference* between the anticipated future state of affairs and that which it could have been predicted would ensue from the initial situation *without the agency of the actor having intervened.*[66]

The model of teacher and student or of therapist and patient as reflected in change has been discussed in Chapter 6. (See Figure 8 in that chapter). As the four exigencies of system action developed, the metaphor of the ship driving at high speed through the sea [67] mentioned in Chapter 6, came at a time when the chief focus of his thinking was upon the adaptive and the integrative exigencies. As the goal attaining and pattern maintaining exigencies became more prominent he expressly states that in investigation "for . . . classificatory purposes, the fundamental starting point is the 'fourfold table' " [68] but frequent usage of *"binary discriminations"* and polar comparisons was retained. In *Economy and Society* (1956) changes in interest rates were made analogous to "a change of a traffic light. A rising interest rate—similar to a red or yellow flash—is less a 'wage increase' and more a signal that rights to intervene are likely to be jeopardized by outright loss, by loss of value through inflation, etc." [69] In this same publication, as noted in Chapter 6, culture was made "analogous to a . . . 'programme' or set of instructions which are 'stored' in . . . [a modern calculating] machine's 'memory.' The programme pattern cannot be derived from the specific operational procedures or vice versa; they are analytically independent facts." [70] Even since the more recent thinking which specifies culture as a component of action the analogy between culture and programme has application since the net result is selective recoverability on demand.

Analyses and explanation of change. Chapter 6 of the present volume deals with Parsons' ideas on social change under the comprehensive processes of boundary maintenance and systemic linkage and under time as a condition of social action. It is worthy of emphasis in the present section that the process of social change as treated by Parsons synthesizes his earlier theoretical contributions concerning the social system with his later preoccupation with the four functional imperatives: the adaptive, the goal attaining, the integrative and the pattern maintaining. It is instructive to note the conceptual emphases in his chapter on social change as presented in *The Social System* (1951) and to compare these with the emphases of concepts central to social change as these are presented a decade later.

Parsons emphasizes in his 1951 work that *"a general theory of the processes of change of social systems is not possible in the present state of knowledge."* [71] Such a theory would presuppose a well established set of laws of systemic process, especially motivation process, a supposition which at that time was without foundation in Parsons' view. Lacking the knowledge from which *laws* of motivational process may be formulated, Parsons posits instead *mechanisms* from which a paradigm of motivational process may be derived. (See Chapter 6, section on status-role.) This paradigm of motivational processes was set forth as operative independently of any particular structuring of roles in an interaction process. It is considered, therefore, to be applicable to a role structuring which is primarily suited to any of the four functional prerequisites of empirical systems which at the time of writing of *The Social System* were identified as kinship systems; instrumental achievement structures and stratification; territoriality, force and integration of the power system; and religion and value-integration. (These four were the forerunners of the four functional imperatives which were later, under slightly different designations, to constitute his much used four-fold table.) The constancy of pattern exhibited by any social system primarily fulfilling one of these four functional prerequisites constitutes an empirical given which justifies other inferences "at least to the extent of saying that if these facts are given the range of variation of other facts about the same system must be limited in certain respects." [72] The mechanisms of motivational processes, then, together with these structural imperatives constitute two of the three categories of knowledge from which conclusions about social change can be drawn. The third such category is the fragmentary knowledge of genuine laws of motivational process which are basic to the motivational paradigm. "For example, the statements to the effect that strain, defined as some combination of one or more of the factors of withdrawal of support, interference with permissiveness, contravention of internalized norms and refusal of approval for valued performance, results in such reactions as anxiety, phantasy, hostile impulses and resort to the defensive-adjustive mechanisms, are definitely statements of laws of motivational process." [73]

Given this cognitive base with the further assumption that the variables inducing change may be abstracted from the biological constitution or the physical environment, Parsons essays in *The Social System* to assemble some generalizations concerning the nature of the process of change within the social system. He terms as the phenomenon of vested interests, the boundary maintaining system which is resistant to change in certain respects. When strain is introduced, there occurs a disturbance in the pattern of expectancy (which latter is an essential part of integration) whereupon re-equilibrating processes are set in motion. Change is not alone "alteration of pattern," but always "alteration by the overcoming of resistance." [74] An analysis of change therefore demands the weighing of the relevant vested interest complex against the mechanisms which overcome the resistance. Parsons sees the possible origins of strain as occurring in any part of the social system as described in structural terms. The very interdependency of those parts means that strain introduced at any one point is an impetus to the change of the whole system. In terms of analysis and prediction the tracing of the repercussions of initial strain is for him more important than the identification of the initiating factors of change. Over-emphasis on the initiating factors (or an over-simplified identification of the prime movers of change) with corresponding neglect of the repercussions can lead to the assumption of a linear trend, an assumption which Parsons believes is seldom valid.[75]

Parsons sees major difficulties in predicting the direction of change despite his conceptualization of action itself as always being oriented, and the further consideration that orientation *is* directional. One major aspect of the directionality of orientation is that of *gratification* which is inherently a state of the personality system of the individual actor, and "There is literally no way of making the transition in gratification-deprivation terms from the individual actor to the social system. There is such a thing as integration of a social system, but most specifically and definitely there is no such thing as a state of gratification of social systems." [76] The second major aspect of directionality of orientation lies in value-realization or the cultural component, which unlike the state of gratification, can be transmitted. "Thus a change in the cultural tradition can be perpetuated and can serve as a base for further change." [77]

Of the three classifications of content of cultural tradition, belief systems, expressive symbols and systems of value-orientation it is the first which is most demonstrably related to direction of change, although there is a a probability that the development of expressive symbolism is also involved as a directional factor. Of the types of cognitive orientation considered by Parsons and discussed in Chapter 6, scientific beliefs and the process of rationalization are prime directional factors. Alterations in scientific beliefs would tend to promote change and such vested interests as traditionalization, authoritarian enforcement and the mechanism of rationalization of the existing order in the psychological sense would tend to retard it.

How these countervailing forces are resolved so that the balance is tipped in one direction or the other is explained at a later date by conceptualizations which were a part of *The Social System* but which were not fully developed or related to each other until some years later with the appearance of *Economy and Soci-*

ety (1956). The explanation utilizes a model of socialization or therapy (discussed in Chapter 6, and constituted of four sequential phases: the permissive phase, the phase of support, the phase of denial of reciprocity, and the phase of manipulation of rewards) together with the four functional exigencies (adaptation, goal attaining, integration and pattern maintenance) and develops the idea of *boundary exchanges* which are, for Parsons, the crux of process. As boundary exchanges are made between the goal attaining (G) cell and the adaptive (A) cell, the latter is provided with facilities which enhance the opportunity to increase goal attainment.

The best-authenticated cases of the importance of this combination lie in the analysis of learning processes of the individual. He must be "motivated" by depriving him of accustomed gratifications if he continues to act in the old ways, and he must be presented with an opportunity, i.e., realistic facilities which can be adapted to new ways of behaving. If there is no goal-attainment deficit there is no motivation to change.[78]

This mode of process analysis (expressed diagramatically in Figure 8 of Chapter 6) was anticipated in important respects in *The Social System* as Parsons traces the repercussions of modified scientific beliefs and technological advance. The roles of the instrumentally oriented economic structure are affected, the character of the organization itself shows changes, and (most germane to the boundary exchange mode of analysis mentioned above) repercussions are evident in the composition of the system of facilities and through it the power structure.[79] These three main channels of repercussions throughout the instrumental complex in turn impinge upon other empirical groupings such as upon the family and upon religious organizations.

A somewhat different set of circumstances marks the revolutionary movement which requires alienative motivation that is sufficiently intense, widely spread and strategically distributed. Should the mechanisms of social control fail to hold such a movement in bounds a deviant sub-cultural group may develop which may be reinforced by already latent alienative motivation present in other sectors of the population. Whether or not it finds such reinforcement is in part dependent upon the successful utilization of at least some of the symbols of the main institutionalized ideology of the society. These latter are rarely perfectly institutionalized; there are generally some inconsistencies between the dominant values of a society and their implementation. The existing system is vulnerable at these points of inconsistency. Sectors of the population committed to the dominant values and aware of their imperfect implementation are potential reinforcements to the deviant sub-culture the values of which may be partially expressed in terms of these widely accepted but imperfectly realized dominant values. As an example Parsons, in *The Social System* (1951) presents the Nazi case which combined the appeals of nationalism and of socialism, hitherto thought of as antithetical.

The genesis of the revolutionary movement and much of its early source of support lies in certain utopian ideologies the promises of which fall far short of fulfillment. (The importance of charisma and charismatic leaders, the routinization of charisma and other consequences follow the general pattern established by Max Weber.) As the utopian ideologies fail to materialize concessions must be made in order to maintain the functional requisites (portrayed in *The Social System* as the kinship systems; the instrumental achievement structures and stratification; territoriality, force and integration of the power system; and religion and value-integration). To the extent that concessions are made which run counter to the original utopianism, the tendencies to radicality are somewhat mitigated. This mitigating tendency, especially as it is considered in relation to the exercise of power, leads Parsons to suggest that:

> there is a sense in which gaining ascendancy over a society has the effect of "turning the tables" on the revolutionary movement. The process of its consolidation as a regime is indeed in a sense the obverse of its genesis as a movement; it is a process of reequilibration of the society; very likely to a state greatly different from what it would have been had the movement not arisen, but *not so greatly* as literal interpretation of the movement's ideology would suggest." [80]

The example of Russia shows an original ideology which was against the family, against differential rewards, against a new system of stratification and against a legal system; subsequent concessions revived all of these. Such ideological compromises suggest to Parsons the existence of a basic societal need for structures suitable for the fulfillment of the functional requirements and of conformity needs associated with the old system. The many points at which the "empirical groupings" and the fundamental functional requirements as identified in *The Social System* enter into his conceptualizations of change in 1951 become even more important as that subject is examined ten years later.[81]

It is noteworthy that the paper upon which is based the more recent aspects of Parsons' concept of social change, is entitled, "Some Considerations on *The Theory* of Social Change." [82] It will be recalled that ten years earlier Parsons was unwilling to label his thoughts on social change as anything definitive enough to be called a theory on the grounds that not enough was known concerning motivational processes. Whereas his earlier work emphasized boundary maintenance his works since that time have increasingly been concerned with boundary exchanges whereby the inputs of one subsystem are the outputs of another (or on a more general level, whereby the inputs and outputs of a system through the agency of its units are interchanges between the system and its environment). Disturbances of sufficient magnitude to withstand the equilibrating mechanisms occasionally appear, channeled through the exogenous influences of the culture and personality systems. Cultural influences such as modifications of the state of empirical knowledge are mentioned but not elaborated in the 1960 paper, in contrast to the central attention given knowledge in relation to change in *The Social System*. Rather, a great deal of attention is given to the boundary exchanges between the social and the personality systems. Thus the motivation of the individual, the very point at which evidence was so inconclusive in 1951 as to cause Parsons to use the term "mechanism" instead of "theory" becomes one pivotal point from which change is now examined.

More important, the institutionalized values of the social system are seen to be institutionizeable only as they are first internalized in the personality of the individual. The typical individual personality is viewed as an integrate of value and motivational commitments which for heuristic purposes is assumed to be stable. The orientation component of the individual actor in a given role expectation is thus thought of as stable with the implication that the institutionalized values are assumed to remain constant for the purposes of analyzing the particular processes of change to which Parsons addresses himself in this paper. The primary variable thus becomes the objects to which the actor is oriented. Although the institutionalized values are assumed to remain constant, "the problem is to account for processes of change in this normative structure, in institutions." [83]

The processes of differentiation are basic to Parsons' analysis. One such differentiation is at the collectivity level where the functional exigencies which were represented by the familiar four empirical groupings are now elaborated as the functional imperatives of adaptation, goal attaining, integration and pattern maintenance as was amply discussed throughout Chapter 6. Differentiation is also observed at the role level whereby the same individual may hold plural roles as, for example, a family member may also be a member of a productive organization in which he has a specific task to perform. As differentiation occurs on both collectivity and role levels, normative patterns governing each of the units and their relations will presumably change. Differentiation of function (at both collectivity and role levels) means loss of function for one unit, new patterns of organization within that unit, new ways of supplying the needs represented by the lost function, ways of handling the risks entailed in the shift to the new situation, ways of balancing the legitimation of both the old and the new units. The crucial question concerning whether or not differentiation will actually take place revolves around the capacities in the system for levels of performance not possible under the undifferentiated state.

Parsons sees the cycle of differentiation starting with a deficit of input at the goal attaining boundaries of the social system which is potentially on the verge of differentiation. If the social system were the family, this deficit of input might be reflected in its productive effectiveness or in its effectiveness at handling the functions of socializing and personality regulation of its members, or in both. The deficit would also be reflected in the boundary exchanges between the family and the other subsystems to which it has a functional relation. The commodity and labor markets, for example, would soon show adverse signs of the family's malfunctioning. The "justification" of the unit's position in society must be made on the unit's ability to furnish what society needs. The facilities allocated to the unit for fulfillment of its societal function will tend to be proportional to the degree to which its output is considered adequate; the rewards allocated to unit members will follow a similar pattern. This latter condition—the allocation of facilities and rewards "is the indispensable condition of the process leading to differentiation." [84]

A summarization of the primary conditions of successful differentiation would include first of all the *opportunity* factor which is essentially "the possibility of institutionalizing the mutual access to facilities"; in the one case making them available to a differentiated social structure which possesses a higher production potential than the residual structure which formerly performed the function; and in the second case, making the goods of production available to the residual unit by means of the exchanges of labor and money through a market mechanism. Also, as a second factor, the kind of integrative support each of the units—the residual and the new—would receive from the community would be included. For example, in the case of the independent peasant or farm owner operator, so long as the community saw merit only in proprietorship, the motivation to exchange labor in factories or elsewhere for money for goods in a clearly differentiated pattern of societal organization would be countered by the motivation on the part of the peasant owner to be thought of as a responsible individual. The essential point necessary for widespread differentiation is that both the new collectivity and the old residual structure be recognized as performing essential functions each in its distinctive way and each worthy of the kind of community support without which the change called for by differentiation would be obstructed. Another component of change which will be represented if differentiation is to prevail to any great extent is a complex of institutionalized norms such as legal norms, standards of performance, of technical adequacy and the like. The new values necessitated by the occurrence of differentiation must be more *extensive* although not necessarily differently patterned than formerly. To the extent that romantic ideologies concerning the felt loss of function of the residual unit are current there is corresponding failure to implement the value-pattern of the differentiated system. The more extensive values may be implemented by specifications concerning their implications for the various levels of the differentiated subsystems. Thus, although economic rationality might be viewed as a value applicable to both newly differentiated system and residual systems, productivity and solvency might be a specification more applicable to the business firm than the family whereas the economic contexts of consumption might be thought of as the special province of the family.

Parsons considers his own thirty page presentation of his recent work on social change as sufficient for only a few highlights of a complex subject. The present summarization of those highlights, reduced in length to one-sixth of the original paper inevitably omits clarifying elaborations. It seems essential, therefore, to report that he now believes the problems of social change to be

. . . soluble in empirical-theoretical terms. Above all we have at our disposal a conceptual scheme which is sufficiently developed so that at least at the level of categorization and of problem statement it is approaching the type of closure . . . which makes *systematic* analysis of interdependencies possible. We can define the main ranges of variability which are essential for empirical analysis, and the main mechanisms through which variations are propagated through the system. We can quantify to the point of designating deficits and surpluses of inputs and outputs, and here and there can come close to specifying threshhold values beyond which equilibrium will break down.[86]

Lest the familiar charges of theory to the exclusion of empiricism be levelled at Parsons' more recent work on social change, it should be mentioned here that change as it occurs or may occur in essentially empirical conditions is examined by Parsons in a variety of essays in the publication, *Structure and Process in Modern Societies* (1960). One essay[87] in that work, for example, tackles the problem of what kind of society is compatible with an industrial economy. In the Weberian tradition, one series of social changes leading to eventual industrialization goes back to *"differentiation* relative to preindustrial institutional systems."[88] A highly differentiated political and industrial organization has to exist, Parsons argues, for the *initial* development of an industrial economy. The opposite situation—a high degree of governmental initiative—is required for those relatively unindustrialized societies to "catch up" in a short time as they implement their goal of increasing industrialization. Although Parsons' operational notes on this paper indicate that his emphasis is structural, and that he has not engaged in any technical analysis of process, "an analysis which I tend to attempt to categorize in terms of input-output interchanges between subsystems," [89] and with the further reservation that space limitations prevented an extended treatment of the pattern-maintenance function and the integrative function, his schematic presentation of the economic complex as differentiated from the political complex seems to the present authors to imply a good deal about possible boundary exchanges (and hence process of change) as concerns the economic and political subsystems.

At any one time the functional imperative emphasized by a society as a social system lends to that society a primacy of a certain organizational structure. As that particular imperative becomes less pressing because the problem it represents is solved or because certain other problems become more pressing, the emphasized feature around which organization centers tends to change. Parsons is willing to be predictive about changes foreseen on the basis of America's functional imperative:

For the past half-century or so, the business man has indeed been the main "community leader" in the United States. I suspect that his heyday is drawing to a close and that the business groups will decline in relative status as the problems of economic production come to be relatively well "solved" and other functions in the society emerge into greater urgency and salience. Functions of government are certainly among these and I look for both a relative rise in prestige of those associated with it and a marked "professionalization" at least of those aspects associated with its administrative functions. Education and research are certainly also among the rising professions, and the recent relative lag which they have been allowed to suffer cannot continue much longer.[90]

The phase aspect of religion as it performs a pattern maintaining function is also related to change. It perhaps represents longer run changes than the economic and political shifts to which the above excerpt is addressed. Parsons, for example, interprets the current salience of religious concern "as part of a more general pattern of periodicities which one expects to find in a rapidly de-

veloping social system, of what Bales calls a 'phase pattern.'" [91]
His attention to change within religious institutions in the United
States and to related changes in other societal institutions [92] is
typically cast in terms of differentiation and integration. Despite
the many differentiated and unintegrated religious elements in
American society Parsons sees the present main trend as moving
in the direction of "greater integration of these various elements
in a viable system which can be a vital part of a larger society. In
this, as in other vital respects, American society is fundamentally
an outgrowth of its European heritage, not an exotic 'sport.'" [93]

ROBERT K. MERTON

Cognitive mapping—conceptualization. The many concepts in
general use in sociology which are identified with Merton's name
attest to his relatively heavy emphasis on what in the present
volume has been called cognitive mapping and validation. From
among the concepts mentioned in Chapter 5, those which are particularly important in the analysis of change are latent and manifest functions; the modes of adaptation in the anomie paradigm,
conformity, innovation, ritualism, retreatism and rebellion; serendipity; problem density; role and status sets and sequences; and
institutional evasion. These and others have been developed in a
setting and by a method of operation which has been so fruitful
that it bears mentioning here. For twenty years his advanced
theory course at Columbia University has been his arena for cognitive mapping where he has "worked up . . . theoretical material." [94] In this setting his interaction with students, a considerable
number of whom are now important sociologists in their own
right, provokes creation, formulation, checking and reconceptualization. The lectures are taped or recorded in other ways so that
for any concept the specific history of its classroom use from inception is available. As one might expect the shelves holding these
lectures which are never the same from year to year are impres-
sively extensive.

A leading research interest of Merton's is the examination of
those processes by which knowledge, particularly sociological
knowledge develops. The mutualities between research and
theory, especially the unanticipated interrelations which led Mer-

ton to apply the word serendipity to some analytical processes as discussed in Chapter 5, bring to mind others' concern with logico-scientific process *per se* such as Homans as he elaborates inductive generalizations and deductive explanation and Braithwaite [95] as he distinguishes the logically contingent (or empirical) from the logically necessary (or theoretical). The serendipity component has frequently led to reconceptualization (and Merton stresses that the syllable *re* in the word reconceptualization is worth emphasizing); he has called attention to many instances of it in his own and others' works. This process of reconceptualization has been outstanding in the studies of bureaucracy by some of his own students among whom may be mentioned Selznick, Lipset, Gould-ner and Blau; [96] and Cloward who called attention to the importance of opportunity for deviancy [97] can be numbered here too.

In contrast to some anthropologists [98] who have shunned so-called action research in which directed change is usually implied, Merton has welcomed participation in it because he thinks that it highlights unanticipated consequences and frequently, as in the case of the study of bureaucracies, leads to reformulation of the conceptual design for the research. In discussing his "Studies in Radio and Film Propaganda" in this light he observes:

When you have specified objectives then the observer can't miss the importance of the unanticipated consequences, it hits him between the eyes. But it's extremely difficult to see it in on-going operations without organization, without specified [expected] outcomes, and therefore it's essential to conceptualize so that you look for it even where it's not obvious.[99]

Besides the considerable number of unanticipated consequences and resultant reconceptualizations which are mentioned in Chapter 5 (see especially the sections on goal attaining and "latent" activity, utilization of facilities and cognitive mapping), the interested reader may be guided by the index listing in Merton's work *Social Theory and Social Structure*.

Merton has become increasingly sensitized to the importance of the cognitive aspects of activity represented in the research situation itself:

It's really startling when you start to investigate articles, books, theories, that have been written with a conscious and deliberate effort to build this into the analysis . . . This is a variable that is assumed one way or another. Now a good example of it is in the length of time it took me to build it in systematically whether dealing with reference group behavior or any type of behavior—this in spite of the manifest-latent functions concept which makes no sense without it.

When Paul [Lazarsfeld] and I did a joint paper on friendship relations, we finally discovered—that's the only way to put it—that in my earlier manuscript on the subject I had made knowledge of the other fellow's values an implicit, not an explicit, variable. . . . I think [this recognition of the importance of the cognitive] came up in our field in an odd way independently in various places, and gradually we began to see that this was a sociological variable . . . [It] came in obviously in recent years through information theory; but independently of information theory it came in through the human relations approach and industrial sociology. It's been inherent in rural sociology in this country from the beginning because when you've got a tie-in between research and planning operations, you can't miss the role of information flow just as you can't miss it in mass communications research. It is implied rather than expressly developed within the whole history of social ecology in this country.[100]

Of the two "empirical generalizations" mentioned at the beginning of the present chapter, a) human behavior as *normatively* oriented and b) behavior as influenced by the interaction of actors with each other, Merton of all the writers reviewed, perhaps, holds the most balanced position with equal emphasis on both components. These two components lie at the base of Merton's explanation of change as revealed by the paradigm for anomie, his orientation in functional analysis and in most of his work. He believes that since sociologists are chiefly interested in studying group processes of interaction, culture enters because of its direct significance for interaction. His own allusions to culture he believes to be overwhelmingly concerned with the definition of status and role.

They are included in culture because they have the same character as a great deal of culture which does not impinge directly on social status or social role. Take for example the cultural values found empirically among the different social strata. Or take the institutional aspects of religion. To some degree they specify and designate norms for religious roles and religious statuses. There is a lot more that is included in religion—theology, for example, which is part of culture . . . Perhaps those in the old tradition of Alfred Weber made a good distinction without knowing it. You do need a three-fold breakdown, although not necessarily the one selected by Alfred Weber. What you need is society (or social system or what-have-you) on the one hand; then culture which should be confined to the resultants of man's activity—in a sense artifacts, value objects; and then a third category or third term to represent those values that exist only in a sense of being the rationale for status definitions and so on . . . The institutional is . . . the bridge category . . . The degree of institutionalization is the extent to which members of a social system both accept and grasp moral legitimacy to a cluster of norms.[101]

Merton distinguishes those patterns to which no one expects literal conformity, "ideal patterns," "religious theologies," and "secular theologies" from those normative patterns which are the actual expectations. Both of these he differentiates from actual behavior. He feels that some intermediate category is needed to designate the phenomena between the first group which are segments of culture and the last which are "actual social relationships." [102]

Another concept of Merton's which is important in the analysis of change is functional analysis, especially since extending its use "to deal with problems of social and cultural change" [103] is a primary concern with him. His now classic treatment of the subject has been briefly reviewed in Chapter 5,[104] where he is quoted as saying *"to seek social change, without due recognition of the manifest and latent functions performed by the social organization undergoing change, is to indulge in social ritual rather than social engineering."* [105] He identifies and criticizes three postulates or "articles of faith" commonly held in functional analysis which he believes to

. . . have proved to be debatable and unnecessary to the functional orientation . . . These postulates hold first, that standardized social activities or cultural items are functional for the *entire* social or cultural system; that *all* such social and cultural items fulfill sociological functions; and third, that these items are consequently *indispensable.*[106]

Reference is also made in Chapter 5 to his treatment of possible ideological biases inherent in functional or any type of analysis as

emphasis upon the study of manifest and latent functions and dis-
functions were considered.

More recently the press toward differentiating causal and
functional analysis has been more insistent. Merton maintains
that functional analysis is not a theory but rather "a theoretical
orientation." [107] He cites Ernest Nagel and others as having demonstrated that the logical syntax of functional and causal analysis
are translatable one into the other.[108] Merton agrees that any
statement cast in functional terms can be translated into causal
terms and vice versa. In both cases, logically, the relationships
between an antecedent and a consequence are being stated. But
what therefore appear to be the same Merton contends are not the
same with regard to the mode of investigation, because it is impossible to arrive at certain statements without a given orientation which leads to that statement.

If you start with the functional orientation you tend to raise certain
questions that give you one set of findings; if you start in the same area
with the causal orientation you come out with another set of findings.
It isn't that they're contradictory; they're different . . . Once you've
got the findings and put them in strictly neutral language, no one could
tell whether your orientation was causal or functional.[109]

If, for example, a political machine were to be studied, two ave-
nues of inquiry might be used: "What brought about the political
machine; what are its causes?"; and "What are the functions of the
political machine for designated groups in a society?". The second
line of questioning inevitably leads, in Merton's opinion, to a relation of the consequences to the stability or instability of the machine. "My only point is [and it is] a matter of record, that as long
as the emphasis is on causal analysis of the political machine, you
get one kind of observation. [With] functional analysis you get
others . . . Functional analysis has always had to have some tacit
notion of feedback and has used various terms to express this." [110]

Analyses and explanation of change. Merton's balance, as
noted above, in judicious emphasis upon behavior which is normatively oriented and which is influenced by the interaction process
itself, is matched by a respect for both the concrete and the
abstract.

Concrete sociological investigations, of course, make at least implicit use of abstract models . . . In order even to depict social change, let alone account for it, one must identify the formally defined elements and patterns of social structure that are changing. Conversely, these models often grow out of and are modified and judged by their applicability to selected aspects of concrete social events.[111]

For Merton, such models would clearly include such concepts as social and cultural goals, social and cultural norms, status and role sets, and many other concepts reviewed in Chapter 5. In his introduction to studies in social and cultural structure he states that "The key concept bridging the gap between statics and dynamics in functional theory is that of strain, tension, contradiction, or discrepancy between the component elements of social and cultural structure." [112]

More recently he has differentiated three particular forms of strain and related these to adaptive mechanisms called "institutional evasion of institutional rules or norms." [113] The three foci of strain he refers to are those on which he believes there is general consensus. They are intended to be illustrative only and are expressed as variables. First is the variable of the rigidity with which people are expected to conform to any particular norm; second is the variable of some degree of cultural inconsistency; and third is the variable of potential conflict to the degree that there is social differentiation in a society composed of different groups with their more or less distinctive subcultures.

Here are three different generalized respects which are illustrative of varying degrees and kinds of stress to which a social system may be subjected. I believe that some mechanisms evolve not to eliminate these pressures but to adapt to them, and which have the effect of reducing them. One such mechanism is empirically observable over and over again, and that's what I refer to as "institutionalized evasion of institutional norms." . . . The reason why I think it's important is that it's another way of cutting into social change. Where there is a cumulative stress situation, you will find institutionalized evasion patterns . . . You have to have the evasion as a kind of cushioning device; if you don't allow it something has to give and you're on the way to social change.[114]

Merton has attempted by various devices to avoid the bias which may result from the sociologist's being an actor (and thereby potentially influenced by various reference systems) at the same time that he is an observer. The assessment of what in fact constitutes nonconformity must be undertaken only with the cautious consideration of the various systems, institutions, power relations and their interconnections. Nonconformity with particular social institutions may represent "the beginning of a new alternative pattern, with its own distinctive claims to moral validity."[115] Common blind spots for the observer are lack of recognition of the important place of power in society[116] and misleading assumptions concerning the extensiveness and inclusiveness and endurance of existing institutions which are legitimized for some groups only.

Most of Merton's observations concerning social change are in some manner related to the sociology of knowledge, social-cultural strain, reference group theory and functional analysis. In addition to the few examples which can be summarized here the reader is referred to the many which were noted in Chapter 5 of the present volume as well as to the fairly comprehensive index in *Social Theory and Social Structure* which has numerous listings under the heading social change. The many aspects of social change which Merton has treated are suggested by the following enumeration of items, all of which will have been encountered before by those who have read Chapter 5 of the present volume:

1. "Relative deprivation" as felt by a class or group, and its importance as a potential in conflict with authority.[117]
2. The distinction between the status-roles of non-conformist and criminal, and the change potential of the former.[118]
3. The possibility that the social scientist's prediction may result in a changed situation, thus falsifying the prediction.[119]
4. "Self-hypnosis" through one's own propaganda and the self-fulfilling prophecy.[120]
5. Conflicting value-orientations in primary groups which may lessen the influence of "the mediating role" of such groups, thus permitting "the influence of the larger society to . . . [become] more binding."[121]
6. The relatively great influence of non-membership groups in social systems having high rates of social mobility.[122]
7. The relative propensity for the "isolated to adopt values of non-membership groups."[123]

8. The relatively isolated mobile individuals who adopt a life style other than the one to which they have been initially socialized.[124]

9. The trickle effect, such as the "trickling-down of fashions and styles in the system of stratification." [125]

Parsons notes [126] that Merton has demonstrated that the dynamics of science in all its institutional manifestations is an agent of change of the highest order. Not only are the universities and other scientific centers creators of knowledge in a sort of quantitative sense, but they perform a function of the utmost importance in its accumulation which develops the "steady move toward reducing what Conant called the 'degree of empiricism.'" [127] Merton specifies four components of the "ethos of science": universalism; communism (by which scientific findings are considered to be common property—not the property of the discoverer); disinterestedness; and organized scepticism. All lead to change, but the last mentioned is the strongest in this respect.[128] "The scientific investigator does not preserve the cleavage between the sacred and the profane, between that which requires uncritical respect and that which can be objectively analyzed." [129]

With this summarizing chapter only a little more than half completed with this section on Merton's works, it is already apparent, as indeed it was at the conclusion of Chapter 8 that although there is considerable consensus among modern theorists when people in all parts of the world who now call themselves social scientists are considered there is even more difference if not dissent among men who are colleagues in a common endeavor. Excerpts from Merton's address to the Fourth World Congress of Sociology (as well as his group property, the potential of fission or unity, see Chapter 5, addendum) have relevance to this state of affairs as well as to the more general theme of social change, and are a fitting finale to this section.

In a final remark on these and the many other lines of cleavage among sociologists, I should like to apply a formulation about the structure of social conflict in relation to the intensity of conflict that was clearly stated by Georg Simmel and Edward Ross. This is the hypothesis, in the words of Ross, that "a society . . . which is riven by a dozen . . . [conflicts] along lines running in every direction, may actually be in less danger of being torn with violence or falling to pieces than one split along just one line. For each new cleavage contributes to narrow and cross clefts, so that one might say that society *is sewn together* by its inner conflicts."

It is an hypothesis borne out by its own history, for since it was set forth by Simmel and by Ross, it has been taken up or independently originated by some scores of sociologists, many of whom take diametrically opposed positions on some of the issues we have reviewed. (I mention only a few of these: Wiese and Becker, Hiller, Myrdal, Parsons, Lewis Coser, Berelson, Lazarsfeld and McPhee, Robin Williams, Dahrendorf, Coleman, Lipset and Zelditch, and among the great number of recent students of "status-discrepancy," Lenski, Adams, Stogdill and Hemphill.) [130]

GEORGE C. HOMANS

Cognitive mapping—conceptualization. "Interaction theorist" is the designation by which Homans has been characterized in the title of Chapter 4. If the two analytically separable components of social action mentioned at the beginning of the present chapter, the normative, and interaction *per se* are considered as poles of a continuum, Homans falls further toward the interaction pole than any of the other writers whose works are considered in the preceding chapters. As Gouldner [131] has observed, Homans has not neglected the normative components but he has increasingly emphasized interaction. Also he has become more interested in interaction as it occurs between two or three individuals.[132]

The most distinguishing feature of Homans' conceptual scheme is its parsimonious use of terms. In *The Human Group* (1950) four components of interaction called elements were differentiated; namely, activities, interaction, sentiment and norms. In *Social Behavior* (1960) he dropped the designation, element, and specified as his primary factor the concept sanction, including reward and punishment.[133] Other commonly used concepts such as those of the PAS Model and his own earlier terms become secondary factors. Since sanctions can be reduced to an amount of activity and to value these latter "can be called elements," but he does not employ the term element frequently in *Social Behavior.*[134] Although this limited repertory of primary factors or central concepts is designed for the analysis of interpersonal interaction Homans does deal with social change, although to a lesser degree than the other theorists here considered, and to a lesser degree in *Social Behavior* than in *The Human Group*. The somewhat narrower focus of *Social Behavior* results in the infrequent use of the concept system, which was frequently employed in *The Human Group*.[135] The concept equilibrium, is also used in later writings (where it is often referred to as practical equilibrium) in a more circumspect manner than in *The Human Group* in which it was called the "bridge to the study of social change."[136] Although some of the mutual interdependencies as deduced from the five propositions presented early in Chapter 4 of the present volume would entitle elementary behavior as studied in *Social Behavior* to be designated as internal system[137] the term internal system is seldom used in *Social Behavior*. Not only have old concepts been discarded or nearly so. There has been an accompanying decline in concern for theory and categorization and a greater interest in explanation and prediction through the use of propositions of the type symbolized by "x varies as y." Not unrelated to these considerations is his disparagement of attempts to specify functional prerequisites or requisites for the survival of societies and groups.[138]

There is no functional prerequisite for the survival of a society except that the society provide sufficient reward for its individual members to keep them contributing activities to its maintenance, and that it reward them not just as members of that society but as men.[139]

In *The Human Group* functionalism was criticized on the grounds that it pays more attention to final than to efficient causes,[140] a point of view which is repeatedly emphasized[141] in Homans' works. Although he concedes that the functional approach offers advantages in opening areas for investigation, he finds greatest fault with the term functional in the sense in which Levi-Strauss used it; namely, that "an institution is what it is because it is good for a society in the sense of creating organic solidarity, and some institutions are, from this point of view, better than others."[142] When he is most critical of functionalism it is usually this form to which he refers and not the "Malinowskian or Radcliffe-Brownian forms,"[143] or the kind represented by

Kingsley Davis' earlier usage which is similar to, if not identical with sociological analyses as mentioned in Chapter 3.

Explanation of social change. Although Homans has stated that *Social Behavior* does not deal with social change [144] this is true only in the formal sense. The parsimonious use of terms, the elevation of sanctions to the sole primary factor in behavior, recent emphasis on deductive explanation and prediction and other aspects of his cognitive mapping just reviewed of course condition and are conditioned by his research targets and results. This could no doubt be illustrated by imagining the inappropriateness of attempting to apply Sorokin's historical studies of ideational, sensate and idealistic cultures, Becker's sacred and secular societies, Parsons' or Williams' studies of societies, or Davis' demographic and theoretical analysis, to elementary social behavior which is his chosen subject. This line of thinking is illustrated by Homans [145] and likewise by Sorokin as each compares research procedures to the use of a fish net, an analogy which illustrates that choice of concepts can not be made independently of research target.

One of the most remarkable characteristics of Homans' writings in both *The Human Group* and in *Social Behavior* is his extreme care not to generalize to society at large from the evidence provided by his studies of small groups and from his analyses of elementary social behavior, and *at the same time* his implications that there are generalizations which could be made. "It is true that a formal leader may be more successful in his own job if he has something of the informal leader about him too— but this only adds to the evidence that the two are not the same." [146] Or, "It is significant how often a group of between eight and a dozen persons crops up under the supervision of a single leader in organizations of many different kinds. The old-fashioned squad in the army is an example." [147] The reader is invited to share what almost appears to be ambivalence on Homans' part as to whether generalizations beyond the small group are justifiable:

We should never assume that the informal group is a microcosm of society at large, that what holds good of the one holds good also for the other . . . And yet, though the resemblances may be superficial, some characteristics of some social-class systems at some times seem to resemble what we have noticed about status in small groups . . .[148]

It must be added, however, that when Homans does at times, even in *Social Behavior,* examine phenomena which properly fall outside the area of elementary social behavior he is generally careful to draw this to the reader's attention.

The last chapter of *Social Behavior,* or what he calls "a primitive orgy after harvest," contains insightful facts concerning social change, the rise of civilization, its possible fall, stagnation, revolution or other results when elementary social behavior is stifled and "generalized reinforcers like money and social approval" [149] become the chief means of exchange. The inevitable resurgence of elementary social behavior from whatever constraints it is subjected to is a predictable source of change.

Elementary social behavior does not grow just in the gaps between institutions; it clings to institutions as to a trellis. It grows everywhere . . . An obvious example is the way in which the soldiers' determination not to let their comrades down contributes more than anything else to the fighting power of an infantry outfit.[150]

Somewhat in contrast to this is the less optimistic tone of *The Human Group* which shows the danger of developing an "internal proletariate" [152] in "civilization [which] is fed on the rot of the village" [152] and kept alive by such "antibodies [as] all sorts of religions." [153]

The cycle is vicious; loss of group membership in one generation may make men less capable of group membership in the next. The civilization that, by its very process of growth, shatters small group life will leave men and women lonely and unhappy . . . Each of the sociologists —Durkheim, LeBon, Figgis, Brooks Adams—who began, just before World War I, to point out the signs of decay in our society, used the same metaphor. They said that society was becoming a dust heap of individuals without links to one another.[154]

In *The Human Group* as in *Social Behavior* broad considerations of change on a societal scale are confined to one final chapter and should not be made to represent more of Homans' thinking as represented by his writings than is actually the case, especially since in the intervening years since the appearance of *The Human*

Group he reports that he has become "increasingly sceptical about the dustheap hypothesis." [155] This scepticism no doubt springs from the perceived ubiquity of elementary social behavior which eventually will break the bonds if too long confined. In *Social Behavior* he expresses this idea thus:

If a poor society must be human because it has nothing else, and a rich society can be human because it has everything else, we moderns are *nouveaux riches* trying to acquire aristocratic tastes. Sometimes the great rebellions and revolutions, cracking the institutional crust, bring out elementary social behavior hot and straight from the fissures. They always appeal, for instance, to the simplest principles of distributive justice: When Adam delved and Eve span, who was then the gentleman? [156]

Homans' dim evaluation of modern civilization in *The Human Group* was not unlike Sorokin's, but this similarity is considerably reduced in *Social Behavior*. And unlike as Homans and Parsons are in their methods and concepts, Parsons' conclusion that "chronic states of tension come to be institutionalized and more or less stabilized" [157] is certainly similar to Homans' position:

The problem need not be solved at all, temporarily or permanently. The society may tear itself apart in conflict without ever creating a new institution that will stick. Still more often the problem may simply persist without issuing in overt conflict but without resolution either ... Yet men have invented one peculiar institution [sometimes called science] that may just conceivably help them get out of their rat race. [158]

The importance of Homans' generalizations, observations, hypotheses and speculations concerning such broad themes as have been touched upon here cannot be measured by the relatively scant treatment accorded them by their author. For the most part those presented so far have emerged less from the use of his rigorously developed sociological conceptual scheme and procedure than from his broad historical studies, knowledge and scholarship. Most of his observations and findings have a more strictly sociological genesis and many have implications for social change whether implied by Homans or not.

The chapter in *Social Behavior* entitled "Status, Conformity and Innovation" reports findings of great relevance for social change, especially that change which Merton calls opportunity for deviance. With due consideration of Homans' reluctance, formally at least, to generalize on a societal level from those findings which are documented on a small group level, his oral statements relating class to conformity-nonconformity may well have wider implications than appear on the surface.

We have established the fact by a number of experiments that both high status people and low status people in ambiguous situations are likely to depart from apparent group opinion . . . It's a risk problem, I think. Risk in the sense . . . that the low status man has got nothing to lose while the other fellow with high status has got a lot to lose, so he can afford to risk some of it. The fellow at the bottom, if he's wrong on this occasion, is no worse off than he was before; so the balance of risk in effect is in favor of his being a deviant.[159]

Homans mentions risk in another sense too, which is related to change, as he notes that specialization requires dependency on someone else for the things that the specialist needs but no longer makes for himself. He risks the chance that another specialist will not do some of these jobs whose products he needs. Both Williams and Parsons, particularly Parsons, also inject the idea of risk taking as differentiation and specialization enter into the process of change. Homans' findings as he relates them, albeit guardedly, to the class system are sure to be of great interest to Marxists and non-Marxists alike.

We are far from arguing that the recognition of status and the secondary mechanisms it brings into play always contribute to social stability They may, on the contrary, introduce important possibilities for further change and innovation.[160]

Homans draws conclusions about group formation and structure from evidence supplied by Helen Jennings and others. The present authors find that one of the most insightful observations in *Social Behavior* is provided as Homans matches hypothetical "model group or toy society" exchanges of choices and sentiments with empirical sociometric results from studies by Jennings, Moreno, Lemann and Soloman. The comparisons reveal more "mutual choice at the very bottom of society" than would be predicted from the "toy" in which "every member chooses other members in order of the value to him of the services they perform." [161]

Certainly the phenomena are common and ask for explanation, for they add up to "companionship in misery" or "the solidarity of the lower class." [162]

Of course, Marxists have their explanation for this. While it is established, as some of the sociometric studies of the senior author have helped to demonstrate,[163] that some of the most sociometrically cohesive groups are made up of persons "whom almost nobody would choose except the other members of the clique," [164] these same findings may instructively be considered along with the "isolate-deviant" observations made by Homans.

The lot of the isolate is often hard . . . [He is apt to give in to persuasion unless there are others]—not just nonconformists but nonconformists of his own stripe . . . Even a single such man seems to be a great comfort, and robs the group at one stroke of the greater part of its power. In this man the nonconformist has a source of support . . .[165]

Homans elsewhere, as has been noted, is at least moderately critical of the industrial society as is each other writer represented in this volume. A question which is in a sense a composite of these evaluations may be put (although it is in no sense being attributed to Homans notwithstanding its inclusion in the present section): Is the industrial proletariate a relatively fertile breeding ground for tight little cliques of "companions in misery"? As will be remembered from Chapter 2 Howard Becker was among the first of American sociologists to pay attention to the misery and alienation of individuals. Sorokin in his classical study of *Social Mobility* and in other connections hypothesized that in industrial societies, contrary to Marxian doctrine, competent individuals are motivated to upward mobility leaving a sort of dreg population to be "companions in misery." A similar theme is the subject of Merton's paradigm of anomie. Obviously more facts are needed but the problem is important and Homans hints at some answers without posing the question.

He suggests that in the South (of the United States) and in England (of the seventeenth century) the lower classes and upper classes were less restrained in gambling, drink, and sex freedom and more indulgent in the sensual pleasures than the middle classes. He notes that although in seventeenth century England the members of the middle class were more apt to be puritanical than lower-class and upper-class members, the middle class were innovators in their way. It was they who were the religious reformers. He observes that in the seventeenth century,

When King and Commons faced one another in arms in the Civil War, middle-class people were specially likely to support Parliament, while the other two classes . . . tended to identify themselves with one another and with the king.[166]

The importance of class in the study of change is further highlighted in Parsons' account of the rise of the Nazis to power in Germany as related in Chapter 6. Homans' observations concerning the differential effect of inflation upon upper, middle and lower classes in sixteenth century England is likewise instructive for students of change. He reports that monetary inflation elevated the middle class farm owner operators because they got more for the produce they sold, but spent very little more because their market needs were few. Laborers, therefore, suffered, more than the middle class owner operators. Aristocratic land owners who lived from rents suffered from the inflation. Thus in this case upper and lower classes could commiserate together.

In summary, it would appear that Homans has more to say about change than his avowed disinterest in the subject (from the point of focus of *Social Behavior*) would lead one to suspect, although the impingements of small group behavior on broad social change are seldom spelled out. Where they are spelled out he drops the purely scientific and logical methods of science for the conjectures and postulates of the historian and social observer, a position he is admirably able to assume since his earliest proficiency was in the field of social history.

KINGSLEY DAVIS

Cognitive mapping—conceptualization. On the analytical continuum ranging from one pole of emphasis on the *normative* to another with emphasis on *interaction per se,* Davis' position as reflected in his early writing and in *Human Society* (1949) would fall toward the normative pole.

A social system is always normative. Its integration rests upon the fact that its members carry in their heads, as part of the cultural heritage, the notion that they *ought* or *ought not* to do certain things . . . An evaluative attitude, an attitude of praise and blame, of accusation and justification, thus pervades every human society.[167]

As was seen in Chapter 3, Davis in *Human Society* distinguishes between the factual and the normative. His conception of role includes actual performance which is seen to be far from normless. That the normative is still strong in his thinking is illustrated by the following more recent statements:

Social orders seem to be made up of people who go around with a kind of ideal situation in mind . . . We hold up a standard of military virtues . . . or duties, then we reward men for going beyond the call of duty implying that there is the expected but that actually performance can be higher . . . Also performance can be lower. You can do less than your duty.[168]

His criticism of Marxism likewise is based on normative considerations:

What is the Marxist fallacy? Well, one version of it is that you derive everything from means—you derive the goals from means . . . the idea that you can get an ethic out of science, for example.[169]

This stress on the normative does not preclude the distinct possibility that Davis' position in this regard has shifted somewhat from the normative pole and on the continuum mentioned above now stands closer to Homans than was earlier the case. Various signs point to such a shift such as his insistence that the feeling of obligation and expectation as differentiated from statistical regularity "are not necessarily mutually exclusive," [170] but that standards of efficiency and norms of moral obligation should be designated by different terms.[171] Even more indicative is his scepticism of value studies as explanations of social change:

I think where you find differences of value from a sociological view, you can't take these as in any way a final explanation because you then have to ask: Why the values? . . . You have to go back into the conditions, situations lying behind these. I never like to take values as a kind of ultimate in explanation and I have a lot of trouble with sociology students today because they all tend to do that . . . I am very suspicious of a sociological analysis that comes to rest on values, just as I am equally suspicious of an analysis that comes to rest on sheer calculation . . . We calculate all the time, and that's why I've come much more in recent years, when I talk about norms, to stress . . . sanctions.[172]

Asked why he thought the social should be distinguished from the cultural his reply gives further support for the inference that his emphasis on the non-normative is considerable:

[You should distinguish them] for the very reason that a society in action is much more than just the culture of that society . . . Real human beings are in action . . . To describe its cultural patterns is not going to give you the real action. Otherwise a lot of my distinctions [such as that between status and role] would be utterly useless. To describe the cultural pattern isn't to describe what's actually going to be accomplished in society. And furthermore, how are you going to explain a change in culture? One of the great difficulties in what I [believe to be] . . . the unfruitful situation with respect to a theory of social change now, is the dominance of . . . [some] anthropologists and their cultural explanations.[173]

Central to Davis' considerations of change as focusing on "the stresses and strains" is the concept of equilibrium, a concept he still believes to be useful if it is not reified. With the quilibrium model he, of course, uses his own conceptual scheme centering in the social system as portrayed in Chapter 3.

It is only in terms of equilibrium that most sociological concepts make sense. Either tacitly or explicitly anyone who thinks about society tends to use the notion . . . It is usually phrased in static terms, but as soon as the element of time is added it alludes to a moving equilibrium.[174]

In the employment of the equilibrium model outside impingements which may alter it and likewise forces within the society which tend to restore it are the focus of interest.[175] Davis sees the chief danger in the use of this or other models as that of reification or reductionism, the latter resulting in the failure to retain independence of elements of a conceptual scheme or reducing all phenomena to too few components or even to a single component. The Marxist fallacy was mentioned above. In the same vein Davis asks, "What is the idealistic fallacy? It is reducing the means to goals. [For the idealist] everything is explicable in terms of goals."[176]

Not much more needs be written about Davis' position on functionalism than what appears in Chapter 3. He finds the term objectionable, and unlike Merton, sees no advantage in retaining it. Although obviously what he had previously designated by the term in his own work matches that which is similarly designated by Merton and Parsons, Davis proposes to drop the term (although not the concept embodied in the term) because a good deal of confusion surrounds its use.

If you look over *Human Society* you'll find that I used the terms sociological analysis and functional analysis synonymously. But . . . in my opinion . . . the terminology . . . got out of hand. . . . Much of the confusion over social function [took place] after that book was written.[177]

As indicated in the preceding section on Homans, Davis' earlier and Parsons' and Merton's present usage differs from that of Levy-Straus whose usage for many epitomizes the term's significance and whose usage for many is not acceptable.

The models and concepts which Davis uses are comparable to those of the writers whose works have already been summarized. His expert use of the means-end schema was discussed in Chapter 3. However, since he is the only specialist in demography among the writers treated here, his use of the "transition model"[178] deserves greater attention here than other models and concepts which are well represented. He describes the demographic transition model in simple terms illustrating some of the dangers in its employment.

The demographic transition [describes] . . . a shift from a regime of negligible population growth characterized by *high* birth and death rates to one of equally little growth based on *low* birth and death rates, during which there is a rapid increase in numbers due to "demographic gap," the lag of fertility decline behind mortality decline.[179]

It has been approximated in many countries but it has never actually happened.[180] Clearly the demographic transition, despite its fruitfulness as an organizing idea, should not be viewed as inevitable or as a predictive instrument.[181]

The model, based upon past experience tempts its users to employ it as though nations entering "transition" would follow patterns of those nations whose experience forms the basis of the model. As Davis remarks:

. . . some demographers have acted as if you could take countries and place them in this transition and call them types, as if it was all very concrete . . . That's the nature of models . . . and this doesn't keep it . . . when properly used and not reified [from being] the controlling idea in population research. The danger of reification [comes when one says] "Well, [India for example] is just in the early stages of the demographic transition. Now, in fifty years or so it will complete the transition." This is a way of dismissing problems.[182]

The advanced countries . . . have not really experienced the full cycle . . . The truth is that no country of India's type has ever yet completed the transition.[183]

To illustrate the difficulties connected with using the model, Davis notes that if India is compared with Great Britain there is a current birth rate in India which was like the birth rate of Great Britain in 1875-1880. The current death rate of India, however, is like the Great Britain death rate of 1800. If the birth rate of Great Britain in 1875-1880 were alone extrapolated in terms which would apply to India of today, by the year 2005 India would have about 540 million people (if the transition took from 55 to 60 years). But on the basis of the 135 years which it took for Great Britain to reduce her birth rate from the high of 1800 to the present level, India in 135 years or by about 2080 would have about 1.5 billion population.[184]

Davis with Judith Blake made an analysis of social structure in relation to fertility which focuses on systemic variations in different societies, of sexual unions and the corresponding variations in fertility rates. This analysis is reviewed in Chapter 3 under the heading systemic linkage. The comprehensiveness of the conceptual scheme used by the Davises in this analysis is demonstrated by the fact that practically all of the considerations of the PAS Model are matched in one way or another in the Davis analysis, although frequently with different terminology. The effort demonstrates the value of a comprehensive *a priori* conceptual scheme which in this case resulted in an outstanding contribution to the field of demography in particular and to the field of sociology in general.

Explanation of change. As mentioned in Chapter 3 Davis differentiates between social and cultural change. The former he exemplifies by the rise of organized labor in capitalistic society and the latter by the systematic sound shifts in the Indo-European languages. He sees cultural change as much broader than social change, the former including science, art, technology, philosophy and the norms of social organization. His conceptualization and analyses in this regard do not differ essentially from the position of some of the other writers reported above and summarized in this chapter under the section devoted to Williams' works. The summarization of Davis' position appears in Chapter 3.

As a student of demography and social change Davis does not see a placid, peaceful road ahead for humanity. His coining of the now popular term "population explosion" reveals the chief reason for his pessimistic views. Something of the explosive quality which Davis sees attached to demographic events may be gleaned from the following:

Mexico's population is growing faster now than the United States population ever did in its heyday with the help of massive immigration. Mexico has no immigration . . . [she] probably has a net out-migration.[185]

It is being demonstrated in country after country that widespread diseases such as malaria, yaws, syphilis, trachoma, cholera, plague, and typhoid can be controlled on a mass basis at low cost . . . The amazingly accelerated reduction of mortality in underdeveloped areas in recent years has thus been accomplished by international disease control, not by economic development in these areas themselves.[186]

Confronted with astronomical population changes, little space for migration, and the difficulties of introducing birth control on a large scale "we are left . . . with the only apparent solution . . . rapid industrialization . . . [but] it seems utopian to look for a smooth transition to modernism." [187]

HOWARD P. BECKER

Problems of cognitive mapping—conceptualization. Although conduct, for Becker was always normative,[188] it was neither socially nor culturally determined.[189] Becker was the only theorist, of those considered here, to make change itself a part of the conceptual device by which change is analyzed. For him reluctance to change or willingness to change was a central component and focus of his continuum which ranges from the sacred at one pole to the secular at the other. To place his writings in terms of their emphasis on change on the sacred-secular continuum would of course be a meaningless tautology. It is not too different from attempting to place his writings on the continuum posited throughout this chapter which in terms of an ideal typological continuum ranges from the pole of completely normative behavior to behavior which arises solely out of interaction. The differentiations on the sacred-secular continuum carry emphasis on both the kind and the saliency of norms, but its author also differentiated between "the process of acquiring culture and the process of developing sociation," [190] and for him both processes were always normative. At the beginning of his sociological career, as exemplified by the Wiese-Becker volume (1932) he was concerned with the classification of forms and processes of interaction. However, in this same volume and in his University of Chicago Ph. D. dissertation (1930) he began his study of the process of *secularization* and the development of the ideal typology, the sacred and the secular which eventually became the continuum of constructed types ranging from the sacred to the secular. Later he became interested in *sacralization* and toward the end of his career wrote about "normative reactions to normlessness." [191] His presidential address to the American Sociological Society, prepared just before his death and read to the society a few months after his death by his son, carried that title. Few sociologists have made norms and the normative more central to their analyses.

The final formulation of Becker's famous sacred-secular continuum is presented in Chapter 2. Although his interests were broad and his writings many, the development and use of the sacred-secular typology was almost always at the center of his scientific activities. Because of the constancy of this theme in his thirty years of sociological writing, and because the core idea of that theme coincided with the core idea of this summarizing chapter—social change, it is appropriate that it be elaborated here somewhat more than have been the works of the other writers herein considered. Such an elaboration is made possible only because a few days before Becker's death the authors had a full day's discussion with him. His remarks were initially addressed to a version of Chapter 2 which, on the basis of his criticism, takes the form as presented in this volume. They fanned out, however, to cover a wide range of sociological phenomena. The tape recording of that interview represents some of his last thinking which in the nature of the case is not elsewhere available. A fuller utilization of that interview than of those of the other authors herein represented will therefore be made, especially since the subject of social change and its conceptualization was an especially strong theme among the many subjects which were discussed on that day in May of 1960.

Becker dwelt at considerable length on the changes he had made in the sacred-secular typology since he first presented one form of it in his University of Chicago Ph. D. dissertation in 1930 and as later published in the Wiese-Becker volume (1932). He traced the influence of other sociologists, especially as they had influenced him in the development of the typology. As a background for a detailed treatment of the typology, his own verbal summary statement may be quoted:

"Park as I look back on it [had the greatest influence on me] being a terrifically effective catalyst, and certainly his hints about sacred-secular were of great importance. Although I certainly took [much] from him . . . the notions and hints coming from Everett Hughes also play a very great part because Hughes, in my judgment, began to pick up some of Park's hints and to formulate them more fruitfully than Park himself did." [192]

As mentioned in his article "Current Sacred-Secular Theory" [193] to which in the interview he referred as the correct statement of the background of his thinking, he stressed the influence of Florian Znanieki and W. I. Thomas, noting in the interview that direct German influences came later. Specifying his indebtedness to George H. Mead he notes, "I took Mead's famous course at Chicago and I have the full notes . . . I got my original notes in 1928." In the development of his master's thesis on bereavement he noted the influences of his major professor Tom Elliot, both in his personal and professional development. As evidenced in the interview and as noted by Becker's colleagues, he was at once interested in the broad aspects of historical events in the tradition of Max Weber, Sorokin, and Toynbee and in rigorous statistical methods; not unlike Homans he stressed the importance of prediction which he symbolized as "x varies as y" or "if and when" statements.[194]

In discussion and in his writing he continually refers to his having begun his occupational life as a mechanical engineer. He touched on this in the interview:

You never break lose from some of your earlier concrete experiences ... I've got to admit to the fact that I came up through the machine shop ... working with concrete phenomena ... I did construct quite elaborate special machines subject to all sorts of mathematical computations—strength of materials, and so forth. Many younger engineers ... out of the ordinary ... academic situation ... would devise types of machinery that were simply pure figments of the imagination. My math is on the whole pretty good [but] I distrust mathematization if it is not coupled with a keen sense of the actual empirical evidence against which it may be validated. There may be an initial bias here and it is a deep-rooted one. I sometimes argue with my younger colleagues. I say, "Young man, I am not talking about something that I am skimming off the top of my head. This *works*." (*tape*)

Perhaps precisely because of his own requirements that theory be heavily grounded in the empirical world, he felt a heavy sense of duty that his students be exposed to a wide range of sociological theory:

Feeling as I do about the great vogue of Parsonian theory, if I were to put students through an obligatory course for the Master's degree in sociological theory and did not get them fully familiar at first hand with Parsons I feel I should be doing them an injustice. The consequence is that I do not fully enough develop other theoretical points of view, including my own. (*tape*)

The development of Becker's thinking through the years is reflected in the changes of the sacred-secular typology from its inception in 1930 to its final form. Its original form, as part of his Ph. D. thesis (1930) and as published in Wiese-Becker in 1932 was re-published in Becker's *Man in Reciprocity* (1956) in juxtaposition with Parsons' pattern variables which appeared in 1950, twenty years after the first appearance of Becker's typology. The comparison afforded by this juxtaposition is included in Appendix

1 of the present chapter. The Becker part thereof provides a bench mark against which his subsequent conceptualizations may be checked, a subject to which a considerable portion of the recorded discussion is devoted. In the interview Becker referred to his own typology of 1930 and Parsons' pattern variables of 1950 as follows:

All I am trying to do [with this combination] is to indicate certain parallels, certain similarities. Since this was for a lecture to an introductory class, I could not go into the details of type construction.

In the original formulation I fell prey to [the notion of thinking up] a model . . . In other words, I had stricken out, in the construction of the accessible secular society a great deal of the qualifying empirical evidence . . . I was building a model, a purely deductive model. I say, "topographical irregularities being 'ideally' absent, zones of population distribution arise that in their spatial patterning reflect exactly the competitive order." What is being done here is to construct a type —construct a model that has no remote probability of empirical approximation. This is the essential point. I go on to say, "It has a complex metropolitan economy, with a territorial as well as an occupational division of labor. Trade is carried on with all parts of the world; there are no political barriers, such as protective tariffs or immigration restructions, of any kind." [See above quoted material in ¶ 3 and ¶ 4 in Appendix below]:

Straight through then, as I said, this becomes a deductive model, and in my recent work I have more and more come to the position that the type must not be a type the empirical approximation of which is inherently nil. There must be, even if only one instance in ten thousand, some probability of a close empirical approximation. Max Weber's methodological statements (not his empirical work) misled me on this. (*tape*)

Becker sees virtually all of his recent work as possessing empirical validity. The isolated sacred society as originally typed in 1930 needed little modification in this regard, and even the isolated secular construct which ideally possesses no topographic irregularities can be matched in urban scenes in which there is a minimum of topographical irregularity. The conviction that it was impermissable to "let your fantasy have free play," "to construct an Airedale with a cast-iron stomach and castors for feet" increasingly guided him in the modifications made on his original typology. The caution thus engendered extended to his ideas of polarity in types:

Some place in the manuscript you spoke of polarized types—sacred and secular. I would say that the term polarization is not utterly out of place, since I would want to give some stress to certain extremes— let us say, holy over here and thrilling over there—but actually I am trying to build a continuum. Earlier it appeared in polarized fashion, but later I became concerned with the possibility of misinterpretation, and I have come more frequently to speak of a continuum than a set of polarisms. (*tape*)

A development that Becker had not foreseen, but which was facilitated by the deemphasis of polarities was the near-circularity of the continuum. The protest against the pro-normless situation, channeled through charismatic leaders results in "new" norms which often are quite archaistic, but are viewed as new by the participants. The result may be "a quick flip back to an old orientation." (Figure 1, Chapter 2.)

Incidentally, I might mention the fact that it was Ruth Useem who put a flea in my ear with regard to what I formerly called the normless society. She said "After everything else you've been talking about it is obvious that you are using a complete contradiction in terms. There can be no such thing as a normless society, if you are insisting that there be empirical grounding for this material." I said, "You're quite right." So then I switched to this term, pronormless. Having done that I was really glad because it gave me four terms that all began with P's and easy to remember. (*tape*)

It was because of the growing insistence that concrete evidence be taken into account that the major constructs composing the sacred-secular continuum were broken down into subordinate units. The actual perceived differences in societies which generally could be categorized as sacred led to the "absolute essential" of the break-down into the holy, loyalistic, intimate, moralistic, fitting and appropriate. Similar considerations concerning societies which were secular led to the pursuant, consequent, comfortable and thrilling. (Figure 1, Chapter 2). Becker was careful to distinguish, however, between the actual empirical instance and the construct representing that empirical instance.

For example, suppose I make a construct out of this body of empirical evidence in which I introduce, say, twelve criteria. [Suppose] I find that all of these twelve criteria are adequately reflected in appropriate empirical configurations and organizations. All right, I have then achieved a very close approximation of the empirical instance. Obviously the empirical instance includes a tremendous amount more than is in the twelve criteria . . . There is always this great gulf fixed between the construct and the empirical instance. The construct can be matched with an empirical instance but the empirical instance always contains vastly more than any construct can ever contain. (*tape*)

Becker considered that the best statement of the sacred-secular continuum was in the Becker-Boskoff publication in the chapter entitled "Current Sacred-Secular Theory," except that he would later have preferred a slight modification of the definitions contained therein in line with his later definitions he had prepared for the *UNESCO Dictionary of Social Science*. This modification was worked into the revision of *Social Thought from Lore to Science*. The new edition of that work with Becker as senior and Harry Elmer Barnes as junior author, he noted, carried the UNESCO material in the first chapter and more of the "sacred-secular framework" throughout. As he discussed the various changes in terminology which the sacred-secular continuum had undergone from its original formulation as represented in Appendix 1 to that in Figure 1, Chapter 2, Becker stressed the finality of the version as it appears in the Becker-Boskoff book and in the *UNESCO Dictionary of Social Science*. "I don't think I am ever going to change it now, but I have changed too much." (*tape*)

His work, *Through Values to Sociological Interpretation* (1950) came out in a German version which was not so complete as the English version but was more up to date. The German version, *Soziologie als Wissenschaft vom sozialen Handeln* (Wuerzburg: Holzner Verlag, undated) did not include Chapter 5 of the English version with the charts comparing other typologies with the sacred-secular continuum. The many subtypes of the sacred and secular societies included in Chapter 5 are also omitted from the German edition. This is one respect in which the German edition is more up to date, because the numerous subtypes represented his earlier emphasis upon taxonomies which was largely deemphasized in his later thinking. After 1950 he moved toward emphasis on fewer categories and more analysis. Those analyses which were facilitated by such concepts as vicinal isolation and related ideas left him indebted to Ellen C. Semple to whom he attributed the concept.[195] The authors asked Becker whether he considered the processes detailed in Wiese-Becker as analytical or taxonomical. He replied that they were mainly a taxonomy which had its utility in a number of ways. "When you have a sufficient body of empirical evidence at your disposal and you are employing such a taxonomy you can see certain possibilities that you otherwise might not see." (*tape*)

Becker's development of the cult-ecclesia continuum when at the University of Pennsylvania early in 1929 was influenced directly by H. Richard Niebuhr, and only indirectly by Troeltsch and Max Weber. He reported that Niebuhr's book *The Social Sources of Denominationalism* made quite an impact on him. Other influences were reported in the interview:

Park had been telling me a lot about what he called the various cults that met in the loop in Chicago, and held Sunday services with cult leaders in theater buildings and so on. To these everyone could come. There was no sect there, nothing rigidly selective, no clear-cut doctrine . . . Weber's influence comes in later and I began to include the idea of allegiance to a personal leader, highly personalized allegiance. Weber speaks of standards as being personal, the leader embodying the standards . . . The best formulation is in MIR.[196] (*tape*)

As Chapter 2 indicates, Becker treated Thomas' wishes as ends and used them in conjunction with the sacred-secular continuum, in the Max Weber tradition. The pattern of influence which Becker traced in this connection shows him to be unusually sensitive to the personal as well as to the intellectual impacts which scholar makes upon scholar.

There was, of course, some influence from Wiese here. If you examine the German original, however, from which I adapted and which I also augmented, you will note that I threw out a number of Wiese's formulations that in my opinion carried him a little too far over toward instincts. He has a long section, for example, in which he accepts McDougall. Some of his treatment of wishes carried him so far over in the instinct direction that I was compelled to qualify, though even here in the Wiese-Becker adaptation, I didn't feel I could go too far, because after all, he had to give his final approval.[197] I would say that Thomas through Znaniecki finally led me over to this classification. I cannot say as I look back that Weber made a strong impact on me until as late as 1929. I knew a little about Weber as a result of my work with Wiese, but Wiese was quite aloof with regard to Weber.[198] . . . You'll find references to Weber in Wiese-Becker all right but Wiese treats Weber in terms of Weber's formulations of 1920 and a little later. Although there's no sacred-secular in Weber there is the notion of insoluble dilemmas—the secularization. [Thomas under Znaniecki's influence] removed the instincts, substituting the term, tendencies. Later he threw them out completely . . . I felt I had to withdraw from their treatment as wishes. Instead I treat them as ends, leaving the wish to much more intensive analysis along social-psychological lines. These ends are not strictly psychological. (*tape*)

Concerning his use of the term value, Becker emphasized that for all practical purposes value is equivalent to object. "Value and object are synonymous terms." *(tape)* The term "needs" is used reciprocally with value, and is equivalent to Parsons' term need disposition, although in Becker's opinion the "tacking on" of the word disposition was superfluous. "You will find that the term need is used in my work in 1948, before the Parsonian need disposition appears in 1950. It was in the introductory chapter in that book on the family. . . . I just wanted to say I was there first." (*tape*)

Asked if his interpretative sociology [199] represented in fact a convergence of Max Weber's *verstehende* sociology, George H. Mead's taking the role of the other, C. H. Cooley's sympathetic introspection, and/or W. I. Thomas' "definition of the situation," as some analysts have claimed, Becker responded that this was a very difficult question for him to answer and would require that he discuss sociation and enculturation.

I have come more and more to make a real working distinction between the process of acquiring culture and the process of developing sociation. Culture is the more inclusive term. There is ample evidence now that children acquire a substantial amount of culture in terms of role responses, in terms of a host of things at an early age before a definite and clear-cut distinction between self and other develops. Piaget produced evidence to this effect but there are many others who also have. Enculturation of the child does occur at a period before the child is capable of sociation in a strict sense. I use sociation—definite association and/or dissociation of self defined as self with other defined as others. The self-and-other differentiation of the child must take place before it is capable of sociation and may not appear until it is three to three-and-a-half. Prior to this there is socialization and enculturation but sociation has not yet become important. So I would tell the social psychologists and the students of culture that they can deal with the child in the enculturative period and this very early socialization period which in certain senses are synonymous. The sociologist really begins when the child as subject sharply differentiates between self and others and who in this full sense can symbolically associate, dissociate, or both. This is a development in my own thinking during the last five years. (*tape*)

Explanation of change. Becker like most of the sociologists writing at mid-century and beyond had begun to question both equilibrium models and structural-functional analysis. He used an equilibrium model, both static and moving, in his Ph. D. dissertation at the University of Chicago and in early publications, including several sections he himself added to the Wiese-Becker publication,[200] as indicated in Appendix 1 of the present chapter. Important for the conceptualization of change is Hertzler's [201] adaptation of Becker's conceptualization which follows:

SCHEMATIC PRESENTATION OF THE EQUILIBRIUM CYCLE

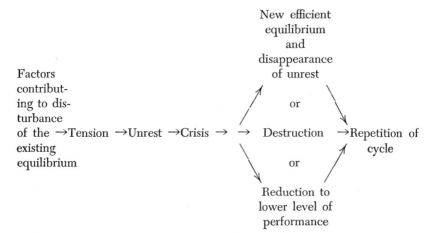

The manner in which Becker adapted ideas from W. I. Thomas and others in the development of his early analysis of change is mentioned in Chapter 2. Crisis and equilibrium were central to this early formulation. In the interview he quoted from the 1930 Ph. D. dissertation, saying that there were no extra copies of the statement in this form. It is appropriate that this quotation with his oral insertions be included here both as a background for consideration of change in general, but particularly for his treatment of equilibrium.

. . . this paper on equilibrium theory and the rejection of certain aspects of equilibrium theory, stem in part from my own reflections on the Chapter four in Wiese-Becker, in which the problem of *part* and *whole* is discussed. Somewhat unguardedly I used an equilibrium analogy in the first formulation of this article on the processes of secularization. It appears in the British version of that article and it also appears in my own doctoral dissertation, although I cut it out of the adaptation of the British version. You will note here in this old doctoral dissertation of 1930—may I read this passage?

"First, the equilibrium of the isolated sacred society is maintained by defining in social terms the vague organic impulses of its accruing members.

Second, the equilibrium is disturbed when intrusive factors, that is to say, external influences, disorganize the community by rendering its adaptive adjustments inadequate for the satisfaction of the impulses it has defined in its members.

Third, because these impulses are consequently blocked or thwarted in one way or another, tension and unrest develop among those members of the community who are most affected.

Fourth, this tension and unrest may lead to various attempts at relief. Movement or change of geographical location (my terminology was here still loose) is often the general form chosen. And as this pattern and/or unusual facilities for the movement of individuals exists, such movement or dispersion may be the specific form chosen. When this dispersion takes the individual concerned into an area markedly different from the isolated sacred society, in terms of which his organic impulses have been conditioned, and if there are no factors tending to conserve the attitudes derived from that society, crisis results.

Fifth, this crisis, while unresolved, generates still more unrest and tension, and some resolving adjustment becomes imperative. The individual accordingly concerned makes an attempt at adjustment which may be successful or unsuccessful.

Sixth, the degree of success or failure can be determined only when the ensuing processes of individuation and differentiation have brought about personality reorganization that increases or lessens tension and unrest. If these indices of maladjustment increase, the adjustment, is by definition, unsuccessful; if they lessen, it has been successful. For all purposes, no other criterion applies.

Seventh, personality change that eventually increases tension and unrest is usually the result of regression to a simpler level. Personality change that lessens tension and unrest is usually reorganization on a more complex level. A number of different personality types result from such regression and reorganization that cannot be described here.

Eighth, when the reorganization is regulative in nature, the ensuing equilibrium is static; when the reorganization is liberative, the ensuing equilibrium is dynamic. Both types of equilibrum are usually much more secular in nature than the personality produced by the isolated sacred society from which the cycle began. The transition from sacred to secular, even at a minimal form, has made its appearance."

The only reason that I have dragged out this early formulation of equilibrium theory is that I see this as an occasion to qualify it. I had begun to get more and more uneasy with the equilibrium theory, and some of the implications deriving from it, so that together with a graduate student named Walter Buckley I formulated a critique of equilibrium theory which I shall make available to you. I should say with regard to this critique of equilibrium that a large number of the formulations are Buckley's. It is really his job. In the preparation of his dissertation we went over this again and again, back and forth, hither and yon, and he then worked this out. This was not all incorporated in his dissertation, so I then worked this thing up, modified it slightly, but the essential language is still Buckley's. I simply made it more precise in a few spots, inserted an additional reference or two, but I would say that this should be viewed as Buckley's paper, coming out of earlier to-and-fro discussions with me and representing a point of view with which I would align myself and which is quite consonant with the earlier qualifications that I began to introduce to the equilibrium formulations that appear in this earlier stuff. I read this, giving due credit to Buckley at the Washington meetings three years ago, if I recall correctly. (*tape*)

This paper, the collaborative efforts of Buckley and Becker, was read at the 1958 meetings of the American Sociological Society. In it the use of mechanical and organic models are blamed for stalemates in the development of current social science. It is noted that the stalemate is especially prevalent when the analogies and homologies of former times are allowed to influence studies of social and psychological tensions, structural change, innovation, communication and the role of ideas. In this use of the equilibrium concept Parsons was the center of criticism. The chief objection to the Parsonian theory as treated in this paper is based upon the claim that equilibrium in Parsons' thinking is identified with the legitimized structure or *status quo* and this taken as the reference point from which deviance occurs. The equilibrium model as used by Parsons, according to Becker and Buckley, does not include structured or institutionalized deviance and patterned strains. (Although some of Parsons' works dealing with "boundary exchanges" which he views as the crux of the process of change, were available at the time, they are not cited. Of course many of the works cited in Chapter 6 and in the section of the present chapter on Parsons either had not been written or were not available in printed form.) As Becker and Buckley saw it, Parsons' equilibrium model differed from equilibrium models as used in astronomy in that the latter have built into the model the deviations themselves such as those planetary orbits which deviate from the perfect ellipse. In astronomy such deviations are only subjectively thought of as deviations but are as much a part of the total system as the elliptical path followed by a given planet. Lewis Coser's [202] parallel criticism is cited. The manuscript attempts to incorporate what its authors consider to be the strong features of Homans' system as presented in *The Human Group*, other features from general systems theory,[203] and various original additions.

The closed system (identified as Parsons' model) which maintains equilibrium is rejected in favor of what is called an open system which maintains a "steady state." Becker and Buckley characterized their model of the social system in a statement which may be paraphrased as follows: An "open" system must be made explicit in the postulate in which through boundaries of a semipermeable nature, energy or materials, are involved in continuous transfer as it is related to its environment. Like Homans, Becker and Buckley join in condemning the notion of functional prerequisites or requisites for a society.[204]

The central idea of the Becker-Buckley model is integration. This is indeed interesting in view of the strong credit they give Homans for their organizing ideas, when it is remembered that Homans in *Social Behavior* carefully avoids the term, integration. Matching the four elements employed by Homans in *The Human Group* (namely, norms, activities, interaction and sentiments) four forms of integration for societies generally are developed. These are 1) normative integration, 2) functional integration, 3) communicative integration and 4) motivational integration. Louis Wirth's emphasis on value-consensus as a major component of normative integration is stressed. Change in one element or relation is counteracted by changes in others so that "safety-valve" mechanisms such as witchcraft and thrill-seeking, or coercion, ideological manipulation, etc. may be expected. Change results in further changes and even restoration of the original condition may be expected to leave the system in a permanently altered state. Thus decision making results in the impossibility of restoring the original structure. There is no tendency to maintain a given internal structure. If a social system manifests a large measure of integration great internal or external changes may be met with little dissociation or disruption of the system or its components. Systems with a small measure of integration may be disrupted, dissociated, or disintegrated by change.

In terms of Beckers' sacred-secular continuum (Figure 1, Chapter 2) the principial system manifests the characteristics of a well-integrated system being characterized by both stability and flexibility capable of abrupt reorganization, elaboration of structure, progressive change or stability. A proverbially or prescriptively sacred society with rigidly traditional and static internal structure, with value systems that do not readily change is not considered as having a large measure of integration. In short, in terms of cybernetics and in the terms used by Homans in *The Human Group* the well integrated system is provided with efficient feed-back mechanisms. Great emphasis is placed upon indeterminancy and wide differences in goals and goal paths in social change. The discussion terminates with what is called a sociological truth; namely, that structural and functional alternatives in Merton's terms must replace functional and structural necessities.

APPENDIX

PATTERN VARIABLES AND CULTURAL CONTEXT *

The cultural contexts represented by two constructed types of sacred and secular societies, in many respects less adequate than the more extended typology heretofore presented, but having the advantage of brevity, were offered in some of my earlier articles and books, beginning about 1930. Independently thereof, Parsons and Shils developed five pairs of "pattern variables"; these are for most practical purposes the same as the idea of cultural context. They group as follows: one set comprises particularism, collectivity-orientation, diffuseness, quality-orientation (ascription), and affectivity; the other includes universalism, ego-orientation, specificity, performance-orientation (achievement), and affective neutrality. It is a little hard, without the thorough analysis provided by the writers mentioned, to show just what these two groups of pattern variables mean, but perhaps if I read to you my two constructed types, interjecting wherever relevant one or several of the pattern variables [indicated below in italics within brackets] you can see how the latter can be applied in such ways as to specify cultural contexts of social actions along lines somewhat similar to those we have been following:

(1) The isolated sacred society is isolated in three ways: vicinally, socially, and mentally. Vicinal isolation leads, among other things, to the fixation of motor habits and intense opposition to change [*affectivity*]; social isolation leads to habitual relationships

* Source: Howard Becker, *Man in Reciprocity* (New York: Frederick A. Praeger, 1956) pp. 191 ff. The authors of the present volume have prepared a hectographed version of this appendix with terms and interpretations based on the PAS Model inserted. It is available from the authors upon request and upon payment of cost of materials and mailing. Fifty cents in stamps or currency should accompany orders.

of withdrawal and the fixation of attitudes toward the in-group
and out-group [*particularism*]; mental isolation, as in the case of
underprivileged classes or races, rigid sects, etc., may be the result of illiteracy, early indoctrination, language handicap, real or
imputed psychological inferiority, etc., is usually associated with
social isolation, and leads to similar results. . . .

(2) In addition to being isolated this society is completely
sacred (in the special sense here given the latter term). No comparison, classification, analysis, and abstraction, habitual or otherwise, is practiced [*no universalism and specificity*]; everything is
unique, concrete, and personal, for all contacts are primary [*particularism, diffuseness*]. The organism is so thoroughly adjusted
to definite motor habits, attitudes inculcated in childhood, and
certain types of association between sense impressions and definite activities that there arises "a feeling of impropriety of certain
forms, of a particular social or religious value, or of superstitious
fear of change" [*affectivity*]. Traditon and ceremonial play a large
part in the life of the society, and every situation is defined in
customary and sacred terms [*particularism, affectivity*]; Tarde's
"custom-imitation" prevails. The folkways and mores rule [*particularism*]; there is a minimum of rationalistic criticism [*of
universalism, affective neutrality, specificity, and performance-
orientation*], and of individuation [*ego-orientation*] a similar minimum. Even the maintenance folkways and the material objects
associated with them are under the sacred sanction; as in the
cases of some pastoral nomads and some simple agriculturalists,
the herd animals are sacred and the soil is sacred [*particularism,
affectivity, quality-orientation*]. In other words, rational and
utilitarian considerations do not have wide scope even in one of
the most organically "utilitarian" of all activities, that of gaining
a livelihood. This dominance of sacred sanctions is facilitated by
the fact that the isolated sacred society is economically self-sufficient; there is no foreign trade nor any other opportunity for the
intrusion of pecuniary valuation and the development of detached
economic attitudes [*of affective neutrality*]. Inasmuch as there is
no trade, the division of labor is simple, and there is no town,
urban, or metropolitan economy; further, no strangers, with their
detached, critical attitudes [*with affective neutrality, specificity,
performance-orientation*] leading to disregard of or contempt for

sacred matters, are tolerated. What is sacred is kept sacred; isolation has a powerful ally in the emotional resistance [*affectivity*] to change it engenders. The form of the kinship group is that of the large family, the *Grossfamilie*, the *genos* [*collectivity-orientation*], and is completely under the control of sacred sanctions. Production and consumption are exclusively community matters [*collectivity-orientation*], and as such are similarly controlled. Property is largely subject to collective and sacred considerations [*collectivity-orientation*]; "rights" of testation are strictly although unconsciously limited as a consequence. There is, however, a minimum of social control by physical force, and even of overt control; offenses against the mores are punished by general aversion, indignation, and traditional and spontaneous verbal or corporal chastisement [*diffuseness*], and not by attempts at the Guilt-Punishment equation [*no specificity*]. Gossip is the most powerful medium of social control within the isolated sacred society, which perforce closely resembles the Polish *okolica* or region within which "a man is talked about" [*particularism, diffuseness, collectivity-orientation*]. Verbal or even tacit "understanding" usually prevails [*diffuseness, particularism*] instead of formal, written contract; when unusually binding obligations are entered into, the promise given in the presence of the whole society [*collectivity-orientation*] or of its traditionally delegated, especially sacred representatives is the method followed. The home or familiar domestic environment, as well as the *milieu natale* or place of birth and up-bringing, are closely linked with fixed motor habits and the correlated emotional responses lending them a strongly sacred character [*particularism, affectivity*]; pecuniary valuation [*specificity, affective neutrality*] is altogether excluded, and change of such environment is attended by marked emotional resistance [*affectivity*]. The function of training the children is completely under sacred control; parenthood is a cultural far more than a biological fact. Irrationalism and supernaturalism, whether traditionally religious in derivation or otherwise, are completely dominant; rationalism [*universalism*] and scepticism are only potentially present. Rational science is unknown.

Here, then, is one of our ideal types, the isolated sacred society.

(3) The accessible secular society, its methodological an-

tithesis, is accessible in three ways (all of them secondary); vicinally, socially, and mentally. Its vicinal accessibility is the result of geographical location that furthers to the utmost limit all the cultural factors leading to such accessibility; terrestrial, maritime, and atmospheric conditions make possible the fullest utilization of all the devices of rapid transportation. In this way the fixation of any dominant proportion of motor habits is rendered practically impossible among a large proportion of the population; there is a premium upon change of every kind, and Tarde's "mode-imitation" prevails. The social accessibility of this secular society is the result of the complete absence of occupational, professional, class, caste, racial, religious, or moral barriers [*affective neutrality, universalism*]; there is nothing whatever to hinder social circulation. Competition is consequently unrestricted, for there are no non-competing groups [*performance-orientation*]; topographical irregularities being "ideally" absent, zones of population distribution arise that in their spatial patterning reflect exactly the competitive order, and the free movement made possible by vicinal accessibility facilitates the spatial allocation of the members of such a society in strict accordance with their economic status [*performance-orientation*]. The mental accessibility of this society is the result of common basic education, complete literacy and lack of language barriers, popularized science and scholarship, a press or similar agency that distributes uniform news to all [*universalism*], etc. etc. . . .

(4) In addition to its accessibility this society is completely secular (in the special sense here given the latter term). Every relationship is treated as a means to an elusive end, "happiness" as consciously defined in terms of the strictly egoistic wishes of the individual [*ego-orientation*], and never as an end in itself. Comparison, analysis, classification, and abstraction [*universalism, specificity*] are habitually practiced; the unique, concrete, and personal [*particularism, diffuseness*] are completely set aside. Nothing is sacred, for the lack of fixed motor habits and the continual contact with new sensual values puts a premium upon change; instead of inability to respond to the new there is inability to refrain from responding to the new—one aspect of mental mobility. Tradition and ceremonial play no part in the life of such a society, and every situation is defined in rationalistic and sec-

ular terms [*universalism, affective neutrality*]. The readily perceivable folkways and mores give ground to rational constructs [*universalism*]; there is a maximum of rationalistic criticism [*universalism, affective neutrality, specificity, performance-orientation*], and of individuation [*ego-orientation*] a similar maximum. The maintenance folkways are subjected to rational analysis, and are changed with whatever frequency and completeness such analysis shows to be necessary [*universalism, affective neutrality, performance-orientation*]. None of the domestic animals is sacred, nor is the soil exempt from thoroughgoing pecuniary evaluation [*specificity, affective neutrality*]. This dominance of secular standards is reinforced by reason of the fact that the accessible secular society is highly differentiated economically; it has a complex metropolitan economy, with a territorial as well as an occupational division of labor [*specificity*]. Trade is carried on with all parts of the world; there are no political barriers, such as protective tariffs or immigration restrictions, of any kind [*universalism*]. The stranger is free to come and go as he will, inasmuch as everyone is more or less a stranger [*specificity*], cosmopolitanism acquires prestige value [*universalism*] and becomes a further aid to the detachment characteristic of the stranger [*affective neutrality, specificity*]. . . . The kinship group is reduced to the particularistic family [*universalism*], and all the production and almost if not all the consumption functions of the latter are taken over by the metropolitan economy [*performance-orientation*]. Property is entirely free of collective and sacred considerations [*ego-orientation*]; rights of testation are unlimited, and the individual can "do what he will with his own." There is a minimum of informal social control; offences against the laws frequently involve no social ostracism [*affective neutrality*], and the Guilt=Punishment equation has full sway [*specificity*]. Inasmuch as the metropolitan economy with its anonymity and differentiation prevails, social control in the form of gossip has little or no power; men do not fear being "talked about" [*universalism, affective neutrality, specificity, ego-orientation*]. Formal, secular, legal contracts are the rule [*universalism, specificity*]; even the marriage relationship is cast in the form of a secular contract between two individuals—a contract in which the kinship bond plays no conditioning part [*ego-orientation*]. The home has no sacred character, but is a

secular stopping-place changed without emotional reluctance—
indeed, with gratification [*specificity, performance-orientation*].
The function of training the children is under the complete control of secular agencies. Irrationalism and supernaturalism of traditionally religious derivation are not found, rationalism and
naturalism have prestige value [*universalism*], and all irrationalism
and supernaturalism must seem to be their opposite, i.e., "scientific." Genuine science [*universalism, affective neutrality, performance-orientation, specificity*] has great power and wide range.

Here, then, is . . . the accessible secular society.

BOILING IT ALL DOWN. Recognizing, of course that the pattern variables have not been presented in their own right, as it
were, but rather have been indirectly illustrated, we may still have
succeeded in getting some idea of what they're all about. Let us
now schematize the whole business, bearing in mind the fact that
what has been said about the evaluation continuum of social
change, implicitness and explicitness, codification and the lack
thereof, accreteness and discreteness, nonrationality and rationality, and folk, prescribed, principled, and normless societies cannot be condensed into the following schema: ·

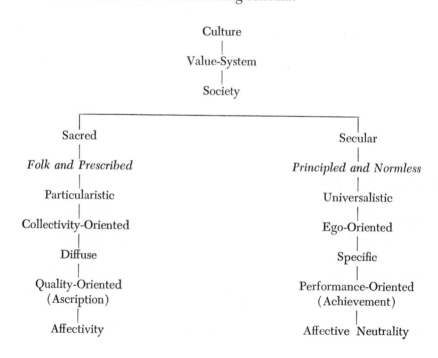

Culture
|
Value-System
|
Society

Sacred | Secular
Folk and Prescribed | Principled and Normless
Particularistic | Universalistic
Collectivity-Oriented | Ego-Oriented
Diffuse | Specific
Quality-Oriented (Ascription) | Performance-Oriented (Achievement)
Affectivity | Affective Neutrality

Note, now, that the sanctioned rationality of prescribed societies doesn't quite fit this arrangement, that the same is true of the affective nonrationality of normless societies, and that no account is taken of the problem of social change.

NOTES

1. *The Point Four Program,* Publication 3347, Economic Cooperation Series 23, Division of Publications, Department of State (Washington, D. C.: Government Printing Office).

2. See for example, Lyle W. Shannon, ed., *Underdeveloped Areas—A Book of Readings and Research* (New York: Harper and Bros., 1957); Godfrey and Monica Wilson, *The Analysis of Social Change Based on Observations in Central Africa* (Cambridge: Cambridge University Press, 1954); Edward C. Banfield, *The Moral Basis of a Backward Society* (Glencoe, Ill.: The Free Press, 1958) p. 163; Wilbert E. Moore and Arnold S. Feldman, eds. *Labor Commitment and Social Change in Developing Areas,* (New York: Social Science Research Council, 1960); various periodicals such as *Economic Development and Cultural Change* and *Community Development Review.*

3. Charles P. Loomis, *Social Systems: Essays on Their Persistence and Change* (Princeton, New Jersey: D. Van Nostrand Company, 1960).

4. Ferdinand Toennies, *Community and Society—Gemeinschaft und Gesellschaft;* translated and introduced by Charles P. Loomis (East Lansing, Michigan: Michigan State University Press, 1957).

5. Pitirim A. Sorokin in the Foreword to Ferdinand Toennies, *op. cit.*

6. Julian H. Steward, *Theory of Culture Change: The Methodology of Multilinear Evolution* (Urbana, Ill.: University of Illinois Press, 1955); H. G. Barnett, *Innovation: The Basis of Cultural Change* (New York: McGraw-Hill Book Co., 1953).

7. Alvin W. Gouldner, "Some Observations on Systematic Theory, 1945-55" in Hans L. Zetterberg, ed. *Sociology in the United States of America* (UNESCO: Paris, 1956), pp. 34-5.

8. Tape recorded discussion with Williams of an earlier version of Chapter 8 of present volume, April, 1960.

9. Heinrich Hertz, *Die Principien der Mechanik* (Leipzig, 1894) as cited in R. B. Braithwaite, *Scientific Explanation* (New York: Harper and Brothers, 1960), pp. 91 and 96.

10. Robin M. Williams, Jr., *American Society: A Sociological Interpretation* (New York: Alfred A. Knopf, 1960), p. 567.

11. Tape recorded discussion with Williams, April, 1960.

12. *Ibid.*

13. Winston White, "Some Comments on Williams' Discussion of American Values," mimeo. p. 2.

14. Tape recorded discussion with Williams, April, 1960.

15. See Chapter 4 of present text; fn. 106.

16. Robin M. Williams, Jr., *op. cit.,* p. 574.

17. Tape recorded discussion with Williams, April, 1960.

18. Robin M. Williams, Jr., *op. cit.*, p. 374.

19. *Ibid.*, p. 515.

20. Robin M. Williams, Jr., "Continuity and Change in Sociological Study," *American Sociological Review*, Vol. 23 (December, 1958), pp. 627-8.

21. Robin M. Williams, Jr., *American Society*, *op. cit.*, p. 570.

22. *Ibid.*, p. 366.   23. *Ibid.*, p. 153.

24. *Ibid.*, p. 571.

25. Robin M. Williams, Jr., *The Reduction of Intergroup Tensions: A Survey of Research on Problems of Ethnic, Racial, and Religious Group Relations* (New York: Social Science Research Council, 1947), p. 47.

26. *Ibid.*, pp. 43-6.

27. Robin M. Williams, Jr., "Racial and Cultural Relations," in Joseph B. Gittler, ed., *Review of Sociology: Analysis of a Decade* (New York: John Wiley and Sons, 1957), p. 430.

28. Robin M. Williams, Jr., "Continuity and Change in Sociological Study," *op. cit.*, pp. 626-7.

29. *Ibid.*, pp. 625-6.

30. Pitirim Sorokin, *Social and Cultural Dynamics*, rev. and abridged in one vol. (Boston: Porter Sargent, c1957), p. 690. Also see Chapter 7 of present volume, fn. 9 for Sorokin's "generic" model of sociocultural phenomena. As Gouldner observes, Sorokin early combined the "normative-meaningful and interaction foci." Alvin W. Gouldner, *op. cit.*, p. 38.

31. Pitirim Sorokin, *Sociocultural Causality, Space, Time* (Durham: Duke Univ. Press, 1943), p. 230, 1st note.

32. See Chapter 7 of present volume, fn. 9. See also Gouldner, *op. cit.*, p. 38.

33. Robert K. Merton, *Social Theory and Social Structure;* rev. and enlarged ed., (Glencoe: The Free Press, 1957), p. 476.

34. Pitirim A. Sorokin, *Society, Culture, and Personality: Their Structure and Dynamics* (New York: Harper and Brothers, 1947), p. 663.

35. Pitirim Sorokin, *Social and Cultural Dynamics*, *op. cit.*, p. 669.

36. *Ibid.*, pp. 667-8.

37. Arthur K. Davis, *Lessons from Sorokin*, manuscript prepared in honor of Sorokin for the proposed Festschrift, ed. by Edward Tiryakian.

38. Pitirim A. Sorokin, *Society, Culture, and Personality*, *op. cit.*, pp. 704, 706.

39. *Ibid.*, p. 696.   40. *Ibid.*, p. 700.

41. *Ibid.*, p. 704.   42. *Ibid.* p. 701.

43. Pitirim Sorokin, *Social and Cultural Dynamics*, *op. cit.*, p. 661.

44. Pitirim Sorokin, *Society, Culture, and Personality*, *op. cit.*, p. 659.

45. *Ibid.*, p. 666.

46. *Ibid.*, p. 660. Here it is seen that his combining of the social and cultural is more complex than and different from what Gouldner assumes. Alvin Gouldner, *op. cit.*, p. 38.

47. Pitirim Sorokin, *Society, Culture, and Personality*, *op. cit.*, p. 662.

48. *Ibid.*, p. 657.   49. *Ibid.*

50. *Ibid.*, p. 638.

51. Pitirim Sorokin, *Social and Cultural Dynamics*, *op. cit.*, pp. 4-7.

52. *Ibid.*, p. 4.   53. *Ibid.*, pp. 5-6.

54. *Ibid.*, p. 7.   55. *Ibid.*, p. 8.

56. *Ibid.*   57. *Ibid.*

58. Pitirim A. Sorokin, *Society, Culture and Personality, op. cit.*, p. 93. See also *ibid.*, p. 335 for the distinction between integration and solidarity.

59. *Ibid.*, p. 93.   60. *Ibid.*, p. 655.

61. Talcott Parsons, *The Social System* (Glencoe: The Free Press, 1951).

62. Alvin Gouldner, *op. cit.*, p. 39.

63. *Ibid.*

64. Talcott Parsons, "Some Considerations on the Theory of Social Change," *Rural Sociology*, Vol. 26, No. 3. Paper read Nov. 2, 1960, to the North Central Regional Rural Sociological Committee of the Farm Foundation, Chicago, Illinois.

65. *Ibid.*

66. Talcott Parsons, *The Structure of Social Action* (Glencoe: The Free Press, 1949, 2nd ed.), pp. 48-9.

67. Talcott Parsons and R. F. Bales, *Family, Socialization and Interaction Process* (Glencoe: The Free Press, 1955), p. 381.

68. Talcott Parsons, "An Approach to Psychological Theory in Terms of the Theory of Action," in Sigmund Koch, ed., *Psychology: A Science* (New York: McGraw-Hill, 1959), p. 701.

69. Talcott Parsons and Neil J. Smelser, *Economy and Society* (Glencoe: The Free Press, 1956), p. 76.

70. *Ibid.*, pp. 69-70.

71. Talcott Parsons, *The Social System, op. cit.*, p. 486.

72. *Ibid.*, p. 484.   73. *Ibid.*, p. 485.

74. *Ibid.*, p. 491.   75. *Ibid.*, p. 494.

76. *Ibid.*, p. 497.   77. *Ibid.*, p. 498.

78. Talcott Parsons, *Economy and Society, op. cit.*, pp. 257-8.

79. Talcott Parsons, *The Social System, op. cit.*, pp. 506-9.

80. *Ibid.*, pp. 528-9.

81. Talcott Parsons, "Some Considerations on the Theory of Social Change," *op. cit.*

82. *Ibid.*, Italics added.

83. *Ibid.*, p. 11.   84. *Ibid.*, p. 16.

85. *Ibid.*, p. 25.   86. *Ibid.*, p. 29.

87. Talcott Parsons, *Structure and Process in Modern Societies* (Glencoe: The Free Press, 1960), Chapter IV.

88. *Ibid.*, p. 162.   89. *Ibid.*, p. 164.

90. *Ibid.*, p. 288.   91. *Ibid.*, p. 319.

92. *Ibid.*, Chapter X.   93. *Ibid.*, p. 321.

94. Tape recorded interview with Robert K. Merton on earlier version of Chapter 5 of present manuscript, December, 1959.

95. R. B. Braithwaite, *op. cit.*

96. See pertinent articles and bibliographical citations for these men in *Reader in Bureaucracy*, ed. by Robert K. Merton, et. al. (Glencoe: The Free Press, 1952).

97. Richard A. Cloward, "Illegitimate Means, Anomie, and Deviant Behavior," *American Sociological Review*, Vol. 24, (April, 1959), pp. 164-176.

98. Research in the field of applied anthropology has often elicited the

criticism that the researcher's identification with program has produced blind spots for the investigator.

99. Tape recorded interview with Robert K. Merton on earlier version of Chapter 5 of present manuscript, December, 1959.

100. *Ibid.*   101. *Ibid.*

102. *Ibid.*

103. Robert K. Merton, *Social Theory and Social Structure, op. cit.*, p. 122.

104. See footnote 9 of Chapter 5 of present volume for investigator's descriptive protocol of the paradigm for functional analysis.

105. Robert K. Merton, *Social Theory and Social Structure, op. cit.*, p. 80.

106. *Ibid.*, p. 25.

107. He lists the following six types of work which are often regarded as comprising sociological theory: 1) methodology; 2) general sociological orientations; 3) analysis of sociological concepts; 4) *post factum* sociological interpretations; 5) empirical generalizations in sociology and 6) sociology theory. Robert K. Merton, *Social Theory and Social Structure, op. cit.*, p. 86.

108. Ernest Nagel, "A Formalization of Functionalism—With Special Reference to Its Application in the Social Sciences," Planning Project for Advance Training in Social Research, Columbia University, October, 1953, Document No. 112.

109. Tape recorded interview with Robert K. Merton on earlier version of Chapter 5 of present manuscript, December, 1959.

110. *Ibid.*

111. Robert K. Merton, "Social Conflict Over Styles of Sociological Work," Paper presented at the Fourth World Congress of Sociology, September, 1959. Stresa. MS. p. 35.

112. Robert K. Merton, *Social Theory and Social Structure, op. cit.*, p. 122.

113. This is a concept to which Robin M. Williams, Jr., devotes a chapter in his *American Society, op. cit.*, and an idea for which he gives Merton credit. See also Wilbert E. Moore, *Industrial Relations and the Social Order* (New York: Macmillan, 1951, rev. ed). Here Moore likewise gives Merton credit for the idea, and refers to Robert K. Merton, "Bureaucratic Structure and Personality," *Social Forces* (1940), vol. 18, pp. 560-8.

114. Tape recorded interview with Robert K. Merton on earlier version of Chapter 5 of present manuscript, December, 1959.

115. Robert K. Merton, *Social Theory and Social Structure, op. cit.*, p. 122.

116. *Ibid.*   117. *Ibid.*, p. 305.
118. *Ibid.*, pp. 360-1.   119. *Ibid.*, p. 129.
120. *Ibid.*, p. 427.   121. *Ibid.*, p. 335.
122. *Ibid.*, p. 293.   123. *Ibid.*, p. 305.
124. *Ibid.*

125. *Ibid.*, p. 184, fn. 40a.

126. Talcott Parsons, *Structure and Process in Modern Societies, op. cit.*, p. 283-4.

127. Robert K. Merton, George G. Reader, and Patricia L. Kendall, *The*

Student-Physician: Introductory Studies in the Sociology of Medical Education (Cambridge, Massachusetts, Harvard University Press, 1957), p. 33.

128. Robert K. Merton, *Social Theory and Social Structure, op. cit.,* pp. 552 ff.

129. *Ibid.,* p. 560.

130. This idea, presented only as an hypothesis by Merton, in the view of the present authors is close to an article of faith which smacks of wishful thinking. The two authors (Simmel and Ross) to whom the statement is credited came from countries which were segmented in the one case by many political parties and in the other by many ethnic and other subgroups. Yet both countries experienced major schisms—the Nazi-Communist schism of Germany and the South pro-slavery North industrial anti-slavery schism of the United States. Preston James who uses the same line of argument to explain political cohesion in some Latin American countries later saw these same countries torn and divided. Preston James, *Latin America* (New York: The Odyssey Press, 1942), p. 80. See also Chapter 5 of the present volume, fn. 197. A contrary and perhaps more realistic hypothesis concerning size and heterogeniety of systems is advanced by Sorokin: "When both of these factors increase, the stratification tends to increase still more and vice versa." See Chapter 7 of present volume, fn. 131.

131. Alvin Gouldner, *op. cit.,* p. 35. Gouldner mentions sentiments and values. In *Social Behavior* written after the appearance of the Gouldner article, sentiment is absorbed by activity. George C. Homans, *Social Behavior: Its Elementary Forms* (New York: Harcourt, Brace & World, 1961).

132. In responding to the statement "The avoidance pattern of the Navajo . . . is a mechanism which insures the social system against undue strain of interaction between incumbents of conflicting status-roles," Homans says, "It insures *individuals* against the undue strain. . . . It's *men* that are important, not *society.*" This theme is found throughout *Social Behavior.*

133. George C. Homans, *Social Behavior, op. cit.* Homans half facetiously states that the motto for *Social Behavior* should be "What's there in it for me?" Taped interview.

134. In Homans' words, "It's perfectly easy to cut up human behavior into a set of categories; no one ever failed who tried and all the sets are different. . . . What's difficult is to specify not the categories but the variables, and to state and demonstrate true propositions of the form "x varies as y" between variables. Tape recorded interview with Homans on earlier version of Chapter 4 of present volume, April, 1960.

135. George C. Homans, *Social Behavior, op. cit.* In George C. Homans, *The Human Group* (New York: Harcourt, Brace, 1950), Homans states "The group will be treated as an organic whole, or social system surviving in an environment," p. 6.

136. George C. Homans, *The Human Group, op. cit.,* p. 449.

137. Tape recorded interview with George C. Homans on earlier version of Chapter 4 of present volume, April, 1960.

138. *Ibid.* To illustrate the futility of specifying functional prerequisites for a society he cites the case of a group in Tierra del Fuego for whose society the functional prerequisites for survival had been laid out by an anthropologist. Despite the fact that the society met all the specifications it did not survive because the group caught the measles and died. Manipu-

lations of logic can also render specifications of functional prerequisites useless. A list of prerequisites may be drawn up, and then it is ascertained that "a new way a society can die [is] by failing to meet the definition of a society." *Ibid.*

139. George C. Homans, *Social Behavior, op. cit.*, p. 384.

140. George C. Homans, *The Human Group, op. cit.*, pp. 271 and 321.

141. See, for example, George C. Homans and David M. Schneider, *Marriage, Authority, and Final Causes* (Glencoe: The Free Press, 1955).

142. *Ibid.*, p. 16. He acknowledges that "Functional theories have been helpful in the sense that they have made people look for all sorts of things they might not otherwise have looked for." Tape recorded interview with Homans on earlier version of Chapter 4 of present volume, April, 1960. In this he seems to agree with Merton.

143. George C. Homans and David M. Schneider, *op. cit.*, pp. 16-7. Here Homans writes, "We are not forced to choose between Malinowski's and Radcliffe-Brown's approach. We need both. Our quarrel is in fact with scholars who try to explain social behavior with one of these theories alone."

144. Tape recorded interview with Homans on earlier version of Chapter 4 of present volume, April, 1960.

145. George C. Homans, *The Human Group, op. cit.*, p. 357. "Effectiveness [of procedure] lies in its regularity, like a net that makes sure that if any fish are lost they will be small . . ."

146. George C. Homans, *Social Behavior, op. cit.*, p. 380.

147. George C. Homans, *The Human Group, op. cit.*, p. 103.

148. George C. Homans, *Social Behavior, op. cit.*, p. 357.

149. *Ibid.*, p. 388.   150. *Ibid.*, p. 391.

151. George C. Homans, *The Human Group, op. cit.*, p. 462.

152. *Ibid.*, p. 367.   153. *Ibid.*, pp. 457-8.

154. *Ibid.*, p. 457.

155. A marginal note made by Homans on the final draft of the ms. for the present chapter.

156. George C. Homans, *Social Behavior, op. cit.*, pp. 397-8.

157. Talcott Parsons, *The Social System, op. cit.*, p. 496.

158. George C. Homans, *Social Behavior, op. cit.*, pp. 396-8.

159. Tape recorded interview with Homans on earlier version of Chapter 4 of present volume, April, 1960.

160. George C. Homans, *Social Behavior, op. cit.*, p. 338.

161. *Ibid.*, pp. 129, 165, 169 and 229 ff. What Homans calls "companionship in misery" or "the solidarity of the lower class" is accounted for on three bases: 1) ecology; i.e., rooming or living together, 2) sharing of the same values and, 3) "the problem of justice . . . the upper class not only deprived them of approval but unjustly deprived them [resulting in] hostility." *Ibid.*, p. 229. Perhaps because of the relatively slight emphasis given to the *cognitive* aspects of action he does not include this as even partial explanation. The present authors following Toennies and others would hypothesize that the lower class member may not know "the value of the services" persons above him have to offer him or knowing it may not possess the rationality or "know how" necessary to avail himself of them. This would square with Sorokin's conclusion in *Social Mobility, op. cit.*, to the effect that the most intelligent and competent are removed from the lower class

by vertical mobility. The relatively great emphasis on the cognitive aspects of action in the works of all the writers discussed in the present volume except Homans and Merton's increasing interest in it (see reference 100 above) would no doubt lead to varying interpretations of this phenomenon. Davis' reaction is worth quoting and taken with the above considerations may emphasize the need for more research to explain the possible relationship between "companionship in misery" and the "solidarity of the lower class": "Why does Herb Hyman find that the lower classes have lesser aspirations than the middle classes. . . . ? They've got some sense, that's the reason." Tape.

162. SB., pp. 165-166 and 230. For literature and findings on alienation see Melvin Seeman, "The Meaning of Alienation," *American Sociological Review*, Vol. 24, No. 6 (December, 1954), pp. 783-791. See also Fritz Pappenheim, *The Alienation of Modern Man* (New York: Monthly Review Press, 1959). See fn. 242, Ch. 2 above for Becker's earlier observations on "companions in misery."

163. Charles P. Loomis *et al.*, *Turrialba: Social Systems and the Strategy of Change* (Glencoe: The Free Press, 1953).

164. George C. Homans, *Social Behavior, op. cit.*, p. 169.

165. *Ibid.*, p. 118.

166. Tape recorded interview with Homans on earlier version of Chapter 4 of present volume, April, 1960.

167. Kingsley Davis, *Human Society* (New York: The MacMillan Company, 1949), p. 10.

168. Tape recorded interview with Davis on earlier version of Chapter 3 of present volume, June, 1960.

169. *Ibid.*   170. *Ibid.*

171. *Ibid.* Among the many references to value appearing in *Human Society* is one of particular interest to students of change: "Yet we find great differences between one society and another in the degree to which resistance to change represents a central value. Modern society, no matter how much it may resist a particular innovation, has as one of its chief dogmas the doctrine of progress—the belief that *this world* can be made a better place by the constant application of empirical knowledge to our material and human resources. It is consequently committed in principle to the value of change." Kingsley Davis, *Human Society, op. cit.*, p. 444.

172. Tape recorded interview with Davis on earlier version of Chapter 3 of present volume, June, 1960. He is also critical of the emphasis on the explanation of deviancy without a corresponding emphasis on the concept of sanctions, and of a relatively too great attention to cultural goals and institutionalized means. *Ibid.*

173. *Ibid.*

174. Kingsley Davis, *Human Society, op. cit.*, p. 634. Another use of models is of interest: "Our courtship system is analogous to our economic system . . . the courtship process is highly competitive." Kingsley Davis, Harry C. Bredemeier and Marion J. Levy, Jr., eds., *Modern American Society, Readings in the Problems of Order and Change* (New York: Rinehart and Company, Inc., 1949).

175. Kingsley Davis, *Human Society, op. cit.*, p. 634.

176. Tape recorded interview with Davis on earlier version of Chapter 3 of present volume, June, 1960.

177. *Ibid.*

178. *Ibid.;* faulty prediction due to reification of models is discussed in Chapter 3 of present chapter under the heading cognitive mapping.

179. Kingsley Davis, "Fertility Control and the Demographic Transition in India"; reprinted from *The Interrelations of Demographic, Economic, and Social Problems in Selected Underdeveloped Areas, Proceedings of the 1953 Annual Conference* (New York: Milbank Memorial Fund), pp. 66-89. (The quotation cited in text is from pp. 1 and 2 of the reprint which does not follow the pagination of the original).

180. Tape recorded interview with Davis on earlier verson of Chapter 3 of present volume, June, 1960.

181. Kingsley Davis, "Fertility Control and the Demographic Transition in India," *op. cit.*, p. 3.

182. Tape recorded interview with Davis on earlier version of Chapter 3 of present volume, June, 1960.

183. Kingsley Davis, "Fertility Control and the Demographic Transition in India," *op. cit.*, pp. 2, 3.

184. *Ibid.*, pp. 5, 6.

185. Tape recorded interview with Davis on earlier version of Chapter 3 of present volume, June, 1960.

186. Kingsley Davis, "The Unpredicted Pattern of Population Change," *The Annals of the American Academy of Political and Social Science,* (May, 1956), pp. 56-7.

187. Kingsley Davis, "Population Change in Backward Areas," in Lyle W. Shannon, ed., *op. cit.*, p. 69.

188. Howard Becker, *Through Values to Social Interpretation* (Durham, N. C.: Duke University Press, 1950), p. 8.

189. *Ibid.*, p. 20.

190. Tape recorded interview with Becker on earlier version of Chapter 2 of present volume, May, 1960; see also Howard Becker, *Through Values to Social Interpretation, op. cit.*, pp. 10 ff.

191. Howard Becker, "Normative Reactions to Normlessness," *American Sociological Review*, Vol. 25, No. 6 (December, 1960), pp. 603 ff.

192. Tape recorded interview with Becker on earlier version of Chapter 2 of present volume, May, 1960. Excerpts from tape recording hereafter cited in text will not be carried in footnotes, but will bear the legend (*tape*) immediately after excerpt.

193. Howard Becker, "Current Sacred-Secular Theory," *Modern Sociological Theory*, ed. by Howard Becker and Alvin Boskoff (New York: The Dryden Press, 1957).

194. Howard Becker, *Through Values to Social Interpretation, op. cit.*, p. 285, fn. In this publication the indexed subjects of prediction and social change have a relatively long list of page entries.

195. This indebtedness was acknowledged in the tape recorded interview, but is also adequately represented in Becker's written works. See Howard Becker, *Through Values to Social Interpretation, op. cit.*, p. 47, and Howard Becker, *Current Sacred Secular Theory, op. cit.*, p. 164; also

Howard Becker, *Man in Reciprocity* (New York: Frederick A. Praeger, 1956), p. 458.

196. MIR refers of course to Howard Becker, *Man in Reciprocity, op. cit.*

197. A projected work for which he had bundles of manuscript at the time of his death would have recast the processes of the Wiese-Becker work into a form more consistent with current sacred-secular theory. It would have been a companion volume, with emphasis on process, to *Man in Reciprocity, op. cit.*, the emphasis of which was on structure.

198. Becker implies that the overlapping in time during which both Weber and Wiese did their principal work fostered a competitive situation which made it impossible for either to embrace the works and ideas of the other completely. His close association with Wiese convinced him that at least from Wiese's point of view this competitive situation prevailed.

199. Howard Becker, *Through Values to Social Interpretation, op. cit.*, Chapter 4. See also Howard Becker, *Man in Reciprocity, op. cit.*, p. 108. For references to the terms employed by the writers mentioned see the item, interpretative sociology in Howard Becker and Alvin Boskoff, eds., *op. cit.*, and the relevant discussions in the same volume by Alvin Boskoff, William L. Kolb, and John C. McKinney.

200. See the Wiese-Becker work, Howard Becker, *Systematic Sociology —on the Basis of the Beziehungslehre und Gebildelehre of Leopold von Wiese* (New York: Wiley, 1932); see also Howard Becker, "Processes of Secularization," *Sociological Review* (British), Vol. 24, (1932); see also Howard Becker, "Systematic Sociology and Leopold von Wiese," in J. L. Moreno, *Sociometry and the Science of Man* (New York: Beacon House, 1956), for a listing of the separate contributions Becker made to the Wiese-Becker publication.

201. Joyce O. Hertzler, *Society in Action* (New York: The Dryden Press, 1954), pp. 59 ff.

202. Lewis Coser, *The Functions of Social Conflict* (Glencoe: The Free Press, 1956), pp. 21-3.

203. Ludwig von Bertalanffy and Anatol Rapoport, eds., *General Systems* (Yearbook of the Society for the Advancement of General Systems Theory), Vol. 1 (1956).

204. For an interesting discussion of what is called a "multi-sided polemic" in American sociology between "secularized" research methodologists and theorists and their opponents see Seymour M. Lipset and Neil Smelser, "Change and Controversy in Recent American Sociology," *The British Journal of Sociology*, Vol. 12, No. 1, March 1961. Pitirim A. Sorokin, Robert MacIver, Robert S. Lynd, Talcott Parsons, Paul Lazarsfeld and their students "along with . . . [men] like Guttman and Stouffer" are given credit for the development of this "secularized" science. Against this are pitted men like C. Wright Mills, Barrington Moore, Jr., and, ironically, both Sorokin and Lynd who did their share to initiate the trends they now deplore. The criticism of "excessive abstraction and overpreoccupation with esoteric methodology" alleges one or all of the following: insufficient attention to historical interpretation and too much attention to "system," insufficient attention to a dialectic view of change (particularly directed at C. Wright Mills, Lewis Feuer and Ralf Dahrendorf, and equally applicable to the Neo-Marxian Herbert Marcuse although not mentioned by the authors), and too sterile

and conservative attitudes toward politics. The authors conclude: "To attempt to dichotomize the study of society into the study of the 'imperatives' inherent in social systems on the one hand, and the study of historic sources of specific—often politically significant—patterns of behavior on the other [is] . . . erroneous." *Ibid.*, p. 46.

This article (*Ibid.*, p. 50, fn. 11) like the book, *Sociology, The Progress of a Decade, A Collection of Articles* (Englewood Cliffs, N. J.: Prentice-Hall, Inc., 1961). p. 4, fn. 9 edited by the same authors carries a footnote with an unfortunate and untrue statement: "Sorokin . . . in a mimeographed document . . . asserted that Parsons studied under him . . ." The document to which the note refers states no such thing. Certainly the sociologists who, like the senior author, owe most to both of these creative and independent men know that neither was a student of the other in the formal sense. Perhaps the footnotes 264 (in ch. 2) and 69 (in ch. 7) and relevant textual material of the present volume best describe the situation.

BIBLIOGRAPHY *

HOWARD P. BECKER **

1928

"Future of Man," tr. of Max Scheler, *The Monthly Criterion* (London, Feb. 1928), pp. 100-119.

"Sargasso Iceberg: A Study in Cultural Lag and Institutional Disintegration," (study of a German [Hunsrück] peasant village) *American Journal of Sociology*, Vol. 34, No. 3, Nov. 1928, pp. 492-506.

"Early African Culture as an Indication of Present Negro Potentialities," tr. of Leo Frobenius, *Annals of the American Academy of Political and Social Science*, Vol. 140, Nov. 1928, pp. 153-165.

"Sociology: Its Methods and Laws," tr. of Eugenio Rignano, Part I., *American Journal of Sociology*, Vol. 24, No. 3, Nov. 1928, pp. 429-450; Part II. *Ibid.*, No. 4, Jan. 1929, pp. 605-622.

1929

Military Training in the Schools and Colleges of Illinois; with E. J. Webster, pam. distributed by Illinois Committee on Military Training in Education, 1929, 37p.

"The Technique of Criminal Investigation in Germany," tr. of Robert Heindl, *Annals of the American Academy of Political and Social Science*, Vol. 146, Nov. 1929, pp. 223-236.

1930

"Distribution of Space in the American Journal of Sociology, 1895-1927," *American Journal of Sociology*, Vol. 36, No. 3, Nov. 1930, pp. 461-466. (Content analysis).

"Systematic Sociology as the Science of Interhuman Behavior," tr. of Leopold von Wiese, *Sociology and Social Research*, Vol. 15, No. 2, Nov.-Dec. 1930, pp. 103-115.

1931

"Forms of Population Movement," Part I., *Social Forces*, Vol. 9, No. 2, Dec. 1930, pp. 147-160; Part II., *Ibid.*, No. 3, Mar. 1931, pp. 351-361.

* The contents of the bibliographies appear here as submitted by the respective authors. Arrangement and bibliographical form has been somewhat altered in the interests of uniformity. No attempt has been made by the present authors to check the accuracy of all bibliographic entries nor to ascertain their inclusiveness. A comparison of the seven sections of this bibliography with the corresponding chapter bibliographies in this volume will show the selectivity of the latter.

** For several recent additional citations not listed below see *Sociological Abstracts*, items 7731, 8527, 8812 and 9424.

"Les théories du conflit el l'origine de l'Etat," with Leon Smelo, *Revue de Synthèse*, Vol. 1, No. 1, Mar. 1931, pp. 15-38.

"Some Forms of Sympathy: A Phenomenological Analysis," *Journal of Abnormal and Social Psychology*, Vol. 26, No. 1, April-June, 1931.

"Pastoral Nomadism and Social Change," *Sociology and Social Research*, Vol. 15, No. 5, May-June, 1931, pp. 417-427.

"Conflict Theories and the Origin of the State," with Leon Smelo, *Sociological Review* (British), Vol. 13, No. 2, July, 1931, pp. 65-79.

"Conquest by Pastoral Nomads," *Sociology and Social Research*, Vol. 15, No. 6, July-Aug. 1931, pp. 511-526.

"The Meaning of Mental Health," *The Survey*, midmonthly, Aug. 1931, pp. 462-463.

"Abstracts of Committee Reports on Mental Deficiency and on Mental Ill-Health," *The White House Conference: Addresses and Abstracts of Committee Reports* (New York: Century, 1931), pp. 303-316.

"Unrest, Culture Contact, and Release During the Middle Ages and the Renaissance," *Southwestern Social Science Quarterly*, Vol. 12, No. 2, Sept. 1931, pp. 1-13.

"Attitudes toward Death and the Dead and Some Possible Causes of Ghost Fear," with D. K. Bruner, *Mental Hygiene*, Vol. 15, No. 4, Oct. 1931, pp. 828-837.

"A Practical Mental Health Program with Especial Reference to the Mental Hygiene of Childhood and to the Local Community," *Psyche*, Vol. 12, No. 2, Oct. 1931, pp. 62-82.

"A Sociological Study of Spartan Culture," with Leon Smelo, *Social Science*, Vol. 6, No. 4, Oct. 1931, pp. 353-361.

"Origines possibles de l'animisme" with D. K. Bruner, *Revue Internationale de Sociologie*, Vol. 39, Nos. 11-12, Nov.-Dec. 1931, pp. 569-580.

1932

Systematic Sociology on the Basis of the Beziehungslehre and Gebildelehre of Leopold von Wiese (New York: Wiley, 1932). Reissued, with 1950 preface, (Norman Paul Press, 1148 St. Joseph St., Gary, Indiana, 1950.) For a detailed account describing Becker's translations, his augmentations, and his substantive additions to the original von Wiese work see *Sociometry*, Vol. 18, No. 4, pp. 518-524 or its replication, J. L. Moreno, ed., *Sociometry and the Science of Man* (New York: Beacon House, 1956), pp. 262-268.

"Säkularisationsprozesse, I. Teil," *Kölner Vierteljahrshefte für Soziologie*, Jan. 1932, pp. 283-294. "II. Teil, *Ibid.*," June 1932, pp. 256-259.

"Mental Subnormality and the Local Community: An Outline of a Practical Program," *The Social Service Review*, Vol. 6, No. 2, June 1932, pp. 256-259.

"Space Apportioned Forty-eight Topics in the American Journal of Sociology," *American Journal of Sociology*, Vol. 38, No. 1, July 1932, pp. 71-78. (Content analysis).

"Processes of Secularization: An Ideal-typical Analysis with Special Reference to Personality Change as Affected by Population Movement, Part I," *Sociological Review* (British), April-July 1932, pp. 135-154. "Part II, *Ibid.*" Oct. 1932, pp. 266-286.

"Some Aspects of Taboo and Totemism," with D. K. Bruner, *Journal of Social Psychology*, Vol. 3, No. 3, Aug. 1932, pp. 337-353.

"Early Generalizations Concerning Population Movement and Culture Contact," (Japanese), *Sociology* (H. Juri Tanabe and Kiyoto Furuno, eds.), Vol. 3, July-Aug. 1932, pp. 39-80.

"Lilienfeld-Toailles, Pavel Fedorovich," *Encyclopedia of the Social Sciences*, Vol. 9, 1932–.

"Geistige Minderwertigkeit," *Deutsche Zeitschrift für Wohlfahrtspflege*, Vol. 7, No. 42, 1932? Accepted for publication, but because of Nazi raids on the journal, its appearance in print is not ascertained.

1933

"Problems of Mental Health" and "Problems of Mental Deficiency." *The Handicapped Child: Report of the Committee on the Physically and Mentally Handicapped*. The White House Conference (New York: Century, 1933), pp. 271-390.

"Tabu and Totemismus: Versuch einer neuen Hypothese ihrer Ursprünge und ihrer Entwicklung," with D. K. Bruner, *Kölner Vierteljahrshefte für Soziologie*, Vol. 12, No. 1, 1933, pp. 52-69.

"Ionia and Athens: Studies in Secularization," *Abstract of Dissertation, The University of Chicago Abstract Series*, 1933.

"The Sorrow of Bereavement," *Journal of Abnormal and Social Psychology*, Vol. 27, No. 4, Jan.-March 1933, pp. 391-410.

"Vicinal Isolation and Mental Immobility," *Social Forces*, Vol. 11, No. 3, Mar. 1933, pp. 326-334.

"Early Generalizations Concerning Population Movement and Culture Contact, Part I," *Sociological Review* (British) Vol. 25, No. 1, April 1933, pp. 45-55. Part II., *Ibid.*, No. 3, Oct. 1933, pp. 218-232.

"Social Thought of Preliterate Peoples, Part I," *Revista di Sociologia*, Vol. 6, (Series 2), No. 4, May-June, 1933, pp. 290-310. Part II, *Ibid.*, Vol. 6, No. 4, July-Oct. 1933, pp. 392-409.

"Historical Sociology," (Czech), *Sociologicka Revue*, Vol. 4, No. 3, 1933, pp. 346-367.

"Le Part du sentiment dans les origines de la croyance a l'immortalité," *Revue Internationale de Sociologie*, Vol. 41, Nos. 9-10, Sept.-Oct. 1933, pp. 487-511.

"Social Thought of Preliterate Peoples," Part I. (Japanese), *Studies of Social Science*, (Tokyo, Hosei University), Vol. 1, No. 2, Oct. 1933, pp. 126-147. Part II, *Ibid.*, Vol. 1, No. 3, Nov. 1933, pp. 64-78.

"Sociologie historique," *Revue de Synthese*, Vol. 5, No. 3, Dec. 1933, pp. 237-50.

"Historical Sociology," L. L. Bernard, ed., *Fields and Problems of Sociology* (New York: Ray Long and R. R. Smith, 1933). Chapter II.

1934

"Sociology and Suffering," tr. with intro. of section from Leopold von Wiese's *Beziehungslehre* (1924), *International Journal of Ethics*, Vol. 44, No. 2, Jan. 1934, pp. 222-235.

"Mental Mobility and Secularization in Hellenic History: a Study of Some

Effects of Migration and Culture Contact," *Revista di Sociologia,* Vol. 7, No. 1, Jan.-March 1934, pp. 14-30.

"British Sociology," (Czech), *Sociologicka Revue,* Vol. 5, No. 4, 1934, pp. 251-270.

"Culture Case Study and Ideal-Typical Method, with Special Reference to Max Weber," *Social Forces,* Vol. 12, No. 3, March 1934, pp. 399-405.

1936

"A New Classification of Culture," (discussion of paper by James W. Woodard), *American Sociological Review,* Vol. 1, No. 1, Feb. 1936, pp. 102-104.

"Sociology in Japan," *American Sociological Review,* Vol. 1, No. 3, June 1936, pp. 455-471.

1938

Social Thought from Lore to Science: Vol. I. A History and Interpretation of Man's Ideas about Life with his Fellows; Vol. II. *Sociological Trends throughout the World;* with Harry Elmer Barnes (Boston: D. C. Heath & Co., 1938). Second ed., 1952, with new introductory note, 1951 preface, value-system commentary, and 1937-1950 appendix (Washington, C. D.: Harren Press, 1952). Portuguese and Spanish translations. Third ed., 1961, revised to include additional comment for each chapter, Encyclopedia Britannica Yearbook articles to 1960, expanded bibliography, and new prefaces. (New York: Dover Publications, 1960). Polish and Italian translations in process.

1939

"Irrational Factors in International Relations," Brown, Hodges and Roucek, eds., *Contemporary World Problems* (New York: Wiley, 1939), Chapter 27, pp. 572-583.

"La Tipologia Constructiva en la Ciencias Sociales," *Revista Mexicana de Sociología,* Vol. 1, Nos. 4-5, Sept.-Dec. 1939, pp. 65-98.

1940

"Constructive Typology in the Social Sciences," *American Sociological Review,* Vol. 5, No. 1, Feb. 1940, pp. 40-55.

Contemporary Social Theory, a symposium, Howard Becker, Frances Bennett Becker and Harry Elmer Barnes, eds., (New York: Appleton-Century, 1940). Chapters II and XV.

1941

"Supreme Values and the Sociologist," *American Sociological Review,* Vol. 6, No. 2, April 1941, pp. 155-172.

"The Limits of Sociological Positivism," *Journal of Social Philosophy,* Vol. 6, No. 4, July 1941, pp. 362-370.

"After the Deluge," Henry P. Jordan, ed., *Problems in Post-War Re-Construction* (Washington, D. C.: American Council on Public Affairs), Ch. 4.

"The Social Sciences and Education," with William L. Kolb; Joseph S. Roucek, ed., *Contemporary Europe* (New York: 1941), Chapter 31, pp. 597-609.

1942

"Introductory chapter," Howard Becker and Reuben Hill, eds., *Marriage and the Family* (Boston: Heath, 1942).

"Sociological Analysis of the Dyad," with Ruth Hill Useem, *American Sociological Review*, Vol. 7, No. 2, Feb. 1942, pp. 13-26.

"Max Scheler's Sociology of Knowledge," with Helmut Otto Dahlke, *Philosophy and Phenomenological Research*, Vol. 2, No. 3, March 1942, pp. 309-322.

"Sacred and Secular Aspects of Human Sociation," with Robert C. Myers, *Sociometry*, Vol. 5, No. 3, Aug. 1942, pp. 207-229.

"Sociology in 1941," *Encyclopaedia Britannica Yearbook for 1942*. The first of a series of such overviews, subsequent articles appearing in successive yearbooks through 1960.

1943

"Befuddled Germany: A Glimpse of Max Scheler," *American Sociological Review*, Vol. 8, No. 2, April 1943, pp. 207-211.

"Monuments: German Personality Types Foreshadowing the Collapse of the Weimar Republic," *American Sociological Review*, Vol. 8, No. 5, October 1943, pp. 525-530.

1945

"Los Pueblos de Alemania," *Revista Mexicana de Sociología*, Vol. 7, No. 1, Jan.-April, 1945, pp. 23-67.

"Interpretative Sociology and Constructive Typology," Gurvitch and Moore, eds., *Twentieth Century Sociology* (New York: Philosophical Library, 1945), Chapter 4, pp. 70-95.

"Peoples of Germany," T. C. McCormick, ed., *Problems of the Postwar World* (New York: McGraw-Hill, 1945), Chapter 16, pp. 342-390.

"What Should Be Our Policy in Germany?" (WGN-Mutual broadcast with Robert V. Jones and others, later issued as pamphlet), *The Reviewing Stand*, Northwestern University, Vol. 5, No. 25, Nov. 25, 1945, 12 pages.

1946

German Youth: Bond or Free (London: Routledge Kegan Paul, 1946); (New York: Oxford University Press, 1947); (Wiesbaden Germany: Verlag Der Greif, 1949); Latter edition in German, bearing title *Vom Barette Schwankt die Feder* includes two additional chapters. British edition reissued 1950, 1954. Most recent American issue: (New York: The Humanities Press, Inc., 1957).

"Maurice Halbwachs," *American Sociological Review*, Vol. 11, No. 2, April, 1946, pp. 233-235.

1947

"Sociology and Related Social Sciences, 1937-1946," *Ten Eventful Years*, special volume issued by *Encyclopaedia Britannica*, 1947.

"Czech and Slovak Sociology," (Czech), 15 page pamphlet on sociology in Czechoslovakia (Prague: V komisi knihkupectvi J. Samce, 1947).

1948

"Max Scheler," *Encyclopaedia Britannica,* 14th ed. revised, 1948.

"Leopold von Wiese and Kaiservaldau," *Ibid.*

"Max Scheler," *Collier's Encyclopedia,* rev. ed., 1948.

"Introductory Chapter," Howard Becker and Reuben Hill, eds., *Family, Marriage, and Parenthood* (Boston: Heath, 1948).

"Politische Gebilde und Aussenkonflikt," *Kölner Zeitschrift für Soziologie,* Vol. 1, No. 1, 1948-49, pp. 5-16.

1949

"Die jüngste Entwicklung der Soziologie," *Universitas,* Vol. 4, No. 7, 1949, pp. 793-799.

"Werte als Werkzeuge sociologischer Analyse," Gottfried Eisermann, ed., *Gegenwartsprobleme der Sociologie: Alfred Vierkandt zum 80. Geburtstag* (Potsdam: Athenaion, 1949), Chapter 7, pp. 116-140.

"The Nature and Consequences of Black Propaganda," *American Sociological Review,* Vol. 14, No. 2, April, 1949, pp. 221-235.

"How Can You Make Your Marriage a Success?" (WGN-Mutual broadcast with Robert F. Winch and others, later issued as pamphlet) *The Reviewing Stand,* Northwestern University, Vol. 12, No. 24, June 19, 1949, 12 pages.

"The Regimented Man: Interviews with German Officials under the Nazis," *Social Forces,* Vol. 28, No. 1, October 1949, pp. 19-24.

1950

Through Values to Social Interpretation: Essays on Social Contexts, Actions, Types, and Prospects (Durham, N. C.: Duke University Press, 1950). Unabridged and revised versions of six articles previously published in abridged form. Extensive bibliography by Hopkins and Mills added.

"Sacred and Secular Societies Considered with Reference to Folk-State and Similar Classifications," *Social Forces,* Vol. 28, No. 4, May 1950, pp. 361-376.

"Changes in the Social Stratification of Contemporary Germany," *American Sociological Review,* Vol. 15, No. 3, June 1950, pp. 333-342.

"In Defense of Morgan's 'Grecian Gens': Ancient Kinship and Stratification," *Southwestern Journal of Anthropology,* Vol. 6, No. 3, Autumn 1950, pp. 309-339.

1951

"Intellectuals, Concentration Camps, and Black Propaganda," *American Journal of Economics and Sociology,* Vol. 10, No. 2, Jan. 1951, pp. 139-144.

"What the Hitler Youth Inherited," *Phylon,* Vol. 12, No. 1, March 1951, pp. 39-54.

"Propaganda and the Impotent German Intellectual," *Social Forces,* Vol. 29, No. 3, March 1951, pp. 273-276.

"Max Weber, Assassination, and German Guilt," *American Journal of Economics and Sociology,* Vol. 10, No. 4, July 1951, pp. 401-406.

"German Families Today," Hans J. Morgenthau, ed., *Germany and the*

Future of Europe (Chicago: Univ. of Chicago Press, 1951), Chapter II, pp. 12-24. This is an abridged version, minus about twenty single-spaced typed pages of an earlier treatment of German family themes and related matters in the hectographed *Proceedings of the Twenty-Sixth Institute of the Norman Waite Harris Memorial Foundation,* University of Chicago, May 29 to June 1, 1950. The editor of this latter work notes on page iii, "the discussions were off the record, and consequently this volume is not for general circulation and is sent only to the participants and a select group of experts." Nevertheless, the unabridged version is not in the strict sense unpublished.

1952

"General Features of Sacred and Secular Societies," K. G. Specht, ed., *Soziologische Forschung in unserer Zeit: Leopold von Wiese zum 75. Geburtstag* (Köln and Opladen: Westdeutscher Verlag, 1952), pp. 64-74. Now superseded by chapter 1 of *Through Values to Social Interpretation* (see 1950 publications above).

"Science, Culture, and Society," *Philosophy of Science,* Vol. 19, No. 4, October 1952, pp. 273-287.

1954

"Anthropology and Sociology," John Gillin, ed., *For a Science of Social Man: Convergences in Anthropology, Sociology and Psychology* (New York: Macmillan, 1954), Chapter 5.

"Vitalizing Sociological Theory," *American Sociological Review,* Vol. 19, No. 4, August 1954, pp. 377-388.

1955

Family, Marriage, and Parenthood, rev. ed., with Reuben Hill, eds., with the assistance of Marguerita Steffenson (Boston: Heath, 1955). Introductory chapter by Howard Becker, revised.

1956

Man in Reciprocity (New York: Frederick A. Praeger, Inc., 1956).

Societies Around the World, with Irwin T. Sanders and associates, eds., (New York: Dryden Press, 1956).

"Systematic Sociology and Leopold von Wiese," J. S. Moreno, ed., *Sociometry and the Science of Man* (New York: Beacon House, 1956), pp. 262-268. Also appears in *Sociometry,* Vol. 18, No. 4, pp. 518-524.

"A Sacred-Secular Evaluation Continuum of Social Change," *Proceedings of the Third International Congress of Sociology* (Amsterdam, Holland: August, 1956), Chapter 6, pp. 19-41.

"Empathy, Sympathy, and Scheler," *International Journal of Sociometry* (New York: Beacon House, September, 1956), pp. 15-22.

"Church and State in the Cosmos of Crete," *International Review of Social History* (Amsterdam) Vol. 1, No. 2, October 1956, pp. 253-295.

"Field Work Among Scottish Shepherds and German Peasants: 'Wholes' and Their Handicaps," *Social Forces,* Vol. 35, No. 1, October 1956, pp. 10-15.

"Leopold von Wiese zum 80. Geburtstag," *Kölner Zeitschrift für Soziologie und Sozialpsychologie*, Vol. 8, No. 4, 1956, pp. 535-539.

1957

"Current Sacred-Secular Theory and Its Development," Becker and Boskoff, eds., *Modern Sociological Theory in Continuity and Change* (New York: The Dryden Press, Inc., 1957), Chapter 6.

1958

"Deutsches Gedankengut in der amerikanischen Socialpsychologie und Soziologie der Gegenwart," *Jahrbuch für Amerikastudien* (Heidelberg: Carl Winter, Universitätsverlag, 1958), Band 3, pp. 15-21.

"Culture Case Study and Greek History: Comparison Viewed Sociologically," *American Sociological Review*, Vol. 23, No. 5, October 1958, pp. 489-504.

1959

"On Simmel's Philosophy of Money," Kurt H. Wolff, ed., *Georg Simmel, 1858-1918* (Columbus: Ohio State University Press, 1959), pp. 216-233.

"Deutsche Beiträge zu der amerikanischen Socialpsychologie und Soziologie der Gegenwart," Alexander Busch, ed. *Soziologie und moderne Gesellschaft: Verhandlungen des 14. Deutschen Soziologentages* (Stuttgart: Ferdinand Enke, 1959), pp. 90-99.

"Das Deutschlandbild in Amerika," *Politische Studien*, Heft 115, 10. Jahrgang, pp. 740-757. (München: Monatschrift der Hochschule für Politische Wissenschaften, Nov. 1959), pp. 737-747.

Soziologie als Wissenschaft vom sozialen Handeln (Würzburg: Holzner Verlag, 1959).

KINGSLEY DAVIS

1934

"An Attempt to Discover Change in Moral Attitudes of High School Students," with Joseph K. Johnson, *International Journal of Ethics*, Vol. 44, No. 2, January 1934, pp. 244-251.

1935

Youth in the Depression (Chicago: University of Chicago Press, 1935).

1936

"Jealousy and Sexual Property," *Social Forces*, Vol. 14, March 1936, pp. 395-405.

"The Application of Science to Personal Relations," *American Sociological Review*, Vol. 1, April 1936, pp. 236-247.

1937

"Structural Analysis of Kinship," with W. Lloyd Warner, *American Anthropologist*, Vol. 39, No. 2, April-June 1937, pp. 291-313.

"Parents Go on Strike," *North American Review,* Vol. 245, June 1937, pp. 221-239.

"Reproductive Institutions and the Pressure for Population," *Sociological Review* (British), Vol. 29, No. 3, July 1937, pp. 1-18.

"The Sociology of Prostitution," *American Sociological Review,* Vol. 2, No. 5, Oct. 1937, pp. 744-755.

1938

"Mental Hygiene and the Class Structure," *Psychiatry,* Vol. 1, No. 1, Feb. 1938, pp. 55-65.

1939

"Illegitimacy and the Social Structure," *American Journal of Sociology,* Vol. 45, No. 2, Sept. 1939, pp. 215-233.

"The Forms of Illegitimacy," *Social Forces,* Vol. 18, No. 1, Oct. 1939, pp. 77-89.

1940

"Extreme Social Isolation of a Child," *American Journal of Sociology,* Vol. 45, Jan. 1940, pp. 554-565.

"The Sociology of Parent-Youth Conflict," *American Sociological Review,* Vol. 5, No. 4, Aug. 1940, pp. 523-535.

"The Child and the Social Structure," *Journal of Educational Sociology,* Vol. 14, Dec. 1940, pp. 217-229.

1941

"Intermarriage in Caste Societies," *American Anthropologist,* Vol. 43, No. 3, July-Sept. 1941, pp. 376-395.

"Social Psychiatry," E. B. Reuter, *Handbook of Sociology* (New York: Dryden Press, 1941).

1942

"Foreword," J. A. L. Singh and Robert M. Zingg, *Wolf Children and Feral Man* (New York: Harper & Bros., 1942), pp. xxi-xxiii.

"Changing Modes of Marriage: Contemporary Family Types," Howard Becker and Reuben Hill, eds., *Marriage and the Family* (Boston: D. C. Heath, 1942), pp. 92-120.

"A Conceptual Analysis of Stratification," *American Sociological Review,* Vol. 7, No. 3, June 1942, pp. 309-321.

"Political Ambivalence in Latin America," *Journal of Legal and Political Sociology,* Vol. 1, Oct. 1942, pp. 127-150.

1943

"The Population of India," *Far Eastern Survey,* Vol. 12, April 19, 1943, pp. 76-79.

1944

"Children of Divorced Parents: A Sociological and Statistical Analysis," *Law and Contemporary Problems,* Summer 1944, pp. 700-720.

"Demographic Fact and Policy in India," *Milbank Memorial Fund Quarterly,* Vol. 22, July 1944, pp. 256-278. Reprinted in Milbank Memorial

Fund, *Demographic Studies of Selected Areas of Rapid Growth* (New York: Milbank Fund, 1944), pp. 35-57.

"Adolescence and the Social Structure," *The Annals of the American Academy of Political and Social Science*, Vol. 236, Nov. 1944, pp. 8-16.

"Refleciones sobre las instituciones políticas," *Jornadas*, Vol. 47 (Mexico, D.F.: El Colegio de México, 1944).

1945

"World Population in Transition," Editor, *Annals of the American Academy of Political and Social Science*, Vol. 237, Jan. 1945. Translated into Spanish as *Corrientes Demograficas Mundiales* (Mexico, D. F.: Fondo de Cultura Economica, 1950).

"The World Demographic Transition," *The Annals of the American Academy of Political and Social Science*, Vol. 237, Jan. 1945, pp. 1-11. Translated and reprinted as La Transición demográfica del mundo," in *La Revista Belga*, Vol. 11, May 1945, pp. 1-11.

"Some Principles of Stratification," with Wilbert E. Moore, *American Sociological Review*, Vol. 10, No. 2, April 1945, pp. 242-249.

1946

Urbanization in Latin America, with Ana Casis (New York: Milbank Memorial Fund, 1946). First appeared in *Milbank Memorial Fund Quarterly* in two parts: Part I, Vol. 24, April 1946, pp. 186-207; Part II, Vol. 24, July 1946, pp. 292-314. Translated into Spanish as "Concentración y desarrollo urbano en América Latina" in *El Trimestre Económico* (Mexico: Vol. 14, Oct.-Dec. 1947), pp. 406-456.

"The Shifting Balance of World Population," Part I, *Forum*, Vol. 105, Jan. 1946, pp. 419-426; Part II, *Ibid.* Feb. 1946, pp. 493-498.

"Human Fertility in India," *American Journal of Sociology*, Vol. 52, No. 3, Nov. 1946, pp. 243-254.

"Population Trends and Policies in Latin America," *Some Economic Aspects of Postwar Inter-American Relations* (Austin: Institute of Latin American Studies, University of Texas, 1946), pp. 25-46.

1947

"Future Migration into Latin America," *Milbank Memorial Fund Quarterly*, Vol. 25, No. 1, Jan. 1947, pp. 44-62. Reprinted in Milbank Memorial Fund, *Postwar Problems of Migration* (New York: Milbank Fund, 1947), pp. 30-48.

"Final Note on a Case of Extreme Isolation," *American Journal of Sociology*, Vol. 52, No. 5, March 1947, pp. 432-437.

"Latin America's Multiplying Peoples," *Foreign Affairs*, Vol. 25, July 1947, pp. 643-654.

"Divorce," Morris Fishbein and Ernest W. Burgess, eds., *Successful Marriage* (Garden City, New York: Doubleday, 1947), pp. 458-465.

1948

"Puerto Rico's Population Problem: Research and Policy," *Milbank Memorial Fund Quarterly*, Vol. 26, No. 3, July 1948, pp. 300-308.

"Population and Resources in the Americas," *Proceedings of the InterAmerican Conference on Conservation of Renewable Natural Resources,* Denver, 1948 (Washington, D. C.: Department of Economic and Social Affairs, Pan American Union, 1950), pp. 88-97.

1949

Modern American Society, with Bredemeier and Levy, eds. (New York: Rinehart & Company, Inc., 1949).

Human Society (New York: The Macmillan Company, 1949).

"Immigration from the Western Hemisphere," with Clarence Senior, *The Annals of the American Academy of Political and Social Science,* Vol. 262, March 1949, pp. 70-81.

"Sociologic Approach: Discussion I," Paul H. Hoch and Joseph Zubin, eds., *Psychosexual Development in Health and Disease* (New York: Grune & Stratton, 1949), pp. 267-271.

"Values, Population and the Supernatural: A Critique," George F. Mair, ed., *Studies in Population* (Princeton: Princeton University Press, 1949), pp. 135-139.

"India and Pakistan: The Demography of Partition," *Pacific Affairs,* Vol. 22, No. 3, Sept. 1949, pp. 254-264.

1950

People on the Move, with Julius Isaac (London: Bureau of Current Affairs, UNESCO, 1950). Translated into Spanish as *Poblaciones en Movimiento* (Buenos Aires: Editorial Sudamericana, 1951).

"The Sociology of an Aging Population," with Jerry W. Combs, Jr., *The Social and Biological Challenge of Our Aging Population* (New York: Columbia University Press, 1950), pp. 146-170.

"The Economic Demography of India and Pakistan," Phillips Talbot, ed., *South Asia in the World Today* (Chicago: University of Chicago Press, 1950), pp. 86-107.

"Population and Development," *Journal of International Affairs,* Vol. 4, No. 2, Spring 1950, pp. 43-49.

"Statistical Perspective on Marriage and Divorce," *The Annals of the American Academy of Political and Social Science,* Vol. 272, Nov. 1950, pp. 9-21.

1951

The Population of India and Pakistan (Princeton: Princeton University Press, 1951).

"Apreciación Critica de Malthus," T. R. Malthus, *Ensayo Sobre el Principio de la Poblacion* (Mexico: Fondo de Cultura Economica, 1951), pp. vii-xli. (This is a critical introduction to the Spanish edition of Malthus' *Essay.*) Published by the District of Columbia Sociological Society in mimeographed form, "An attempt to Lay the Ghost of Malthus," October 18, 1951. Reprinted in large part in P. F. Lazarsfeld and M. Rosenberg, *The Language of Social Research* (Glencoe, Ill.: Free Press, 1955).

"Introduction," William J. Goode, *Religion Among the Primitives* (Glencoe, Ill.: Free Press, 1951), pp. 11-17.

"Population and the Further Spread of Industrial Society," *Proceedings of American Philosophical Society,* Vol. 95, No. 1, Feb. 1951, pp. 8-19.

"The Pattern of Puerto Rican Fertility," with Jerry W. Combs, Jr., *Population Studies,* Vol. 4, No. 4, March 1951, pp. 364-379.

"Population and Progress in Puerto Rico," *Foreign Affairs,* July 1951, pp. 625-636.

"The American Family: What It Is—and Isn't," *New York Times Magazine,* Sept. 30, 1951, pp. 18, 41-42.

"Differential Fertility in Puerto Rico," with Jerry W. Combs, Jr., *Population Studies,* Vol. 5, No. 2, Nov. 1951, pp. 104-116.

1952

"The Controversial Future of Underdeveloped Areas," Paul K. Hatt, ed., *World Population and Future Resources* (New York: American Book Company, 1952), pp. 14-24.

"The Demographic Foundations of World Organization," Lyman Bryson, et al., eds., *Foundations of World Organization* (New York: Harper & Bros., 1952), pp. 61-70.

1953

"Puerto Rico: A Crowded Island," *Annals of the American Academy of Political and Social Science,* Vol. 285, Jan. 1953, pp. 116-122. Reprinted in translation as "Puerto Rico: Una Isla Superpoblada," *La Torre,* Vol. 1, No. 2, April-June 1953, pp. 129-140.

"Future Population Trends and Their Significance," *Transactions of the Eighteenth North American Wildlife Conference* (Washington: Wildlife Management Institute, 1953).

1954

"The Demographic Foundations of National Power," Morroe Berger, et al., eds., *Freedom and Control in Modern Society* (New York: Van Nostrand, 1954), pp. 206-242.

"Fertility Control and the Demographic Transition in India," Milbank Memorial Fund, *Interrelations of Demographic, Economic, and Social Problems in Selected Underdeveloped Areas* (New York: Milbank Fund, 1954). Proceedings of the 1953 Annual Conference of the Milbank Fund.

"The World Distribution of Urbanization," with Hilda Hertz, *Bulletin of the International Statistical Institute,* Vol. 33, Part 4, pp. 227-242. Proceedings of the International Statistical Conferences, New Delhi and Calcutta, 1951.

"Small Families Are Still the Fashion," *New York Times Magazine,* July 11, 1954, pp. 17, 35.

"Urbanization and the Development of Pre-Industrial Areas," with Hilda Hertz, *Economic Development and Cultural Change,* Vol. 3, Oct. 1954, pp. 6-26.

1955

"The Origin and Growth of Urbanization in the World," *American Journal of Sociology,* Vol. 60, March 1955, pp. 429-437.

"Blankes Aleen: Race and Caste in Africa," *Yale Review,* Vol. 64, Spring 1955, pp. 469-476.

"Institutional Patterns Favoring High Fertility in Underdeveloped Areas," *Eugenics Quarterly,* Vol. 2, March 1955, pp. 33-39.

"Malthus and the Theory of Population," Paul F. Lazarsfeld and Morris Rosenberg, eds., *The Language of Social Research* (Glencoe, Ill.: Free Press, 1955), pp. 540-553.

"How Much Do We Know About Divorce?" *Look Magazine,* July 26, 1955, pp. 65-69.

"Divorce Downswing," *New York Times Magazine,* May 8, 1955, p. 67.

"United States Immigration and Food Exports in Relation to World Population Problems," with Fairfield Osborn, *World Population and Resources* (London: Political and Economic Planning, 1955), pp. 158-164.

"Food and People," with Fairfield Osborn, *Wall Street Journal,* April 7, 1955. (A reprint in part of the preceding article.)

" 'Ideal Size' for Our Population," *New York Times Magazine,* May 1, 1955, pp. 12, 30, 32, 34, 37.

"Preface," William Petersen, *Planned Migration: The Social Determinants of the Dutch-Canadian Movement* (Berkeley: University of California Press, 1955), pp. 263-315.

"Social and Demographic Aspects of Economic Development in India," Simon Kuznets, Wilbert E. Moore, and Joseph J. Spengler, eds., *Economic Growth: Brazil, India, Japan* (Durham, N. C.: Duke University Press, 1955), pp. 263-315.

"Internal Migration and Urbanization in Relation to Economic Development," *United Nations, World Population Conference,* 1954, Papers (New York: United Nations, 1955), Vol. II, pp. 783-801.

1956

"Social Structure and Fertility: An Analytic Framework," with Judith Blake, *Economic Development and Cultural Change,* Vol. 4, April 1956, pp. 211-235.

"The Unpredicted Pattern of Population Change," *Annals of the American Academy of Political and Social Science,* Vol. 305, May 1956, pp. 53-59.

"The Amazing Decline of Mortality in Underdeveloped Areas," *Papers and Proceedings of the Annual Meeting of the American Economic Association,* (New York: December 28-30, 1955). The Proceedings are published as Vol. 44, May 1956, of the *American Economic Review* in which the Davis article appears on pp. 305-318.

"Population Analysis [of Jordan]," Raphael Patai, ed., *The Hashemite Kingdom of Jordan* (New Haven: Human Relations Area Files, 1956), pp. 42-53.

"Population Analysis [of Syria]," Raphael Patai, ed., *The Republic of Syria* (New Haven: Human Relations Area Files, 1956), Vol. 1, pp. 49-80.

"Population Analysis [of Lebanon]," Raphael Patai, ed., *The Republic of Lebanon* (New Haven: Human Relations Area Files, 1956), pp. 42-53.

1957

"Introduction," George W. Roberts, *The Population of Jamaica* (Cambridge: University Press, 1957), pp. xvii-xxii.

"Analysis of the Population Explosion," *New York Times Magazine*, Sept. 22, 1957, pp. 15, 77, 78, 79.

"Divorce and Its Effects," Morris Fishbein and R. J. R. Kennedy, eds., *Modern Marriage and Family Living* (New York: Oxford University Press, 1957), pp. 100-112.

"Introduction," Joseph A. Kahl, *The American Class Structure* (New York: Rinehart, 1957), pp. v-vii.

1958

"A Crowding Hemisphere: Population Change in the Americas," ed., *Annals of the American Academy of Political and Social Science*, Vol. 316, March 1958.

"The Political Impact of New Population Trends," *Foreign Affairs*, Vol. 36, Jan. 1958, pp. 293-301.

"Urban Demography and Ecology: Research Problems with Special Reference to Metropolitan Affairs in California," *Alpha Kappa Deltan*, Vol. 28, Winter 1958, pp. 9-27.

"Recent Population Trends in the New World: An Over-all View," *Annals of the American Academy of Political and Social Science*, Vol. 216, March 1958, pp. 1-10.

"The Demographic Consequences of Changes in Productive Technology: An Essay on the Problem of Measurement," *Social, Economic and Technological Change* (Paris: International Social Science Council, UNESCO, 1958), pp. 193-227.

"The Early Marriage Trend," *What's New*, No. 207, Fall 1958, pp. 2-6.

"Conventional versus Metropolitan Data in the International Study of Urbanization," with Jack P. Gibbs, *American Sociological Review*, Vol. 23, Oct. 1958, pp. 504-514. Appears in Spanish as "Caracteristicas de los Datos Utilizables en un Estudio Internacional Sobre la Urbanizacion," *Revista Mexicana de Sociología*, Vol. 20, Sept.-Dec. 1958), pp. 649-667.

1959

The World's Metropolitan Areas (Berkeley: University of California Press, 1959).

"The Sociology of Demographic Behavior," Robert K. Merton, Leonard Broom, and Leonard S. Cottrell, Jr., eds., *Sociology Today: Problems and Prospects* (New York: Basic Books, 1959), Chapter 14, pp. 309-333.

"People: Too Many Too Soon?" *The Rotarian*, Vol. 94, April 1959, pp. 10-12.

"The Other Scare: Too Many People," *New York Times Magazine*, March 15, 1959, pp. 13, 108, 110, 112, 114. Reprinted in Milwaukee Journal, April 26, 1959, Part 5, pp. 1, 3.

"The Abominable Heresy: A Reply to Dr. Buckley," *American Sociological Review*, Vol. 24, Feb. 1959, pp. 82-3.

"The Myth of Functional Analysis as a Special Method in Sociology and Anthropology," *American Sociological Review*, Vol. 24, Dec. 1959, pp. 757-782.

1960

"Population and Welfare in Industrial Societies," *Health Education Monographs*, No. 9, 1960, pp. 2-19. (This was the Fourth Annual Dorothy

Nyswander Lecture given April 6, 1960, at the School of Public Health, University of California, Berkeley.)

"Colonial Expansion and Urban Diffusion in the Americas," *International Journal of Comparative Sociology,* Vol. 1, March 1960, pp. 43-66.

"Birth Control and Public Policy," with Judith Blake, *Commentary,* Vol. 29, Feb. 1960, pp. 115-121.

"Past and Future Growth of the Nation's Capital," *Transportation Plan for the National Capitol Region,* Hearings before the Joint Committee on Washington Metropolitan Problems, Congress of the United States, 86th Congress, November 9-14, 1959 (Washington: Government Printing Office, 1960), pp. 40-45. See also the oral testimony by the author, pp. 31-39.

1961

"Population and Sex," *The Encyclopedia of Sexual Behavior* (New York: Hawthorn Books, 1961), Vol. II, pp. 841-847.

"Prostitution," Robert K. Merton and Robert A. Nisbet, eds., *Contemporary Social Problems* (New York: Harcourt, Brace & World, 1961), pp. 262-288.

"The World's Population Crisis," *Ibid.,* pp. 291-323.

"American Society: Its Group Structure," *Contemporary Civilization* (Chicago: Scott, Foresman, 1961), No. 2, pp. 171-186.

GEORGE CASPAR HOMANS

1930

Massachusetts on the Sea, with S. E. Morison (Boston: Massachusetts Tercentenary Commission, 1930).

1932

"The Dark Angel: The Tragedy of Herman Melville," *New England Quarterly,* Vol. 5, 1932, pp. 699-730.

1934

An Introduction to Pareto, with C. P. Curtis (New York: Knopf, 1934).

1936

"Men and Land in the Middle Ages," *Speculum,* Vol. 11, 1936, pp. 338-351.

"Terroirs ordonnés et champs orientés: une hypothèse sur le village anglais," *Annales d'histoire économique et sociale,* Vol. 8, 1936, pp. 438-448.

1937

"Partible Inheritance of Villagers' Holdings," *Economic History Review,* Vol. 8, 1937, pp. 48-56.

1938

English Villagers of the Thirteenth Century (Cambridge, Mass.: Harvard University Press, 1941); (New York: Russell and Russell, 1960).

Fatigue of Workers (New York: Reinhold, 1941).
"Free Bull," *Review of English Studies*, Vol. 14, 1938, pp. 447-449.

1940

"The Puritans and the Clothing Industry in England," *New England Quarterly*, Vol. 13, 1940, pp. 519-529.

1941

"Anxiety and Ritual: The Theories of Malinowski and Radcliffe-Brown," *American Anthropologist*, Vol. 43, 1941, pp. 164-172.

1946

"The Small Warship," *American Sociological Review*, Vol. 11, 1946, pp. 294-300.

1947

"A Conceptual Scheme for the Study of Social Organization," *American Sociological Review*, Vol. 12, 1947, pp. 13-26.
"Reflections on the Wildcat Strikes," with J. F. Scott, *American Sociological Review*, Vol. 12, 1947, pp. 278-287.

1948

The Society of Fellows, with O. T. Bailey (Cambridge, Mass.: Harvard University Press, 1948).

1949

"The Strategy of Industrial Sociology," *American Journal of Sociology*, Vol. 54, 1949, pp. 330-337.

1950

The Human Group (New York: Harcourt, Brace, 1950).

1953

"Status Among Clerical Workers," *Human Organization*, Vol. 12, 1953, pp. 5-10.
"The Rural Sociology of Medieval England," *Past and Present*, No. 4, 1953, pp. 32-43.

1954

"The Cash Posters: A Study of a Group of Working Girls," *American Sociological Review*, Vol. 19, 1954, pp. 724-733.
"Industrial Harmony as a Goal," A. Kornhauser, R. Dubin, and A. M. Ross, *Industrial Conflict* (New York: McGraw-Hill, 1954), pp. 48-58.
"Psychological Aspects of Social Structure," with H. L. Riecken; G. Lindzey, ed., *Handbook of Social Psychology* (Cambridge, Mass.: Addison-Wesley, 1954), Vol. 2, pp. 786-832.

1955

Marriage, Authority, and Final Causes, with D. M. Schneider (Glencoe, Ill.: The Free Press, 1955).

"Kinship Terminology and the American Kinship System," with D. M. Schneider, *American Anthropologist,* Vol. 57, 1955, pp. 1194-1208.

"The Sociologist's Contribution to Management in the Future," *The Manager,* Vol. 23, 1955, pp. 1033-1036, 1085.

1956

"Giving a Dog a Bad Name," *The Listener,* Vol. 56, 1956, pp. 232-233.

1957

"Bureaucracy as Big Brother," *The Listener,* Vol. 58, 1957, pp. 731-732.

"La Congruence du Status," *Journal de Psychologie Normale et Pathologique,* Vol. 56, 1957, pp. 22-34.

"The Frisians in East Anglia," *Economic History Review,* 2nd Series, Vol. 10, 1957, pp. 189-206.

"The Anglo-Saxon Invasions Reconsidered," *Proceedings of the Massachusetts Historical Society,* Vol. 71, 1953-1957, pp. 37-49.

1958

"Social Behavior as Exchange," *American Journal of Sociology,* Vol. 63, 1958, pp. 597-606.

1959

"Sociology at Cambridge," *Cambridge Review,* Vol. 70, 1959, pp. 461-463.

1961

Social Behavior: Its Elementary Forms (New York: Harcourt, Brace and World, 1961).

"The Humanities and the Social Sciences," *American Behavioral Scientist,* Vol. 4, 1961, pp. 3-6.

1962

Sentiments and Activities: Essays in Social Science (New York: The Free Press of Glencoe, 1962).

ROBERT K. MERTON

1934

"Durkheim's Division of Labor in Society," *American Journal of Sociology,* Vol. 40, pp. 319-328.

"Recent French Sociology," *Social Forces,* Vol. 12, pp. 537-545.

1935

"The Course of Arabian Intellectual Development, 700-1300 A. D.," with P. A. Sorokin, *Isis,* Vol. 22, pp. 516-524.

"Fluctuations in the Rate of Industrial Invention," *Quarterly Journal of Economics,* Vol. 49, pp. 454-474.
"Science and Military Technique," *Scientific Monthly,* Vol. 41, pp. 542-545.

1936

"Civilization and Culture," *Sociology and Social Research,* Vol. 21, pp. 103-113.
"Puritanism, Pietism and Science," *Sociological Review,* Vol. 28, pp. 1-30.
"The Unanticipated Consequences of Purposive Social Action," *American Sociological Review,* Vol. 1, pp. 894-904.

1937

"Some Economic Factors in Seventeenth Century English Science," *Scientia: Rivista di Scienza,* pp. 142-152.
"Science, Population and Society," *Scientific Monthly,* Vol. 44, pp. 165-171.
"Social Time: A Methodological and Functional Analysis," with P. A. Sorokin, *American Journal of Sociology,* Vol. 42, pp. 615-629.
"Sociological Aspects of Invention, Discovery and Scientific Theories," with P. A. Sorokin; P. A. Sorokin, *Social and Cultural Dynamics* (New York: American Book Company), pp. 125-180; 439-476.
"The Sociology of Knowledge," *Isis,* Vol. 27, pp. 493-503.

1938

Science, Technology and Society in Seventeenth Century England; in Osiris: Studies on the History and Philosophy of Science, and on the History of Learning and Culture, George Sarton, ed. (Bruges, Belgium: The Saint Catherine Press Ltd.)
"Science and the Social Order," *Philosophy of Science,* Vol. 5, pp. 321-337.
"Social Structure and Anomie," *American Sociological Review,* Vol. 3, pp. 672-682.

1939

"Science and the Economy of 17th Century England," *Science and Society,* Vol. 3, pp. 1-30.

1940

"Bureaucratic Structure and Personality," *Social Forces,* Vol. 18, pp. 560-568.
"Crime and the Anthropologist," with M. F. Ashley Montagu, *American Anthropologist,* Vol. 42, pp. 384-408.
"Fact and Factitiousness in Ethnic Opinionnaires," *American Sociological Review,"* Vol. 5, pp. 13-28.

1941

"Intermarriage and the Social Structure: Fact and Theory," *Psychiatry,* Vol. 4, pp. 361-374.
"Karl Mannheim and the Sociology of Knowledge," *Journal of Liberal Religion,* Vol. 2, pp. 125-147.
"Znaniecki's The Social Role of the Man of Knowledge: A Review Article," *American Sociological Review,* Vol. 6, pp. 111-115.

1942

"The Formation of Socio-Economic Scales: A Comment," with G. Knupfer, *Rural Sociology*, Vol. 8, pp. 236-239.

"A Reanalysis of Documents on the Family Encounters the Depression," with E. W. Burgess, et al. (New York: Social Science Research Council), hectographed.

"Science and Technology in a Democratic Order," *Journal of Legal and Political Sociology*, Vol. 1, pp. 115-126.

1943

"Studies in Radio and Film Propaganda," with P. F. Lazarsfeld, *Transactions*, New York Academy of Sciences, Series II, Vol. 6, pp. 58-79.

1944

"The Boomerang Response," with P. L. Kendall, *Channels*, National Publicity Council for Health and Welfare Service, Vol. 21, pp. 1-7.

"Paternal Status and the Economic Adjustment of High School Graduates," with Bryce Ryan, *Social Forces*, Vol. 22, pp. 302-306.

"The Value of High School Scholarship on the Labor Market," with Bryce Ryan, *Journal of Educational Sociology*, Vol. 17, pp. 524-534.

1945

"Role of the Intellectual in Public Bureaucracy," *Social Forces*, Vol. 23, pp. 405-415.

"Sociological Theory," *American Journal of Sociology*, Vol. 50, pp. 462-473.

"The Sociology of Knowledge," G. Gurvitch and W. E. Moore, eds., *Twentieth Century Sociology* (New York: Philosophical Library), pp. 366-405.

1946

Mass Persuasion, with M. Fiske and A. Curtis (New York: Harper & Brothers).

"The Focused Interview," with P. L. Kendall, *American Journal of Sociology*, Vol. 51, pp. 541-557.

1947

"The Machine, the Worker and the Engineer," *Science*, Vol. 105, pp. 79-84.

"Selected Problems of Field Work in the Planned Community," *American Sociological Review*, Vol. 12, pp. 304-312.

1948

"The Bearing of Empirical Research upon the Development of Sociological Theory," *American Sociological Review*, Vol. 13, pp. 505-515.

"Discrimination and the American Creed," R. M. Mac Iver, ed., *Discrimination and National Welfare* (New York: Harper & Brothers), pp. 99-126.

"A Note on Mass Persuasion," *International Journal of Opinion and Attitude Research*, Spring issue, pp. 101-108.

"Mass Communication, Popular Tastes and Organized Social Action," with

P. F. Lazarsfeld; Lyman Bryson, ed., *Communication of Ideas* (New York: Harper and Brothers), pp. 95-118.

"The Position of Sociological Theory: Discussion," *American Sociological Review*, Vol. 13, pp. 164-168.

"The Self-Fulfilling Prophecy," *The Antioch Review*, Summer, pp. 193-210.

"Social Psychology of Housing," Wayne Dennis, ed., *Current Trends in Social Psychology* (University of Pittsburgh Press), pp. 163-217.

"What Do We Know About Prejudice?" *University of Chicago Round Table*, No. 528, May 2d.

1949

Social Theory and Social Structure (Glencoe, Ill.: The Free Press); revised and enlarged ed., 1957. Translations: *Eléments de méthode sociologique* (Paris: Librairie Plon, 1953); *Teoria e Struttura Sociale* (Bologna: Società Editrice Il Mulino, 1959).

"Election Polling Forecasts and Public Images of Social Science," with Paul K. Hatt, *Public Opinion Quarterly*, Vol. 13, pp. 185-222.

"Social Structure and Anomie: Revisions and Extensions," Ruth N. Anshen, ed., *The Family: Its Function and Destiny* (New York: Harper & Brothers), pp. 224-257.

"Patterns of Influence: A Study of Interpersonal Influence and Communications Behavior in a Local Community," P. F. Lazarsfeld and F. Stanton, eds., *Communications Research 1948-49* (New York: Harper & Brothers), pp. 180-219.

"The Role of Applied Social Science in the Formation of Policy," *Philosophy of Science*, Vol. 16, pp. 161-181.

"Foreword," Logan Wilson and W. L. Kolb, *Sociological Analysis* (New York: Harcourt, Brace), pp. xi-xiii.

1950

Continuities in Social Research: Studies in the Scope and Method of The American Soldier, with P. F. Lazarsfeld (Glencoe, Ill.: The Free Press).

"Contributions to the Theory of Reference Group Behavior," with A. S. Kitt; R. K. Merton and P. F. Lazarsfeld, eds., *Continuities in Social Research, Ibid.*

"Foreword," George C. Homans, *The Human Group* (New York: Harcourt, Brace), pp. xvii-xxiii.

1951

Social Policy and Social Research in Housing, with P. S. West, M. Jahoda and H. C. Selvin, eds. *The Journal of Social Issues*, Vol. 7, Nos. 1 & 2.

"Social Scientists and Research Policy," with D. Lerner; Daniel Lerner and H. D. Lasswell, eds., *The Policy Sciences* (Stanford University Press), pp. 282-307.

"Large-Scale Community Research in the Epidemiology of Essential Hypertension in Man," *Symposium on Essential Hypertension* (Boston: Commonwealth of Massachusetts Recess Commission on Hypertension), pp. 327-334.

1952

Reader in Bureaucracy, with A. P. Gray, B. Hockey and H. C. Selvin, eds., (Glencoe, Ill.: The Free Press).

"Brief Bibliography for the Sociology of Science," with B. Barber, *Proceedings*, American Academy of Arts and Sciences, Vol. 80, Part 2, pp. 140-154.
"An Horrific Caricature," *The American Scholar*, Vol. 21, pp. 356-358.
"Foreword," Bernard Barber, *Science and the Social Order* (Glencoe, Ill.: The Free Press), pp. xi-xxiii.

1953

"Foreword," Hans Gerth and C. W. Mills, *Character and Social Structure* (New York: Harcourt, Brace), pp. vii-ix.

1954

"Friendship as Social Process: A Substantive and Methodological Analysis," with P. F. Lazarsfeld; M. Berger, T. Abel and C. Page, eds., *Freedom and Control in Modern Society* (New York: Van Nostrand), pp. 18-66.

1955

"The Socio-cultural Environment and Anomie," H. L. Witmer and R. Kotinsky, eds., *New Perspectives for Research on Juvenile Delinquency* (Washington: U. S. Government Printing Office), pp. 24-50.
"Discussion: The Knowledge of Man," Lewis Leary, ed., *The Unity of Knowledge* (New York: Doubleday), pp. 150-154.

1956

The Focused Interview, with M. Fiske and P. L. Kendall (Glencoe, Ill.: The Free Press).
"Studies in the Sociology of Medical Education," with S. Bloom and N. Rogoff, *Journal of Medical Education*, Vol. 31, pp. 552-565.

1957

The Freedom to Read, with R. McKeon and W. Gellhorn (New York: R. R. Bowker Co.).
The Student-Physician: Introductory Studies in the Sociology of Medical Education, with G. G. Reader and P. L. Kendall (Cambridge, Mass.: Harvard University Press).
"Some Preliminaries to a Sociology of Medical Education," *Ibid.*, pp. 3-79.
"The Role-Set: Problems in Sociological Theory," *British Journal of Sociology*, Vol. 8, No. 2, pp. 106-120.
"Priorities in Scientific Discovery: A Chapter in the Sociology of Science," *American Sociological Review*, Vol. 22, No. 6, pp. 635-659.

1958

"Procedures for the Sociological Study of the Value Climate of Medical Schools," with R. Christie; H. H. Gee and R. J. Glaser, eds., *The Ecology of the Medical Student* (Evanston, Ill.: Association of American Medical Colleges), pp. 125-153.
"Medical Education as Social Process," with P. L. Kendall; E. G. Jaco, ed.,

Patients, Physicians and Illness (Glencoe, Ill.: The Free Press), pp. 321-350.
"The Functions of the Professional Association," *American Journal of Nursing*, Vol. 58, pp. 50-54.
"Issues in the Growth of a Profession," *Proceedings*, 41st Convention of American Nurses Association, pp. 295-306.
"Foreword," Blaine E. Mercer, *The Study of Society* (New York: Harcourt, Brace), pp. v-vi.

1959

Sociology Today: Problems and Prospects, with L. Broom and L. S. Cottrell, Jr., eds. (New York: Basic Books).
"Notes on Problem-Finding in Sociology," *Ibid.*, pp. ix-xxxiv.
"Social Conformity, Deviation and Opportunity-Structures," *American Sociological Review*, Vol. 24, No. 2, pp. 177-189.
"The Scholar and the Craftsman: A Commentary," Marshall Clagett, ed., *Critical Problems in the History of Science* (Madison: The University of Wisconsin Press), pp. 24-29.

1960

"The Ambivalence of Le Bon's The Crowd; Introduction," Gustave Le Bon, *The Crowd* (New York: Viking Press, Compass Ed.) pp. v-xxxix.
"The Recognition of Excellence," *Recognition of Excellence*, Working Papers of the Edgar Stern Fund (Glencoe: The Free Press), pp. 297-328.
"The Search for Professional Status," *American Journal of Nursing.*
"Foreword," Harry M. Johnson, *Sociology* (New York: Harcourt, Brace), pp. iii-v.
"The Mosaic of the Behavioral Sciences, Parts I and II." *Revista de Ciencias Sociales* de la Universidad de Puerto Rico (forthcoming).
"The Conference on the History of Quantification in the Sciences," *Items*, Social Science Research Council.
"Social Conflict over Styles of Sociological Work. *Fourth World Congress of Sociology*, September 1959 (forthcoming).
"The Corporation: Its Coexistence with Men," Melvin Anshen and G. L. Bach, eds., *Management and Corporations 1985* (New York: McGraw-Hill Book Co.), pp. 57-61.
"Some Thoughts on the Professions in American Society"; Brown University Convocation Address, June 6, 1960.
"Singletons and Multiples in Scientific Discovery," *Proceedings of the American Philosophical Society* (forthcoming).

TALCOTT PARSONS

1928-29

" 'Capitalism' in Recent German Literature: Sombart and Weber," *Journal of Political Economy*, Vol. 36, pp. 641-661; Vol. 37, pp. 31-51.

1930

Translation of Weber, Max, *The Protestant Ethic and the Spirit of Capitalism* (London and New York: Allen and Unwin, and Scribners).

1931

"Wants and Activities in Marshall," *Quarterly Journal of Economics,* Vol. 46, pp. 101-140.

"Economics and Sociology: Marshall in Relation to the Thought of His Time," *Quarterly Journal of Economics,* Vol. 46, pp. 316-347.

1933

"Malthus," *Encyclopedia of the Social Sciences,* Vol. 10, pp. 68-69.

"Pareto," *Ibid.,* Vol. 11, pp. 576-8.

1934

"Some Reflections on 'The Nature and Significance of Economics'," *Quarterly Journal of Economics,* Vol. 48, pp. 511-545.

"Society," *Encyclopedia of the Social Sciences,* Vol. 14, pp. 225-231.

"Sociological Elements in Economic Thought, I." *Quarterly Journal of Economics,* Vol. 49, pp. 414-453.

1935

"Sociological Elements in Economic Thought, II." *Quarterly Journal of Economics,* Vol. 49, pp. 645-667.

"The Place of Ultimate Values in Sociological Theory," *International Journal of Ethics,* Vol. 45, pp. 282-316.

"H. M. Robertson on Max Weber and His School," *Journal of Political Economy,* Vol. 43, pp. 688-696.

1936

"Pareto's Central Analytical Scheme," *Journal of Social Philosophy,* Vol. 1, pp. 244-262.

"On Certain Sociological Elements in Professor Taussig's Thought," Jacob Viner, ed., *Explorations in Economics: Notes and Essays contributed in honor of F. M. Taussig* (New York: McGraw-Hill, 1936), pp. 359-379.

1937

The Structure of Social Action (New York: McGraw-Hill).

"Education and the Professions," *International Journal of Ethics,* Vol. 47, pp. 365-369.

1938

"The Role of Theory in Social Research," *American Sociological Review,* Vol. 3, pp. 13-20.

‡° "The Role of Ideas in Social Action," *American Sociological Review,* Vol. 3, pp. 653-664.

1939

‡° "The Professions and Social Structure," *Social Forces,* Vol. 17, pp. 457-467.

"Comte," *Journal of Unified Science,* Vol. 9, pp. 77-83.

‡ Also in *Essays in Sociological Theory,* 1st ed., 1949.
° Also in *Essays in Sociological Theory,* Rev. ed., 1954.

1940

#* "An Analytical Approach to the Theory of Social Stratification," *American Journal of Sociology,*" Vol. 45, pp. 841-862.
#* "Motivation of Economic Activities," *Canadian Journal of Economics and Political Science,* Vol. 6, pp. 187-203. Also published in C. W. M. Hart, ed., *Essays in Sociology,* and in Robert Dubin, *Human Relations in Administration: The Sociology of Organization.*

1942

"Max Weber and the Contemporary Political Crisis," *Review of Politics,* Vol. 4, pp. 61-76, 155-172.
"The Sociology of Modern Anti-Semitism," J. Graeber and Steuart Henderson Britt, eds., *Jews in a Gentile World* (New York, Macmillan).
#* "Age and Sex in the Social Structure of the United States," *American Sociological Review,* Vol. 7, pp. 604-616. Republished in several places, notably, Wilson and Kolb, *Sociological Analysis,* and Kluckhohn and Murray, *Personality in Nature, Society and Culture,* 1st and 2nd editions.
#* "Propaganda and Social Control," *Psychiatry,* Vol. 5, pp. 551-572.
* "Democracy and the Social Structure in Pre-Nazi Germany," *Journal of Legal and Political Sociology,* Vol. 1, pp. 96-114.
* "Some Sociological Aspects of the Fascist Movements," *Social Forces,* Vol. 21, pp. 138-147.

1943

#* "The Kinship System of the Contemporary United States," *American Anthropologist,* Vol. 45, pp. 22-38.

1944

#* "The Theoretical Development of the Sociology of Religion," *Journal of the History of Ideas,* Vol. 5, pp. 176-190.

1945

#* "The Present Position and Prospects of Systematic Theory," Georges Gurvitch and Wilbert E. Moore, eds., *Twentieth Century Sociology, A Symposium* (New York: Philosophical Library, 1945).
#* "The Problem of Controlled Institutional Change: An Essay on Applied Social Science," *Psychiatry,* Vol. 8, pp. 79-101.
"Racial and Religious Differences as Factors in Group Tensions," Louis Finkelstein et al., eds., *Unity and Difference in the Modern World* (New York: The Conference on Science, Philosophy and Religion in Their Relation to the Democratic Way of Life, Inc., 1945).

1946

"The Science Legislation and the Role of the Social Sciences," *American Sociological Review,* Vol. 11, pp. 653-666.

Also in *Essays in Sociological Theory,* 1st ed., 1949.
* Also in *Essays in Sociological Theory,* Rev. ed., 1954.

Bibliography 685

* "Population and Social Structure [of Japan]," Douglas G. Haring, ed., *Japan's Prospect* (Cambridge, Harvard University Press, 1946).

1947

Max Weber: The Theory of Social and Economic Organization, ed. and tr. with A. M. Henderson (Oxford University Press, 1947). ‡ Introduction by Talcott Parsons. Reprinted by the Free Press, 1957.
‡* "Certain Primary Sources and Patterns of Aggression in the Social Structure of the Western World," *Psychiatry,* Vol. 10, pp. 167-181. (Prepared for the Conference on Science, Philosophy and Religion at its September 1946 meeting in Chicago, Ill., and also published in the volume issued by the Conference.)
"Some Aspects of the Relations Between Social Science and Ethics," *Social Science,* Vol. 22, pp. 213-217.
"Science Legislation and the Social Sciences," *Political Science Quarterly,* Vol. 62, No. 2, June 1947; *Bulletin of Atomic Scientists,* January, 1947.

1948

"Sociology, 1941-46," with Bernard Barber, *American Journal of Sociology,* Vol. 53, pp. 245-257.
‡ "The Position of Sociological Theory," *American Sociological Review,* Vol. 13, pp. 156-171.

1949

"Essays in Sociological Theory Pure and Applied (Glencoe, Ill.: The Free Press, 1949).
"The Rise and Decline of Economic Man," *Journal of General Education,* Vol. 4, pp. 47-53.
* "Social Classes and Class Conflict in the Light of Recent Sociological Theory," *American Economic Review,* Vol. 39, pp. 16-26.

1950

* "The Prospects of Sociological Theory," *American Sociological Review,* Vol. 15, pp. 3-16.
* "Psychoanalysis and the Social Structure," *The Psychoanalytic Quarterly,* Vol. 19, pp. 371-384.
"The Social Environment of the Educational Process," *Centennial* (Washington: American Association for the Advancement of Science), pp. 36-40.

1951

The Social System (Glencoe, Ill.: The Free Press, 1951).
Toward a General Theory of Action, ed. and contributor with Edward A. Shils (Cambridge: Harvard University Press, 1951).
"Graduate Training in Social Relations at Harvard," *Journal of General Education,* Vol. 5, pp. 149-157.
"Illness and the Role of the Physician: A Sociological Perspective," *Ameri-*

‡ Also in *Essays in Sociological Theory,* 1st ed., 1949.
* Also in *Essays in Sociological Theory,* Rev. ed., 1954.

can Journal of Orthopsychiatry, Vol. 21, pp. 452-460. Reprinted in Kluckhohn and Murray, 2nd ed.

1952

"The Superego and the Theory of Social Systems," *Psychiatry,* Vol. 15, pp. 15-25. Reprinted in Parsons, Bales, and Shils, *Working Papers;* see 1953 entries.

"Religious Perspectives in College Teaching: Sociology and Social Psychology," Hoxie N. Fairchild, ed., *Religious Perspectives in College Teaching* (New York: The Ronald Press Company, 1952), pp. 286-337.

* "A Sociologist Looks at the Legal Profession," *Conference on the Profession of Law and Legal Education,* Dec. 4, 1952, Conference Series Number II, The Law School, University of Chicago; pp. 49-63.

1953

Working Papers in the Theory of Action, with Robert F. Bales and Edward A. Shils (Glencoe, Ill.: The Free Press, 1953).

"Psychoanalysis and Social Science with Special Reference to the Oedipus Problem," Franz Alexander and Helen Ross, eds., *Twenty Years of Psychoanalysis* (New York: W. W. Norton and Co., Inc., 1953).

* "A Revised Analytical Approach to the Theory of Social Stratification," Reinhard Bendix and Seymour M. Lipset, eds., *Class, Status and Power: A Reader in Social Stratification* (Glencoe, Ill.: The Free Press, 1953).

"Illness, Therapy and the Modern Urban American Family," with Renee Fox, *Journal of Social Issues,* Vol. 8, pp. 31-44.

"Some Comments on the State of the General Theory of Action," *American Sociological Review,* Vol. 18, No. 6, Dec. 1953, pp. 618-631.

1954

Essays in Sociological Theory; rev. ed. (Glencoe, Ill.: The Free Press).

"The Father Symbol: An Appraisal in the Light of Psychoanalytic and Sociological Theory," Bryson, Finkelstein, MacIver and McKeon, eds., *Symbols and Values: An Initial Study,* 13th Symposium of the Conference on Science, Philosophy and Religion (New York: Harper & Bros., 1954), pp. 523-544.

"Psychology and Sociology," John P. Gillin, ed., *For a Science of Social Man* (New York: Macmillan Co.) pp. 67-102.

"The Incest Taboo in Relation to Social Structure and the Socialization of the Child," *British Journal of Sociology,* Vol. 5, No. 2, June 1954, pp. 101-117.

1955

Family, Socialization and Interaction Process, with Robert F. Bales, James Olds, Morris Zelditch and Philip E. Slater (Glencoe, Ill.: The Free Press).

‡ " 'McCarthyism' and American Social Tension: A Sociologist's View," *Yale Review,* Winter 1955, pp. 226-245. Reprinted under title, "Social Strains

* Also in *Essays in Sociological Theory,* Rev. ed., 1954.
‡ Also in *Structure and Process in Modern Societies;* see 1960 publications.

in America," Daniel Bell, ed., *The New American Right* (New York: Criterion Books, 1955).

1956

Economy and Society, with Neil J. Smelser (London: Routledge and Kegan Paul and Glencoe, Ill.: The Free Press).

Éléments pour une théorie de l'action, with introd. by François Bourricaud (Paris: Plon).

‡ "A Sociological Approach to the Theory of Organizations," *Administrative Science Quarterly,* I. June 1956, pp. 63-85; II. Sept. 1956, pp. 225-239.

"A Sociological Model for Economic Development," with Neil J. Smelser, *Explorations in Entrepreneurial History,* Harvard University.

1957

‡ "The Distribution of Power in American Society," *World Politics,* Vol. 10, Oct. 1957, pp. 123-143.

"Malinowski and the Theory of Social Systems," Raymond Firth, ed., *Man and Culture* (London: Routledge and Kegan Paul).

"Man in His Social Environment—As Viewed by Modern Social Science," *Centennial Review of Arts and Science,* Michigan State University, Winter 1957, pp. 50-69.

"The Mental Hospital as a Type of Organization," Milton Greenblatt, Daniel J. Levinson and Richard H. Williams, eds., *The Patient and the Mental Hospital* (Glencoe, Ill.: The Free Press).

"Reflexions sur les Organizations Religieuses aux Etats-Unis," *Archives de Sociologie des Religions,* January-June, pp. 21-36.

Sociologia di dittatura (Bologna: Il Molino).

1958

‡ "Authority, Legitimation, and Political Action," C. J. Friedrich, ed., *Authority* (Cambridge, Mass.: Harvard University Press).

"The Definitions of Health and Illness in the Light of American Values and Social Structure," E. Gartly Jaco, ed., *Patients, Physicians, and Illness* (Glencoe, Ill.: The Free Press).

"Social Structure and the Development of Personality," *Psychiatry,* November 1958, pp. 321-340.

"General Theory in Sociology," Robert K. Merton, Leonard Broom, and Leonard S. Cottrell, Jr., eds., *Sociology Today* (New York: Basic Books).

‡ "Some Ingredients of a General Theory of Formal Organization," Andrew W. Halpin, ed., *Administrative Theory in Education* (Chicago: Midwest Administration Center, University of Chicago).

‡ "Some Reflections on the Institutional Framework of Economic Development," *The Challenge of Development: A Symposium* (Jerusalem: The Hebrew University).

‡ "Some Trends of Change in American Society: Their Bearing on Medical Education," *Journal of the American Medical Association,* May 1958, pp. 31-36.

‡ "The Pattern of Religious Organization in the United States," *Daedalus,* Summer 1958, pp. 65-85.

‡ Also in *Structure and Process in Modern Societies;* see 1960 publications.

1959

"An Approach to Psychological Theory in Terms of the Theory of Action," Sigmund Koch, ed., *Psychology: A Science,* Vol. III. (New York: Mc-Graw-Hill).

"The Principal Structures of Community: A Sociological View," C. J. Friedrich, ed., *Community* (New York: The Liberal Arts Press).

" 'Voting' and the Equilibrium of the American Political System," Eugene Burdick and Arthur Brodbeck, eds., *American Voting Behavior* (Glencoe, Ill.: The Free Press).

"Durkheim's Contribution to the Theory of Integration of Social Systems," Kurt H. Wolff, ed., *Emile Durkheim, 1858-1917: A Collection of Essays, with Translations and Bibliography* (Columbus, Ohio: The Ohio State University Press).

"Implications of the Study," (on Marjorie Fiske's study, "Book Selection and Retention in California Public and School Libraries") *The Climate of Book Selection,* a symposium of the University of California School of Librarianship. (Berkeley: The University of California Press).

"Some Problems Confronting Sociology as a Profession," *American Sociological Review,* August, 1959.

"The School Class as a Social System," *Harvard Educational Review,* Fall, 1959.

"An Approach to the Sociology of Knowledge," (Read at the Fourth World Congress of Sociology at Milan, Italy, September, 1959).

1960

Structure and Process in Modern Societies, (A collection of essays) (Glencoe, Ill.: The Free Press).

"Mental Illness and 'Spiritual Malaise': the Roles of the Psychiatrist and of the Minister of Religion," Hans Hofmann, ed., *Making the Ministry Relevant Today.*

"Pattern Variables Revisited: A Response to Professor Dubin's Stimulus," *American Sociological Review,* August, 1950.

"Toward a Healthy Maturity," *Journal of Health and Human Behavior,* Fall, 1960.

"Social Structure and Political Orientation," *World Politics,* October, 1960. (This is a review of S. M. Lipset, *Political Man,* and William Kornhauser, *The Politics of Mass Society.*)

"A Review," *American Sociological Review,* October, 1960. (This is a review of Reinhard Bendix, *Max Weber: An Intellectual Portrait.*)

"The Place of Law in Social Systems," Harry C. Bredemeier, ed., *Sociology and Law* (New Brunswick, N. J.: Rutgers University Press).

1961

Theories of Society, with Edward A. Shils, Kaspar D. Naegele, and Jesse R. Pitts, eds., 2 vols. (Glencoe, Ill.: The Free Press).

"Some Principal Characteristics of Industrial Societies," C. E. Black, ed., *The Transformation of Russian Society Since 1861* (Cambridge, Mass.: Harvard University Press).

"Christianity and Modern Industrial Society," Edward A. Tiryakian, ed., *Festschrift for Pitirim A. Sorokin* (Glencoe, Ill.: The Free Press).

"The Link Between Character and Society," with W. R. White; S. M. Lipset and L. Lowenthal, eds. *Culture and Social Character; The Work of David Riesman,* (Glencoe: The Free Press).

"Some Considerations on the Theory of Social Change," *Rural Sociology,* Vol. 26, No. 3.

"The Contribution of Psychoanalysis to the Social Sciences," *Science and Psychoanalysis,* 1961.

"The Cultural Background of American Religious Organization," (To be published in the proceedings of the Conference on Science, Philosophy and Religion, at which it was read in August, 1960).

PITIRIM A. SOROKIN *

1910

"Istoriko-Statistichesky Ocherk Zyrian," with K. Jakov, *Trudy expedizii po isledovaniu semli Pechorskago kraia* (St. Petersburg: 1910).

"K voprosu ob evoluzii i progresse," *Vestnik Psykhologii i Kriminalnoi Antropologii,* September 1911.

"Glavneishia teorii progressa," *Vestnik Znania,* September 1911.

"K. Hamsun i E. Verhaern," *Vseobschiy Journal,* September 1911.

"Perejitki animisma u Zyrian"; "K voprocu ob evolusii semiy i braka u Zyrian"; "Sovremmennyie Zyriane"; *Isvestia Archangelskago Obschestva Isuchenia Russkago Severa,* 1910, 1911, 1912.

1911

"Granitzy i predmet soziologii," *Novyie Idei v Soziologii,* No. 1. "Obsor teoriy i osnovnykh problem progressa," *Ibid.,* No. 3. (St. Petersburg, 1911).

1914

Prestuplenie i kara, podvig i nagrada (St. Petersburg: Isdatelstvo Dolbysheva, 1914).

"E. Durkheim ob religii," *Novyie Idei v Soziologii,* No. 4. (St. Petersburg, 1914).

"Sakony rasvitia nakazaniy s toshky zrenia psychologicheskoi teorii prava L. I. Petrajitzkago," *Novyie Idei v Pravovedenii,* No. 3. (St. Petersburg, 1914).

1915

L. N. Tolstoi, kak filosof (Moscow: Isdatelstvo Posrednik, 1915).

"'Tretia' shkola i spor 'klassikov' s 'soziologami' s ugolovnom prave," *Iuridicheski Vestnik,* No. 11, 1915.

* Author's note: The bibliography appearing here is comprehensive for books, but selective for articles. Of several hundred editorials and essays published in papers such as *Delo Naroda, Volia Naroda,* and other popular periodicals, and of some 200 papers published in the scientific journals of various countries, appearing here are selected articles typical of the kind of problems discussed in these papers.

1916

"Kategoria 'doljnago' i eia primenimost k izucheniu sozialnykh iavleniy," *Iuridicheski Vestnik,* 1916.

1917

Problema sozialnago ravenstva (St. Petersburg: isdatelstvo Revoluzionnaia Mysl, 1917).

Pracheshnaia Tchelovecheskikh dush (St. Petersburg: Ejemesiachnyi Journal, 1917).

"Struktura sovremennoi dogmatiki ugolovnago prava," *Vestnik Psykhologii, Kriminalnoi Antropologii i Pedagogiki,* Vol. 13, Nos. 1-5, 1917.

1919

Uchebnik obechey teorii prava (Iaroslavl: Isdatelstvo Iaroslavskago Soyuza Kooperativov, 1919).

1920

Obschedostupnuy uchebnik soziologii (Iaroslavl: Isdatelstvo Iaroslavskago Soyuza Kooperativov, 1920).

Sistema sociologii, 2 vols. (St. Petersburg: Isdatelstvo Kolos, 1920).

"Osnovnuis problemy sociologii P. L. Lavrova," *Sbornik Pamiaty Lavrova* (Petrograd· Kolos, 1920).

1921

Golod kak factor (St. Petersburg: Isdatelstvo Kolos, 1921). (This title was destroyed by the Soviet Government).

"Vliyanie professi na povedenie liudey i reflexologia professionalnykh group," *Journal Psychologii, Nevrologii i Reflexologii,* 1921.

1922

Sovremennoie sostoianie Rossii (Praga: Kooperativnoie Isdatelstvo, 1922).

"Golod i ideologia obschestva," *Ekonomist,* Nos. 4-5, 1922.

1923

Popularnuye ocherki sozialnoi pedagogiki i politiki (Ujgorod: isdanie Komiteta delovodchikov i narodnoprosvetitelnukh rad Podkarpatskoi Rusi, 1923).

1924

Leaves from a Russian Diary (New York: E. P. Dutton & Co., 1924); (Boston: Beacon Press, 1950).

"The New Soviet Codes and Soviet Justice," *Michigan Law Review,* November, 1924.

1925

Sociology of Revolution (Philadelphia and London: Lippincott Co., 1925). Translations: *Die Soziologie der Revolution* (München: Lehmanns Verlag, 1928) Latvian edition (Riga: 1934).

"American Millionaires and Multimillionaires," *Social Forces*, May 1925.
"Monarchs and Rulers," *Social Forces*, September 1925, March 1926.

1926

"Changes in Occupations and Economic Status of American Families During Four Generations," *Publications of American Sociological Society*, Vol. 32, 1926.
"Impoverishment and the Expansion of Governmental Control," *American Journal of Sociology*, September 1926.
"Die Russische Soziologie im Zwanzigsten Jahrhundert," *Jahrbuch für Soziologie*, Vol. 2, 1926.

1927

Social Mobility (New York: Harper & Brothers, 1927); *Social and Cultural Mobility* (Glencoe: The Free Press, 1959). Translations: Chinese edition (Shanghai: Shanghai World Publishing Co., 1933); Spanish edition: *Estratificacion y Movilidad Social* (Mexico: Instituto de Investigaciones Sociales de la Universidad Nacional, 1956); Japanese edition (in part), 1928.
"Leaders of Labor and Radical Movements in the United States and Foreign Countries," *American Journal of Sociology*, November, 1927.
"Sociology and Ethics," W. Ogburn and A. Goldenweiser, *The Social Sciences* (Boston: Houghton Mifflin Co., 1927).
"Soziale Bewegungsvorgänge," *Kölner Vierteljahrshefte für Soziologie*, Jahrgang VI., Heft 2, 1927.
"Stratification sociale et intelligence," *Revue Intern de Sociologie*, No. 9-10, 1927.
"A Survey of the Cyclical Conceptions of Social and Historical Process," *Social Forces*, September 1927.
"Russian Sociology in the Twentieth Century," *American Journal of Sociology*, Vol. 31, 1927.

1928

Contemporary Sociological Theories (New York: Harper & Brothers, 1928). Translations: *Soziologische Theorien* (München: C. H. Beck Verlag, 1931); *Sociologija* (Belgrad: isd. Geze Kona, 1932-33); *Sociologicke Nauky* (Prague: Jan Laichter, 1936); Chinese editions, 1932, 1936; *Yuzyilimizin Sosyoloji Nazariyeleri* (Istanbul: Huanubiat Basimevi, 1949); 2nd Turkish ed. 1950; *Teorias Sociológicas Contemporáneas* (Buenos Aires: Editorial Depalma, 1951); Hindi edition (Prasad & Sons, 1961); Japanese edition (in part) 1930.
"Arbeitsleistung und Entlohnung," *Kölner Vierteljahrshefte für Soziologie*, Jahrgang 7, Heft 2, 1928.
"Experimente zur Soziologie," *Zeitschrift für Völkerpsychologie und Soziologie*, March 1928.
"Farmer Leaders in the United States," *Social Forces*, September 1928.

1929

Principles of Rural-Urban Sociology, with C. C. Zimmerman (New York: Henry Holt Co., 1929). Translation: Japanese (in part), 1931-32.

"Die Politische Einstellung der Farmer and Bauern," *Zeitschrift für Völker-psychologie und Soziologie,* March 1929.
"Some Contrasts of Contemporary European and American Sociology," *Social Forces,* September 1929.

1930

A Systematic Source Book in Rural Sociology, with C. C. Zimmerman and C. J. Galpin, 3 vols. (Minneapolis:. University of Minnesota Press, 1930-32).
"An Experimental Study of Efficiency of Work under Various Specified Conditions," *American Journal of Sociology,* March 1930.
"Die Soziologie als Spezialwissenschaft," *Zeitschrift für Völkerpsychologie und Soziologie,* March 1930.

1932

"An Experimental Study of the Influence of Suggestion on the Discrimination and Valuation of People," *American Journal of Sociology,* March 1932.
"Metabolism of the Different Strata of Social Institutions and Institutional Continuity," *Metron,* Nos. 1, 2, 1932.

1933

"Studien zur Soziologie der Kunst," *Sociologus,* March 1933.
"Recent Social Trends: A Criticism," *Journal of Political Economy,* April-June, 1933.

1935

"The Course of Arabian Intellectual Development, 700-1300 A. D.," with Robert K. Merton, *Isis,* February 1935.

1936

"The Fluctuation of Idealism and Materialism, From 600 B. C. to 1920 A. D.," *Reine und Angewandte Soziologie, Eine Festgabe für F. Toennies* (Leipzig: H. Buske Verlag, 1936).
"Forms and Problems of Culture Integration and Methods of Their Study," *Rural Sociology,* September 1936.

1937

Social and Cultural Dynamics, (New York: American Book Co., 1937-41) 4 vols. abridged one volume edition (Boston: Porter Sargent, 1957).
"Le Concept d'équilibre: est il necessaire aux sciences sociales," *Revue Intern de Sociologie,* Vol. 44, 1937.
"Social Time: Methodological and Functional Analysis," with Robert K. Merton, *American Journal of Sociology,* March 1937.

1938

"A Neglected Factor of War," *American Sociological Review,* August, 1938.
"Pseudo-Sociologos," *Journal of Social Philosophy,* July 1938.
"Histrionics," *The Southern Review,* Winter, 1938.

1939

Time-Budgets of Human Behavior, with C. Q. Berger (Cambridge: Harvard University Press, 1939).
"Les phases socio-culturelles dans la culture Euro-Americaine," *Melanges Offerts a Emilie Witmeur* (Paris: Sirey, 1939)

1940

"Arnold J. Toynbee's Philosophy of History," *Journal of Modern History,* September 1940.

1941

Crisis of Our Age (New York: E. P. Dutton Co., 1941). Translations: *A Crise do Nosso Tempo* (Sao Paulo: Editora Universitaria, 1945), *La Crisis de Nuestra Era* (Buenos Aires: Espasa-Calpe, 1948); *De Crisis Onser Eeuw* (Deventer: N. Kluwer, 1950); *Aikamme Kriisi* (Porvoo-Helsinki: Werner Soederstroem Osakeyhtioe, 1952); *Die Krise Unserer Zeit* (Frankfurt am Main: Joachim Henrich-Verlag, 1950); Japanese edition (Tokyo: Kitaro Sekine, 1952); Norwegian edition (Oslo: Statistik Sentralbyra, 1948).

1942

Man and Society in Calamity (New York: E. P. Dutton Co., 1942).
"La Influencia de las Calamidades sobre Organizacion Politica, Economica y Social," *Revista Mexicana de Sociologia,* No. 3, 1942.

1943

Sociocultural Causality, Space, Time (Durham: Duke University Press, 1943).

1944

Russia and the United States (New York: E. P. Dutton Co., 1944); revised English ed. (London: Stevens & Sons, 1950). Translations: *Rússia e Estados Unidos* (Sao Paulo: Editora Universitaria, 1944) Japanese edition (Tokyo: Toyo Keizai Shimpo Sha, 1953).
"Dinamica Socio Cultural y Evolucionismo," *Revista Mexicana de Sociología,* No. 2, 1944.
"The Cause and Factors of War," *Annual Report of the American Historical Association for 1942,* Washington, 1944.
"The Conditions and Prospects for a World without War," *American Journal of Sociology,* March, 1944.

1945

"O Papel da Semelhanca e Dessemelhanca na Solidariedade e Antagonismo Sociais," *Service Social,* March 1945.
"Sociocultural Dynamics and Evolutionism," G. Gurvitch and Wilbert E. Moore, eds., *Twentieth Century Sociology* (New York: Philosophical Library, 1945).
"War and Post-War Changes in Social Stratification," *American Sociological Review,* April 1945.

1947

Society, Culture and Personality (New York: Harper and Brothers, 1947). Translations: *Sociedad, Cultúra y Personalidad* (Madrid: Aguilar, 1960). "Qu'est-ce q'une Class Sociale?" *Cahiers Internationals de Sociologie,* No. 2, 1947.

1948

Reconstruction of Humanity (Boston: Beacon Press, 1948). Translations: *Menneskehetens Gjenreisning* (Oslo: Olaf Norlis Forlag, 1953) Japanese edition (Tokyo: Bungei-Shunju-Shinsha, 1951) *Die Wiederherstellung der Menschenwürde* (Frankfurt am Main: Joachim Henrich-Verlag, 1952) India edition (Bombay: Bharatiya Vidya Bhavan, 1958). Hindi edition, 1961.

1949

"Concept, Tests, and Energy of Spontaneity-Creativity," *Sociometry,* Nos. 1-3.
"Lasting and Dying Factors in the World's Cultures," F. S. C. Northrop, ed., *Ideological Differences and World Order* (New Haven: Yale University Press, 1949).
"The Real Causes of the Russian-American Conflict," *World Affairs,* April 1949.

1950

Explorations in Altruistic Love and Behavior: Symposium (Boston: Beacon Press, 1950).
Altruistic Love: A Study of American Good Neighbors and Christian Saints (Boston: Beacon Press, 1950).
Social Philosophies of an Age of Crisis (Boston: Beacon Press, 1950). Translations: *Kulturkrise und Gesellschaftsphilosophie* (Suttgart-Wien: Humboldt Verlag, 1953). *Las Filosofias Sociales de Nuestra Epoca de Crisis* (Madrid: Aguilar, 1954).
"Notes on the Interdependence of Philosophy and Sociology," *Revue Internationale de Philosophie,* July 1950.

1951

S. O. S. The Meaning of Our Crisis (Boston: Beacon Press, 1951).
"Amitology as Applied Science of Amity and Unselfish Love," *Soziologische Forschung in unserer Zeit,* Ein Sammelwerk L. v. Wiese zum 75. Geburtstag (Köln, 1951).
"Polarizacion en la Frustracion y en las Crisis, *Revista Internacional de Sociologia,* July-September 1951.

1952

Estructura Mental y Energias del Hombre (Mexico: Instituto de Investigaciones Sociales, Universidad Nacional, 1952).

1953

"El Supraconsciente," *Revista Internacional de Sociologia,* January-March 1953.

1954

Forms and Techniques of Altruistic and Spiritual Growth: Symposium (Boston: Beacon Press, 1954).
The Ways and Power of Love (Boston: Beacon Press, 1954).
"Les Travaux du Centre de Recherches de Harvard sur l'altruisme créateur," *Cahiers Internationals de Sociologie*, 1954.

1955

"Remarks on J. L. Moreno's Theory of Spontaneity-Creativity," *Sociometry and the Science of Man*, December 1955.
"Testomania," *Harvard Educational Review*, Fall, 1955.

1956

Fads and Foibles in Modern Sociology and Related Sciences (Chicago: Henry Regnery, 1956). Translations: *Achaques y Manias de la Sociologia Moderna y Ciencias Afines* (Madrid: Aguilar, 1957) *Tendances et Deboires de la Sociologie Americaine* (Paris: Aubier, 1959). Some chapters have been translated into Japanese and German.
"Leon Petrazycki's Law and Morality," *Harvard Law Review*, April 1956.
"Fifty years of Change in Sociology," *Sociology and Social Research*, July-August, 1956.
"This is My Faith," S. G. Cole, ed. *This Is My Faith* (New York: Harper and Brothers, 1956).

1957

The American Sex Revolution (Boston: Porter Sargent, 1957). Translations: *La Revolutión Sexual en los Estados Unidos de America* (Mexico: Instituto de Investigaciones Sociales, Universidad Nacional, 1958); *Sex-Besatt Vaesterland* (Stockholm: Tidningarnas Artikelvoerland, 1959); Japanese edition (Tokyo: Gigi Tsushinsha, 1957); India edition under the title: *Sane Sex Order* (Bombay: Bharatiya Vidya Bhavan, 1960); Portuguese edition (Rio de Janeiro: Editora Funda de Cultura, 1961).
"The Fine Arts in the College Curriculum," *Bulletin of Association of American Colleges*, Mar. 1957.
"Integralism Is My Philosophy," Whit Burnett, ed. *This Is My Philosophy* (New York: Harper and Brothers, 1957).
"Sociology and the Advances of Natural Science," *The National Academy of Economics and Political Science*, Special Publications Series No. 13 (Washington, 1957).
"Foreword," Ferdinand Toennies, *Community & Society (Gemeinschaft und Gesellschaft)*, tr. and ed. by Charles P. Loomis (East Lansing, Michigan: The Michigan State University Press, 1957).

1958

"Physicalist and Mechanistic School in Sociology," J. S. Roucek, ed., *Contemporary Sociology* (New York: Philosophical Library, 1958).

1959

Power and Morality (Boston: Porter Sargent, 1959); India edition (Bombay: Bharatiya Vidya Bhavan, 1960).
"The Integral Theory of Values," A. Maslow, ed., *New Knowledge in Human Values* (New York: Harper and Brothers, 1959).
"Theses on Moral Transformation of Mankind," *Indian Sociologist*, March 1959.
"Studies of Harvard Research Center in Creative Altruism," (Harvard University Press, 1959).

1960

"How Are Sociological Theories Conceived, Developed, and Validated," *Social Science*, April 1960.
"Three Basic Trends of Our Times," *Main Currents in Modern Thought*, Nos. 3-4, 1960.
"The Mysterious Energy of Love," *Akten des XVIII. Kongresses des Institut International de Sociologie*, Vol. 1. (Meisenheim/Glan: Verlag Anton Hain K. G., 1960).
"A Quest for Integral System of Sociology," *Mémoire du XIXe Congres International de Sociologie*, Vol. 1 (Mexico: Comite Organisateur du XIXe Congrés, 1960).
"Mutual Convergence of the United States and the Soviet Russia towards Third Intermediary Type," *Memoire du XIXe Congres*, Vol. 1 (Mexico, 1960).
"Theses on Creativity," *Syracuse University Symposium on Creativity*, 1960.
"Variations on Spencerian Theme of Militant and Industrial Types of Society," *Social Science*, April 1961.
Recordings: "The Mysterious Energy of Love," "Three Basic Trends of Our Times," three-hour lectures recorded in *Campus Library* by Campus World, Inc.

ROBIN M. WILLIAMS, JR.

1936

"Farm Tenancy in North Carolina, 1860-1955," with Olaf Wakefield, Mimeographed Bulletin, North Carolina Agricultural Experiment Station, 1936.
"Farm Tenancy Programs in North Carolina," *Journal of Land and Public Utility Economics*, 1936.

1939

"Rural Youth Studies in the United States," *Rural Sociology*, June 1939.
"Rural Youth in North Carolina," North Carolina Agricultural Experiment Station *Bulletin*, June 1939.

1941

"Concepts of Marginality in Rural Population Studies," *Rural Sociology*, Vol. 5, Sept. 1941.
"Comment on the paper 'Status Systems and the Socialization of the Child' by Allison Davis," *American Sociological Review*, Vol. 6, June 1941.

"Planning for People," *Land Policy Review*, Vol. 4, Jan. 1941.
"Community Land-Use Planning Committee: Organization, Leadership, Attitudes, Carrard County, Kentucky 1931," with H. W. Beers, J. S. Page, and D. Ensminger, Kentucky Agricultural Experiment Station *Bulletin 417*, June 1941.

1942

"Social Stratification in the Ante-Bellum South," with Wilbert E. Moore, *American Sociological Review*, Vol. 7, June 1942.

1943

"Farmers on Local Planning Committees in Three Kentucky Counties, 1939-1940," with Howard W. Beers, Kentucky Agricultural Experiment Station *Bulletin 443*, May 1943.
"Attitudes Toward Rural Migration and Family Life in Johnson and Robertson Counties, Kentucky 1941," with Howard W. Beers, Kentucky Agricultural Experiment Station *Bulletin 452*, 1943.

1944

"Age Structure of Kentucky Population, 1940," with Howard W. Beers, Kentucky Agricultural Experiment Station *Bulletin 465*, June 1944.

1946

"Review of Current Research in Rural Sociology," *Rural Sociology*, Vol. 11, June 1946.
"Some Observations on Sociological Research in Government During World War II," *American Sociological Review*, Vol. 11, Oct. 1946.

1947

"The Reduction of Intergroup Tensions," Social Science Research Council *Bulletin 57*, 1947.

1948

"Discussion of 'Concerning Ethnic Research,'" *American Sociological Review*, Vol. 13, April 1948.

1949

The American Soldier, with S. A. Stouffer and others (Princeton, N. J.: Princeton University Press, 1949). Vol. I and II.

1951

American Society: A Sociological Interpretation (New York: Alfred A. Knopf, 1951).

1953

"Application of Research to Practice in Intergroup Relations," *American Sociological Review*, Vol. 18, Feb. 1953.
"Reactions of College Students to Manpower Policies and the Military Service Prospect," with Edward A. Suchman and Rose K. Goldsen, *The Educational Record*, Vol. 34, April 1953.

"Student Reaction to Impending Military Service," *American Sociological Review*, Vol. 18, June 1953.

"College Students and the Korean War," with Edward A. Suchman and Rose K. Goldsen, *Public Opinion Quarterly*, Summer 1953.

1954

Schools in Transition, with Margaret W. Ryan (Chapel Hill, N. C.: University of North Carolina Press, 1954).

1955

"Preface" with Gilbert Shapiro; Charles Winick, *Trends in Human Relations Research* (New York: Anti-Defamation League of B'nai B'rith, 1955).

1956

Friendship and Social Values in a Suburban Community, with associates (Eugena, Oregon: University of Oregon, 1956). Processed.

"Situational Patterning in Intergroup Relations," with Melvin L. Kohn, *American Sociological Review*, Vol. 21, April 1956.

"Factors Associated with the Development of Cross-Cultural Social Interaction," with Rose K. Goldsen and Edward A. Suchman, *The Journal of Social Issues*, Vol. 12, 1956.

"Religion, Value-Orientations and Intergroup Conflict," *Journal of Social Issues*, Vol. 12, 1956.

"Educational Desegregation as a Context for Research," with Burton Fisher and Irving Janis, *American Sociological Review*, Vol. 21, Oct. 1956.

1957

"Some Consequences of Religious Heterogeneity in America," J. Milton Yinger, *Religion, Society and the Individual* (New York: Macmillan Co., 1957.)

"Unity and Diversity in Modern America," *Social Forces*, Vol. 36, Oct. 1957.

"Racial and Cultural Relations," Joseph B. Gittler, *Review of Sociology: Analysis of a Decade* (New York: John Wiley & Sons, 1957).

1958

"Continuity and Change in Sociological Study," *American Sociological Review*, Vol. 23, Dec. 1958.

1959

"Friendship and Social Values in a Suburban Community," *The Pacific Sociological Review*, Vol. 2, Spring 1959.

"Rural Sociology in a Changing Society," *Rural Sociology in a Changing Society*, proceedings of a North Central Rural Sociology Committee (NCr-5) Seminar, November 11, 1959, Chicago, Illinois. (Columbus, Ohio: Ohio Agricultural Extension Service, Ohio State University), pp. 1-11.

1960

What College Students Think, with Rose K. Goldsen, Morris Rosenberg, and Edward A. Suchman (New York: D. Van Nostrand Co., 1960).

American Society: A Sociological Interpretation (New York: Alfred A. Knopf, rev. ed., 1960).

1961

"The Sociological Theory of Talcott Parsons," Max Black, ed., *The Social Theories of Talcott Parsons* (Englewood Cliffs, N. J.: Prentice-Hall, Inc., 1961), pp. 64-99.

Index of Names

701

Subject Index

Accessibility, 52-53, 72-73, 76; *See also* sections in chapters 2-8 designated by heading Territoriality

Achievement:
as rank determinant, 60-63, 133-134, 136, 207, 394-395, 539-540
as related to status-role allocation, 62, 138-139
as related to atrophy of talent, 62
presence of in all societies, 134, 136
characteristics of, 343
and "success" as major American value orientation, 522, 551, 554
See also Ascription, Horizontal mobility, Performance, Quality, Rank, Vertical mobility

Activity:
definitions of, 1-2, 183-184
social, 116
as goal directed, 116-117, 194, 196, 265, 462-463
scarcity and value of as related to rank, 134, 136, 207
correlation of with value, 177, 184
inclusive of sentiments, 183
frequency of, 176-177, 184, 200-201
as response to sanctions, 217-218, 406, 550
instrumental-consummatory, 332, 335-336
and work as major American value orientation, 557

Actor:
as element in social action, 116
orientation of, 344-345

Adaptive function, 337, 347-348, 349, 350-351; *See also* Economy

Affective neutrality:
function of, 259, 369-370, 513-514, 534
vs. affectivity, 342, 434
acquisition of, 421

Affective nonrationality, *See* Mode(s) of evaluation

Affectivity, vs. affective neutrality, 342, 434

Allocation of status-roles, 13; *See also* Rank, as well as sections in chapters 2-8 designated by heading Allocation of status-roles

American value system, 263-264, 387, 396, 504-505, 557-560

Anomie paradigm:
and implications for change, 273, 316
vs. institutionalization, 422

Antagonistic relations, 454-459

Application of sanctions as process, 14; *See also* sections in chapters 2-8 designated by heading Application of sanctions

Appropriateness, as value on sacred-secular continuum, 43

Artist as communicator of sentiment, 373-374, 460-461

Ascetic Protestantism:
emapthy of with capitalism, 25, 41, 285-286, 572

707